MOTIVATION AND WORK BEHAVIOR

McGraw-Hill Series in Management

Fred Luthans and Keith Davis, Consulting Editors

MOTIVATION AND WORK BEHAVIOR

FOURTH EDITION

Richard M. Steers

College of Business Administration
University of Oregon

Lyman W. Porter

Graduate School of Management
University of California, Irvine

McGRAW-HILL BOOK COMPANY

New York   St. Louis   San Francisco   Auckland   Bogotá
Hamburg   London   Madrid   Mexico   Milan   Montreal
New Delhi   Panama   Paris   São Paulo   Singapore   Sydney   Tokyo   Toronto

MOTIVATION AND WORK BEHAVIOR

234567890   DOCDOC   8943210987

ISBN 0-07-060948-9

This book was set in Times Roman by Automated Composition Service, Inc.
The editor was Kathleen L. Loy;
the production supervisor was Joe Campanella;
the cover was designed by Laura Stover. New drawings
were done by Volt Information Sciences, Inc.
R. R. Donnelley & Sons Company was printer and binder.

Library of Congress Cataloging-in-Publication Data

Steers, Richard M.
  Motivation and work behavior.

  (McGraw–Hill series in management)
  Includes bibliographies and indexes.
  1. Employee motivation. 2. Psychology, Industrial.
I. Porter, Lyman W. II. Title. III. Series.
HF 5549.5.M63S73   1987   658.3′14   86-27865
ISBN 0-07-060948-9

CONTENTS

PART FOUR   MOTIVATION THEORY IN PERSPECTIVE

PREFACE

Interest in the topic of motivation in work organizations has risen steadily in recent years. Some 30 years ago the level of knowledge and research in the area consisted largely of classic, though singular, efforts to set forth some basic theoretical generalizations based on only fragmentary research data. Beginning in the early 1960s, however, interest in motivational problems of organizations increased significantly. This trend has continued through the 1970s and into the 1980s. It is difficult to pick up a current research journal in organizational behavior, industrial psychology, or the general area of management without finding at least one selection dealing with motivational problems at work.

Such intense interest in the field is a healthy sign that increased knowledge will be gained on this important topic. Simultaneously, however, a potential problem exists in ensuring that the various research efforts are somehow integrated and synthesized so that we can maximize our understanding of the main issues involved. This book is largely the result of our concern for this potential problem. Several major theories of motivation have been advanced and tested during the past decade or so. Moreover, while a great deal has been written concerning the relation of motivational processes to various other important organizational factors (such as job design and group dynamics), this literature has also been largely fragmentary. Our hope in organizing this book, then, is to bring together in one volume the major contemporary theories, research, and applications in the area of motivation and work behavior.

It is our belief that a thorough knowledge of motivation as it affects organizational processes requires at least three important inputs. First, the reader must gain a general knowledge of what is meant by the concept of motivation, as well as of historical approaches to the study of motivation. Also, the reader needs a fairly comprehensive framework for analyzing the various theories and applications that exist. We have attempted to deal with these matters in Part One of the book. Second, it is our contention that the serious student of motivation must be conversant with the major theories that exist in the field today. These theories—and the research associated with them—are described in Part Two. This part in the fourth edition focuses particularly on cognitive and reinforcement theories. Finally, we feel that theories alone are of little value unless the student can understand how motivational processes relate to other organizational variables. Such interrelationships are covered in detail in Parts Three and Four. In Part Three of this edition, new sections have been added on careers in organizations, managing marginal performance, and motivation in other contexts. Part Four then attempts to review and synthesize what has been learned concerning the role of motivation in organizational settings.

Throughout the fourth edition, readings have been updated. This edition includes 13 new selections. In addition, the text has also been updated and expanded somewhat.

The approach taken here is to integrate text materials with selections authored by some of the foremost scholars in the field. The major focus in the text and readings is on a blend of theoretical formulations with practical applications. Thus, the chapters (especially in Part Three) generally contain some major theoretical propositions, some research evidence relevant to the theories, and some examples of how such models have been or could be applied in existing organizations. Furthermore, each chapter contains a set of questions to stimulate discussion and analysis of the major issues.

This book is designed primarily for students of organizational behavior, industrial psychology, and general management. It also should be useful for managers who wish to gain an increased understanding of problems of work motivation. It is assumed that the reader has had some previous exposure to organizational behavior, perhaps through an introductory course. This volume attempts to build upon such knowledge and to analyze general organizational processes, using the concept of motivation as the basic unit of analysis.

We wish to express our sincere appreciation to all those who have contributed to the realization of this project in its various editions. In particular, our thanks go to Keith Davis, Arizona State University; Peter Dubno, New York University; Mark Fichman, Carnegie-Mellon University; Jerald Greenberg, Ohio State University; Ralph Katerberg, University of Cincinnati; Terence Mitchell, University of Washington; Richard Mowday, University of Oregon; Greg Oldham, University of Illinois at Urbana-Champaign; and Eugene Stone, Bowling Green University for their helpful comments and suggestions. We are also indebted to Cindy P. Lindsay and Janet Black for their valuable assistance in preparing the manuscript for publication. In addition, we are grateful to our respective schools, the University of Oregon and the University of California, Irvine, for providing stimulating motivational environments in which to work. Finally, a special note of appreciation is due our wives, Sheila and Meredith, for their support and encouragement throughout the project.

Richard M. Steers
Lyman W. Porter

PART **ONE**

INITIAL CONSIDERATIONS

CHAPTER 1

THE ROLE OF MOTIVATION IN ORGANIZATIONS

The topic of motivation at work has received considerable and sustained attention in recent years among both practicing managers and organizational researchers. One has only to ask first-level supervisors what their most taxing work problems are for evidence of the importance of the concept to management. Likewise, one can observe the large number of empirical articles relating to the topic in psychological and management journals for evidence of its importance to researchers. Several factors appear to account for the prominence of this topic as a focal point of interest.

To begin with, managers and organizational researchers cannot avoid a concern with the *behavioral* requirements of an organization. In addition to the necessity to acquire financial and physical resources, every organization needs people in order to function. More specifically, Katz and Kahn (1966) have posited that organizations have three behavioral requirements in this regard: (1) people must be attracted not only to join the organization but also to remain in it; (2) people must perform the tasks for which they are hired, and must do so in a dependable manner; and (3) people must go beyond this dependable role performance and engage in some form of creative, spontaneous, and innovative behavior at work (Katz, 1964; Katz & Kahn, 1966). In other words, for an organization to be effective, according to this reasoning, it must come to grips with the motivational problems of stimulating both the decision to participate and the decision to produce at work (March & Simon, 1958).

A second and related reason behind the attention directed toward motivation centers around the pervasive nature of the concept itself. Motivation as a concept represents a highly complex phenomenon that affects, and is affected by, a multitude of factors in the organizational milieu. A comprehensive understanding of the way in which organizations function requires that at least some attention be directed toward the question of why people behave as they do on the job (that is, the determinants of employee work behavior *and* the ramifications of such behavior for an organization). An understanding of the topic of motivation is thus essential in order to comprehend more fully the effects of variations in other factors (such as leadership style, job redesign, and salary systems) as they relate to performance, satisfaction, and so forth.

Third, given the ever-tightening constraints placed on organizations by governmental regulations, increased foreign and domestic competition, citizens' lobbies, and the like, management has had to look for new mechanisms to increase—and in some cases just to maintain—its level of organizational effectiveness and efficiency. Much of the ''slack'' that organizations could depend upon in the past has disappeared in the face of these new environmental types of constraints. Because of this, management must ensure that it is deriving full potential benefit from those resources—including human resources—that it does have at its disposal. Thus, organizational effectiveness becomes to some degree a question of management's ability to motivate its employees to direct at least a reasonable effort toward the goals of the organization.

A fourth reason can be found in the nature of present and future technology required for production. As technology increases in complexity, machines tend to become necessary *yet insufficient* vehicles of effective and efficient operations. Modern technology can no longer be considered synonymous with the term ''automation.'' Consider the example of the highly technologically based aerospace programs in the United States. While mastery of the technological aspects of engineering is a prerequisite for developing complex projects, a second and equally important ingredient is the ability of organizations to bring together thousands of employees, who often must work at peak capacity to *apply* the technology required for success. In other words, it becomes necessary for an organization to ensure that it has employees who are both capable of using and willing to use the advanced technology to achieve organizational objectives.

Finally, while organizations have for some time viewed their financial and physical resources from a long-term perspective, only recently have they begun seriously to apply this same perspective to their human resources. Many organizations are now beginning to pay increasing attention to developing their employees as future resources (a ''talent bank'') upon which they can draw as they grow and develop. Evidence for such concern can be seen in the recent growth of management and organization development programs, in the increased popularity of ''assessment center'' appraisals, in recent attention to personnel planning, and in the emergence of ''human resource accounting'' systems. More concern is being directed, in addition, toward stimulating employees to enlarge their job skills (through training, job design, job rotation, and so on) at both the blue-collar and the white-collar levels in an effort to ensure a continual reservoir of well-trained and highly motivated people.

In summary, then, there appear to be several reasons why the topic of motivation has been receiving increased attention by both those who study organizations and those who manage them. The old simplistic, prescriptive guidelines concerning "economic man" are simply no longer sufficient as a basis for understanding human behavior at work. New approaches and greater understanding are called for to deal with the complexities of contemporary organizations.

Toward this end, this book will attempt to assist the serious student of motivation to obtain a more comprehensive and empirically based knowledge of motivation at work. This will be done through a combination of explanatory text and readings on current theories, research, and applications in the field. Before discussing some of the more current approaches to motivation, however, some consideration is in order concerning the nature of basic motivational processes. This consideration is followed by a brief history of early psychological and managerial approaches to the topic. Finally, a conceptual framework is presented to aid in the comprehension and evaluation of the various theories and models that follow. Throughout this book, emphasis is placed on the comparative approach; that is, we are primarily concerned with similarities among—and differences between— the various theories and models rather than with the presentation and defense of one particular theory. Moreover, because of the pervasive nature of the topic, we feel that the concept of motivation can best be understood only by considering its role as it affects—and is affected by—other important variables which constitute the work environment. Thus, special emphasis is placed throughout on the study of *relationships* between major variables (for example, motivation as it relates to reward systems, group influences, and job design) rather than on the simple enumeration of facts or theories.

THE NATURE OF MOTIVATION

The term "motivation" was originally derived from the Latin word *movere*, which means "to move." However, this one word is obviously an inadequate definition for our purposes here. What is needed is a description which sufficiently covers the various aspects inherent in the process by which human behavior is activated. A brief selection of representative definitions indicates how the term has been used:

> . . . the contemporary (immediate) influences on the direction, vigor, and persistence of action. (Atkinson, 1964)
>   . . . how behavior gets started, is energized, is sustained, is directed, is stopped, and what kind of subjective reaction is present in the organism while all this is going on. (Jones, 1955)
>   . . . a process governing choices made by persons or lower organisms among alternative forms of voluntary activity. (Vroom, 1964)
>   . . . motivation has to do with a set of independent/dependent variable relationships that explain the direction, amplitude, and persistence of an individual's behavior, holding constant the effects of aptitude, skill, and understanding of the task, and the constraints operating in the environment. (Campbell & Pritchard, 1976)

These definitions appear generally to have three common denominators which may be said to characterize the phenomenon of motivation. That is, when we discuss motivation, we are primarily concerned with: (1) what energizes human behavior; (2) what directs or channels such behavior; and (3) how this behavior is maintained or sustained. Each of these three components represents an important factor in our understanding of human behavior at work. First, this conceptualization points to energetic forces within individuals that *drive* them to behave in certain ways and to environmental forces that often trigger these drives. Second, there is the notion of goal orientation on the part of individuals; their behavior is directed *toward* something. Third, this way of viewing motivation contains a *systems orientation*; that is, it considers those forces in the individuals and in their surrounding environments that feed back to the individuals either to reinforce the intensity of their drive and the direction of their energy or to dissuade them from their course of action and redirect their efforts. These three components of motivation appear again and again in the theories and research that follow.

THE MOTIVATIONAL PROCESS: BASIC CONSIDERATIONS

Building upon this definition, we can now diagram a *general* model of the motivational process. While such a model is an oversimplification of far more complex relationships, it should serve here to represent schematically the major sets of variables involved in the process. Later, we can add to this model to depict how additional factors may affect human behavior at work.

The basic building blocks of a generalized model of motivation are (1) needs or expectations, (2) behavior, (3) goals, and (4) some form of feedback. The interaction of these variables is shown in Exhibit 1. Basically, this model posits that individuals possess in varying strengths a multitude of needs, desires, and expectations. For example, they may have a high need for affiliation, a strong desire for additional income, or an expectation that increased effort on the job would lead to a promotion. These "activators" are generally characterized by two phenomena. First, the emergence of such a need, desire, or expectation generally creates a state of disequilibrium within the individuals which they will try to reduce; hence, the energetic component of our definition above. Second, the presence of such needs, desires, or expectations is generally associated with an anticipation or belief that certain actions will lead to the reduction of this disequilibrium; hence, the goal-orientation component of our definition.

In theory, the following is presumed to be the chain of events: On the basis of some combination of this desire to reduce the internal state of disequilibrium and the anticipation or belief that certain actions should serve this purpose,

EXHIBIT 1
A generalized model of the basic motivation process. (After Dunnette & Kirchner, 1965.)

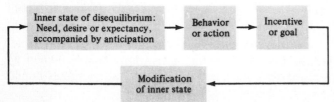

individuals act or behave in a certain manner that they believe will lead to the desired goal. The initiation of this action then sets up a series of cues, either within the individuals or from their external environment, which feed information back to the individuals concerning the impact of their behavior. Such cues may lead them to modify (or cease) their present behavior, or they may reassure them that their present course of action is correct.

An example should clarify this process. Individuals who have a strong desire to be with others (that is, have a high "need for affiliation") may attempt to increase their interactions with those around them (behavior) in the hope of gaining their friendship and support (goal). On the basis of these interactions, they may eventually reach a point where they feel they have enough friends and may then direct their energies toward other goals. Or, conversely, they may receive consistent negative feedback that informs them that their behavior is not successful for goal attainment, and they may then decide to modify such behavior. In either case, we can see the important moderating effect of feedback on subsequent behavior and goals.

The general model of the motivational process appears fairly simple and straightforward. Such is not the case, however. Several complexities exist which tend to complicate the theoretical simplicity. Dunnette and Kirchner (1965) and others have identified four such complications. First, motives can really only be *inferred*; they cannot be seen. Thus, when we observe individuals putting in a great deal of overtime, we really do not know whether they are doing it because of the extra income they receive or simply because they enjoy their work. In fact, at least five reasons have been identified for why it is difficult to infer motives from observed behavior: (1) any single act may express several motives; (2) motives may appear in disguised forms; (3) several motives may be expressed through similar or identical acts; (4) similar motives may be expressed in different behavior; and (5) cultural and personal variations may significantly moderate the modes of expression of certain motives (Hilgard & Atkinson, 1967).

A second complication of the model centers around the dynamic nature of motives. Any individual at any one time usually has a host of needs, desires, and expectations. Not only do these motives change but they may also be in conflict with each other. A desire to put in extra hours at the office to "get ahead" may be in direct conflict with a desire to spend more time with one's family. Thus, given the changing nature of an individual's particular set of motives, and given their often conflicting nature, it becomes exceedingly difficult to observe or measure them with much certainty.

Third, considerable differences can exist among individuals concerning the manner in which they select certain motives over others and the intensity with which they pursue such motives. A salesperson who has a strong need for achievement may in large measure satisfy this need by one big sale and then turn his or her attention to other needs or desires. A second salesperson, however, may be spurred on by such a sale to increase his or her achievement motive and to try for an even bigger sale in the near future. Or, as found by Atkinson and Reitman (1956), a high need for achievement may be related to performance only when certain other needs (such as need for affiliation) were not aroused. In other words, it is important to realize that individual differences exist among employees which can significantly affect what they desire and how they pursue such desires.

A final complication of the model is the impact of goal attainment on subsequent motives and behavior. The intensity of certain motives (such as hunger, thirst, sex) is generally considerably reduced upon gratification. When this happens, other motives come to the forefront as primary motivating factors. However, the attainment of certain other goals may lead to an *increase* in the intensity of some motives. For example, as Herzberg, Mausner, and Snyderman (1959) and others have argued, giving a person a pay raise does not long "satisfy" the desire for more money; in fact, it may even heighten this desire. Similarly, promoting an employee to a new and more challenging job may intensify the drive to work harder in anticipation of the *next* promotion. Thus, while the gratification of certain needs, desires, and expectations may at times lead individuals to shift their focus of attention toward different motives, at other times such gratification can serve to increase the strength of the motive.

In conclusion, it must be remembered that the above description of motivational processes represents a very general model of human behavior. As will be seen in the following chapters, considerable research has been done in an attempt to more rigorously define the nature of the relationships between the major variables in this process, particularly as they relate to behavior in the work situation. We have reviewed this general model in an effort to provide a basic framework for the understanding and analysis of the more specific theories that follow. However, before proceeding with these theories, we shall first review very briefly some early psychological approaches to motivation, and then follow our review with a discussion of some traditional management approaches to motivating employees.

PSYCHOLOGICAL APPROACHES TO MOTIVATION

Most psychological theories of motivation, both early and contemporary, have their roots—at least to some extent—in the principle of *hedonism*.[1] This principle, briefly defined, states that individuals tend to seek pleasure and avoid pain. Hedonism assumes a certain degree of conscious behavior on the part of individuals whereby they make intentional decisions or choices concerning future actions. In theory, people rationally consider the behavioral alternatives available to them and act to maximize positive results and to minimize negative results. The concept of hedonism dates back to the early Greek philosophers; it later reemerged as a popular explanation of behavior in the eighteenth and nineteenth centuries, as seen in the works of such philosophers as Locke, Bentham, Mill, and Helvetius. Bentham even went so far as to coin the term "hedonic calculus" in 1789 to describe the process by which individuals calculate the pros and cons of various acts of behavior.

Toward the end of the nineteenth century, motivation theory began moving from the realm of philosophy toward the more empirically based science of psy-

---

[1]For a more detailed discussion of early psychological models of motivation, see Cofer & Appley (1964) and Atkinson (1964).

chology. As consideration of this important topic grew, it became apparent to those who attempted to use the philosophically based concept of hedonism that several serious problems existed. Vroom explained this dilemma as follows:

> There was in the doctrine no clear-cut specification of the type of events which were pleasurable or painful, or even how these events could be determined for a particular individual; nor did it make clear how persons acquired their conceptions of ways of attaining pleasure and pain, or how the source of pleasure and pain might be modified by experience. In short the hedonistic assumption has no empirical content and was untestable. Any form of behavior could be explained, after the fact, by postulating particular sources of pleasure or pain, but no form of behavior could be predicted in advance [1964, p. 10].

In an effort to fill this void, several theories of motivation began evolving which attempted to formulate empirically verifiable relationships among sets of variables which could be used to predict behavior. The earliest such theory centered on the concept of instinct.

Instinct Theories

While not rejecting the notion of hedonism, psychologists like James, Freud, and McDougall argued that a more comprehensive explanation of behavior was necessary than simply assuming a rational person pursuing his or her own best interest. In short, they posited that two additional variables were crucial to our understanding of behavior: instinct and unconscious motivation.

Instead of seeing behavior as being highly rational, these theorists saw much of it as resulting from instinct. McDougall, writing in 1908, defined an instinct as "an inherited or innate psychophysical disposition which determines its possessor to perceive, or pay attention to, objects of a certain class, to experience an emotional excitement of a particular quality upon perceiving such an object, and to act in regard to it in a particular manner, or at least, to experience an impulse to such an action." However, while McDougall saw instinct as purposive and goal-directed, other instinct theorists, like James, defined the concept more in terms of blind and mechanical action. James (1890) included in his list of instincts the following: locomotion, curiosity, sociability, love, fear, jealousy, and sympathy. Each person was thought by James and McDougall to have such instincts in greater or lesser degree and these instincts were thought to be the prime determinants of behavior. In other words, individuals were seen as possessing automatic *predispositions* to behave in certain ways, depending on internal and external cues.

The second major concept associated with instinct theories is that of unconscious motivation. While the notion of unconscious motivation is implicit in the writings of James, it was Freud (1915) who most ardently advocated the existence of such a phenomenon. On the basis of his clinical observations, Freud argued that the most potent behavioral tendencies were not necessarily those that individuals *consciously* determined would be in their best interests. Individuals were not always aware of all their desires and needs. Rather, such unconscious phenomena as dreams, slips of the tongue ("Freudian slips"), and neurotic symptoms were seen by Freud as manifestations of the hedonistic principle on an *unconscious* level. Thus, a major factor in human motivation was seen here as resulting from forces unknown even to the individual.

The instinct theory of motivation was fairly widely accepted during the first quarter of this century. Then, beginning in the early 1920s, it came under increasing attack on several grounds (Hilgard & Atkinson, 1967; Morgan & King, 1966). First, there was the disturbing fact that the list of instincts continued to grow, reaching nearly six thousand in number. The sheer length of such a list seriously jeopardized any attempt at parsimony in the explanation of motivation. Second, the contention that individuals varied greatly in the strengths or intensities of their motivational dispositions was becoming increasingly accepted among psychologists, adding a further complication to the ability of instinct theory to explain behavior fully. Third, some researchers found that at times there may be little relation between the strengths of certain motives and subsequent behavior. Fourth, some psychologists came to question whether the unconscious motives as described by Freud were really instinctive or whether they were *learned* behavior. In fact, this fourth criticism formed the basis of the second "school" of motivation theorists, who later became known as "drive" theorists.

Drive and Reinforcement Theories

Researchers who have been associated with drive theory typically base their work on the influence that learning has on subsequent behavior. Thus, such theories have a historical component, which led Allport (1954) to refer to them as "hedonism of the past"; that is, drive theories generally assume that decisions concerning present behavior are based in large part on the consequences, or rewards, of past behavior. Where past actions led to positive consequences, individuals would tend to repeat such actions; where past actions led to negative consequences or punishment, individuals would tend to avoid repeating them. This position was first elaborated by Thorndike in his "law of effect." Basing his "law" on experimental observations of animal behavior, Thorndike posited:

> Of several responses made to the same situation, those which are accompanied or closely followed by satisfaction to the animal will, other things being equal, be more firmly connected with the situation, so that when it recurs, they will be more likely to occur; those which are accompanied or closely followed by discomfort to the animal will, other things being equal, have their connections with that situation weakened, so that when it recurs, they will be less likely to occur. The greater the satisfaction or discomfort, the greater is the strengthening or weakening of the bond [1911, p. 244].

While this law of effect did not explain why some actions were pleasurable or satisfying and others were not, it did go a long way toward setting forth an empirically verifiable theory of motivation. Past learning and previous "stimulus-response" connections were viewed as the major causal variables of behavior.

The term "drive" was first introduced by Woodworth (1918) to describe the reservoir of energy that impels an organism to behave in certain ways. While Woodworth intended the term to mean a general supply of energy within an organism, others soon modified this definition to refer to a host of specific energizers (such as hunger, thirst, sex) toward or away from certain goals. With the introduction of the concept of drive, it now became possible for psychologists to predict in advance—at least in theory—not only what goals an individual would strive toward but also the strength of the motivation toward such goals. Thus, it became feasible for researchers to attempt to test the theory in a fairly rigorous fashion, a task that was virtually impossible for the earlier theories of hedonism and instinct.

A major theoretical advance in drive theory came from the work of Cannon in the early 1930s. Cannon (1939) introduced the concept of "homeostasis" to describe a state of disequilibrium within an organism which existed whenever internal conditions deviated from their normal state. When such disequilibrium occurred (as when an organism felt hunger), the organism was motivated by internal drives to reduce the disequilibrium and to return to its normal state. Inherent in Cannon's notion was the idea that organisms exist in a dynamic environment and that the determining motives for behavior constantly change, depending upon where the disequilibrium exists within the system. Thus, certain drives, or motives, may move to the forefront and then, once satisfied, retreat while other drives become paramount. This concept can be seen to a large extent in the later works of Maslow and Murray (see Chapter 2).

The first comprehensive—and experimentally specific—elaboration of drive theory was put forth by Hull. In his major work *Principles of Behavior*, published in 1943, Hull set down a specific equation to explain an organism's "impetus to respond": Effort = Drive × Habit. "Drive" was defined by Hull as an energizing influence which determined the intensity of behavior, and which theoretically increased along with the level of deprivation. "Habit" was seen as the strength of relationship between past stimulus and response (S-R). Hull hypothesized that habit strength depended not only upon the closeness of the S-R event to reinforcement but also upon the magnitude and number of such reinforcements. Thus, Hull's concept of habit draws very heavily upon Thorndike's "law of effect." Hull argued that the resulting effort, or motivational force, was a *multiplicative* function of these two central variables.

If we apply Hull's theory to an organization setting, we can use the following example to clarify how drive theory would be used to predict behavior. A person who has been out of work for some time (high deprivation level) would generally have a strong need or desire to seek some means to support himself or herself (goal). If, on the basis of *previous* experience, this person draws a close association between the securing of income and the act of taking a job, we would expect him or her to search ardently for employment. Thus, the motivation to seek employment would be seen, according to this theory, as a multiplicative function of the intensity of the need for money (drive) and the strength of the feeling that work has been associated with the receipt of money in the past (habit).

Later, in response to empirical evidence which was inconsistent with the theory, Hull (1952) modified his position somewhat. Instead of positing that behavior was wholly a function of antecedent conditions (such as past experiences), he added an incentive variable to his equation. His later formulation thus read: Effort = Drive × Habit × Incentive. This incentive factor, added in large measure in response to the attack by the cognitive theorists (see below), was defined in terms of anticipatory reactions to future goals. It was thus hypothesized that one factor in the motivation equation was the size of, or attraction to, future potential rewards. As the size of the reward varied, so too would the motivation to seek such a reward. This major revision by Hull (as amplified by Spence, 1956) brought drive theory into fairly close agreement with the third major category of motivational theories, the cognitive theories. However, while cognitive theories have generally been applied to humans, including humans at work, drive theory research has continued by and large to study animal behavior in the laboratory.

Just as drive theory draws upon Thorndike's "law of effect," so do modern reinforcement approaches (e.g., Skinner, 1953). The difference is that the former theory emphasizes an internal state (i.e., drive) as a necessary variable to take into account, while reinforcement theory does not. Rather, the reinforcement model places total emphasis on the *consequences* of behavior. Behavior initiated by the individual (for whatever reason) that produces an effect or consequence is called *operant* behavior (i.e., the individual has "operated" on the environment), and the theory deals with the contingent relationships between this operant behavior and the pattern of consequences. It ignores the inner state of the individual and concentrates solely on what happens to a person when he or she takes some action. Thus, strictly speaking, reinforcement theory is not a theory of motivation because it does not concern itself with what energizes or initiates behavior. Nevertheless, since a reinforcement approach provides a powerful means of analysis of what controls behavior (its direction and maintenance), it is typically considered in discussions of motivation and will be given prominent attention later in this book (Chapters 4 and 5).

Cognitive Theories

The third major line of development in psychological approaches to motivation is the cognitive theories. Whereas drive theories viewed behavior largely as a function of what happened in the past, cognitive theories saw motivation as a sort of "hedonism of the future." The basic tenet of this theory is that a major determinant of human behavior is the beliefs, expectations, and anticipations individuals have concerning future events. Behavior is thus seen as purposeful and goal-directed, and based on conscious intentions.

Two of the most prominent early researchers in this field were Edward Tolman and Kurt Lewin. While Tolman studied animal behavior and Lewin human behavior, both took the position that organisms make conscious decisions concerning future behavior on the basis of cues from their environment. Such a theory is largely *ahistorical* in nature, as opposed to the historical notion inherent in drive theory. Tolman (1932) argued, for example, that learning resulted more from changes in beliefs about the environment than from changes in the strengths of past habits. Cognitive theorists did not entirely reject the concept that past events may be important for present behavior, however. Lewin (1938), whose work is characterized by an ahistorical approach, noted that historical and ahistorical approaches were in some ways complementary. Past occurrences could have an impact on present behavior to the extent that they modified present conditions. For example, the past experience of a child who burned a finger on a hot stove may very likely carry over into the present to influence behavior. In general, however, the cognitive theorists posit that it is the "events of the day" that largely influence behavior; past events are important only to the extent that they affect present and future beliefs and expectations.

In general, cognitive theories, or expectancy/valence theories (also called "instrumentality" theories) as they later became known (see Chapter 3), view motivational force as a multiplicative function of two key variables: expectancies and valences. "Expectancies" were seen by Lewin (1938) and Tolman (1959) as beliefs individuals had that particular actions on their part would lead to certain outcomes. "Valence" denoted the amount of positive or negative value placed on the outcomes by an individual. Individuals were viewed as engaging in some form of choice behavior where they first determined the potential outcomes of various acts of behavior and the value they attached to each of these outcomes. Tolman (1959) refers to this as a "belief-value matrix." Next, individuals selected that mode of behavior which maximized their potential benefits. When put into equation form, such a formulation reads: Effort = Expectancy × Valence.

This conceptualization of the motivational process differs from drive theory in several respects. First, as has already been mentioned, while drive theory emphasizes past stimulus-response connections in the determination of present behavior, expectancy/valence theory stresses anticipation of response-outcome connections.

Second, as pointed out by Atkinson (1964), a difference exists between the two theories with regard to what is activated by a drive (in drive theory) or expectation (in expectancy/valence theory). In drive theory, the magnitude of the goal is seen as a source of *general* excitement; that is, it represents a nonselective influence on performance. In expectancy/valence theory, on the other hand, *positively* valent outcomes are seen as acting *selectively* to stimulate particular forms of behavior that should lead to these outcomes.

Third, a subtle difference exists concerning the nature in which outcomes and rewards acquire their positive or negative connotations. The difference has been described by Porter and Lawler as follows:

> For drive theory, this has traditionally come about through their ability to reduce the tension associated with the deprivation of certain physiologically based drives. It also states that some outcomes acquire their rewarding or adverse properties through their association with primary reinforcers. Outcomes that gain their values this way are typically referred to as secondary reinforcers. Expectancy theory has been much less explicit on this point. However, expectancy theorists seem typically to have included more than just physiological factors as determinants of valence. For example, needs for esteem, recognition, and self-actualization have been talked about by expectancy theory with explaining performance. Drive theory, on the other hand, has focused largely on learning rather than performance and has not found it necessary to deal with motives like self-actualization in order to explain this learning [1968, p. 11].

However, while several differences can thus be found between drive theories and cognitive theories, Atkinson (1964) has emphasized that the two approaches actually share many of the same concepts. Both stress the importance of some form of goal orientation; that is, both posit the existence of some reward or outcome that is desired and sought. Moreover, both theories include the notion of a learned connection between central variables; drive theory posits a learned stimulus-response association, while cognitive theories see a learned association between behavior and outcome.

Just as there has been an evolutionary process in psychological theories of motivation, so too have there been major developments and trends in the way managers in work organizations approach motivation in the work situation. With these general psychological theories in mind, we shall now shift our attention to the workplace and review some of these early managerial approaches to motivating employees. It will be noted in the discussion below that, although psychological and managerial models of motivation developed, roughly, during the same period, there are few signs of any cross-fertilization of ideas until relatively recently.

MANAGERIAL APPROACHES TO MOTIVATION

Despite the fact that large-scale, complex organizations have existed for several hundred years, managerial attention to the role of motivation in such organizations is a most recent phenomenon. Before the industrial revolution, the major form of "motivation" took the form of fear of punishment—physical, financial, or social. However, as manufacturing processes became more complex, large-scale factories emerged which destroyed many of the social and exchange relationships which had existed under the "home industries," or "putting-out," system of small manufacturing. These traditional patterns of behavior between workers and their "patron" were replaced by the more sterile and tenuous relationship between employees and their company. Thus, the industrial revolution was a revolution not only in a production sense but also in a social sense.

The genesis of this *social* revolution can be traced to several factors. First, the increased capital investment necessary for factory operation required a high degree of efficiency in order to maintain an adequate return on investment. This meant that an organization had to have an efficient work force. Second, and somewhat relatedly, the sheer size of these new operations increased the degree of impersonalization in superior-subordinate relationships, necessitating new forms of supervising people. Third, and partly as a justification of the new depersonalized factory system, the concept of social Darwinism came into vogue. In brief, this philosophy argued that no person held responsibility for other people and that naturally superior people were destined to rise in society, while naturally inferior ones would eventually be selected out of it. In other words, it was "every man for himself" in the workplace.

These new social forces brought about the need for a fairly well defined *philosophy* of management. Many of the more intrinsic motivational factors of the home industry system were replaced by more extrinsic factors. Workers—or, more specifically, "good" workers—were seen as pursuing their own best economic self-interests. The end result of this new approach in management was what has been termed the "traditional" model of motivation.

Traditional Model

This model is best characterized by the writings of Frederick W. Taylor (1911) and his associates in the scientific management school. Far from being exploitative in intent, these writers viewed scientific management as an economic boon to the worker as well as to management. Taylor saw the problem of inefficient production as a problem primarily with management, not workers. It was management's responsibility to find suitable people for a job and then to train them in the most efficient methods for their work. The workers having been thus well trained, management's next responsibility was to install a wage incentive system whereby workers could maximize their income by doing exactly what management told them to do and doing it as rapidly as possible. Thus, in theory, scientific management represented a joint venture of management and workers to the mutual benefit of both. If production problems arose, they could be solved either by altering the technology of the job or by modifying the wage incentive program.

This approach to motivation rested on several very basic contemporary assumptions about the nature of human beings. Specifically, workers were viewed as being typically lazy, often dishonest, aimless, dull, and, most of all, mercenary. To get them into the factories and to keep them there, an organization had to pay a "decent" wage, thus outbidding alternative forms of livelihood (e.g., farming). To get workers to produce, tasks were to be simple and repetitive, output controls were to be externally set, and workers were to be paid bonuses for beating their quotas. The manager's major task was thus seen as closely supervising workers to ensure that they met their production quotas and adhered to company rules. In short, the underlying motivational assumption of the traditional model was that, for a price, workers would tolerate the routinized, highly fractionated jobs of the factory. These assumptions and expectations, along with their implied managerial strategies, are summarized in Exhibit 2.

As this model became increasingly applied in organizations, several problems began to arise. To begin with, managers, in their quest for profits, began modifying the basic system. While jobs were made more and more routine and specialized (and "efficient" from a mass-production standpoint), management began putting severe constraints on the incentive system, thereby limiting worker income. Soon, workers discovered that, although their output was increasing, their wages were not (at least not proportionately). Simultaneously, fear of job security arose. As factories became more "efficient," fewer workers were needed to do the job and layoffs and terminations became commonplace. Workers responded to the situation through elaborate and covert methods of restriction of output in an attempt to optimize their incomes, while at the same time protecting their jobs. Unionism began to rise, and the unparalleled growth and efficiency that had occurred under scientific management began to subside.

In an effort to overcome such problems, some organizations began to reexam-

EXHIBIT 2
GENERAL PATTERNS OF MANAGERIAL APPROACHES TO MOTIVATION
(After Miles, Porter, & Craft, 1966)

Traditional model	Human relations model	Human resources model
Assumptions 1 Work is inherently distasteful to most people. 2 What they do is less important than what they earn for doing it. 3 Few want or can handle work which requires creativity, self-direction, or self-control.	Assumptions 1 People want to feel useful and important. 2 People desire to belong and to be recognized as individuals. 3 These needs are more important than money in motivating people to work.	Assumptions 1 Work is not inherently distasteful. People want to contribute to meaningful goals which they have helped establish. 2 Most people can exercise far more creative, responsible self-direction and self-control than their present jobs demand.
Policies 1 The manager's basic task is to closely supervise and control subordinates. 2 He or she must break tasks down into simple, repetitive, easily learned operations. 3 He or she must establish detailed work routines and procedures, and enforce these firmly but fairly.	Policies 1 The manager's basic task is to make each worker feel useful and important. 2 He or she should keep subordinates informed and listen to their objections to his or her plans. 3 The manager should allow subordinates to exercise some self-direction and self-control on routine matters.	Policies 1 The manager's basic task is to make use of "untapped" human resources. 2 He or she must create an environment in which all members may contribute to the limits of their ability. 3 He or she must encourage full participation on important matters, continually broadening subordinate self-direction and control.
Expectations 1 People can tolerate work if the pay is decent and the boss is fair. 2 If tasks are simple enough and people are closely controlled, they will produce up to standard.	Expectations 1 Sharing information with subordinates and involving them in routine decisions will satisfy their basic needs to belong and to feel important. 2 Satisfying these needs will improve morale and reduce resistance to formal authority — subordinates will "willingly cooperate."	Expectations 1 Expanding subordinate influence, self-direction, and self-control will lead to direct improvements in operating efficiency. 2 Work satisfaction may improve as a "by-product" of subordinates making full use of their resources.

ine the simplicity of their motivational assumptions about employees and to look for new methods to increase production and maintain a steady work force. It should be pointed out, however, that the primary economic assumption of the traditional model was not eliminated in the newer approaches and that it remains a central concept of many motivational approaches today. Recent studies among both managers and workers indicate that money is a primary motivational force and that many workers will, in fact, select jobs more on the basis of salary prospects than job content (Mahoney, 1964; Opinion Research Corporation, 1947; Opsahl & Dunnette, 1966). (See Chapter 6.) However, newer approaches have tended to view the role of money in more complex terms as it affects motivational force. Moreover, these newer theories argue that additional factors are also important inputs into the decision to produce. One such revisionist approach to motivation at work is the "human relations" model.

Human Relations Model

Beginning in the late 1920s, initial efforts were begun to discover why the traditional model was inadequate for motivating people. The earliest such work, carried out by Mayo (1933, 1945) and Roethlisberger and Dickson (1939), pointed the way to what was to become the human relations school of management by arguing that it was necessary to consider the "whole person" on the job. These researchers posited that the increased routinization of tasks brought about by the industrial revolution had served to drastically reduce the possibilities of finding satisfaction in the task itself. It was believed that, because of this change, workers began seeking satisfaction elsewhere (such as from their coworkers). On the basis of this early research, some managers began replacing many of the traditional assumptions with a new set of propositions concerning the nature of human beings (see Exhibit 2). Bendix (1956, p. 294) best summarized this evolution in managerial thinking by noting that the "failure to treat workers as human beings came to be regarded as the cause of low morale, poor craftsmanship, unresponsiveness, and confusion."

The new assumptions concerning the "best" method of motivating workers were characterized by a strong social emphasis. It was argued here that management had a responsibility to make employees *feel* useful and important on the job, to provide recognition, and generally to facilitate the satisfaction of workers' social needs. Attention was shifted away from the study of worker-machine relations and toward a more thorough understanding of interpersonal and group relations at work. Behavioral research into factors affecting motivation began in earnest, and morale surveys came into vogue in an attempt to measure and maintain job satisfaction. The basic ingredient that typically was *not* changed was the nature of the required tasks on the job.

The motivational strategies which emerged from such assumptions were several. First, as noted above, management felt it had a new responsibility to make workers feel important. Second, many organizations attempted to open up vertical communication channels so employees would know more about the organization and would have greater opportunity to have their opinions heard by management. Company newsletters emerged as one source of downward communication; employee "gripe sessions" were begun as one source of upward communication. Third, workers were increasingly allowed to make routine decisions concerning their own jobs. Finally, as managers began to realize the existence of informal groups with their own norms and role prescriptions, greater attention was paid to employing *group* incentive systems. Underlying all four of these developments was the presumed necessity of viewing motivation as largely a social process.

Supervisory training programs began emphasizing the idea that a supervisor's role was no longer simply that of a taskmaker. In addition, supervisors had to be understanding and sympathetic to the needs and desires of their subordinates. However, as pointed out by Miles (1965), the basic goal of management under this strategy remained much the same as it had been under the traditional model; that is, both strategies aimed at securing employee compliance with managerial authority.

Human Resources Models

More recently, the assumptions of the human relations model have been challenged, not only for being an oversimplified and incomplete statement of human behavior at work, but also for being as manipulative as the traditional model. These later models have been proposed under various titles, including McGregor's (1960) "Theory Y," Likert's (1967) "System 4," Schein's (1972) "Complex Man," and Miles' (1965) "Human Resources" model. We shall adopt the latter term here as being more descriptive of the underlying philosophy inherent in these newer approaches.

Human resources models generally view humans as being motivated by a complex set of interrelated factors (such as money, need for affiliation, need for achievement, desire for meaningful work). It is assumed that different employees often seek quite different goals in a job and have a diversity of talent to offer. Under this conceptualization, employees are looked upon as reservoirs of potential talent and management's responsibility is to learn how best to tap such resources.

Inherent in such a philosophy are several fairly basic assumptions about the nature of people. First, it is assumed that people want to contribute on the job. In this sense, employees are viewed as being somewhat "premotivated" to perform. In fact, the more people become involved in their work, the more meaningful the job can often become. Second, it is assumed that work does not necessarily have to be distasteful. Many of the current efforts at job enrichment and job redesign are aimed at increasing the potential meaningfulness of work by adding greater amounts of task variety, autonomy, responsibility, and so on. Third, it is argued that employees are quite capable of making significant and rational decisions affecting their work and that allowing greater latitude in employee decision making is actually in the best interests of the organization. Finally, it is assumed that this increased self-control and direction allowed on the job, plus the completion of more meaningful tasks, can in large measure determine the level of satisfaction on the job. In other words, it is generally assumed that good and meaningful performance leads to job satisfaction and not the reverse, as is assumed in the human relations model.

Certain implied managerial strategies follow naturally from this set of assumptions. In general, this approach would hold that it is management's responsibility to first understand the complex nature of motivational patterns. On the basis of such knowledge, management should attempt to determine how best to use the potential resources available to it through its work force. It should assist employees in meeting some of their own *personal* goals within the organizational context. Moreover, such a philosophy implies a greater degree of participation by employees in relevant decision-making activities, as well as increased autonomy over task accomplishment. Thus, in contrast to the traditional and human relations models, management's task is seen not so much as one of manipulating employees to accept managerial authority as it is of setting up conditions so that employees can meet their own goals at the same time as meeting the organization's goals.

In conclusion, it should be pointed out that the human resources approach to motivation has only lately begun to receive concentrated attention. Many organizations have attempted to implement one or more aspects of it, but full-scale adoptions of such models, including the multitude of strategic implications for managers, are still relatively rare. In fact, when one looks across organizations, it becomes readily apparent that all three models have their advocates, and empirical evidence supportive of a given approach can be offered in defense of one's preferred strategy. In recent years, in fact, the notion of a multiple strategy— using all three approaches at one time or another depending upon the nature of the organization, its technology, its people, and its goals and priorities—has come to be labeled a "contingency approach" to management. In effect, a contingency perspective allows one to dispense with the unlikely assumption that a single approach will be equally effective under any and all circumstances, and rather substitutes an emphasis on diagnosis of the situation to determine which approach will be most useful and appropriate under the *particular* circumstances.

A FRAMEWORK FOR ANALYSIS

Before proceeding to a consideration of some of the more highly developed or widely accepted contemporary theories of motivation, we should place this complex topic within some meaningful conceptual framework. Such a framework would serve as a vehicle not only for organizing our thoughts concerning human behavior at work but also for evaluating the ability of each of the theories that follows to deal adequately with all the factors in the work situation. In other words, it should provide a useful beginning for later analyses by pointing to several important factors to look for in the theoretical approaches that follow.

The conceptual model we wish to pose here (after Porter & Miles, 1974) consists of two parts. First, it assumes that motivation is a complex phenomenon that can best be understood within a multivariate framework: that is *several* important—and quite often distinct—factors must be taken into account when explaining motivational processes. Second, the model proposed here argues that these motivationally relevant factors must be viewed within a systems framework; we must concern ourselves with interrelationships and interactive effects among the various factors. It is our belief, then, that a full comprehension of the intricacies of human behavior at work requires the student of motivation to consider both parts of this equation: a multivariate conceptual approach and an integrating systems framework. Let us briefly examine each part of this proposed framework for analysis.

Multivariate Conceptual Approach

If motivation is concerned with those factors which energize, direct, and sustain human behavior, it would appear that a comprehensive theory of motivation at work must address itself to at least three important sets of variables which constitute the work situation. First, some consideration must be given to the characteristics of the individual; second, some thought should be directed toward the behavioral implications of the required job tasks; and third, some concern should be shown for the impact of the larger organizational environment. These three sets of variables, along with examples of each, are depicted in Exhibit 3.

Characteristics of the Individual   The natural starting point for discussing any theory of motivation is the nature of the individual. We are concerned with what the employee *brings to* the work situation. Considerable research (see, for example, Atkinson, 1964; Vroom, 1964) has demonstrated that differences in individuals can at times account for a good deal of the variance in effort and performance on a job. Thus, when we examine the factors constituting the motivational force equation, we must ask how large an input is made by these variations within people themselves. At least three major categories of individual difference characteristics have been shown to affect the motivational process: interests, attitudes, and needs.

"Interests" refers to the direction of one's attention. It appears likely that the nature of an employee's interest would affect both the manner and the extent to which external stimuli (like money) would affect behavior. Consider the example of two people working side by side on the same job and earning identical salaries. Person A is highly interested in the work; person B is not. In this example, person A can be seen as "self-motivated" to some degree because he or she is pursuing a central interest (his or her work), and we would expect this person to derive considerable satisfaction from the activity. If person A were offered a pay raise to take a less interesting job, he or she would be faced with making a decision on whether to keep the more interesting job or to earn more money, and it is not inconceivable that the intrinsic rewards of the present job would be motivation enough *not* to accept the transfer. Person B, however, who is not interested in the work, has no such conflict of choice in our simplified example; there is no motivation to stay on the present job and the added income of the new job could be a strong incentive for change. Some empirical research exists in support of our hypothetical example. Several studies have shown that an employee's motivation to participate (stay on the job) is to a large extent determined by the degree of fit between his or her vocational interests and the realities of the job. Thus, interests may be considered one factor that individuals generally bring to the organization that, at least to some extent, can affect how they behave at work.

In addition to interests, employees' attitudes or beliefs may also play an important role in their motivation to perform. Individuals who are very dissatisfied with their jobs, or with their supervisor, or any number of other things, may have little desire to put forth much effort. Several theories of motivation have encompassed the notion of attitudes as they relate to performance behavior at work. For exam-

EXHIBIT 3
VARIABLES AFFECTING THE MOTIVATIONAL PROCESS IN ORGANIZATIONAL SETTINGS
(After Porter & Miles, 1974)

I. Individual characteristics	II. Job characteristics (examples)	III. Work environment characteristics
1 Interests	Types of intrinsic rewards	1 Immediate work environment
2 Attitudes (examples)	Degree of autonomy	• Peers
		• Supervisor(s)
• Toward self	Amount of direct performance feedback	2 Organizational actions
• Toward job		• Reward practices
• Toward aspects of the work situation	Degree of variety in tasks	• Systemwide rewards
3 Needs (examples)		• Individual rewards
• Security		• Organizational climate
• Social		
• Achievement		

Note: These lists are not intended to be exhaustive, but are meant to indicate some of the more important variables influencing employee motivation.

ple, Korman (1970, 1971) has proposed a theory of motivation centering around one's attitudes about oneself (that is, one's self-image). This theory posits that individuals attempt to behave in a fashion consistent with their own self-image. If employees see themselves as failures on the job, they will not put forth much effort and their resulting performance will probably be poor. Such action will then reinforce the negative self-image. Two important points can be made here. First, various attitudes (in this case, attitudes about oneself) can play an important role in motivational force to perform. Second, in this example, there is a specific implied managerial strategy to improve employee effort: the manager should attempt to modify the employees' self-image. If the employees in our example were proud to work for the XYZ Company and if they saw themselves as effective contributors to the company's goals, they would, in theory, be more likely to perform at a higher level.

The individual characteristic that has received the most widespread attention in terms of motivation theory and research is the concept of "needs." A need may be defined as an internal state of disequilibrium which causes individuals to pursue certain courses of action in an effort to regain internal equilibrium. For example, individuals who have a high need for achievement might be motivated to engage in competitive acts with others so they can "win," thereby satisfying this need. The theories of Maslow and of McClelland and Atkinson use this concept of need as the basic unit of analysis. While further discussion of these types of theories is reserved for the following chapter, suffice it to say that variations in human needs can be significant factors in the determination of effort and performance.

Characteristics of the Job   A second set of variables to be considered when viewing the motivational process involves those factors relating to the attributes of an individual's job. We are concerned here with what an employee *does* at work. Factors such as the variety of activities required to do the job, the significance of the tasks, and the type of feedback one receives as a consequence of performing the job all have a role to play in motivation. Later in the book (Chapter 10) a model developed by Hackman and Oldham (1976) will be presented that attempts to provide a theoretical explanation of how these types of job-related variables interact to affect motivation and performance. Other parts of that chapter will provide additional evidence on the role that job design changes can play in determining employee behavior. In effect, whether jobs are designed well or poorly (from either the organization's or the employee's point of view), they are crucial in their impact on the motivational process in the work setting.

Characteristics of the Work Environment   The final set of variables under our analytical framework that appears to be relevant to the motivational process is concerned with the nature of the organizational, or work, environment. Work environment factors can be divided for our purposes into two major categories: those associated with the immediate work environment (the work group), and those associated with the larger problem of organizationwide actions. Both categories, however, focus primarily on *what happens to* the employee at work.

As indicated in Exhibit 3, there are at least two major factors in the immediate work environment that can affect work behavior. The first is the quality of peer-group interactions. Research dating from the Hawthorne studies (Roethlisberger & Dickson, 1939) indicates that peer-group influence can significantly influence an employee's effort. Such influence can occur at both ends of the productivity continuum: peers can exert pressure on "laggards" to contribute their fair share of output, or they can act to curb the high productivity of the "rate-buster." These considerations are discussed in Chapter 6. Similarly, supervisory or leadership style can influence effort and performance under certain circumstances. Immediate supervisors can play an important role in motivation because of their control over desired rewards (such as bonuses, raises, feedback) and because of their central role in the structuring of work activities. In other words, supervisors have considerable influence over the ability or freedom of employees to pursue their own personal goals on the job.

The second major category of work environment variables—organizationwide actions—are concerned with several factors which are common throughout the organization and are largely determined by the organization itself. Such factors would include both systemwide rewards (like fringe benefits) and individual rewards (such as overall salary system and allocation of status). Moreover, the emergent organizational climate that pervades the work environment would also fall into this category. Factors such as openness of communication, perceived relative emphasis on rewards versus punishment, degree of interdepartmental cooperation, and so forth, may at times influence individuals' decisions to produce on the job.

Interactive Effects

The foregoing discussion makes it apparent that a multitude of variables throughout the organizational milieu can be important inputs into the motivational force equation. Such a conclusion forces us to take a broad perspective when we attempt to understand or explain why employees behave as they do at work. However, this simple enumeration of motivationally relevant factors fails to recognize how these variables may interact with one another within a systems type of framework to determine work behavior. In other words, the second half of our conceptual framework stresses the fact that we must consider motivational models from a dynamic perspective. For example, an individual may have a strong desire to perform well on the job, but he or she may lack a clear understanding of his or her proper role. The employee may thus waste or misdirect effort and thereby fail to receive expected rewards. Similarly, an employee may truly want to perform at a high level, but simply lack the necessary ability for good performance on his or her particular job. The important point here is that, when viewing various approaches to motivation, it becomes clear that one must be aware of the interactive or "system" dynamics between major sets of variables that may influence resulting effort and performance.

Each of the theories of work motivation that will be considered in the following chapters has focused on *at least* one of these three major factors: the individual, the job, or the organizational environment. Several of the theories have included more than one factor. Moreover, some of the more highly developed models have placed such variables within a systems framework and have studied the interactive effects between the major sets of variables. Hopefully, the framework for analysis presented here will aid in understanding the pervasive nature of motivation and in evaluating the adequacy of each of the major theories to explain human behavior at work.

A note of caution is in order, however. When evaluating the theories and the research evidence that follow, the student of motivation must determine whether it is helpful to try to find the "one best way" to motivate individuals in the work situation or whether different approaches may be more or less relevant, depending upon the uses for which the theory is employed. That is, as with theories of management in general, both practicing managers and organizational researchers must decide whether they want to search for an ultimate universal theory of motivation which can be applied in all types of situations, or whether they want to adopt a contingency approach and select that theory which appears most pertinent to the specific problem at hand. In this connection, it is well to keep in mind that many of the theories, concepts, and approaches that will be discussed throughout the book are in fact complementary to one another, and therefore the search for understanding and for practical application is as much one of trying to seek out integration as it is one of making choices.

PLAN OF BOOK

In the selection that follows in this introductory chapter, Mitchell provides a relatively recent broad overview of current thinking about the field of motivation.

In particular, he briefly reviews the range of current theoretical approaches to motivation and some of the practical problems that are involved when organizations attempt to implement them in practice. He concludes with some guidelines and directions for future research. This article will give the reader additional perspectives on the field as a whole and will serve to highlight some important issues that need to be kept in mind when reading articles dealing with theory presented in Part Two.

The remainder of the book consists of three parts. Part Two introduces the student to major contemporary theories of motivation as they relate to the work situation. Each chapter includes an introductory section which lays the foundation for an understanding of the articles that follow. The particular articles within each chapter not only cover the theoretical propositions of each model but also review some of the research associated with each theory. The articles, when taken together, will, it is hoped, present both the strengths and the weaknesses of the various theories.

Part Three concentrates on the study of the relationship of motivation to various other important phenomena found in the work situation. Emphasis is placed on interrelationships among various factors (e.g., the relation between job design and motivation), and each chapter presents a broad survey of the relevant theories and research on the topic.

Finally, in Part Four we summarize and integrate what has been learned here. Consideration is given not only to how the various issues in motivation relate to one another but also to how they relate to the broader concerns of organizational behavior. The implications of such information for managerial practice are also discussed.

REFERENCES AND SUGGESTED ADDITIONAL READINGS

Allport, G. W. The historical background of modern social psychology. In G. Lindzey (Ed.), *Handbook of social psychology.* Cambridge, Mass.: Addison-Wesley, 1954.

Atkinson, J. W. *An introduction to motivation.* Princeton, N.J.: Van Nostrand, 1964.

Atkinson, J. W., & Reitman, W. R. Performance as a function of motive strength and expectancy of goal attainment. *Journal of Abnormal Social Psychology,* 1956, **53,** 361–366.

Bendix, R. *Work and authority in industry.* New York: Wiley, 1956.

Campbell, J. P., & Pritchard, R. D. Motivation theory in industrial and organizational psychology. In M. D. Dunnette (Ed.), *Handbook of industrial and organizational psychology.* Chicago: Rand McNally, 1976.

Cannon, W. B. *The wisdom of the body.* New York: Norton, 1939.

Cofer, C. N., & Appley, M. H. *Motivation: Theory and research.* New York: Wiley, 1964.

Dunnette, M. D., & Kirchner, W. K. *Psychology applied to industry.* New York: Appleton-Century-Crofts, 1965.

Freud, S. The unconscious. In *Collected papers of Sigmund Freud,* Vol. IV (First Published in J. Riviere, trans.). London: Hogarth, 1949. (1915.)

Hackman, J. R., & Oldham, G. R. Motivation through the design of work: Test of a theory. *Organizational Behavior and Human Performance,* 1976, **16,** 250–279.

Herzberg, F., Mausner, B., & Snyderman, B. B. *The motivation to work.* New York: Wiley, 1959.

Hilgard, E. R., & Atkinson, R. C. *Introduction to psychology.* New York: Harcourt, Brace & World, 1967.

Hull, C. L. *Principles of behavior.* New York: Appleton-Century-Crofts, 1943.

Hull, C. L. *A behavior system: An introduction to behavior theory concerning the individual organism.* New Haven, Conn.: Yale University Press, 1952.

James, W. *The principles of psychology,* Vols. I and II. New York: Henry Holt, 1890.

Jones, M. R. (Ed.) *Nebraska symposium on motivation.* Lincoln: University of Nebraska Press, 1955.

Katz, D. The motivational basis of organizational behavior. *Behavioral Science,* 1964, **9,** 131–146.

Katz, D., & Kahn, R. *The social psychology of organizations.* New York: Wiley, 1966.

Korman, A. K. Toward an hypothesis of work behavior. *Journal of Applied Psychology,* 1970, **54,** 31–41.

Korman, A. K. Expectancies as determinants of performance. *Journal of Applied Psychology,* 1971, **55,** 218–222.

Lewin, K. *The conceptual representation and the measurement of psychological forces.* Durham, N.C.: Duke University Press, 1938.

Likert, R. *The human organization.* New York: McGraw-Hill, 1967.

Mahoney, T. A. Compensation preference of managers. *Industrial Relations,* 1964, **3,** 135–144.

March, J. G., & Simon, H. A. *Organizations.* New York: Wiley, 1958.

Mayo, E. *The human problems of an industrial civilization.* New York: Macmillan, 1933.

Mayo, E. *The social problems of an industrial civilization.* Cambridge, Mass.: Harvard University Press, 1945.

McDougall, W. *An introduction to social psychology.* London: Methuen, 1908.

McGregor, D. *The human side of enterprise.* New York: McGraw-Hill, 1960.

Miles, R. E. Human relations or human resources? *Harvard Business Review,* 1965, **43**(4), 148–163.

Miles, R. E., Porter, L. W., & Craft, J. A. Leadership attitudes among public health officials. *American Journal of Public Health,* 1966, **56,** 1990–2005.

Morgan, C. T., & King, R. A. *Introduction to psychology.* New York: McGraw-Hill, 1966.

Opinion Research Corporation. *Public opinion index for industry,* 1947.

Opsahl, R. L., & Dunnette, M. D. The role of financial compensation in industrial motivation. *Psychological Bulletin,* 1966, **66,** 94–118.

Porter, L. W., & Lawler, E. E., III. *Managerial attitudes and performance.* Homewood, Ill.: Irwin, 1968.

Porter, L. W., & Miles, R. E. Motivation and management. In J. W. McGuire (Ed.), *Contemporary management: Issues and viewpoints.* Englewood Cliffs, N.J.: Prentice-Hall, 1974.

Roethlisberger, F., & Dickson, W. J. *Management and the worker.* Cambridge, Mass.: Harvard University Press, 1939.

Schein, E. *Organizational psychology.* Englewood Cliffs, N.J.: Prentice-Hall, 1972.

Skinner, B. F. *Science and human behavior.* New York: Macmillan, 1953.

Spence, K. W. *Behavior theory and conditioning.* New Haven, Conn.: Yale University Press, 1956.

Taylor, F. W. *Scientific management.* New York: Harper, 1911.

Thorndike, E. L. *Animal intelligence: Experimental studies.* New York: Macmillan, 1911.

Tolman, E. C. *Purposive behavior in animals and men*. New York: Appleton-Century-Crofts, 1932.

Tolman, E. C. Principles of purposive behavior. In S. Koch (Ed.), *Psychology: A Study of a science*, Vol. 2. New York: McGraw-Hill, 1959.

Vroom, V. H. *Work and motivation*. New York: Wiley, 1964.

Woodworth, R. S. *Dynamic psychology*. New York: Columbia University Press, 1918.

Motivation: New Directions for Theory, Research, and Practice

Terence R. Mitchell

Over the last five years various professional commitments have led this author to look at the field of motivation from both a theory-research perspective as well as a practical or applied perspective. The analysis of the theoretical and research literature has resulted in detailed and comprehensive review papers (Mitchell, 1979; Mitchell, in press). The attempts to deal with applications and implications were prompted by field research endeavors (Latham, Mitchell, & Dossett, 1978) and the writing and revision of a textbook (Mitchell, 1978). Several ideas have emerged from these activities.

First, from the reviews of motivation theory and research (Campbell & Pritchard, 1976; Korman, Greenhaus, & Badin, 1977; Locke, 1975; Staw, 1977), it became clear that some shifts in the field were occurring. The overwhelming percentage of current papers are concerned with information processing or social-environmental explanations of motivation (Salancik & Pfeffer, 1977, 1978) rather than need-based approaches or approaches that focus on individual differences. These latter approaches, represented by people like Maslow, have almost disappeared in the literature.

The information processing approaches are illustrated by the large amount of work on expectancy theory, goal setting, and equity theory. Theories focusing on the job environment, such as operant conditioning or job enrichment, and theories emphasizing social cues and social evaluations also have been important. These approaches have all been helpful in increasing the understanding of motivation.

A second trend, however, has not been so widely recognized. More specifically, when one reviews this research, it becomes readily apparent that most of the studies investigate only one theory in depth. Many studies set out to demonstrate that goal setting, operant conditioning, or expectancy theory work. In other cases the research is concerned with fine tuning the theory (e.g., Is participative or assigned goal setting better? Should expectancies be added to or multiplied by valences? Is a variable or continuous schedule of reinforcement best?). These questions are important, but few studies have been designed to integrate theories, to test them competitively, or to analyze the settings in which different theories work best.

Several issues also emerged from the practical experiences and attempts to summarize applied principles. First, there are some preliminary questions that must be answered and requirements that need to be met before implementing any motivational system. These questions and requirements revolve around (1) how people are evaluated and (2) the demands of the task. In other words, to apply motivational principles, one must do some preliminary work involving other organizational factors.

From *Academy of Management Review*, 1982, *7*, 80–88. Reprinted by permission.

Second, in attempting to apply motivational principles in an organization, one often runs into mitigating circumstances. There are situations and settings that make it exceptionally difficult for a motivational system to work. These circumstances may involve the kinds of jobs or people present, the technology, the presence of a union, and so on. The factors that hinder the application of motivational theory have not been articulated either frequently or systematically. The purpose of this paper is to review what is currently known about motivation, describe some theoretical areas in which ambiguity exists, and identify some situational constraints on the utilization of this knowledge.

The goal of this paper is not to provide a comprehensive source of references on the topic of motivation. Vast resources are already available for that purpose. There are whole books devoted to the topic (Korman, 1974; Lawler, 1973; Ryan, 1970; Vroom, 1964; Weiner, 1972), books of readings (McClelland & Steele, 1973; Steers & Porter, 1979; Tosi, House, & Dunnette, 1972), and many review articles (Campbell & Pritchard, 1976; Korman et al., 1977; Locke, 1975; Mitchell, 1979; Staw, 1977). The material and principles discussed in this paper will be dealt with at a fairly global level. This is not to say that the ideas are not supportable or that a detailed level of analysis is not important. In most cases, at least one representative citation will be provided. However, the objective of the paper is to stimulate debate and interest in some issues about motivation that (1) have been said infrequently or (2) have recently emerged and need to be highlighted.

BACKGROUND

Many nonacademics would probably describe motivation as the degree to which an individual wants and tries hard to do well at a particular task or job. Dictionary definitions describe motivation as the goad to action. The more technical definitions given by social scientists suggest that motivation is the psychological processes that cause the arousal, direction, and persistence of behavior (Atkinson, 1964; Campbell, Dunnette, Lawler, & Weick, 1970; Huse & Bowditch, 1977; Kast & Rosenzweig, 1979; Korman, 1974; Luthans, 1977). Many authors add a voluntary component or goal directed emphasis to that definition (Hellriegel & Slocum, 1976; Lawler, 1973; Ryan, 1970; Vroom, 1964). Thus motivation becomes those psychological processes that cause the arousal, direction, and persistence of voluntary actions that are goal directed.

Although there is some disagreement about the importance of different aspects of this definition (e.g., whether arousal or choice is more important), there is consensus about some underlying properties of this definition. First, motivation traditionally has been cast as an *individual* phenomenon. Each individual is unique and all of the major motivational theories allow in one way or another for this uniqueness to be demonstrated (e.g., different people have different needs, expectations, values, attitudes, reinforcement histories, and goals). Second, motivation usually is described as *intentional*. That is, motivation supposedly is under the employee's control. Most behaviors that are seen as influenced by motivation (e.g., effort on the job) typically are viewed as actions the individual has chosen to do.

A third point is that motivation is *multifaceted*. The two factors of greatest importance have been the arousal (activation, energizers) and direction (choice) of behavior. The question of persistence has been of minor importance, partly because the issue of maintenance of behavior (once it is started and directed) has received less attention and partly because some authors have defined persistence simply as the reaffirmation of the initial choice of action (March & Simon, 1958).

The arousal question has focused on what gets people activated. What are the circumstances that arouse people so they want to do well? The second question, that of choice, deals with the force on the individual to engage in desired behaviors. Given that the person is aroused, what gets them going in a particular direction? These distinctions are reflected in much of the writing on motivation.

The fourth point to make is that the purpose of motivational theories is to predict *behavior*. Motivation is concerned with action and the internal and external forces that influence one's choice of action. Motivation is not the behavior itself, and it is not performance. The behavior is the criterion—that which is chosen. And in some cases the chosen action will be a good reflection of performance. But the psychological processes, the actual behavior, and performance are all different things, and the confusion of the three frequently has caused problems in analysis, interpretation, and application.

So, given these elaborations, a definition of motivation becomes somewhat more detailed. Motivation becomes the degree to which an individual wants and chooses to engage in certain specified behaviors. Different theories propose different reasons, but almost all of them emphasize an individual, intentional choice of behavior analysis.

PRELIMINARY QUESTIONS

Given that one understands what motivation is, the next question concerns why it is important to management. Most organizations function under the principle of rationality (Scott & Hart, 1979). That is, the primary goal of management is to increase efficiency by getting the greatest output at the lowest cost. Therefore, any behaviors that contribute to greater efficiency will be actions that management will want to encourage. These actions might be coming to work, being punctual, or exerting a lot of effort. Because these behaviors often are assumed by management to be motivated—voluntary choices controlled by the individual—management often establishes what it calls a motivational system. This system is intended to influence the factors that cause the behavior in question.

The important point to make is that one must be clear in distinguishing between this motivation system and the definition of motivation as a cognitive, individual, intentional phenomenon. The motivational system is imposed from the outside. It is constructed according to the assumptions held by management about (1) what behaviors are important for effectiveness and (2) the factors that influence these behaviors. To make sure these assumptions are correct, some preliminary work should be done before any system is tried.

Performance Appraisal

Although many organizational factors contribute to effectiveness, such as turnover, absenteeism, and technology, probably the factor that is described as most important and one that management feels it can influence is job performance. Job performance typically is viewed as partially determined by the motivation to work hard and, therefore, increases in motivation should result in greater effort and higher performance. However, to have any idea about the effects of a motivational system, one must have a good performance appraisal instrument. Changes in performance must be detectable and demonstrable. There is not enough space to go into the merits of various appraisal procedures (Kane & Lawler, 1979; Kavangh, 1981; Landy & Farr, 1980), but there are some generalizations that can be made about appraisal and its relationship to motivation.

First, it goes without question that a both reliable and valid system is needed— not only for issues of motivation but for issues of selection, promotion, counseling, and adherence to legal guidelines. In short, a second appraisal device is necessary for many personnel functions.

But besides the methodological properties of the device, there are some substantive issues as well. The more closely a performance appraisal device fits with the definition of motivation, the easier it will be to assess the effects of motivational interventions or strategies. More specifically, if performance is defined in behavioral and individual terms and so is motivation, then the concepts and their measures show correspondence. They are less likely to be confounded by other factors.

This distinction is very important. Some appraisals use group or team goals as performance criteria as opposed to individual performance. Also, some appraisals emphasize outcomes (policies sold) as opposed to behavior (clients visited). The further away one gets from individual behavior, the more difficult it is to infer directly and unambiguously a change in motivation rather than a change in performance.

To some extent, however, the type of appraisal may be dictated by the technology or task with which people are engaged. In some cases group performance or outcomes may be the best one can do. This is a point that will be covered later, but at this juncture it is sufficient to mention that (1) a good performance appraisal device is necessary and (2) the closer this device is to measuring individual behavior, the easier it is to evaluate the effects of motivational systems or technologies introduced by management.

Factors Influencing Performance

Given that a good performance appraisal system is in place and that it measures individual behavior, the next question is: Does motivation make a difference for performance? Many years ago Vroom suggested the equation: performance = ability × motivation; and somewhat later the term role perceptions was added to the right side of that equation (Porter & Lawler, 1968). More recently, Campbell and Pritchard (1976) expanded that definition to performance = f(aptitude level × skill level × understanding of the task × choice to expend effort ×

choice of degree of effort × choice to persist × facilitating and inhibiting conditions not under the control of the individual). These authors recognized that performance is caused by at least four and maybe more factors. In order to do well one must (1) know what is required (role expectations), (2) have the ability to do what is required, (3) be motivated to do what is required, and (4) work in an environment in which intended actions can be translated into behavior.

The implication is that there probably are some jobs for which trying to influence motivation will be irrelevant for performance. These circumstances can occur a variety of ways. There may be situations in which ability factors or role expectation factors are simply more important than motivation. For example, the best predictor of high school grades typically is intellectual endowment, not hours spent studying. In a paper entitled "Performance Equals Ability and What," Dunnette concluded that "ability differences still are empirically the most important determiners of differences in job performance" (1973, p. 22). Some of the problems referred to in this quote pertain to inadequate performance measures or poorly articulated theories of motivation, but part of the problem is that performance on some tasks simply is controlled more by ability than by motivation.

Another circumstance may occur in which performance is controlled by technological factors. For example, on an assembly line, given that minimally competent and attentive people are there to do the job, performance may not vary from individual to individual. Exerting effort may be irrelevant for performance.

One way to gain information about these issues is through a thorough job analysis. This type of analysis can help to determine what behaviors contribute to performance and the extent to which these behaviors are controlled voluntarily (motivated) or controlled by ability factors, social factors, or technology. Except for some recent work by Hackman (Hackman & Morris, 1975; Hackman & Oldham, 1980), this in infrequently discussed.

The implications of the points about job analysis, performance appraisal, and the factors that contribute to performance appraisal, and the factors that contribute to performance boil down to one crucial point: *Performance is not the same as motivation.* If one wants to assess changes in motivation or the influence of interventions on motivation, then one must measure motivation and its contribution to behavior. If performance is assessed globally or nonbehaviorally, then performance is not a good indicator of motivation. Even when performance is individually and behaviorally assessed, motivation may control substantially less than 100 percent of the variance in performance. That is, behaviors may be jointly determined by ability and motivation or some other combination of factors. When either of these two circumstances is true, the researcher or practitioner should seek to define and assess motivation separately. This point is infrequently recognized (Lawler, 1973) and almost never practiced.

In summary, before any motivation system is installed, one must be sure (a) that there is a good performance appraisal system available, (b) that motivation is an important contributor to performance, and (c) that where motivation clearly is not the major contributor to performance, a separate measure of motivation or of behaviors clearly caused by motivation is developed. When these three conditions are not being met, there is little point in pursuing the topic further. If they do exist, then one has the opportunity to put into practice what has been learned from previous research on motivation.

RESEARCH REVIEW

As mentioned earlier, theories of motivation typically are concerned with the questions of arousal and behavioral choice. The purpose of a review of these topics is not to criticize the different motivational theories. All of them have revealed some aspects of motivation that have empirical support. But some of the *factors controlling behavior* that they emphasize are more or less applicable in various situations. It is hoped that an understanding of these mitigating circumstances can serve as an initial step in developing contingency models of motivation: models that describe when and where certain motivational systems will be most effective.

Theories of Arousal

The most popular theories of arousal for many years have been those that emphasize needs. Theories that emphasize individual needs (e.g., need achievement) or groups of needs (e.g., need hierarchies) all postulate that the arousal process is due to need deficiencies. That is, people want certain things in their jobs and they will work to fulfill those needs.

The major implications of this research have been two-fold. First, these theories clearly recognize and make central the idea of individual differences (Alderfer, 1977). Different people are motivated by different things. The second widely accepted point is that organizations generally have overlooked upper level needs. The works of such people as Maslow, McGregor, Herzberg, and Alderfer all suggest that, in general, organizations spend much more time being concerned with the fulfillment of lower level needs (e.g., through motivational systems emphasizing pay, hours of work, and the physical setting) than with the fulfillment of upper level needs (e.g., through systems emphasizing autonomy, recognition, creativity, and variety).

In recent years there has been a shift away from these need-based theories of arousal (Salancik & Pfeffer, 1977, 1978; Weiner, 1972) to approaches that emphasize processes such as social facilitation or evaluation apprehension (Ferris, Beehr, & Gilmore, 1978). These theories suggest that people are aroused by the presence of others and the knowledge that other people are evaluating them. The social cues in the form of expectations given off by subordinates, co-workers, and supervisors become important causes of arousal.

Other current approaches emphasize some ideas of cognitive inconsistency—for example, Korman's (1976) work on self-esteem—or the match between task related needs and the characteristics of the job. An example of this latter approach is Hackman and Oldham's (1980) theory of job enrichment suggesting that an enriched job is motivating only for those who have high needs for growth.

What almost all of these theories emphasize in one way or another is that arousal is seen as (1) current and (2) highly related to the social or task environment. Thus, instead of deep-seated needs developed a long time ago that reside solely within the individual, a much more external and present frame of reference is emerging. Central to almost all of the new approaches is the idea that the individual cognitively processes and evaluates a lot of information and that motivation is linked strongly to this information processing activity.

In summary, the arousal theories say (1) attend to individual differences, (2) try to attend to upper level (intrinsic) needs, (3) note that social expectations have powerful effects, and (4) note that current information is extremely important. In attempting to implement these ideas, however, difficulties often arise. Some of these obstructions are as follows.

First, there is a whole set of organizational factors that make it difficult to individualize rewards and emphasize upper level intrinsic needs. The larger the organization and the more heterogeneous the work force, the more difficult it becomes. Ideally one would like to let employees have some choice in their compensation—for example, cafeteria style plans (Lawler, 1976)—and let managers have greater flexibility in the administration of rewards. But in practice these strategies are hard to implement. Dealing with unions also tends to restrict this flexibility because their striving for equity often leads to solidifying reward systems rather than increasing the latitude of management.

The theories that focus on social cues and expectations require that people be observed and that management have some influence on social norms. One idea that strives to let evaluation apprehension operate at the appropriate level is to match the level of appraisal with those people who most frequently observe the work of the individual. So, for example, if supervisors do not directly observe the work of subordinates, but co-workers or their subordinates do observe this individual, then have peer or subordinate evaluations be part of the appraisal process.

Influencing social norms is more problematical. Factors like organizational climate are known to be important, and processes such as team building may help to instill norms or expectations for hard work. However, very little theory or research exists that uses these norms as dependent variables. This is an area for further work.

In summary, some important things have been learned about arousal as an individualized process and one that is frequently related to current social cues. However, practical limitations such as organization size, unions, or heterogeneity of personnel may limit attempts to implement the knowledge. Also, further work is needed on understanding how one can influence social norms and expectations.

Theories of Choice

The major theories of behavioral choice are goal setting, expectancy theory, operant conditioning, and equity theory. The research on goal setting is quite clear. People work harder with goals than without goals. This is especially true if the goals are specific and difficult and if feedback exists (Locke, 1978; Steers & Porter, 1974; Yukl & Latham, 1978). The areas of ongoing research emphasize such issues as whether participative or assigned goal setting works best, whether rewards directly influence motivation, or whether they influence motivation by changing the level of the goal.

Expectancy theory and operant conditioning are very different in underlying philosophy (cognitive versus noncognitive), but they generate similar principles of application. Both approaches argue that (1) rewards should be closely tied to behavior, (2) reward administration should be frequent and consistent, and (3) people are motivated by outcomes (expected or past).

Reviews of expectancy theory (Connolly, 1976; Mitchell, 1980; Schwab, Olian-Gottlieb, & Heneman, 1979) and operant conditioning or social learning (Babb & Kopp, 1978; David & Luthans, 1980) are available. People doing research on both theories are concerned with issues that have to do with how to tie rewards to behavior, what sorts of schedules to use, how to measure various theoretical components, and so on. But, except for some minor disagreements (Mawhinney & Behling, 1973), the approaches are in agreement about principles of application.

Equity theory (Carrell & Dittrich, 1978; Goodman, 1977) suggests that people are motivated by a desire for fairness. When they believe they are being treated unfairly, they will behave in ways that they believe will restore their sense of equity. Although overreward (getting more than one should) and underreward (getting less than one should) are similar from a theoretical perspective, the research suggests otherwise. People are more comfortable (less likely to change their behavior) with overreward than with underreward. If people feel that they are underrewarded and can do little about directly influencing their rewards, they are liable to be dissatisfied, work less, and be absent more frequently than when they feel that they are being treated equitably.

Without getting into detailed analyses, one can point out some important differences and similarities between these approaches. The most striking difference is the basic underlying motivational mechanism postulated as the cause of behavior. There are (1) intentions to reach a goal, (2) expectations of maximum payoff, (3) past reinforcement histories, and (4) a desire for fairness. The similarities are that all four approaches define motivation as an individual, intentional process. Also, except for the operant approach, all three of the others focus on relatively current information processing. In this respect, the arousal and choice models seem to be headed in a similar direction. Finally, three of the models define motivation as directly influenced by outcomes (expectancy, operant, and equity approaches); goal setting sees outcomes as indirectly influencing motivation through goal level and intentions.

In order to utilize the information generated from these approaches, one must be able to set specific individual goals, tie rewards to individual behavior, and treat people fairly and equitably. As usual, this is easier said than done. A number of circumstances or situations make it difficult to implement these ideas.

One major problem is that many jobs involve considerable interdependence (Lawler, 1973). People frequently must work with others in order for the job to be accomplished successfully. This interdependence often makes it difficult to specify or tease out individual contributions. To the extent to which there is failure to assess individual behavioral contributions accurately, there will be trouble with individual goal setting and reward administration. Either group goals or rewards may be used.

A second important factor is observability. Individual feedback and reward administration both depend on the extent to which one knows what employees are doing. In many cases, people work alone, or in relatively isolated situations (e.g., within offices, on the road). To the extent that there is poor information about what people actually do, there will be difficulty with implementation.

A third problem has to do with change. In certain situations, jobs and people change fairly rapidly. The changes in jobs may be due to changes in technology, and the changes in people may be due to turnover. Note, again, that motivation emphasizes an individualized behavioral approach. Changes in jobs and people necessitate changes in the motivation system in the form of different behaviors to observe and different rewards to administer.

Finally, the heterogeneity of jobs causes difficulty as well. Each different type of job ideally should require a different job description, different behaviors, and, therefore, different reward systems. These last two points focus on the compromise often required in implementing motivational principles. In many cases people or jobs must be lumped together. However, it should be recognized that, to the extent to which there is deviation from the individual behavioral conceptualization of motivation, there probably will be a reduction in the effectiveness of the motivational program and the ability to measure its impact.

DISCUSSION

An analysis of both the theory and practice described above results in some important statements about where research on the topic of motivation should go from here. In terms of theoretical development, it appears as if three things are needed.

First, more integration is needed. Except for a few papers—for example, Locke (1978); and Wofford (1979)—very little theoretical work has been done to suggest the additive or interactive effects of the various approaches. The empirical studies that do compare or combine approaches suggest that combining various factors can lead to an increase in motivation. For example, a paper by White, Mitchell, and Bell (1977) demonstrates that evaluation apprehension, goal setting, and social pressure all have significant effects on motivation and that these effects might be additive.

A second implication that follows the above line of reasoning is that contingency type models of motivation need to be developed and tested. More specifically, the question is no longer whether goal setting or operant approaches work, it is where and when they work best. The mitigating circumstances that were described make it more difficult for one theory to work than another. For example, social cues and evaluation apprehension may increase in importance with interdependence, and goal setting and expectancy or operant approaches may become less feasible. With interdependence comes more social interaction and the chance to observe the behavior of others. Social cues and evaluation apprehension should be more salient. On the other hand, interdependence may make it more difficult to specify individual contributions and reward them. At this point there is almost nothing in the literature that suggests when and where different motivational strategies will be most appropriate.

The third issue complements the other two. Because many jobs are, in fact, interdependent, social, and subject to change, more theory and research needs to be generated on how group processes effect motivation. Strategies such as team building or other interventions designed to increase commitment and motivation need to be studied as motivational models. An understanding is needed of the effects of such interventions on motivated behaviors and how these behaviors contribute to performance. It is hoped that more attention to the above issues will result in a more comprehensive understanding of not only the causes of motivation, but how and when and where different strategies should be used.

Hand in hand with these changes in theory and research should come changes in practice. One of the first things that should be developed is a set of diagnostic questions that any manager should ask about the motivational process. A flow chart or decision tree could be developed such as the one presented in Exhibit 1. To some extent this looks like the Vroom and Yetton (1973) model. Unfortunately, the Vroom and Yetton model is vastly superior in its level of detail, analysis, and support. For example, the weighting of factors 3 through 7 in Exhibit 1 is still unknown. There is little to guide one as to the order in which to ask the questions. But, more importantly, there is little guidance about what to do if the answers to 3 through 7 are yes. If what people do can be observed, if various rewards can be utilized, and if rewards can be tied to individual behavior without concern for social pressures or changes in the job, then systems are available that are ready to go. However, the situation is more ambiguous if the reverse of these conditions holds. The knowledge about how to influence motivation when correct behaviors are hard to define and observe, constantly

EXHIBIT 1
A FLOW DIAGRAM OF QUESTIONS ABOUT MOTIVATION

---

1 Can performance be defined in individual, behavioral terms? If not, develop a separate measure of motivation.
2 Is motivation important for performance, or are abilities and situational factors more important? If motivation is important, but not the same as performance, develop a separate measure of motivation.
If one cannot meet the requirements of questions 1 and 2, it may not be worth it to proceed further. If, however, motivation is important for performance and performance is a good reflection of motivation or a good measure of motivation exists, then proceed with the analysis.
3 Is the reward system rigid and inflexible? In other words, are people and tasks grouped into large categories for reward purposes?
4 Is it difficult to observe what people are actually doing on the job?
5 Is an individual's behavior dependent heavily on the actions of others?
6 Are there lots of changes in people, jobs, or expected behavior?
7 Are social pressures the major determinants of what people are doing on the job?
If questions 3 through 7 are answered with a no, then some system combining a needs analysis with goal setting, operant, expectancy, and equity ideas should be effective.

---

changing, and under the control of interdependencies or social pressures is severely limited.

The obvious implication for the practitioner is that the cost of implementing one of the more traditional motivation systems (e.g., MBO, behavior modification) might outweigh the benefit under these latter conditions. Until there are better answers to the question of how to influence motivation when these conditions exist, it will be difficult to develop any sort of comprehensive strategy for enhancing motivation. Thus, although the focus of current research is coming to recognize the importance of social processes, changes in jobs or people (Katz, 1980), and problems in flexibility and ability to give feedback (Ilgen, Fisher, & Taylor, 1979; Nadler, 1979), few remedies for these problems have been developed. Until this is done, a substantial inadequacy will remain in the ability to understand and influence motivation on the job.

REFERENCES

Alderfer, C. P. A critique of Salancik and Pfeffer's examination of need satisfaction theories. *Administrative Science Quarterly*, 1977, 22, 658–669.

Atkinson, J. W. *An introduction to motivation*. Princeton, N. J.: Van Nostrand, 1964.

Babb, H. W., & Kopp, D. G. Applications of behavior modification in organizations: A review and critique. *Academy of Management Review*, 1978, 3, 281–290.

Campbell, J. P., & Pritchard, R. D. Motivation theory in industrial and organizational psychology. In M. D. Dunnette (Ed.), *Handbook of industrial and organizational psychology*. Chicago: Rand McNally, 1976, 62–130.

Campbell, J. P., Dunnette, M. D., Lawler, E. E., III, & Weick, K. E., Jr. *Managerial behavior, performance, and effectiveness*. New York: McGraw-Hill, 1970.

Carroll, M. R., & Dittrich, J. E. Equity theory: The recent literature, methodological considerations, and new directions. *Academy of Management Review*, 1978, 3, 202–210.

Connolly, T. Some conceptual and methodological issues in expectancy models of work performance motivation. *Academy of Management Review*, 1976, 1 (4), 37–47.

Davies, T. R. V., & Luthans, F. A social learning approach to organizational behavior. *Academy of Management Review*, 1980, 5, 281–290.

Dunnette, M. D. Performance equals ability and what? Center for the Study of Organizational Performance and Human Effectiveness, University of Minnesota, Technical Report No. 4009, Minneapolis, 1973.

Ferris, G. R., Beehr, T. A., & Gilmore, D. C. Social facilitation: A review and alternative conceptual model. *Academy of Management Review*, 1978, 3, 338–347.

Goodman, P. S. Social comparison process in organizations. In B. M. Staw & G. R. Salancik (Eds.), *New directions in organizational behavior* (Vol. 1). Chicago: St. Clair Press, 1977, 97–132.

Hackman, J. R., & Morris, G. G. Group tasks, group interaction process, and group performance effectiveness. In L. Berkowitz (Ed.), *Advances in experimental social psychology* (Vol. 7). New York: Academic Press, 1975.

Hackman, J. R., & Oldham, G. R. *Work redesign*. Reading, Mass.: Addison-Wesley, 1980.

Hellriegel, D., & Slocum, J. W., Jr. *Organizational behavior: Contingency views.* St. Paul, Minn: West Publishing, 1976.

Huse, E. F., & Bowditch, J. L. *Behavior in organizations: A systems approach to managing.* Reading, Mass.: Addison-Wesley, 1977.

Ilgen, D. R., Fisher, C. D., & Taylor, M. S. Consequences of individual feedback on behavior in organizations. *Journal of Applied Psychology*, 1979, 64, 349–371.

Kane, J. S., & Lawler, E. E. Performance appraisal effectiveness: Its assessment and determinants. In B. Staw (Ed.), *Research in organizational behavior* (Vol. 1). Greenwich, Conn.: JAI Press, 1979, 425–478.

Kast, F. E., & Rosenzweig, J. E. *Organization and management: A systems approach.* New York: McGraw-Hill, 1979.

Katz, R. Time and work: Toward an integrative perspective. In B. M. Staw & L. L. Cummings (Eds.), *Research in organizational behavior* (Vol. 2). Greenwich, Conn.: JAI Press, 1980, 81–128.

Kavanagh, M. J. Performance appraisal. In K. Rowland & G. Ferris (Eds.), *Personnel management.* Boston, Mass.: Allyn and Bacon, 1981.

Korman, A. K. *The psychology of motivation.* Englewood Cliffs, N. J.: Prentice-Hall, 1974.

Korman, A. K. Hypothesis of work behavior revisited and an extension. *Academy of Management Review*, 1976, 1 (1), 50–63.

Korman, A. K., Greenhaus, J. H., & Badin, I. J. Personnel attitudes and motivation. *Annual Review of Psychology*, 1977, 28, 175–196.

Landy, F. J., & Farr, J. L. Performance rating. *Psychological Bulletin*, 1980, 87, 72–107.

Latham, G. P., Mitchell, T. R., & Dossett, D. L. The importance of participative goal setting and anticipated rewards on goal difficulty and job performance. *Journal of Applied Psychology*, 1978, 63, 163–171.

Lawler, E. E., III. *Motivation in work organizations.* Monterey, Cal.: Brooks/Cole, 1973.

Lawler, E. E., III. New approaches to pay administration. *Personnel*, 1976, 53, 11–23.

Locke, E. A. Personnel attitudes and motivation. *Annual Review of Psychology*, 1975, 26, 457–480.

Locke, E. A. The ubiquity of the techniques of goal setting in theories and approaches to employee motivation. *Academy of Management Review*, 1978, 3, 594–601.

Luthans, F. *Organizational behavior.* New York: McGraw-Hill, 1977.

March, J. G., & Simon, H. A. *Organizations.* New York: Wiley, 1958.

Mawhinney, T. C., & Behling. O. Differences in predictions of work behavior from expectancy and operant models of individual motivation. *Proceedings of the Academy of Management*, 1973, 383–388.

McClelland, D. C., & Steele, R. S. *Human motivation: A book of readings.* Morristown, N. J.: General Learning Press, 1973.

Mitchell, T. R. Organizational behavior. *Annual Review of Psychology*, 1979, 30, 243–281.

Mitchell, T. R. Expectancy-value models in organizational psychology. In N. Feather (Ed.), *Expectancy, incentive and action.* Hillsdale, N. J.: Erlbaum and Associates, 1980.

Mitchell, T. R. Motivational strategies. In K. Rowland & G. Ferris (Eds.), *Personnel management.* Boston, Mass.: Allyn and Bacon, in press.

Mitchell, T. R. *People in organizations: Understanding their behavior.* New York: McGraw-Hill, 1978.

Nadler, D. A. The effects of feedback on task group behavior: A review of the experimental research. *Organizational Behavior and Human Performance*, 1979, 23, 309–338.

Porter, L. W., & Lawler, E. E., III. *Managerial attitudes and performance*. Homewood, Ill.: Dorsey, 1968.

Ryan, T. A. *Intentional behavior: An approach to human motivation*. New York: Ronald Press, 1970.

Salancik, G. R., & Pfeffer, J. An examination of need satisfaction models of job attitudes. *Administrative Science Quarterly*, 1977, 22, 427–456.

Salancik, G. R., & Pfeffer. J. A social information processing approach to job attitudes and task design. *Administrative Science Quarterly*, 1978, 23, 224–253.

Schwab, D. P., Olian-Gottlieb, J. D., & Heneman, H. G., III. Between subjects expectancy theory research: A statistical review of studies predicting effort and performance. *Psychological Bulletin*, 1979, 86, 139–147.

Scott, W. G., & Hart, D. K. *Organizational America*, Boston: Houghton Mifflin, 1979.

Staw, B. M. Motivation in organizations: Toward synthesis and redirection. In B. M. Staw & G. R. Salancik (Eds.), *New directions in organizational behavior* (Vol. 1). Chicago: St. Clair Press, 1977, 54–95.

Steers, R. M., & Porter, L. W. The role of task-goal attributes in employee performance. *Psychological Bulletin*, 1974, 81, 434–452.

Steers, R. M., & Porter, L. W. *Motivation and work behavior*. New York: McGraw-Hill, 1979.

Tosi, H. L., House, R. J., & Dunnette, M. D. *Managerial motivation and compensation: A selection of readings*. East Lansing, Mich.: MSU Business Studies, 1972.

Vroom, V. H. *Work and motivation*. New York: Wiley, 1964.

Vroom, V. H., & Yetton, P. W. *Leadership and decision making*. Pittsburgh: University of Pittsburgh Press, 1973.

Weiner, B. *Theories of motivation: From mechanism to cognition*. Chicago: Rand McNally, 1972.

White, S., Mitchell, T. R., & Bell, C. H. Goal setting, evaluation apprehension and social cues as determinants of job performance and job satisfaction in a simulated organization. *Journal of Applied Psychology*, 1977, 62, 665–673.

Wofford, J. C. A goal-energy-effort requirement model (GEER) of work motivation. *Academy of Management Review*, 1979, 4, 193–201.

Yukl, G. A., & Latham, G. P. Interrelationships among employee participation, individual differences, goal difficulty, goal acceptance, instrumentality and performance. *Personnel Psychology*, 1978, 31, 305–324.

QUESTIONS FOR DISCUSSION

1 Exactly what is meant by the term "motivation"?

2 Describe the basic motivational process.

3 What similarities are there in the development of psychological theories of motivation compared with the development of managerial theories? What differences?

4 What are the basic differences between drive or reinforcement models of motivation and cognitive models? Which approach seems more applicable to motivation in work settings?

5 What is the real difference between the human resources model and the earlier human relations model?

6 What value is there from a managerial standpoint in taking a comprehensive approach to motivational problems, as suggested in this chapter?

7 Why do many people casually equate motivation with performance? Can you think of situations where the two variables would be virtually equivalent?

8 Think of a job situation with which you are familiar and use it to answer questions 3 to 7 in Mitchell's flow diagram (Exhibit 1). Which question was the toughest to answer? Why?

PART TWO

THEORETICAL APPROACHES TO MOTIVATION

NEED THEORIES
OF MOTIVATION

One of the most pervasive notions in the area of work motivation has been the concept of human needs. This concept can be found as an element of other, more complex, models of work motivation, and it is often utilized in typical descriptions of work situations, for example, the case of an employee who is seen by others in the organization as having a high need for achievement, only a moderate need for power, or a low need for affiliation. Although need theories are currently not generating a great deal of research (as Mitchell noted in the article in Chapter 1), they still represent a potentially useful way of attaining a broader and deeper understanding of the complex phenomenon that we call "motivation." As noted in Chapter 1, they focus on what the individual *brings to* the work situation. For these reasons, we devote a chapter to an examination of the major need theories.

Several need theories can be identified in the literature. Of primary importance here are three such models, those of Maslow, Alderfer, and Murray. All three of these models, while differing in some respects, argue that human needs represent the primary driving force behind employee behavior in organizational settings. Let us briefly examine each of these models.

MASLOW'S NEED HIERARCHY THEORY

One of the most popular theories of work motivation today is Abraham Maslow's need hierarchy theory. From the time of its introduction in the mid-1940s until the late 1950s, the theory remained primarily in the realm of clinical psychology, where Maslow did most of his developmental work. As more attention began to be focused on the role of motivation at work, however, the need hierarchy theory emerged in the early 1960s as an appealing model of human behavior in organizations. Largely because of the popularization of the model by Douglas McGregor

(1967), this theory became widely discussed and used by both organizational psychologists and managers.

Maslow's model consists of two fundamental premises. The first premise states that individuals are primarily "wanting" creatures, motivated by a desire to satisfy certain specific types of needs. On the basis of his clinical observations, Maslow (1943, 1954) posited that most individuals pursue with varying intensities the following needs:

1 *Physiological needs* These needs are thought to be the most basic needs and include the needs for food, water, and sex.

2 *Safety needs* The second set of needs centers around the need to provide a safe and secure physical and emotional environment, an environment that is free from threats to continued existence.

3 *Belongingness needs* These needs relate to one's desire to be accepted by one's peers and to develop friendship.

4 *Esteem needs* Esteem needs focus on one's desire to have a positive self-image and to receive recognition, attention, and appreciation from others for one's contributions.

5 *Self-actualization needs* The highest need category is the need for self-actualization. Here the individual is concerned primarily with developing his or her full potential as an individual and with becoming all that it is possible to become.

According to Maslow, those needs that are largely unsatisfied tend to create tension within people that leads them to behave in ways that are aimed at reducing the tension and restoring internal equilibrium. Once a certain need or set of needs becomes satisfied, it loses its potency as a motivating force until it again becomes manifest (or activated). For instance, when a person's physiological needs (say, for food) have been met, they will no longer motivate behavior until the person again becomes hungry. Until such time, according to Maslow, the individual would be motivated by other needs. In other words, many of these needs are cyclical. In this regard, the model is similar to other "need" theories of motivation and personality (such as Murray's theory).

Unique to Maslow, however, is his second fundamental premise. Specifically, Maslow argues that the needs which individuals pursue are universal across various populations and that they are arranged sequentially in hierarchical form. That is, once the lower-order needs are satisfied, the individual moves up the hierarchy one level at a time and attempts to satisfy the next higher-order needs.

Parenthetically, it is of interest to note that Maslow (1954) discussed two additional needs in his earlier work: cognitive and aesthetic. *Cognitive* needs are the needs to know and understand. Examples of cognitive needs include the need to satisfy one's curiosity and the desire to learn. *Aesthetic* needs include the desire to move toward beauty and away from ugliness. These two needs were not included in Maslow's hierarchical arrangement, however, and have generally been omitted from discussions of his concepts as they relate to organizational settings.

ALDERFER'S MODIFIED NEED HIERARCHY THEORY

In response to criticism of the original formulation (see the selection by Wahba and Bridwell), Clayton Alderfer has proposed a modified need hierarchy theory that essentially collapses Maslow's five hierarchical levels into three. This model has become known as the ''ERG theory'' (or existence-relatedness-growth theory). Specifically, Alderfer (1969) suggests the following three need levels:

1 *Existence needs* These needs include those required to sustain human existence. Therefore, this category would include both physiological and safety needs.

2 *Relatedness needs* This category concerns how people relate to their surrounding social environment and includes the needs for meaningful social and interpersonal relationships.

3. *Growth needs* This category, thought to be the highest need category, includes the needs for self-esteem and self-actualization.

In general, then, Alderfer suggests that individuals move up the hierarchy from existence needs to relatedness needs to growth needs, as the lower-level needs become satisfied. In this respect, Alderfer's model is quite similar to that proposed by Maslow.

Alderfer's theory differs from Maslow's original formulation, however, in two important respects. First, Maslow argued that progression from one level in the hierarchy to the next was based on the satisfaction of the lower-order need; hence, individuals progress up the hierarchy as a result of satisfaction. Alderfer's ERG theory, in contrast, suggests that in addition to this satisfaction-progression process, there is also a frustration-regression process, as shown in Exhibit 1. That is, when an individual is continually frustrated in attempts to satisfy growth needs, relatedness needs may reemerge as primary and the individual may redirect his or her efforts toward these lower-order needs.

A second major difference is that unlike Maslow's original formulation, Alder-

EXHIBIT 1
Satisfaction-progression, frustration-regression components of ERG theory (Landy & Trumbo, 1980, p. 341).

Need Frustration	Desire Strength	Need Satisfaction

Key

Satisfaction-progression ————

Frustration-regression — — — —

fer's model suggests that more than one need may be operative, or activated, at the same time. This assumption suggests a less rigid model of the motivational process and bears a resemblance in this regard to Murray's manifest needs model.

MURRAY'S MANIFEST NEEDS THEORY

In addition to the models of Maslow and Alderfer, there is a third theory· which uses the concept of human needs as the basic unit of analysis. This is Murray's manifest needs theory. This model had its origin in the early work of Henry A. Murray and his associates at the Harvard Psychological Clinic during the 1930s. On the basis of several years of clinical observations, Murray (1938) wrote his classic *Explorations in Personality*, in which he argued that individuals could be classified according to the strengths of various personality-need variables. These needs were believed to represent a central motivating force, in terms of both the intensity and the direction of goal-directed behavior. A need was defined as "a construct . . . which stands for a force . . . in the brain region, a force which organizes perception, apperception, intellection, conation and action in such a way as to transform in a certain direction an existing, unsatisfying situation" (1938, p. 123). A somewhat briefer definition has been offered by McClelland (1971, p. 13): "a recurrent concern for a goal state." Needs were not something that could be observed by the researcher. On the contrary, Murray (1938, p. 54) stated that the analysis of such needs was "a hypothetical process, the occurrence of which is imagined in order to account for certain objective and subjective facts." In other words, one could only *infer* needs from observed behavior.

Moreover, needs were viewed as largely learned behavior—rather than innate tendencies—which was activated by cues from the external environment. This conception closely resembles the concepts of "motive" and "drive" and can be likened to a state of disequilibrium. According to Murray, each need was composed of two factors: (1) a qualitative or directional component, which represents the object toward which the motive is directed, and (2) a quantitative or energetic component, which represents the strength of intensity of the motive toward the object.

While much of the research attention relating to this theory has concerned the need for achievement, it is important to point out that Murray viewed an individual's personality as being composed of many divergent, and often conflicting, needs which had the potential of motivating human behavior. This list of needs included the needs for achievement, affiliation, power, autonomy, nurturance, and deference (see Exhibit 2). Thus, for example, individuals with a strongly aroused need for achievement would typically attempt to engage in activities where they could excel and accomplish something important to them. According to this model, needs may be manifest ("activated") or latent. To say that a need is latent does not imply that the need is not strong, but only that it has been inhibited and has found no overt form of expression. Thus, a person may have a high need for achievement, but such a need may not be strongly aroused because of impediments in the environment (such as the lack of a challenging task). The result would theoretically be poor performance. If sufficient arousal of the need

EXHIBIT 2
MURRAY'S NEEDS

Need	Characteristics
Achievement	Aspires to accomplish difficult tasks; maintains high standards and is willing to work toward distant goals; responds positively to competition; willing to put forth effort to attain excellence.
Affiliation	Enjoys being with friends and people in general; accepts people readily; makes efforts to win friendships and maintain associations with people.
Aggression	Enjoys combat and argument; easily annoyed; sometimes willing to hurt people to get his or her way; may seek to "get even" with people perceived as having harmed him or her.
Autonomy	Tries to break away from restraints, confinement, or restrictions of any kind; enjoys being unattached, free, not tied to people, places, or obligations; may be rebellious when faced with restraints.
Endurance	Willing to work long hours; doesn't give up quickly on a problem; persevering, even in the face of great difficulty; patient and unrelenting in his or her work habits.
Exhibition	Wants to be the center of attention; enjoys having an audience; engages in behavior which wins the notice of others; may enjoy being dramatic or witty.
Harm avoidance	Does not enjoy exciting activities, especially if danger is involved; avoids risk of bodily harm; seeks to maximize personal safety.
Impulsivity	Tends to act on the "spur of the moment" and without deliberation; gives vent readily to feelings and wishes; speaks freely; may be volatile in emotional expression.
Nurturance	Gives sympathy and comfort; assists others whenever possible; interested in caring for children, the disabled, or the infirm; offers a "helping hand" to those in need; readily performs favors for others.
Order	Concerned with keeping personal effects and surroundings neat and organized, dislikes clutter, confusion, lack of organization; interested in developing methods for keeping materials methodically organized.
Power	Attempts to control the environment and to influence or direct other people; expresses opinions forcefully; enjoys the role of leader and may assume it spontaneously.
Succorance	Frequently seeks the sympathy, protection, love, advice, and reassurance of other people; may feel insecure or helpless without such support; confides difficulties readily to a receptive person.
Understanding	Wants to understand many areas of knowledge; values synthesis of ideas, verifiable generalization, logical thought, particularly when directed at satisfying intellectual curiosity.

Source: Adapted from D. N. Jackson, *Personality Research Form Manual.* Goshen, N.Y.: Research Psychologists Press, 1967.

were attained (by providing a challenging job), we would expect the resulting drive to energize achievement-oriented behavior.

While Murray was concerned with an entire set of needs, most current research in this area has focused on the specific need for achievement, particularly as it relates to performance in organizational settings. (Some recent research has also been carried out on the needs for power and affiliation.) The two most prominent contemporary investigators in the need for achievement (abbreviated "*n Ach*") research are David C. McClelland and John Atkinson. McClelland and Atkinson view the achievement motive as a relatively stable predisposition to strive for success. More specifically, *n Ach* is defined as "behavior toward competition with a standard of excellence" (McClelland, Atkinson, Clark, & Lowell, 1953). The basis or reward for such a motive is posited to be the positive affect associated with successful performance. McClelland, Atkinson, and their associates present a series of primarily laboratory studies indicative of a strong positive relation between high need for achievement and high levels of performance and executive success (Atkinson & Feather, 1966; McClelland, 1951; McClelland et al., 1953). More recent studies both in the field and in the laboratory have tended to support such a conclusion. However, Cofer and Appley (1964, p. 374) caution that "the theory McClelland and his coworkers have developed is neither compelled by nor directly derived from their data, but is presumably consistent with the data."

IMPLICATIONS FOR MANAGEMENT

Although Maslow's original concern centered on the development of a model that was generally descriptive of the relation between motivation and personality, he later focused his attention specifically on the motivational problems of employees in work settings (Maslow, 1965). When the need hierarchy concept is applied to work organizations, the implications for managerial actions become obvious. Managers have the responsibility, according to this line of reasoning, to create a "proper climate" in which employees can develop to their fullest potential. This proper climate might include increasing the opportunities for greater autonomy, variety, responsibility, and so forth, so that employees could work toward higher-order need satisfaction. Failure to provide such a climate would theoretically increase employee frustration and could result in poorer performance, lower job satisfaction, and increased withdrawal from the organization.

Somewhat similarly, the achievement motivation model of Murray, McClelland, and Atkinson focuses largely on individual characteristics as they relate to motivational force. The implicit managerial strategy here would be to design the work environment so that it "cues" the achievement motive. Hence, as noted in the selection by Steers in this chapter, high *n Ach* employees should be given challenging work assignments. Such assignments provide them with opportunities to accomplish something with a standard of excellence, thereby leading to need satisfaction. On the other hand, other motivational strategies may be more appropriate for motivating those with low needs for achievement.

In addition, some research suggests that need for achievement can influence the relationship between performance and job satisfaction (Steers, 1975). Specifically, it was found in one study among managers that a fairly strong relationship existed between performance and satisfaction for employees high in need for achievement. No such relationship was found for low *n Ach* employees. These findings suggest that good performance represents one form of need satisfaction for high *n Ach* employees, thus leading to feelings of general job satisfaction. For low *n Ach* employees, on the other hand, other needs (such as for affiliation or power) are probably more important, and there is little reason to believe that good performance would necessarily help satisfy these other needs. One implication of these findings concerns supervisory style. That is, low *n Ach* employees may require closer supervision than high *n Ach* employees because high *n Ach* employees are motivated by need level to perform. They are ''self-motivated.'' Other techniques (e.g., closer supervision and incentive systems) may be necessary to a greater extent to ensure good task performance for low *n Ach* employees.

Finally, in a separate field study, it was found that managers who have a high need for achievement also tend to be more participative; that is, they tend to allow their subordinates to have a greater voice in decisions affecting their jobs (Steers, 1977). No such findings emerged for employees with high needs for affiliation or power. This suggests that when successful task accomplishment requires the coordinated efforts of several people (such as in a research laboratory), it would be important to select a group manager who had a high need for achievement and who would work through others to ensure task accomplishment.

OVERVIEW

Two readings follow. The first, by Wahba and Bridwell, outlines the basic premises of Maslow's model as well as relevant research on the model. It concludes by analyzing the conceptual and methodological difficulties involved in empirically testing the theory. The second selection, by Steers, summarizes the basic propositions of Murray's manifest needs theory. Particular emphasis is given to the managerial implications of need theories of motivation.

REFERENCES

Alderfer, C. P. A new theory of human needs. *Organizational Behavior and Human Performance*, 1969, **4**, 142–175.

Alderfer, C. P. *Existence, relatedness, and growth.* New York: Free Press, 1972.

Atkinson, J. W., & Feather, N. T. *A theory of achievement motivation.* New York: Wiley, 1966.

Cofer, C. N., & Appley, M. H. *Motivation: Theory and research.* New York: Wiley, 1964.

Landy, F., & Trumbo, D. *Psychology and work behavior.* Homewood, Ill.: Dorsey, 1980.

Maslow, A. H. A theory of human motivation. *Psychological Review*, 1943, **50**, 370–396.

Maslow, A. H. *Motivation and personality.* New York: Harper, 1954.

Maslow, A. H. *Eupsychian management.* Homewood, Ill.: Irwin, 1965.

McClelland, D. C. *Personality.* New York: Dryden Press, 1951.

McClelland, D. C., Atkinson, J. W., Clark, R. A., & Lowell, E. L. *The achievement motive*. New York: Appleton-Century-Crofts, 1953.

McClelland, D. C. & Winter, D. G. *Motivating economic achievement*. New York: Free Press, 1971.

McGregor, D. *The professional manager*. New York: McGraw-Hill, 1967.

Murray, H. A. *Explorations in personality*. New York: Oxford University Press, 1938.

Steers, R. M. Effects of need for achievement on the job performance–job attitude relationship. *Journal of Applied Psychology*, 1975, **60**, 678–682.

Steers, R. M. Antecedents and outcomes of organizational commitment. *Administrative Science Quarterly*, 1977, **22**, 46–56.

Maslow Reconsidered: A Review of Research on the Need Hierarchy Theory

Mahmoud A. Wahba
Lawrence G. Bridwell

PURPOSE AND BACKGROUND

Maslow's Need Hierarchy Theory [references 21; 22; 24] presents the student of work motivation with an interesting paradox: the theory is widely accepted, but there is little research evidence to support it. Since Maslow first published his theory thirty years ago, it has become one of the most popular theories of motivation in the management and organizational behavior literature. Furthermore, the theory has provided an a priori conceptual framework to explain diverse research findings. [26] Such widespread acceptance of the Need Hierarchy Theory is rather surprising in light of the fact that until the mid-sixties [1; 7; 14] little empirical evidence existed that tested predictions of the theory. It has become a tradition for writers to point out the discrepancy between the popularity of the theory and the lack of clear and consistent empirical evidence to support it. [6; 9; 10; 30]

Recently, the interest in Maslow's Need Hierarchy Theory has been revived, due to the publication of a number of empirical studies testing some predictions of the theory. As yet, however, no known review of the literature compares and integrates the findings of these studies. The purpose of this paper is to review and evaluate the empirical research related to Maslow's Need Hierarchy Theory, thereby assessing the empirical validity of the theory itself.

Several constraints were imposed on this review. First, the review will deal only with the test of Maslow's theory in the work situation. [For a review of the empirical evidence in other situations, see reference 10.] Second, this review will include only studies that used statistical rather than clinical methodology. [25] Third, this review will deal only with what is considered to be the core or the main elements of Maslow's theory as it relates to work motivation.

MASLOW'S NEED HIERARCHY THEORY: A BRIEF DESCRIPTION

Part of the appeal of Maslow's Need Hierarchy Theory is that it provides both a theory of human *motives* by classifying basic human needs in a hierarchy, and a theory of *human motivation* that relates these needs to general behavior. As a theory of motives or needs, Maslow proposed that basic needs are structured in a hierarchy of prepotency and probability of appearance. The hierarchy of needs is as follows (in ascending order of prepotency): the physiological needs, the safety needs, the belongingness or love needs, the esteem needs, and the need for self-actualization.

As a theory of motivation, Maslow utilized the two concepts of deprivation and

From *Proceedings of the Thirty-third Annual Meeting of the Academy of Management*, 1973, pp. 514–520. Reprinted by permission of the Academy of Management and the authors.

gratification to provide the dynamic forces that linked needs to general behavior. He used the deprivation concept to establish "dominance" within his hierarchy of needs. He postulated that deprivation or dissatisfaction of a need of high prepotency will lead to the domination of this need over the organism's personality.

Following the satisfaction of a dominating need, the second element of the dynamic force in Maslow's Theory will then take place. Relative gratification of a given need submerges it and "activates" the next higher need in the hierarchy. The activated need then dominates and organizes the individual's personality and capacities so that instead of the individual's being hunger obsessed, he now becomes safety obsessed.

This process of deprivation → domination → gratification → activation continues until the physiological, safety, affiliation, and esteem needs have all been gratified and the self-actualization need has been activated. In a later work [23], Maslow modified the gratification/activation idea by proposing that gratification of the self-actualization need causes an increase in its importance rather than a decrease. Maslow also acknowledged numerous exceptions to his theory. Notably, he pointed out that long deprivation of a given need may create a fixation for that need. Also, higher needs may emerge not after gratification, but rather after long deprivation, renunciation, or suppression of lower needs. Maslow emphasized again and again that behavior is multi-determined and multi-motivated. From this general approach Maslow dealt with a wide range of consequences to his theory.

The present paper will review the research literature that attempted to test Maslow's theory or parts of it. The review will be divided into three related sections, each section dealing with one main element of Maslow's Need Hierarchy Theory. These elements are:

1 Maslow's Need Classification scheme;
2 The Deprivation/Domination proposition;
3 The Gratification/Activation proposition.

Maslow's Need Classification Scheme

Most of the research dealing with Maslow's need classification scheme has utilized factor analytic techniques. In the literature, eight factor analytic studies attempted explicitly to test Maslow's need classification scheme. These studies raised three related questions:

1 Does the factor analysis yield five factors that can be interpreted conceptually in terms of Maslow's five need categories?
2 Are Maslow's need categories independent from each other or do they overlap? What is the pattern of overlapping? Is the overlapping between adjacent or non-adjacent categories?
3 Are Maslow's need categories independent from supposedly unrelated items or factors?

The samples in these studies were composed of various groups (professionals, nonprofessionals, students, managers, males, and females) and four different measuring scales were used. A modified Porter [27] Need Satisfaction Question-naire (NSQ) was the research instrument in four studies. Although it was designed basically to reflect Maslow's need classification scheme, the NSQ appears to suffer from a number of methodological problems particularly due to response bias. Subjects filling out the instrument give the fulfillment and importance ratings almost simultaneously. This produces a high correlation between fulfillment and importance. [3] Also, Lawler and Suttle [19] pointed out that the correlations among the NSQ items in the same category were not high and that all items correlated with each other. As a result the NSQ may not accurately reflect Maslow's need classification scheme.

Three researchers [3; 5; 17] used three different scales. Huizinga's 24-item questionnaire appears to be the best designed scale for several reasons. One, it reflects all of Maslow's categories including the physiological needs. Two, the questionnaire is oriented to work motivation in general rather than being specific to the employee's present job. The questions were placed in the context of how important each of the items would be in the respondent's evaluation of *any* job. Unlike the NSQ, this minimizes the situational aspects of the current job affecting the answers of respondents. Three, it contains both positive and negative items to reflect the concepts of gratification and deprivation. Fourth, the scale was well validated by various methods. However, the scale did have one weakness; no reliability figures were reported.

The following conclusions can be drawn from the results of the factor analytic studies testing Maslow's need classification scheme.

1 None of the studies has shown *all* of Maslow's five need categories as independent factors. Only Beer's study showed four independent factors reflecting four needs; the fifth need overlapped with an unrelated factor.

2 In some studies, lower-order needs and higher-order needs clustered together independently from each other.

3 Self-actualization needs emerged as an independent factor in some studies, and in other studies, they overlapped with other need categories.

4 Two studies using two samples each showed no support for Maslow's need categories.

Another type of evidence related to the test of Maslow's need classification scheme comes from studies that attempted to classify human needs empirically by factor analysis techniques without an a priori theoretical framework. [8; 12; 28] These studies do not show need categories similar to those proposed by Maslow.

Taken together, the empirical results of the factor analytic studies provide no consistent support for Maslow's need classification as a whole. There is no clear evidence that human needs are classified into five distinct categories, or that these categories are structured in a special hierarchy. Some evidence exists for possibly two types of needs, higher- and lower-order needs, even though this categorization is not always operative. Self-actualization needs may emerge as an independent category. However, it is not possible to assess from the studies reviewed whether self-actualization is, in fact, a need or simply a social desirability response resulting from certain cultural values. [6] There is some empirical evidence to substantiate this latter conclusion. [17]

The Deprivation/Domination Proposition

The deprivation/domination proposition is closely related to the gratification/acti-vation proposition. Consequently, some studies have provided a test of both prop-ositions at the same time. However, to allow for careful examination of both prop-ositions, it was decided to review each proposition independently.

The deprivation/domination proposition can be interpreted as follows: the higher the deprivation or deficiency of a given need, the higher its importance, strength, or desirability. Deficiency is usually measured as the difference between what is expected and what is attained. The evidence to test this proposition is derived from two groups of studies. The first group of studies utilizes the Porter NSQ in the measurement of job satisfaction, and the second group of studies investigates the relationship between satisfaction and the judged importance of environmental and job characteristics.

The samples for the first group of studies consisted mostly of managers. These studies utilized the Porter NSQ or a modified variation of it. Although these stud-ies were not originally designed to test Maslow's ideas, they provide the neces-sary data to test the deprivation/domination proposition. In particular, these stud-ies present a measure of need deficiency and a measure of need importance. According to Maslow's theory, the most deficient need should be the most domi-nant or important need. Consequently, the rank in order of both need deficiency and need importance should correspond to each other. In particular, the most deficient need should be ranked as the most important need. The results generally showed that the deprivation/domination proposition is partially supported with regard to self-actualization and autonomy needs; but the results do not support the proposition with regard to security, social and esteem needs. Findings of other studies utilizing different scales or methodologies are generally consistent with the Porter type studies. [1; 2; 3; 14; 17; 19; 29] These studies show directly or indi-rectly that the proposition of deprivation/domination is not always supported.

It is difficult to assess whether the higher order needs (autonomy and self-actualization) are ranked more important in the Porter type studies because they are deficient, or reported deficient because they are important. Some evidence for the latter conclusion comes from another group of studies dealing with satisfaction and the judged importance of environmental and job characteristics. Two studies [13; 20] showed a V-curve relationship between satisfaction and judged impor-tance. That is, the higher the satisfaction *or* the dissatisfaction, the higher the ranked importance. Another study [11] showed that this relationship is limited to cases where a Likert-type scale is used. Under an alternative scale of measure-ment (e.g., Job Descriptive Index) only high satisfaction is correlated to impor-tance which is the opposite of Maslow's hypothesis. These studies indicate that the issue of need deprivation and the domination of behavior may not be as simple as suggested by Maslow.

The Gratification/Activation Proposition

The gratification/activation proposition has been mostly operationalized in two ways:

1 Need satisfaction should be generally decreasing going up in the Maslow need hierarchy:
2 The higher the satisfaction with a given need:
  a the lower the importance of the need, *and*
  b the higher the importance of the need at the next level of the hierarchy.

Several studies that used the original or modified version of the NSQ provide a test of the idea that need satisfaction should decrease going up in Maslow's need hierarchy. The samples consisted mostly of managers and also included professionals and workers. The results indicate that either self-actualization or security are the least satisfied needs, and social needs are the most satisfied. The degree of satisfaction of other needs varies widely: it is difficult to determine their general pattern. These trends are not in agreement with those proposed by Maslow.

Four cross-sectional studies explicitly tested the proposition, the higher the satisfaction with a given need, the lower the importance of this need *and* the higher the importance of the need at the next level in the hierarchy. Two studies [29; 32] produced findings opposite to Maslow's proposition. Two others [2; 3] showed limited support for individual needs of the hierarchy, and no support for other needs.

Two longitudinal studies [14; 19] also tested the gratification/activation proposition. The longitudinal studies are based on the assumption that changes in need satisfaction and need strength or importance can only be studied over time using longitudinal data. The proposition tested is that the satisfaction of needs in one category should correlate negatively with the importance of these same needs and positively with the importance of needs in the next higher level of the hierarchy. The longitudinal studies used a cross-lagged correlational analysis in addition to static correlational analysis. The former technique makes it possible to test with some confidence the strength and direction of causal relationships by using longitudinal data and correlational analysis. The two longitudinal studies indicate no support for Maslow's propositions. The two studies, however, provide the most appropriate methodology to test Maslow's theory in general and its dynamic aspects in particular.

General Evaluation and Conclusion

This literature review shows that Maslow's Need Hierarchy Theory has received little clear or consistent support from the available research findings. Some of Maslow's propositions are totally rejected, while others receive mixed and questionable support at best. The descriptive validity of Maslow's Need Classification scheme is not established, although there are some indications that low-order and high-order needs may form some kind of hierarchy. However, this two-level hierarchy is not always operative, nor is it based upon the domination or gratification concepts. No strong evidence supports the deprivation/domination proposition except with regard to self-actualization. Self-actualization, however, may not be a basic need, but rather a romantic throwback to the eighteenth century notion of the "noble savage." [6] That is, it may be based more on wishes of what man should be than on what he actually is. Furthermore, a number of competing theories explain self-actualization with more rigor than does Maslow's theory. [10] Longitudinal data does not support Maslow's gratification/activation proposition, and the limited support received from cross-sectional studies is questionable because of numerous measurement and control problems.

Do these findings invalidate Maslow's Need Hierarchy Theory? The answer to this question is rather difficult, partly because of the nature of the theory, which defies empirical testing, and partly because of the conceptual, methodological and measurement problems of the research reviewed. Maslow's Need Hierarchy Theory is almost a non-testable theory. This is evident by the relatively limited research that has sought to test it, and the difficulty of interpreting and operationalizing its concepts. For example, what behavior should or should not be included in each need category? How can a need be gratified out of existence? What does dominance of a given need mean? What are the conditions under which the theory is operative? How does the shift from one need to another take place? Do people also go down the hierarchy as they go up in it? Is there an independent hierarchy for each situation or do people develop a general hierarchy for all situations? What is the time span for the unfolding of the hierarchy? These and similar questions are not answered by Maslow and are open for many interpretations.

The most problematic aspect of Maslow's theory, however, is that dealing with the concept of need itself. There is ample evidence that people seek objects and engage in behavior that are in no way related to the satisfaction of needs. [15; 31] Cofer and Appley [10] concluded that this is probably true also for animals. Vroom [30] does not use the concept of needs in his discussion of motivation. Lawler [18] limits the use of the term to certain stimuli (or outcomes) that can be grouped together because they are sought by people. Even if we accept such a limited view of needs, the remaining question should be, why should needs be structured in a fixed hierarchy? Does this hierarchy vary for different people? What happens to the hierarchy over time? How can we have a fixed hierarchy when behavior is multi-determinate? These and other logical arguments have been raised about Maslow's theory by many writers [e.g., 6] and have resulted in some attempts to reformulate the theory which have shown some validity. [e.g., 1; 2; 3; 4; 16]

The research reviewed in this paper is not free from weakness. In particular, there are two drawbacks in most of the research reviewed; the interpretation and operationalization of the theory, and the measurement problems. The variations in interpretations are evident by the hypotheses and the operational definitions attached to Maslow's main concepts by different authors. Methodologically, Maslow's theory is a clinically derived theory and its unit of analysis is the individual. Most of the research used the group as the unit of analysis. The theory is a dynamic theory, while most of the research, except the two longitudinal studies, dealt with the theory as a static theory. Maslow's theory is based upon a causal logic, while most of the studies were correlational (again except for the dynamic correlations used by the two longitudinal studies). The dependent variables in most of the research varied and were measured usually by self-reporting techniques, but none of the studies included observable behavior. Although there are six different scales designed especially to reflect Maslow's ideas, there are many measurement problems associated with these scales. Some of the scales do not show acceptable reliability coefficients and their construct validity is questionable.

Future research dealing with Maslow's theory should concentrate upon the areas that show some promise and ignore those areas that received little support. It is possible to develop further some of the ideas that received some support from the empiric research and improve its predictive validity, e.g., two-level hierarchy, gratification concept, and self-actualization needs. These areas should be clarified and operationalized to facilitate the formulation of testable hypotheses. The dynamic aspects of the theory should be subjected to further tests, and scales of measurements should be more refined to allow more reliable and valid tests of the theory.

REFERENCES

1 Alderfer, C. P. Differential importance of human needs as a function of satisfaction obtained in the organization. Ph.D. diss., Yale University, 1966.

2 Alderfer, C. P. An empirical test of a new theory of human needs. *Organizational Behavior and Human Performance,* 1969, 4, 142–75.

3 Alderfer, C. P. *Existence, relatedness, and growth.* New York: Free Press, 1972.

4 Barnes, L. B. *Organizational systems and engineering groups.* Boston: Harvard Graduate School of Business, 1960.

5 Beer, M. *Leadership, employee needs and motivation.* Columbus: Bureau of Business Research, Ohio State University, 1966.

6 Berkowitz, L. Social motivation. In Lindzey, G., and Aronson, E. (Eds.), *Handbook of social psychology,* 2nd ed., vol. 3. Reading, Mass.: Addison-Wesley, 1969.

7 Blai, B., Jr. An occupational study of job satisfaction and need satisfaction. *Journal of Experimental Education,* 1964, 32, 383–88.

8 Centers, R. Motivational aspects of occupational stratification. *Journal of Social Psychology,* 1948, 28, 187–217.

9 Clark, J. B. Motivation in work groups: A tentative view. *Human Organization,* 1960–61, 13, 198–208.

10 Cofer, C. N., and Appley, M. H. *Motivation: Theory and research.* New York: Wiley, 1964.

11 Dachler, H. P., and Hulin, C. L. A reconsideration of the relationship between satisfaction and judged importance of environmental and job characteristics. *Organizational Behavior and Human Performance,* 1969, 4, 252–66.

12 Friedlander, F. Underlying sources of job satisfaction. *Journal of Applied Psychology,* 1963, 47, 246–50.

13 Friedlander, F. Comparative work value systems. *Personnel Psychology,* 1965, 18, 1–20.

14 Hall, D. T., and Nougaim, K. E. An examination of Maslow's need hierarchy in an organizational setting. *Organizational Behavior and Human Performance*, 1968, 3, 12–35.

15 Harlow, H. F. Mice, monkeys, men, and motives. *Psychological Review*, 1953, 60, 23–32.

16 Harrison, R. *A conceptual framework for laboratory training*. Unpublished manuscript, 1966.

17 Huizinga, G. *Maslow's need hierarchy in the work situation*. The Netherlands: Wolters-Noordhoff nv Groningen, 1970.

18 Lawler, E. E. *Pay and organizational effectiveness: A psychological review*. New York: McGraw-Hill, 1971.

19 Lawler, E. E., and Suttle, J. L. A causal correlation test of the need hierarchy concept. *Organizational Behavior and Human Performance*, 1972, 7, 265–87.

20 Locke, E. A. Importance and satisfaction in several job areas. Paper delivered at American Psychological Association convention, New York, 1961.

21 Maslow, A. H. A theory of human motivation. *Psychological Review*, 1943, 50, 370–96.

22 Maslow, A. H. *Motivation and personality*. New York: Harper, 1954.

23 Maslow, A. H. *Eupsychian management*. Homewood, Ill.: Irwin-Dorsey, 1965.

24 Maslow, A. H. *Motivation and personality*, 2nd ed. New York: Harper and Row, 1970.

25 Meehl, P. E. *Clinical vs. statistical prediction*. Minneapolis: University of Minnesota Press, 1954.

26 Miner, J. B., and Dachler, H. P. Personnel attitudes and motivation. *Annual Review of Psychology* (in press).

27 Porter, L. W. Job attitudes in management: I. Perceived deficiencies in need fulfillment as a function of job level. *Journal of Applied Psychology*, 1962, 46, 375–84.

28 Schaffer, R. H. Job satisfaction as related to need satisfaction in work. *Psychological Monographs*, 1953, 47, Whole no. 364.

29 Trexler, J. T., and Schuh, A. J. Longitudinal verification of Maslow's motivation hierarchy in a military environment. *Experimental Publication System*. Washington, D.C.: American Psychological Association, 1969, Manuscript no. 020A.

30 Vroom, V. H. *Work and motivation*. New York: Wiley, 1964.

31 White, R. W. Motivation reconsidered: The concept of competence. *Psychological Review*, 1959, 66, 297–333.

32 Wofford, J. C. The motivational basis of job satisfaction and job performance. *Personnel Psychology*, 1971, 24, 501–18.

Murray's Manifest Needs Theory

Richard M. Steers

The second need theory of motivation [after Maslow] was developed by Henry A. Murray (1938) and is called the *manifest needs theory* (or the need-press model). While the initial formulations were developed by Murray in the 1930s and 1940s, the model has been considerably developed and extended by David McClelland and John Atkinson (Atkinson, 1964; McClelland et al., 1953).

BASIC PREMISES OF THE MANIFEST NEEDS MODEL

Like Maslow, Murray felt that individuals could be classified according to the strengths of various needs. People were thought to possess at any one time a variety of divergent—and often conflicting—needs which influence behavior. A *need* was defined as a "recurrent concern for a goal state" (McClelland, 1971, p. 13). Each need was believed to be composed of two components: 1) a qualitative, or directional, component which includes the object toward which the need is directed; and 2) a quantitative, or energetic, component which consists of the strength or intensity of the need toward the object. Needs were thus viewed as the central motivating force for people in terms of both direction and intensity.

Overall, Murray posited that individuals possess about two dozen needs, including the needs for achievement, affiliation, power, and so forth. Murray believed that needs are mostly learned, rather than inherited, and are activated (or manifested) by cues from the external environment. For example, an employee who had a high need for achievement would only be expected to pursue that need (that is, to try to achieve something) when the environmental conditions were appropriate (e.g., when he was given a challenging task). Only then would the need become *manifest*. When the need was not cued, the need was said to be *latent*, or not activated.

MASLOW VS. MURRAY

The manifest theory resembles Maslow's model in that both theories identify a set of needs and goals toward which behavior is directed. The two models differ, however, in two important respects. First, Murray does not suggest that needs are arranged in an hierarchical form as does Maslow. And, second, Murray's model allows for more flexibility in describing people. Maslow's need hierarchy model places individuals on one level at a time in the hierarchy (e.g., esteem needs). Using Murray's manifest needs model, on the other hand, we can describe an individual as having high needs for achievement and autonomy and low needs for affiliation and power—all at the same time. Hence, we are able to be more specific in describing people, instead of merely claiming they have "higher-order need strengths" as is the case with Maslow.

While the manifest needs model encompasses an entire set of needs, most research in organizational settings has focused on the four needs of achievement, affiliation, autonomy, and power. These four needs seem to be particularly important for understanding people at work. Therefore, we shall consider each of these needs as they relate to work settings.

NEED FOR ACHIEVEMENT

Basic Concepts

By far the most prominent need from the standpoint of studying organizational behavior is the need for achievement (also known as *n Ach* or n Achievement). Need for achievement is defined as "behavior toward competition with a standard of excellence" (McClelland et al., 1953). High need for achievement is characterized by: 1) a strong desire to assume personal responsibility for finding solutions to problems; 2) a tendency to set moderately difficult achievements goals and take calculated risks; 3) a strong desire for concrete feedback on task performance; and 4) a single-minded preoccupation with task and task accomplishment. Low need for achievement, on the other hand, is typically characterized by a preference for low risk levels on tasks and for shared responsibility on tasks.

Need for achievement is an important motive in organizations because many managerial and entrepreneurial positions require such drive in order to be successful. Thus, when a manager who has a high *n Ach* is placed on a difficult job, the challenging nature of the task serves to cue the achievement motive which, in turn, activates achievement-oriented behavior. However, it is important to point out that when high need achievers are placed on routine or non-challenging jobs, the achievement motive will probably not be activated. Hence, there would be little reason to expect them to perform in a superior fashion under such conditions (McClelland, 1961; Steers and Spencer, 1977).

The concept of need for achievement is important, not only for understanding human behavior in its own right, but also for understanding how people respond to the work environment. As such, the concept has important implications for job design. Enriching an employee's job by providing greater amounts of variety, autonomy, and responsibility would probably enhance performance only for those employees who were challenged by such a job (that is, high need achievers). Low need achievers, on the other hand, may be frustrated by the increased personal responsibility for task accomplishment and, as such, may perform poorly or may even withdraw from the situation.

Need for Achievement and Economic Development

McClelland (1961) has applied the notion of n Achievement to the study of economic development in underdeveloped countries. These studies are described in an interesting book entitled *The Achieving Society*.

As a result of several years of study, two general findings emerged. First, according to McClelland, there is a fairly consistent correlation between a country's current state of economic development and measurable mean levels of n Achievement in that country. Higher mean levels of *n Ach* are found in more prosperous nations, while lower levels are found in the less prosperous. Second, when McClelland examined the literature of ancient cultures for references to achievement-oriented aspirations and behaviors, he found some evidence that increases in the achievement motive preceded subsequent economic development in those civilizations.

Based on these findings, McClelland argues that economic development and prosperity at a national level can be influenced to some extent by the achievement strivings of a nation's people. Such findings have important implications for current efforts to assist underdeveloped nations in that they suggest a need to instill the achievement motive in the population (in addition to economic aid) in order to facilitate development.

Developing n Achievement

Need for achievement, like other needs, is apparently learned at an early age and is influenced largely by the independence training given children by their parents. As Sanford and Wrightsman (1970, p. 212) point out, "the relatively demanding parent who clearly instigates self-reliance in the child and who then rewards independent behavior is teaching the child a need for achievement."

Since it is estimated that only about 10 percent of the population are high need achievers, questions are logically raised concerning how one becomes a high need achiever. McClelland's (1965) answer to this question is that achievement motivation can be taught to adults with moderate success. Achievement motivation training consists of four steps:

1 Teach participants how to think, talk, and act like a person with high need achievement.

2 Stimulate participants to set higher, but carefully planned and realistic, work goals for themselves.

3 Give the participants knowledge about themselves.

4 Create a group *esprit de corps* from learning about each others' hopes and fears, successes and failures, and from going through an emotional experience together.

To date, the evidence appears to support the usefulness of such training programs for increasing *n Ach*. With few exceptions, managers in various countries who attended such programs received more rapid promotions, made more money, and expanded their businesses more quickly after completing the course than did control groups. It is important to note here, however, that such managers were consistently chosen from entrepreneurial-type jobs thought to be most suited for high need achievers. The success of such programs on employees who perform routine, clerical, or automated tasks remains very doubtful because such jobs are not designed to activate the achievement motive.

NEED FOR AFFILIATION

In contrast to the need for achievement, relatively little is known about the behavioral consequences of the need for affiliation, despite the fact that this need has been widely recognized since early in this century (Trotter, 1916). The need for affiliation (n Aff) may be defined as an "attraction to another organism in order to feel reassured from the other that the self is acceptable" (Birch and Veroff, 1966, p. 65). This need should not be confused with being sociable or popular; instead, it is the need for human companionship and reassurance.

People with a high need for affiliation are typified by the following: 1) a strong desire for approval and reassurance from others; 2) a tendency to conform to the wishes and norms of others when pressured by people whose friendship they value; and 3) a sincere interest in the feelings of others. High n Aff individuals tend to take jobs characterized by a high amount of interpersonal contact, like sales, teaching, public relations, and counseling.

How does n Aff influence employee behavior? Some evidence suggests that individuals with a high need for affiliation have better attendance records than those with a low n Aff (Steers and Braunstein, 1976). Moreover, some research suggests that high n Aff employees perform somewhat better in situations where personal support and approval is tied to performance. Support for this position comes from French (1958) who found in a laboratory experiment that, while high n Ach individuals performed better when given *task-related* feedback, high n Aff individuals performed better when given *supportive* feedback. Effort and performance for those high in n Aff can also be enhanced somewhat under a cooperative work norm where pressure for increased output is exerted by one's *friends* only (French, 1955; Atkinson and Raphelson, 1956; DeCharms, 1957). The implications of such findings for leadership or supervisory behavior are fairly clear. To the extent that supervisors can create a cooperative, supportive work environment where positive feedback is tied to task performance, we would expect high n Aff employees to be more productive. The reason for this is simple: working harder in such an environment would lead to the kinds of need satisfaction desired by those high in n Aff.

NEED FOR AUTONOMY

Need for autonomy (n Aut) is a desire for independence and for freedom from any kind of constraint. Individuals with a high need for autonomy prefer situations where they: 1) work alone; 2) control their own work pace; and 3) are not hampered by excessive rules or procedures governing their work behavior (Birch and Veroff, 1966).

The effects of a high need for autonomy on employee behavior can be significant. For instance, it has been found that high n Aut individuals: 1) tend not to react to external pressures for conformity to group norms (Kasl, Sampson, and French, 1964); 2) tend to be poor performers unless they are allowed to participate in the determination of their tasks (Vroom, 1959); 3) are not committed to the goals and objectives of the organization; and 4) are typically found among craft and tradespeople and lower-echelon employees, not managers (Vroom, 1959). This last finding may be explained by the fact that managerial success is in large measure determined by a manager's ability to interact successfully with others, to cooperate, and compromise. Individuals with a high need for autonomy typically refuse to do this.

NEED FOR POWER

A final need that has proved important for understanding organizational behavior is an individual's need for power (or dominance). Need for power represents a desire to influence others and to control one's environment. It has a strong social connotation, in contrast to n Autonomy, in that a high *n Pow* employee will try to control (or lead) those around him.

Interest in the power motive dates from the early work of Alfred Adler (1930), who believed that power was the major goal of all human activity. Adler saw human development as a process by which people learn to exert control over the forces that have power over them. Hence, a person's ultimate satisfaction comes with his or her ability to have influence over the environment. While the subsequent work of Murray (1938), McClelland (1975), and others do not see power as an all-consuming drive as Adler did, they nevertheless view it as an important need.

In summarizing the research on need for power, here's how Litwin and Stringer (1968, p. 18) describe individuals high in *n Pow:*

> . . . They usually attempt to influence directly—by making suggestions, by giving their opinions and evaluations, and by trying to talk others into things. They seek positions of leadership in group activities; whether they become leaders or are seen only as "dominating individuals" depends on other attributes such as ability and sociability. They are usually verbally fluent, often talkative, sometimes argumentative.

Additional recent research demonstrates that employees with high needs for power or dominance tend to be superior performers, have above average attendance records, and tend to be in supervisory positions (Steers and Braunstein, 1976). Moreover, such individuals were rated by others as having good leadership abilities.

Two Faces of Power

McClelland (1976) notes that n Power can take two forms among managers: personal power and institutionalized power. Employees with a *personal-power* orientation strive for dominance almost for the sake of dominance. Personal conquest is very important to them. Moreover, such individuals tend to reject institutional responsibilities. McClelland likens personal-power types to conquistadors or feudal chieftans; that is, they attempt to inspire their subordinates to heroic performance but want their subordinates to be responsible to their leader, not to the organization.

The *institutionalized-power* manager, on the other hand, is far more concerned with problems of the organization and what he or she can do to facilitate goal attainment. McClelland (1976) describes institutionalized-power types as follows: 1) they are organization-minded and feel personal responsibility for building up the organization; 2) they enjoy work and getting things done in an orderly fashion; 3) they seem quite willing to sacrifice some of their own self-interest for the welfare of the organization; 4) they have a strong sense of justice or equity; and 5) they are more mature (i.e., they are less defensive and more willing to seek expert advice when necessary).

MANIFEST NEEDS AND MANAGERIAL EFFECTIVENESS

Based on the foregoing discussion of the various needs, questions are logically raised concerning the influence various manifest needs have on managerial behavior and effectiveness. Is it possible to build a profile of a successful manager based on these needs? Recent research by McClelland (1975, 1976) suggests that such a profile is possible on a very general level.

McClelland's (1976, p. 102) argument begins by asking what we mean by managerial success:

> Almost by definition, a good manager is one who, among other things, helps subordinates feel strong and responsible, who rewards them properly for good performance, and who sees that things are organized in such a way that subordinates feel they know what they should be doing. Above all, managers should foster among subordinates a strong sense of team spirit, of pride in working as part of a particular team. If a manager creates and encourages this spirit, his subordinates certainly should perform better.

Based on this description, what type of manager is most suited to the tasks of managing? A manager with a high need for achievement? need for affiliation? need for power? McClelland argues persuasively that the best manager is one who has a high need for power! Let's examine why.

Managers who have a high need for *achievement* concentrate their efforts on personal accomplishment and improvement. They tend to be highly independent individuals who want to assume responsibility (and credit) for task accomplishment and who want short-term concrete feedback on their performance so they know how well they are doing. These characteristics are often closely associated with *entrepreneurial* success (such as an independent business person). However, these same characteristics can be detrimental where the individual has to manage others. In complex organizations, managers obviously cannot perform all the tasks necessary for success; teamwork is necessary. Moreover, feedback on the group's effort and performance is often vague and delayed. Hence, the managerial environment is not totally suitable to stimulate the achievement motive in managers.

Managers who have a high need for *affiliation* fare no better. Affiliative managers have a high need for group acceptance and, partly as a result of this, they often tend to be indecisive in decision-making for fear of alienating one faction or another. Moreover, this concern for maintaining good interpersonal relationships often results in their attention being focused on keeping subordinates happy instead of on work group performance. McClelland (1976, p. 104) summed up his research findings on the affiliative manager by noting:

> The manager who is concerned about being liked by people tends to have subordinates who feel that they have very little personal responsibility, that organizational procedures are not clear, and that they have little pride in their work groups.

In contrast, managers with a high need for *institutionalized* power were found in McClelland's (1976) study to supervise work groups that were both more productive and more satisfied than other managers. (McClelland also found that managers high in need for *personal* power were far less successful managers than those with a need for institutionalized power.) Several reasons exist for the success of the n Power manager. One explanation is suggested by Zaleznik (1970, p. 47):

> Whatever else organizations may be (problem-solving instruments, sociotechnical systems, reward systems, and so on), they are political structures. This means that organizations operate by distributing authority and setting a stage for the exercise of power. It is no wonder, therefore, that individuals who are highly motivated to secure and use power find a familiar and hospitable environment in business.

In other words, power-oriented managers, when truly concerned about the organization as a whole (instead of themselves) provide the structure, drive, and support necessary to facilitate goal-oriented group behavior. In this sense, they fit very nicely into the definition of managerial success noted above. However, as noted by McClelland (1976), a power-oriented manager pays a price in terms of personal health. He measured need for power among a group of Harvard graduates over twenty years ago. Twenty years later in a follow-up study, McClelland found that 58% of those rated high in power in the earlier study either had high blood pressure or had died of heart failure!

One final point needs to be discussed before leaving the topic of needs and managerial success. This concerns the *interactive* effects of the various needs on performance. In particular, a study by Andrews (1967) looked at both n Power and n Achievement in two Mexican companies. Company A was a dynamic and rapidly growing organization characterized by high employee morale and enthusiasm. Company B, on the other hand, had shown almost no growth despite large initial investments and a favorable market; moreover, Company B had serious problems of employee dissatisfaction and turnover. An assessment of the various need strengths among managers in both companies revealed several interesting findings. To begin with, the upper management of Company A (the more dynamic firm) were much higher on n Achievement than managers in Company B. The presidents of both companies were extremely high in n Power. However, in Company A, the president's n Power was combined with a moderately high n Achievement. This was not the case in the less successful Company B. Hence, based on these findings, it would appear that the most successful managers may be those who combine a power-orientation *with* an achievement-orientation.

REFERENCES

Adler, A. Individual psychology. Translated by S. Langer in C. Murchison (ed.), *Psychologies of 1930.* Worcester, Mass.: Clark University Press, 1930, 398–399.

Andrews, J. D. W. The achievement motive and advancement in two types of organizations. *Journal of Personality and Social Psychology,* 1967, *6,* 163–168.

Atkinson, J. W. *An introduction to motivation.* Princeton, N.J.: Van Nostrand, 1964.

Atkinson, J. W., & Raphelson, A. C. Individual differences in motivation and behavior in particular situations. *Journal of Personality,* 1956, *24,* 349–363.

Birch, D., & Veroff, J. *Motivation: A study of action.* Monterey, Ca.: Brooks/Cole, 1966.

DeCharms, R. C. Affiliation motivation and productivity in small groups. *Journal of Abnormal and Social Psychology,* 1957, *55,* 222–276.

French, E. Some characteristics of achievement motivation. *Journal of Experimental Psychology,* 1955, *50,* 232–236.

French, E. Effects of the interaction of motivation and feedback on task performance. In J. W. Atkinson (ed.), *Motives in fantasy, action, and society.* Princeton, N.J.: Van Nostrand, 1958, 400–408.

Kasl, S. V., Sampson, E. E., & French, J. R. P. The development of a projective measure of the needs for independence: A theoretical statement and some preliminary evidence. *Journal of Personality,* 1964, *32,* 566–586.

Litwin, G. H., & Stringer, R. A., Jr. *Motivation and organizational climate.* Boston: Division of Research, Graduate School of Business Administration, Harvard University, 1968.

McClelland, D. C. Power is the great motivation. *Harvard Business Review,* 1976, *54*(2), 100–110.

McClelland, D. C. *Power: The inner experience.* New York: Irvington, 1975.

McClelland, D. C. *Assessing human motivation.* New York: General Learning Press, 1971.

McClelland, D. C. Toward a theory of motive acquisition. *American Psychologist,* 1965, *20,* 321–333.

McClelland, D. C. *The achieving society.* Princeton, N.J.: Van Nostrand, 1961.

McClelland, D. C., Atkinson, J. W., Clark, R. A., & Lowell, E. L. *The achievement motive.* New York: Appleton-Century-Crofts, 1953.

Murray, H. A. *Explorations in personality.* New York: Oxford University Press, 1938.

Sanford, F. H., & Wrightsman, L. S., Jr. *Psychology,* Third edition. Monterey, Ca.: Brooks/Cole, 1970.

Steers, R. M., & Braunstein, D. N. A behaviorally based measure of manifest needs in work settings. *Journal of Vocational Behavior,* 1976, *9,* 251–266.

Steers, R. M., & Spencer, D. G. The role of achievement motivation in job design. *Journal of Applied Psychology,* 1977, *4,* 472–479.

Trotter, W. *Instincts of the herd in peace and war.* New York: Macmillan, 1916.

Vroom, V. H. Some personality determinants of the effects of participation. *Journal of Abnormal and Social Psychology,* 1959, *59,* 322–327.

Zaleznik, A. Power and politics in organizational life. *Harvard Business Review,* 1970, May-June, 47–60.

QUESTIONS FOR DISCUSSION

1 Why do you think Maslow's theory of motivation has been so popular among both managers and organizational researchers?

2 Is Maslow's need hierarchy a theory of motivation or a theory of personality?

3 Considering the disconfirming research evidence on Maslow's theory, what aspects of Maslow's hierarchy of needs would you consider useful to the practicing manager?

4 If needs are activated by the environment, what complications does this suggest for the design of jobs and organizations?

5 As a manager, how would you utilize the knowledge that an employee of yours has a high need for achievement (*n Ach*)?

6 How would you go about improving the performance of an employee who has a low need for achievement?

7 If high need for achievement people tend to be superior performers, why not simply increase organizational performance by hiring only high *n Ach* employees?

8 Researchers have found that a person with high need for achievement may simultaneously have a low need for affiliation. What are the implications of this type of finding?

9 McClelland argues that the best manager is one who has a high need for power. Under what circumstances might it be more beneficial to have a manager with high *n Ach*, high *n Aff*, high *n Aut*?

10 What do you think is the optimal need profile for a typical blue-collar worker?

CHAPTER 3

COGNITIVE APPROACHES TO MOTIVATION

The second major approach to the study of work motivation is represented by a constellation of cognitive theories. As noted in Chapter 1, cognitive theories generally assume that individuals engage in some form of conscious behavior on the job. That is, people are seen as being reasoning, thinking individuals who often consider the consequences of their actions at work. Thus, cognitive theorists attempt to develop models concerning the thought processes people go through as they decide to participate and perform in the workplace.

In this chapter, we consider three related cognitive theories of motivation: (1) expectancy theory (also called "valence-instrumentality-expectancy theory," or "VIE theory"), (2) equity theory, and (3) goal-setting theory. (Strictly speaking, goal-setting has been labeled by its principal proponents as a "technique" rather than a "theory." However, it has a strong conceptual base and is commonly referred to by many in the field as "goal-setting theory.") The reader will want to focus on how these three cognitively based approaches compare with one another and especially with reinforcement and social learning approaches, discussed in Chapter 4.

Because of the nature of the material presented in the readings that follow, it would be redundant to elaborate on each of the cognitive theories here. In the first article, Pinder provides a comprehensive overview of expectancy theory, with particular emphasis on the three concepts—valence, instrumentality, and expectancy—that constitute the essence of this way of thinking about motivation. In the second article, Mowday reviews the key formulations and relevant research pertaining to equity theory. The following two articles—the first by Locke and the second by Latham and Locke—show how the goal-setting technique relates to other motivational theories and how it has been applied in "real-world" work settings.

Valence-Instrumentality-Expectancy Theory
Craig C. Pinder

Probably the most popular theory of work motivation among organizational scientists in recent years has been that which is referred to as Valence-Instrumentality-Expectancy Theory or Expectancy Theory (Locke, 1975). Actually, there are a variety of theories included under these general titles, although the similarities among them are more important than are the differences. Each of these theories has its modern roots in Vroom's (1964) book on work motivation, although earlier theory in psychology relating to general human motivation quite clearly predates Vroom's interpretation for organizational science (e.g., Atkinson, 1958; Davidson, Suppes, and Siegel, 1957; Lewin, 1938; Peak, 1955; Rotter, 1955; Tolman, 1959), and an early study by Georgopoulos, Mohoney, and Jones (1957) demonstrated the relevance of the theory for work behavior.

Since Vroom's book was published, there have been a number of variations and revisions of his basic concepts, although most of the theoretical work has been vastly superior to the numerous empirical attempts to test the theory in all of its various forms. In fact, it can be defensibly argued that, in spite of the numerous studies conducted since 1964 that have ostensibly sought to test versions of the theory, very little is known about its validity. This is because, as has been the case with so much research on employee motivation, studies directed at VIE Theory have been fraught with serious flaws—flaws which make it almost impossible to conclude whether the theory, in any of its forms, holds any scientific merit (Arnold, 1981; Campbell and Pritchard, 1976; Locke, 1975; Pinder, 1977). Nevertheless, let's take a look at the theory in its most basic form—that proposed by Vroom (1964) for application to work settings.

VROOM'S ORIGINAL THEORY

Vroom's theory assumes that ". . . the choices made by a person among alternative courses of action are lawfully related to psychological events occurring contemporaneously with the behavior" (1964, pp. 14–15). In other words, people's behavior results from conscious choices among alternatives, and these choices (behaviors) are systematically related to psychological processes, particularly perception and the formation of beliefs and attitudes. The purpose of the choices, generally, is to maximize pleasure and minimize pain. Like Equity Theory then, VIE Theory assumes that people base their acts on perceptions and beliefs, although we need not anticipate any one-to-one relationships between particular beliefs and specific behaviors (such as job behaviors).

To understand why Vroom's theory and those which have followed it are referred to as *VIE Theory*, we must examine the three key mental components

Excerpted from Chapter 7 of C. C. Pinder, *Work motivation*. Glenview, Ill.: Scott, Foresman, 1984. Reprinted by permission.

that are seen as instigating and directing behavior. Referred to as Valence, Instrumentality, and Expectancy, each of these components is, in fact, a *belief*.

The Concept of Valence

VIE theory assumes that people hold preferences among various outcomes or states of nature. For example, the reader probably prefers, other things equal, a higher rate of pay for a particular job over a lower rate of pay. Here, pay level is the *outcome* in question, and the preference for high pay over low pay reflects the strength of the reader's basic underlying need state. Likewise, some people hold preferences among different types of outcomes (as opposed to greater or lesser amounts of a particular outcome). For example, many employees would seem to prefer an opportunity to work with other people, even if the only jobs featuring high levels of social interaction entail less comfortable surroundings, lower pay, or some other trade-off. The point is that people have more or less well-defined preferences for the outcomes they derive from their actions.

Vroom uses the term *valence* to refer to the affective (emotional) orientations people hold with regard to outcomes. An outcome is said to be positively valent for an individual if she would prefer having it to not having it. For example, we would say that a promotion is positively valent for an employee who would rather be promoted than not be promoted. Likewise, we say that an outcome which a person would prefer to avoid has negative valence for her, or simply that it is negatively valent. For example, fatigue, stress, and layoffs are three outcomes that are usually negatively valent among employees. Finally, it is sometimes the case that an employee is indifferent toward certain outcomes; in such cases, the outcome is said to hold zero valence for that individual.

The most important feature of people's valences concerning work-related outcomes is that they refer to the level of satisfaction the person *expects* to receive from them, *not from the real value the person actually derives from them*. So, for example, the reader may be enrolled in a program of business management because she expects that the outcomes to follow (an education and a diploma, among others) will be of value to her when she is finished. It may be the case, however, that when the student graduates there will be little or no market demand for the services she has to offer the world of business and administration, so the degree may have little real value. The point here is that people attribute either positive or negative preferences (or indifference) to outcomes according to the satisfaction or dissatisfaction they *expect* to receive from them. It is often the case that the true value of an outcome (such as a diploma) is either greater or lesser than the valence (expected value) that outcome once held for the individual who was motivated to either pursue it or avoid it. As a final example, consider the individual who fears being fired, but learns after actually being dismissed from a job that she is healthier, happier, and better off financially in the new job she acquired after having been terminated by her former employer. In this case, being fired was a negatively valent outcome before it occurred, but eventually turned out to be of positive value after it occurred.

Performance as an Outcome Of the many outcomes that follow an employee's work effort, one of the most important, of course, is the level of performance that is accomplished. In fact, for the sake of understanding Vroom's theory, the strength of the connection in the mind of the employee between his effort and the performance level he achieves is very important, as we will see shortly. Further, the degree to which the employee believes that his performance will be connected to other outcomes (such as pay, for example) is also critical. The point here is that work effort results in a variety of outcomes, some of them directly, others indirectly. The level of job performance is the most important outcome for understanding work motivation from a VIE Theory perspective. So, *V* stands for valence—the expected levels of satisfaction and/or dissatisfaction brought by work-related outcomes.

The Concept of Instrumentality

We have just stated that outcomes carry valences for people. But what determines the valence of a particular outcome for an employee? For example, we noted that performance level is an important outcome of a person's work effort, but what determines the valence associated with a given level of performance? For Vroom, the answer is that a given level of performance is positively valent if the employee believes that it will lead to other outcomes, which are called *second-level outcomes*. In other words, if an employee believes . . . that a high level of performance is *instrumental* for the acquisition of other outcomes that he expects will be gratifying (such as a promotion, for example), and/or if he believes that a high performance level will be instrumental for avoiding other outcomes that he wishes to avoid (such as being fired), then that employee will place a high valence upon performing the job well.

Consider the meaning of the adjective *instrumental*. The author's typewriter at the present time is instrumental in the preparation of this book. It contributes to the job; it helps. Something is said to be instrumental if it is believed to lead to something else, if it helps achieve or attain something else. Hence, studying is commonly seen by students as instrumental for passing exams. In turn, passing exams is often *believed* instrumental for the acquisition of diplomas, which, in turn, are *believed* to be instrumental for landing jobs in tight labor market conditions.

Vroom (1964) suggests that we consider instrumentality as a probability belief linking one outcome (performance level) to other outcomes, ranging from 1.0 (meaning that the attainment of the second outcome is certain if the first outcome is achieved), through zero (meaning that there is no likely relationship between the attainment of the first outcome and the attainment of the second), to -1.0 (meaning that the attainment of the second outcome is certain without the first and that it is impossible with it). For example, bonus pay that is distributed at random would lead to employee instrumentality perceptions linking bonus pay to performance equal to zero. ("Performance and pay have no connection around here!") On the other hand, commission pay schemes which tie pay directly to performance, and only to performance, are designed to make employees perceive that performance is positively instrumental for the acquisition of money. Finally, an employee who has been threatened with dismissal for being drunk on the job may be told by his supervisor, in effect, that lack of sobriety at work is negatively instrumental for continued employment, or, alternatively, that further imbibing will be positively instrumental for termination. (The notion of negative instrumentalities makes Vroom's original formulation of VIE Theory somewhat more difficult and cumbersome than it might otherwise be, so subsequent versions of the theory have avoided using it, choosing instead to speak only of positive instrumentalities.)

Consider the case of an employee who perceives that high performance will *not* lead to things he desires, but that it will be more instrumental for attaining outcomes to which he attributes negative valences. High performance will not be positively valent for such a person, so we would not expect to see him striving to perform well. As a further example, an employee might perceive that taking a job as a traveling salesman will be instrumental for attaining a number of outcomes, some of which he expects will be positive, some of which he believes will be negative. On the positively valent side, meeting new people and seeing the countryside may be appealing to him, because he expects that these outcomes will be instrumental for satisfying his relatedness and growth needs, while the possible threat to his family life may be aversive to him, the popularly acknowledged exploits to traveling salesmen notwithstanding!

In short, the *I* in VIE Theory stands for instrumentality—an outcome is positively valent if the person believes that it holds high instrumentality for the acquisition of positively valent consequences (goals or other outcomes), and the avoidance of negatively valent outcomes. But in order for an outcome to be positively valent, the outcomes to which the person believes it is connected must themselves, in turn, be seen as positively valent. If an employee anticipates that high levels of performance will lead primarily to things he dislikes, then high performance will not be positively valent to him. Likewise, if the individual perceives that high performance is generally rewarded with things he desires, he will place high valence on high performance and—other things being equal—he will strive for high performance. Of course, the valence of such second-level-outcomes is determined by the nature of the person's most salient needs and values.

Already, the reader should be able to distill a few implications for the design of reward systems in organizations: if management wants high performance levels, it must tie positively valent outcomes to high performance *and be sure that employees understand the connection*. Likewise, low performance must be seen as connected to consequences that are of either zero or negative valence.

The Concept of Expectancy

The third major component of VIE Theory is referred to as *expectancy*. Expectancy is the strength of a person's belief about whether a particular outcome is possible. The author, for example, would place very little expectancy on the prospect of becoming an astronaut. The reasons are, of course, personal, but the point is that he doesn't believe that any amount of trying on his part will see him aboard the space shuttle! If a person believes that he can achieve an outcome, he will be more motivated to try for it, assuming that other things are equal (the other things, of course, consist of the person's beliefs about the valence of the outcome, which, in turn, is determined by the person's beliefs about the odds that the outcome will be instrumental for acquiring and avoiding those things he either wishes to acquire or avoid, respectively).

Vroom (1964) spoke of expectancy beliefs as *action-outcome* associations held in the minds of individuals, and suggested that we think of them in probability terms ranging from zero (in the case where the person's subjective probability of attaining an outcome is psychologically zero—"I can't do it") through to 1.0, indicating that the person has no doubt about his capacity to attain the outcome. In practice, of course, people's estimates tend to range between these two extremes.

There are a variety of factors that contribute to an employee's expectancy perceptions about various levels of job performance. For example, his level of confidence in his skills for the task at hand, the degree of help he expects to receive from his supervisor and subordinates, the quality of the materials and equipment available, the availability of pertinent information and control over sufficient budget, are common examples of factors that can influence a person's expectancy beliefs about being able to achieve a particular level of performance. Previous success experiences at a task and a generally high level of self-esteem also strengthen expectancy beliefs (Lawler, 1973). The point is that an employee's subjective estimate of the odds that he can achieve a given level of performance is determined by a variety of factors, both within his own control and beyond it.

The Concept of Force

Vroom (1964) suggests that a person's beliefs about expectancies, instrumentalities, and valences interact psychologically to create a motivational force to act in those ways that seem most likely to bring pleasure or to avoid pain. "Behavior on the part of a person is assumed to be the result of a field of forces each of which has a direction and magnitude" (p. 18). Vroom likens his concept of force to a variety of other metaphorical concepts, including things such as *performance vectors* and *behavior potential*. We can think of the force as representing the strength of a person's *intention* to act in a certain way. For example, if a person elects to strive for a particular level of job performance, we might say that the person's beliefs cause the greatest amount of force to be directed toward that level, or that he intends to strive for that level rather than for other levels.

Symbolically, Vroom (1964, p. 18) summarizes his own theory as follows:

$$F_i = f \sum_{i=1}^{n} (E_{ij}V_j) \quad \text{and} \quad V_j = f\left[\sum_{j=1}^{n} I_{jk}V_k\right]$$

where F_i = the psychological force to perform an act (i) (such as strive for a
          particular level of performance)

E_{ij} = the strength of the expectancy that the act will be followed by the
          outcome j

V_j = the valence for the individual of outcome j

I_{jk} = instrumentality of outcome j for attaining second-level outcome k

V_k = valence of second-level outcome k

or, in his words:

> The force on a person to perform an act is a monotonically increasing function of the
> algebraic sum of the products of the valences of all outcomes and the strength of his
> expectancies that the act will be followed by the attainment of these outcomes.

So people choose from among the alternative acts the one(s) corresponding to
the strongest positive (or weakest negative) force. People attempt to maximize
their overall best interest, using the information available to them and their
evaluations of this information. *In the context of work motivation, this means
that people select to pursue that level of performance that they believe will
maximize their overall best interest* (or *subjective expected utility*).

Notice from the formula above that there will be little or no motivational force
operating on an individual to act in a certain manner if any of three conditions
hold: (1) if the person does not believe that she can successfully behave that way
(that is, if her expectancy of attaining the outcome is effectively zero); (2) if she
believes that there will be no positively valent outcomes associated with behaving
in that manner; (3) if she believes the act will result in a sufficient number of
outcomes that are negatively valent to her.

The Choice of a Performance Level   When we think of the levels of job
performance that an employee might strive for as the outcome of interest, Vroom's
theory suggests that the individual will consider the valences, instrumentalities,
and expectancies associated with each level of the entire spectrum of performance
levels and will elect to pursue the level that generates the greatest positive force
(or lowest negative force) for him. If the person sees more good outcomes than
bad ones associated with performing at a high level, he will strive to perform at
that level. On the other hand, if a lower level of performance results in the
greatest degree of psychological force, we can anticipate that he will settle for
such a level. The implication is that low motivation levels result from employee
choices to perform at low levels, and that these choices, in turn, are the result
of beliefs concerning the valences, instrumentalities and expectancies held in the
mind of the employee.

REFINEMENTS TO THE THEORY

Since the publication of Vroom's book in 1964, there has been a considerable
amount of both theoretical and empirical attention paid to expectancy-type models
of work motivation. Aside from attempting to test the validity of the theory in

its simple form, most of these efforts have sought to study the characteristics of people and organizations that influence valence, instrumentality, and expectancy beliefs, or to examine the types of conditions within which VIE-type predictions of work motivation can be expected to apply. A complete discussion of these refinements could easily constitute an entire book—well beyond our present purposes. The reader who is interested in pursuing major theoretic advances in VIE Theory is referred to the following sources: Campbell, Dunnette, Lawler, and Weick, 1970; Dachler and Mobley, 1973; Feldman, Reitz, and Hiterman, 1976; Graen, 1969; House, Shapiro, and Wahba, 1974; Kopelman, 1977; Kopelman and Thompson, 1976; Lawler, 1971, 1973; Naylor, Pritchard, and Ilgen, 1980; Porter and Lawler, 1968; Reinharth and Wahba, 1976; Staw, 1977; and Zedeck, 1977. Thorough reviews of the *research evidence* pertaining to VIE Theory are provided by Heneman and Schwab, (1972), Mitchell and Biglan (1971), and Campbell and Pritchard (1976).

For the purpose of the present discussion, only one of the many theoretical advancements of VIE Theory will be presented, followed by a brief summary of the validity of the theory and a number of difficulties that have been encountered in determining its validity. Finally, we will conclude with a discussion of the major implications of VIE Theory for the practice of management. So, to begin, let's take a look at one of the most important modifications and extensions offered to Vroom's work—the model offered by Porter and Lawler (1968).

The Porter/Lawler Model

Vroom's (1964) statement of VIE Theory left a number of questions unanswered. Perhaps the most important of these concerned the origins of valence, instrumentality, and expectancy beliefs, and the nature of the relationship, if any, between employee attitudes toward work and job performance. Porter and Lawler (1968) developed a theoretic model and then tested it, using a sample of managers, and revised it to explore these issues. The revised statement of their model is provided in schematic form in Figure 1.

In a nutshell, their theory suggests the following. *Employee effort* is jointly determined by two key factors: the *value* placed on certain outcomes by the individual, and the *degree to which the person believes that his effort will lead to the attainment of these rewards.* As predicted by Vroom, Porter and Lawler found that these two factors interact to determine effort level; in other words, they found that people must both positively value outcomes and believe that these outcomes result from their effort for any further effort to be forthcoming.

However, effort may or may not result in *job performance*, which they defined as the accomplishment of those tasks that comprise a person's job. The reason? The level of *ability* the person has to do his job, and his *role clarity*, the degree of clarity of the understanding the person has concerning just what his job consists of. Thus, a person may be highly motivated (putting out a lot of effort), but that effort will not necessarily result in what can be considered performance, unless he has both the ability to perform the job as well as a clear understanding of the ways in which it is appropriate to direct that effort. The student reader is probably

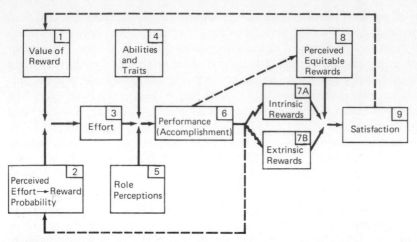

FIGURE 1
The revised Porter/Lawler model.

familiar with at least one colleague who has high motivation to learn and succeed in university, but who lacks either the ability or the *savior faire* needed to direct his energy into what can be considered performance in the academic context: learning and self-development. In short, all three ingredients are needed to some degree, and if any of them is absent, performance cannot result.

Next, what is the relationship between performance (at whatever level is accomplished) and *job satisfaction*? As reflected in Figure 1, Porter and Lawler argue that performance and satisfaction may or may not be related to one another, depending upon a number of factors. First, they note that it is not always the case that performance results in rewards in organizations. Further, they recognize that there are at least two types of rewards potentially available from performance: intrinsic and extrinsic. Porter and Lawler recognize that intrinsic rewards can be much more closely connected with good performance than extrinsic rewards, because the former result (almost automatically) from performance itself, whereas the latter depend upon outside sources (both to recognize that performance has been attained and to administer rewards accordingly).

Porter and Lawler suggest that the level of performance a person believes she has attained will influence the level of rewards that she believes will be *equitable*. So, if an employee believes that her efforts have resulted in a high degree of performance, she will expect a greater level of reward than would be the case if she believes that her performance is not as high. As a result, a particular reward, if any is forthcoming, will be assessed in terms of its level of equity in the mind of the employee, rather than in terms of its absolute level. We sometimes hear statements such as "That pay increase was an insult, considering all I do for this company," reflecting Porter and Lawler's belief that it is not the absolute amount of reward that follows performance which determines whether it is satisfying; rather, the amount, however large or small, must be seen by the employee as equitable in order for it to be satisfying.

Satisfaction was defined in Porter and Lawler's research as ". . . the extent to which rewards actually received meet or exceed the perceived equitable level of rewards" (p. 31). And, as suggested by the feedback loop at the top of Figure 1, the level of satisfaction or dissatisfaction experienced by the person as a result of his treatment by the organization helps determine the value he places in the future on the rewards in question. Moreover, notice the feedback loop at the bottom of the diagram. It suggests that the strength of the person's belief that effort will result in rewards is also determined through experience.

Comments and Criticisms of Porter and Lawler

A number of points must be made about this model. First, the primary focus of the research that accompanied its development was upon *pay* and the role of pay in employee motivation. Although the authors limited their consideration of outcomes other than pay, they argued that the general model should be relevant for consequences other than pay. In addition, since pay was the focus, the emphasis was upon positive consequences only rather than upon both positive and negative consequences (such as fatigue, demotions, or various forms of punishment).

Secondly, Porter and Lawler tested the propositions they derived from their model *cross-sectionally* (rather than over time), and using only managers from the extreme ends of the distributions on the important variables in that model, excluding those individuals who fell near the middle in each case. This is a common practice in research, but one that causes overestimates of the validity of the model being tested (Taylor and Griess, 1976). Additionally, they measured job satisfaction using a technique that is also commonly used, but one which has subsequently been shown to be inappropriate, probably reducing the apparent validity of the model (Johns, 1981).

A third point is that although their model posits the importance of ability as an interactive factor with motivation as a determinant of job performance, Porter and Lawler's *own research* did not pay much attention to examining the specific role of ability. However, other researchers have addressed this issue, and the results seem to suggest that while ability has an important influence on performance, it may not *interact* with motivation in the manner believed by Vroom (1964) and Porter and Lawler (cf. Terborg, 1977).

Fourthly, while Porter and Lawler use the term *value* rather than *valence*, it seems clear that they had the same concept in mind as Vroom. The reader is reminded again of the importance of distinguishing between valence and value when considering motivation from a VIE Theory perspective: it is the anticipated value (valence) of an outcome that is crucial in determining effort, not actual value, per se.

Another point has to do with the way the connection between effort and rewards was conceptualized and measured. Current theories recognize that employee beliefs about the strength of the connection between effort and reward distribution can usefully be broken down into two components: (1) the strength of the belief that a person's effort will result in job performance; and (2) the strength of the person's belief that performance, if achieved, will eventuate into rewards. Porter and Lawler acknowledge the prospect for breaking this overall cognition down into its component parts, and subsequent work by Lawler (1973) and others maintains this distinction.

Performance and Satisfaction (Again) A major contribution of the Porter-Lawler model consists of the implications it holds for the issue concerning the relationship between performance and satisfaction. Consider the diagram in Figure 1. According to the theory, will satisfaction and performance be related to one another? If so, when? The figure suggests that these two factors may or may not be related to one another, but that when they are, the order of causality is far from simple.

First, how might satisfaction be a contributing determinant of performance levels? A number of conditions must hold.

1 That satisfaction must leave the person desirous of attaining more of the same outcome(s). Satisfied needs tend to lose their capacity to motivate behavior, although growth need satisfaction seems to increase the strength of these needs.

2 Even if the reward maintains its valence, effort will result only if the person believes that effort results in the attainment of the reward (which, as we have discussed, is not always the case).

3 In order for the individual's effort to result in performance, the person must have the ability to perform, as well as have a clear idea concerning how to try to perform—where to direct his effort.

4 The performance must result in rewards, and these rewards must be perceived as equitable, for the reasons discussed earlier.

In short, in order for satisfaction to be a contributing cause of performance, as was believed during the days of the human relations movement (and as is still commonly believed by managers and people on the street), all of the foregoing individual and organizational conditions must apply. Rather complicated, to say the least.

Can performance be a cause of satisfaction? The model implies that it can. First, as already noted, high performance can be an immediate cause of intrinsic satisfaction, assuming that the job provides sufficient challenge to appeal to growth needs. Secondly, however, performance can contribute to extrinsic satisfaction if at least three conditions hold:

1 Desired rewards must be tied to that performance (as opposed to being tied to chance or other factors).

2 The person must perceive the connection between his performance and the rewards he receives.

3 The person must believe that the rewards he receives for his performance are equitable.

Again, not a very simple relationship, but Porter and Lawler's model helps explain why the relationships observed between performance and satisfaction have traditionally been so low, although, in their research, the two factors were found to be more strongly connected than is usually the case.

In conclusion, Porter and Lawler have provided a useful elaboration of the fundamental concepts of VIE Theory as presented only a few years earlier by Vroom. The dynamic features of their model (as reflected in the feedback loops) indicate the ongoing nature of the motivation process, and sheds some light on why some employees are more productive than others, why some employees are more satisfied with their work than others, and when we can expect to find a relationship between employee attitudes and performance.

THE VALIDITY OF VIE THEORY

In spite of the fact that there have been innumerable tests of the scientific validity of VIE Theory, only recently have researchers begun to perform studies that can be considered fair or appropriate, given the claims made by the theory itself. In fact, Campbell and Pritchard (1976) have identified at least twelve common problems in the many studies conducted to that time.

The Between/Within Issue

Probably the most important of these problems has had to do with testing the theory as if it were intended to make behavioral and attitudinal predictions *across* individuals, as opposed to *within* individuals (Arnold, 1981; Kopelman, 1977; Mitchell, 1974). In other words, the theory is intended to make predictions about which behavioral alternatives an individual will choose from among those that confront him. The theory states that the alternative which is perceived to maximize the individual's overall expected utility and satisfaction will be the one selected. On the other hand, a major proportion of the investigations reported to date have ignored or violated this assumption by computing expected levels of motivational force (or effort) for a number of people using those peoples' scores on VIE factors, and then correlating these predicted scores, across individuals, with ratings on some other form of score representing actual behavior or attitudes.

To illustrate more completely, suppose we were to compute expected effort scores for a sample of twenty people, using the information these people provide us through interviews or questionnaires. We would calculate these scores using some form of $E(\Sigma VI)$ formula. Then suppose we rank ordered these people on the basis of the magnitude of this overall predicted effort level. Next, we gather supervisory ratings of the actual typical effort levels of these same people and rank order them again, this time on the basis of their supervisory ratings. Finally, assume we correlate these *actual* effort scores with our predicted effort scores, attempting to determine whether the people with the highest predicted scores tended to have the highest supervisory ratings, and whether those with the lowest predicted scores also had the lowest ratings.

The approach just described is referred to as a between-individual one, for apparent reasons. This has been the methodology which has been erroneously used so many times, and the results generated from this type of research design have appeared not to support the theory, because, in fact, there has tended not to be very strong relationships between predicted effort and rated effort, when the data were compiled in this fashion. Accordingly, researchers have concluded that, by and large, the theory is only moderately valid.

Consider the mistake being made in studies conducted this way. The theory merely purports to make predictions concerning *single* individuals, one at a time, about the decision alternatives each of them will select. So, for example, Parker and Dyer (1976) were able to make better than chance predictions about the decisions reached by naval officers as to whether or not to retire voluntarily. Likewise, Arnold (1981) made predictions supportive of the theory concerning the choices of jobs made by undergraduate students; Matsui, Kagawa, Nagamatsu, and Ohtsuka (1977) predicted which of six insurance policies agents would prefer to sell; while Nebeker and Mitchell (1974) and Matsui and Ohtsuka (1978) predicted the leadership styles of supervisors in different settings and in different cultures.*

What is wrong with the between-individual approach for testing the theory? It does not take into account differences between people in ability, the difficulty of the jobs they perform, differences in the level of rewards they receive for their work, and various other things. The difference between these two approaches is subtle when first considered, but incredibly significant for the conclusions one reaches about the validity of the theory. Moreover, the between-individuals approach assumes that people who hold identical valence, instrumentality, and expectancy beliefs will respond identically to instruments designed to assess these constructs. Clearly, this assumption is dubious (Mitchell, 1974). As noted by Atkinson (1964) and Kopelman (1977), the last person in a family to arrive at the dinner table is not necessarily the least hungry! So, to conclude that the theory is not very valid on the basis of research that utilizes an across (or between) individuals approach hardly seems fair.

Other Research Difficulties

In addition to the between/within problem just described, there have been a variety of other typical mistakes made by researchers interested in VIE Theory (Campbell and Pritchard, 1976). A complete discussion of these is beyond our present purpose, but brief mention can be made of a few:

1 The use of incorrect mathematical procedures for testing the interaction effects between effort and ability posited by the theory (see Arnold, 1981 for a way of dealing with this problem).

2 The use of supervisory ratings of *performance* as the criterion against which predictions of employee force is compared. The use of performance rather than effort has occurred because of the difficulty of assessing the latter. But since the theory purports to predict effort, and because effort is only one determinant of performance, the results of these studies have been negatively biased against the theory.

---

*The interested student reader may wish to read of a study in which the researchers utilized a VIE model to predict the academic effort and performance of a sample of college students, employing a statistical technique to control for the between/within person problem (Mitchell and Nebeker, 1973).

3 Low validity and reliability of valence, instrumentality, and expectancy measures (see de Leo and Pritchard, 1974). The effect of these problems has been to cause underestimates of the validity of the theory.

4 The use of cross-sectional research designs, in spite of the fact that the theory speaks of changes, at one point in time, of V, I, and E perceptions being predictive of changes of effort at some subsequent point in time (see Mayes, 1978a for a discussion of this problem and Lawler and Suttle, 1973 and Kopelman, 1979 for attempts to get around it).

5 Assuming that the valence, instrumentality, and expectancy beliefs people hold are independent of one another, then multiplying these scores algebraically. It may be that these three beliefs are not in fact independent of one another, such that people may place higher valence upon outcomes that are believed more difficult to attain. Multiplication assumes independence.

6 Assuming that people are, in fact, as rational as the theory would suggest, for all aspects of their behavior, when, in fact, we know that people have limited cognitive capacities and that much of human behavior is habitual and subconscious (Locke, 1975; Mayes, 1978b; Staw, 1977; Simon, 1957).

Conclusion

The self-correcting cycle of research activity has raised questions about these and other common problems in the research on VIE Theory, and the more recent studies have taken many of them into account. As a result, it appears that VIE Theory may be a more valid representation of work-related attitudes and behaviors than has been concluded by many authors who have surveyed studies that were fraught with the problems identified above. In short, we conclude that the situation for VIE Theory may be similar to that for Maslow's need hierarchy theory, Equity Theory, and maybe even Herzberg's two-factor theory: although there have been many studies conducted with the intention of testing its validity, only recently have there been many appropriately-conducted studies, leaving us with grounds for optimism that the theory is a reasonably valid model of the causes of work behavior.

IMPLICATIONS OF VIE THEORY FOR MANAGEMENT

Beliefs about work (or about life in general) are based on the individual's perceptions of the surrounding environment, and these perceptions are influenced by information stored in the person's memory. It is assumed here that valence, instrumentality, and expectancy beliefs are established and influenced in the same manner as are other beliefs. Therefore, it also follows that because beliefs may not be valid or accurate, the person's behavior may not seem appropriate to observers. And it also follows that because these three beliefs are merely beliefs (as opposed to intentions), they may not result in behavior at all, or at least, they may not result in any specifically predictable behaviors. They should, however, influence an individual's *intentions* to act certain ways. Accordingly, a number of implications follow from VIE Theory for any supervisor who wishes to try to "motivate" his staff.

Expectancy-Related Factors

First, in order to generate positive expectancy forces, the supervisor must assign his personnel to jobs for which they are trained, and which they are capable of performing. This requires that the supervisor understand the skills, strengths, and weaknesses of each of his subordinates, as well as the nature of the skill requirements of the jobs to which he is assigning them. If people are assigned to tasks that they are not capable of performing, according to VIE Theory, their expectancy perceptions will be low, and we will not expect to see them trying to perform.

Consider how difficult it is, in practice, for supervisors completely to appreciate the skill requirements of the jobs their employees must perform, and to recognize that it is the level of skills of the *employees* vis à vis the jobs, not their own skill levels, that matter. Jobs often change with time and as incumbents come and go, making it difficult to keep track of what they require. In addition, supervisors who have performed some or all of the jobs under their purview may forget how difficult these jobs are to newcomers, so they may either overestimate or underestimate the difficulty level of jobs for any of these reasons. Finally, it is important to recognize that employees' skills and abilities change over time, both as a result of formal training and education, as well as from the natural consequences of maturation and simple work experiences.

But adequate skill levels are not sufficient to assure positive expectancy perceptions. In addition, the employee must *believe* that the other circumstances surrounding his effort are favorable and conducive to his success. For example, the supervisor must be sure that machinery and equipment are in good repair, and that the employee's own staff, if any, are trained and capable of being of assistance. Likewise, there must be sufficient budget to make successful performance possible. In short, the job must be capable of being performed by an employee if we are to expect the employee to try to perform it, and—more importantly—the person must perceive that it is so. But countless practical factors can combine to make it very difficult for any supervisor to accurately estimate the expectancy beliefs held by particular employees about specific jobs; accordingly, they make it difficult for supervisors to fully implement the implications that follow from the expectancy component of VIE Theory.

Of particular importance for supervisors is the structuring of the expectancy beliefs of newcomers to a work setting (Hall, 1976). Managers often take a ''sink or swim'' approach with new employees, assigning them work duties that are too difficult, given their relative lack of familiarity with the rules, procedures, and the myriad other circumstances that must be understood in order to make work efforts successful. An alternative approach is to under-challenge newcomers, requiring them to work through a tedious series of trivial jobs before being given any real challenge. Recent college graduates often complain of this treatment upon landing their first jobs after graduating, and, as a result, turnover among recent graduates is usually very high (Mobley, 1982). A third approach, the desired one, is to strike a balance using a combination of achievement-oriented, supportive, and directive leadership styles (as defined in the previous section), attempting to make the newcomer's initial experiences challenging and successful. Success experiences are necessary for developing strong expectancy beliefs, and for maintaining a positive self-concept about one's work—a feeling of competence, self-determination, and high self-esteem (cf. Deci, 1975; Hall, 1976; Korman, 1970, 1976).

Instrumentality-Related Factors

In order to operationalize the concepts of instrumentality and valence, supervisors must make sure that positively valent rewards are associated with good job performance, *and that their employees perceive this connection.* In practice, this also is difficult for a number of reasons. Most supervisors have a limited stock of rewards available to them for distribution to their subordinates. Company policies with regard to pay and benefits are usually restrictive, for the good reasons of control and the maintenance of equity. Further, union contracts are generally quite clear about the bases of reward distribution and often require that pay and other rewards be based on seniority rather than merit, further restricting the capacity of individual supervisors always to know who their meritorious employees are. This problem is especially common among managerial, professional, and technical personnel, in whose jobs good performance is normally very hard to measure, even when someone tries diligently to do so. As a result of these and other practical difficulties, implementing the instrumentality implications of VIE is often (perhaps usually) very difficult.

Valence-Related Factors

Where does the notion of valence fit into practice? VIE Theory would prescribe that those rewards which are distributed for good performance should be the types of things that employees desire. All that we know from common sense, as well as that which we have learned from research into human needs, tells us that different people have different need profiles at different times, so it follows that different outcomes will be rewarding for different people at different times. Hence, even the same outcome (such as a job transfer to another city) may be positively valent for some people, while being negatively valent for others. And to the extent that satisfied needs tend to lose their capacity to motivate behavior, we can expect certain organizationally-distributed rewards to be satisfying and perhaps motivating for a particular individual in some circumstances, but not so in other circumstances. Hence, older employees often have no desire to meet and befriend new employees on the job: their relatedness needs are already well met and secured by interactions with old friends and acquaintances. In short, implementing VIE, with regard to providing valent outcomes for work, can be very difficult in practice.

Individual Organizations

One leading authority has discussed the importance of attempting to reward individuals with outcomes that are best suited to their individual needs (Lawler,

1973, 1976). His suggestions entail comprehensive analyses of both the employees and the jobs in organizations, followed by the careful assignment of people to those jobs in which they will find outcomes they desire, *especially as a consequence of good performance*.

A notable attempt to structure rewards on a more-or-less individualized basis can be found in the concept of *cafeteria-style* compensation plans (Lawler, 1966; Nealy, 1963; Schuster, 1969). The general design of these plans is for the individual employee to be allotted a fixed dollar sum of compensation that she can distribute according to her own preferences across a variety of forms of compensation, including salary, and any of a number of fringe benefits, deferred earnings, stock options, and the like.

Cafeteria-style plans have not, however, been widely adopted; in large measure because of a number of practical considerations that were discussed above (Belcher, 1974). For example, these plans tend to make payroll accounting procedures more complicated and more expensive to administer (Hettenhouse, 1971). In addition, there seems to be some belief on the part of management groups that employees should be required to invest their earnings in at least some amount of protection from insecurity (such as long-term disability and health insurance), whether they desire to do so or not. Another problem concerns the fact that many group life and health insurance plans are priced according to the number of persons in an organization who subscribe to them. Therefore, any sort of compensation system that allows some people to opt out of a group plan may result in higher premiums for those who opt into group coverage, thereby discouraging the individual decisions to opt out. Yet another difficulty that can arise from cafeteria-style plans results when employees elect to take all or most of their compensation in the form of cash, thereby threatening the relationship of internal equity between job level and pay level in the eyes of the employees involved. Finally, Belcher (1974) suggests that some of the negative reactions to cafeteria plans arise from a fear that if compensation were completely individualized, the infinite number of combinations and blends that are possible would be completely unmanageable, but that it should be possible to offset this fear by arranging a limited number of combinations from which individuals may choose. It may be, according to Belcher, that it is not necessary to *totally* individualize compensation plans. In fact, a study by Mahoney (1964) supports this view.

Another problem usually encountered by managerial attempts to individualize employee rewards in a fashion consistent with VIE Theory concerns the difficulty of accurately determining the actual *needs* of individual employees. . . . Managers simply may not be able to accurately determine the needs of their employees, so they must rely on techniques such as attitude surveys and one-on-one discussions to learn about employee *values*.

The distinction between needs and values may appear academic, but it is more than that. Rewards may be satisfying, according to Locke (1976), as long as they correspond with employee values and are not inconsistent with employee needs. But when employee values deviate from needs (meaning that people desire things that are not actually conducive to their best interests), organizational reward systems aimed at fulfilling employee values may not be at all beneficial, for either the individuals involved or for the organization as a whole. So, for example, certain employees may indicate that they desire greater responsibility and decision making power in their jobs. This stated preference reflects first a value—something the individuals *believe* will be good for themselves. In many cases, this value, if attained, will in fact satisfy needs—in this case, greater responsibility may be instrumental for fulfilling growth needs. In other cases, however, employees find that greater responsibility on their jobs is burdensome, stressful, and very frustrating: not everybody benefits from having responsible jobs.

The point of all this is that attempts to structure organizational reward systems in accordance with VIE Theory require that managers determine, somehow, what their subordinates want, and that they then proceed to tie job performance to the distribution of those outcomes. As noted above, systematic attempts to do this are frequently undertaken with the aid of employee attitude surveys; therefore VIE Theory may serve to guide the construction of such surveys, as we will see.

The Content of Employee Surveys

While a complete discussion of the design and use of employee attitude surveys is beyond our present purpose, VIE Theory clearly has a number of implications for this process. Specifically, rather than including only questions dealing with employee attitudes (as is commonly the case), greater benefit can be gained from seeking insight into the nature of employee beliefs, particularly beliefs about whether people feel it is typically possible to convert effort into performance, and whether rewards are seen as being tied to performance and as being equitable (Lawler, 1967b). In addition, more can be learned from enquiring *why* employees hold high or low expectancy and instrumentality beliefs, as well as why they believe the distribution of rewards is seen as inequitable, should that be the case.

The reader who is interested in greater detail about the construction of employee surveys is referred to recent books by Nadler (1977) and Dunham and Smith (1979). Detail concerning the administration of surveys in organizational settings is provided by Williams, Seybolt, and Pinder (1975).

Summary

The point here is that even those managers and supervisors who understand VIE Theory, and who are capable of distilling practical implications from it for application on their jobs, are usually severely handicapped by countless practical features of organizations, work groups, union contracts, standard practices and policies, history, and precedents. More importantly however, we must remember that even if managers are able to structure work settings and reward distribution systems so as to comply with the implications of VIE Theory, they will not be successful unless their policies and practices result in beliefs and perceptions, on the part of employees, which are consistent with high performance levels. For example, employees might not realize that rewards are, in fact, distributed in accordance with merit, even if that is actually the case. Likewise, employees may underestimate their chances of succeeding at a task, because they are not aware of the help that is available to them at the time. According to VIE Theory, it is beliefs that ultimately determine employee behavior, so unless managerial practices translate into beliefs that are favorable toward high job performance, beliefs will not result in employee intentions to perform well.

To conclude, VIE Theory offers a number of elegant implications for managerial practices aimed at generating and sustaining high levels of employee motivation. But putting these implications into practice can be difficult, because managers are often quite limited in the degree of control they have over the practical factors that must be manipulated in order to totally determine their employees' expectancy, valence, and instrumentality beliefs, and thereby influencing their intentions to perform well.

REFERENCES

Arnold, H. J. A test of the validity of the multiplicative hypothesis of expectancy-valence theories of work motivation. *Academy of Management Journal*, 1981, *24*, 128–41.

Atkinson, J. W. Towards experimental analysis of human motivation in terms of motives, expectancies, and incentives. In J. W. Atkinson (Ed.) *Motives in fantasy, action, and society*. Princeton: Van Nostrand, 1958.

Atkinson, J. W. *An introduction to motivation*. Princeton, N.J.: Van Nostrand, 1964.

Belcher, D. *Compensation administration*. Englewood Cliffs, N.J.: Prentice-Hall, 1974.

Campbell, J. P., Dunnette, M. D., Lawler III, E. E. and Weick, K. E. *Managerial behavior, performance and effectiveness*. N.Y.: McGraw-Hill, 1970.

Campbell, J. P. & Pritchard, R. D. Motivation theory in industrial and organizational psychology. In M. D. Dunnette (Ed.) *Handbook of industrial and organizational psychology*. Chicago: Rand McNally, 1976.

Dachler, H. P. & Mobley, W. Construct validation of an instrumentality-expectancy-task-goal model of work motivation: Some theoretical boundary conditions. *Journal of Applied Psychology*, 1973, *58*, 397–418.

Davidson, D., Suppes, P. & Siegel, S. *Decision making: An experimental approach*. Stanford: Stanford University Press, 1957.

Deci, E. L. *Intrinsic motivation*. N.Y.: Plenum Press, 1975.

deLeo, P. J. & Pritchard, R. D. An examination of some methodological problems in testing expectancy-valence models with survey techniques. *Organizational Behavior and Human Performance*, 1974, *12*, 143–148.

Dessler, G. & Valenzi, E. R. Initiation of structure and subordinate satisfaction: A path analysis test of Path-Goal Theory. *Academy of Management Journal*, 1977, *20*, 251–260.

Downey, H. K., Sheridan, J. E. & Slocum, J. W. The Path-Goal Theory of leadership: A longitudinal analysis. *Organizational Behavior and Human Performance*, 1976, *16*, 156–176.

Dunham, R. B. & Smith, F. J. *Organizational surveys: An internal assessment of organizational health*. Glenview, Ill.: Scott, Foresman and Co., 1979.

Evans, M. G. The effects of supervisory behavior on the path-goal relationship. *Organizational Behavior and Human Performance*, 1970, *5*, 277–298.

Evans, M. G. Extensions of a path-goal theory of motivation. *Journal of Applied Psychology.*

Faltermayer, E. Who will do the dirty work tomorrow? *Fortune*, 1974, *89*(1), 132–138.

Feldman, J. M., Reitz, H. J. & Hiterman, R. J. Alternatives to optimization in expectancy theory. *Journal of Applied Psychology*, 1976, *61*, 712–720.

Georgopoulos, B. C., Mahoney, G. M. & Jones, N. W. A path-goal approach to productivity. *Journal of Applied Psychology*, 1957, *41*, 345–353.

Graen, G. Instrumentality theory of work motivation: Some experimental results and suggested modifications. *Journal of Applied Psychology Monograph*, 1969, *53*, No.2, Part 2.

Greene, C. N. Questions of causation in the path-goal theory of leadership. *Academy of Management Journal*, 1979, *22*, 22–41.

Hall, D. T. *Careers in organizations.* Pacific Palisades, Calif.: Goodyear, 1976.

Heneman, H. G. III & Schwab, D. P. Evaluation of research on expectancy theory predictions of employee performance. *Psychological Bulletin*, 1972, *78*(1), 1–9.

Hettenhouse, G. W. Compensation cafeteria for top executives. *Harvard Business Review*, 1971, *49*(5), 113–119.

House, R. J. A path-goal theory of leadership. *Administrative Science Quarterly*, 1971, *16*, 321–338.

House, R. J. & Dessler, G. The path-goal theory of leadership: Some post hoc and a priori tests. In J. G. Hunt (Ed.) *Contingency approaches to leadership.* Carbondale, Ill.: Southern Illinois University Press, 1974.

House, R. J. & Mitchell, T. R. Path-goal theory of leadership, *Journal of Contemporary Business*, 1974, *3*, 81–98.

House, R. J., Shapiro, H. J., & Wahba, M. A. Expectancy theory as a predictor of work behavior and attitude: A reevaluation of empirical evidence. *Decision Sciences*, 1974, 5, 481–506.

Johns, G. Difference score measures of organizational behavior variables: A critique. *Organizational Behavior and Human Performance*, 1981, *27*, 443–463.

Kopelman, R. E. Across-individual, within-individual and return on effort versions of expectancy theory. *Decision Sciences*, 1977, *8*, 651–662.

Kopelman, R. E. A causal correlational test of the Porter and Lawler framework. *Human Relations*, 1979, *32*, 545–556.

Kopelman, R. E. & Thompson, P. H. Boundary conditions for expectancy theory predictions of work motivation and job performance. *Academy of Management Journal*, 1976, *19*, 237–258.

Korman, A. K. Toward a hypothesis of work behavior. *Journal of Applied Psychology*, 1970, *54*, 31–41.

Korman, A. K. Hypothesis of work behavior revisited and an extension. *Academy of Management Review*, 1976, *1*, 50–63.

Lawler, E. E. The mythology of management compensation. *California Management Review*, 1966, *9*, 11–22.

Lawler, E. E. Attitude surveys and job performance. *Personnel Administration*, 1967b, *30* (5), 3–5, 22–24.

Lawler, E. E. *Pay and organization effectiveness: A psychological view.* New York: McGraw-Hill, 1971.

Lawler, E. E. *Motivation in work organizations.* Monterey, California. Brooks/Cole, 1973.

Lawler, E. E. Individualizing Organizations: A Needed Emphasis in Organizational Psychology. In H. Meltzer and F. R. Wickert (Eds.) *Humanizing organizational behavior.* Springfield, Ill.: Charles C. Thomas, 1976.

Lawler, E. E. & Suttle, J. L. Expectancy theory and job behavior. *Organizational Behavior and Human Performance*, 1973, *9*, 482–503.

Lewin, K. The conceptual representation and the measurement of psychological forces. *Contributions to Psychological Theory*, Durham, N.C.: Duke University Press, 1938, 1, No. 4.

Locke, E. A. The Nature and Causes of Job Satisfaction. In M. D. Dunnette (Ed.) *Handbook of industrial and organizational psychology*. Chicago, Rand McNally, 1976.

Locke, E. A. Personnel attitudes and motivation. *Annual Review of Psychology*, 1975, *26*, 457–480.

Mahoney, T. A. Compensation preferences of managers. *Industrial Relations*, 1964, *3*, 135–144.

Matsui, T., Kagawa, M., Nagamatsu, J. & Ohtsuka, Y. Validity of expectancy theory as a within-personal behavioral choice model for sales activities. *Journal of Applied Psychology*, 1977, *62*, 764–767.

Matsui, T. and Ohtsuka, Y. Within-person expectancy theory predictions of supervisory consideration and structure behavior. *Journal of Applied Psychology*, 1978, *63*, 128–131.

Mayes, B. T. Incorporating time-lag effects into the expectancy model of motivation: A reformulation of the model. *Academy of Management Review*, 1978a, *3*, 374–379.

Mayes, B. T. Some boundary conditions in the application of motivation models. *Academy of Management Review*, 1978b, *3*, 51–58.

Mitchell, T. R. Expectancy models of satisfaction, occupational preference and effort: A theoretical, methodological and empirical appraisal. *Psychological Bulletin*, 1974, *81*, 1053–1077.

Mitchell, T. R. & Biglan, A. Instrumentality theories: Current uses in psychology. *Psychological Bulletin*, 1971, *76*, 432–454.

Mitchell, T. R. & Nebeker, D. M. Expectancy theory predictions of academic effort and performance. *Journal of Applied Psychology*, 1973, *57*, 61–67.

Mobley, W. H. *Employee turnover: Causes, consequences, and control*. Reading, Mass.: Addison-Wesley, 1982.

Nadler, D. A. *Feedback and organization development: Using data-based methods*. Reading, Mass.: Addison-Wesley, 1977.

Naylor, J. D., Pritchard, R. D., & Ilgen, D. R. *A theory of behavior in organizations*. New York: Academic Press, 1980.

Nealey, S. M. Pay and benefit preference. *Industrial Relations*, 1963, *3*, 17–28.

Nebeker, D. M. & Mitchell, T. R. Leader behavior: An expectancy theory approach. *Organizational Behavior and Human Performance*, 1974, *11*, 355–367.

Parker, D. F. & Dyer, L. Expectancy theory as a within person behavioral choice model: An empirical test of some conceptual and methodological refinements. *Organizational Behavior and Human Performance*, 1976, *17*, 97–117.

Peak, H. Attitude and motivation. In M. R. Jones (Ed.) *Nebraska Symposium on Motivation*. Lincoln: University of Nebraska Press, 1955.

Pinder, C. C. Concerning the application of human motivation theories in organizational settings. *Academy of Management Review*, 1977, 2, 384–397.

Porter, L. W. & Lawler, E. E. *Managerial Attitudes and Performance*. Homewood, Illinois: Dorsey Press, 1968.

Reinharth, L. & Wahba, M. A. A test of alternative models of expectancy theory. *Human Relations*, 1976, *29*, 257–272.

Rotter, J. B. The Role of the Psychological Situation in Determining the Direction of Human Behavior. In M. R. Jones (Ed.) *Nebraska Symposium on Motivation*, Lincoln: University of Nebraska Press, 1955.

Schriesheim, C. A. & DeNisi, A. S. Task dimensions as moderators of the effects of instrumental leadership: A two-sample replicated test of path-goal leadership theory. *Journal of Applied Psychology*, 1981, *66*, 589–597.

Schriesheim, C. & Von Glinow, M. A. The path-goal theory of leadership: A theoretical and empirical analysis. *Academy of Management Journal*, 1977, 398–405.

Schriesheim, J. F. & Schriesheim, C. A. A test of the path-goal theory of leadership and some suggested directions for future research. *Personnel Psychology*, 1980, *33*, 349–370.

Schuster, J. R. Another look at compensation preferences. *Industrial Management Review*, 1969, *10*, 1–18.

Simon, H. A. *Administrative behavior.* (2nd ed.) New York: Macmillan, 1957.

Staw, B. M. Motivation in Organizations: Toward Synthesis and Redirection. In B. M. Staw and G. R. Salancik (Eds.) *New directions in organizational behavior.* Chicago: St. Clair Press, 1977.

Taylor, E. K. & Griess, T. The missing middle in validation research. *Personnel Psychology*, 1976, *29*, 5–11.

Terborg, J. R. Validation and extension of an individual differences model of work performance. *Organizational Behavior and Human Performance*, 1977, *18*, 188–216.

Tolman, E. C. Principles of Purposive Behavior. In S. Koch (Ed.) *Psychology: A Study of a Science.* Vol. 2. New York: McGraw-Hill, 1959.

Vroom, V. H. *Work and motivation.* New York: Wiley, 1964.

Walter, G. A. & Marks, S. E. *Experiential learning and change.* New York: Wiley, 1981.

Williams, L. K., Seybolt, J. W., & Pinder, C. C. On administering questionnaires in organizational settings. *Personnel Psychology*, 1975, *28*, 93–103.

Zedeck, S. An information processing model and approach to the study of motivation. *Organizational Behavior and Human Performance*, 1977, *18*, 47–77.

Equity Theory Predictions of Behavior in Organizations

Richard T. Mowday

Employees are seldom passive observers of the events that occur in the workplace. They form impressions of others and the events that affect them and cognitively or behaviorally respond based on their positive or negative evaluations. A great deal of theory and research in the social sciences has been devoted to understanding these evaluative processes. More specifically, research has attempted to uncover the major influences on individual reactions in social situations and the processes through which these reactions are formed. One useful framework for understanding how social interactions in the workplace influence employee reactions to their jobs and participation in the organization is provided by theories of

This paper was written especially for this volume. Support for the preparation of the manuscript was partially provided by a grant from the Office of Naval Research, Contract No. N00014-76-C-0164, NR 170-812. The assistance of Thom McDade in the early stages of preparing the paper is gratefully acknowledged.

social exchange processes (Adams, 1965; Homans, 1961; Jaques, 1961; Patchen, 1961; Simpson, 1972).

Exchange theories are based on two simple assumptions about human behavior. First, there is an assumed similarity between the process through which individuals evaluate their social relationships and economic transactions in the market. Social relationships can be viewed as exchange processes in which individuals make contributions (investments) for which they expect certain outcomes. Individuals are assumed to have expectations about the outcomes that should result when they contribute their time or resources in interaction with others.

The second assumption concerns the process through which individuals decide whether or not a particular exchange is satisfactory. Most exchange theories assign a central role to social comparison processes in terms of how individuals evaluate exchange relationships. Information gained through interaction with others is used to determine whether an exchange has been advantageous. For example, individuals may compare their outcomes and contributions in an exchange with the outcomes and contributions of the person with whom they are interacting. Where there is relative equality between the outcomes and contributions of both parties to an exchange, satisfaction is likely to result from the interaction.

The popularity of social exchange theories may be attributable to their agreement with commonsense observations about human behavior in social situations. Exchange theories suggest that individuals in social interaction behave in a manner similar to the ''economic man'' of classical economics. Most theories of motivation assume that individuals are motivated to maximize their rewards and minimize their costs (Vroom, 1964; Walster, Bercheid, & Walster, 1976). The major difference between assumptions made about economic man and social exchange theories is that the latter recognize that individuals exist in environments characterized by limited and imperfect information. The ambiguity present in most social situations results in individuals relying heavily on information provided by others to evaluate their actions and those of others (Darley & Darley, 1973). Social interactions therefore play a central role in providing information to individuals on the quality of their relationships with others. Our reliance upon others for valued information, however, may place constraints on how we behave in our interactions with others. In order to maintain our social relationships it may be necessary to conform to certain social norms that prevent us from maximizing our outcomes without regard to the outcome of others.

The purpose of this paper is to examine one prominent theory of social exchange processes: Adams' (1963a, 1965) theory of equity. Although Adams' theory is only one of several exchange theories that have been developed, it deserves special attention for several reasons. First, Adams' theory is perhaps the most rigorously developed statement of how individuals evaluate social exchange relationships. The careful formulation of the theory has led to considerable research interest in testing its specific predictions. The large number of studies available on equity theory provides evidence upon which to evaluate the adequacy of social exchange models. Second, the majority of research on equity theory has investigated employee reactions to compensation in employer-employee exchange relationships. The theory and supporting research are therefore highly relevant to increasing our understanding of behavior in organizational settings.

In the sections that follow, Adams' equity theory will be briefly summarized and the research evidence reviewed. The major empirical and conceptual questions surrounding the theory will then be discussed. Finally, the generalizability of the theory will be considered and suggestions made for applying equity theory to several previously neglected areas of organizational behavior.

EQUITY THEORY

Antecedents of Inequity

The major components of exchange relationships in Adams' theory are inputs and outcomes. Inputs or investments are those things a person contributes to the exchange. In a situation where a person exchanges his or her services for pay, inputs may include previous work experience, education, effort on the job, and training. Outcomes are those things that result from the exchange. In the employment situation, the most important outcome is likely to be pay. In addition, other outcomes such as supervisory treatment, job assignments, fringe benefits, and status symbols may also be considered in evaluating the exchange. To be considered in evaluating exchange relationships, inputs and outcomes must meet two conditions. First, the existence of an input or outcome must be recognized by one or both parties to the exchange. Second, an input or outcome must be considered relevant to the exchange (i.e., have some marginal utility). Unless inputs or outcomes are both recognized and considered relevant, they will not be considered in evaluating an exchange relationship.

Adams suggests that individuals weight their inputs and outcomes by their importance to the individual. Summary evaluation of inputs and outcomes are developed by separately summing the weighted inputs and weighted outcomes. In the summation process, inputs and outcomes are treated as independent even though they may be highly related (e.g., age and previous work experience would be considered as separate inputs). The ratio of an individual's (called "person's") outcomes to inputs is compared to the ratio of outcomes to inputs of another individual or group (called "other"). Other may be a person with whom you are engaged in a direct exchange, another individual engaged in an exchange with a common third party, or person in a previous or anticipated work situation. The selection of comparison others is discussed in more detail below. The important consideration at this point is that person evaluates his or her outcomes and inputs by comparing them with those of others.

Equity is said to exist whenever the ratio of person's outcomes to inputs is equal to the ratio of other's outcomes and inputs.

$$\frac{O_p}{I_p} = \frac{O_o}{I_o}$$

Inequity exists whenever the two ratios are unequal.

$$\frac{O_p}{I_p} < \frac{O_o}{I_o} \quad \text{or} \quad \frac{O_p}{I_p} > \frac{O_o}{I_o}$$

Several important aspects of this definition should be recognized. First, the conditions necessary to produce equity or inequity are based on the individual's perceptions of inputs and outcomes. In behavioral terms, the objective characteristics of the situation are of less importance than the person's perceptions. Second, inequity is a relative phenomenon. Inequity does not necessarily exist if person has high inputs and low outcomes as long as the comparison other has a similar ratio. Employees may therefore exhibit satisfaction on a job that demands a great deal and for which they receive very little if their comparison other is in a similar position. Third, inequity exists when a person is relatively underpaid and relatively overpaid. It is this implication of Adams' theory that has generated the most attention since it suggests that people will react in a counterintuitive fashion when they are overpaid. Research evidence indicates, however, that the threshold for underpayment is lower than that associated with overpayment (Levanthal, Weiss, & Long, 1969). As might be expected, individuals are somewhat more willing to accept overpayment in an exchange relationship than they are to accept underpayment. The relationship between the ratios of outcomes to inputs of person and other might best be considered along a continuum reflecting different degrees of inequity ranging from overpayment on one extreme to underpayment on the other. The midpoint of the continuum represents the point at which the two ratios are equal. Equity is defined as a zone which is asymmetric about the midpoint. The asymmetry reflects the fact that the thresholds for overpayment and underpayment may differ.

One final aspect of Adams' formulation should be mentioned. Walster et al. (1976) have shown that the formula relating the two ratios of person and other is inadequate in situations where inputs might be negative. Following their example, consider the situation where person's inputs have a value of 5 and outcomes are −10 while other's inputs and outcomes are −5 and 10, respectively. Using Adams' formula, these two ratios are equal and thus a condition of equity would be said to exist.

$$\frac{O_p}{I_p} = \frac{-10}{5} = -2 \text{ and } \frac{O_o}{I_o} = \frac{10}{-5} = -2$$

Obviously, a situation in which person makes positive inputs but receives negative outcomes is inequitable when compared to another who makes negative inputs but receives positive outcomes. Walster et al. (1976) have proposed an alternative formulation that overcomes this problem. Equity and inequity are defined by the following relationship.

$$\frac{\text{Outcomes}_p - \text{Inputs}_p}{(|\text{Inputs}_p|)^{k}{}_p} \text{ compared with } \frac{\text{Outcomes}_o - \text{Inputs}_o}{(|\text{Inputs}_o|)^{k}{}_o}$$

The reader interested in pursuing this subject further can find a more detailed discussion of this formula and its terms in Walster et al. (1976).

Consequence of Inequity

The motivational aspects of Adams' theory are derived from the hypothesized consequences of perceived inequity. The major postulates of the theory can be summarized simply: (1) perceived inequity creates tension in the individual; (2) the amount of tension is proportional to the magnitude of the inequity; (3) the tension created in the individual will motivate him or her to reduce it; and (4) the strength of the motivation to reduce inequity is proportional to the perceived inequity (Adams, 1965). In other words, the presence of inequity motivates the individual to change the situation through behavioral or cognitive means to return to a condition of equity.

The methods through which individuals reduce inequity are referred to as methods of inequity resolution. Adams describes six alternative methods of restoring equity: (1) altering inputs; (2) altering outcomes; (3) cognitively distorting inputs or outcomes; (4) leaving the field; (5) taking actions designed to change the inputs or outcomes of the comparison other; or (6) changing the comparison other. The choice of a particular method of restoring equity will depend upon the characteristics of the inequitable situation. Adams suggests, however, that the person will attempt to maximize positively valent outcomes and minimize increasingly effortful inputs in restoring equity. In addition, person will resist changing the object of comparison and distorting inputs that are considered central to the self-concept. In general, it is considered easier to distort other's inputs and outcomes than the person's own inputs or outcomes. Finally, leaving the field (e.g., turnover from an organization) as a method of reducing inequity will only be considered in extreme cases of inequity.

RESEARCH ON EQUITY THEORY PREDICTIONS OF EMPLOYEE REACTIONS TO PAY

Considerable research interest has been generated in testing predictions from Adams' theory. The most recent review of equity theory research summarized the results from over 160 investigations (Adams & Freedman, 1976). Although equity considerations are relevant to a number of different types of social relationships (cf., Walster et al., 1976), most early research focused attention on the employer-employee exchange relationship. These studies were generally laboratory investigations in which subjects were hired to perform relatively simple tasks such as proofreading or interviewing. The simple nature of the tasks suggests that differences found between subjects in the quantity or quality of performance would be attributable to motivation levels rather than differences in skills or abilities. Perceived inequity was induced by either manipulating the subject's perceived qualifications to be hired for the task (qualifications manipulation) or by actual differences in pay rates (manipulation by circumstances).

Predictions from equity theory about employee reactions to pay distinguish between two conditions of inequity (underpayment versus overpayment) and two methods of compensation (hourly versus piece rate). Specific predictions are summarized for each condition in Table 1. The methodology and results of selected studies designed to test these predictions are presented in Table 2. More extensive

TABLE 1
EQUITY THEORY PREDICTIONS OF EMPLOYEE REACTIONS TO INEQUITABLE PAYMENT

	Underpayment	Overpayment
Hourly payment	Subjects underpaid by the hour produce less or poorer-quality output than equitably paid subjects	Subjects overpaid by the hour produce more or higher-quality output than equitably paid subjects.
Piece-rate payment	Subjects underpaid by piece rate will produce a large number of low-quality units in comparison with equitably paid subjects	Subjects overpaid by piece rate will produce fewer units of higher quality than equitably paid subjects

reviews of this literature can be found in Adams and Freedman (1976), Campbell and Pritchard (1976), Goodman and Friedman (1971), Lawler (1968a), Opsahl and Dunnette (1966), and Pritchard (1969).

A review of the studies summarized in Table 2 suggests general support for equity theory predictions. In the overpayment-hourly condition, a number of studies have provided some support for the prediction that overpaid subjects will produce higher quantity than equitably paid subjects (Adams & Rosenbaum, 1962); Arrowood, 1961; Goodman & Friedman, 1968; Lawler, 1968b; Pritchard, Dunnette, & Jorgenson, 1972; Wiener, 1970). Several studies have either failed to support or provided mixed support for equity theory predictions in this condition, although they often differed from the supporting studies in the manner in which perceived inequity was experimentally manipulated (Anderson & Shelly, 1970; Evans & Simmons, 1969; Friedman & Goodman, 1967; Valenzi & Andrews, 1971). In the overpayment-piece-rate condition, support for the theory has been found by Adams (1963b), Adams and Jacobsen (1964), Adams and Rosenbaum (1962), Andrews (1967), and Goodman and Friedman (1969). Mixed or marginal support for the theory was provided by Lawler, Koplin, Young, and Fadem (1968) and Wood and Lawler (1970). Although fewer studies have examined the under-payment conditions, support for both the hourly and piece-rate predictions have been reported (Andrews, 1967; Evans & Simmons, 1969; Lawler & O'Gara, 1967; Pritchard et al., 1972).

Although the support for Adams' theory appears impressive, several questions concerning the interpretation of the study results need to be considered. Following Vroom (1964), Goodman and Friedman (1971) suggest that the following concepts must be operationalized to provide a complete and unambiguous test of equity theory: (1) person's evaluation of his or her inputs; (2) person's perception of the relevance of the inputs for task performance; (3) person's perception of the experimenter's perception of the inputs; (4) person's perception of other's out-come-input ratio; (5) person's perception of future outcomes; (6) person's perception of the outcomes relative to alternative outcomes (e.g., past outcomes); and (7) relative importance person attaches to using 4, 5, and 6 as comparison objects. Control over these factors is central to ensuring a high degree of internal validity for the results of experimental studies. To the extent these factors may remain uncontrolled, conclusive tests of the theory become very difficult and alternative explanations for the study results can be raised. It should be apparent that many of these factors remain uncontrolled in even the most rigorous laboratory experiment. For example, Goodman and Friedman (1971) point out that the comparison other used by subjects is ambiguous in most studies. To the extent subjects use different comparison others than intended by the experimenter, interpretation of the study results becomes problematic.

A number of writers have been critical of research on equity theory precisely because several alternative explanations may exist for observed differences in the performance of subjects, particularly in the overpayment condition (Campbell & Pritchard, 1976; Goodman & Freidman, 1971; Lawler, 1968a; Pritchard, 1969). Two problems are commonly raised in interpreting the results of research on overpayment inequity, and both have to do with experimental manipulations of perceived inequity. Inequity is commonly induced in subjects by challenging their qualifications for the job. Subjects are led to believe they do not possess the necessary experience or training to qualify for the rate of pay they are to receive. Although seldom verified, it is assumed that this will result in experienced overpayment inequity (i.e., subjects believe they are being paid more than they should receive given their qualifications).

Challenging the qualifications of subjects, however, may also be experienced as threatening their self-esteem or perceived job security. Subjects may therefore work harder to prove to themselves (and to the experimenter) that they are capable of performing the task or to protect their job security. In other words, subjects may perform as predicted by the theory for reasons related to the experimental treatment but not to perceived inequity. Support for these alternative explanations for results of research on overpayment inequity comes from several sources. Andrews and Valenzi (1970) had subjects role-play an overpayment inequity situation in which subject qualifications to perform the task were challenged. When asked to indicate how they would respond in this situation, none of the subjects responded in terms of wage inequity. A majority of subjects, however, responded in terms of their self-image as a worker. In another study, Wiener (1970) found that overpaid subjects produced more than equitably paid subjects only when the task was ego-involving (i.e., task performance was central to the self concept). Based on this finding, he argued that the performance of subjects in the overpayment condition was more highly attributable to devalued self-esteem brought about by challenges to their qualifications than to feelings of inequity. In studies where perceived inequity has been manipulated by means other than challenging the subject's qualifications (e.g., by actual changes in pay rates), less support is commonly found for equity theory predictions (Evans & Simmons, 1969; Pritchard et al., 1972; Valenzi & Andrews, 1971).

Several writers have seriously questioned the extent to which overpayment in work organizations may lead to perceived inequity. Locke (1976), for example, argues that employees are seldom told they are overpaid or made to feel incompetent to perform their job duties as is the case in laboratory experiments. He argues that employees are more likely to simply adjust their idea of equitable payment to justify what they are getting. This raises the possibility that employees in organizations use their pay rates as a primary source of information about their contribu-

TABLE 2
SUMMARY OF EQUITY THEORY RESEARCH ON EMPLOYEE REACTIONS TO PAY

Study	Equity condition	Method of induction	Task	Dependent variables	Results
Adams (1963b)	Overpayment: hourly and piece rate	Qualifications	Interviewing	Productivity, work quality	Hourly-overpaid subjects produced greater quantity and piece-rate—overpaid subjects produced higher quality and lower quantity than equitably paid subjects.
Adams and Jacobsen (1964)	Overpayment: piece rate	Qualifications	Proofreading	Productivity, work quality	Overpaid subjects produced less quantity of higher quality.
Adams and Rosenbaum (1962)	Overpayment: hourly and piece rate	Qualifications	Interviewing	Productivity	Hourly-overpaid subjects produced more quantity while piece-rate—overpaid subjects produced less quantity.
Anderson and Shelly (1970)	Overpayment: hourly	Qualifications, importance of task	Proofreading	Productivity, work quality	No differences were found between groups
Andrews (1967)	Overpayment and underpayment: piece rate	Circumstances, previous wage experiences	Interviewing Data checking	Productivity, work quality	Overpaid subjects produced higher quality and underpaid subjects produced greater quantity and lower quality.

Study					
Arrowood (1961)	Overpayment: hourly	Qualifications, work returned	Interviewing	Productivity	Overpaid subjects had higher productivity.
Evans and Simmons (1969)	Overpayment and underpayment: hourly	Competence, authority	Proofreading	Productivity, work quality	Underpaid subjects produced more of poorer quality in competence condition. No differences found in other conditions.
Friedman and Goodman (1967)	Overpayment: hourly	Qualifications	Interviewing	Productivity	Qualifications induction did not affect productivity. When subjects were classified by perceived qualifications, unqualified subjects produced less than qualified subjects.
Goodman and Friedman (1968)	Overpayment and underpayment: hourly	Qualifications, quantity versus quality emphasis	Questionnaire coding	Productivity, work quality	Overpaid subjects produced more than equitably paid subjects. Emphasis on quantity versus quality affected performance.
Goodman and Friedman (1969)	Overpayment: piece rate	Qualifications, quantity versus quality emphasis	Questionnaire scoring	Productivity, work quality	Overpaid subjects increased productivity or work quality, depending upon induction.
Lawler (1968b)	Overpayment: hourly	Qualifications, circumstances	Interviewing	Productivity, work quality	Overpaid (unqualified) subjects produced more of lower quality. Subjects overpaid by circumstances did not differ from equitably paid group.

TABLE 2
SUMMARY OF EQUITY THEORY RESEARCH ON EMPLOYEE REACTIONS TO PAY (CONTINUED)

Study	Equity condition	Method of induction	Task	Dependent variables	Results
Lawler, Koplin, Young, and Fadem (1968)	Overpayment: piece rate	Qualifications	Interviewing	Productivity, work quality	Overpaid subjects produced less of higher quality in initial work session. In later sessions, subject's perceived qualifications and productivity increased. The need for money was related to productivity for both groups.
Lawler and O'Gara (1967)	Underpayment: piece rate	Circumstances	Interviewing	Productivity, work quality	Underpaid subjects produced more of lower quality and also perceived their job as more interesting but less important and complex.
Pritchard, Dunnette, and Jorgenson (1972)	Overpayment and underpayment: hourly and piece rate	Circumstances, actual change in payment	Clerical task	Performance satisfaction	Circumstances induction did not result in performance differences for piece rate, but some support was found for hourly overpay and underpay.

Study	Independent variable	Independent variable (2)	Task	Dependent variables	Results
Valenzi and Andrews (1971)	Overpayment and underpayment: hourly	Circumstances	Clerical task	Productivity, work quality	Changes in pay rate supported hourly predictions. Some support found for piece-rate—overpayment prediction but not for underpayment.
Wiener (1970)	Overpayment: hourly	Qualifications, inputs versus outcomes, ego-oriented versus task-oriented	Word manipulation	Productivity, work quality	No significant differences found between conditions. 27 percent of underpaid subjects quit. No other subjects in other conditions quit. Outcome-overpayment subjects produced more. Input-overpaid subjects produced more only on ego-oriented task.
Wood and Lawler (1970)	Overpayment: piece rate	Qualifications	Reading	Amount of time reading, quality	Overpaid subjects produced less, but this could not be attributed to striving for higher quality.

tions (e.g., "if the organization is willing to pay this much, I must be making a valuable contribution"). Campbell and Pritchard (1976) also point out that employer-employee exchange relationships are highly impersonal when compared to exchanges between two close friends. Perceived overpayment inequity may be more likely in the latter exchange relationship than in the former. Individuals may react to overpayment inequity only when they believe their actions have led to someone else's being treated unfairly (Campbell & Pritchard, 1976; Walster et al., 1976). From the employee's standpoint in work organizations, there may be little objective evidence that the organization feels it is being treated unfairly.

In summary, predictions from Adams' theory about employee reactions to wage inequities have received some support in the research literature. Research support for the theory appears to be strongest for predictions about underpayment inequity. Although there are fewer studies of underpayment than of overpayment, results of research on underpayment are relatively consistent and subject to fewer alternative explanations. There are both theoretical and empirical grounds for being cautious in generalizing the results of research on overpayment inequity to employee behavior in work organizations. Where such studies have manipulated perceived inequity by challenging subjects' qualifications for the job, observed differences in performance can be explained in ways that have little to do with inequity. Where other methods of inducing overpayment inequity are used, considerably less support is often found for the theory. Predicted differences in productivity and satisfaction due to overpayment inequity are often in the predicted direction but fail to reach acceptable levels of statistical significance.

Conceptual Issues in Equity Theory

In addition to the methodological considerations discussed with respect to research on equity theory, several writers have also raised questions about the conceptual adequacy of the theory (e.g., Weick, 1967). Since theories or models of social processes are ways of making sense out of our environment by simplifying relationships between variables, it should not be surprising that any given theory fails to capture the complexity we know to exist in the real world. Consequently, there are usually a number of limitations that can be pointed out in any given theory, and equity theory is no different from other motivation approaches in this regard. The conceptual issues to be discussed below point to several limitations of the present formulation of equity theory, and they should be viewed as areas in which the theory may be clarified or extended through further research.

Concept of Equity

The concept of equity is most often interpreted in work organizations as a positive association between an employee's effort or performance on the job and the pay he or she receives (Goodman, 1977). In other words, it is believed that employees who contribute more to the organization should receive higher amounts of the rewards the organization has to offer. This belief is often referred to as the "equity norm." Adams (1965) suggests that individual expectations about equity or "fair" correlations between inputs and outcomes are learned during the process of socialization (e.g., in the home or at work) and through comparison with the inputs and outcomes of others. Although few would question the existence of an equity norm governing social relationships, the derivation of this norm and its pervasiveness remain somewhat unclear. In addition, it is important to determine the extent to which the equity norm is defined by an individual's effort and performance or by other types of contributions they may make to organizations.

Walster et al. (1976) suggest the norm of equity originates in societal attempts to develop methods of allocating rewards that maximize the amount of collective reward. Through evolving ways to "equitably" distribute rewards and costs among its members, groups or organizations can maximize the total rewards available. Groups therefore induce their members to behave equitably and establish reinforcement systems to ensure this norm is followed in social relationships. It should be apparent, however, that groups or society in general frequently deviate from the equity norm in distributing rewards. Social welfare programs and old-age medical assistance, for example, are instances in which resources are distributed on the basis of need rather than an assessment of the individual's contribution to the larger group.

The equity norm appears to be only one of several norms that govern the distribution of rewards in social relationships. An important question concerns what factors influence the extent to which rewards are distributed equitably or allocated on some other basis. In an analysis of reward allocation in small groups, Leventhal (1976) suggests that the particular distribution rule adopted in allocating rewards is related to both the goals of the reward system and characteristics of the allocator. Table 3 contrasts three decision rules that can be used in allocating rewards (equity, equality, and responsiveness to needs) and the situations where each rule is most likely to be used. The equity norm appears to be most closely associated with the goal of maximizing productivity in a group, while rewards are most likely to be distributed equally when the goal is to minimize group conflict.

Distribution rules represent an important concept in understanding reward systems (Cook, 1975; Goodman, 1977). Distribution rules identify the association between any dimension of evaluation and the levels of outcomes to be distributed. A consideration of distribution rules suggests both that different norms may govern the distribution of rewards in organizations and that different factors may weight more heavily in allocating rewards using any given norm. For example, in organizations where an equity norm is followed, it is common to find that an individual's contribution in terms of seniority is a more important basis for rewards than is actual job performance. Our ability to predict how individuals react to reward systems therefore depends upon identifying the particular norm they believe should be followed and the specific dimension (i.e., input) they feel is most important in allocating rewards. Equity theory often assumes that rewards should be given in relation to a person's contribution and, further, that performance is the most important contribution in the work setting. The accuracy of our predictions of employee reactions to reward systems can be increased, however, by recognizing the existence of several norms governing the distribution of rewards and the differential importance that may be attached to employee inputs.

TABLE 3
DISTRIBUTION RULES FOR ALLOCATING REWARDS

Distribution rule	Situations where distribution rule is likely to be used	Factors affecting use of distribution rule
Equity/contributions (outcomes should match contributions)	1 Goal is to maximize group productivity. 2 A low degree of cooperation is required for task performance.	1 What receiver is expected to do 2 What others receive 3 Outcomes and contributions of person allocating rewards 4 Task difficulty and perceived ability 5 Personal characteristics of person allocating rewards and person performing
Social responsibility/needs (outcomes distributed on the basis of needs)	1 Allocator of rewards is a close friend of the receiver, feels responsible for the well-being of the receiver, or is successful or feels competent.	1 Perceived legitimacy of needs 2 Origin of need (e.g., beyond control of the individual)
Equality (equal outcomes given to all participants)	1 Goal is to maximize harmony, minimize conflict in group. 2 Task of judging performer's needs or contribution is difficult. 3 Person allocating rewards has a low cognitive capacity. 4 A high degree of cooperation is required for task performance. 5 Allocator anticipates future interactions with low-input member.	1 Sex of person allocating rewards (e.g., females more likely to allocate rewards equally than males) 2 Nature of task

Source: Adapted from Leventhal (1976).

Choice of a Method of Inequity Resolution

Although the several factors Adams (1965) suggested individuals will take into consideration in choosing among alternative methods of reducing inequity make the theory more testable, they do not allow a totally unequivocal set of predictions to be made from the theory (Wicklund & Brehm, 1976). In any situation, a given method of restoring inequity may satisfy one of these rules while at the same time violating another. Cognitively distorting inputs as a method of reducing inequity, for example, may allow the individual to maximize positively valent outcomes, but at the expense of threatening aspects central to his or her self-concept. When such a conflict occurs, it is difficult to specify how an individual will react to inequity. Opsahl and Dunnette (1966) have pointed out that the inability to predict how individuals will react to inequity makes conclusive tests of the theory problematic. If an overcompensated group fails to respond to inequity by increasing inputs, can this be interpreted as a disconfirmation of the theory or as an instance in which other methods of reducing inequity (e.g., cognitively distorting your own or other's inputs or outcomes) are being used? This ambiguity associated with equity theory appears to result in a situation where almost any result of empirical research can be explained in terms of the theory.

Many of the studies of equity theory have failed to capture the complexity of inequity resolution processes (Adams & Freedman, 1976). It is common in such studies to set up an inequitable situation and determine the extent to which subjects reduce inequity by changing work quantity or quality. In more personal exchange relationships, however, the method of reducing inequity chosen may be sensitive to cues from the other party to the exchange (Adams & Freedman, 1976). For example, in overpayment situations, an organization may suggest employees increase their skills and abilities through further education rather than increasing their effort on the job. Research also suggests that strategies for reducing inequity are dynamic and may change over time. Lawler et al. (1968) found that subjects reduced overpayment-piece-rate inequity by increasing work quality in an initial work session but increased their perceived qualifications to perform the task in subsequent sessions. Cognitively changing perceived inputs (qualifications) may have allowed subjects to reduce the overpayment inequity in a manner that permitted increased quantity of production and thus increased rewards to be received.

The way in which individuals reduce perceived inequity appears to be a complex process. A greater understanding of this process is essential to increasing the accuracy of predictions from equity theory.

Choice of a Comparison Other

One area of recent concern in equity theory is to develop a greater understanding of how individuals choose comparison standards against which to evaluate inputs and outcomes. Adams (1965) suggested that comparison others may be the other party to the exchange or another individual involved in an exchange with the same third party. Until recently, little has been known about the actual comparison standards people use or the process through which alternative comparisons are chosen.

Goodman (1974) differentiated between three classes of referents: (1) others, (2) self-standards, and (3) system referents. Others are people who may be involved in a similar exchange either with the same organization or with some other organization. Self-standards are unique to the individual but different from his or her current ratio of outcomes and inputs; for example, individuals may compare their current ratio against inputs and outcomes associated with an earlier job. System referents are implicit or explicit contractual expectations between an employer and employee. At the time of being hired, an employee may be promised future rewards and this can become a basis for evaluating the exchange. In a study of 217 managers, Goodman (1974) found each of these referents was used in determining the degree of satisfaction with pay. Perhaps his most important finding was that a majority of managers reported using multiple referents in assessing their satisfaction. For example, 28 percent of the managers indicated they compared their present situation against both those of others and self-standards. He also found that higher levels of education were associated with choosing a comparison referent outside the organization.

Based on his research, Goodman (1977) has developed a model of the factors that may influence the selection of comparison person or standard. This model is presented in Figure 1. He postulates that the choice of a referent is a function of both the availability of information about the referent and the relevance or attractiveness of the referent for the comparison. Availability of information about referents is primarily determined by the individual's propensity to search and his or her position in an organization (i.e., access to information). The relevance or attractiveness of a referent is determined jointly by the instrumentality of the referent for satisfying the individual's comparison needs and the number and strength of needs related to a referent. A more detailed discussion of this model can be found in Goodman (1977).

Goodman's (1974, 1977) work represents an important step in increasing our understanding of how social comparison processes are made. If his model is supported by subsequent research, it will provide an important tool for both researchers and managers in determining who or what employees use in making comparisons about their present level of rewards.

FIGURE 1
Factors influencing the selection of a referent in social comparison processes. (Adapted from Goodman, 1977.)

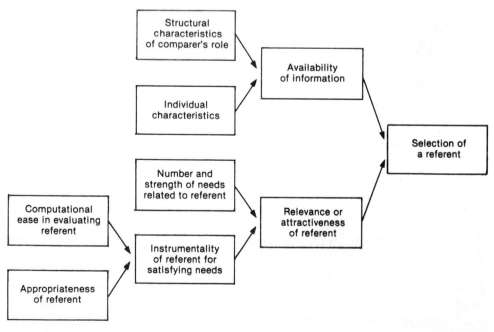

Individual and Situational Differences in Reactions to Inequity

One area of research on equity theory that has received little attention is the impact of individual and situational differences on employee perceptions and reactions to inequity. The importance of considering individual differences was first demonstrated by Tornow (1971). Recognizing that the classification of something as an input or an outcome is often ambiguous in equity comparisons, he suggested that individuals may have a stable tendency to classify ambiguous job elements as either inputs or outcomes. Using the data collected by Pritchard et al. (1972), he subsequently classified subjects as either input- or outcome-oriented and found this factor had an impact on their reactions to inequity. For example, outcome-oriented individuals were found to be more sensitive to overpayment than were subjects with an input orientation. Individual differences were therefore having an effect on how individuals reacted to perceived inequity. This is an area in which more research is needed to isolate the stable traits of individuals that can affect inequity perceptions. One variable that may be promising is the individual's level of internal/external control (Rotter, 1966). It is possible that individuals who believe events that happen to them are under their control (internals) would have a greater propensity to attempt to reduce perceived inequity than individuals who believe events are largely beyond their control (externals).

The importance of considering situational factors in employee reactions to inequity has already been noted in discussing Campbell and Pritchard's (1976) personal-impersonal exchange continuum. In the overpayment situation, employees may not react strongly to perceived inequity since the exchange with the larger organization is quite impersonal. However, where exchanges are between two close friends, both parties to the exchange may be highly sensitive to any inequities. Walster et al. (1976) have noted that an individual who feels responsible for an inequitable situation may express greater tension than someone who inadvertently finds himself or herself in an inequitable relationship. The locus of cause for a perceived inequity may therefore represent an important consideration in how individuals react to perceived inequity, particularly when the inequity is favorable to themselves.

RELATIONSHIP OF EQUITY THEORY TO EXPECTANCY THEORY

Much of the original interest in equity theory came from the fact that it made predictions about individual behavior that were difficult to incorporate into existing theories of motivation (Weick, 1967). For example, in the overpayment-piece-rate situation equity theory predicted that employees will increase quality and reduce quantity of performance. In contrast, expectancy theory appears to suggest that individual attempt to maximize the attainment of valued outcomes and that motivation levels should be high whenever attractive outcomes (e.g., pay) are made directly contingent upon performance. Considerable research interest has been generated in trying to test these seemingly competing predictions.

Lawler (1968a) was one of the first to suggest that equity theory and expectancy theory may not be irreconcilable in terms of their predictions. A review of the equity theory literature led Lawler to conclude that the results of studies of the hourly payment condition could be explained equally well by expectancy theory. In the piece-rate conditions, expectancy theory could make the same predictions as equity theory if it was assumed that perceived inequity influenced the valence or attractiveness of rewards. It is possible that increasingly large piece-rate rewards have a decreasing valence for employees and that the amount of reward that has been received influences the valence of additional amounts of the reward. Lawler felt that if perceived equity were explicitly recognized as one of the factors affecting the valence of outcomes, expectancy theory could explain the results of equity theory research. Lawler (1973) and others (Campbell & Pritchard, 1976) have therefore concluded that equity considerations could be subsumed under the more general expectancy theory of motivation.

Although the two theories do not really appear to be in conflict, it is unclear whether this reflects genuine similarity or the ambiguity with which the theories are stated. As noted by Campbell and Pritchard (1976), both theories are somewhat ambiguous and thus it always is possible to come up with some previously unrecognized outcome that will reconcile competing predictions. In addition, the effects of perceived inequity on the valence of outcomes remains to be demonstrated. Although Lawler et al. (1968) found that the need for money correlated more highly with productivity for overpaid subjects than for equitably paid subjects, need for money was not experimentally manipulated and thus the direction of causality is difficult to establish. In addition, a composite measure of need for money was constructed based on measures taken both before and after the manipulation of perceived overpayment. Consequently, the effects of the inequity manipulation on the subject's need for money (an indicator of valence of money) cannot be determined.

In view of the ambiguity surrounding the two theories and the lack of evidence concerning the effects of perceived inequity on the valence of outcomes, it is perhaps premature to conclude that equity theory can be incorporated into expectancy theory. As Adams (1968) has argued, it may be less useful to debate which theory can be incorporated into the other than to identify the conditions in which individual behavior is guided by either equity or expectancy considerations.

CONCLUSIONS AND DIRECTIONS FOR FUTURE RESEARCH

Evaluating the current status of equity theory presents something of a dilemma; depending upon the particular body of literature one examines, very different conclusions can be drawn. On the one hand, researchers interested in organizations have largely moved away from equity theory to other motivation approaches in explaining behavior in the workplace. After a high level of initial research interest, organization researchers appear to have followed the arguments of Lawler (1973) and others that equity theory can be incorporated into expectancy theory. Consequently, research involving applications of equity theory to organizational settings has decreased in recent years. If the current literature in social psychology is examined, on the other hand, a very different picture emerges. Walster et al.

(1976) recently introduced a reformulation of Adams' original theory, and it has been heralded as a general theory of social behavior capable of integrating a number of the minitheories (e.g., reinforcement theory, cognitive consistency theory) that currently exist. Berkowitz and Walster (1976, p. xi) go so far as to talk about "a new mood of optimism" emerging in social psychology, at least in part attributable to the promise of equity theory for developing a more comprehensive understanding of social behavior.

Has equity theory largely outlived its usefulness as a theory of motivation in organizations, or is it a theory capable of providing general explanations of behavior in a number of different social settings? This is a difficult question to answer at the present time. However, it appears that equity theory has more to contribute to our understanding of organizational behavior than previous research would suggest. The early emphasis of organizational research on equity theory predictions of employee reactions to pay was perhaps both its greatest strength and weakness. On the positive side, focusing on monetary rewards provided a research setting in which the variables were easily quantifiable and the predictions were relatively unambiguous (or so it seemed at the time). On the negative side, exclusive interest in employee reactions to pay prevented the extension of equity theory to other areas of social relationships in organizations. Adams (1965) was careful to note that equity theory was relevant to any social situations in which exchanges may take place (e.g., between coworkers, between superiors and subordinates, etc.). With the exception of Goodman's (1977) recent work on social comparison process in organizations, the extension of the theory to a broad range of social relationships has been left to social psychologists (see Berkowitz & Walster, 1976). Several areas of behavior in organizations that might profitably be examined in equity theory terms are discussed below.

Previous research on equity theory has largely been concerned with individual reactions to perceived inequity. What appears to have been neglected are the instrumental uses of inequity in interpersonal relationships (Adams & Freedman, 1976). Individuals in organizations, for example, may purposely create perceived inequity in social relationships as a way of improving their situation or achieving certain goals. Supervisors may routinely attempt to convince employees that they are not contributing as much as another employee or at a level expected for the pay they receive. Creating perceptions of overpayment inequity may therefore be viewed as a strategy designed to increase the level of employee performance. Just as routinely, employees may attempt the same strategy, but in reverse. Ingratiation attempts (Wortman & Linsenmeier, 1977) may be viewed as strategies on the part of lower-status employees to increase the outcomes of those in higher level positions. To the extent that those in higher positions perceive an inequity in their social relationships with lower-level employees, they will feel obligated to reciprocate. Research evidence that individuals may create perceived inequity in social relationships as a means of accomplishing certain objectives was presented by Leventhal and Bergman (1969). They found that subjects who were moderately underrewarded attempted to reduce the inequity by taking some of their partner's money when given the opportunity. Subjects who were extremely underrewarded, however, increased the discrepancy between their own rewards and those of their partner by increasing his or her advantage. By intensifying the inequity, subjects may have been following a deliberate strategy designed to convince their partner that a more equitable distribution of rewards was necessary.

Campbell, Dunnette, Lawler, and Weick (1970) have suggested the importance of viewing leadership processes in terms of exchanges between superiors and subordinates. In describing what they call the "unilateral fiction" in leadership research, they point out that managers are most often viewed as initiating the action of others and that superior-subordinate interactions are assumed to end when the manager issues a directive. Relationships between superiors and subordinates in organizations, however, are more accurately characterized by reciprocal-influence processes. A great deal of interaction between managers and employees in organizations may involve bargaining processes in which the terms of an exchange are established to the satisfaction of each party. When the manager issues a directive that is carried out by the employee, it is reasonable to assume that expectations of repayment are formed in the employee. Furthermore, when employees do a favor for the manager it may result in a perceived obligation to reciprocate on the part of the manager. Reciprocal relationships between managers and employees can be described in terms of equity theory; taking such a perspective may increase our understanding of the leadership process.

Equity theory appears to offer a useful approach to understanding a wide variety of social relationships in the workplace. Additional research is needed to extend predictions from the theory beyond simple questions about how employees react to their pay. As Goodman and Friedman (1971) have noted, equity theory predictions about employee performance levels may be one of the less interesting and useful applications of the theory. The effects of perceived inequity on employee performance levels are often slight and of limited time duration. The utility of equity theory may be greatest for increasing our understanding of interpersonal interactions at work (e.g., supervisory-subordinate relationships). In this regard, researchers interested in organizations may want to follow the lead of social psychologists in extending applications of the theory.

REFERENCES

Adams, J. S. Toward an understanding of inequity. *Journal of Abnormal and Social Psychology,* 1963, **67**, 422–436. (a)

Adams, J. S. Wage inequities, productivity and work quality. *Industrial Relations,* 1963, **3**, 9–16. (b)

Adams, J. S. Inequity in social exchange. In L. Berkowitz (Ed.), *Advances in experimental social psychology.* Vol. 2. New York: Academic Press, 1965. Pp. 267–299.

Adams, J. S. Effects of overpayment: Two comments on Lawler's paper. *Journal of Personality and Social Psychology,* 1968, **10**, 315–316.

Adams, J. S., & Freedman, S. Equity theory revisited: Comments and annotated bibliography. In L. Berkowitz & E. Walster (Eds.), *Advances in experimental social psychology,* Vol. 9. New York: Academic Press, 1976. Pp. 43–90.

Adams, J. S., & Jacobsen, P. R. Effects of wage inequities on work quality. *Journal of Applied Psychology,* 1964, **69**, 19–25.

Adams, J. S., & Rosenbaum, W. B. The relationship of worker productivity to cognitive dissonance about wage inequities. *Journal of Applied Psychology,* 1962, **46**, 161–164.

Anderson, B., & Shelly, R. K. Reactions to inequity, II: A replication of the Adams experiment and a theoretical reformulation. *Acta Sociologica,* 1970, **13**, 1–10.

Andrews, I. R. Wage inequity and job performance: An experimental study. *Journal of Applied Psychology,* 1967, **51**, 39–45.

Andrews, I. R., & Valenzi, E. Overpay inequity or self-image as a worker: a critical examination of an experimental induction procedure. *Organizational Behavior and Human Performance,* 1970, **53**, 22–27.

Arrowood, A. J. Some effects on productivity of justified and unjustified levels of reward under public and private conditions. Unpublished doctoral dissertation, University of Minnesota, 1961.

Berkowitz, L., & Walster, E. (Eds.), *Advances in experimental social psychology,* Vol. 9. New York: Academic Press, 1976.

Campbell, J. P., Dunnette, M. D., Lawler, E. E., & Weick, K. E. *Managerial behavior, performance, and effectiveness.* New York: McGraw-Hill, 1970.

Campbell, J., & Pritchard, R. D. Motivation theory in industrial and organizational psychology. In M. Dunnette (Ed.), *Handbook of industrial and organizational psychology.* Chicago: Rand McNally, 1976. Pp. 63–130.

Cook, K. S. Expectations, evaluations and equity. *American Sociological Review,* 1975, **40**, 372–388.

Darley, J. M., & Darley, S. A. *Conformity and deviation.* Morristown, N.J.: General Learning Press, 1973.

Evans, W. M., & Simmons, R. G. Organizational effects of inequitable rewards: Two experiments in status inconsistency. *Administrative Science Quarterly,* 1969, **14**, 224–237.

Friedman, A., & Goodman, P. Wage inequity, self-qualifications, and productivity. *Organizational Behavior and Human Performance,* 1967, **2**, 406–417.

Goodman, P. S. An examination of referents used in the evaluation of pay. *Organizational Behavior and Human Performance,* 1974, **12**, 170–195.

Goodman, P. S. Social comparison processes in organizations. In B. Staw & G. Salancik (Eds.), *New directions in organizational behavior.* Chicago: St. Clair, 1977. Pp. 97–132.

Goodman, P. S., & Freidman, A. An examination of the effect of wage inequity in the hourly condition. *Organizational Behavior and Human Performance,* 1968, **3**, 340–352.

Goodman, P. S., & Friedman, A. An examination of quantity and quality of performance under conditions of overpayment in piece-rate. *Organizational Behavior and Human Performance,* 1969, **4**, 365–374.

Goodman, P. S., & Friedman, A. An examination of Adams' theory of inequity. *Administrative Science Quarterly,* 1971, **16**, 271–288.

Homans, G. C. *Social behavior: Its elementary forms.* New York: Harcourt, Brace & World, 1961.

Jaques, E. *Equitable payment.* New York: Wiley, 1961.

Lawler, E. E. Equity theory as a predictor of productivity and work quality. *Psychological Bulletin,* 1968, **70**, 596–610. (a)

Lawler, E. E. Effects of hourly overpayment on productivity and work quality. *Journal of Personality and Social Psychology,* 1968, **10**, 306–313. (b)

Lawler, E. E. *Motivation in work organizations.* Belmont, Calif.: Brooks/Cole, 1973.

Lawler, E. E., Koplin, C. A., Young, T. F., & Fadem, J. A. Inequity reduction over time and an induced overpayment situation. *Organizational Behavior and Human Performance,* 1968, **3**, 253–268.

Lawler, E. E., & O'Gara, P. W. Effects of inequity produced by underpayment on work output, work quality, and attitudes toward the work. *Journal of Applied Psychology,* 1967, **51**, 403–410.

Leventhal, G. S. Fairness in social relationships. In J. Thibaut, J. Spence, & R. Carson

(Eds.), *Contemporary topics in social psychology*. Morristown, N.J.: General Learning Press, 1976.

Leventhal, G. S., & Bergman, J. T. Self-depriving behavior as a response to unprofitable inequity. *Journal of Experimental Social Psychology*, 1969, **5**, 153–171.

Leventhal, G. S., Weiss, T., & Long, G. Equity, reciprocity, and reallocating rewards in the dyad. *Journal of Personality and Social Psychology*, 1969, **13**, 300–305.

Locke, E. A. The nature and causes of job satisfaction. In M. Dunnette (Ed.), *Handbook of industrial and organizational psychology*. Chicago: Rand McNally, 1976. Pp. 1297–1349.

Opsahl, R. L., & Dunnette, M. The role of financial compensation in industrial motivation. *Psychological Bulletin*, 1966, **66**, 94–118.

Patchen, M. *The choice of wage comparisons*. Englewood Cliffs, N.J.: Prentice-Hall, 1961.

Pritchard, R. D. Equity theory: A review and critique. *Organizational Behavior and Human Performance*, 1969, **4**, 176–211.

Pritchard, R. D., Dunnette, M. D., & Jorgenson, D. O. Effects of perceptions of equity and inequity on worker performance and satisfaction. *Journal of Applied Psychology*, 1972, **56**, 75–94.

Rotter, J. B. Generalized expectancies for internal versus external control of reinforcement. *Psychological Monographs*, 1966, **80** (1, Whole No. 609).

Simpson, R. L. *Theories of social exchange*. Morristown, N.J.: General Learning Press, 1972.

Tornow, W. W. The development and application of an input-outcome moderator test on the perception and reduction of inequity. *Organizational Behavior and Human Performance*, 1971, **6**, 614–638.

Valenzi, E. R., & Andrews, I. R. Effect of hourly overpay and underpay inequity when tested with a new induction procedure. *Journal of Applied Psychology*, 1971, **55**, 22–27.

Vroom, V. H. *Work and motivation*. New York: Wiley, 1964.

Walster, E., Bercheid, E., & Walster, G. W. New directions in equity research. In L. Berkowitz & E. Walster (Eds.), *Advances in experimental social psychology*, Vol. 9. New York: Academic Press, 1976. Pp. 1–42.

Weick, K. E. The concept of equity in the perception of pay. *Administrative Science Quarterly*, 1967, **2**, 414–439.

Wicklund, R. A., & Brehm, J. W. *Perspectives on cognitive dissonance*. Hillsdale, N.J.: Lawrence Erlbaum, 1976.

Wiener, Y. The effects of "task-" and "ego-oriented" performance on 2 kinds of overcompensation inequity. *Organizational Behavior and Human Performance*, 1970, **5**, 191–208.

Wood, I., & Lawler, E. E. Effects of piece-rate overpayment on productivity. *Journal of Applied Psychology*, 1970, **54**, 234–238.

Wortman, C. B., & Linsenmeier, J. A. W. Interpersonal attraction and methods of ingratiation in organizational settings. In B. M. Staw & G. R. Salancik (Eds.), *New directions in organizational behavior*. Chicago: St. Clair, 1977. Pp. 133–178.

The Ubiquity of the Technique of Goal Setting in Theories of and Approaches to Employee Motivation

Edwin A. Locke

In an earlier article, this author wrote:

> A cardinal attribute of the behavior of living organisms is goal-directedness. It may be observed at all levels of life: in the assimilation of food by an amoeba, in the root growth of a tree or a plant, in the stalking of prey by a wild animal, and in the activities of a scientist in a laboratory (20, p. 991).

Goal-directedness can also be observed in the behavior of an employee at work. Most employee behavior is not only goal directed, it is *consciously* goal directed, i.e., purposeful. [All goal directed action is not purposeful—the actions of the heart and digestive system are goal directed but are not consciously regulated. For the purposes of this article, the terms "goal directed" and "purposeful" are used interchangeably. For a detailed epistemological analysis of these concepts, see Locke (20).] While purposeful action is required for a human being to survive, such action is not automatic; it is determined neither by instinct nor by environmental conditioning (24). To consciously direct one's actions toward an end requires an act of choice. One must focus one's thought on what one wants to achieve and on the means to attain it.

Since productive work requires purposeful action and since the setting of conscious purpose is a volitional process, all organizations face the necessity of persuading employees to set goals which will further organizational objectives. While virtually all existing theories of and approaches to work motivation have recognized this necessity, the nature, degree, and form of this recognition has varied widely from theory to theory. One can divide such theories and approaches into three categories based on the degree to which they have emphasized explicitly goal-setting as a method of directing employee activities. (Certainly there are differing points of view within each of the theoretical approaches or schools to be discussed here, but these differences are not considered in this article; the focus is on identifying the essential elements of each school, i.e., elements common to virtually all advocates.)

One group of theories, Scientific Management and Management by Objectives (MBO), has explicitly recognized the importance of goal-setting in both theory and practice. A second group, Human Relations and Valence-Instrumentality-Expectancy (VIE) theory, denied the importance of goal-setting in earlier versions but acknowledged its importance, in both theory and practice, in later versions. The third group, Job Enrichment and Organizational Behavior Modification (OB Mod), has consistently refused to concede the relevance of goal setting in formal

From *Academy of Management Review*, 1978, *3*, 594–601. Reprinted by permission.

theoretical statements, but has acknowledged its importance implicitly by actually encouraging goal-setting when these theories are put into practice.

Let us examine each group of theories in turn.

SCIENTIFIC MANAGEMENT AND MANAGEMENT BY OBJECTIVES

Nowhere was the importance of goal setting more explicitly recognized than in Scientific Management which attained popularity in the first two decades of this century. Its founder, Frederick W. Taylor, preferred the term "task" to "goal" (38). Task referred to the specific amount of work assigned to the worker each day.

Taylor wrote:

> Perhaps the most important law belonging to this class [pertaining to the motives which influence people], in its relation to scientific management, is the effect which the task idea has upon the efficiency of the workman. This, in fact, has become such an important element of the mechanism of scientific management, that by a great number of people scientific management has come to be known as 'task management,' (38, p. 120).

Taylor acknowledged that the task idea was not new, noting that it was routinely used in education, the task being the assignment given each day by the teacher.

The original contribution of Taylor and other advocates of Scientific Management to the task concept lay in the development of methods of estimating a proper day's task for a worker. Motion study, popularized by Gilbreth, focused on eliminating wasted motions from the work, while time study, systematized by Taylor, enabled experts to determine how much work should be accomplished by a carefully selected and trained worker using the most efficient motions (the "one best way"). Each worker was given daily feedback regarding performance in relation to task with respect to both quantity and quality. This was supplemented when necessary with coaching and encouragement by supervisors (38).

To obtain the worker's commitment to the assigned task, which involved learning radically new work methods as well as attaining substantially higher productivity, a differential, or two-tiered, piece rate system was employed. This method of payment resulted in a substantially higher rate of pay (e.g., 70%) for attaining the task than for failure to attain it. Since attaining the task resulted, in effect, in the worker's receiving a monetary bonus, Taylor's colleague, Henry Gantt, called it a "task and bonus" system. (Technically the differential piece rate and task and bonus incentive systems are not identical, but the minor differences are irrelevant here.)

Management by Objectives (6), which stresses goal setting by definition, did not become popular until about forty years after the alleged demise of Scientific Management. MBO can be viewed, in large part, as Scientific Management applied to a managerial context. For example, the tasks or goals of managers under MBO are determined by organizational goals rather than by time study, a procedure which is not applicable to managerial work. Similarly, in line with the longer range time perspective of managerial jobs, the goals under MBO programs refer to the work to be accomplished within the following three to twelve months rather than the work to be accomplished each day as in the case of manual work.

The counterpart, in MBO, of training the worker in the use of standardized tools and motions, is the action plan which is tailored to each manager's unique skills and problems. In contrast to repetitive manual work, the "one best way" to accomplish managerial objectives cannot always be known in advance since it will differ with each manager's particular circumstances.

Like Scientific Management, an effective MBO program integrates the MBO system with the reward system so that individuals are rewarded for reaching their goals. Due to the greater complexity of the manager's job, MBO does not usually employ pre-determined bonuses for specific accomplishments.

HUMAN RELATIONS AND VIE THEORY

Scientific Management reached the peak of its popularity by about 1920. The following decade saw a continuing interest in bonuses but markedly less interest in tasks, the main exception being the laboratory work on goal-setting by Mace (28). The British Industrial Health and Fatigue Research Boards (as well as American Industrial Psychologists of the 1920s) did extensive studies of the effects of incentives, illumination, rest pauses, hours of work, ventilation, noise, and music on performance and morale (23).

The following two decades ushered in a shift in emphasis from physical conditions of work to social conditions, due, of course, to the influence of the Hawthorne studies (33) which marked the beginning of the Human Relations school. To the degree that goal-setting was considered at all by the Hawthorne investigators, it was viewed primarily as a factor which limited production rather than one which motivated production, and such limiting, in turn, was seen as being caused by the social conditions of work, e.g., group norms.

The well documented existence of restriction of output (30, 33, 43) was widely interpreted by Human Relations advocates as showing the inadequacy of "task and bonus" systems in industry. It was asserted by the Hawthorne researchers that employees were either too stupid or too irrational to understand incentive systems or too disinterested in money, in comparison to social rewards, for it to be a motivator of production (33, pp. 531ff). Despite the fact that actual evidence from the Hawthorne studies themselves supported the view that the workers were most responsive to financial incentives (5) and restricted output, quite rationally in their context, so as not to lose future earnings (37), the main conclusion drawn from the studies was that social incentives (such as belonging to a cohesive work group) were more potent than monetary ones.

While more recent advocates of the Human Relations school necessarily share this emphasis on the importance of social factors, some acknowledge the importance of "task and bonus" factors as well. This acknowledgment was initially largely implicit, in that it was revealed mainly in the *practices* of Human Relations advocates. For example, both performance standards and incentives were used in the famous Harwood studies (29). Many studies of participation confounded the effects of participation with those of goal setting by urging participative groups to set high goals (17, 19, 36, 40, p. 167). Recent research indicates that the motivational effects of participation, when they occur, may be due partly to its association with goal setting, since participation often has no effect on performance when goal setting, including goal level, is controlled (11, 31).

Most contemporary Human Relations advocates openly concede the importance of task and bonus factors. A recent book on the Scanlon Plan, a participative, Human Relations oriented plan which uses economic rewards to motivate employees, asserts that:

> . . . standards are not inconsistent with a Scanlon Plan if they are used as a tool for meeting the cost and not for restrictive control. Everyone needs a benchmark and a set of criteria to evaluate himself . . . (10, p. 121).

Similarly, Likert, while emphasizing the importance of managers acting supportively toward subordinates, acknowledges that:

> Superiors in System 4 organizations . . . should have high performance aspirations, but this is not enough. Every *member* should have high performance aspirations as well, (18, p. 51).

This emphasis is taken seriously in practice, as demonstrated in a report of the application of System 4 to GM's Lakewood assembly plant (8). Higher management set explicit goals for such areas as production, scrap, grievances, and labor costs, and then had employees set their own goals on the basis of higher management input and their own knowledge of operation. With respect to feedback concerning goal accomplishment, "Employees at Lakewood were given more information about how they were doing and were given it more frequently than ever before" (8, p. 36).

The main difference between the theories of Likert and Taylor with respect to goals lies in the methods by which they are set. Taylor attempted to use a scientific approach, time and motion study, while Likert favors participation, e.g., group decision-making. These different methods reflect the different theoretical orientations of the Scientific Management and Human Relations philosophies. Scientific Management was primarily concerned with facts, i.e., the best way to do the job, including the objective determination of a proper day's work, while the Human Relations school has been primarily concerned with feelings, i.e., what will make the worker happiest.

Most contemporary Human Relations advocates acknowledge that successful managers must be concerned with both facts (concern for production), and feelings (concern for people) (3).

VIE, or valence-instrumentality-expectancy theory, which became popular in the 1960s, also failed to recognize the importance of goal setting in its early versions (41). Its initial disregard of goal setting is probably explained by its hedonistic emphasis. Its major focus was on the way in which people's beliefs and feelings (allegedly) lead them to choose a particular course of action. (In this respect, VIE theory resembles Human Relations theory.) The major premise of VIE theory is that in making choices, an individual mentally sums the expected pleasures to be derived from each possible alternative, subtracts the sum of the expected pains, and chooses the alternative with the highest positive net value.

The hedonistic and other assumptions of VIE theory have been sufficiently criticized in detail elsewhere (22). Suffice it to say that more recent models have put less stress on hedonism, and, more pertinent to the present discussion, have expanded VIE theory to include an explicit goal setting stage (4, pp. 345ff). Recent research has shown that one possible way to integrate some of the VIE constructs with goal setting is to view values and expectancies as factors which influence the goals an individual chooses, while viewing goals themselves as the more direct determinants of action (7). (Even this model of motivation is grossly incomplete, and there are still unresolved conflicts between VIE theory and goal setting theory, e.g., the relationship of expectancy of success to level of performance.)

COGNITIVE GROWTH AND OB MOD

The last two theories of employee motivation to be discussed have never shown any explicit theoretical recognition of the relevance of goal setting to employee motivation. Both schools have recognized its importance implicitly, since when these theories are put into practice, goal setting is virtually always involved, directly or indirectly.

The Cognitive Growth School, associated mainly with Maslow and Herzberg (12, 14), began in the early 1960s and emphasized man's psychological or growth needs (e.g., knowing more, integrating one's knowledge, being creative, being effective in ambiguity, developing a genuine sense of self-worth, etc.). It was asserted that this need could be best satisfied through work. According to Herzberg, jobs which did not allow for such growth needed to be enriched by providing the employee with increased responsibility and autonomy.

Herzberg never mentioned goal setting as an element of job enrichment. In fact, the idea was rejected by him (13, pp. 98–99) and his followers (9, p. 28), due probably to its association with Scientific Management whose emphasis on extreme division of labor Herzberg disparages (12).

In practice, goal setting was smuggled into the procedure of job enrichment under another name, namely, feedback. The explicit purpose of feedback in job enrichment programs is to increase the employee's feeling of achievement and to provide him or her with a sense of personal responsibility for the work. Two obvious questions that arise in this context are: How does an employee know when he or she has achieved something? How does he or she know when he or she has adequately or successfully fulfilled his/her responsibility? The answer must be: When the feedback is compared, by management or by the employee, with some standard of appropriate performance, i.e., when the feedback is appraised in terms of some goal. Thus whenever management gives its employees feedback, one can be confident that some performance standard is involved, implicitly if not explicitly.

Numerous studies have shown that feedback, in itself, does *not* have the power to motivate performance directly (1, 25). It has been argued that feedback motivates action only indirectly, through its relationship to goal setting. For example, if the feedback shows that one's prior performance was below the desired standard, one can increase one's subsequent effort, or change one's tactics, in order to meet the standard in the future.

In practice, job enrichment has involved so many different types of job changes, often within the same study, that isolating specific effects of the different elements is virtually impossible (22). Noticeable progress in this direction was made recently in a simulated field study by Umstot, Bell, and Mitchell (39). They found that job enrichment procedures from which goal setting elements had been specifically deleted led to increased job satisfaction but failed to improve productivity. In contrast, assigning the employees explicit, challenging goals accompanied by feedback led to higher productivity even in the absence of job enrichment. When goal setting and job enrichment were combined, both productivity and satisfaction improved. In some recent studies alleged to involve job enrichment, employee goal setting has been advocated explicitly (42).

It is possible that increases in the quantity or quality of productivity found in job enrichment studies (9, 16) are at least partially attributable to an implicit goal-setting element. Locke, Sirota, and Wolfson (26), in their field study of job enrichment, attributed some of the performance improvement found to goals and feedback, but also suggested that productivity might increase under such programs as a result of the elimination of unnecessary tasks or of a more efficient use of manpower—as when employees are allowed to work where they are needed rather than where they are arbitrarily assigned by a supervisor. [For a list of additional factors that may be involved in job enrichment programs, see Locke (22).]

If the practice of goal smuggling has been subtle and inconspicuous among advocates of the Cognitive Growth School, it is much more obvious among advocates of a more recent school, Organizational Behavior Modification, which became popular as a method of motivating employees in the 1970s. The OB Mod technique of goal smuggling consists of openly advocating the use of "performance standards," a term used as a synonym for goal, accompanied by feedback and possibly praise and/or money, but describing these procedures at the theoretical level in behavioristic language. Thus performance standards or goals become "controlling stimuli" or "discriminative stimuli," and feedback, praise, and money become "reinforcers" (2, 24, 27).

While this behavioristic jargon adds nothing to our understanding of how or why these techniques actually modify employee behavior (21), it enables OB Mod advocates to pretend that they are basing their procedures on Skinner's model of man. By removing any reference to human consciousness (e.g., human knowledge, values, feelings) when discussing terms like goals, feedback, and money and by asserting that these "stimuli" or "reinforcers" automatically condition employees to behave in a certain way, Behavior Mod advocates can remain, theoretically, within a behavioristic framework.

While the OB Mod philosophy is not applicable to people (21), the practices employed by its advocates do often succeed in improving employee performance. But most of these practices are the same as those used by advocates of Scientific Management and (to a smaller extent) Human Relations (24).

CONCLUSION

The most striking aspect of the history of the technique of goal setting in theories of employee motivation is that none of them were able to escape it. Theories which rejected it initially were compelled to acknowledge its importance later. Approaches which denied its importance in theory inevitably recognized it in practice.

The ubiquity of goal setting in these theories is no accident. It is not due to coincidence nor to the irresistible power of social pressures within the scientific community, but to an explicit or implicit recognition of a basic fact of reality: rational human action is goal directed. All competent managers recognize this and quite logically attempt to influence (by instructions, persuasion, etc.) the nature and difficulty of the goals their employees set in order to further organizational goals.

This should not be taken to imply that goal setting is the only element in these theories that helps to motivate employee performance, but only that it is one very important element. (Other motivational elements include such factors as incentives, participation, and autonomy which could affect the employee's commitment to and willingness to set goals and which can also affect motivation subconsciously.)

The concept of goal is not the most fundamental motivational concept; it does not provide an ultimate explanation of human action. The concepts of need and value are the more fundamental concepts (23) and are, along with the individual's knowledge and premises, what determine goals. Goal setting is simply the most directly useful motivational approach in a *managerial* context, since goals are the most immediate regulators of human action and are more easily modified than values of sub-conscious premises. The impressive results obtained by Latham and others in increasing productivity through the use of goal setting in industrial settings testifies to the practical utility of this concept (15).

Many people (including the author) have been surprised at the ease with which employers have been able to get employees to accept assigned goals [as in the field studies summarized by Latham and Yukl (15)]. Many of us assumed that most employees would reject assigned goals unless they were accompanied by substantial monetary incentives or by "good" Human Relations techniques such as participation. We failed to realize that the "demand characteristics" (32) involved in the employer-employee relationship are very similar to, if not stronger than, those involved in an experimenter-subject relationship. Just as a subject is hired to do the bidding of an experimenter, an employee is hired to perform tasks for an employer. The employee's mental "set" upon accepting a job is: "What do you want me to do?" In short, it is the same mental set as that of an experimental subject.

This is not to say that the employer's power is unlimited. It is not. The ease with which employers can get employees to accept assigned goals depends upon numerous factors, including: fairness and difficulty of the goals, values of the employees, their trust of management, and the perceived legitimacy of management's demands.

Nor should it be assumed that setting specific quantitative goals is inevitably beneficial. For example, stressing goal achievement in certain areas might lead to neglect of performance in other areas where the results are not so easily measurable. It may also lead to falsifying data. If the process of setting goals and formulating action plans does not include a measure of the costs of achieving the goals, they may be attained at a greater cost than the organization is really willing to pay. The process of goal setting must always be considered in relation to the wider organizational context.

In conclusion, Latham's studies of goal setting were simulated by the laboratory work of Locke (19), who was in turn influenced by Ryan (34, 35) whose basic motivational concept, the task or intention, is almost identical to Taylor's (38). In view of his widespread influence, it would not be unjustified to view Taylor as the father of employee motivation theory. Despite the decades of outrageous criticisms which Taylor's theories have had to endure, made often by writers who seem not to have read his actual writings, he has had the last word.

REFERENCES

1 Annett, J. *Feedback and Human Behavior* (Baltimore: Penguin, 1969).
2 "At Emery Air Freight: Positive Reinforcement Boosts Performance," *Organizational Dynamics,* Vol. 1, No. 3 (1973), 41–50.
3 Blake, R. R., and J. S. Mouton. *The Managerial Grid* (Houston: Gulf Publishing Co., 1964).
4 Campbell, J. P., M. D. Dunnette, E. E. Lawler, and K. E. Weick. *Managerial Behavior, Performance, and Effectiveness* (New York: McGraw-Hill, 1970).
5 Carey, A. "The Hawthorne Studies: A Radical Criticism." *American Sociological Review,* Vol. 32 (1967), 403–416.
6 Carroll, S. J., and H. L. Tosi. *Management by Objectives* (New York: Macmillan, 1973).
7 Cartledge, N. D. "An Experimental Study of the Relationship Between Expectancies, Goal Utility, Goals and Task Performance," (Ph.D. Thesis, University of Maryland, 1973).
8 Dowling, W. F. "At General Motors: System-4 Builds Performance and Profits," *Organizational Dynamics,* Vol. 3, No. 3 (1975), 23–38.
9 Ford, R. N. *Motivation Through the Work Itself* (New York: American Management Association, 1969).
10 Frost, C. F., J. H. Wakeley, and R. A. Ruh. *The Scanlon Plan for Organizational Development: Identity, Participation, and Equity* (East Lansing, Mich.: Michigan State University, 1974).
11 Hannan, R. L. "The Effects of Participation in Goal Setting on Goal Acceptance and Performance: A Laboratory Experiment," (Master's Thesis, University of Maryland, 1975).

12 Herzberg, F. *Work and the Nature of Man* (Cleveland: World Publishing Co., 1966).

13 Herzberg, F. "One More Time: How Do You Motivate Employees?" in R. M. Steers and L. W. Porter (Eds.), *Motivation and Work Behavior* (New York: McGraw-Hill, 1975).

14 Herzberg, F., B. Mausner, and B. B. Snyderman. *The Motivation to Work* (New York: Wiley, 1959).

15 Latham, G. P., and G. A. Yukl. "A Review of Research on the Application of Goal Setting in Organizations," *Academy of Management Journal*, Vol. 18 (1975), 824–845.

16 Lawler, E. E. "Job Design and Employee Motivation," in V. H. Vroom and E. L. Deci (Eds.), *Management and Motivation* (Baltimore: Penguin, 1970).

17 Lawrence, L. C., and P. C. Smith. "Group Decision and Employee Participation," *Journal of Applied Psychology*, Vol. 39 (1955), 334–337.

18 Likert, R. *The Human Organization* (New York: McGraw-Hill, 1967).

19 Locke, E. A. "Toward a Theory of Task Motivation and Incentives," *Organizational Behavior and Human Performance*, Vol. 3 (1968), 157–189.

20 Locke, E. A. "Purpose without Consciousness: A Contradiction," *Psychological Reports*, Vol. 25 (1969), 991–1009.

21 Locke, E. A. "Critical Analysis of the Concept of Causality in Behavioristic Psychology," *Psychological Reports*, Vol. 31 (1972), 175–197.

22 Locke, E. A. "Personnel Attitudes and Motivation," *Annual Review of Psychology*, Vol. 26 (1975), 457–480.

23 Locke, E. A. "The Nature and Causes of Job Satisfaction," in M. D. Dunnette (Ed.), *Handbook of Industrial and Organizational Psychology* (Chicago: Rand McNally, 1976).

24 Locke, E. A. "The Myths of Behavior Mod in Organizations," *Academy of Management Review*. Vol. 2 (1977), 543–553.

25 Locke, E. A., N. Cartledge, and J. Koeppel. "Motivational Effects of Knowledge of Results: A Goal Setting Phenomenon?" *Psychological Bulletin*, Vol. 70 (1968), 474–485.

26 Locke, E. A., D. Sirota, and A. D. Wolfson. "An Experimental Case Study of the Successes and Failures of Job Enrichment in a Government Agency," *Journal of Applied Psychology*, Vol. 61 (1976), 701–711.

27 Luthans, F., and R. Kreitner. *Organizational Behavior Modification* (Glenview, Ill.: Scott Foresman, 1975).

28 Mace, C. A. "Incentives: Some Experimental Studies," *Report No. 72* (Great Britain: Industrial Health Research Board, 1935).

29 Marrow, A. J., D. G. Bowers, and S. E. Seashore, *Management by Participation* (New York: Harper, 1967).

30 Mathewson, S. B. *Restriction of Output Among Unorganized Workers* (New York: Viking, 1931).

31 Meyer, H. H., E. Kay, and J. R. P. French. "Split Roles in Performance Appraisal," *Harvard Business Review*, Vol. 43 (Jan./Feb. 1965), 123–129.

32 Orne, M. T. "On the Social Psychology of the Psychological Experiment with Particular Reference to Demand Characteristics," *American Psychologist*, Vol. 17 (1962), 776–783.

33 Roethlisberger, F. J., and W. J. Dickson. *Management and the Worker* (Cambridge: Harvard University Press, 1939).

34 Ryan, T. A. *Intentional Behavior* (New York: Ronald, 1970).

35 Ryan, T. A., and P. C. Smith. *Principles of Industrial Psychology* (New York: Ronald, 1954).

36 Sorcher, M. *Motivating the Hourly Employee* (General Electric: Behavioral Research Service, 1967).
37 Sykes, A. J. M. "Economic Interest and the Hawthorne Researches," *Human Relations,* Vol. 18 (1965), 253–263.
38 Taylor, F. W. *The Principles of Scientific Management* (New York: Norton, 1911/1967).
39 Umstot, D. D., C. H. Bell, and T. R. Mitchell. "Effects of Job Enrichment and Task Goals on Satisfaction and Productivity: Implications for Job Design," *Journal of Applied Psychology,* Vol. 61 (1976), 379–394.
40 Viteles, M. S. *Motivation and Morale in Industry* (New York: Norton, 1953).
41 Vroom, V. H. *Work and Motivation* (New York: Wiley, 1964).
42 Walters, R. W. "Job Enrichment: Challenge of the Seventies," in W. W. Suojanen, M. J. McDonald, G. L. Swallow, and W. W. Suojanen (Eds.), *Perspectives on Job Enrichment and Productivity* (Atlanta: Georgia State Univ., 1975).
43 Whyte, W. F. *Money and Motivation* (New York: Harper, 1955).

Goal Setting—A Motivational Techinque That Works

Gary P. Latham
Edwin A. Locke

The problem of how to motivate employees has puzzled and frustrated managers for generations. One reason the problem has seemed difficult, if not mysterious, is that motivation ultimately comes from within the individual and therefore cannot be observed directly. Moreover, most managers are not in a position to change an employee's basic personality structure. The best they can do is try to use incentives to direct the energies of their employees toward organizational objectives.

Money is obviously the primary incentive, since without it few if any employees would come to work. But money alone is not always enough to motivate high performance. Other incentives, such as participation in decision making, job enrichment, behavior modification, and organizational development, have been tried with varying degrees of success. A large number of research studies have shown, however, that one very straightforward technique—goal setting—is probably not only more effective than alternative methods, but may be the major mechanism by which these other incentives affect motivation. For example, a recent experiment on job enrichment demonstrated that unless employees in enriched jobs set higher, more specific goals than do those with unenriched jobs, job enrichment has absolutely no effect on productivity. Even money has been found most effective as a motivator when the bonuses offered are made contingent on attaining specific objectives.

From *Organizational Dynamics*, 1979, **8**(2), 68–80. © 1979 by AMACOM, a division of American Management Associations. All rights reserved.

THE GOAL-SETTING CONCEPT

The idea of assigning employees a specific amount of work to be accomplished—a specific task, a quota, a performance standard, an objective, or a deadline—is not new. The task concept, along with time and motion study and incentive pay, was the cornerstone of scientific management, founded by Frederick W. Taylor more than 70 years ago. He used his system to increase the productivity of blue collar workers. About 20 years ago the idea of goal setting reappeared under a new name, management by objectives, but this technique was designed for managers.

In a 14-year program of research, we have found that goal setting does not necessarily have to be part of a wider management system to motivate performance effectively. It can be used as a technique in its own right.

Laboratory and Field Research

Our research program began in the laboratory. In a series of experiments, individuals were assigned different types of goals on a variety of simple tasks—addition, brainstorming, assembling toys. Repeatedly it was found that those assigned hard goals performed better than did people assigned moderately difficult or easy goals. Furthermore, individuals who had specific, challenging goals outperformed those who were given such vague goals as to "do your best." Finally, we observed that pay and performance feedback led to improved performance only when these incentives led the individual to set higher goals.

While results were quite consistent in the laboratory, there was no proof that they could be applied to actual work settings. Fortunately, just as Locke published a summary of the laboratory studies in 1968, Latham began a separate series of experiments in the wood products industry that demonstrated the practical significance of these findings. The field studies did not start out as a validity test of laboratory theory, but rather as a response to a practical problem.

In 1968, six sponsors of the American Pulpwood Association became concerned about increasing the productivity of independent loggers in the South. These loggers were entrepreneurs on whom the multimillion-dollar companies are largely dependent for their raw material. The problem was twofold. First, these entrepreneurs did not work for a single company; they worked for themselves. Thus they were free to (and often did) work two days one week, four days a second week, five half-days a third week, or whatever schedule they preferred. In short, these workers could be classified as marginal from the standpoint of their productivity and attendance, which were considered highly unsatisfactory by conventional company standards. Second, the major approach taken to alleviate this problem had been to develop equipment that would make the industry less dependent on this type of worker. A limitation of this approach was that many of the logging supervisors were unable to obtain the financing necessary to purchase a small tractor, let alone a rubber-tired skidder.

Consequently, we designed a survey that would help managers determine "what makes these people tick." The survey was conducted orally in the field with 292 logging supervisors. Complex statistical analyses of the data identified three basic types of supervisor. One type stayed on the job with their men, gave them instructions and explanations, provided them with training, read the trade magazines, and had little difficulty financing the equipment they needed. Still, the productivity of their units was at best mediocre.

The operation of the second group of supervisors was slightly less mechanized. These supervisors provided little training for their workforce. They simply drove their employees to the woods, gave them a specific production goal to attain for the day or week, left them alone in the woods unsupervised, and returned at night to take them home. Labor turnover was high and productivity was again average.

The operation of the third group of supervisors was relatively unmechanized. These leaders stayed on the job with their men, provided training, gave instructions and explanations, and in addition, set a specific production goal for the day or week. Not only was the crew's productivity high, but their injury rate was well below average.

Two conclusions were discussed with the managers of the companies sponsoring this study. First, mechanization alone will not increase the productivity of logging crews. Just as the average tax payer would probably commit more mathematical errors if he were to try to use a computer to complete his income tax return, the average logger misuses, and frequently abuses, the equipment he purchases (for example, drives a skidder with two flat tires, doesn't change the oil filter). This increases not only the logger's downtime, but also his costs which, in turn, can force him out of business. The second conclusion of the survey was that setting a specific production goal combined with supervisory presence to ensure goal commitment will bring about a significant increase in productivity.

These conclusions were greeted with the standard, but valid, cliché, "Statistics don't prove causation." And our comments regarding the value of machinery were especially irritating to these managers, many of whom had received degrees in engineering. So one of the companies decided to replicate the survey in order to check our findings.

The company's study placed each of 892 independent logging supervisors who sold wood to the company into one of three categories of supervisory styles our survey had identified—namely, (1) stays on the job but does not set specific production goals; (2) sets specific production goals but does not stay on the job; and (3) stays on the job and sets specific production goals. Once again, goal setting, in combination with the on-site presence of a supervisor, was shown to be the key to improved productivity.

TESTING FOR THE HAWTHORNE EFFECT

Management may have been unfamiliar with different theories of motivation, but it was fully aware of one label—the Hawthorne effect. Managers in these wood products companies remained unconvinced that anything so simple as staying on the job with the men and setting a specific production goal could have an appreciable effect on productivity. They pointed out that the results simply reflected the positive effects any supervisor would have on the work unit after giving his crew attention. And they were unimpressed by the laboratory experiments we cited—

experiments showing that individuals who have a specific goal solve more arithmetic problems or assemble more tinker toys that do people who are told to "do your best." Skepticism prevailed.

But the country's economic picture made it critical to continue the study of inexpensive techniques to improve employee motivation and productivity. We were granted permission to run one more project to test the effectiveness of goal setting.

Twenty independent logging crews who were all but identical in size, mechanization level, terrain on which they worked, productivity, and attendance were located. The logging supervisors of these crews were in the habit of staying on the job with their men, but they did not set production goals. Half the crews were randomly selected to receive training in goal setting; the remaining crews served as a control group.

The logging supervisors who were to set goals were told that we had found a way to increase productivity at no financial expense to anyone. We gave the ten supervisors in the training group production tables developed through time-and-motion studies by the company's engineers. These tables made it possible to determine how much wood should be harvested in a given number of manhours. They were asked to use these tables as a guide in determining a specific production goal to assign their employees. In addition, each sawhand was given a tallymeter (counter) that he could wear on his belt. The sawhand was asked to punch the counter each time he felled a tree. Finally, permission was requested to measure the crew's performance on a weekly basis.

The ten supervisors in the control group—those who were not asked to set production goals—were told that the researchers were interested in learning the extent to which productivity is affected by absenteeism and injuries. They were urged to "do your best" to maximize the crew's productivity and attendance and to minimize injuries. It was explained that the data might be useful in finding ways to increase productivity at little or no cost to the wood harvester.

To control for the Hawthorne effect, we made an equal number of visits to the control group and the training group. Performance was measured for 12 weeks. During this time, the productivity of the goal-setting group was significantly higher than that of the control group. Moreover, absenteeism was significantly lower in the groups that set goals than in the groups who were simply urged to do their best. Injury and turnover rates were low in both groups.

Why should anything so simple and inexpensive as goal setting influence the work of these employees so significantly? Anecdotal evidence from conversations with both the loggers and the company foresters who visited them suggested several reasons.

Harvesting timber can be a monotonous, tiring job with little or no meaning for most workers. Introducing a goal that is difficult, but attainable, increases the challenge of the job. In addition, a specific goal makes it clear to the worker what it is he is expected to do. Goal feedback via the tallymeter and weekly recordkeeping provide the worker with a sense of achievement, recognition, and accomplishment. He can see how well he is doing now as against his past performance and, in some cases, how well he is doing in comparison with others. Thus the worker not only may expend greater effort, but may also devise better or more creative tactics for attaining the goal than those he previously used.

NEW APPLICATIONS

Management was finally convinced that goal setting was an effective motivational technique for increasing the productivity of the independent woods worker in the South. The issue now raised by the management of another wood products company was whether the procedure could be used in the West with the company logging operations in which the employees were unionized and paid by the hour. The previous study had involved employees on a piece-rate system, which was the practice in the South.

The immediate problem confronting this company involved the loading of logging trucks. If the trucks were underloaded, the company lost money. If the trucks were overloaded, however, the driver could be fined by the Highway Department and could ultimately lose his job. The drivers opted for underloading the trucks.

For three months management tried to solve this problem by urging the drivers to try harder to fill the truck to its legal net weight, and by developing weighing scales that could be attached to the truck. But this approach did not prove cost effective, because the scales continually broke down when subjected to the rough terrain on which the trucks traveled. Consequently, the drivers reverted to their former practice of underloading. For the three months in which the problem was under study the trucks were seldom loaded in excess of 58 to 63 percent of capacity.

At the end of the three-month period, the results of the previous goal setting experiments were explained to the union. They were told three things—that the company would like to set a specific net weight goal for the drivers, that no monetary reward or fringe benefits other than verbal praise could be expected for improved performance, and that no one would be criticized for failing to attain the goal. Once again, the idea that simply setting a specific goal would solve a production problem seemed too incredible to be taken seriously by the union. However, they reached an agreement that a difficult, but attainable, goal of 94 percent of the truck's legal net weight would be assigned to the drivers, provided that no one could be reprimanded for failing to attain the goal. This latter point was emphasized to the company foremen in particular.

Within the first month, performance increased to 80 percent of the truck's net weight. After the second month, however, performance decreased to 70 percent. Interviews with the drivers indicated that they were testing management's statement that no punitive steps would be taken against them if their performance suddenly dropped. Fortunately for all concerned, no such steps were taken by the foremen, and performance exceeded 90 percent of the truck's capacity after the third month. Their performance has remained at this level to this day, seven years later.

The results over the nine-month period during which this study was conducted

saved the company $250,000. This figure, determined by the company's account-
ants, is based on the cost of additional trucks that would have been required to
deliver the same quantity of logs to the mill if goal setting had not been implemented. The dollars-saved figure is even higher when you factor in the cost of the
additional diesel fuel that would have been consumed and the expenses incurred
in recruiting and hiring the additional truck drivers.

Why could this procedure work without the union's demanding an increase in
hourly wages? First, the drivers did not feel that they were really doing anything
differently. This, of course, was not true. As a result of goal setting, the men
began to record their truck weight in a pocket notebook, and they found themselves bragging about their accomplishments to their peers. Second, they viewed
goal setting as a challenging game: "It was great to beat the other guy."

Competition was a crucial factor in bringing about goal acceptance and commitment in this study. However, we can reject the hypothesis that improved performance resulted solely from competition, because no special prizes or formal recognition programs were provided for those who came closest to, or exceeded, the
goal. No effort was made by the company to single out one "winner." More important, the opportunity for competition among drivers had existed before goal
setting was instituted; after all, each driver knew his own truck's weight, and the
truck weight of each of the 36 other drivers every time he hauled wood into the
yard. In short, competition affected productivity only in the sense that it led to the
acceptance of, and commitment to, the goal. It was the setting of the goal itself
and the working toward it that brought about increased performance and decreased costs.

PARTICIPATIVE GOAL SETTING

The inevitable question always raised by management was raised here: "We know
goal setting works. How can we make it work better?" Was there one best method
for setting goals? Evidence for a "one best way" approach was cited by several
managers, but it was finally concluded that different approaches would work best
under different circumstances.

It was hypothesized that the woods workers in the South, who had little or no
education, would work better with assigned goals, while the educated workers in
the West would achieve higher productivity if they were allowed to help set the
goals themselves. Why the focus on education? Many of the uneducated workers
in the South could be classified as culturally disadvantaged. Such persons often
lack self-confidence, have a poor sense of time, and are not very competitive. The
cycle of skill mastery, which in turn guarantees skill levels high enough to prevent
discouragement, doesn't apply to these employees. If, for example, these people
were allowed to participate in goal setting, the goals might be too difficult or they
might be too easy. On the other hand, participation for the educated worker was
considered critical in effecting maximum goal acceptance. Since these conclusions appeared logical, management initially decided that no research was necessary. This decision led to hours of further discussion.

The same questions were raised again and again by the researchers. What if the logic were wrong? Can we afford to implement these decisions without evaluating them systematically? Would we implement decisions regarding a new approach to tree planting without first testing it? Do we care more about trees than we do about people? Finally, permission was granted to conduct an experiment.

Logging crews were randomly appointed to either participative goal setting, assigned (nonparticipative) goal setting, or a do-your-best condition. The results were startling. The uneducated crews, consisting primarily of black employees who participated in goal setting, set significantly higher goals and attained them more often than did those whose goals were assigned by the supervisor. Not surprisingly, their performance was higher. Crews with assigned goals performed no better than did those who were urged to do their best to improve their productivity. The performance of white, educationally advantaged workers was higher with assigned rather than participatively set goals, although the difference was not statistically significant. These results were precisely the opposite of what had been predicted.

Another study comparing participative and assigned goals was conducted with typists. The results supported findings obtained by researchers at General Electric years before. It did not matter so much *how* the goal was set. What mattered was *that* a goal was set. The study demonstrated that both assigned and participatively set goals led to substantial improvements in typing speed. The process by which these gains occurred, however, differed in the two groups.

In the participative group, employees insisted on setting very high goals regardless of whether they had attained their goal the previous week. Nevertheless, their productivity improved—an outcome consistent with the theory that high goals lead to high performance.

In the assigned-goal group, supervisors were highly supportive of employees. No criticism was given for failure to attain the goals. Instead, the supervisor lowered the goal after failure so that the employee would be certain to attain it. The goal was then raised gradually each week until the supervisor felt the employee was achieving his or her potential. The result? Feelings of accomplishment and achievement on the part of the worker and improved productivity for the company.

These basic findings were replicated in a subsequent study of engineers and scientists. Participative goal setting was superior to assigned goal setting only to the degree that it led to the setting of higher goals. Both participative and assigned-goal groups outperformed groups that were simply told to "do your best."

An additional experiment was conducted to validate the conclusion that participation in goal setting may be important only to the extent that it leads to the setting of difficult goals. It was performed in a laboratory setting in which the task was to brainstorm uses for wood. One group was asked to "do your best" to think of as many ideas as possible. A second group took part in deciding with the experimenter, the specific number of ideas each person would generate. These goals were, in turn, assigned to individuals in a third group. In this way, goal difficulty was held constant between the assigned-goal and participative groups. Again, it was found that specific, difficult goals—whether assigned or set through partici-pation—led to higher performance than did an abstract or generalized goal such as "do your best." And, when goal difficulty was held constant, there was no significant difference in the performance of those with assigned as compared with participatively set goals.

These results demonstrate that goal setting in industry works just as it does in the laboratory. Specific, challenging goals lead to better performance than do easy or vague goals, and feedback motivates higher performance only when it leads to the setting of higher goals.

It is important to note that participation is not only a motivational tool. When a manager has competent subordinates, participation is also a useful device for in-creasing the manager's knowledge and thereby improving decision quality. It can lead to better decisions through input from subordinates.

A representative sample of the results of field studies of goal setting conducted by Latham and others is shown in Figure 1. Each of these ten studies compared the performance of employees given specific challenging goals with those given "do best" or no goals. Note that goal setting has been successful across a wide variety of jobs and industries. The effects of goal setting have been recorded for as long as seven years after the onset of the program, although the results of most studies have been followed up for only a few weeks or months. The median im-provement in performance in the ten studies shown in Figure 1 was 17 percent.

FIGURE 1
REPRESENTATIVE FIELD STUDIES OF GOAL SETTING

Researcher(s)	Task	Duration of study or of significant effects	Percent of change in performance[a]
Blumenfeld & Leidy	Servicing soft drink coolers	Unspecified	+27
Dockstader	Keypunching	3 mos.	+27
Ivancevich	Skilled technical jobs	9 mos.	+15
Ivancevich	Sales	9 mos.	+24
Kim and Hamner	5 telephone service jobs	3 mos.	+13
Latham and Baldes	Loading trucks	9 mos.[b]	+26
Latham and Yukl	Logging	2 mos.	+18
Latham and Yukl	Typing	5 weeks	+11
Migliore	Mass production	2 years	+16
Umstot, Bell, and Mitchell	Coding land parcels	1–2 days[c]	+16

[a]Percentage changes were obtained by subtracting pre-goal-setting performance from post-goal-setting perfor-mance and dividing by pre-goal-setting performance. Different experimental groups were combined where appropriate. If a control group was available, the percentage figure represents the difference of the percentage changes between the experimental and control groups. If multiple performance measures were used, the median improvement on all measures was used. The authors would like to thank Dena Feren and Vicki McCaleb for performing these calcula-tions.
[b]Performance remained higher for seven years.
[c]Simulated organization.

A CRITICAL INCIDENTS SURVEY

To explore further the importance of goal setting in the work setting, Dr. Frank White conducted another study in two plants of a high-technology, multinational corporation on the East Coast. Seventy-one engineers, 50 managers, and 31 clerks were asked to describe a specific instance when they were especially productive and a specific instance when they were especially unproductive on their present jobs. Responses were classified according to a reliable coding scheme. Of primary interest here are the external events perceived by employees as being responsible for the high-productivity and low-productivity incidents. The results are shown in Figure 2.

The first set of events—pursuing a specific goal, having a large amount of work, working under a deadline, or having an uninterrupted routine—accounted for more than half the high-productivity events. Similarly, the converse of these— goal blockage, having a small amount of work, lacking a deadline, and suffering work interruptions—accounted for nearly 60 percent of the low-productivity events. Note that the first set of four categories are all relevant to goal setting and the second set to a lack of goals or goal blockage. The goal category itself—that of pursuing an attainable goal or goal blockage—was the one most frequently used to describe high- and low-productivity incidents.

The next four categories, which are more pertinent to Frederick Herzberg's motivator-hygiene theory—task interest, responsibility, promotion, and recognition—are less important, accounting for 36.8 percent of the high-productivity in-

FIGURE 2
EVENTS PERCEIVED AS CAUSING HIGH AND LOW PRODUCTIVITY*

Event	Percent of times event caused	
	High productivity	Low productivity
Goal pursuit/Goal blockage	17.1	23.0
Large amount of work/Small amount of work	12.5	19.0
Deadline or schedule/No deadline	15.1	3.3
Smooth work routine/Interrupted routine	5.9	14.5
Intrinsic/Extrinsic factors	50.6	59.8
Interesting task/Uninteresting task	17.1	11.2
Increased responsibility/Decreased responsibility	13.8	4.6
Anticipated promotion/Promotion denied	1.3	0.7
Verbal recognition/Criticism	4.6	2.6
People/Company conditions	36.8	19.1
Pleasant personal relationships/Unpleasant personal relationships	10.5	9.9
Anticipated pay increase/Pay increased denied	1.3	1.3
Pleasant working conditions/Unpleasant working conditions	0.7	0.7
Other (miscellaneous)	—	9.3

*N = 152 in this study by Frank White.

cidents (the opposite of these four categories accounted for 19.1 percent of the lows). The remaining categories were even less important.

Employees were also asked to identify the responsible agent behind the events that had led to high and low productivity. In both cases, the employees themselves, their immediate supervisors, and the organization were the agents most frequently mentioned.

The concept of goal setting is a very simple one. Interestingly, however, we have gotten two contradictory types of reaction when the idea was introduced to managers. Some claimed it was so simple and self-evident that everyone, including themselves, already used it. This, we have found, is not true. Time after time we have gotten the following response from subordinates after goal setting was introduced: "This is the first time I knew what my supervisor expected of me on this job." Conversely, other managers have argued that the idea would not work, precisely *because* it is so simple (implying that something more radical and complex was needed). Again, results proved them wrong.

But these successes should not mislead managers into thinking that goal setting can be used without careful planning and forethought. Research and experience suggest that the best results are obtained when the following steps are followed:

Setting the goal. The goal set should have two main characteristics. First; it should be specific rather than vague: "Increase sales by 10 percent" rather than "Try to improve sales." Whenever possible, there should be a time limit for goal accomplishment: "Cut cost by 3 percent in the next six months."

Second, the goal should be challenging yet reachable. If accepted, difficult goals lead to better performance than do easy goals. In contrast, if the goals are perceived as unreachable, employees will not accept them. Nor will employees get a sense of achievement from pursuing goals that are never attained. Employees with low self-confidence or ability should be given more easily attainable goals than those with high self-confidence and ability.

There are at least five possible sources of input, aside from the individual's self-confidence and ability, that can be used to determine the particular goal to set for a given individual.

The scientific management approach pioneered by Frederick W. Taylor uses time and motion study to determine a fair day's work. This is probably the most objective technique available, but it can be used only where the task is reasonably repetitive and standardized. Another drawback is that this method often leads to employee resistance, especially in cases where the new standard is substantially higher than previous performance and where rate changes are made frequently.

More readily accepted, although less scientific than time and motion study, are standards based on the average past performance of employees. This method was used successfully in some of our field studies. Most employees consider this approach fair but, naturally, in cases where past performance is far below capacity, beating that standard will be extremely easy.

Since goal setting is sometimes simply a matter of judgment, another technique we have used is to allow the goal to be set jointly by supervisor and subordinate. The participative approach may be less scientific than time and motion study, but it does lead to ready acceptance by both employee and immediate superior in addition to promoting role clarity.

External constraints often affect goal setting, especially among managers. For example, the goal to produce an item at a certain price may be dictated by the actions of competitors, and deadlines may be imposed externally in line with contract agreements. Legal regulations, such as attaining a certain reduction in pollution levels by a certain date, may affect goal setting as well. In these cases, setting the goal is not so much the problem as is figuring out a method of reaching it.

Finally, organizational goals set by the board of directors or upper management will influence the goals set by employees at lower levels. This is the essence of the MBO process.

Another issue that needs to be considered when setting goals is whether they should be designed for individuals or for groups. Rensis Likert and a number of other human relations experts argue for group goal setting on grounds that it promotes cooperation and team spirit. But one could argue that individual goals better promote individual responsibility and make it easier to appraise individual performance. The degree of task interdependence involved would also be a factor to consider.

Obtaining Goal Commitment   If goal setting is to work, then the manager must ensure that subordinates will accept and remain committed to the goals. Simple instruction backed by positive support and an absence of threats or intimidation were enough to ensure goal acceptance in most of our studies. Subordinates must perceive the goals as fair and reasonable and they must trust management, for if they perceive the goals as no more than a means of exploitation, they will be likely to reject the goals.

It may seem surprising that goal acceptance was achieved so readily in the field studies. Remember, however, that in all cases the employees were receiving wages or a salary (although these were not necessarily directly contingent on goal attainment). Pay in combination with the supervisor's benevolent authority and supportiveness were sufficient to bring about goal acceptance. Recent research indicates that whether goals are assigned or set participatively, supportiveness on the part of the immediate superior is critical. A supportive manager or supervisor does not use goals to threaten subordinates, but rather to clarify what is expected of them. His or her role is that of a helper and goal facilitator.

As noted earlier, the employee gets a feeling of pride and satisfaction from the experience of reaching a challenging but fair performance goal. Success in reaching a goal also tends to reinforce acceptance of future goals. Once goal setting is introduced, informal competition frequently arises among the employees. This further reinforces committment and may lead employees to raise the goals spontaneously. A word of caution here, however: We do not recommend setting up formal competition, as this may lead employees to place individual goals ahead of company goals. The emphasis should be on accomplishing the task, getting the job done, not "beating" the other person.

When employees resist assigned goals, they generally do so for one of two reasons. First, they may think they are incapable of reaching the goal because they lack confidence, ability, knowledge, and the like. Second, they may not see any personal benefit—either in terms of personal pride or in terms of external rewards like money, promotion, recognition—in reaching assigned goals.

There are various methods of overcoming employee resistance to goals. One possibility is more training designed to raise the employee's level of skill and self-confidence. Allowing the subordinate to participate in setting the goal—deciding on the goal level—is another method. This was found most effective among uneducated and minority group employees, perhaps because it gave them a feeling of control over their fate. Offering monetary bonuses or other rewards (recognition, time off) for reaching goals may also help.

The last two methods may be especially useful where there is a history of labor-management conflict and where employees have become accustomed to a lower level of effort than currently considered acceptable. Group incentives may also encourage goal acceptance, especially where there is a group goal, or when considerable cooperation is required.

Providing Support Elements   A third step to take when introducing goal setting is to ensure the availability of necessary support elements. That is, the employee must be given adequate resources—money, equipment, time, help—as well as the freedom to utilize them in attaining goals, and company policies must not work to block goal attainment.

FIGURE 3
Goal-setting model.

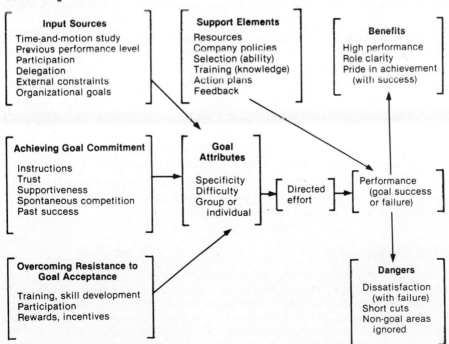

Before turning an employee loose with these resources, however, it's wise to do a quick check on whether conditions are optimum for reaching the goal set. First, the supervisor must make sure that the employee has sufficient ability and knowledge to be able to reach the goal. Motivation without knowledge is useless. This, of course, puts a premium on proper selection and training and requires that the supervisor know the capabilities of subordinates when goals are assigned. Asking an employee to formulate an action plan for reaching the goal, as in MBO, is very useful, as it will indicate any knowledge deficiencies.

Second, the supervisor must ensure that the employee is provided with precise feedback so that he will know to what degree he's reaching or falling short of his goal and can thereupon adjust his level of effort or strategy accordingly. Recent research indicates that, while feedback is not a sufficient condition for improved performance, it is a necessary condition. A useful way to present periodic feedback is through the use of charts or graphs that plot performance over time.

Elements involved in taking the three steps described are shown in Figure 3, which illustrates in outline form our model of goal setting.

CONCLUSION

We believe that goal setting is a simple straightforward and highly effective technique for motivating employee performance. It is a basic technique, a method on which most other methods depend for their motivational effectiveness. The currently popular technique of behavior modification, for example, is mainly goal setting plus feedback, dressed up in academic terminology.

However, goal setting is no panacea. It will not compensate for underpayment of employees or for poor management. Used incorrectly, goal setting may cause rather than solve problems. If, for example, the goals set are unfair, arbitrary, or unreachable, dissatisfaction and poor performance may result. If difficult goals are set without proper quality controls, quantity may be achieved at the expense of quality. If pressure for immediate results is exerted without regard to how they are attained, short-term improvement may occur at the expense of long-run profits. That is, such pressure often triggers the use of expedient and ultimately costly methods—such as dishonesty, high-pressure tactics, postponing of maintenance expenses, and so on—to attain immediate results. Furthermore, performance goals are more easily set in some areas than in others. It's all too easy, for example, to concentrate on setting readily measured production goals and ignore employee development goals. Like any other management tool, goal setting works only when combined with good managerial judgment.

SELECTED BIBLIOGRAPHY

A summary of the early (mainly laboratory) research on goal setting may be found in E. A. Locke's "Toward a Theory of Task Motivation and Incentives" (*Organization Behavior and Human Performance,* May 1968). More recent reviews that include some of the early field studies are reported by G. P. Latham and G. A. Yukl's "Review of Research on the Application of Goal Setting in Organizations" (*Academy of Management Journal,* December 1975) and in R. M. Steers and L. W. Porter's "The Role of Task-Goal Attributes in Employee Performance" (*Psychological Bulletin,* July 1974).

An excellent historical discussion of management by objectives, including its relationship to goal-setting research, can be found in G. S. Odiorne's "MBO: A Backward Glance" (*Business Horizons,* October 1978).

A thorough review of the literature on participation, including the relationship of participation and goal setting, can be found in a chapter by E. A. Locke and D. M. Schweiger, "Participation in Decision-Making: One More Look," in B. M. Staw's edited work, *Research in Organizational Behavior* (Vol. 1, Greenwich, JAI Press, 1979). General Electric's famous research on the effect of participation in the appraisal interview is summarized in H. H. Meyer, E. Kay, and J. R. P. French, Jr.'s "Split Roles in Performance Appraisal" (*Harvard Business Review,* January-February 1965).

The relationship of goal setting to knowledge of results is discussed in E. A. Locke, N. Cartledge, and J. Koeppel's "Motivational Effects of Knowledge of Results: A Goal Setting Phenomenon?" (*Psychological Bulletin,* December 1968) and L. J. Becker's "Joint Effect of Feedback and Goal Setting on Performance: A Field Study of Residential Energy Conservation" (*Journal of Applied Psychology,* August 1978). Finally, the role of goal setting in virtually all theories of work motivation is documented in E. A. Locke's "The Ubiquity of the Technique of Goal Setting in Theories of and Approaches to Employee Motivation" (*Academy of Management Review,* July 1978).

QUESTIONS FOR DISCUSSION

1 What boundary conditions would you propose as the limitations within which expectancy (VIE) theory is an effective model of motivation?

2 As a manager, which of the cognitive theories would you find most useful for dealing with a subordinate who has a low sales productivity? What theory would be most useful for dealing with high absenteeism? Why? What different actions might you take if you analyzed these situations with some other theory of motivation?

3 Using expectancy theory, outline ways in which a manager might directly affect each component of the model.

4 How would you compare expectancy theories with need theories of motivation?

5 Some managerial behaviors are well planned, and others may be merely the by-products of personal style or habit. What incidental managerial behaviors might affect valence, instrumentality, and expectancy calculations by subordinates?

6 What implications does the Porter and Lawler definition of satisfaction ("a derivative variable") have for determining rewards?

7 How would you evaluate the research evidence in support of equity theory?

8 Why do you think equity theory has been largely ignored by many managers and writers working in the field of organizational behavior?

9 What can line managers learn from equity theory that could help them improve their supervisory abilities?

10 How do the prescriptions for effective managerial behavior which follow from equity theory differ from those derived from Murray's needs theory?

11 Suggest some new applications for equity theory in work organizations in addition to those in the area of pay.

12 Why should it *not* "be assumed that setting specific quantitative goals is inevitably beneficial"?

13 Locke asserts that "rational human action is goal directed." Do you agree with this statement? What actions in organizations do you expect would *not* conform to Locke's aphorism?

14 Discuss the similarity in the practices used by advocates of O.B. mod., scientific management, and human relations theories to which Locke alludes.

15 The study by Umstot, Bell, and Mitchell found that goal-setting led to higher productivity, while job enrichment resulted in increased satisfaction. Goal-setting combined with job enrichment produced improvements in both productivity and satisfaction. What underlying theory of motivation would you propose to explain these results?

16 Locke explains the difference in the approaches with respect to goals of scientific management and human relations theories. Are the types of goals set and the process of goal-setting under each approach likely to be different? Explain.

17 Would the general principles of operant conditioning be as applicable to solving the problems of turnover or absenteeism as they would to solving those of performance? Why or why not? Cite examples to illustrate your answer.

CHAPTER 4

REINFORCEMENT AND SOCIAL LEARNING APPROACHES TO MOTIVATION

In this chapter, we address the important role of reinforcement-based processes in work motivation. The basic difference between the reinforcement approach and other approaches (e.g., need theories and cognitive theories) was discussed in Chapters 1 and 3. In the present chapter, an effort will be made to examine reinforcement types of theories in more detail.

In particular, we will see that there are, in fact, several reinforcement models, not just one. (A similar situation was shown for cognitive theories.) Two reinforcement models will be covered here. First, behavior modification as an operant technique of reinforcement will be examined. This is followed by a discussion of recent adaptations of social learning theory to the workplace.

BEHAVIOR MODIFICATION

Although Skinner's (1953) research on the effects of positive reinforcement, or behavior modification, on behavior has been widely publicized in the psychological literature, it is only recently that attention has been paid to the application of such principles to work settings in organizations. In the last decade or so, management researchers have experimented with these techniques in such diverse areas as job design, compensation, and organizational climate.

The basic concept of behavior modification is simple. Briefly, it assumes that human behavior can be engineered, shaped, or altered by manipulating the reward structures of various forms of behavior. This process is called "positive reinforcement." Performance standards are clearly set, and improvement results—at least in theory—from the application of frequent *positive* feedback and from recognition for satisfactory behavior. Negative feedback is not generally used. It is assumed that the employee's desire for the rewards of positive feedback and recognition will in large measure motivate him or her to perform satisfactorily in anticipation of such rewards.

According to Luthans and Kreitner (1975), three fundamental principles underlie behavior modification. First, it is necessary to deal exclusively with observable behavioral events, not attitudes, perceptions, or feelings. Second, one should measure behavior in terms of response frequency, or the extent to which desired behaviors are repeated by individuals. Third, since behavior is viewed as a function of its consequences (according to advocates of behavior modification), clear contingency relationships must be established for employees between acts or behaviors and subsequent rewards or outcomes. The ramifications of these three principles are discussed in detail in the reading selections in this chapter.

Advocates of behavior modification point to several advantages that purportedly result from the use of operant conditioning techniques. For such benefits to result, however, major responsibility is placed on managers to control the work environment and reward contingencies. Without such control, the major benefits of the program are lost. Hence, managerial behavior is seen as crucial for the success of such programs.

A variety of managerial implications emerge from recent work on behavior modification (Luthans & Kreitner, 1975). First, it is important that managers clearly inform subordinates concerning which behaviors are desirable and get rewarded and which behaviors do not get rewarded. Second, performance can be improved by providing continuous feedback to employees concerning the nature and quality of their work. This would include pointing out errors made by employees as well as noting ways of overcoming such errors. Third, it is important that the rewards or consequences offered for good performance equal behaviors exhibited by employees. That is, if an employee is doing a good job, he or she should be told this. Supervisors often find this hard to do, but the importance of recognizing good behavior is crucial to behavior modification. Fourth, managers should ensure that all employees are not rewarded equally; that is, rewards should be differentiated by performance levels. If employees fail to see a clear relationship between performance and rewards, there is little reason to believe they will exert increased energies for task accomplishment. As can be seen from these managerial implications, behavior modification as a theory of work motivation requires significant administrative effort in managing reward contingencies. When examining this approach, it would be useful to compare both the theory and the managerial implications with the more cognitive theories of motivation.

While behavior modification in work organizations may appear appealing on the surface, it has not been universally accepted. Whyte (1972), for example, points out that most of the research in support of Skinner's theory is laboratory-based, using primarily animals under highly controlled conditions. He argues that such principles may not apply when one attempts to use them in the more complex world of organizations. While not completely rejecting Skinner, Whyte raises four problems with applying his principles to "real-life" behavior.

First, much of Skinner's research has ignored complex social processes that can moderate any incentive system. If group performance norms are set in contravention to the positive reinforcement incentive system for improving performance, such incentives may have little impact.

Second, there is the problem of conflicting stimuli. For example, the use of positive reinforcement to gain increased productivity may stimulate employees' desires to improve output and yet simultaneously arouse their fears that this improved output will only lead to the permanent establishment of still higher performance standards.

Third, there is the traditional problem of obtaining employees' belief that management is truly acting with the employees' interests in mind and not simply trying to exploit them.

Fourth, there is what Whyte terms the "one-body problem." An employee is motivated by experiences and anticipations that come from a variety of sources (family, friends, coworkers, and so on). If behavior modification principles are to be effectively implemented, Whyte argues, all these forms of input would need to be controlled simultaneously so that a unified system of positive reinforcement could be attained. This would certainly be no easy task.

SOCIAL LEARNING THEORY

The second reinforcement approach to be considered here is social learning theory. This theory incorporates the interactive nature of the major variables of organizational behavior: the behavior itself, the environment, and the person (or internal cognitions). Thus, this approach is broader than behavior modification, primarily because of its inclusion of the recognition of cognitive processes in behavior.

OVERVIEW

In the readings that follow, several aspects of reinforcement-based approaches to motivation are examined. First, Hamner discusses the basic principles of operant conditioning and its relationship to developing reinforcement contingencies on the job. Behavior modification is thus the focus of this paper. In the next article, Hamner and Hamner review a series of field tests of behavior modification. They begin with a summary of the four basic stages essential to positive reinforcement programs, and then they examine 10 specific organizational applications of such programs in a variety of work settings. The final selection, by Kreitner and Luthans, provides an overview of social learning theory and shows how that theory builds both on reinforcement principles and on knowledge about cognitive processes. The theory, as will be seen in the article by Kreitner and Luthans, stresses the reciprocal interaction of the person, behavior, and the environment. This article concludes with a set of action steps that managers can take to implement an approach consistent with the fundamentals of social learning theory.

REFERENCES

Luthans, F., & Kreitner, R. *Organizational behavior modification*. Glenview, Ill.: Scott, Foresman, 1975.

Skinner, B. F. *Science and human behavior*. New York: Free Press, 1953.

Whyte, W. F. Skinnerian theory in organizations. *Psychology Today*, April 1972, 67–68, 96, 98, 100.

Reinforcement Theory and Contingency Management in Organizational Settings

W. Clay Hamner

Traditionally management has been defined as the process of getting things done through other people. The succinctness of this definition is misleading in that, while it may be easy to say *what* a manager does, it is difficult to describe the determinants of behavior, i.e. to tell *how* the behavior of the manager influences the behavior of the employee toward accomplishment of a task. Human behavior in organizational settings has always been a phenomenon of interest and concern. However, it has only been in recent years that a concerted effort has been made by social scientists to describe the principles of reinforcement and their implications for describing the determinants of behavior as they relate to the theory and practice of management (e.g. see Nord, 1969; Wiard, 1972; Whyte, 1972; Jablonsky and DeVries, 1972; Hersey and Blanchard, 1972; and Behling, Schriesheim, and Tolliver, in press).[1]

Organizational leaders must resort to environmental changes as a means of influencing behavior. Reinforcement principles are the most useful method for this purpose because they indicate to the leader how he might proceed in designing or modifying the work environment in order to effect specific changes in behavior (Scott and Cummings, 1973). A reinforcement approach to management does not consist of a bag of tricks to be applied indiscriminately for the purpose of coercing unwilling people (Michael & Meyerson, 1962). Unfortunately, many people who think of Skinnerian applications (Skinner, 1969) in the field of management and personnel think of manipulation and adverse control over employees. Increased knowledge available today of the positive aspects of conditioning as applied to worker performance should help to dispel these notions.

The purpose of this paper is to describe the determinants of behavior as seen from a reinforcement theory point of view, and to describe how the management of the contingencies of reinforcement in organizational settings is a key to successful management. Hopefully, this paper will enable the manager to understand how his behavior affects the behavior of his subordinates and to see that in most cases the failure or success of the worker at the performance of a task is a direct function of the manager's own behavior. Since a large portion of the manager's time is spent in the process of modifying behavior patterns and shaping them so that they will be more goal oriented, it is appropriate that this paper begin by describing the processes and principles that govern behavior.

LEARNING AS A PREREQUISITE FOR BEHAVIOR

Learning is such a common phenomenon that we tend to fail to recognize its occurrence. Nevertheless, one of the major premises of reinforcement theory is that all behavior is learned—a worker's skill, a supervisor's attitude and a secretary's manners. The importance of learning in organizational settings is asserted by Costello and Zalkind when they conclude:

> Every aspect of human behavior is responsive to learning experiences. Knowledge, language, and skills, of course; but also attitudes, value systems, and personality characteristics. All the individual's activities in the organization—his loyalties, awareness of organizational goals, job performance, even his safety record have been learned in the largest sense of that term (1963, p. 205).

There seems to be general agreement among social scientists that learning can be defined as *a relatively permanent change in behavior potentiality that results from reinforced practice or experience.* Note that this definition states that there is change in behavior potentiality and not necessarily in behavior itself. The reason for this distinction rests on the fact that we can observe other people responding to their environments, see the consequences which accrue to them, and be vicariously conditioned. For example, a boy can watch his older sister burn her hand on a hot stove and "learn" that pain is the result of touching a hot stove. This definition therefore allows us to account for "no–trial" learning. Bandura (1969) describes this as imitative learning and says that while behavior can be *acquired* by observing, reading, or other vicarious methods, "*performance* of observationally learned responses will depend to a great extent upon the nature of the reinforcing consequences to the model or to the observer" (p. 128).

Luthans (1973, p. 362) says that we need to consider the following points when we define the learning process:

1 Learning involves a change, though not necessarily an improvement, in behavior. Learning generally has the connotation of improved performance, but under this definition bad habits, prejudices, stereotypes, and work restrictions are learned.

2 The change in behavior must be relatively permanent in order to be considered learning. This qualification rules out behavioral changes resulting from fatigue or temporary adaptations as learning.

3 Some form of practice or experience is necessary for learning to occur.

4 Finally, practice or experience must be reinforced in order for learning to occur. If reinforcement does not accompany the practice or experience, the behavior will eventually disappear.

From this discussion, we can conclude that learning is the acquisition of knowledge, and performance is the translation of knowledge into practice. The primary effect of reinforcement is to strengthen and intensify certain aspects of ensuing behavior. Behavior that has become highly differentiated (shaped) can be understood and accounted for only in terms of the history of reinforcement of that behavior (Morse, 1966). Reinforcement generates a reproducible behavior process in time. A response occurs and is followed by a reinforcer, and further responses occur with a characteristic temporal patterning. When a response is reinforced it subsequently occurs more frequently than before it was reinforced. Reinforce-

ment may be assumed to have a characteristic and reproducible effect on a particular behavior, and usually it will enhance and intensify that behavior (Skinner,
1938; 1953).

TWO BASIC LEARNING PROCESSES

Before discussing in any detail exactly how the general laws or principles of reinforcement can be used to predict and influence behavior, we must differentiate
between two types of behavior. One kind is known as *voluntary* or *operant* behavior, and the other is known as *reflex* or *respondent* behavior. Respondent behavior takes in all responses of human beings that are *elicited* by special stimulus
changes in the environment. An example would be when a person turns a light on
in a dark room (stimulus change), his eyes contract (respondent behavior).

Operant behavior includes an even greater amount of human activity. It takes
in all the responses of a person that may at some time be said to have an effect
upon or do something to the person's outside world (Keller, 1969). Operant behavior *operates* on this world either directly or indirectly. For example, when a person presses the up button at the elevator entrance to "call" the elevator, he is
operating on his environment.

The process of learning or acquiring reflex behavior is different from the processes of learning or acquiring voluntary behavior. The two basic and distinct
learning processes are known as *classical conditioning* and *operant conditioning*.
It is from studying these two learning processes that much of our knowledge of
individual behavior has emerged.

Classical Conditioning[2]

Pavlov (1902) noticed, while studying the automatic reflexes associated with di-
gestion, that his laboratory dog salivated (unconditioned response) not only when
food (unconditioned stimulus) was placed in the dog's mouth, but also when other
stimuli were presented before food was placed in the dog's mouth. In other words,
by presenting a neutral stimulus (ringing of a bell) every time food was presented
to the dog, Pavlov was able to get the dog to salivate to the bell alone.

A stimulus which is not a part of a reflex relationship (the bell in Pavlov's
experiment) becomes a *conditioned stimulus* for the response by repeated, temporal pairing with an *unconditioned* stimulus (food) which already elicits the response. This new relationship is known as a conditioned reflex, and the pairing
procedure is known as classical conditioning.

While it is important to understand that reflex behavior is conditioned by a
different process than is voluntary behavior, classical conditioning principles are
of little use to the practicing manager. Most of the behavior that is of interest to
society does not fit in the paradigm of reflex behavior (Michael and Meyerson,
1962). Nevertheless, the ability to generalize from one stimulus setting to another
is very important in human learning and problem solving, and for this reason,
knowledge of the classical conditioning process is important.

Operant Conditioning[3]

The basic distinction between classical and operant conditioning procedures is in terms of the *consequences* of the conditioned response. In classical conditioning, the sequence of events is independent of the subject's behavior. In operant conditioning, consequences (rewards and punishments) are made to occur as a consequence of the subject's response or failure to respond. The distinction between these two methods is shown in Figure 1.

In Figure 1, we see that classical conditioning involves a three stage process. In the diagram, let *S* refer to *stimulus* and *R* to *response*. We see that in stage 1, the unconditioned stimulus (food) elicits an unconditioned response (salivation). In stage 2, a neutral stimulus (bell) elicits no known response. However, in stage 3, after the ringing of the bell is repeatedly paired with the presence of food, the bell alone becomes a conditioned stimulus and elicits a conditioned response (salivation). The subject has no control over the unconditioned or conditioned response, but is "at the mercy" of his environment and his past conditioning history.

Note, however, that for voluntary behavior, the consequence is dependent on the behavior of the individual in a given stimulus setting. Such behavior can be said to "operate" (Skinner, 1969) on the environment, in contrast to behavior which is "respondent" to prior eliciting stimuli (Michael and Meyerson, 1962). Reinforcement is not given every time the stimulus is presented, but is *only* given when the correct response is made. For example, if an employee taking a work break puts a penny (R) in the soft drink machine (S), nothing happens (consequence). However, if he puts a quarter (R) in the machine (S), he gets the soft drink (consequence). In other words, the employee's behavior is *instrumental* in determining the consequences which accrue to him.

The interrelationships between the three components of (1) *stimulus* or environment, (2) *response* or performance, and (3) consequences or *reinforcements* are known as the *contingencies* of reinforcement. Skinner (1969) says "The class of responses upon which a reinforcer is *contingent* is called an operant, to suggest the action on the environment followed by reinforcements (p. 7)." Operant conditioning presupposes that human beings explore their environment and act upon it.

FIGURE 1
Classical vs. operant conditioning.

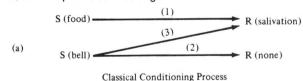

(a)

Classical Conditioning Process

————————(S = stimulus, R = responses, arrow = leads to)—————————

S ——→ R (voluntary behavior) ——→ Consequences

(b)

Operant Conditioning Process

This behavior, randomly emitted at first, can be constructed as an operant by making a reinforcement contingent on a response. Any stimulus present when an operant is reinforced acquires control in the sense that the rate of response for that individual will be higher when it is present. "Such a stimulus does not act as a *goal*; it does not elicit the response (as was the case in classical conditioning of reflex behavior)[4] in the sense of forcing it to occur. It is simply an essential aspect of the occasion upon which response is made and reinforced (Skinner, 1969, p. 7)."

Therefore, an adequate formulation of the interaction between an individual and his environment must always specify three things: (1) the occasion upon which a response occurs, (2) the response itself and (3) the reinforcing consequences. Skinner holds that the consequences determine the likelihood that a given operant will be performed in the future. Thus to change behavior, the consequences of the behavior must be changed, i.e. the contingencies must be rearranged (the ways in which the consequences are related to the behavior) (Behling, *et al.,* in press). For Skinner, this behavior generated by a given set of contingencies can be accounted for without appealing to hypothetical inner states (e.g. awareness or expectancies). "If a conspicuous stimulus does not have an effect, it is not because the organism has not attended to it or because some central gatekeeper has screened it out, but because the stimulus plays no important role in the prevailing contingencies (Skinner, 1969, p. 8)."

Arrangement of the Contingencies of Reinforcement

In order to *understand* and *interpret* behavior, we must look at the interrelationship among the components of the contingencies of behavior. If one expects to influence behavior, he must also be able to manipulate the consequences of the behavior (Skinner, 1969). Haire (1964) reports the importance of being able to manipulate the consequences when he says,

> Indeed, whether he is conscious of it or not, the superior is bound to be constantly shaping the behavior of his subordinates by the way in which he utilizes the rewards that are at his disposal, and he will inevitably modify the behavior patterns of his work group thereby. For this reason, it is important to see as clearly as possible what is going on, so that the changes can be planned and chosen in advance, rather than simply accepted after the fact.

After appropriate reinforcers that have sufficient incentive value to maintain stable responsiveness have been chosen, the contingencies between specific performances and reinforcing stimuli must be arranged (Bandura, 1969). Employers intuitively use rewards in their attempt to modify and influence behavior, but their efforts often produce limited results because the methods are used improperly, inconsistently, or inefficiently. In many instances considerable rewards are bestowed upon the workers, but they are not made conditional or contingent on the behavior the manager wishes to promote. Also, "long delays often intervene between the occurrence of the desired behavior and its intended consequences; special privileges, activities, and rewards are generally furnished according to fixed time schedules rather than performance requirements; and in many cases, positive reinforcers are inadvertently made contingent upon the wrong type of behavior" (Bandura, 1969, pp. 229–230).

One of the primary reasons that managers fail to "motivate" workers to perform in the desired manner is due to a lack of understanding of the power of the contingencies of reinforcement over the employee and of the manager's role in arranging these contingencies. The laws or principles for arranging the contingencies are not hard to understand, and if students of behavior grasp them firmly, they are powerful managerial tools which can be used to increase supervisory effectiveness.

As we have said, operant conditioning is the process by which behavior is modified by manipulation of the contingencies of the behavior. To understand how this works, we will first look at various *types* (arrangements) of contingencies, and then at various *schedules* of the contingencies available. Rachlin (1970) described the four basic ways available to the manager of arranging the contingencies—*positive reinforcement, avoidance learning, extinction,* and *punishment.* The difference among these types of contingencies depends on the consequence which results from the behavioral act. Positive reinforcement and avoidance learning are methods of strengthening *desired* behavior, and extinction and punishment are methods of weakening *undesired* behavior.

Positive Reinforcement   "A positive reinforcer is a stimulus which, when added to a situation, strengthens the probability of an operant response (Skinner, 1953, p. 73)." The reason it strengthens the response is explained by Thorndike's (1911) Law of Effect. This law states simply that behavior which appears to lead to a positive consequence tends to be repeated, while behavior which appears to lead to a negative consequence tends not to be repeated. A positive consequence is called a reward.

Reinforcers, either positive or negative, are classified as either: (1) unconditioned or primary reinforcers, or (2) conditioned or secondary reinforcers. Primary reinforcers such as food, water, and sex are of biological importance in that they are innately rewarding and have effects which are independent of past experiences. Secondary reinforcers such as job advancement, praise, recognition, and money derive their effects from a consistent pairing with other reinforcers (i.e., they are conditioned). Secondary reinforcement, therefore, depends on the individual and his past reinforcement history. What is rewarding to one person may not be rewarding to another. Managers should look for a reward system which has maximal reinforcing consequences to the group he is supervising.

Regardless of whether the positive reinforcer is primary or secondary in nature, once it has been determined that the consequence has reward value to the worker, it can be used to increase the worker's performance. So the *first step* in the successful application of reinforcement procedures is to select reinforcers that are sufficiently powerful and durable to "maintain responsiveness while complex patterns of behavior are being established and strengthened" (Bandura, 1969, p. 225).

The *second step* is to design the contingencies in such a way that the reinforcing events are made contingent upon the desired behavior. This is the rule of reinforcement which is most often violated. Rewards must result from performance, and the greater the degree of performance by an employee, the greater should be his reward. Money as a reinforcer will be discussed later, but it should be noted that money is not the only reward available. In fact, for unionized employees, the supervisor has virtually no way to tie money to performance. Nevertheless, other forms of rewards, such as recognition, promotion and job assignments, can be made contingent on good performance. Unless a manager is willing to discriminate between employees based on their level of performance, the effectiveness of his power over the employee is nil.

The arrangement of positive reinforcement contingencies can be pictured as follows:

Stimulus → Desired response → Positive consequences
$(S \rightarrow R \rightarrow R^+)$

The stimulus is the work environment which leads to a response (some level of performance). If this response leads to positive consequences, then the probability of that response being emitted again increases (Law of Effect). Now, if the behavior is undesired, then the supervisor is conditioning or teaching the employee that undesired behavior will lead to a desired reward. It is important therefore that the reward administered be equal to the performance input of the employee. Homans (1950) labels this as the rule of distributive justice and stated that this reciprocal norm applies in both formal (work) and informal (friendship) relationships. In other words, the employee *exchanges* his services for the rewards of the organization. In order to maintain desired performance, it is important that the manager design the reward system so that the level of reward administered is proportionately contingent on the level of performance emitted.

The *third step* is to design the contingencies in such a way that a reliable procedure for eliciting or inducing the desired response patterns is established; otherwise, if they never occur there will be few opportunities to influence the desired behavior through contingent management. If the behavior that a manager wishes to strengthen is already present, and occurs with some frequency, then contingent applications of incentives can, from the outset, increase and maintain the desired performance patterns at a high level. However, as Bandura (1969) states, "When the initial level of the desired behavior is extremely low, if the criterion for reinforcement is initially set too high, most, if not all, of the person's responses go unrewarded, so that his efforts are gradually extinguished and his motivation diminished (p. 232)."

The nature of the learning process is such that acquiring the new response patterns can be easily established. The principle of operant conditioning says that an operant followed by a positive reinforcement is more likely to occur under similar conditions in the future. Through the process of *generalization,* the more nearly alike the new situation or stimulus is to the original one, the more the old behavior is likely to be emitted in the new environment. For example, if you contract with an electrician to rewire your house, he is able to bring with him enough old behavioral patterns which he generalized to this unfamiliar, but similar, stimulus setting (the house) in order to accomplish the task. He has learned through his past reinforcement history that, when in a new environment, one way to speed up the correct behavior needed to obtain reward is to generalize from similar settings with which he has had experience. Perhaps one reason an employer wants a person with work experience is because the probability of that person emitting the correct behavior is greater and thus the job of managing that person simplified.

Just as generalization is the ability to react to similarities in the environment, *discrimination* is the ability to react to differences in a new environmental setting. Usually when an employee moves from one environment (a job, a city, an office) to another he finds that only certain dimensions of the stimulus conditions change. While all of the responses of the employee in this new setting will not be correct, by skilled use of the procedures of reinforcement currently being discussed, we can bring about the more precise type of stimulus control called discrimination. When we purchase a new car, we do not have to relearn how to drive a car (generalizable stimulus). Instead we need only learn the differences in the new car and the old car so that we can respond to these differences in order to get reinforced. This procedure is called *discrimination training*. "If in the presence of a stimulus a response is reinforced, and in the absence of this stimulus it is extinguished, the stimulus will control the probability of the response in high degree. Such a stimulus is called a *discriminative stimulus* (Michael and Meyerson, 1962)."

The development of effective discriminative repertoires is important for dealing with many different people on an interpersonal basis. Effective training techniques will allow the supervisor to develop the necessary discriminative repertoires in his new employees (e.g., see Bass and Vaughan, 1966, *Training in Industry: The Management of Learning*).

Using the principles of generalization and discrimination in a well-designed training program allows the manager to accomplish the third goal of eliciting or inducing the desired response patterns. Training is a method of *shaping* desired behavior so that it can be conditioned to come under the control of the reinforcement stimuli. Shaping behavior is necessary when the response to be learned is not currently in the individual's repertoire and when it is a fairly complex behavior. In shaping, we teach a desired response by reinforcing the series of successive steps which lead to the final response. This method is essentially the one your parents used when they first taught you to drive. You were first taught how to adjust the seat and mirror, fasten the seat belt, turn on the lights and windshield wipers, and then how to start the engine. Each time you successfully completed each stage you were positively reinforced by some comment. You then were allowed to practice driving on back roads and in empty lots. By focusing on one of these aspects at a time and reinforcing proper responses, your parents were able to shape your driving behavior until you reached the final stage of being able to drive. After your behavior was shaped, driving other cars or driving in new territories was accomplished successfully by the process of generalization and discrimination. This same process is used with a management trainee who is rotated from department to department for a period of time until he has "learned the ropes." After his managerial behavior has been minimally shaped, he is transferred to a managerial position where, using the principles of generalization and discrimination, he is able to adjust to the contingencies of the work environment.

Avoidance Learning   The second type of contingency arrangement available to the manager is called escape, or avoidance learning. Just as with positive reinforcement, this is a method of strengthening desired behavior. A contingency arrangement in which an individual's performance can terminate an already noxious stimulus is called *escape* learning. When behavior can prevent the onset of a noxious stimulus the procedure is called *avoidance learning*. In both cases, the result is the development and maintenance of the desired operant behavior (Michael and Meyerson, 1962).

An example of this kind of control can be easily found in a work environment. Punctuality of employees is often maintained by avoidance learning. The noxious stimulus is the criticism by the shop steward or office manager for being late. In order to avoid criticism other employees make a special effort to come to work on time. A supervisor begins criticizing a worker for "goofing off." Other workers may intensify their efforts to escape the criticism of the supervisor.

The arrangement of an escape reinforcement contingency can be diagrammed as follows:

Noxious stimulus $\rightarrow$ Desired response $\rightarrow$ Removal of noxious stimulus
$(S^- \rightarrow R \nrightarrow S^-)$

The distinction between the process of strengthening behavior by means of positive reinforcement techniques and avoidance learning techniques should be noted carefully. In one case, the individual works hard to gain the consequences from the environment which result from good work, and in the second case, the individual works hard to avoid the noxious aspects of the environment itself. In both cases the same behavior is strengthened.

While Skinner (1953) recognizes that avoidance learning techniques can be used to condition desired behavior, he does not advocate their use. Instead a Skinnerian approach to operant conditioning is primarily based on the principles of positive reinforcement.

Extinction   While positive reinforcement and avoidance learning techniques can be used by managers to strengthen desired behavior, extinction and punishment techniques are methods available to managers for reducing undesired behavior. When positive reinforcement for a learned or previously conditioned response is withheld, individuals will continue to exhibit that behavior for an extended period of time. Under repeated nonreinforcement, the behavior decreases and eventually disappears. This decline in response rate as a result of nonrewarded repetition of a task is defined as *extinction*.

The diagram of the arrangement of the contingency of extinction can be shown as follows:

(1) Stimulus $\rightarrow$ Response $\rightarrow$ Positive consequences
     $(S \rightarrow R \rightarrow R^+)$

(2) Stimulus → Response → Withholding of positive consequences
  (S → R $\not\to$ R⁺)

(3) Stimulus → Withholding of response
  (S $\not\to$ R)

   The behavior which was previously reinforced because (a) it was desired or (b) by poor reinforcement practices is no longer desired. To extinguish this behavior in a naturally recurring situation, response patterns sustained by positive reinforcement (Stage 1) are frequently eliminated (Stage 3) by discontinuing the rewards (Stage 2) that ordinarily produce the behavior. This method when combined with a positive reinforcement method is the procedure of behavior modification recommended by Skinner (1953). It leads to the least negative side effects and when the two methods are used together, it allows the employee to get the rewards he desires and allows the organization to eliminate the undesired behavior.

   Punishment   A second method of reducing the frequency of undesired behavior is through the use of punishment. Punishment is the most controversial method of behavior modification, and most of the ethical questions about operant methods of control center around this technique. "One of the principal objections to aversive control stems from the widespread belief that internal, and often unconscious, forces are the major determinant of behavior. From this perspective, punishment may temporarily suppress certain expressions, but the underlying impulses retain their strength and press continuously for discharge through alternative actions (Bandura, 1969, p. 292)." While Skinner (1953) discounts the internal state hypothesis, he recommends that extinction rather than punishment be used to decrease the probability of the occurrence of a particular behavior.
   Punishment is defined as presenting an aversive or noxious consequence contingent upon a response, or removing a positive consequence contingent upon a response. Based on the Law of Effect, as rewards strengthen behavior, punishment weakens it. This process can be shown as follows:

(1) Stimulus → Undesired behavior → Noxious consequence or withholding of
  (S → R → R⁻)   positive consequence
  (or $\not\to$ R⁺)

(2) Stimulus → Undesired behavior
  (S $\not\to$ R)

Notice carefully the difference in the withholding of rewards in the punishment process and the withholding of rewards in the extinction process. In the extinction process, we withhold rewards for behavior that has previously been administered the rewards because the behavior was desired. In punishment, we withhold a reward because the behavior is undesired, has never been associated with the reward before, and is in fact a noxious consequence. For example, if your young son began imitating an older neighborhood boy's use of profanity and you thought it was "cute," you might reinforce the behavior by laughing or by calling public attention to it. Soon, the son learns one way to get the recognition he craves is to use profanity—even though he may have no concept of its meaning. As the child reaches an accountable age, you decide that his use of profanity is no longer as cute as it once was. To stop the behavior you can do one of three things: (1) You can withhold the previous recognition you gave the child by ignoring him (extinction), (2) You can give the child a spanking (punishment by noxious consequence), or (3) You can withhold his allowance or refuse to let him watch television (punishment by withholding of positive consequences not previously connected with the act.)

It should be noted that method 2 and perhaps method 3 would be considered cruel because of the parent's own inconsistencies. Punishment should rarely be used to extinguish behavior that has previously been reinforced if the person administering the punishment is the same person who previously reinforced the behavior. However, had the parent failed to extinguish the use of profanity prior to sending the child out in society (e.g. school, church), it is possible that the society may punish the child for behavior that the parent is reinforcing or at least tolerating. It is often argued therefore that the failure to use punishment early in the life of a child for socially unacceptable behavior (e.g., stealing, driving at excessive speeds, poor table manners) is more cruel than the punishment itself, simply because the society will withhold rewards or administer aversive consequences for the behavior which the parents should have extinguished.

The use of aversive control is frequently questioned on the assumption that it produces undesirable by-products. In many cases this concern is warranted. Bandura (1969) states that it depends on the circumstances and on the past reinforcement history of the reinforcement agent and the reinforcement target as to whether punishment or extinction should be used. He says:

> Many of the unfavorable effects, however, that are sometimes associated with punishment are not necessarily inherent in the methods themselves but result from the faulty manner in which they are applied. A great deal of human behavior is, in fact, modified and closely regulated by natural aversive contingencies without any ill effects. On the basis of negative consequences people learn to avoid or to protect themselves against hazardous falls, flaming or scalding objects, deafening sounds, and other hurtful stimuli. . . . In instances where certain activities can have injurious effects, aversive contingencies *must* be socially arranged to ensure survival. Punishment is rarely indicated for ineffectiveness or deleterious side effects when used, for example, to teach young children not to insert metal objects into electrical outlets, not to cross busy thoroughfares . . . Certain types of negative sanctions, if applied considerately, can likewise aid in eliminating self-defeating and socially detrimental behavior without creating any special problems (p. 294).

Rules for Using Operant Conditioning Techniques   Several rules concerning the arrangement of the contingencies of reinforcement should be discussed. While these rules have common sense appeal, the research findings indicate that these rules are often violated by managers when they design control systems.

Rule 1. Don't reward all people the same. In other words, differentiate the rewards based on performance as compared to some defined objective or stand-ard. We know that people compare their own performance to that of their peers to determine how well they are doing ("Social Comparison Theory," Festinger, 1954) and they compare their rewards to the rewards of their peers ("Equity The-ory," Adams, 1965) in order to determine how to evaluate their rewards. While some managers seem to think that the fairest system of compensation is one where everyone in the same job classification gets the same pay, employees want differ-entiation so that they know their importance to the organization. Based on social comparison and equity theory assumptions, it can be argued that managers who reward all people the same are encouraging, at best, only average performance. Behavior of high performance workers is being extinguished (ignored) while the behavior of average performance and poor performance workers is being strength-ened by positive reinforcement.

Rule 2. Failure to respond has reinforcing consequences. Managers who find the job of differentiating between workers so unpleasant that they fail to respond must recognize that failure to respond modifies behavior. "Indeed, whether he is conscious of it or not, the superior is bound to be constantly shaping the behavior of his subordinates by the way in which he utilizes the rewards that are at his disposal, and he will inevitably modify the behavior of his work group (Haire, 1964)." Managers must be careful that they examine the performance conse-quence of their non-action as well as their action.

Rule 3. Be sure to tell a person what he can do to get reinforced. By making clear the contingencies of reinforcement to the worker, a manager may be actually increasing the individual freedom of the worker. The employee who has a stand-ard against which to measure his job will have a built-in feedback system which allows him to make judgments about his own work. The awarding of the rein-forcement in an organization where the worker's goal is specified will be associ-ated with the performance of the worker and not based on the biases of the super-visor. The assumption is that the supervisor rates the employee accurately (see Scott and Hamner, 1973a) and that he then reinforces the employee based on his ratings (see Scott and Hamner, 1973b). If the supervisor fails to rate accurately or administer rewards based on performance, then the stated goals for the worker will lose stimulus control, and the worker will be forced to search for the "true" contingencies, i.e., what behavior should he perform in order to get rewarded (e.g., ingratiation? loyalty? positive attitude?).

Rule 4. Be sure to tell a person what he is doing wrong. As a general rule, very few people find the act of failing rewarding. One assumption of behavior therefore is that a worker wants to be rewarded in a positive manner. A supervisor should never use extinction or punishment as a sole method for modifying behavior, but if used judiciously in conjunction with other techniques designed to promote more effective response options (Rule 3) such combined procedures can hasten the change process. If the supervisor fails to specify why a reward is being withheld, the employee may associate it with past desired behavior instead of the undesired behavior that the supervisor is trying to extinguish. The supervisor then extin-guishes good performance while having no effect on the undesired behavior.

Rules 3 and 4, when used in combination, should allow the manager to control behavior in the best interest of reaching organizational goals. At the same time they should give the employee the clarity he needs to see that his own behavior and not the behavior of the supervisor controls his outcomes.

Rule 5. Don't punish in front of others. The reason for this rule is quite simple. The punishment (e.g., reprimand) should be enough to extinguish the undesired behavior. By administering the punishment in front of the work group, the worker is doubly punished in the sense that he is also put out of face (Goffman, 1959). This additional punishment may lead to negative side-effects in three ways. First, the worker whose self-image is damaged may feel that he must retaliate in order to protect himself. Therefore, the supervisor has actually increased undesired responses. Secondly, the work group may misunderstand the reason for the punishment and through "avoidance learning" may modify their own behavior in ways not intended by the supervisor. Third, the work group is also being punished in the sense that observing a member of their team being reprimanded has noxious or aversive properties for most people. This may result in a decrease in the performance of the total work group.

Rule 6. Make the consequences equal to the behavior. In other words be fair. Don't cheat the worker out of his just rewards. If he is a good worker, tell him. Many supervisors find it very difficult to praise an employee. Others find it very difficult to counsel an employee about what he is doing wrong. When a manager fails to use these reinforcement tools, he is actually reducing his effectiveness. When a worker is overrewarded he may feel guilty (Adams, 1965) and based on the principles of reinforcement, the worker's current level of performance is being conditioned. If his performance level is less than others who get the same reward, he has no reason to increase his output. When a worker is underrewarded, he becomes angry with the system (Adams, 1965). His behavior is being extinguished and the company may be forcing the good employee (underrewarded) to seek employment elsewhere while encouraging the poor employee (overrewarded) to stay.

An Argument for Positive Reinforcement

Most workers enter the work place willingly if not eagerly. They have a sense of right and wrong and have been thoroughly conditioned by their parents and by society. By the time they reach adulthood, it can be assumed that they are mature. For these reasons, it is argued here as well as by others (Skinner, 1953; Wiard, 1972), that the only tool needed for worker motivation is the presence or absence of positive reinforcement. In other words, managers do not, as a general rule, need to use avoidance learning or punishment techniques in order to control behavior.

Whyte (1972) says "positive reinforcers generally are more effective than negative reinforcers in the production and maintenance of behavior" (p. 67). Wiard (1972) points out, "There may be cases where the use of punishment has resulted in improved performance, but they are few and far between. The pitfalls of punishment can be encountered with any indirect approach" (p. 16). However, a positive reinforcement program is geared toward the desired results. It emphasizes what needs to be done, rather than what should not be done. A positive reinforcement program is result oriented, rather than process oriented. A well designed program encourages individual growth and freedom, whereas negative approach (avoidance learning and punishment) encourages immaturity in the individual and therefore eventually in the organization itself.

The reason organizations are ineffective according to Skinner (1969) is because they insist on using avoidance learning or punishment techniques, and because they fail to use a positive reinforcement program in an effective manner. He says:

> The contingencies of positive reinforcement arranged by governmental and religious agencies are primitive, and the agencies continue to lean heavily on the puritanical solution. Economic reinforcement might seem to represent an environmental solution, but it is badly programmed and the results are unsatisfactory for both the employer (since not much is done) and the employee (since work is still work). Education and the management of retardates and psychotics are still largely aversive. In short, as we have seen, the most powerful forces bearing on human behavior are not being effectively used. . . . Men are happy in an environment in which active, productive, and creative behavior is reinforced in effective ways (pp. 63–64).

Schedules of Positive Reinforcement

The previous discussion was primarily concerned with methods of arranging the contingencies of reinforcement in order to modify behavior. Two major points were discussed. First, some type of reinforcement is necessary in order to produce a change in behavior. Second, a combined program of positive reinforcement and extinction are more effective for use in organizations than are programs using punishment and/or avoidance learning techniques. The previous discussion thus tells what causes behavior and why it is important information for the manager, but it does not discuss the several important issues dealing with the scheduling or administering of positive reinforcement.

According to Costello and Zalkind (1963), "The speed with which learning takes place and also how lasting its effects will be is determined by the timing of reinforcement" (p. 193). In other words, the effectiveness varies as a function of the schedule of its administration. A reinforcement schedule is a more-or-less formal specification of the occurrence of a reinforcer in relation to the behavioral sequence to be conditioned, and effectiveness of the reinforcer depends as much upon its scheduling as upon any of its other features (magnitude, quality and degree of association with the behavioral act) (Adam and Scott, 1971).

There are many conceivable arrangements of a positive reinforcement schedule which managers can use to reward workers (Ferster and Skinner, 1957). Aldis (1961) identifies two basic types of schedules which have the most promise concerning possible worker motivation. These schedules are *continuous* and *partial reinforcement* schedules.

Continuous Reinforcement Schedule   Under this schedule, every time the correct operant is emitted by the worker, it is followed by a reinforcer. With this schedule, behavior increases very rapidly but when the reinforcer is removed (extinction) performance decreases rapidly. For this reason it is not recommended for use by the manager over a long period of time. It is also difficult or impossible for a manager to reward the employee continuously for emitting desired behavior. Therefore a manager should generally consider using one or more of the partial reinforcement schedules when he administers both financial and nonfinancial rewards.

Partial Reinforcement Schedules   Partial reinforcement, where reinforcement does not occur after every correct operant, leads to slower learning but stronger retention of a response than total or continuous reinforcement. "In other words, *learning is more permanent when we reward correct behavior only part of the time*" (Bass and Vaughan, 1966, p. 20). This factor is extremely relevant to the observed strong resistance to changes in attitudes, values, norms, and the like.

Ferster and Skinner (1957) have described four types of partial reinforcement schedules for operant learning situations. They are:

1   Fixed Interval Schedule   Under this schedule a reinforcer is administered only when the desired response occurs after the passage of a specified period of time since the previous reinforcement. Thus a worker paid on a weekly basis would receive a full pay check every Friday, assuming that the worker was performing minimally acceptable behavior. This method offers the least motivation for hard work among employees (Aldis, 1961). The kind of behavior often observed with fixed interval schedules is a pause after reinforcement and then an increase in rate of responding until a high rate of performance occurs just as the interval is about to end. Suppose the plant manager visits the shipping department each day at approximately 10:00 A.M. This fixed schedule of supervisory recognition will probably cause performance to be at its highest just prior to the plant manager's visit and then performance will probably steadily decline thereafter and not reach its peak again until the next morning's visit.

2   Variable Interval Schedule   Under this schedule, reinforcement is administered at some variable interval of time around some average. This schedule is not recommended for use with a pay plan (Aldis, 1961), but it is an ideal method to use for administering praise, promotions, and supervisory visits. Since the reinforcers are dispensed unpredictably, variable schedules generate higher rates of response and more stable and consistent performance (Bandura, 1969). Suppose our plant manager visits the shipping department on an *average* of once a day but at randomly selected time intervals, i.e., twice on Monday, once on Tuesday, not on Wednesday, not on Thursday, and twice on Friday, all at different times during the day. Performance will be higher and have less fluctuation than under the fixed interval schedule.

3   Fixed-Ratio Schedule   Here a reward is delivered only when a fixed number of desired responses take place. This is essentially the piece-work schedule for pay. The response level here is significantly higher than that obtained under any of the interval (or time-based) schedules.

4   Variable Ratio Schedule   Under this schedule, a reward is delivered only after a number of desired responses with the number of desired responses changing from the occurrence of one reinforcer to the next, around an average. Thus a person working on a 15 to 1 variable ratio schedule might receive reinforcement after ten responses, then twenty responses, then fifteen responses, etc., to an average of one reinforcer per fifteen responses. Gambling is an example of a variable ratio reward schedule. Research evidence reveals that of all the variations in scheduling procedures available, this is the most powerful in sustaining behavior (Jablonsky and DeVries, 1972). In industry, this plan would be impossible to use as the only plan for scheduling reinforcement. However, Aldis (1961) suggests how this method could be used to supplement other monetary reward schedules:

> Take the annual Christmas bonus as an example. In many instances, this "surprise" gift has become nothing more than a ritualized annual salary supplement which everybody expects. Therefore, its incentive-building value is largely lost. Now suppose that the total bonus were distributed at irregular intervals throughout the year and in small sums dependent upon the amount of work done. Wouldn't the workers find their urge to work increased? (p. 63)

An important point to remember is that to be effective a schedule should always include the specification of a contingency between the behavior desired and the occurrence of a reinforcer. In many cases it may be necessary to use each of the various schedules for administering rewards—for example, base pay of a fixed interval schedule, promotions and raises on a variable interval schedule, recognition of above average performance with a piece-rate plan (fixed ratio) and supplementary bonuses on a variable ratio schedule. The effect of each of the types of reinforcement schedules and the various methods of arranging reinforcement contingencies on worker performance is summarized in Table 1.

The necessity for arranging appropriate reinforcement contingencies is dramatically illustrated by several studies in which rewards were shifted from a response-contingent (ratio) to a time-contingent basis (interval). During the period in which rewards were made conditional upon occurrence of the desired behavior, the appropriate response patterns were exhibited at a consistently high level. When the same rewards were given based on time and independent of the worker's behavior, there was a marked drop in the desired behavior. The reinstatement of the performance-contingent reward schedule promptly restored the high level of responsiveness (Lovaas, Berberich, Perloff, and Schaeffer, 1966; Baer, Paterson, and Sherman, 1967). Similar declines in performance were obtained when workers were provided rewards in advance without performance requirements (Ayllon and Azrin, 1965; Bandura and Perloff, 1967).

Aldis (1961) encourages businessmen to recognize the importance of a positive reinforcement program. He also says that experimentation with various schedules of positive reinforcement is the key to reducing job boredom and increasing worker satisfaction. He concludes:

> Most of us fully realize that a large proportion of all workers hold jobs that are boring and repetitive and that these employees are motivated to work not by positive rewards but by various oblique forms of threat. . . . The challenge is to motivate men by positive rewards rather than by negative punishment or threats of punishments. . . . Businessmen should recognize how much their conventional wage and salary systems essentially rely on negative reinforcement.

TABLE 1
OPERANT CONDITIONING SUMMARY

Arrangement of reinforcement contingencies	Schedule of reinforcement contingencies	Effect on behavior when applied to the individual	Effect on behavior when removed from the individual
	Continuous reinforcement	Fastest method to establish a new behavior	Fastest method to extinguish a new behavior
	Partial reinforcement	Slowest method to establish a new behavior	Slowest method to extinguish a new behavior
	Variable partial reinforcement	More consistent response frequencies	Slower extinction rate
	Fixed partial reinforcement	Less consistent response frequencies	Faster extinction rate
Positive reinforcement Avoidance reinforcement		Increased frequency over preconditioning level	Return to preconditioning level
Punishment extinction		Decreased frequency over preconditioning level	Return to preconditioning level

Source: Adapted from Behling et al., reprinted with permission of the author from "Present Theories and New Directions in Theories of Work Effort," *Journal Supplement and Abstract Service* of the American Psychological Corporation.

Thus the promise of newer methods of wage payments which rely on more immediate rewards, on piece-rate pay, and greater randomization does not lie only in the increase in productivity that might follow. The greater promise is that such experiments may lead to happier workers as well (p. 63).

MANAGEMENT AND THE DISSEMINATION OF KNOWLEDGE

Previously we defined *learning* as the acquisition of knowledge (by the process of operant conditioning), and performance as the translation of knowledge into behavior (depending on the consequences). It can be argued therefore that what managers do is disseminate knowledge to those they manage in order to gain the desired level of performance. The question that remains to be answered is "What is knowledge, i.e., what information should one disseminate to control behavior?"

There are two types of knowledge according to Skinner (1969). *Private knowledge* (Polanyi, 1960; Bridgeman, 1959) is knowledge established through experience with the contingencies of reinforcement. Skinner says, "The world which establishes contingencies of reinforcement of the sort studied in an operant analysis is presumably 'what knowledge is about.' A person comes to know that world and how to behave in it in the sense that he acquires behavior which satisfies the contingencies it maintains" (1969, p. 156). The behavior which results from private knowledge is called *contingency-shaped* behavior. This is the knowledge which one must possess in order to perform correctly in order to get rewarded. This knowledge does not assume any awareness on the part of the person but is based entirely on the person's past reinforcement history. A person can "know how" to play golf, for example, as indicated by a series of low scores—yet it is an entirely different thing to be able to tell others how to play golf. A machine operator may be an excellent employee, but make a poor foreman. One reason may be that, while he possesses private knowledge about his job, he is unable to verbalize the contingencies to other people.

Public knowledge, then, is the ability to derive rules from the contingencies, in the form of injunctions or descriptions which specify occasions, responses, and consequences (Skinner, 1969, p. 160). The behavior which results from public knowledge is called *rule-governed* behavior.

The reason the possession of public knowledge is important to the manager is simple. The employee looks to the manager for information about what behavior is required, how to perform the desired behavior, and what the consequences of the desired behavior will be. Before a manager can give correct answers to these questions, he must understand the true contingencies himself, since his business is not in doing, but in telling others how to do. The point is to be able to analyze the contingencies of reinforcement found in the organization and "to formulate rules or laws which make it unnecessary to be exposed to them in order to behave appropriately" (Skinner, 1969, p. 166).

After living in a large city for a long time, a person is able to go from Point A to Point B with little trouble. The knowledge of how to get around in the city was shaped by the past history with the environment. This behavior is an example of contingency-shaped behavior. If a stranger arrives in the same city and desires to go from Point A to Point B he too will have little trouble. He will look at a map of the city, and follow the path specified by the map. This behavior is an example of rule-governed behavior. Whether or not a person will continue to follow the map (rule) in the future is dependent on the consequences of following the map in the past. If the rule specified the correct contingencies, he probably will continue to use the map, but if a person found the map to be in error, then he will probably look to other sources of information (e.g., asking someone with private knowledge). The same thing happens in industry. If a manager is correct in the specification of the rules, i.e., the new worker follows the rules and receives a reward, then the worker will probably follow the other rules specified by the manager. If the manager specifies incorrect rules, then the worker may look to his peers or to other sources for information (e.g., the union steward) and specification of rules which describe behavior that will be rewarded.

There are two kinds of rules the manager can specify to the employee. A command or *mand* is a rule that specifies behavior and consequences of the behavior, where the consequences are arranged by the person giving the command. The specified or implied consequences for failure to act are usually aversive in nature and the judgment of the correctness of the behavior is made by the person given the command. A foreman who tells the worker to be on time for work is giving the worker a command. The implied consequence is that if the employee fails to report on time, the foreman will take action.

Advice and warnings are called *tacts* and involve rules which specify the reinforcements contingent on prior stimulations from rules, or laws. They specify the same contingencies which would directly shape behavior (private knowledge). The specifications of the tact speeds up the conditioning process. If a secretary tells her boss he should take an umbrella when he goes to lunch she is describing a tact. She has no control over the consequences (getting wet) of the behavior (not carrying the umbrella). Instead it is determined by the environment itself (weather). Skinner (1969) says:

> Go west, young man is an example of advice (tacting) when the behavior it specifies will be reinforced by certain consequences which do not result from action taken by the advisor. We tend to follow advice because previous behavior in response to similar verbal stimuli has been reinforced. Go west, young man is a command when some consequences of the specified action are arranged by the commander—say, the aversive consequences arranged by an official charged with relocating the inhabitants of a region. When maxims, rules, and laws are advice, the governed behavior is reinforced by consequences which might have shaped the same behavior directly in the absence of the maxims, rules, and laws. When they are commands, they are effective only because special reinforcements have been made contingent upon them (p. 148).

While a manager must possess public knowledge as well as private knowledge in order to accomplish his task of "getting things done through other people" in keeping with a plea for positive reinforcement and unbiased reward systems, tacting is the method of rule specification recommended. Skinner (1969) recommends that by specifying the contingencies in such a way that the consequences are positive in nature and failure to respond is met with the withholding of a reward rather than by aversive stimuli, "the 'mand' may be replaced by a 'tact' describing conditions under which specific behavior on the part of the listener will be reinforced (p. 158)." Instead of saying "Give me that report" say "I need the report." "The craftsman begins by ordering his apprentice to behave in a given way; but he may later achieve the same effect simply by describing the relation between what the apprentice does and the consequences" (Skinner, 1969, p. 158). Thus, the technique which managers use to direct the employee can make a lot of difference in the acceptance of the rule by the employee. A mand operates from an avoidance learning base while a tact operates from a positive reinforcement base. A tact is more impersonal and gives the employee freedom in that it does not "enjoin anyone to behave in a given way, it simply describes the contingencies under which certain kinds of behavior will have certain kinds of consequences" (Skinner, 1969, p. 158).

CONTROVERSIES SURROUNDING AN OPERANT APPROACH TO MANAGEMENT

The reinforcement approach to the study and control of human behavior has met with resistance and criticism, primarily through a lack of understanding of its recommended uses and limitations. Goodman (1964) said, "Learning theory has two simple points to make and does so with talmudic ingenuity, variability, intricacy, and insistence. They are reinforcement and extinction. What has to be left out . . . is thought."

While the criticisms would be too numerous to mention here, an attempt will be made to examine three of the major controversies surrounding an operant approach to the management of people in organizational settings.

1 *The application of operant conditioning techniques ignores the individuality of man.* Ashby (1967) said "now the chief weakness of programmed instruction is that it rewards rote learning, and worse than that—it rewards only those responses which are in agreement with the programme." Proponents of an operant approach to contingency management recognize that a poorly designed program can lead to rigidity in behavior. This is one of the major reasons that they recommend a program of reinforcement, which best fits the group or individuals being supervised. It is untrue, however, that behaviorists ignore the individuality of man. Each man is unique based on his past reinforcement history. When personnel psychologists build sophisticated selection models to predict future performance, they are actually trying to identify those applicants who will perform well under the contingencies of that particular organization. That does not mean that a person rejected cannot be motivated, but only that the current reward system of that organization is better suited for another applicant.[5]

In other words, the problem a manager faces is not to design contingencies that will be liked by all men, "buy a way of life which will be liked by those who live it" (Skinner, 1969, p. 4). As Hersey and Blanchard (1972) point out, "Positive reinforcement is anything that is rewarding to the individual being reinforced. Reinforcement, therefore, depends on the individual (p. 22)." What is reinforcing to one may not be reinforcing to someone else based on the person's past history of satiation, deprivation and conditioning operations. A manager can do two things to ensure that the contingencies of reinforcement are designed to support the individuality of the worker. First, as noted earlier he can strive to hire the worker who desires the rewards offered by the firm; i.e., can the person be happy or satisfied with this firm? Second, if it seems that the contingencies are ineffective, the manager can change the contingencies by using a democratic process— letting the employees design their own reward structure within the limits set by the organization. "Democracy is an effort to solve the problem by letting the people design the contingencies under which they are to live or—to put it another way—by insisting that the designer himself live under the contingencies he designs" (Skinner, 1969, p. 43).

In summary, therefore, it can be concluded that a voluntary society, where man has freedom to move from one organization to another, operant methods of control should not ignore the individuality of man. Instead man should seek work where his individuality can best be appreciated and industries should select employees who can best be motivated by the contingencies available to them. It should be noted, however, that through the unethical application of conditioning principles, some employers may exploit workers. The overall evidence would seem to indicate that this is not due to the weakness in behavioral theory, but due to the weakness of man himself.

2 *The application of operant conditioning techniques restricts freedom of choice.*

> Discussion of the moral implications of behavioral control almost always emphasizes the Machiavellian role of change agents and the self-protective maneuvers of controllers. . . . The tendency to exaggerate the powers of behavioral control by psychological methods alone, irrespective of willing cooperation by the client, and the failure to recognize the reciprocal nature of interpersonal control obscure both the ethical issues and the nature of the social influence processes (Bandura, 1969, p. 85).

Kelman (1965) noted that the primary criterion that one might apply in judging the ethical implications of social influence approaches is the degree to which they promote freedom of choice. If individualism is to be guaranteed, it must be tempered by a sense of social obligation by the individual and by the organization.

Bandura (1969) noted that a person is considered free insofar as he can partly influence future events by managing his own behavior. A person in a voluntary society can within limits exert some control over the variables that govern his own choices. Skinner (1969) noted that "Men are happy in an environment in which active, productive, and creative behavior is reinforced in effective ways" (p. 64). One method of effectively reinforcing behavior is by allowing the employee some determination in the design of the reinforcement contingencies. Another method is to design self-control reinforcement systems in which individuals regulate their own activities (Ferster, Nurenberger and Levitt, 1962; Harris, 1969).

While it cannot be denied that reinforcers which are "all too abundant and powerful" (Skinner, 1966) can restrict freedom of choice, it is not true that a behavioral or Skinnerian approach is against freedom of choice; the opposite is true. As Bandura noted, "Contrary to common belief, behavioral approaches not only support a humanistic morality, but because of their relative effectiveness in establishing self-determination these methods hold much greater promise than traditional procedures for enhancement of behavioral freedom and fulfillment of human capabilities" (p. 88).

3 *Operant theory, through its advocacy of an external reward system, ignores the fact that individuals can be motivated by the job itself.* Deci (1971, 1972) among others (Likert, 1967; Vroom and Deci, 1970) criticizes behaviorists for advocating a system of employee motivation that only utilizes externally mediated rewards, i.e., rewards such as money and praise administered by someone other than the employee himself. In so doing, according to Deci, management is attempting to control the employee's behavior so he will do what he is told. The limitations of this method of worker motivation, for Deci, is that it only satisfies man's "lower-order" needs (Maslow, 1943) and does not take into account man's "higher-order" needs for self-esteem and self-actualization. Deci states, "It follows that there are many important motivators of human behavior which are not under the direct control of managers and, therefore, cannot be contingently administered in a system of piece-rate payments" (1972, p. 218).

Deci recommends that we should move away from a method of external control, and toward a system where individuals can be motivated by the job itself. He says that this approach will allow managers to focus on higher-order needs where the rewards are mediated by the person himself (intrinsically motivated). To motivate employees intrinsically, tasks should be designed which are interesting, creative and resourceful, and workers should have some say in decisions which concern them "so they will feel like causal agents in the activities which they engage in" (Deci, 1972, p. 219). Deci concludes his argument against a contingency approach to management by saying:

> . . . It is possible to pay workers and still have them intrinsically motivated. Hence the writer favors the prescription that we concentrate on structuring situations and jobs to arouse intrinsic motivation, rather than trying to structure piece-rate and other contingency payment schemes. Workers would be intrinsically motivated and would seek to satisfy their higher-order needs through effective performance. The noncontingent payments (or salaries) would help to satisfy the workers and keep them on the job, especially if the pay were equitable (Adams, 1965; Pritchard, 1969) (1972, p. 227).

Deci levels criticism at a positive reinforcement contingency approach on the basis of four issues: (1) advocating that external rewards be administered by someone else, (2) ignoring the importance of the task environment, (3) ignoring the importance of internal rewards, and (4) advocating a contingent payment plan. Deci makes two errors, from a reinforcement theory point of view, when he advocates noncontingent equitable pay plans. First, equity theory (Adams, 1965) assumes that rewards are based on performance. If they weren't, then the pay would be equal, not equitable. Second, and more crucial, is Deci's assumption that a pay plan can be noncontingent. Bandura notes that "all behavior is inevitably controlled, and the operation of psychological laws cannot be suspended by romantic conceptions of human behavior, any more than indignant rejection of the law of gravity as antihumanistic can stop people from falling" (1969, p. 85). Homme and Tosti (1965) made the point that, "either one manages the contingencies or they get managed by accident. Either way there will be contingencies, and they will have their effect" (p. 16). In other words, if managers instituted a pay plan that was "noncontingent," they would in fact be rewarding poor performance and extinguishing good performance (see Rules 1, 2, and 6).

The assertion that a contingency approach advocates that the rewards always be administered by someone else is false. Skinner specifically (1969, p. 158) recommends that manding behavior be replaced by tacting methods for achieving the same effect. Skinner suggested that one safeguard against exploitation is to make sure that the design of the contingencies never controls. In addition to recommending that the contingencies be so designed that they are controlled by the environment (tacting), operant theories have advocated self-control processes in which individuals regulate their own behavior by arranging appropriate contingencies for themselves (Ferster, Nurenberger and Levitt, 1962). Bandura (1969) concluded that:

> The selection of well-defined objectives, both intermediate and ultimate, is an essential aspect of any self-directed program of change. The goals that individuals choose for themselves must be specified in sufficiently detailed behavioral terms to provide adequate guidance for the actions that must be taken daily to attain desired outcomes. . . .

Individuals can, therefore, utilize objective records of behavioral changes as an additional source of reinforcement for their self-controlling behavior (p. 255).

Studies which have explored the effect of self-reinforcement on performance have shown that systems which allowed workers to keep a record of their own output to use as a continuous feedback system and for reinforcement purposes helped the workers to increase their performance (Kolb, Winter and Berlew, 1968; Fox, 1966). Michigan Bell Telephone Company and the Emery Air Freight Corporation are two of several firms which are currently using self-reinforcement programs in order to increase worker motivation and performance. Both programs have been immensely successful (see *Business Week,* December 18, 1971, and December 2, 1972).

It should be noted that even though the individual is determining his own reward in the self-feedback program, the reinforcers are both externally (money, recognition, praise) and internally (self-feedback) mediated. According to Skinner (1957) and Bem (1967) the self-report feedback is a "tract" or description of an internal feeling state. In both cases, the rewards must be contingent on performance for effective control of the behavior to take place.

Deci's recommendation that jobs should be designed so that they are interesting, creative, and resourceful is wholeheartedly supported by proponents of a positive reinforcement program. Skinner (1969) warns managers that too much dependency on force and a poorly designed monetary reward system may actually reduce performance, while designing the task so that it is automatically reinforcing can have positive effects on performance. Skinner says:

> The behavior of an employee is important to the employer, who gains when the employee works industriously and carefully. How is he to be induced to do so? The standard answer was once physical force: men worked to avoid punishment or death. The byproducts were troublesome, however, and economics is perhaps the first field in which an explicit change was made to positive reinforcement. Most men now work, as we say, 'for money.'
>
> Money is not a natural reinforcer; it must be conditioned as such. Delayed reinforcement, as in a weekly wage, raises a special problem. No one works on Monday morning because he is reinforced by a paycheck on Friday afternoon. The employee who is paid by the week works during the week to avoid losing the standard of living which depends on a weekly system. Rate of work is determined by the supervisor (with or without the pacing stimuli of a production line), and special aversive contingencies maintain quality. The pattern is therefore still aversive. It has often been pointed out that the attitude of the production-line worker toward his work differs conspicuously from that of the craftsman, who is envied by workers and industrial managers alike. One explanation is that the craftsman is reinforced by more than monetary consequences, but another important difference is that when a craftsman spends a week completing a given set object, each of the parts produced during the week is likely to be automatically reinforcing because of its place in the complete object (p. 18).

Skinner (1969) also agrees with Deci that the piece-rate may actually reduce performance in that it is so powerful it is most often misused, and "it is generally opposed by those concerned with the welfare of the worker (and by workers themselves when, for example, they set daily quotas)" (p. 19).

It appears therefore, that critics of operant conditioning methods misunderstand the recommendations of behaviorists in the area of worker motivation. Operant theory does advocate interesting job design and self-reinforcement feedback systems, where possible. It does not advocate force or try to control the employee's behavior by making the employee "do what he is told." It is not against humanistic morality; rather it advocates that workers be rewarded on their performance and not on their needs alone.

While other controversies about operant conditioning could be reviewed, the examination of these three issues should give the reader a flavor of the criticisms which surround the use of a contingency approach to behavioral control.

ETHICAL IMPLICATIONS FOR WORKER CONTROL

The deliberate use of positive and negative reinforcers often gives rise to ethical concern about harmful effects which may result from such practices. Poorly designed reward structures can interfere with the development of spontaneity and creativity. Reinforcement systems which are deceptive and manipulative are an insult to the integrity of man. The employee should be a willing party to the influence attempt, with both parties benefiting from the relationship.

The question of whether man should try to control human behavior is covered in a classic paper by Rogers and Skinner (1956). The central issue discussed was one of personal values. Rogers contends that "values" emerge from the individual's "freedom of choice," a realm unavailable to science. Skinner, in rebuttal, points out that the scientific view of man does not allow for such exceptions, and that choice and the resulting values are, like all behavior, a function of man's biology and his environment. Since biology and environment lie within the realm of science, "choice" and "value" must be accessible to scientific inquiry. Skinner and Rogers are both concerned with abuse of the power held by scientists, but Skinner is optimistic that good judgment will continue to prevail. Krasner (1964) agrees with Skinner that we should apply scientific means to control behavior, but warns that behavioral control can be horribly misused unless we are constantly alert to what is taking place in society.

Probably few managers deliberately misuse their power to control behavior. Managers should realize that the mismanagement of the contingencies of reinforcement is actually self-defeating. Workers will no longer allow themselves to be pushed around, but instead will insist that the work environment be designed in such a way that they have a chance at a better life. The effective use of a positive reinforcing program is one of the most critical challenges facing modern management.

The first step in the ethical use of behavioral control in organizations is the understanding by managers of the determinants of behavior. Since reinforcement is the single most important concept in the learning process, managers must learn how to design effective reinforcement programs that will encourage creative, productive, satisfied employees. This paper has attempted to outline the knowledge available for this endeavor.

NOTES

1 The author is indebted to Professor William E. Scott, Jr., Graduate School of Business, Indiana University for sharing with him his Skinnerian philosophy.

2 Classical conditioning is also known as respondent conditioning and Pavlovian conditioning.

3 Operant conditioning is also known as instrumental conditioning and Skinnerian conditioning.

4 Parentheses added.

5 This is true because the criterion variable is some measure of performance, and performance is directly tied to the reinforcement consequences for the current employees used to derive the selection model.

REFERENCES

Adam, E. E., and Scott, W. E., The application of behavioral conditioning procedures to the problems of quality control, *Academy of Management Journal,* 1971, **14**, 175–193.

Adams, J. S., Inequity in social exchange, in L. Berkowitz (ed.), *Advances in Experimental Psychology,* Academic Press, 1965, 157–189.

Aldis, O., Of pigeons and men, *Harvard Business Review,* 1961, **39**, 59–63.

Ayllon, T., and Azrin, N. H., The measurement and reinforcement of behavior of psychotics, *Journal of the Experimental Analysis of Behavior,* 1965, **8**, 357–383.

Ashby, Sir Eric, Can education be machine made?, *New Scientist,* February 2, 1967.

Baer, D. M., Peterson, R. F., and Sherman, J. A., The development of imitation by reinforcing behavioral similarity to a model, *Journal of the Experimental Analysis of Behavior,* 1967, **10**, 405–416.

Bandura, A., and Perloff, B., The efficacy of self-monitoring reinforcement systems, *Journal of Personality and Social Psychology,* 1967, **7**, 111–116.

Bandura, A., *Principles of Behavior Modification,* Holt, Rinehart and Winston, Inc., New York, 1969.

Bass, B. M., and Vaughan, J. A., *Training in Industry: The Management of Learning,* Wadsworth Publishing Company, Belmont, Calif., 1966.

Behling, O., Schriesheim, C., and Tolliver, J., Present theories and new directions in theories of work effort, *Journal Supplement Abstract Service* of the American Psychological Corporation, in press.

Bem, D. J., Self-perception: An alternative interpretation of cognitive dissonance phenomena, *Psychological Review,* 1967, **74**, 184–200.

Bridgeman, D. W., *The Way Things Are,* Harvard Press, Cambridge, Mass., 1959.

Costello, T. W., and Zalkind, S. S., *Psychology in Administration,* Prentice-Hall, Inc., Englewood Cliffs, N.J., 1963.

Deci, E. L., The effects of externally mediated rewards on intrinsic motivation, *Journal of Personality and Social Psychology,* 1971, **18**, 105–115.

Deci, E. L., The effects of contingent and noncontingent rewards and controls on intrinsic motivation, *Organizational Behavior and Human Performance,* 1972, **8**, 217–229.

Festinger, L., A theory of social comparison processes, *Human Relations,* 1954, **7**, 117–140.

Ferster, C. B., and Skinner, B. F., *Schedules of Reinforcement,* Appleton-Century-Crofts, New York, 1957.

Ferster, C. B., Nurenberger, J. I., and Levitt, E. B., The control of eating, *Journal of Mathematics,* 1962, **1**, 87– 109.

Fox, L., The use of efficient study habits, In R. Ulrich, T. Stachnik, and J. Mabry (eds.), *Control of Human Behavior,* Scott, Foresman, Glenview, Ill., 1966, 85–93.

Goffman, E., *The Presentation of Self in Everyday Life,* Doubleday, New York, 1959.

Goodman, Paul, *Compulsory Mis-education,* Horizon Press, New York, 1964.

Haire, Mason, *Psychology in Management,* 2nd ed., McGraw-Hill, New York, 1964.

Harris, M. B., A self-directed program for weight control: A pilot study, *Journal of Abnormal Psychology,* 1969, **74**, 263–270.

Henry, Jules, Review of human behavior: An inventory of scientific findings by Bernard Berelson and Gary A. Steiner, *Scientific American,* July, 1964.

Hersey, P., and Blanchard, K. H., The management of change: Part 2, *Training and Development Journal,* February, 1972, 20–24.

Hilgard, E. R., *Theories of Learning,* 2nd ed., Appleton-Century-Crofts, New York, 1956.

Homme, L. E., and Tosti, D. T., Contingency management and motivation, *Journal of the National Society for Programmed Instruction,* 1965, **4**, 14– 16.

Jablonsky, S., and DeVries, D., Operant conditioning principles extrapolated to the theory of management, *Organizational Behavior and Human Performance,* 1972, **7**, 340–358.

Keller, F. S., *Learning: Reinforcement Theory,* Random House, New York, 1969.

Kelman, H. C., Manipulation of human behavior: An ethical dilemma for the social scientist, *Journal of Social Issues,* 1965, **21**, 31–46.

Kolb, D. A., Winter, S. K., and Berlew, D. E., Self-directed change: Two studies, *Journal of Applied Behavioral Science,* 1968, **4**, 453–471.

Krasner, L., Behavior control and social responsibility, *American Psychologist,* 1964, **17**, 199–204.

Likert, R., *New Patterns of Management,* McGraw-Hill, New York, 1961.

Lovass, O. I., Berberich, J. P., Perloff, B. F., and Schaeffer, B., Acquisition of imitative speech for schizophrenic children, *Science,* 1966, **151**, 705–707.

Luthans, F., *Organizational Behavior,* McGraw-Hill, New York, 1973.

Maslow, A. H., A theory of human motivation, *Psychological Review,* 1943, **50**, 370–396.

McGregor, D., *The Human Side of Enterprise,* New York, McGraw-Hill, 1960.

Michael, J., and Meyerson, L., A behavioral approach to counseling and guidance, *Harvard Educational Review,* 1962, **32**, 382–402.

Morse, W. H., Intermittent reinforcement, in W. K. Honig (ed.), *Operant Behavior,* Appleton-Century-Crofts, New York, 1966.

New tool: Reinforcement for good work, *Business Week,* December 18, 1971, 68–69.

Nord, W. R., Beyond the teaching machine: The neglected area of operant conditioning in the theory and practice of management, *Organizational Behavior and Human Performance,* 1969, 375–401.

Pavlov, I. P., *The Work of the Digestive Glands* (translated by W. H. Thompson), Charles Griffin, London, 1902.

Polanyi, M., *Personal Knowledge,* University of Chicago Press, 1960.

Rachlin, H., *Modern Behaviorism,* W. H. Freeman and Co., New York, 1970.

Rogers, Carl R., and Skinner, B. F., Some issues concerning the control of human behavior: A symposium, *Science,* 1956, **124**, 1057–1066.

Scott, W. E., and Cummings, L. L., *Readings in Organizational Behavior and Human Performance,* Revised Edition, Irwin, Homewood, Ill., 1973.

Scott, W. E., and Hamner, W. Clay, The effects of order and variance in performance on supervisory ratings of workers, Paper presented at the *45th Annual Meeting,* Midwestern Psychological Association, Chicago, 1973.

Scott, W. E., and Hamner, W. Clay, The effect of order and variance in performance on the rewards given workers by supervisory personnel, mimeograph, Indiana University, 1973.

Scott, W. E., Activation theory and task design. *Organizational Behavior and Human Performance*, 1966, **1**, 3–30.

Skinner, B. F., *The Behavior of Organisms*, New York, Appleton-Century, 1938.

Skinner, B. F., *Walden Two*, New York, The Macmillan Company, 1948.

Skinner, B. F., Are theories of learning necessary? *Psychological Review*, 1950, **57**, 193–216.

Skinner, B. F., *Science and Human Behavior*, New York, The Macmillan Company, 1953.

Skinner, B. F., Freedom and the control of men, *American Scholar*, 1956, **25**, 47–65.

Skinner, B. F., Some issues concerning the control of human behavior, *Science*, 1956, **124**, 1056–1066.

Skinner, B. F., *Verbal Behavior*, New York, Appleton-Century-Crofts, 1957.

Skinner, B. F., Behaviorism at fifty, *Science*, 1963a, **134**, 566–602.

Skinner, B. F., Operant behavior, *American Psychologist*, 1963b, **18**, 503–515.

Skinner, B. F., *Contingencies of Reinforcement*, Appleton-Century-Crofts, New York, 1969.

Skinner, B. F., *Beyond Freedom and Dignity*, Alfred A. Knopf, New York, 1971.

Thorndike, E. L., *Animal Intelligence*, Macmillan, New York, 1911.

Vroom, V. H., and Deci, E. L., An overview of work motivation. In V. H. Vroom and E. L. Deci (eds.), *Management and Motivation*, Penguin Press, Baltimore, 1970, 9–19.

Wiard, H., Why manage behavior? A case for positive reinforcement, *Human Resource Management*, Summer, 1972, 15–20.

Where Skinner's theories work, *Business Week*, December, 1972, 64–65.

Whyte, W. F., Skinnerian theory in organizations, *Psychology Today*, April, 1972, 67–68, 96, 98, 100.

Behavior Modification on the Bottom Line

W. Clay Hamner
Ellen P. Hamner

SETTING UP A POSITIVE REINFORCEMENT PROGRAM IN INDUSTRY

Many organizations are setting up formal motivational programs in an attempt to use the principles of positive reinforcement to increase employee productivity.

A positive reinforcement approach to management differs from traditional motivational theories in two basic ways. First, . . . a positive reinforcement program calls for the maximum use of reinforcement and the minimum use of punishment. Punishment tends to leave the individual feeling controlled and coerced. Second, a positive reinforcement program avoids psychological probing into the worker's

Abridged and reprinted by permission of the publisher from *Organizational Dynamics*, Spring 1976, **4**(4), 8–21. © 1976 by AMACOM, a division of American Management Associations. All rights reserved.

attitudes as a possible cause of behavior. Instead, the work situation itself is analyzed, with the focus on the reward contingencies that cause a worker to act the way in which he does.

A positive reinforcement program, therefore, is results-oriented rather than process-oriented. Geary A. Rummler, president of Praxis Corporation, a management consultant firm, claims that the motivational theories of such behavioral scientists as Herzberg and Maslow, which stress workers' psychological needs, are impractical. "They can't be made operative. While they help classify a problem, a positive reinforcement program leads to solutions."

STAGES IN PROGRAM DEVELOPMENT

Positive reinforcement programs currently used in industry generally involve at least four stages. The *first stage,* according to Edward J. Feeney, formerly vice-president, systems, of Emery Air Freight Corporation, is to define the behavioral aspects of performance and do a performance audit. This step is potentially one of the most difficult, since some companies do not have a formal performance evaluation program, especially for nonmanagerial employees, and those that do have a program often rate the employee's behavior on nonjob-related measures (such as friendliness, loyalty, cooperation, overall attitude, and so on). But once these behavioral aspects are defined, the task of convincing managers that improvement is needed and of persuading them to cooperate with such a program is simplified. Feeney asserts, "Most managers genuinely think that operations in their bailiwick are doing well; a performance audit that proves they're not comes as a real and unpleasant surprise."

The *second state* in developing a working positive reinforcement program is to develop and set specific goals for each worker. Failure to specify concrete behavioral goals is a major reason many programs do not work. Goals should be expressed in such terms as "decreased employee turnover" or "schedules met," rather than only in terms of "better identification with the company" or "increased job satisfaction." The goals set, therefore, should be in the same terms as those defined in the performance audit, goals that specifically relate to the task at hand. Goals should be reasonable—that is, set somewhere between "where you are" (as spelled out in the performance audit) and some ideal.

While it is important for the manager to set goals, it is also important for the employee to accept them. An approach that tends to build in goal acceptance is to allow employees to work with management in setting work goals. According to John C. Emery, president of Emery Air Freight Corporation, the use of a participatory management technique to enlist the ideas of those performing the job not only results in their acceptance of goals, but also stimulates them to come up with goals.

The *third stage* in a positive reinforcement program is to allow the employee to keep a record of his or her own work. This process of self-feedback maintains a continuous schedule of reinforcement for the worker and helps him obtain intrinsic reinforcement from the task itself. Where employees can total their own results, they can see whether they are meeting their goals and whether they are improving over their previous performance level (as measured in the performance audit stage). In other words, the worker has two chances of being successful—either by beating his previous record or by beating both his previous record and his established goal. E. D. Grady, general manager-operator services for Michigan Bell, maintains that the manager should set up the work environment in such a way that people have a chance to succeed. One way to do this, he says, is to "shorten the success interval." Grady says, "If you're looking for success, keep shortening the interval of measurement so you can get a greater chance of success which you can latch on to for positive reinforcements." Instead of setting monthly or quarterly goals, for example, set weekly or daily goals.

The *fourth stage*—the most important step in a positive reinforcement program—is one that separates it from all other motivation plans. The supervisor looks at the self-feedback report of the employee and/or other indications of performance (sales records, for example) and then praises the positive aspects of the employee's performance (as determined by the performance audit and subsequent goal setting). This extrinsic reinforcement should strengthen the desired performance, while the withholding of praise for substandard performance should give the employee incentive to improve that performance level. Since the worker already knows the areas of his or her deficiencies, there is no reason for the supervisor to criticize the employee. In other words, negative feedback is self-induced, whereas positive feedback comes from both internal and external sources.

. . . This approach to feedback follows the teachings of B. F. Skinner, who believes that use of positive reinforcement leads to a greater feeling of self-control, while the avoidance of negative reinforcement keeps the individual from feeling controlled or coerced. Skinner says, "You can get the same effect if the supervisor simply discovers things being done right and says something like 'Good, I see you're doing it the way that works best.' "

While the feedback initially used in step four of the positive reinforcement program is praise, it is important to note that other forms of reinforcement can have the same effect. M. W. Warren, the director of organization and management development at the Questor Corporation, says that the five "reinforcers" he finds most effective are (1) money (but only when it is a consequence of a specific performance and when the relation to the performance is known); (2) praise or recognition; (3) freedom to choose one's own activity; (4) opportunity to see oneself become better, more important, or more useful; and (5) power to influence both coworkers and management. Warren states, "By building these reinforcers into programs at various facilities, Questor is getting results." The need for using more than praise after the positive reinforcement program has proved effective is discussed by Skinner.

> It does not cost the company anything to use praise rather than blame, but if the company then makes a great deal more money that way, the worker may seem to be getting gypped. However, the welfare of the worker depends on the welfare of the company, and if the company is smart enought to distribute some of the fruits of positive reinforcement in the form of higher wages and better fringe benefits, everybody gains from the supervisor's use of positive reinforcements (*Organizational Dynamics*, Winter, 1973, p. 35).

EARLY RESULTS OF POSITIVE REINFORCEMENT PROGRAMS IN ORGANIZATIONS, 1969–1973

Companies that claimed to be implementing and using positive reinforcement programs such as the one described above include Emery Air Freight, Michigan Bell Telephone, Questor Corporation, Cole National Company in Cleveland, Ford Motor Company, American Can, Upjohn, United Air Lines, Warner-Lambert, Addressograph-Multigraph, Allis-Chalmers, Bethlehem Steel, Chase Manhattan Bank, IBM, IT&T, Proctor and Gamble, PPG Industries, Standard Oil of Ohio, Westinghouse, and Wheeling-Pittsburgh Steel Corporation (see *Business Week*, December 18, 1971, and December 2, 1972). Because such programs are relatively new in industrial settings (most have begun since 1968), few statements of their relative effectiveness have been reported. In the Winter 1973 issue of *Organizational Dynamics* (p. 49), it was stated that "there's little objective evidence available, and what evidence there is abound in caveats—the technique will work under the proper circumstances, the parameters of which are usually not easily apparent."

In the area of employee training, Northern Systems Company, General Electric Corporation, and Emery Air Freight claim that positive reinforcement has improved the speed and efficiency of their training program. In their programmed learning program, the Northern Systems Company structures the feedback system in such a way that the trainee receives positive feedback only when he demonstrates correct performance at the tool station. The absence of feedback is experienced by the trainee when he fails to perform correctly. Therefore, through positive reinforcements, he quickly perceives that correct behaviors obtain for him the satisfaction of his needs, and that incorrect behaviors do not. Emery has designed a similar program for sales trainees. *Business Week* reported the success of the program by saying:

> It is a carefully engineered, step-by-step program, with frequent feedback questions and answers to let the salesman know how he is doing. The course contrasts with movies and lectures in which, Feeney says, the salesman is unable to gauge what he has learned. The aim is to get the customer on each sales call to take some kind of action indicating that he will use Emery services. Significantly, in 1968, the first full year after the new course was launched, sales jumped from $62.4 million to $79.8 million, a gain of 27.8 percent compared with an 11.3 percent rise the year before.

Since 1969, Emery has instituted a positive reinforcement program for all of its employees and credits the program with direct savings to the company of over $3 million in the first three years and indirectly with pushing 1973 sales over the $160 million mark. While Emery Air Freight is and remains the biggest success story for a positive reinforcement program to date, other companies also claim improvements as a result of initiating similar programs. At Michigan Bell's Detroit office, 2,000 employees in 1973 participated in a positive reinforcement program. Michigan Bell credits the program with reducing absenteeism from 11 percent to 6.5 percent in one group, from 7.5 percent to 4.5 percent in another group, and from 3.3. percent to 2.6 percent for all employees. In addition, the program has resulted in the correct completion of reports on time 90 percent of the time as compared with 20 percent of the time before the program's implementation. The Wheeling-

Pittsburgh Steel Corporation credits its feedback program with saving $200,000 a month in scrap costs.

In an attempt to reduce the number of employees who constantly violated plant rules, General Motors implemented a plan in one plant that gave employees opportunities to improve or clear their records by going through varying periods of time without committing further shop violations. They credit this positive reinforcement plan with reducing the number of punitive actions for shop-rule infractions by two-thirds from 1969 to 1972 and the number of production-standard grievances by 70 percent during the same period.

While there was a great deal of interest in applying behavior modification in industrial settings after the successes of Emery Air Freight and others who followed suit were made known in 1971, the critics of this approach to worker motivation predicted that it would be short-lived. Any success would owe more to a "Hawthorne Effect" (the positive consequences of paying special attention to employees) than to any real long-term increase in productivity and/or worker satisfaction. The critics pointed out—quite legitimately, we might add—that most of the claims were testimonial in nature and that the length of experience between 1969-73 was too short to allow enough data to accumulate to determine the true successes of positive reinforcement in improving morale and productivity. With this in mind, we surveyed ten organizations, all of which currently use a behavior modification approach, to see if the "fad" created by Emery Air Freight had died or had persisted and extended its gains.

Specifically, we were interested in knowing (1) how many employees were covered; (2) the kinds of employees covered; (3) specific goals (stages 1 & 2); (4) frequency of self-feedback (stage 3); (5) the kinds of reinforcers used (stage 4); and (6) results of the program. A summary of companies surveyed and the information gained is shown in Figure 1.

CURRENT RESULTS OF POSITIVE REINFORCEMENT PROGRAMS IN ORGANIZATIONS

The ten organizations surveyed included Emery Air Freight, Michigan Bell-Operator Services, Michigan Bell-Maintenance Services, Connecticut General Life Insurance Company, General Electric, Standard Oil of Ohio, Weyerhaeuser, City of Detroit, B. F. Goodrich Chemical Company, and ACDC Electronics. In our interviews with each of the managers, we tried to determine both the successes and the failures they attributed to the use of behavior modification or positive reinforcement techniques. We were also interested in whether the managers saw this as a fad or as a legitimate management technique for improving the productivity and quality of work life among employees.

Emery Air Freight

Figure 1 shows Emery Air Freight still using positive reinforcement as a motivational tool. John C. Emery commented: "Positive reinforcement, always linked to feedback systems, plays a central role in performance improvement at Emery Air Freight. *All* managers and supervisors are being trained via self-instructional, pro-

FIGURE 1
RESULTS OF POSITIVE REINFORCEMENT AND SIMILAR BEHAVIOR MODIFICATION PROGRAMS IN ORGANIZATIONS IN 1976

Organization & person surveyed	Length of program	Number of employees covered/total employees	Type of employees	Specific goals	Frequency of feedback	Reinforcers used	Results
Emery Air Freight John C. Emery, Jr., President Paul F. Hammond, Manager—Systems Performance	1969–1976	500/2,800	Entire workforce	(a) Increase productivity (b) Improve quality of service	Immediate to monthly, depending on task	Previously only praise and recognition; others now being introduced	Cost savings can be directly attributed to the program
Michigan Bell— Operator Services E. D. Grady, General Manager— Operator Services	1972–1976	2,000/5,500	Employees at all levels in operator services	(a) Decrease turnover & absenteeism (b) Increase productivity (c) Improve union-management relations	(a) Lower level— weekly & daily (b) Higher level— monthly & quarterly	(a) Praise & recognition (b) Opportunity to see oneself become better	(a) Attendance performance has improved by 50% (b) Productivity and efficiency have continued to be above standard in areas where positive reinforcement (PR) is used

Organization	Years	Ratio	Participants	Goals	Timing	Feedback	Results
Michigan Bell—Maintenance Services Donald E. Burwell, Division Superintendent Maintenance & Services Dr. W. Clay Hamner, Consultant	1974–1976	220/5,500	Maintenance workers, mechanics, & first & second-level supervisors	Improve (a) productivity (b) quality (c) safety (d) customer-employee relations	Daily, weekly, and quarterly	(a) Self-feedback (b) Supervisory feedback	(a) Cost efficiency increase (b) Safety improved (c) Service improved (d) No change in absenteeism (e) Satisfaction with superior & coworkers improved (f) Satisfaction with pay decreased
Connecticut General Life Insurance Co. Donald D. Illig, Director of Personnel Administration	1941–1976	3,000/13,500	Clerical employees & first-line supervisors	(a) Decrease absenteeism (b) Decrease lateness	Immediate	(a) Self-feedback (b) System-feedback (c) Earned time off	(a) Chronic absenteeism & lateness has been drastically reduced (b) Some divisions refuse to use PR because it is "outdated"

FIGURE 1
RESULTS OF POSITIVE REINFORCEMENT AND SIMILAR BEHAVIOR MODIFICATION PROGRAMS IN ORGANIZATIONS IN 1976 (CONTINUED)

Organization & person surveyed	Length of program	Number of employees covered/total employees	Type of employees	Specific goals	Frequency of feedback	Reinforcers used	Results
General Electric[1] Melvin Sorcher, Ph.D., formerly Director of Personnel Research Now Director of Management Development, Richardson-Merrell, Inc.	1973–1976	1,000	Employees at all levels	(a) Meet EEO objectives (b) Decrease absenteeism & turnover (c) Improve training (d) Increase productivity	Immediate—uses modeling & role playing as training tools to teach interpersonal exchanges & behavior requirements	Social reinforcers (praise, rewards, & constructive feedback)	(a) Cost savings can be directly attributed to the program (b) Productivity has increased (c) Worked extremely well in training minority groups and raising their self-esteem (d) Direct labor cost decreased
Standard Oil of Ohio T. E. Standings, Ph.D., Manager of Psychological Services	1974	28	Supervisors	Increase supervisor competence	Weekly over 5 weeks (25-hour) training period	Feedback	(a) Improved supervisory ability to give feedback judiciously (b) Discontinued because of lack of overall success

| Weyerhaeuser Company Gary P. Latham, Ph.D., Manager of Human Resource Research | 1974–1976 | 500/40,000 | Clerical production (tree planters) & middle-level management & scientists | (a) To teach managers to minimize criticism & to maximize praise (b) To teach managers to make rewards contingent on specified performance levels (c) To use optimal schedule to increase productivity | Immediate—daily & quarterly | (a) Pay (b) Praise & recognition | (a) Use money, obtained 33% increase in productivity with one group of workers, and 18% increase with a second group, and an 8% decrease in a third group (b) Currently experimenting with goal setting & praise and/or money at various levels in organization (c) With a lottery-type bonus, the cultural & religious values of workers must be taken into account |

FIGURE 1
RESULTS OF POSITIVE REINFORCEMENT AND SIMILAR BEHAVIOR MODIFICATION PROGRAMS IN ORGANIZATIONS IN 1976 (CONTINUED)

Organization & person surveyed	Length of program	Number of employees covered/total employees	Type of employees	Specific goals	Frequency of feedback	Reinforcers used	Results
City of Detroit Garbage Collectors[2]	1973–1975	1,122/1,930	Garbage collectors	(a) Reduction in paid manhour per ton (b) Reduction on overtime (c) 90% of routes completed by standard (d) Effectiveness (quality)	Daily & quarterly based on formula negotiated by city & sanitation union	Bonus (profit sharing) & praise	(a) Citizen complaints declined significantly (b) City saved $1,654,000 first year after bonus paid (c) Worker bonus = $307,000 first year or $350 annually per man (d) Union somewhat dissatisfied with productivity measure and is pushing for more bonus to employee (e) 1975 results not yet available

						Praise & recognition; freedom to choose one's own activity	Production has increased over 300%
B. F. Goodrich Chemical Co. Donald J. Barnicki, Production Manager	1972–1976	100/420	Manufacturing employees at all levels	(a) Better meeting of schedules (b) Increase productivity	Weekly		
ACDC Electronics Division of Emerson Electronics Edward J. Feeney, Consultant	1974–1976	350/350	All levels	(a) 96% attendance (b) 90% engineering specifications met (c) Daily production objectives met 95% of time (d) Cost reduced by 10%	Daily & weekly feedback from foreman to company president	Positive feedback	(a) Profit up 25% over forecast (b) $550,000 cost reduction on $10M sales (c) Return of 1900% on investment including consultant fees (d) Turnaround time on repairs went from 30 to 10 days (e) Attendance is now 98.2% (from 93.5%)

1. Similar programs are now being implemented at Richardson-Merrell under the direction of Dr. Sorcher and at AT&T under the direction of Douglas W. Bray, Ph.D., director of management selection and development, along with several other smaller organizations (see A. P. Goldstein, Ph.D. & Melvin Sorcher, Ph.D. *Changing Supervisor Behavior,* Pergamon Press. 1974).

2. From *Improving Municipal Productivity: The Detroit Refuse Incentive Plan.* The National Commission on Productivity, April 1974.

grammed instruction texts—one on reinforcement and one on feedback. No formal off-the-job training is needed. Once he has studied the texts, the supervisor is encouraged immediately to apply the learning to the performance area for which he is responsible."

Paul F. Hammond, Emery's manager of system performance and the person currently in charge of the positive reinforcement program, said that there are a considerable number of company areas in which quantifiable success has been attained over the last six or seven years. Apart from the well-publicized container savings illustration (results of which stood at $600,000 gross savings in 1970 and over $2,000,000 in 1975), several other recent success stories were noted by Emery and Hammond. They include:

• Standards for customer service on the telephone had been set up and service was running 60 to 70 percent of standard. A program very heavily involved with feedback and reinforcement was introduced a few years ago and increased performance to 90 percent of objectives within three months—a level that has been maintained ever since.

• Several offices have installed a program in which specified planned reinforcements are provided when targeted levels of shipment volume are requested by Emery customers. All offices have increased revenue substantially; one office doubled the number of export shipments handled, and another averages an additional $60,000 of revenue per month.

• A program of measuring dimensions of certain lightweight shipments to rate them by volume rather than weight uses reinforcement and feedback extensively. All measures have increased dramatically since its inception five years ago, not the least of which is an increase in revenue from $400,000 per year to well over $2,000,000 per year.

While this latest information indicates that positive reinforcement is more than a fad at Emery Air Freight, Emery pointed out that a major flaw in the program had to be overcome. He said, "Inasmuch as praise is the most readily available no-cost reinforcer, it tends to be the reinforcer used most frequently. However, the result has been to *dull* its effect as a reinforcer through its sheer repetition, even to risk making praise an *irritant* to the receiver." To counter this potential difficulty, Emery managers and supervisors have been taught and encouraged to expand their reinforcers beyond praise. Among the recommended reinforcers have been formal recognition such as a public letter or a letter home, being given a more enjoyable task after completing a less enjoyable one, invitations to business luncheons or meetings, delegating responsibility and decision making, and tying such requests as special time off or any other deviation from normal procedure to performance. Thus it seems that Skinner's prediction made in 1973 about the need for using more than praise after the reinforcement program has been around for a while has been vindicated at Emery Air Freight.

Michigan Bell-Operator Service

The operator services division is still actively using positive reinforcement feedback as a motivational tool. E. D. Grady, general manager for Operator Services, said, "We have found through experience that when standards and feedback are not provided, workers generally feel their performance is at about the 95 percent level. When the performance is then compared with clearly-defined standards, it is usually found to meet only the 50th percentile in performance. It has been our experience, over the past ten years, that when standards are set and feedback provided in a positive manner, performance will reach very high levels—perhaps in the upper 90th percentile in a very short period of time. . . .We have also found that when positive reinforcement is discontinued, performance returns to levels that existed prior to the establishment of feedback." Grady said that while he was not able at this time to put a specific dollar appraisal on the cost savings from using a positive reinforcement program, the savings were continuing to increase and the program was being expanded.

In one recent experiment, Michigan Bell found that when goal setting and positive reinforcement were used in a low-productivity inner-city operator group, service promptness (time to answer call) went from 94 percent to 99 percent of standard, average work time per call (time taken to give information) decreased from 60 units of work time to 43 units of work time, the percentage of work time completed within ideal limits went from 50 percent to 93 percent of ideal time (standard was 80 percent of ideal), and the percentage of time operators made proper use of references went from 80 percent to 94 percent. This led to an overall productivity index score for these operators that was significantly higher than that found in the control group where positive reinforcement was not being used, even though the control group of operators had previously (six months earlier) been one of the highest producing units.

Michigan Bell-Maintenance Services

Donald E. Burwell, Division Superintendent of Maintenance and Services at Michigan Bell, established a goal-setting and positive reinforcement program in early 1974. He said, "After assignment to my present area of responsibility in January, I found that my new department of 220 employees (maintenance, mechanics, and janitorial services), including managers, possessed generally good morale. However, I soon became aware that 1973 performances were generally lower than the 1973 objectives. In some cases objectives were either ambiguous or nonexistent."

With the help of a consultant, Burwell overcame the problem by establishing a four-step positive reinforcement program similar to the one described earlier in this article. As a result, the 1974 year-end results showed significant improvements over the 1973 base-year average in all areas, including safety (from 75.6 to 89.0), service (from 76.4 to 83.0), cost performance/hour (from 27.9 to 21.2, indexed), attendance (from 4.7 to 4.0) and worker satisfaction and cooperation (3.01 to 3.51 on a scale of 5), and worker satisfaction with the supervisors (2.88 to 3.70, also on a scale of 5); 1975 figures reflect continuing success.

While Burwell is extremely pleased with the results of this program to date, he adds a word of caution to other managers thinking of implementing such a program: "I would advise against accepting any one method, including positive reinforcement, as a panacea for all the negative performance trends that confront managers. On the other hand, positive reinforcement has aided substantially in performance improvement for marketing, production, and service operators. Nevertheless, the manager needs to know when the positive effects of the reinforcement program have begun to plateau and what steps he should consider taking to maintain his positive performance trends."

Connecticut General Life Insurance Company

The Director of Personnel Administration at Connecticut General Life Insurance Company, Donald D. Illig, stated that Connecticut General has been using positive reinforcement in the form of an attendance bonus system for 25 years with over 3,200 clerical employees. Employees receive one extra day off for each ten weeks of perfect attendance. The results have been outstanding. Chronic absenteeism and lateness have been drastically reduced, and the employees are very happy with the system. Illig noted, however, that, "Our property and casualty company, with less than half the number of clerical employees countrywide, has not had an attendance-bonus system . . . and wants no part of it. At the crux of the problem is an anti-Skinnerian feeling, which looks at positive reinforcement—and thus an attendance-bonus system—as being overly manipulative and old-fashioned in light of current theories of motivation."

General Electric

A unique program of behavior modification has been introduced quite successfully at General Electric as well as several other organizations by Melvin Sorcher, formerly director of personnel research at G.E. The behavior modification program used at G.E. involves using positive reinforcement and feedback in training employees. While the first program centered primarily on teaching male supervisors how to interact and communicate with minority and female employees and on teaching minority and female employees how to become successful by improving their self-images, subsequent programs focused on the relationship between supervisors and employees in general. By using a reinforcement technique known as behavior modeling, Sorcher goes beyond the traditional positive reinforcement ("PR") program. The employee is shown a videotape of a model (someone with his own characteristics—that is, male or female, black or white, subordinate or superior) who is performing in a correct or desired manner. Then, through the process of role playing, the employee is encouraged to act in the successful or desired manner shown on the film (that is, he is asked to model the behavior). Positive reinforcement is given when the goal of successful display of this behavior is made in the role-playing session.

Sorcher notes that this method has been successfully used with over 1,000 G.E. supervisors. As a result, productivity has increased, the self-esteem of hard-core employees has increased, and EEO objectives are being met. He says, "The positive results have been the gratifying changes or improvements that have occurred, especially improvements that increase over time as opposed to the usual erosion of effort after most training programs have passed their peak. . . . On the negative side, some people and organizations are calling their training 'behavior modeling' when it does not fit the criteria originally defined for such a program. For example, some programs not only neglect self-esteem as a component, but show little evidence of how to shape new behaviors. . . . Regarding the more general area of behavior modification and positive reinforcement, there is still a need for better research. There's not a lot taking place at present, which is unfortunate because on the surface these processes seem to have a lot of validity."

Standard Oil of Ohio

T. E. Standings, manager of psychological services at SOHIO, tried a training program similar to the one used by Sorcher at General Electric. After 28 supervisors had completed five weeks of training, Standings disbanded the program even though there were some short-term successes. He said, "My feelings at this point are that reinforcement cannot be taught at a conceptual level in a brief period of time. (Of course, the same comments can no doubt be made about Theory Y, MBO, and TA.) I see two alternatives: (1) Identify common problem situations, structure an appropriate reinforcement response for the supervisor, and teach the response through the behavioral model, or (2) alter reinforcement contingencies affecting defined behaviors through direct alternatives in procedural and/or informational systems without going through the supervisor directly."

Weyerhaeuser Company

Whereas Emery Air Freight has the longest history with applied reinforcement theory, Weyerhaeuser probably has the most experience with controlled experiments using goal setting and PR techniques. The Human Resource Research Center at Weyerhaeuser, under the direction of G. P. Latham, is actively seeking ways to improve the productivity of all levels of employees using the goal-setting, PR feedback technique.

According to Dr. Latham, "The purpose of our positive reinforcement program is threefold: (1) To teach managers to embrace the philosophy that 'the glass is half-full rather than half-empty.' In other words, our objective is to teach managers to minimize criticism (which is often self-defeating since it can fixate the employee's attention on ineffective job behavior and thus reinforce it) and to maximize praise and hence fixate both their and the employee's attention on effective job behavior. (2) To teach managers that praise by itself may increase job satisfaction, but that it will have little or no effect on productivity unless it is made contingent upon specified job behaviors. Telling an employee that he is doing a good job in no way conveys to him what he is doing correctly. Such blanket praise can inadvertently reinforce the very things that the employee is doing in a mediocre way. (3) To teach managers to determine the optimum schedule for administering a reinforcer—be it praise, a smile, or money in the employee's pocket."

Weyerhaeuser has found that by using money as a reinforcer (that is, a bonus over and above the worker's hourly rate), they obtained a 33 percent increase in productivity with one group of workers, an 18 percent increase in productivity with a second group of workers, and an 8 percent decrease in productivity with a third group of workers. Latham says, "These findings point out the need to measure and document the effectiveness of any human resource program. The results obtained in one industrial setting cannot necessarily be expected in another setting.''

Latham notes that because of its current success with PR, Weyerhaeuser is currently applying reinforcement principles with tree planters in the rural South as well as with engineers and scientists at their corporate headquarters. In the latter case, they are comparing different forms of goal setting (assigned, participative, and a generalized goal of ''do your best'') with three different forms of reinforcement (praise or private recognition from a supervisor, public recognition in terms of a citation for excellence, and a monetary reward). Latham adds, ''The purpose of the program is to motivate scientists to attain excellence. Excellence is defined in terms of the frequency with which an individual displays specific behaviors that have been identified by the engineers/scientists themselves as making the difference between success and failure in fulfilling the requirements of their job.''

City of Detroit, Garbage Collectors

In December, 1972, the City of Detroit instituted a unique productivity bonus system for sanitation workers engaged in refuse collection. The plan, which provides for sharing the savings for productivity improvements efforts, was designed to save money for the city while rewarding workers for increased efficiency. The city's Labor Relations Bureau negotiated the productivity contract with the two unions concerned with refuse collection: The American Federation of State, County and Municipal Employees (AFSCME), representing sanitation laborers (loaders), and the Teamsters Union, representing drivers. The two agreements took effect on July 1, 1973.

The bonus system was based on savings gained in productivity (reductions in paid man-hours per ton of refuse collected, reduction in the total hours of overtime, percentage of routes completed on schedule, and effectiveness or cleanliness). A bonus pool was established and the sanitation laborers share 50-50 in the pool with the city—each worker's portion being determined by the number of hours worked under the productivity bonus pool, exclusive of overtime.

By any measure, this program was a success. Citizen complaints decreased dramatically. During 1974, the city saved $1,654,000 after the bonus of $307,000 ($350 per man) was paid. The bonus system is still in effect, but the unions are currently disputing with the city the question of what constitutes a fair day's work. Both unions involved have expressed doubts about the accuracy of the data used to compute the productivity index or, to be more precise, how the data are gathered and the index and bonus computed. Given this expected prenegotiation tactic by the unions, the city and the customers both agree that the plan has worked.

B. F. Goodrich Chemical Company

In 1972, one of the production sections in the B.F. Goodrich Chemical plant in Avon Lake, Ohio, as measured by standard accounting procedures, was failing. At that time, Donald J. Barnicki, the production manager, introduced a positive reinforcement program that included goal setting and feedback about scheduling, targets, costs, and problem areas. This program gave the information directly to the foreman on a once-a-week basis. In addition, daily meetings were held to discuss problems and describe how each group was doing. For the first time the foreman and their employees were told about costs that were incurred by their group. Charts were published that showed area achievements in terms of sales, cost, and productivity as compared with targets. Films were made that showed top management what the employees were doing, and these films were shown to the workers so they would know what management was being told.

According to Barnicki, this program of positive reinforcement turned the plant around. "Our productivity has increased 300 percent over the past five years. Costs are down. We had our best startup time in 1976 and passed our daily production level from last year the second day after we returned from the holidays."

ACDC Electronics

Edward J. Feeney, of Emery Air Freight fame, now heads a consulting firm that works with such firms as General Electric, Xerox, Braniff Airways, and General Atomic in the area of positive reinforcement programs. One of Mr. Feeney's current clients is the ACDC Electronics Company (a division of Emerson Electronics). After establishing a program that incorporated the four-step approach outlined earlier in this article, the ACDC Company experienced a profit increase of 25 percent over the forecast; a $550,000 cost reduction on $10 million in sales; a return of 1,900 percent on investment, including consultant fees; a reduction in turnaround time on repairs from 30 to 10 days; and a significant increase in attendance.

According to Ken Kilpatrick, ACDC President, "The results were as dramatic as those that Feeney had described. We found out output increased 30–40 percent almost immediately and has stayed at that high level for well over a year." The results were not accomplished, however, without initial problems, according to Feeney. "With some managers there were problems of inertia, disbelief, lack of time to implement, interest, difficulty in defining output for hard-to-measure areas, setting standards, measuring past performance, estimating economic payoffs, and failure to apply all feedback or reinforcement principles." Nevertheless, after positive results began to surface and initial problems were overcome, the ACDC management became enthused about the program.

CONCLUSION

This article has attempted to explain how reinforcement theory can be applied in organizational settings. We have argued that the arrangement of the contingencies of reinforcement is crucial in influencing behavior. Different ways of arranging these contingencies were explained, followed by a recommendation that the use of positive reinforcement combined with oral explanations of incorrect behaviors, when applied correctly, is an underestimated and powerful tool of management. The correct application includes three conditions. *First,* reinforcers must be selected that are sufficiently powerful and durable to establish and strengthen behavior; *second,* the manager must design the contingencies in such a way that the reinforcing events are made contingent on the desired level of performance; *third,* the program must be designed in such a way that it is possible to establish a reliable training procedure for inducing the desired response patterns.

To meet these three conditions for effective contingency management, many firms have set up a formal positive reinforcement motivational program. These include firms such as Emery Air Freight, Michigan Bell, Standard Oil of Ohio, General Electric, and B. F. Goodrich, among others. Typically, these firms employ a four-stage approach in designing their programs: (1) A performance audit is conducted in order to determine what performance patterns are desired and to measure the current levels of that performance; (2) specific and reasonable goals are set for each worker; (3) each employee is generally instructed to keep a record of his or her own work; and (4) positive aspects of the employee's performance are positively reinforced by the supervisor. Under this four-stage program, the employee has two chances of being successful—he can beat his previous level of performance or he can beat that plus his own goal. Also under this system, negative feedback routinely comes only from the employee (since he knows when he failed to meet the objective), whereas positive feedback comes from both the employee and his supervisor.

While we noted that many firms have credited this approach with improving morale and increasing profits, several points of concern and potential shortcomings of this approach should also be cited. Many people claim that you cannot teach reinforcement principles to lower-level managers very easily and unless you get managers to understand the principles, you certainly risk misusing these tools. Poorly designed reward systems can interfere with the development of spontaneity and creativity. Reinforcement systems that are deceptive and manipulative are an insult to employees.

One way in which a positive reinforcement program based solely on praise can be deceptive and manipulative occurs when productivity continues to increase month after month and year after year, and the company's profits increase as well, but employee salaries do not reflect their contributions. This seems obviously unethical and contradictory. It is unethical because the workers are being exploited and praise by itself will not have any long-term effect on performance. Emery Air Freight, for example, has begun to experience this backlash effect. It is contradictory because the manager is saying he believes in the principle of making intangible rewards contingent on performance but at the same time refuses to make the tangible monetary reward contingent on performance. Often the excuse given is that "our employees are unionized." Well, this is not always the case. Many firms that are without unions, such as Emery, refuse to pay on performance. Many other firms with unions have a contingent bonus plan. Skinner in 1969 warned managers that a poorly designed monetary reward system may actually reduce performance. The employee should be a willing party to the influence attempt, with both parties benefitting from the relationship.

Peter Drucker's concern is different. He worries that perhaps positive reinforcers may be misused by management to the detriment of the economy. He says,

"The carrot of material rewards has not, like the stick of fear, lost its potency. On the contrary, it has become so potent that it threatens to destroy the earth's finite resources if it does not first destroy more economies through inflation that reflects rising expectations." In other words, positive reinforcement can be too effective as used by firms concerned solely with their own personal gains.

Skinner in an interview in *Organizational Dynamics* stated that a feedback system alone may not be enough. He recommended that the organization should design feedback and incentive systems in such a way that the dual objective of getting things done and making work enjoyable is met. He says what must be accomplished, and what he believes is currently lacking, is an effective training program for managers. "In the not-too-distant future, however, a new breed of industrial managers may be able to apply the principles of operant conditioning effectively."

We have evidence in at least a few organizational settings that Skinner's hopes are on the way to realization, that a new breed of industrial managers are indeed applying the principles of operant conditioning effectively.

SELECTED BIBLIOGRAPHY

For an understandable view of Skinner's basic ideas in his own words, see B. F. Skinner's *Contingencies of Reinforcement* (Appleton-Century-Crofts, 1969) and Carl R. Rogers and B. F. Skinner's "Some Issues Concerning the Control of Human Behavior" (*Science*, 1965, Vol. 24, pp. 1057–1066). For Skinner's views on the applications of his ideas in industry see "An Interview with B. F. Skinner" (*Organizational Dynamics*, Winter 1973, pp. 31–40).

For an account of Skinner's ideas in action, see the same issue of *Organizational Dynamics* (pp. 41–50) and "Where Skinner's Theories Work" (*Business Week*, December 2, 1972, pp. 64–69).

An article highly critical of the application of Skinner's ideas in industry is W. F. Whyte's "Pigeons, Persons, and Piece Rates" (*Psychology Today*, April 1972, pp. 67–68). For a more sympathetic and more systematic treatment see W. R. Nord's "Beyond the Teaching Machine: The Negative Area of Operant Conditioning" in *The Theory and Practice of Management, Organizational Behavior and Human Performance* (1969, No. 4, pp. 375–401).

For comments on behavior modification by the author, see W. Clay Hamner's "Reinforcement Theory and Contingency Management" in L. Tosi and W. Clay Hamner, eds., *Organizational Behavior and Management: A Contingency Approach* (St. Clair Press, 1974, pp. 188–204) and W. Clay Hamner's "Worker Motivation Programs: Importance of Climate Structure and Performance Consequences."

Last, the best discussion of the general subject of pay and performance is Edward E. Lawler III's *Pay and Organizational Effectiveness* (McGraw-Hill, 1971).

A Social Learning Approach to Behavioral Management: Radical Behaviorists "Mellowing Out"

Robert Kreitner
Fred Luthans

We are said to be living in an age of synthesis, a time when emphasis has shifted from analyzing isolated details to studying the whole picture. Although we have learned a great deal by taking things apart and analyzing them, much remains to be understood about complex interrelations in phenomena such as the human body, organizations, and ecosystems; for example, it is difficult to fully appreciate a day at the beach by staring at a single grain of sand. There comes a time in every discipline when essential pieces of information need to be synthesized into meaningful wholes. Many areas of management have already moved in this direction: strategic planning, manufacturing-resources planning, and career planning are some examples. Unfortunately, human resources management lags in this regard; a bits-and-pieces approach and conflicting models are still commonplace in this field.

An overview of the conceptual development of organizational behavior quickly reveals that analysis has been emphasized to the near exclusion of synthesis. As indicated on the right-hand pendulum of Exhibit 1, traditional motivation theories have long been preoccupied with a host of complex internal causes of behavior such as needs, satisfaction, and expectations. Then, about a decade ago, we suggested a significantly different model of organizational behavior carrying the label *organizational behavior modification* (O.B. Mod.). This alternative perspective was anchored in B. F. Skinner's technology of operant conditioning and his underlying philosophy of radical behaviorism. The original conceptualization of O.B. Mod. was to make specific, on-the-job behavior occur more or less often by systematically managing *antecedent conditions* (that serve to cue the target behavior) and/or by managing *contingent consequences* that serve to encourage or discourage repetition of the target behavior. Unlike the then popular motivation theories that dealt with unobservable internal states, the external O.B. Mod. approach suggested that managers should focus on actual behavior and on factors in the environment that controlled behavior.

Both the internal and external theories of organizational behavior have made contributions to understanding and managing employees. Those who wish to manage employee behavior need to consider relevant cognitive processes such as expectations and attributions in addition to such internal states as needs and satisfaction. Similarly, behavior and its environmental cues and consequences should be considered. But because internal and external theorists alike have focused too much on analysis and not enough on synthesis, a realistic picture of

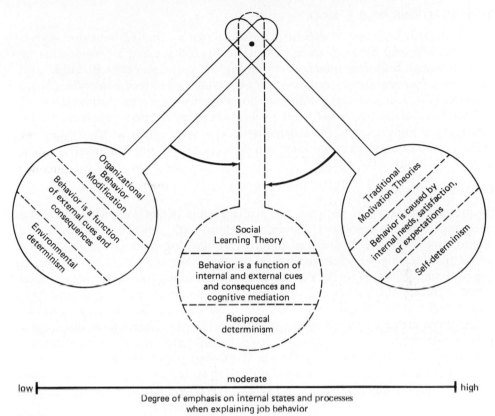

EXHIBIT 1
Conceptual pendulum of organizational behavior.

employee behavior still has not emerged. Neither the internal nor the external perspective, taken alone, gives a complete picture of why employees behave as they do; more important from a managerial standpoint, neither provides adequate guidelines for improved performance at all levels of modern organizations. This is why *social learning theory*, the middle position in Exhibit 1, provides both an academically sound framework for research and a practical framework for improved human performance at work.

In taking a social learning perspective, we are not abandoning objective, observable behavior as the primary unit of analysis. However, cognitive processes that result in expectations, self-evaluative standards, and causal attributions will be used to explain how employee behavior is acquired and maintained. Covert (or internal) cues, behavior, and consequences all play an important role. It is our hope that the social learning approach will lead to a comprehensive understanding and better practical control of today's human resources. Before exploring the particulars of this new approach, however, a brief review of the O.B. Mod. approach is necessary.

CONTRIBUTIONS OF O.B. MOD.

Organizational behavior modification (also known as applied behavior analysis and organizational behavior management) seems to have had a considerable impact on human resources management during the past decade. O.B. Mod.'s primary contributions are (1) emphasis on observable employee behavior; (2) recognition of the impact that contingent consequences have on performance; (3) recognition that positive reinforcement is more effective than punishment when managing employees; and (4) a demonstrated, causal effect on the bottom-line performance of employees working in a wide variety of organizations.

Behavior Is the Key

By making instances of *behavior* the primary units of analysis, O.B. Mod. has encouraged human resources managers to deal with something they can see, record, and later use to measure progress. Managing behavior is much more useful than dealing with inferred internal states, when the aim is to improve the quantity and quality of work. For instance, which of the following managers has a better chance of affecting job performance: manager A, who says, "Joe has a bad attitude; he better shape up or ship out!" or manager B, who says, "Joe has failed to use the new computerized work station for six different tasks this week"? By pinpointing a specific behavior problem, manager B has the comparative advantage. This behavioral orientation is gaining popularity in other areas as well. For example, behaviorally anchored rating scales (BARS) are recommended for performance appraisal.

Consequences Influence Behavior

The basic premise of O.B. Mod. has been that behavior is a function of its consequences. For managers preoccupied with cognition (internal processes connected with needs, valences, or expectations), the notion of focusing on contingent environmental consequences to explain behavior is quite foreign. Yet everyday experience confirms the influence of contingent consequences. For example, busy executives give difficult assignments to their best people because they want quick results. These overworked middle managers soon learn that being a go-getter doesn't pay off, so they cut back. A manager familiar with the relationship between consequences and behavior would realize that the assignment of extra work is punishing rather than reinforcing and may bring about a decline in performance.

Behavior that is reinforced either positively (something desirable is presented) or negatively (something undesirable is withdrawn) tends to be repeated. On the other hand, behavior that is ignored or punished (something undesirable is presented, or something of value is withdrawn) tends to be replaced by behavior that pays off. As the previous example of the go-getter illustrates, the haphazard management of behavioral consequences can detract from rather than improve job performance and goal attainment.

Taking a Positive Approach

How can we improve employees' performance as well as enhance their dignity and feeling of self-worth? O.B. Mod.'s method is to increase desirable behaviors (those that contribute to goal attainment) with positive reinforcement instead of decreasing undesirable behaviors (those that diminish goal attainment) with punishment. Positive reinforcement, a term rarely heard in executive boardrooms and management circles a decade ago, has become a widely known technique. Popular books like *In Search of Excellence* and *The One Minute Manager*, which extol the virtues of positive reinforcement, have been labeled mandatory reading by enlightened executives.

Desirable and undesirable behavior (for example, being prompt versus being tardy) are reciprocal sides of the same coin; only one side can show at a time. The manager who positively reinforces desirable behaviors among employees eventually achieves the same performance improvement that the punitive manager seeks, but without the erosion of trust and goodwill and without any attendant fear, suspicion, and revenge.

One does not have to go far to uncover horror stories about punitive managers. For instance, a field sales representative recently told us how his manager had tried to "motivate" people by making the low seller for the month take home a live goat for a weekend. The implication was that the laggard was "goat of the month," and the hope was that the unfortunate employee, embarrassed by questions from neighbors and relatives, would be bullied into improved performance. Of course, the manager's punitive approach precipitated mistrust and turnover but failed to improve sales. Taking on O.B. Mod. approach, the sales representative convinced his boss to institute a pilot program of positive reinforcement (a small cash bonus) for a specific behavior (calling the office three times a day). Significant positive results were achieved immediately. A desirable side-effect was that people felt better about themselves, their boss, and the company.

Impact on Performance Behaviors

Unlike most approaches to human resources management, O.B. Mod. has been demonstrated to have a *causal* impact on the performance behaviors of employees in a wide variety of organizations. Starting with the widely publicized Emery Air Freight experience, there have been a growing number of reported successful applications of O.B. Mod. Some of these reports are based on anecdotal or testimonial evidence—for example, the Emery Air Freight experience and most of the applications described in the recent *Handbook of Organizational Behavior Management*—but sophisticated research also shows the impact of O.B. Mod. in areas such as employee productivity, absenteeism, tardiness, safety, and sales.

Along with a number of colleagues, we focused our own research in the past ten years on the application of O.B. Mod. in manufacturing plants (small, medium, and large), retail stores, and hospitals as well as on a number of individual managers using self-management at every level in many kinds of organizations. Using such experimental designs as control groups, reversal, and multiple base lines, we found that O.B. Mod. had a dramatic, positive impact on the quantity and quality of output in manufacturing plants, on the sales performance and absence from the work station of department store clerks, and on a host of hospital performance measures, both medical (procedures accomplished, patient through-put, retake rates, posting or filing errors) and nonmedical areas (average time to repair, product waste, time to admit, and systems log-on time).

Experimental research studies have shown that executives using self-management techniques can deliberately alter their own behaviors in the areas of notifying someone when leaving the office, depending upon the boss to make decisions, spending time on the phone, filling out daily expense forms, writing a plan, following a plan, reducing stress, processing paperwork, and meeting deadlines. It has been amply demonstrated that O.B. Mod. does improve performance at different levels and in different types of organizations.

LIMITATIONS OF THE O.B. MOD. MODEL

Although the O.B. Mod. model produces positive results, it does have two limitations: (1) it excludes important cognitive processes; and (2) it does not treat the influence of antecedents on behavior. The first limitation much more than the second has led critics to call O.B. Mod. mechanistic and to question its long-term value as a realistic approach to human resources management.

Exclusion of Cognitive Processes

According to Skinner, the search for inner causes of behavior merely distracts one from identifying the environmental factors that are actually responsible for directing, shaping, and altering behavior. On the other hand, cognitive theorists insist that any theory of human behavior is deficient if it does not take into account a person's unique ability to remember, anticipate, and symbolize. After all, they argue, we are not empty-headed automatons blindly reacting to environmental stimulation. We perceive, judge, and choose; hence any approach to behavioral management should take these cognitive processes into account.

Ignored Antecedents of Behavior

Unlike the first limitation, the second limitation has been pinpointed by O.B. Mod. advocates. They note that environmental consequences have been emphasized to the near exclusion of antecedents or cues. In the original formulation of O.B. Mod., we used the three-term contingency, A → B → C (antecedent leads to behavior leads to consequence) to assist the manager in analyzing employee behavior. The antecedent in this model serves as a cue prompting the person to behave in a given way. Yet the behavior is still a function of its contingent consequence. But antecedents cue specific behavior through their association with contingent consequences. When walking down the hall at work, for example, we stop to chat with those who say things that please us and avoid those who are unpleasant. All things considered, antecedents deserve much more attention because they exercise potent *feedforward* control over a great deal of employee behavior. Extending O.B. Mod. with social learning theory overcomes these limitations of our model.

SOCIAL LEARNING THEORY

When Albert Bandura, Stanford's noted behavioral psychologist, was conducting his pioneering experiments on vicarious learning, he became convinced that cognitive functioning must not be overlooked in explaining complex human behavior. He observed that mental cues and memory aids help people learn and retain behavior more efficiently than trial-and-error shaping. This challenged operant conditioning as well as radical behaviorism. A practical example of Bandura's position is the salesperson who relies on a mental image of an apple to remember Applegate, the name of a prospective client. In Bandura's view, this way of learning is more efficient than rote memorization of clients' names in a structured training session. But, unlike the radical cognitive theorists, Bandura gives a great deal of weight to the impact of environmental cues and consequences on actual behavior. Bandura and others such as Michael Mahoney, Donald Meichenbaum, and Walter Mischel have formulated social learning theory, a theory of behavior that takes into account intrapersonal and environmental determinants.

The notion that behavior is a function of both personal and environmental factors appeared in original formulations of the social psychology of Kurt Lewin and others. Today's social learning theorists, however, stress that behavior itself (ignored by traditional social psychologists) as well as cognitive processes and environmental factors are *reciprocal determinants*. This describes a dynamic relationship in which the person neither mechanistically reacts to environmental forces nor exercises unrestricted free will. In the social learning approach, people influence their environment, which in turn influences the way they think and behave. Exhibit 2 is a summary model of the dimensions and relationships of social learning theory (SLT).

Definition of Social Learning

Social learning refers to the fact that we acquire much of our behavior by observing and imitating others within a social context. This is not a one-way flow of influence. According to social learning theory, people's behavior and environment influence each other. For example, at a societal level we are held accountable for obeying unpopular laws until we elect officials who will repeal or amend them (the military draft), practice civil disobedience in order to influence legislators to change laws (Civil Rights Movement), or rise up in revolt (the Boston Tea Party). Inherent in this complex social equation is the reciprocal influence of our behavior, our cognitive processes, and our social environment. Sometimes individual behavior prevails; at other times the environment prevails. Meanwhile, people perceive, judge, choose, and exercise a measure of self-control.

For modern managers who are disenchanted with traditional behavioral theo-

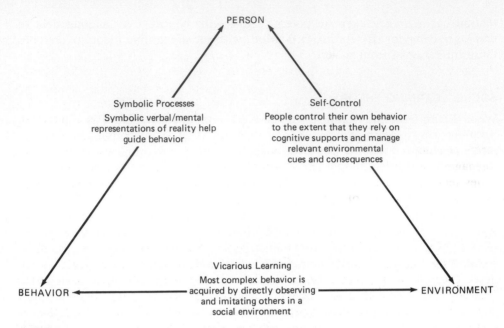

EXHIBIT 2
A basic model of social learning theory.

ries, Bandura's portrayal of SLT is particularly helpful because it improves on popular work motivation theories and extends operant learning theory. Although traditional work motivation theories (like Abraham Maslow's needs hierarchy) do address the employee's need for social interaction, they fail to explain the nature of that interaction. SLT improves upon the traditional theories by assigning a prominent role to vicarious or observational learning. Similarly, SLT extends the operant model of learning—what we have called the external approach—by explaining how the individual processes environmental stimuli. This helps us understand why similar employees in similar situations often behave quite differently; the operant model is limited in its ability to explain such variations.

SLT also is quite different from work-motivation and operant-conditioning theories because it gives attention to three important processes: vicarious learning or modeling, symbolism, and self-control. By understanding the roles these three processes play in the reciprocal triangle illustrated in Exhibit 2, managers can begin to appreciate how social learning theory integrates the internal and external approaches in a way that translates into improved techniques for managing human resources.

Effectiveness of Modeling

Vicarious learning and observational learning are alternative labels for the modeling process of acquiring new behavior within the SLT framework. When compared with tedious operant shaping whereby someone is systematically reinforced for approximating a desired behavior (a machine operator is complimented by the supervisor for getting progressively closer to tolerance), modeling is much more efficient. Complex behavior can be learned quickly through this process. In fact, organizational participants, especially in the executive and managerial ranks, probably acquire far more behavior by observing and imitating behavior models than by trial-and-error shaping. Research shows that people tend to imitate models with whom they personally identify (consider the use of outdated training films). Moreover, modeled behavior that pays off with a desired consequence tends to be readily imitated (consider a ''do-as-I-say, not-as-I-do'' management style). There is also evidence that modeling is valuable in teaching sales techniques and other skills that were traditionally believed to be intuitive or to stem from years of experience.

Use of Symbolism

According to SLT, verbal and mental symbolism helps people to organize and store convenient representations of reality. For instance, the mnemonic phrase ''red—right—returning'' has reminded generations of sailors that vessels returning to port from sea should keep the red buoys on their right-hand side to avoid running aground. Furthermore, it is more efficient and in some cases safer to imagine solutions to problems and to anticipate consequences to actions than to experience everything firsthand. For today's harried executives, imagining the consequences of a stressful and unhealthy life style and taking appropriate preventive steps is certainly a better solution than experiencing a heart attack. Values, goals, beliefs, and rules are convenient symbolic guideposts for appropriate behavior. With this information, executives are challenged to systematically and proactively manage their own and others' symbolic coding and processing rather than simply to leave matters to reaction and chance.

Role of Self-Control

According to SLT, people can control their own behavior if they can cue it, support it, and reward or punish it. In other words, to the extent that we can manage our environment and cognitive processes, we can manage our own behavior. For example, an overweight manager who is tempted to eat a between-meal snack might think of how nice a new, smaller outfit would look and feel. And eliminating all snacks from the immediate work area or offering only low-calorie ones would be a helpful way of altering the environment. Eventually, when the weight goal is reached, purchasing and enjoying the new outfit will be very rewarding.

Beyond the O.B. Mod. Model

As stated earlier, the original model for O.B. Mod. utilized the A → B → C contingency. In this operant paradigm, environmental antecedents (A) were said to cue behaviors (B) that were then followed by positive or negative contingent consequences (C) in the environment. Then, according to the law of effect, a supportive, positive environment increased the frequency and magnitude of behavior whereas unsupportive, negative consequences discouraged behavior. In this model we characterized effective behavioral management as the appropriate arrangement of supportive environmental antecedents and consequences.

Now, by merging the time-honored, cognitive situation-organism-behavior contingency (S-O-B) with the operant A-B-C contingency, we have derived an S↔O↔B↔C model. This expanded model for O.B. Mod. (shown in Exhibit 3) clearly reflects the influence of social learning theory because of the interaction among the situation, organism, behavior, and consequence components. A one-way, linear flow of influence lacks the dynamic interaction emphasized by SLT. It is important to recognize that even in this expanded model, overt behavior remains the primary unit of analysis, but the mediating effects of cognition along with covert cues, behavior, and consequences are now taken into consideration.

In Exhibit 3, three cognitive mediating processes are listed under the Organism portion of our expanded O.B. Mod. model. These are goal acceptance/rejection, expectations, and causal attributions. Because each of them serves as a highly personalized gatekeeper that determines which cues and consequences will prompt which particular behavior, and because they were not part of the original O.B. Mod. model, we will examine them closely.

Goal Acceptance/Rejection   Goals and goal setting have been a central feature of management theory and practice since Peter Drucker coined the term "management by objectives" (MBO) 30 years ago. Researchers like Edwin Locke have proved time and again that people who have goals or objectives (preferably difficult and measurable ones) consistently outperform those who have no goals and those who are instructed to do their best. Nevertheless, conflicting research findings on goal setting still crop up, and MBO is known as both a failure and a success. From a behavioral perspective, a major stumbling block for MBO programs may be goal rejection at the individual level. An imposed goal, no matter how well conceived, is the property of the organization until the individual personally adopts it. To date, the most popular prescription for encouraging members of an organization to accept its goals is to have them help set the goals. Therefore we have included *opportunity to participate in goal setting* as a goal cue under the situation portion of the S-O-B-C model (the expanded O.B. Mod. model).

Expectations   Largely due to the popularity of Victor Vroom's and Lyman Porter and Edward Lawler's expectancy models of work motivation, the concept of expectations is fairly well established in the behavioral-management literature. In terms of probabilities, expectations vary from a low of zero (no chance) to a high of one (virtual certainty). Expectations influence how managers behave and make decisions (e.g., "Will I get a bonus this year so I can buy a new car?" "How will the new electronic office system affect my job?" "Will the new director of personnel significantly change our staffing or training policies?").

Expectancy motivation theorists carefully distinguish between effort-perfor-

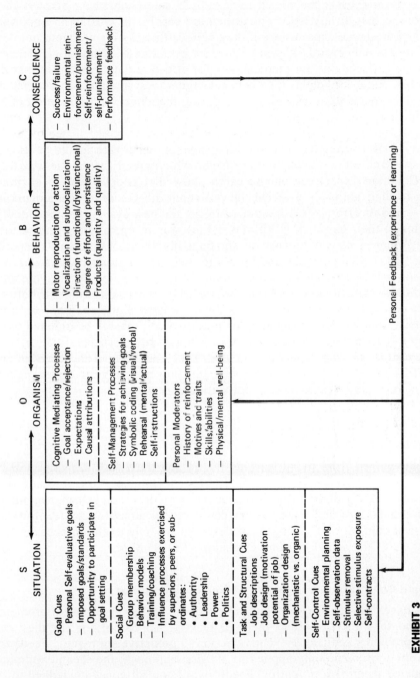

EXHIBIT 3
Expanded model for organizational behavior modification (S-O-B-C model). [Source: Fred Luthans and Robert Kreitner, *Organizational Behavior Modification and Beyond: An Operant and Social Learning Approach* (Scott, Foresman, 1985).]

S
SITUATION

Goal Cues
– Personal Self-evaluative goals
– Imposed goals/standards
– Opportunity to participate in goal setting

Social Cues
– Group membership
– Behavior models
– Training/coaching
– Influence processes exercised by superiors, peers, or sub-ordinates:
  • Authority
  • Leadership
  • Power
  • Politics

Task and Structural Cues
– Job descriptions
– Job design (motivation potential of job)
– Organization design (mechanistic vs. organic)

Self-Control Cues
– Environmental planning
– Self-observation data
– Stimulus removal
– Selective stimulus exposure
– Self-contracts

O
ORGANISM

Cognitive Mediating Processes
– Goal acceptance/rejection
– Expectations
– Causal attributions

Self-Management Processes
– Strategies for achieving goals
– Symbolic coding (visual/verbal)
– Rehearsal (mental/actual)
– Self-instructions

Personal Moderators
– History of reinforcement
– Motives and traits
– Skills/abilities
– Physical/mental well-being

B
BEHAVIOR

– Motor reproduction or action
– Vocalization and subvocalization
– Direction (functional/dysfunctional)
– Degree of effort and persistence
– Products (quantity and quality)

C
CONSEQUENCE

– Success/failure
– Environmental rein-forcement/punishment
– Self-reinforcement/self-punishment
– Performance feedback

Personal Feedback (experience or learning)

193

mance expectations and performance-reward expectations. Taking a social learning perspective, Bandura has labeled the former type *efficacy* expectations and the latter type *outcome* expectations. For example, salespeople have high efficacy expectations if they firmly believe that they are capable of closing an important sale and high outcome expectations if they believe that closing an important deal will lead to desired rewards like pay raises or promotions. Thus, high efficacy and outcome expectations are prerequisites for effective employee performance. The S-O-B-C model is intended to help managers to systematically understand and use such expectancies instead of considering them out of context or ignoring them altogether.

Causal Attributions   It is becoming increasingly clear that people have self-serving cause-and-effect models in their heads which greatly affect the way they behave. Common experience and research show that people tend to attribute successes to their ability (''I solved the problem with the new data processing program'') and/or effort (''I worked hard to get the new system implemented'') and failures to their bad luck (''Murphy's Law was in operation'') and/or task difficulty (''there's no way to work out the bugs in this crazy program''). People who generally attribute success and failure to their own actions have an *internal* locus of control; those with an *external* locus of control generally attribute success and failure to factors beyond their control. Of course, differing attributions will affect how employees interpret and respond to cues. For example, a training film demonstrating how to use a microcomputer would probably be imitated more readily by a person who believes that ability is the key to success than by one who believes that success depends upon luck. Like goal acceptance/rejection and expectations, causal attributions are subtle but powerful cognitive gatekeepers that facilitate or hamper S-O-B-C reciprocation.

NEW O.B. MOD. TECHNIQUES FOR IMPROVING PERFORMANCE AT WORK

The insights gained from social learning theory and the S-O-B-C model will be used to examine some specific, new O.B. Mod. techniques for improving performance at work: feedforward control, feedback control, and self-management. Although elements of self-management could be subsumed under feedforward and feedback control, self-management deserves separate attention because it is a cornerstone of the social learning extension of O.B. Mod.

Feedforward Control and Management of Employee Behavior

Managers have two ways to turn plans into action: (1) they can wait for problems to arise and then try to correct them (a reactive approach); or (2) they can anticipate problems and take preventive action (a proactive approach). Feed*back* control is the term commonly applied to the first approach; the second approach can be labeled feed*forward* control. Feedforward control is acknowledged to be the better approach because it encourages managers to act in anticipation of rather than in response to a problem. Feedforward control makes it easier to prevent grievances, equipment breakdowns, and defects in goods or services. In the expanded O.B. Mod. approach, managers can exercise feedforward control over employee performance by systematically managing goal cues, social cues, and task and structural cues (see *Situation* in Exhibit 3). A supportive situation will increase the chances that the job will be done right the first time.

Goal Cues   Employees with challenging and measurable goals tend to outperform those without goals. Social learning theorists have pointed out that a personal goal serves not only as a target for performance but also as a basis for assessing progress. Unfortunately, personal goals and organizational goals in complex organizations are often at odds with one another. This means that organizations must impose at least some goals on employees. Consequently, participation in goal setting is important because it increases the chances of goal acceptance. Managers and executives should encourage their people to set their own performance goals and accept imposed goals by having them participate. If these personal or participative goals are measurable in behavioral terms, they will serve as the focal point for the entire S-O-B-C process.

Social Cues   Because members of organizations acquire much of their behavior by observing others (social learning), managers can ensure that these people are exposed to constructive rather than destructive behavior models. Transferring a potentially productive employee away from the influence of troublemakers is an obvious way of rearranging the social cues. More formal feedforward control of employee performance can be achieved by incorporating modeling into training programs. Training programs based on observation of behavior models, structured practice of specific behaviors, and positive reinforcement for successful imitation have proved much more effective than lectures or discussions.

Every manager is a powerful behavior model for subordinates, regardless of his or her intentions or desires. "Do-as-I-say, not-as-I-do" managers need to learn the truth of the American Indian lament: "What you do speaks so loudly that I cannot hear what you say." Executives and managers influence subordinates when they exercise authority, leadership, and power. A manager who smokes while leaning against a no-smoking sign but tries to enforce smoking policies loses credibility. High-level Japanese managers who roll up their sleeves and pitch in when necessary understand the value of a "do-as-I-do" approach.

Task and Structural Cues   A healthy measure of feedforward control can be exercised by making sure that employees have a clear idea of what is expected of them. In addition to measurable objectives, clear and concise job descriptions can get employees headed in the right direction. Beyond that, the motivating potential of the work itself can be enhanced through progressive job design. As researchers have pointed out in recent years, meaningful jobs that offer a sense of personal responsibility and knowledge of results tend to cue better performance than do fragmented, boring, and repetitive jobs. Moreover, as it has been forcefully pointed out by the best-selling book, *In Search of Excellence,* employees who desire creative latitude will respond more favorably to fluid and flexible organic structure than to rigid, bureaucratic, mechanistic structures.

Maintaining and Improving Behavior through Feedback Control

The influence of social learning in the expanded O.B. Mod. model is clearly evident in the preceding discussion of feedforward control. Social learning places much emphasis on situational cues. These cues prompt desirable behavior by enhancing goal acceptance, raising efficacy and outcome expectations, and personalizing causal attributions. On the other hand, feedback control reflects the influence of Skinner's operant conditioning, which emphasizes that behavior is a function of its consequences. Feedback control of employee behavior involves the systematic management of consequences.

Four primary sources of consequences are listed in the consequence portion of Exhibit 3. Success, positive reinforcement from relevant others, self-reinforcement, and constructive performance feedback all strengthen behavior. Similarly, behaviors that fail or that are punished or ignored by relevant others, self-punished, or followed by negative or inadequate feedback on performance are weakened. Managers are challenged to arrange, within an S-O-B-C framework, a supportive consequence climate for productive behavior. Good intentions are insufficient, and productive behavior that is ignored or not rewarded eventually gives way to counterproductive behavior that has more immediate payoffs for the individual. Kenneth Blanchard and Spencer Johnson, in *The One Minute Manager,* underscore positive reinforcement in managing behavior when they say, "catch employees doing something *right.*" This is feedback control through positive reinforcement.

The Use of Self-Management

A unique contribution of social learning theory is its emphasis on self-management. This bottom-up approach stands in marked contrast to our conventional, top-down theories of management. Managing has traditionally been conceptualized and practiced as something a superior *does to* an organization, a group, or a subordinate. The attention that leadership theories have received throughout the years clearly shows the entrenchment of this top-down bias. Even the so-called democratic or participative leadership styles fail to break out of the top-down rut because they imply that management *lets* subordinates participate only if and when it is convenient.

The S-O-B-C model is an alternative: it includes a system of cues, cognitive processes, and consequences that help people manage their own behavior. We believe that self-management is the most efficient form of management because it precludes the need for costly, close supervision. With this in mind, let's take a closer look at the ways that managers can use self-control cues, self-management processes, and self-reinforcement/self-punishment.

Self-Control Cues   Members of organizations can do a number of things to create a physical/social environment that cues their own desirable behavior and discourages unwanted behavior. This *environmental planning* can take the form of one or a combination of the following techniques.

1 Self-Observation Data   By observing and recording how often a target behavior occurs, a participant can accomplish two things: (1) obtain an objective measurement of the behavior, and (2) formulate a self-management plan. For example, a manager who is always "putting out fires" and never seems to get anything done might find it instructive to keep track of interruptions by unscheduled phone calls. Hard data would permit an objective assessment of the problem and provide a rationale for schedule adjustments.

2 Stimulus Removal   This self-management technique involves the removal of cues that prompt unwanted behavior. For instance, an engineer who is given to daydreaming may find it helpful to remove pictures of family members or favorite vacation spots and other distracting stimuli from the work area.

3 Selective Stimulus Exposure   Instead of eliminating a disruptive cue from the environment, one can fall back on selective exposure. A manager who is disrupted by unscheduled visits because of an unrestricted open-door policy, for example, might trim the open-door period to a stated hour in the morning and in the afternoon. Similarly, disruptive phone calls can be channeled through a secretary or an answering device.

4 Self-Contracts   A self-contract is an if-then deal with oneself. For instance, an executive might hold off working on a preferred project until a less preferred one is completed. Self-contracts and personal goal setting go hand in hand.

Self-Management Processes   From a social learning perspective of O.B. Mod. there are four cognitive processes that can facilitate self-management.

1 Strategies for Achieving Goals   Goal setting is a recognized prerequisite of effective management, but strategies and action plans need to be formulated if goals are to become reality. Managers at all levels can enhance their self-management skills by systematically considering strategies and formulating action plans aimed at accomplishing their self-improvement goals.

2 Symbolic Coding   Visual and verbal codes can help people remember things of importance. A mental image of a newspaper picture showing someone injured, for example, could serve as a reminder to take out additional employee accident insurance. As a verbal code phrase, like "Monday/Fun day" might remind a manager who is driving home on Friday to file a budget request on Monday.

3 Rehearsal   Whether covert or overt, rehearsal of desired behavior prepares managers to deal with unfamiliar situations. It is no accident that successful salespeople anticipate customer questions or complaints and mentally rehearse replies. Practice, both in one's thoughts and in reality, is a cornerstone of successful selling and other crucial management skills (dealing with problem employees, or selling middle managers on a new idea).

   4 Self-Instruction   Cognitive supports in the form of self-instruction can help managers do the right thing at the right time. Many stress-management programs encourage executives to use self-instruction that prompts them to relax, slow down, do one thing at a time, and stick to priorities.

Self-Reinforcement/Self-Punishment

Both covert and overt behaviors need positive consequences if they are to be sustained and strengthened. When combined with the techniques just discussed, self-granted rewards can lead to self-improvement. But as failed dieters and smokers can attest, there are short-run as well as long-run influences on self-reinforcement. For the overeater, the immediate gratification of eating has more influence over behavior than the promise of a new wardrobe. The same sort of dilemma plagues procrastinators. Consequently, one needs to weave a powerful web of cues, cognitive supports, and internal and external consequences to win the tug-of-war with status-quo payoffs. Primarily because it is so easy to avoid, self-punishment tends to be ineffectual. As with managing the behavior of others, positive instead of negative consequences are recommended for effective self-management.

CONCLUSION

Social learning theory is practical. It provides a framework for *understanding* and *controlling* human resources in today's organizations. This framework includes internal processes as well as the behavior and the antecedent or consequent environmental contingencies. To date, behavioral theories have suffered from an imbalance, and managers have had to rely on disjointed theories and techniques: need theory, job design, expectancy theory, goal setting, operant theory, and positive reinforcement. Now, with social learning theory, we finally have a *balanced* and *systematic* way of understanding employee behavior as well as a set of proven and potentially powerful techniques for controlling employee behavior and self-behavior for the purpose of improved performance.

   American organizations are still among the most productive in the world largely because of our technology. Organizations in the Far East and even in Western Europe have made substantial gains in many industries largely because they are better than we are at human resources management. In the United States the difference between good and excellent organizations can be largely attributed to how people are managed.

   A social learning approach and its accompanying techniques may provide the basis for increasing the productivity of our human resources and thus may provide the impetus for getting us back on track as the industrial leader of the world. For example, modeling can have a revolutionary impact on training at all levels. More objective behavior-based rather than trait-based performance evaluations can be used to revamp the appraisal systems currently under fire. But the real key to improvements may be found in new ways managers and executives look at and actually manage the "front end" (antecedents) and the "back end" (consequences) of their people's performances.

On the front end, managers have traditionally done a good job on task and structural cues. (See Exhibit 3.) Considerable time and energy have been devoted to job descriptions, job design (including quality-of-work-life), and organization design and development. But the goal cues, the social cues, and the self-control cues identified in Exhibit 3 have been largely ignored. Goal setting and participation are practical goal cues; quality circles and team-oriented and group-oriented leadership styles are practical social cues; and screening techniques, data display boards, and self-goals/self-contracts are practical self-control cues.

These new approaches to front-end management, according to social learning theory, provide the setting in which productive behaviors can occur. Once the behaviors are elicited by these cues, however, there must be contingent consequences that sustain and increase the resulting productive behaviors. In other words, the contingent reward systems of the organization and of individual managers are critical to the performance of the people in the organization.

The answer to back-end management is not necessarily in more exotic profit-sharing or bonus plans, but instead may be found in contingent performance-feedback systems that are objective, immediate, positive, and visual; supervisor/manager attention and recognition; and, ultimately, deliberate self-rewards manifested as a sense of accomplishment and the feelings that go with a job well done.

QUESTIONS FOR DISCUSSION

1 Why do operant conditioning principles stress the necessity of avoiding negative feedback?

2 From a managerial standpoint, what is really new and innovative about operant conditioning?

3 What potential drawbacks exist when you attempt to use operant conditioning at work?

4 Would operant conditioning tend to work better among blue- or white-collar employees? Why?

5 Analyze and compare the assumptions behind cognitive and O.B. Mod. theories. Are there some situations in which one set of assumptions would be more valid than the other? Explain.

6 How might predictions about behavior made from social learning theory differ from predictions arising from $B = f(P,E)$?

7 Compare the "vicarious processes" mentioned by Kreitner and Luthans with the observations of equity theory. What insights into human behavior do they share?

8 Social learning theory suggests that behavior may be maintained through direct reinforcement and punishment or through a person's observation (or modeling) of the reinforcing or punishing outcomes of other people's behavior. How might the effects of these two methods (direct and indirect) differ?

9 Compare and contrast expectancy theory with the "cognitive processes" and "self-control processes" of social learning theory.

PART THREE

CENTRAL ISSUES IN MOTIVATION AT WORK

REWARD SYSTEMS IN ORGANIZATIONS

One of the central issues—if not *the* central issue—in considering motivation in work situations concerns the reward systems utilized in and by organizations. Using the concept of reward in its broadest sense as something given in return for good received, we can see that reward systems in organizations involve *exchange* relationships. Organizations or those individuals functioning in their behalf (e.g., managers and supervisors) provide rewards to employees in exchange for "good received," that is, membership, attendance, and performance. The ways in which rewards are distributed within organizations and their relative amounts have considerable impact on the levels of employee motivation. Despite the obvious importance of reward systems to both employers and employees, experience has shown that they are neither simple nor easy to design and implement in ways that both parties will view as mutually beneficial and satisfactory.

TYPES OF REWARDS

There is a wide array of types of rewards that can be obtained in organizational settings, ranging from obvious ones such as pay, fringe benefits, and promotion, to praise, autonomy in decision making, and feelings of accomplishment and competency. These different types of rewards, however, can be classified along two major dimensions: intrinsic/extrinsic and systemwide/individual.

Intrinsic rewards are those that the individual provides himself or herself (e.g., feelings of accomplishment) as a result of performing some task. Extrinsic rewards, on the other hand, are those that are provided *to* the individual by someone else. Much of the conceptual work on intrinsic motivation is incorporated in the work of Deci (1975a, b) and his *cognitive evaluation theory*. Briefly, this theory argues that an individual's level of effort on a task is determined largely by the nature of the rewards available for task accomplishment. Two processes by which rewards influence intrinsic motivation can be identified.

First, there is the notion of *locus of causality*. When behavior is intrinsically motivated, an individual's perceived locus of causality is thought to be internal; that is, individuals feel that task accomplishment is under their own control. Under such circumstances, they will engage in activities for *intrinsic* rewards. On the other hand, when individuals receive *extrinsic* rewards for task behavior, they will perceive their locus of causality to be external and will engage in those activities only when they believe that extrinsic rewards will be forthcoming. The important point here is that, according to Deci, providing extrinsic rewards on an intrinsically satisfying task leads to a shift from internal to external locus of causality. As Deci (1972) states:

> Interpreting these results in relation to theories of work motivation, it seems clear that the effects of intrinsic motivation and extrinsic motivation are not additive. When extrinsic rewards such as money can certainly motivate behavior, they appear to be doing so at the expense of intrinsic motivation; as a result, contingent pay systems do not appear to be compatible with participative management systems (pp. 224–225).

The empirical evidence that has been obtained over the past several years with regard to the hypothesis that providing extrinsic rewards reduces the impact of intrinsic rewards is, however, decidedly mixed (Guzzo, 1979). This appears to be especially so the closer that situations approximate typical work settings.

Second, rewards can also influence intrinsic motivation through changes in feelings of *competence* and *self-determination*. Rewards or outcomes that reassure people they are competent or self-determining tend to increase their intrinsic motivation to perform. However, rewards or outcomes that convince people they are not competent or self-determining tend to decrease intrinsic motivation.

The balance of the chapter will focus primarily on extrinsic rewards, those provided by the organization or some designated official (e.g., supervisor) *to* the individual. In considering extrinsic versus intrinsic rewards, however, the reader should be aware that in the literature on motivation at work these terms sometimes take on other meanings. Guzzo (1979) has made the excellent point that any particular reward has multiple attributes (self-generated or not, immediate or delayed, of long or short duration, etc.). Thus, it is important to keep in mind that there are many variations of types of rewards within the two broad categories of extrinsic and intrinsic. As just one example among many that could be provided, consider that while a simple pat on the back from a supervisor and a promotion to a higher-status job with a significant increase in pay are both extrinsic rewards, their effects on the individual's performance may be quite different.

The other major dimension that can be used to classify types of rewards in organizational settings is the distinction emphasized by Katz (1964): systemwide rewards versus individual rewards. The distinction is this: systemwide rewards are those that are provided by the organization to everyone in a broad category of employees. Examples would be certain fringe benefits (e.g., medical insurance) that everyone in the organization receives simply by being an employee,

	Systemwide	**Individual**
Extrinsic	Example: Insurance benefits	Example: Large merit increase
Intrinsic	Example: Pride in being part of a "winning" organization	Example: Feeling of self-fulfillment

EXHIBIT 1
Types of rewards.

or the dining room facilities provided to all managers above a certain level. Individual rewards, on the other hand, are provided to particular individuals but not to all individuals in a category. Examples would be bonuses and merit increases.

If we combine the two dimensions, intrinsic/extrinsic and systemwide/individual, we have a convenient way of categorizing any particular type of reward, as shown in Exhibit 1. It is useful to keep this classification system in mind when considering the intended functions of reward systems that are discussed in the next section. A particular type of reward will often be very effective for one function, but very ineffective for another function.

FUNCTIONS OF REWARD SYSTEMS

Organizations provide rewards for many reasons. These were discussed briefly at the beginning of Chapter 1 and are summarized in Exhibit 2 (utilizing categorization schemes suggested by March & Simon, 1958, and Katz, 1964). As can be seen, rewards in and from organizations can potentially motivate two broad categories of behavior: participation in the organization and performance in the organization. The first of these categories, participation, can in turn be divided into membership and attendance. "Membership" refers to the act of joining the organization as well as the decision to remain with it, and organizations clearly need to be concerned with both aspects. Thus, they devote considerable effort

EXHIBIT 2
FUNCTIONS OF REWARDS SYSTEMS

A Participation
   1 Membership
      a Joining
      b Remaining
   2 Attendance (i.e., avoidance of absenteeism)
B Performance
   1 "Normal" role (job) performance
   2 "Extra-role behavior" (e.g., innovation, high commitment)

to designing reward systems which will induce individuals to become members of the organization in the first place and which also will instill a strong desire to stay with it once having become a part of it. It should be clear, though, that although the *design* of a reward system affects decisions to join and subsequently remain (or leave), *implementation* of a reward system also affects how long a person will stay with a particular organization. From the organization's perspective, excessive turnover can be a major problem, and thus well-designed reward systems may not be effective because of faulty implementation in practice. The other participation category involves attendance or, in other words, the avoidance of absenteeism. Although absenteeism may not be as severe a problem for many organizations as the difficulties of attracting people to join the organization or the problem of excessive turnover, it is nevertheless a type of behavior that most organizations want to reduce. Therefore, one of the objectives in the design of reward systems is to motivate high levels of attendance.

The other major category of behavior that reward systems are designed to facilitate is that of job performance (or the "decision to produce" in March & Simon's terminology). Here, again, there are two distinct subcategories: "normal" or expected role (job) performance, and what is called "extra-role behavior." The former refers to performance that meets the minimal expected standards that the organization has designated for someone in a particular job. When this standard is met, the organization would consider that the employee's part of the psychological contract has been fulfilled. The employee has, in effect, exchanged adequate job performance for an agreed-upon level of compensation. Typically, to obtain an expected level of job performance the organization devotes considerable attention to the design and implementation of monetary compensation systems. The assumption is that if a pay system is set up in a way that appears fair and equitable in the amount and distribution of compensation, then most individuals in the organization can be depended upon to perform at least adequately if not outstandingly.

Extra-role behavior, on the other hand, goes "above and beyond" what is normally expected (by the organization) in the psychological contract. It is behavior that is spontaneous and innovative (Katz, 1964). Many examples could be offered, of course, such as the clerk who goes out of the way to placate a dissatisfied customer, or the manager who voluntarily stays overtime to solve some particular production problem. The essential point is that most organizations probably would not function very well if the only type of role behavior they received from all employees was routine minimally acceptable job performance. Hence, organizations need to find ways to motivate extra-role behavior from at least some of their employees (and particularly in certain types of circumstances—such as crises—that face organizations at particular times). The problem, from the organization's point of view, is that rewards which may be effective in generating normal job performance (such as certain systemwide rewards) may not be very useful in motivating extra-role behavior. Thus, to the extent that such extraordinary behavior is needed, the organization is presented with a considerable challenge in the design and application of reward systems, particularly as they involve individual extrinsic or intrinsic rewards.

IMPLEMENTATION AND ALLOCATION ISSUES

As noted several times already, the best-designed reward systems can often go awry in producing their intended results because of the manner in which they are implemented. Several of the articles in this chapter (especially the initial article, by Lawler, and also those by Kerr and by Hamner) deal directly with reward allocation and implementation problems. As one reviews the detailed discussions in these articles, it is useful to keep in mind several of the broad issues involved.

One important issue in implementing reward systems, and perhaps the most basic issue of all, concerns the evaluation or appraisal of performance. If rewards are to be distributed in such a way that they have a positive impact on an individual's motivation to participate and to perform, it is crucial that the organization have effective means for assessing the quality and quantity of performance. If the appraisal systems that organizations utilize are unreliable or lack reasonable validity, it can hardly be expected that rewards distributed on the basis of such systems can have much effect in the desired direction.

A second issue involves the questions of how and whether rewards are in fact related to performance. While it might seem obvious, at first glance, that rewards should be distributed directly in relation to differences in performance, there are many reasons organizations do not do so. One reason was discussed above, the problem of accurately appraising performance. Another reason would include the possibility that rewarding a particular type of performance will focus attention away from other desirable aspects of performance. In addition, there is the possibility that rewarding certain individuals or groups for high performance may have a negative effect on other individuals or groups. Also, many organizations believe they are relating rewards directly to performance when, in fact, the relationship is not seen or believed by those receiving the rewards. This, of course, reduces the motivational impact of the reward system. The message here is threefold: first, it is not an easy matter to set up reward systems that relate rewards closely to performance; second, it may not always be desirable to do so, from the organization's perspective; and, third, even when organizations are both willing and able to tie rewards closely to particular types of employee job behavior, the link may not be perceived as close by the recipients of the rewards.

Another issue in reward systems implementation is the question of how well the systems in a particular organization relate to the management style that characterizes that organization (Porter, Lawler, & Hackman, 1975). Organization theorists often distinguish between two broad categories of management style, an open/participative style versus a more traditional/authoritarian style. (Of course, many organizations, if not most, represent a blend of these two styles.) To the extent that a particular firm or agency is managed in accordance with one or the other of these styles, the more likely it is that a reward system will be ineffective if it is implemented in a way that is inconsistent with the particular management style. For example, a participative appraisal system coupled with a highly participative approach in the decisions regarding reward distribution is not likely to work well in an organization that is otherwise run in a very hierarchical, authoritarian manner. Likewise, attempting to have a rigid reward system based only on highly quantified and objective measures of performance is unlikely to have positive effects in an organization that prides itself on its open and participative way of operating.

A final implementation issue revolves around the question of whether there should be relative openness or secrecy regarding various aspects of monetary compensation. This issue is particularly acute in the management parts of organizations, where typically there are fairly wide variations in pay for individuals at roughly the same level of the organization. Organizations vary considerably in how ''open'' the information provided is. Some provide extensive information about how rates of pay are determined but not very much information, if any, about the amount. Other organizations provide relatively little information about either. A minority of organizations (and those usually are in the public sector) provide open information both about methods of determining pay and about amounts. The issue, then, for most organizations (particularly in the private sector) is not so much whether to be open or secret, but rather the degree of openness.

OVERVIEW

The first selection, by Lawler, presents a broad perspective on strategic considerations in the design of reward systems. In this article, the author makes a strong case for relating reward systems to the organization's strategic planning, with special attention given to options available to organizations in their selection of particular features to emphasize in the design of a coordinated system. Lawler also emphasizes that process issues are as important as structural dimensions in constructing a reward system that is internally consistent with other elements of an overall human resources management program.

The fact that rewards that are intended to affect one type of behavior can actually end up encouraging other (nondesired) types of behavior is discussed in the article by Kerr. He illustrates his points with examples from both work organizations and society and concludes with suggestions about how organizations and managers may be able to increase the likelihood that rewards will actually produce their hoped-for effects. The third and fourth readings in this chapter consider pay and compensation. Hamner examines a number of reasons merit pay systems frequently fail to produce higher levels of motivation and offers a set of recommendations for reducing this failure rate. Lawler (in another article in this chapter) reviews four relatively new approaches to total compensation that are likely to be implemented with increasing frequency in the future: an all-salaried work force, skill-based job evaluation systems, lump sum salary increases, and cafeteria benefit programs.

REFERENCES

Deci, E. L. The effects of contingent and non-contingent rewards and controls on intrinsic motivation. *Organizational Behavior and Human Performance*, 1972, **8,** 217–229.

Deci, E. L. *Intrinsic motivation*. New York: Plenum, 1975. (a)

Deci, E. L. Notes on the theory and metatheory of intrinsic motivation. *Organizational Behavior and Human Performance*, 1975 **15**, 130–145. (b)

Guzzo, R. A. Types of rewards, cognitions, and work motivation. *Academy of Management Review*, 1979, **4**, 75–86.

Katz, D. The motivational basis of organizational behavior. *Behavioral Science*, 1964, **9**, 131–146.

March, J. G., & Simon, H. A. *Organizations*. New York: Wiley, 1958.

Porter, L. W., Lawler, E. E., III, & Hackman, J. R. *Behavior in organizations*. New York: McGraw-Hill, 1975.

The Strategic Design of Reward Systems

Edward E. Lawler III

Reward systems are one of the most prominent and frequently discussed features of organizations. Indeed, the literature on organizational behavior and personnel management is replete with examples of their functional as well as their dysfunctional role in organizations (Whyte, 1955). All too often, however, a thorough discussion of how they can be a key strategic factor in organizations is missing. The underlying assumption in this chapter is that when properly designed, the reward systems of an organization can be a key contributor to the effectiveness of the organization. However, for this to occur, careful analysis needs to be made of the role that reward systems can and should play in the strategic plan of the organization.

OBJECTIVES OF REWARD SYSTEMS

The first step in discussing the strategic role of reward systems is to consider what behavioral impact they can have in organizations. That is, we need to first address the outcomes that one can reasonably expect an effective reward system to produce. The research so far on reward systems suggests that potentially they can influence the following factors which, in turn, influence organizational effectiveness.

1 *Attraction and retention* Research on job choice, career choice, and turnover clearly shows that the kind and level of rewards an organization offers influences who is attracted to work for an organization and who will continue to work for it (Mobley, 1982). Overall, those organizations that give the most rewards tend to attract and retain the most people. Research also shows that better performers need to be rewarded more highly than poorer performers in order to be attracted and retained. Finally, the way rewards are administered and distributed influences who is attracted and retained. For example, better performing individuals are often attracted by merit-based reward systems.

2 *Motivation* Those rewards that are important to individuals can influence their motivation to perform in particular ways. People in work organizations tend to behave in whatever way they perceive leads to rewards they value (Lawler, 1973; Vroom, 1964). Thus an organization that is able to tie valued rewards to the behaviors it needs to succeed is likely to find that the reward system is a positive contributor to its effectiveness.

3 *Culture* Reward systems are one feature of organizations that contribute to their overall culture or climate. Depending upon how reward systems are developed, administered, and managed, they can cause the culture of an organization

Based in part on E. E. Lawler III, Reward systems in organizations. In J. Lorsch (Ed.), *Handbook of organizational behavior*. Englewood Cliffs, N.J.: Prentice-Hall, 1983. Partial support of this work was provided by the office of Naval Research under Contract 53 N00014-81-k-0048; NR 170-923.

This version is from C. J. Fombrun, N. Tichy, and M. A. Devanna, *Strategic human resources management*. New York: John Wiley & Sons. Reprinted by permission of John Wiley & Sons, Inc.

to vary quite widely. For example, they can influence the degree to which it is seen as a human resource-oriented culture, an entreprenurial culture, an innovative culture, a competence-based culture, and a participative culture.

4 *Reinforce and define structure* The reward system of an organization can reinforce and define the organization's structure. Often this feature of reward systems is not fully considered in the design of reward systems. As a result, their impact on the structure of an organization is unintentional. This does not mean, however, that the impact of the reward system on structure is usually minimal. Indeed, it can help define the status hierarchy, the degree to which people in technical positions can influence people in line management positions, and it can strongly influence the kind of decision structure that exists. The key features here seem to be the degree to which the reward system is strongly hierarchical and the degree to which it allocates rewards on the basis of movements up the hierarchy.

5 *Cost* Reward systems are often a significant cost factor. Indeed, the pay system alone may represent over 50% of the organization's operating cost. Thus it is important in strategically designing the reward system to focus on how high these costs should be and how they will vary as a function of the organization's ability to pay. For example, a reasonable outcome of a well-designed pay system might be an increased cost when the organization has the money to spend and a decreased cost when the organization does not have the money. An additional objective might be to have lower overall reward system costs than business competitors.

In summary, reward systems in organizations should be looked at from a cost–benefit perspective. The cost can be managed and controlled and the benefits planned for. The key is to identify the outcomes needed in order for the organization to be successful and then to design the reward system in a way that these outcomes will, in fact, be realized.

RELATIONSHIP TO STRATEGIC PLANNING

Figure 1 presents a way of viewing the relationship between strategic planning and reward systems. It suggests that once the strategic plan is developed, the organization needs to focus on the kind of human resources, climate, and be-

FIGURE 1
Reward and strategy implementation.

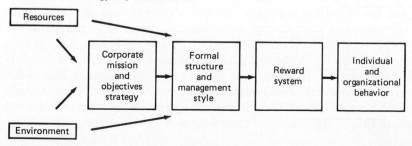

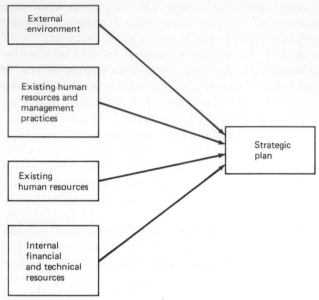

FIGURE 2
Constraints on strategy formulation.

havior that is needed in order to make it effective. The next step is to design reward systems that will motivate the right kind of performance, attract the right kind of people, and create a supportive climate and structure.

Figure 2 suggests another way in which the reward system needs to be taken into consideration in the area of strategic planning. It suggests that before the strategic plan is developed in an existing organization, it is important to assess a number of things including the current reward systems and to determine the kind of behavior, climate, and structure of which they are supportive. This step is needed so that when the strategic plan is developed it is based on a realistic assessment of the current condition of the organization and the changes likely to be needed to implement the new strategic plan. This point is particularly pertinent to organizations that are considering going into new lines of business, developing new strategic plans, and acquiring new divisions.

Often the new lines of business require a different behavior and, therefore, a different reward system. Simply putting the old reward system in place in the new business is often not good enough and, indeed, can lead to failure in the new business. On the other hand, developing a new reward system for the new business can cause problems in the old business because of the type of comparisons that are made between different parts of the same organization. This is not to say that organizations should avoid venturing into new businesses, it is merely to say that a careful assessment of kinds of reward system changes that are needed should take place before organizations enter into new business sectors.

DESIGN OPTIONS

There are almost an infinite number of ways to design and manage reward systems in organizations. This is because there are a host of rewards that can be given and, of course, a large number of ways that they can be distributed. The focus in the remainder of this chapter is on the visible extrinsic rewards that an organization controls and that can as a matter of policy and practice be allocated to members on a specific basis. Included are pay, promotion, status symbols, and perquisites; little attention is given to such intrinsic rewards as feelings of responsibility, competence, and personal growth and development.

A useful dichotomy in thinking about options in the design of reward systems is the process or content one. All organizational systems have a content or structural dimension as well as a process dimension. The structural or content dimension of a reward system refers to the formal mechanisms, procedures, and practices (e.g., the salary structures, the performance appraisal forms), in short, the nuts and bolts of the system. The process side refers to the communication and decision process parts of the system. A key issue here involves the degree of openness with respect to information about how the reward system operates and how people are rewarded. A second issue is the degree of participation that is allowed in the design of the reward system and the ongoing administration of it. Many organizations, without ever choosing to, administer rewards in a top-down secretive way. As is discussed further, this is not the only way that rewards can be administered. The discussion of design choices begins by looking at some key structural choices and then turns to a consideration of some key process choices.

STRUCTURAL DECISIONS

Basis for Rewards

Traditionally, in organizations such rewards as pay and perquisites are based on the type of jobs that people do. Indeed, with the exception of bonuses and merit salary increases, the standard policy in most organizations is to evaluate the job, not the person, and then to set the reward level. This approach is based on the assumption that job worth can be determined and that the person doing the job is worth only as much to the organization as the job itself is worth. This assumption is in many respects valid since through such techniques as job evaluation programs it is possible to determine what other organizations are paying people to do the same or similar jobs. Among the advantages of this system is that it assures an organization that its compensation costs are not dramatically out of line with those of its competitors and it gives a somewhat objective basis to compensation practices.

An alternative to job-based pay which has recently been tried by a number of organizations is to pay individuals for the skills that they possess. In many cases this will not produce dramatically different pay rates than are produced by paying for the nature of the job. After all, the skills that people have usually match reasonably well the jobs that they are doing. It can, however, produce some different results in several respects. Often people have more skills than the job uses and in such cases these individuals are paid more than they would be paid under a job-based system. In other cases individuals do not have the skills when they first enter a job and do not deserve the kind of pay that goes with the job. In these cases individuals have to earn the right to be paid whatever the job-related skills are worth.

Perhaps the most important changes that are introduced when skill-based or competence-based pay is used occur in the kind of climate and motivation it produces in an organization. Instead of people being rewarded for moving up the hierarchy, people are rewarded for increasing their skills and developing themselves. This can create in the organization a climate of concern for personal growth and development and, of course, it can produce a highly talented workforce. In the case of factories where this system has been used it typically means that many people in the organization can perform multiple tasks and thus the workforce is highly knowledgeable and flexible.

In most cases where skills-based pay has been tried it tends to produce an interesting mix of positive and negative features as far as the organization is concerned (Lawler, 1981). Typically, it tends to produce somewhat higher pay levels for individuals but this is usually offset by greater workforce flexibility. This flexibility often leads to lower staffing levels, fewer problems when absenteeism or turnover occur, and, indeed, it often leads to lower absenteeism and turnover itself because people like the opportunity to utilize and be paid for a wide range of skills. On the other hand, skill-based pay can be rather challenging to administer because it is not clear how one goes to the outside marketplace and decides, for example, how much skill is worth. Skill assessment can also be difficult to accomplish. There are a number of well-developed systems for evaluating jobs and comparing them to the marketplace but there are none that really do this with respect to the skills an individual has.

There are no well-established rules to determine which organizational situations fit job-based pay and which fit skill or competence-based pay. In general, skill-based pay seems to fit those organizations that want to have a flexible, relatively permanent workforce that is oriented toward learning, growth, and development. It also seems to fit particularly well new plant start-ups and other situations where the greatest need is for skill development. Despite the newness and the potential operational problems with skill-based pay, it does seem to be a system that more and more organizations will be using especially in slow growth environments.

Pay for Performance

Perhaps the key strategic decision that needs to be made in the design of any reward system is whether it will be based on performance. Once this decision is made, a number of other features of the reward system tend to fall into place. The major alternative to basing pay on performance is to base it on seniority. Many government agencies, for example, base their rates in the job the person does and then on how long they have been in that job. In Japan individual pay is also often based on seniority, although individuals often receive bonuses based on corporate performance.

Most business organizations in the United States say that they reward individual performance and they call their pay system and their promotion system merit-based. Having a true merit pay or promotion system is often easier said than done, however. Indeed, it has been observed that many organizations would be better off if they did not try to relate pay and promotion to performance and relied on other bases for motivating performance.[1] The logic for this statement stems from the difficulty of specifying what kind of performance is desired and then determining whether, in fact, it has been demonstrated. There is ample evidence that a poorly designed and administered reward system can do more harm than good. However, there is evidence that when pay is effectively related to the desired performance, it can help to motivate, attract, and retain outstanding performers. Thus when it is feasible it is usually desirable to relate pay to performance.

There are numerous ways to relate pay to performance and often the most important strategic decision that organizations make is how they do this. The options open to organizations are enormous. The kind of pay reward that is given can vary widely and include such things as stock and cash. In addition, the frequency with which rewards are given can vary tremendously from time periods of a few minutes to many years. Performance can be measured at the individual level so that each individual gets a reward based on his or her performance. Rewards also can be given to groups based on the performance of the group, and rewards can be given based on the performance of total organizations. This gives the same reward to everyone in an organization. Finally, there are many different kinds of performance that can be rewarded. For example, managers can be rewarded for sales increases, productivity volumes, their ability to develop their subordinates, their cost reduction ideas, and so on.

Rewarding some behaviors and not others has clear implications for performance and thus decisions about what is to be rewarded need to be made carefully and with attention to the overall strategic plan of the business (Galbraith and Nathanson, 1978; Salschneider, 1981). Consideration needs to be given to such issues as short versus long-term performance, ROI maximization versus sales growth, and so on. Once the strategic plan has been developed to the point where key performance objectives have been defined, then the reward system needs to be designed to motivate the appropriate performance. Decisions about such issues as whether to use stock options (a long-term incentive), for example, should be made only after careful consideration of whether they are supportive of the kind of behavior that is desired (Crystal, 1978; Ellij, 1982).

It is beyond the scope of this chapter to go into any great detail about the pros and cons of the many approaches to relating pay to performance. Table 1 gives an idea of some of the design features possible in a reward system and some of the pluses and minuses associated with them.

---

[1]See Kerr (1975) for an interesting discussion of reward systems and their unintended consequences.

TABLE 1
RATINGS OF VARIOUS INCENTIVE PLANS[a]

Salary reward		Tie pay to performance	Negative side	Encourage cooperation	Employee acceptance
Individual	Productivity	4	1	1	4
plan	Cost effectiveness	3	1	1	4
	Superior's rating	3	1	1	3
Group plan	Productivity	3	1	2	4
	Cost effectiveness	3	1	2	4
	Superior's rating	2	1	2	3
Organizational	Productivity	2	1	3	4
plan	Cost effectiveness	2	1	2	4
Individual	Productivity	5	3	1	2
plan	Cost effectiveness	4	2	1	2
	Superior's rating	4	2	1	2
Group plan	Productivity	4	1	3	3
	Cost effectiveness	3	1	3	3
	Superior's rating	3	1	3	3
Organizational	Productivity	3	1	3	4
plan	Cost effectiveness	3	1	3	4
	Profit	2	—	—	—

[a]On a scale of 1 to 5, 1 = low and 5 = high.

First, each plan is evaluated in terms of its effectiveness in creating the perception that pay is tied to performance. In general this indicates the degree to which the approach ties pay to performance in a way that leads employees to believe that higher pay will follow good performance. Second, each plan is evaluated in terms of whether it resulted in the negative side effects that often are produced by performance-based pay plans. These include social ostracism of good performers, defensive behavior, and giving false data about performance. Third, each plan is evaluated in terms of the degree to which it encourages cooperation among employees. Finally, employee acceptance of the plan is rated. The ratings range from 1 to 5; a 5 indicates that the plan is generally high on the factor and a 1 indicates it is low. The ratings were developed based on a review of the literature and on my experience with the different types of plans.[2]

A number of trends appear in the ratings. Looking only at the criterion of tying pay to performance, we see that the individual plans tend to be rated highest, group plans are rated next, and organizational plans are rated lowest. This occurs because in group plans, to some extent, and in organizational plans, to a great extent, an individual's pay is not directly a function of his or her behavior. An individual's pay in these situations is influenced by the behavior of many others. In addition, when some types of performance measures (e.g., profits) are used, pay is influenced by external conditions that employees cannot control.

Bonus plans are generally rated higher than pay raise and salary increase plans.

[2]Lawler (1971) discusses this at greater length.

This is because with bonus plans it is possible to substantially vary an individual's pay from time period to time period. With salary increase plans, this is very difficult since past raises tend to become an annuity.

Finally, note that approaches that use objective measures of performance are rated higher than those that use subjective measures. In general, objective measures enjoy higher credibility; that is, employees will often accept the validity of an objective measure, such as sales volume or units produced, when they will not accept a superior's rating. When pay is tied to objective measures, therefore, it is usually clearer to employees that pay is determined by performance. Objective measures are also often publicly measurable. When pay is tied to them, the relationship between performance and pay is much more visible than when it is tied to a subjective, nonverifiable measure, such as a supervisor's rating. Overall, the suggestion is that individually based bonus plans that rely on objective measures produce the strongest perceived connection between pay and performance.

The ratings of the degree to which plans contribute to negative side effects reveal that most plans have little tendency to produce such effects. The notable exceptions here are individual bonus and incentive plans at the nonmanagement level. These plans often lead to situations in which social rejection and ostracism are tied to good performance, and in which employees present false performance data and restrict their production. These side effects are particularly likely to appear where trust is low and subjective productivity standards are used.

In terms of the third criterion—encouraging cooperation—the ratings are generally higher for group and organizational plans than for individual plans. Under group and organizational plans, it is generally to everyone's advantage that an individual work effectively, because all share in the financial fruits of higher performance. This is not true under an individual plan. As a result, good performance is much more likely to be supported and encouraged by others when group and organizational plans are used. If people feel they can benefit from another's good performance, they are much more likely to encourage and help other workers to perform well than if they cannot benefit and may be harmed.

The final criterion—employee acceptance—shows that, as noted earlier, most performance-based pay plans have only moderate acceptance. The least acceptable seems to be individual plans. Their low acceptance, particularly among nonmanagement employees, seems to stem from their tendency to encourage competitive relationships between employees and from the difficulty in administering such plans fairly.

It should be clear that no one performance-based pay plan represents a panacea. It is, therefore, unlikely that any organization will ever be completely satisfied with the approach it chooses. Furthermore, some of the plans that make the greatest contributions to organizational effectiveness do not make the greatest contributions to quality of work life and vice versa. Still the situation is not completely hopeless. When all factors are taken into account, group and organizational bonus plans that are based on objective data and individual level salary increase plans rate high.

Many organizations choose to put individuals on multiple or combination reward systems. For example, they may put individuals on a salary increase system that rewards them for their individual performance while at the same time giving everybody in the division or plant a bonus based on divisional performance. Some plans measure group or company performance and then divide up the bonus pool generated by the performance of a larger group among individuals based on individual performance. This has the effect of causing individuals to be rewarded for both individual and group performance in the hope that this will cause individuals to perform all needed behaviors.

A common error in the design of many pay-for-performance systems is the tendency to focus on measurable short-term operating results because they are quantifiable and regularly obtained anyway. Many organizations reward their top-level managers in particular on the basis of quarterly or annual profitability. This can have the obvious dysfunctional consequence of causing managers to be very short-sighted in their behavior and to ignore strategic objectives important to the long-term profitability of the organization. A similarly grievous error can be the tendency to depend on completely subjective performance appraisals for the allocation of pay rewards. Considerable evidence exists to show that these performance appraisals are often biased and invalid and instead of contributing to positive motivation and a good work climate that improves superior–subordinate relationships they lead to just the opposite.[3] These are just two of the most common errors that can develop in the administration of performance reward systems. Other common errors include the giving of too small rewards, failure to clearly explain systems, and poor administrative practices.

In summary, the decision of whether to relate pay to performance is a crucial one in any organization. The error of automatically assuming that they should be related can be a serious one. Admittedly, the advantages of doing it effectively are significant and can greatly contribute to the organizational effectiveness. What is often overlooked is that doing it poorly can have more negative consequences than positive ones. Specifically, if performance is difficult to measure and/or rewards are difficult to distribute based on performance, the effect of the pay-for-performance system can be the motivation of counterproductive behaviors, lawsuits charging discrimination, and the creation of a climate of mistrust, low credibility, and managerial incompetence. On the other hand, total abandonment of a merit pay system means that the organization gives up a potentially important motivator of performance and, as a result, may condemn itself to a reduced level of performance. The ideal, of course, is to create conditions where pay can be effectively related to performance and as a result have it be an important contributor to the effectiveness of the organization.

Market Position

The reward structure of an organization influences behavior partially as a function of how the amount of rewards given compare to what other organizations give. Organizations frequently have well-developed policies about how their pay levels should compare with the pay levels in other companies. For example, some companies (e.g., IBM) feel it is important to be a leading payer and they con-

[3]See also Latham and Wexley (1981).

sciously set their pay rates at a level that is higher than that of any of the companies they compete with. Other companies are much less concerned about being in the leadership position with respect to pay and as a result are content to focus their pay levels at or below the market for the people they hire. This structural issue in the design of pay systems is a critical one because it can strongly influence the kind of people that are attracted and retained by an organization as well as influence the turnover rate and the selection ratio. Simply stated, those organizations that adopt a more aggressive stance with respect to the marketplace end up attracting and retaining more individuals. From a business point of view this may pay off for them, particularly if turnover is a costly factor in the organization and if a key part of the business strategy demands attracting and retaining highly talented individuals.

On the other hand, if many of the jobs in the organizations are low-skilled and people are readily available in the labor market to do them, then a corporate strategy of high pay may not pay off. It can increase labor costs and produce a minimum number of benefits. Of course, organizations do not have to be high payers for all the jobs. Indeed, some organizations identify certain key skills that they need and adopt the stance of being a high payer for them and an average or below average payer for other skills. This has some obvious business advantages in terms of allowing organizations to attract the critical skills that it needs to succeed and at the same time to control costs.

Although it is not often recognized, the kind of market position that a company adopts with respect to its reward systems can also have a noticeable impact on organization climate. For example, a policy that calls for above market pay can contribute to the feeling in the organization that it is an elite organization, that people must be competent to be there, and that they are indeed fortunate to be there. A policy that splits certain skill groups into a high pay position leaving the rest of the organization at a lower pay level can, on the other hand, contribute to a spirit of elite groups within the organization and cause some divisive social pressures.

Finally, it is interesting to note that some organizations try to be above average in noncash compensation as a way of competing for the talent they need. They talk in terms of producing an above-average quality of work life and stress not only hygiene factors but interesting and challenging work. This stance potentially can be a very effective one, because it puts organizations in the position of attracting people who value these things and could give them a competitive edge at least with these people.

In summary, the kind of market position that an organization has with respect to its total reward package is crucial in determining the behavior of the members as well as the climate of the organization. It needs to be carefully related to the general business strategy of the organization and, in particular, to the kind of human resources that it calls for as well as to the organization climate.

Internal–External Pay Comparison-Oriented

Organizations differ in the degree to which they strive toward internal equity in their pay and reward systems. Those organizations where internal equity is highly valued work very hard to see that individuals doing similar work will be paid the same even though they are in very different parts of the country, and in different businesses. Some corporations (e.g., IBM) set the national pay structure for their organization based on the highest pay that a job receives anywhere in the country. Those organizations that do not stress internal equity typically focus on the labor market as the key determinant of what somebody should be paid and although this does not necessarily produce different pay for people doing the same job, it may. For example, the same job in different industries, electronics and auto, for example, may be paid quite differently.

There are a number of advantages and disadvantages to the strategy of focusing on internal pay comparisons and paying all people in similar jobs the same regardless of where they are in the organization. It can make the transfer of people from one location to another easier since there won't be any pay differences. In addition, it can produce an organizational climate of homogeneity and the feeling that all work for the same company and all are treated well or fairly. It also can reduce or eliminate the tendency of people to want to move to a higher paying division or location and the tendency for rivalry and dissatisfaction to develop within the organization because of poor internal pay comparisons.

On the other hand, a focus on internal equity can be very expensive, particularly if the organization is diversified and as usually happens, pay rates across the corporation get set at the highest level that the market demands anywhere in the corporation (Salschneider, 1981). The disadvantage of this is obvious. It causes organizations to pay a lot more than is necessary in order to attract and retain good people. Indeed, in some situations it can get so severe that organizations become noncompetitive in certain businesses and industries and find that they have to limit themselves to those businesses where their pay structures make their labor costs competitive. Labor costs that are too high have, for example, often make it difficult for auto and oil and gas companies to compete in new business areas.

In summary, the difference between focusing on external equity and internal equity is a crucial one in the design of pay systems. It can determine the cost structure as well as the climate and behavior of organizations. The general rule is that highly diversified companies find themselves pulled more strongly toward an external market orientation, whereas organizations that are single industry or single technology-based typically find themselves more comfortable with an internal equity emphasis.

Centralized–Decentralized Reward Strategy

Closely related to the issue of internal versus external equity is the issue of a centralized versus decentralized reward system strategy. Those organizations that adopt a centralized strategy typically assign to corporate staff groups the responsibility for seeing that such things as pay practices are similar throughout the organization. They typically develop standard pay grades and pay ranges, standardized job evaluation systems, and, perhaps, standardized promotion systems. In decentralized organizations, policy and practice in the area of pay and promotion and other important reward areas is left to local option. Sometimes the corporations have broad guidelines or principles that they wish to stand for but the day-to-day administration and design of the system is left up to the local entity.

The advantages of a centralized structure rest primarily on the expertise that can be accumulated at the central level and the degree of homogeneity produced in the organization. This homogeneity can lead to a clear image of the corporate climate, feelings of internal equity, and the belief that the organization stands for something. It also eases the job of communicating and understanding what is going on in different parts of the organization. The decentralized strategy allows for local innovation and, of course, closely fitting the practices to the particular business.

Just as is true with many other of the critical choices, there is no right choice between a centralized and decentralized approach to reward system design and administration. Overall, the decentralized system tends to make the most sense when the organization is involved in businesses that face different markets and perhaps are at different points in their maturity.[4] It allows those unique practices to surface that can give a competitive advantage to one part of the business but may prove to be a real hindrance or handicap to another. For example, such perquisites as cars are often standard operating procedure in one business, whereas they are not in another. Similarly, extensive bonuses may be needed to attract one group of people (e.g., oil exploration engineers), whereas it makes little sense in attracting other groups (e.g., research scientists). Overall, then, an organization needs to carefully look at its mix of businesses and the degree it wants to stand for a certain set of principles or policies across all its operating divisions and then decide whether a centralized or decentralized reward strategy is likely to be most effective.

Degree of Hierarchy

Closely related to the issue of job-based versus competence-based pay is the strategic decision concerning the hierarchical nature of the reward systems in an organization. Often no formal decision is ever made to have a relatively hierarchical or relatively egalitarian approach to rewards in an organization. An hierarchical approach simply happens because it is so consistent with the general way organizations are run. Hierarchical systems usually pay people greater amounts of money as they move higher up the organization ladder, and give people greater perquisites and symbols of office as they move up. The effect of this approach is to strongly reinforce the traditional hierarchical power relationships in the organization and to create a climate of different status and power levels. In steeply hierarchical reward systems the reward system may have more levels in it than the formal organization chart and, as a result, create additional status differences in the organization.

---

[4]Greiner (1972) discusses the implications of organizational life cycles. See also Galbraith and Nathanson (1978).

The alternative to a hierarchical system is one in which differences in rewards and perquisites that are based only on hierarchical level are dramatically downplayed. For example, in those large corporations (e.g., Digital Equipment Corporation) that adopt an egalitarian stance to rewards, such things as private parking spaces, executive restrooms, and special entrances are eliminated. People from all levels in the organization eat, work, and travel together. Further, individuals can be relatively highly paid by working their way up a technical ladder and do not have to go on to a management ladder in order to gain high levels of pay. This less hierarchical approach to pay and other rewards produces a quite different climate in an organization than does the hierarchical one. It tends to encourage decision-making by expertise rather than by hierarchical position and it draws fewer status differences in the organization.

As with all reward system strategic choices there is no right or wrong answer as to how hierarchical a system should be. In general, a steeply hierarchical system makes the most sense when an organization needs relatively rigid bureaucratic behavior, strong top-down authority, and a strong motivation for people to move up the organizational hierarchy. A more egalitarian approach fits with a more participative management style, and the desire to retain technical specialists and experts in nonmanagement roles or lower-level management roles. It is not surprising, therefore, that many of the organizations that have emphasized egalitarian perquisites are in high technology and knowledge-based industries.

Reward Mix

The kind of rewards that organizations give to individuals can vary widely. The money, for example, that is given can come in many forms varying all the way from stock through medical insurance. Organizations can choose to reward people almost exclusively with cash, downplaying fringe benefits, perquisites, and status symbols. The major advantage of paying in cash is that the value of cash in the eyes of the recipient is universally high. When the cash is translated into fringe benefits, perquisites, and other trappings of office it may lose its value for some people and as a result be a poor investment (Nealy, 1963). On the other hand, certain benefits can best be obtained through mass purchase and, therefore, many individuals want the organization to provide them. In addition, certain status symbols or perquisites may be valued by some individuals beyond their actual dollar cost to the organization and thus represent good buys. Finally, as mentioned earlier, there often are some climate and organizational structure reasons for paying people in the form of perquisites and status symbols.

One interesting development in the area of compensation is the flexible or cafeteria-style benefit program. Here individuals are allowed to make up their own reward package so that it is sure to fit their needs and desires. The theory is that this will lead to organizations getting the best value for their money because they will give people only those things that they desire. It also has the advantage of treating individuals as mature adults rather than as dependent people who need their welfare looked after in a structured way. At the moment this approach has been tried in only a few organizations. The results so far have been favorable, thus there is reason to believe that others may be adopting it in the near future because it can offer a strategic cost–benefit advantage in attracting and retaining certain types of employees.

Overall, the choice of what form of rewards to give individuals needs to be driven by a clear feeling of what type of climate the organization wishes to have. For example, the idea of a flexible compensation package is highly congruent with a participative open organization climate that treats individuals as mature adults and wants to attract talented mature people. An approach that emphasizes rewards may, on the other hand, appeal to people who are very status-oriented, who value position power, and who need a high level of visible reinforcement for their position. This would seem to fit best in a relatively bureaucratic organization that relies on position power and authority in order to carry out its actions.

PROCESS ISSUES AND REWARD ADMINISTRATION

A number of process issues with respect to reward systems design and administration could be discussed here. In some respects process issues come up more often than do structure and content issues because organizations are constantly having to make reward system management, implementation, and communication decisions, whereas structures tend to be relatively firmly fixed in place. However, rather than discussing specific process issues here, the focus is on broad process themes that can be used to characterize the way reward systems are designed and administered.

Communication Policy

Organizations differ widely in how much information they communicate about their reward systems. At one extreme some organizations are extremely secretive, particularly in the area of pay. They forbid people from talking about their individual rewards, give minimal information to individuals about how rewards are decided upon and allocated, and have no publicly disseminated policies about such things as market position, the approach to gathering market data, and potential increases and rewards for individuals. At the other extreme, some organizations are so open that everyone's pay is a matter of public record as is the overall organization pay philosophy. [Many new high involvement plants operate this way (Walton, 1980).] In addition, all promotions are subject to open job postings and in some instances peer groups discuss the eligibility of people for promotion.

The difference between an open and closed communication policy in the area of rewards is enormous. Like all the other choices that must be made in structuring a reward system, there is no clear right or wrong approach. Rather it is a matter of picking a position on the continuum from open to secret that is supportive of the overall climate and types of behavior that are needed for organizational effectiveness. An open system tends to encourage people to ask questions, share data, and ultimately be involved in decisions. A secret system tends to put people in a more dependent position to keep power concentrated at the top and to allow an organization to keep its options open with respect to commitments to individuals. Some negative side effects of secret systems are the existence of considerable distortion about the actual rewards that people get and creation of a low trust environment in which people have trouble understanding the relationship between pay and performance. Thus a structurally sound pay system may end up being rather ineffective because it is misperceived if strong policies are kept in place.

Open systems put considerable pressure on organizations to do an effective job of administering rewards. Thus if policies such as merit pay, which are difficult to defend, are to be implemented, then considerable time and effort need to be invested in pay administration. If they are done poorly, strong pressures usually develop to eliminate the policies and pay everyone the same. Ironically, therefore, if an organization wants to spend little time administrating rewards but still wants to use merit pay, secrecy may be the best policy, although secrecy, in turn, may limit the effectiveness of the merit pay plan.

Decision-Making Practices

Closely related to the issue of communication is the issue of decision-making. Open communication makes possible the involvement of a wide range of people in the decision-making process concerning compensation. Further, if individuals are to be actively involved in decisions concerning reward systems, they need to have information about policy and actual practice.

In discussing the type of decision-making processes that are used in organizations with respect to reward systems, it is important to distinguish between decisions concerning the design of reward systems and decisions concerning the ongoing administration of reward systems. It is possible to have different decision-making styles with respect to each of these two types of decisions. Traditionally, of course, organizations have made both design and ongoing administration decisions in a top-down manner.

Systems typically have been designed by top management with the aid of staff support and administered by strict reliance on the chain of command. The assumption has been that this provides the proper checks and balances in the system and in addition locates decision-making where the expertise rests. In many cases this is a valid assumption and certainly fits well with an organizational management style that emphasizes hierarchy, bureaucracy, and control through the use of extrinsic rewards. It does not fit, however, with an organization that believes in more open communication, higher levels of involvement on the part of people, and control through individual commitment to policies. It also does not fit when expertise is broadly spread throughout the organization. This is often true in organizations that rely heavily on knowledge workers or that spend a great deal of effort training their people to become expert in technical functions.

There have been some reports in the research literature of organizations experimenting with having employees involved in the design of pay systems. For example, employees have been involved in designing their own bonus system in some instances and the results have been generally favorable. When employees are involved it seems to lead them to raising important issues and providing expertise not normally available to the designers of the system. And perhaps more important, once the system is designed the acceptance level of it and the understanding of it tends to be very high. This often leads to a rapid start-up of the system and to a commitment to see it survive long-term. In other cases systems have been designed by line managers rather than by staff support people because of the feeling that they are the ones that need to support it, maintain it, and be committed to it. In the absence of significant design input from line people it often is unrealistic to expect them to have the same level of commitment to the pay system as the staff people have.

There also has been some experimentation with having peer groups and low-level supervisory people handle the day-to-day decision-making about who should receive pay increases and how jobs should be evaluated and placed in pay structures. The most visible examples of this are in the new participative plants that use skill-based pay (Walton, 1980). In these, typically, the work group reviews the performance of the individual and decides whether he or she has acquired the new skills. Interestingly, what evidence there is suggests that this has gone very well. In many respects this is not surprising since the peers often have the best information about performance and thus are in a good position to make a performance assessment. The problem in traditional organizations is that they lack the motivation to give valid feedback and to respond responsibly, thus their expertise is of no use. In more participative open systems this motivational problem seems to be less severe and, as a result, involvement in decision-making seems to be more effective. There also have been isolated instances of executives assessing each other on a peer group reward system and practices (e.g., in Graphic Controls Corporation). Again, there is evidence that this can work effectively when combined with a history of open and effective communication. Deciding on rewards is clearly not an easy task for groups to do and thus should be taken on only when there is comfort with the confrontation skills of the group and trust in their ability to talk openly and directly about each other's performance.

Overall, there is evidence that some participative approaches to reward system design and administration can be effective. The key seems to be articulating the practices in the area of reward systems with the general management style of the organization. In more participative settings there is good reason to believe that participative approaches to reward systems can be effective because of their congruence with the overall style and because the skills and norms to make them effective are already in place. In more traditional organizations the typical top-down approach to reward systems design administration probably remains the best. From a strategic point of view, the decision then about how much participation and reward system design and administration must rest upon whether a participative high involvement type organization is best in order to accomplish the strategic objectives of the business. If so, then participation in pay decisions and reward system decisions should be considered.

REWARD SYSTEM CONGRUENCE

So far each reward system design feature has been treated as an independent factor. This was done for exposition of the concepts but it fails to emphasize the importance of overall reward system congruence. Reward system design features are not stand-alone items. There is considerable evidence that they affect each other and, as such, need to be supportive of the same types of behavior, reflect the same overall managerial philosophy, and be generated by the same business strategy.

Table 2 illustrates one effort to define congruent sets of reward system practices. Here the effort is to show how two different management philosophies call for two very different reward system practices. The two management philosophies portrayed here are a traditional bureaucratic management style and a participative employee involvement strategy. As can be seen from the table, every reward system practice needs to be different in these two cases. The reward system practices that go with traditional bureacratic models tend to be more secretive, more top-down, and oriented toward producing regularity in behavior. The participative practices encourage self-development, openness, employee involvement in reward system allocation decisions, and, ultimately, more innovation and commitment to the organization.

The importance of congruence is not limited to just the reward system in an organization. The reward system needs to fit the other features of the organization

TABLE 2
APPROPRIATE REWARD SYSTEM PRACTICES

	Traditional or Theory X	**Participative or Theory Y**
Reward system		
Fringe benefits	Vary according to organization level	Cafeteria—same for all levels
Promotion	All decisions made by top management	Open posting for all jobs; peer group involvement in decision process
Status symbols	A great many, carefully allocated on the basis of job position	Few present, low emphasis on organization level
Pay		
Type of system	Hourly and salary	All salary
Base rate	Based on job performed; high enough to attract job applicants	Based on skills; high enough to provide security and attract applicants
Incentive plan	Piece rate	Group and organization-wide bonus, lump sum increase
Communication policy	Very restricted distribution of information	Individual rates, salary survey data, all other information made public
Decision-making locus	Top management	Close to location of person whose pay is being set

in order that total human resource management system congruence exists. This means that the reward system needs to fit such things as the way jobs are designed, the leadership style of the supervisors, and the types of career tracks available in the organization, to mention just a few. Unless this kind of fit exists, the organization will be replete with conflicts and, to a degree, the reward system practices will potentially be canceled out by the practices in other areas. To mention just one example, an organization can have a very well-developed performance appraisal system, but in the absence of well-designed jobs and effective supervisory behavior it will be ineffective. Performance appraisal demands interpersonally competent supervisory behavior and jobs that allow for good performance measure.

CONCLUSION

Overall, the design of an effective reward system demands not only a close articulation between the business strategy of an organization and the reward system, but also a clear fit between the reward system and the other design features of the organization. The implication of this for-reward system design is that not only is there no one right set of practices for reward systems, it is also impossible to design an effective reward system in the absence of knowing how other design features of the organization are arrayed. This suggests that the key strategic decisions about the reward system need to be made in an interactive fashion in which tentative reward system design decisions are driven by the business strategy and then are tested against how other features of the organization are being designed. The key, of course, is to ultimately come up with an integrated human resource management strategy that is consistent in the way it encourages people to behave, that attracts the kind of people that can support the business strategy, and that encourages them to behave appropriately.

REFERENCES

Crystal, G. S. *Executive Compensation*. New York: AMACOM, 1978.

Ellij, B. R. *Executive Compensation—A Total Pay Perspective*. New York: McGraw-Hill, 1982.

Galbraith, J. and D. Nathanson. *Strategy Formulation: Analytical Concepts*. St. Paul, MN: West Publishing Co., 1978.

Galbraith, J. and D. Nathanson. *Strategy Implementation: The Role of Structure and Process*. St. Paul, MN: West Publishing, 1978.

Greiner, L. "Evolution and Resolution as Organizations Grow." *Harvard Business Review*, 1972, **50** (4), 37–46.

Kerr, S. "On the Folly of Rewarding A. While Hoping for B." *Academy of Management Journal*, 1975, **18**, 796–783.

Latham, G. P. and K. N. Wexley. *Increasing Productivity Through Performance Appraisal*. Reading, MA: Addison-Wesley, 1981.

Lawler, E. E. *Pay and Organizational Effectiveness: A Psychological View*. New York: McGraw-Hill, 1971.

Lawler, E. E. *Motivation in Work Organizations*. Monterey, CA: Brooks/Cole, 1973.

Lawler, E. E. *Pay and Organization Development*. Reading, MA: Addison-Wesley, 1981.

Mobley, W. H. *Employee Turnover: Causes, Consequences, and Control*. Reading, MA: Addison-Wesley, 1982.

Nealy, S. "Pay and Benefit Preferences." *Industrial Relations*, 1963, **3,** 17–28.

Salschneider, J. "Devising Pay Strategies for Diversified Companies." *Compensation Review*, 1981, 5–25.

Vroom, V. *Work and Motivation*. New York: Wiley, 1964.

Walton, R. E. "Establishing and Maintaining Commitment in Work Organizations." In *The Organizational Life Cycle*. J. Kimberly, and R. H. Miles and Associates (Eds.), San Francisco: Jossey-Bass, 1980.

Whyte, W. F. (Ed.). *Money and Motivation: An Analysis of Incentives on Industry*. New York: Harper, 1955.

On the Folly of Rewarding A, while Hoping for B

Steven Kerr

Whether dealing with monkeys, rats, or human beings, it is hardly controversial to state that most organisms seek information concerning what activities are rewarded, and then seek to do (or at least pretend to do) those things, often to the virtual exclusion of activities not rewarded. The extent to which this occurs of course will depend on the perceived attractiveness of the rewards offered, but neither operant nor expectancy theorists would quarrel with the essence of this notion.

Nevertheless, numerous examples exist of reward systems that are fouled up in that behaviors which are rewarded are those which the rewarder is trying to *discourage,* while the behavior he desires is not being rewarded at all.

In an effort to understand and explain this phenomenon, this paper presents examples from society, from organizations in general, and from profit making firms in particular. Data from a manufacturing company and information from an insurance firm are examined to demonstrate the consequences of such reward systems for the organizations involved, and possible reasons why such reward systems continue to exist are considered.

SOCIETAL EXAMPLES

Politics

Official goals are "purposely vague and general and do not indicate . . . the host of decisions that must be made among alternative ways of achieving official goals and the priority of multiple goals . . . " (8, p. 66). They usually may be relied on to offend absolutely no one, and in this sense can be considered high acceptance, low quality goals. An example might be "build better schools." Operative goals

Reprinted from *Academy of Management Journal*, 1975, **18,** 769–783. Reprinted by permission.

are higher in quality but lower in acceptance, since they specify where the money will come from, what alternative goals will be ignored, etc.

The American citizenry supposedly wants its candidates for public office to set forth operative goals, making their proposed programs "perfectly clear," specifying sources and uses of funds, etc. However, since operative goals are lower in acceptance, and since aspirants to public office need acceptance (from at least 50.1 percent of the people), most politicians prefer to speak only of official goals, at least until after the election. They of course would agree to speak at the operative level if "punished" for not doing so. The electorate could do this by refusing to support candidates who do not speak at the operative level.

Instead, however, the American voter typically punishes (withholds support from) candidates who frankly discuss where the money will come from, rewards politicians who speak only of official goals, but hopes that candidates (despite the reward system) will discuss the issues operatively. It is academic whether it was moral for Nixon, for example, to refuse to discuss his 1968 "secret plan" to end the Vietnam war, his 1972 operative goals concerning the lifting of price controls, the reshuffling of his cabinet, etc. The point is that the reward system made such refusal rational.

It seems worth mentioning that no manuscript can adequately define what is "moral" and what is not. However, examination of costs and benefits, combined with knowledge of what motivates a particular individual, often will suffice to determine what for him is "rational."[1] If the reward system is so designed that it is irrational to be moral, this does not necessarily mean that immorality will result. But is this not asking for trouble?

War

If some oversimplification may be permitted, let it be assumed that the primary goal of the organization (Pentagon, Luftwaffe, or whatever) is to win. Let it be assumed further that the primary goal of most individuals on the front lines is to get home alive. Then there appears to be an important conflict in goals—personally rational behavior by those at the bottom will endanger goal attainment by those at the top.

But not necessarily! It depends on how the reward system is set up. The Vietnam war was indeed a study of disobedience and rebellion, with terms such as "fragging" (killing one's own commanding officer) and "search and evade" becoming part of the military vocabulary. The difference in subordinates' acceptance of authority between World War II and Vietnam is reported to be considerable, and veterans of the Second World War often have been quoted as being outraged at the mutinous actions of many American soldiers in Vietnam.

Consider, however, some critical differences in the reward system in use during the two conflicts. What did the GI in World War II want? To go home. And

---

[1]In Simon's (10, pp. 76–77) terms, a decision is "subjectively rational" if it maximizes an individual's valued outcomes so far as his knowledge permits. A decision is "personally rational" if it is oriented toward the individual's goals.

when did he get to go home? When the war was won! If he disobeyed the orders to clean out the trenches and take the hills, the war would not be won and he would not go home. Furthermore, what were his chances of attaining his goal (getting home alive) if he obeyed the orders compared to his chances if he did not? What is being suggested is that the rational soldier in World War II, *whether patriotic or not,* probably found it expedient to obey.

Consider the reward system in use in Vietnam. What did the man at the bottom want? To go home. And when did he get to go home? When his tour of duty was over! This was the case *whether or not* the war was won. Furthermore, concerning the relative chance of getting home alive by obeying orders compared to the chance if they were disobeyed, it is worth noting that a mutineer in Vietnam was far more likely to be assigned rest and rehabilitation (on the assumption that fatigue was the cause) than he was to suffer any negative consequence.

In his description of the "zone of indifference," Barnard stated that "a person can and will accept a communication as authoritative only when . . . at the time of his decision, he believes it to be compatible with his personal interests as a whole" (1, p. 165). In light of the reward system used in Vietnam, would it not have been personally irrational for some orders to have been obeyed? Was not the military implementing a system which *rewarded* disobedience, while *hoping* that soldiers (despite the reward system) would obey orders?

Medicine

Theoretically, a physician can make either of two types of error, and intuitively one seems as bad as the other. A doctor can pronounce a patient sick when he is actually well, thus causing him needless anxiety and expense, curtailment of enjoyable foods and activities, and even physical danger by subjecting him to needless medication and surgery. Alternatively, a doctor can label a sick person well, and thus avoid treating what may be a serious, even fatal ailment. It might be natural to conclude that physicians seek to minimize both types of error.

Such a conclusion would be wrong.[2] It is estimated that numerous Americans are presently afflicted with iatrogenic (physician *caused*) illnesses (9). This occurs when the doctor is approached by someone complaining of a few stray symptoms. The doctor classifies and organizes these symptoms, gives them a name, and obligingly tells the patient what further symptoms may be expected. This information often acts as a self-fulfilling prophecy, with the result that from that day on the patient for all practical purposes is sick.

Why does this happen? Why are physicians so reluctant to sustain a type 2 error (pronouncing a sick person well) that they will tolerate many type 1 errors? Again, a look at the reward system is needed. The punishments for a type 2 error are real: guilt, embarrassment, and the threat of lawsuit and scandal. On the other hand, a type 1 error (labeling a well person sick) "is sometimes seen as sound clinical practice, indicating a healthy conservative approach to medicine" (9, p. 69). Type 1 errors also are likely to generate increased income and a stream of

[2]In one study (4) of 14,867 films for signs of tuberculosis, 1,216 positive readings turned out to be clinically negative; only 24 negative readings proved clinically active, a ratio of 50 to 1.

steady customers who, being well in a limited physiological sense, will not embarrass the doctor by dying abruptly.

Fellow physicians and the general public therefore are really *rewarding* type 1 errors and at the same time *hoping* fervently that doctors will try not to make them.

GENERAL ORGANIZATIONAL EXAMPLES

Rehabilitation Centers and Orphanages

In terms of the prime beneficiary classification (2, p. 42) organizations such as these are supposed to exist for the "public-in-contact," that is, clients. The orphanage therefore theoretically is interested in placing as many children as possible in good homes. However, often orphanages surround themselves with so many rules concerning adoption that it is nearly impossible to pry a child out of the place. Orphanages may deny adoption unless the applicants are a married couple, both of the same religion as the child, without history of emotional or vocational instability, with a specified minimum income, and a private room for the child, etc.

If the primary goal is to place children in good homes, then the rules ought to constitute means toward that goal. Goal displacement results when these "means become ends-in-themselves that displace the original goals" (2, p. 229).

To some extent these rules are required by law. But the influence of the reward system on the orphanage's management should not be ignored. Consider, for example, that the:

1 Number of children enrolled often is the most important determinant of the size of the allocated budget.

2 Number of children under the director's care also will affect the size of his staff.

3 Total organizational size will determine largely the director's prestige at the annual conventions, in the community, etc.

Therefore, to the extent that staff size, total budget, and personal prestige are valued by the orphanage's executive personnel, it becomes rational for them to make it difficult for children to be adopted. After all, who wants to be the director of the smallest orphanage in the state?

If the reward system errs in the opposite direction, paying off only for placements, extensive goal displacement again is likely to result. A common example of vocational rehabilitation in many states, for example, consists of placing someone in a job for which he has little interest and few qualifications, for two months or so, and then "rehabilitating" him again in another position. Such behavior is quite consistent with the prevailing reward system, which pays off for the number of individuals placed in any position for 60 days or more. Rehabilitation counselors also confess to competing with one another to place relatively skilled clients, sometimes ignoring persons with few skills who would be harder to place. Extensively disabled clients find that counselors often prefer to work with those whose disabilities are less severe.[3]

Universities

Society *hopes* that teachers will not neglect their teaching responsibilities but *rewards* them almost entirely for research and publications. This is most true at the large and prestigious universities. Cliches such as "good research and good teaching go together" notwithstanding, professors often find that they must choose between teaching and research oriented activities when allocating their time. Rewards for good teaching usually are limited to outstanding teacher awards, which are given to only a small percentage of good teachers and which usually bestow little money and fleeting prestige. Punishments for poor teaching also are rare.

Rewards for research and publications, on the other hand, and punishments for failure to accomplish these, are commonly administered by universities at which teachers are employed. Furthermore, publication oriented resumés usually will be well received at other universities, whereas teaching credentials, harder to document and quantify, are much less transferable. Consequently it is rational for university teachers to concentrate on research, even if to the detriment of teaching and at the expense of their students.

By the same token, it is rational for students to act based upon the goal displacement which has occurred within universities concerning what they are rewarded for. If it is assumed that a primary goal of a university is to transfer knowledge from teacher to student, then grades become identifiable as a means toward the goal, serving as motivational, control, and feedback devices to expedite the knowledge transfer. Instead, however, the grades themselves have become much more important for entrance to graduate school, successful employment, tuition refunds, parental respect, etc., than the knowledge or lack of knowledge they are supposed to signify.

It therefore should come as no surprise that information has surfaced in recent years concerning fraternity files for examinations, term paper writing services, organized cheating at the service academies, and the like. Such activities constitute a personally rational response to a reward system which pays off for grades rather than knowledge.

BUSINESS RELATED EXAMPLES

Ecology

Assume that the president of XYZ Corporation is confronted with the following alternatives:

1 Spend $11 million for antipollution equipment to keep from poisoning fish in the river adjacent to the plant; or

[3]Personal interviews conducted during 1972–1973.

2 Do nothing, in violation of the law, and assume a one in ten chance of being caught, with a resultant $1 million fine plus the necessity of buying the equipment.

Under this not unrealistic set of choices it requires no linear program to determine that XYZ Corporation can maximize its probabilities by flouting the law. Add the fact that XYZ's president is probably being rewarded (by creditors, stockholders, and other salient parts of his task environment) according to criteria totally unrelated to the number of fish poisoned, and his probable cause of action becomes clear.

Evaluation of Training

It is axiomatic that those who care about a firm's well-being should insist that the organization get fair value for its expenditures. Yet it is commonly known that firms seldom bother to evaluate a new GRID, MBO, job enrichment program, or whatever, to see if the company is getting its money's worth. Why? Certainly it is not because people have not pointed out that this situation exists; numerous practitioner oriented articles are written each year to just this point.

The individuals (whether in personnel, manpower planning, or wherever) who normally would be responsible for conducting such evaluations are the same ones often charged with introducing the change effort in the first place. Having convinced top management to spend the money, they usually are quite animated afterwards in collecting arigorous vignettes and anecdotes about how successful the program was. The last thing many desire is a formal, systematic, and revealing evaluation. Although members of top management may actually *hope* for such systematic evaluation, their reward systems continue to *reward* ignorance in this area. And if the personnel department abdicates its responsibility, who is to step into the breach? The change agent himself? Hardly! He is likely to be too busy collecting anecdotal "evidence" of his own, for use with his next client.

Miscellaneous

Many additional examples could be cited of systems which in fact are rewarding behaviors other than those supposedly desired by the rewarder. A few of these are described briefly below.

Most coaches disdain to discuss individual accomplishments, preferring to speak of teamwork, proper attitude, and a one-for-all spirit. Usually, however, rewards are distributed according to individual performance. The college basketball player who feeds his teammates instead of shooting will not compile impressive scoring statistics and is less likely to be drafted by the pros. The ballplayer who hits to right field to advance the runners will win neither the batting nor home run titles, and will be offered smaller raises. It therefore is rational for players to think of themselves first, and the team second.

In business organizations where rewards are dispensed for unit performance or

for individual goals achieved, without regard for overall effectiveness, similar attitudes often are observed. Under most Management by Objectives (MBO) systems, goals in areas where quantification is difficult often go unspecified. The
organization therefore often is in a position where it *hopes* for employee effort in
the areas of team building, interpersonal relations, creativity, etc., but it formally
rewards none of these. In cases where promotions and raises are formally tied to
MBO, the system itself contains a paradox in that it "asks employees to set challenging, risky goals, only to face smaller paychecks and possibly damaged careers
if these goals are not accomplished" (5, p. 40).

It is *hoped* that administrators will pay attention to long run costs and opportunities and will institute programs which will bear fruit later on. However,
many organizational reward systems pay off for short run sales and earnings only.
Under such circumstances it is personally rational for officials to sacrifice
long term growth and profit (by selling off equipment and property, or by sti-
fling research and development) for short term advantages. This probably is
most pertinent in the public sector, with the result that many public officials are
unwilling to implement programs which will not show benefits by election
time.

As a final, clear-cut example of a fouled-up reward system, consider the cost-
plus contract or its next of kin, the allocation of next year's budget as a direct
function of this year's expenditures. It probably is conceivable that those who
award such budgets and contracts really hope for economy and prudence in
spending. It is obvious, however, that adopting the proverb "to him who spends
shall more be given," rewards not economy, but spending itself.

TWO COMPANIES' EXPERIENCES

A Manufacturing Organization

A midwest manufacturer of industrial goods had been troubled for some time by
aspects of its organizational climate it believed dysfunctional. For research purposes, interviews were conducted with many employees and a questionnaire was
administered on a companywide basis, including plants and offices in several
American and Canadian locations. The company strongly encouraged employee
participation in the survey, and made available time and space during the workday
for completion of the instrument. All employees in attendance during the day of
the survey completed the questionnaire. All instruments were collected directly
by the researcher, who personally administered each session. Since no one employed by the firm handled the questionnaires, and since respondent names were
not asked for, it seems likely that the pledge of anonymity given was believed.

A modified version of the Expect Approval scale (7) was included as part of the
questionnaire. The instrument asked respondents to indicate the degree of approval or disapproval they could expect if they performed each of the described
actions. A seven point Likert scale was used, with one indicating that the action
would probably bring strong disapproval and seven signifying likely strong approval.

Although normative data for this scale from studies of other organizations are unavailable, it is possible to examine fruitfully the data obtained from this survey in several ways. First, it may be worth noting that the questionnaire data corresponded closely to information gathered through interviews. Furthermore, as can be seen from the results summarized in Table 1, sizable differences between various work units, and between employees at different job levels within the same work unit, were obtained. This suggests that response bias effects (social desirability in particular loomed as a potential concern) are not likely to be severe.

Most importantly, comparisons between scores obtained on the Expect Approval scale and a statement of problems which were the reason for the survey revealed that the same behaviors which managers in each division thought dysfunctional were those which lower level employees claimed were rewarded. As compared to job levels 1 to 8 in Division B (see Table 1), those in Division A claimed a much higher acceptance by management of "conforming" activities. Between 31 and 37 percent of Division A employees at levels 1-8 stated that going along with the majority, agreeing with the boss, and staying on everyone's good side brought approval; only once (level 5-8 responses to one of the three items) did a majority suggest that such actions would generate disapproval.

Furthermore, responses from Division A workers at levels 1-4 indicate that behaviors geared toward risk avoidance were as likely to be rewarded as to be punished. Only at job levels 9 and above was it apparent that the reward system was positively reinforcing behaviors desired by top management. Overall, the same "tendencies toward conservatism and apple-polishing at the lower levels" which divisional management had complained about during the interviews were those claimed by subordinates to be the most rational course of action in light of the existing reward system. Management apparently was not getting the behaviors it was *hoping* for, but it certainly was getting the behaviors it was perceived by subordinates to be *rewarding*.

An Insurance Firm

The Group Health Claims Division of a large eastern insurance company provides another rich illustration of a reward system which reinforces behaviors not desired by top management.

Attempting to measure and reward accuracy in paying surgical claims, the firm systematically keeps track of the number of returned checks and letters of complaint received from policyholders. However, underpayments are likely to provoke cries of outrage from the insured, while overpayments often are accepted in courteous silence. Since it often is impossible to tell from the physician's statement which of the two surgical procedures, with different allowable benefits, was performed, and since writing for clarifications will interfere with other standards used by the firm concerning "percentage of claims paid within two days of receipt," the new hiree in more than one claims section is soon acquainted with the informal norm: "When in doubt, pay it out!"

The situation would be even worse were it not for the fact that other features of

TABLE 1
SUMMARY OF TWO DIVISIONS' DATA RELEVANT TO CONFORMING AND RISK-AVOIDANCE BEHAVIORS
(Extent to Which Subjects Expect Approval)

Dimension	Item	Division and sample	Total responses	Percentage of workers responding		
				1, 2, or 3 Disapproval	4	5, 6, or 7 Approval
Risk avoidance	Making a risky decision based on the best information available at the time, but which turns out wrong.	A, levels 1-4 (lowest)	127	61	25	14
		A, levels 5-8	172	46	31	23
		A, levels 9 and above	17	41	30	30
		B, levels 1-4 (lowest)	31	58	26	16
		B, levels 5-8	19	42	42	16
		B, levels 9 and above	10	50	20	30
	Setting extremely high and challenging standards and goals, and then narrowly failing to make them.	A, levels 1-4	122	47	28	25
		A, levels 5-8	168	33	26	41
		A, levels 9+	17	24	6	70
		B, levels 1-4	31	48	23	29
		B, levels 5-8	18	17	33	50
		B, levels 9+	10	30	0	70
	Setting goals which are extremely easy to make and then making them.	A, levels 1-4	124	35	30	35
		A, levels 5-8	171	47	27	26
		A, levels 9+	17	70	24	6
		B, levels 1-4	31	58	26	16
		B, levels 5-8	19	63	16	21
		B, levels 9+	10	80	0	20

TABLE 1 (Continued)

				Percentage of workers responding		
Dimension	Item	Division and sample	Total responses	1, 2, or 3 Disapproval	4	5, 6, or 7 Approval
Conformity	Being a "yes man" and always agreeing with the boss.	A, levels 1-4	126	46	17	37
		A, levels 5-8	180	54	14	31
		A, levels 9+	17	88	12	0
		B, levels 1-4	32	53	28	19
		B, levels 5-8	19	58	21	11
		B, levels 9+	10	80	10	10
	Always going along with the majority.	A, levels 1-4	125	40	25	35
		A, levels 5-8	173	47	21	32
		A, levels 9+	17	70	12	18
		B, levels 1-4	31	61	23	16
		B, levels 5-8	19	68	11	21
		B, levels 9+	10	80	10	10
	Being careful to stay on the good side of everyone, so that everyone agrees that you are a great guy.	A, levels 1-4	124	45	18	37
		A, levels 5-8	173	45	22	33
		A, levels 9+	17	64	6	30
		B, levels 1-4	31	54	23	23
		B, levels 5-8	19	73	11	16
		B, levels 9+	10	80	10	10

the firm's reward system tend to neutralize those described. For example, annual "merit" increases are given to all employees, in one of the following three amounts:

1 If the worker is "outstanding" (a select category, into which no more than two employees per section may be placed): 5 percent
2 If the worker is "above average" (normally all workers not "outstanding" are so rated): 4 percent
3 If the worker commits gross acts of negligence and irresponsibility for which he might be discharged in many other companies: 3 percent.

Now, since (a) the difference between the 5 percent theoretically attainable through hard work and the 4 percent attainable merely by living until the review date is small and (b) since insurance firms seldom dispense much of a salary increase in cash (rather, the worker's insurance benefits increase, causing him to be further overinsured), many employees are rather indifferent to the possibility of obtaining the extra one percent reward and therefore tend to ignore the norm concerning indiscriminant payments.

However, most employees are not indifferent to the rule which states that, should absences or latenesses total three or more in any six-month period, the entire 4 or 5 percent due at the next "merit" review must be forfeited. In this sense the firm may be described as *hoping* for performance, while *rewarding* attendance. What it gets, of course, is attendance. (If the absence-lateness rule appears to the reader to be stringent, it really is not. The company counts "times" rather than "days" absent, and a ten-day absence therefore counts the same as one lasting two days. A worker in danger of accumulating a third absence within six months merely has to remain ill (away from work) during his second absence until his first absence is more than six months old. The limiting factor is that at some point his salary ceases, and his sickness benefits take over. This usually is sufficient to get the younger workers to return, but for those with 20 or more years' service, the company provides sickness benefits of 90 percent of normal salary tax-free! Therefore. . . .)

CAUSES

Extremely diverse instances of systems which reward behavior A although the rewarder apparently hopes for behavior B have been given. These are useful to illustrate the breadth and magnitude of the phenomenon, but the diversity increases the difficulty of determining commonalities and establishing causes. However, four general factors may be pertinent to an explanation of why fouled up reward systems seem to be so prevalent.

Fascination with an "Objective" Criterion

It has been mentioned elsewhere that:

> Most "objective" measures of productivity are objective only in that their subjective elements are a) determined in advance, rather than coming into play at the time of the formal evaluation, and b) well concealed on the rating instrument itself. Thus industrial firms seeking to devise objective rating systems first decide, in an arbitrary manner, what dimensions are to be rated, . . . usually including some items having little to do with organizational effectiveness while excluding others that do. Only then does Personnel Division churn out official-looking documents on which all dimensions chosen to be rated are assigned point values, categories, or whatever (6, p. 92).

Nonetheless, many individuals seek to establish simple, quantifiable standards against which to measure and reward performance. Such efforts may be successful in highly predictable areas within an organization, but are likely to cause goal displacement when applied anywhere else. Overconcern with attendance and lateness in the insurance firm and with number of people placed in the vocational rehabilitation division may have been largely responsible for the problems described in those organizations.

Overemphasis on Highly Visible Behaviors

Difficulties often stem from the fact that some parts of the task are highly visible while other parts are not. For example, publications are easier to demonstrate than teaching, and scoring baskets and hitting home runs are more readily observable than feeding teammates and advancing base runners. Similarly, the adverse consequences of pronouncing a sick person well are more visible than those sustained by labeling a well person sick. Team-building and creativity are other examples of behaviors which may not be rewarded simply because they are hard to observe.

Hypocrisy

In some of the instances described the rewarder may have been getting the desired behavior, notwithstanding claims that the behavior was not desired. This may be true, for example, of management's attitude toward apple-polishing in the manufacturing firm (a behavior which subordinates felt was rewarded, despite management's avowed dislike of the practice). This also may explain politicians' unwillingness to revise the penalties for disobedience of ecology laws, and the failure of top management to devise reward systems which would cause systematic evaluation of training and development programs.

Emphasis on Morality or Equity Rather than Efficiency

Sometimes consideration of other factors prevents the establishment of a system which rewards behaviors desired by the rewarder. The felt obligation of many Americans to vote for one candidate or another, for example, may impair their ability to withhold support from politicians who refuse to discuss the issues. Similarly, the concern for spreading the risks and costs of wartime military service may outweigh the advantage to be obtained by commiting personnel to combat until the war is over.

It should be noted that only with respect to the first two causes are reward systems really paying off for other than desired behaviors. In the case of the third and fourth causes the system *is* rewarding behaviors desired by the rewarder, and the systems are fouled up only from the standpoints of those who believe the rewarder's public statements (cause 3), or those who seek to maximize efficiency rather than other outcomes (cause 4).

CONCLUSIONS

Modern organization theory requires a recognition that the members of organizations and society possess divergent goals and motives. It therefore is unlikely that managers and their subordinates will seek the same outcomes. Three possible remedies for this potential problem are suggested.

Selection

It is theoretically possible for organizations to employ only those individuals whose goals and motives are wholly consonant with those of management. In such cases the same behaviors judged by subordinates to be rational would be perceived by management as desirable. State-of-the-art reviews of selection techniques, however, provide scant grounds for hope that such an approach would be successful (for example, see 12).

Training

Another theoretical alternative is for the organization to admit those employees whose goals are not consonant with those of management and then, through training, socialization, or whatever, alter employee goals to make them consonant. However, research on the effectiveness of such training programs, though limited, provides further grounds for pessimism (for example, see 3).

Altering the Reward System

What would have been the result if:

1 Nixon had been assured by his advisors that he could not win reelection except by discussing the issues in detail?

2 Physicians' conduct was subjected to regular examination by review boards for type 1 errors (calling healthy people ill) and to penalties (fines, censure, etc.) for errors of either type?

3 The President of XYZ Corporation had to choose between (a) spending $11 million dollars for antipollution equipment, and (b) incurring a fifty-fifty chance of going to jail for five years?

Managers who complain that their workers are not motivated might do well to consider the possibility that they have installed reward systems which are paying off for behaviors other than those they are seeking. This, in part, is what happened in Vietnam, and this is what regularly frustrates societal efforts to bring about honest politicians, civic-minded managers, etc. This certainly is what happened in both the manufacturing and the insurance companies.

A first step for such managers might be to find out what behaviors currently are being rewarded. Perhaps an instrument similar to that used in the manufacturing firm could be useful for this purpose. Chances are excellent that these managers will be surprised by what they find—that their firms are not rewarding what they assume they are. In fact, such undesirable behavior by organizational members as they have observed may be explained largely by the reward systems in use.

This is not to say that all organizational behavior is determined by formal rewards and punishments. Certainly it is true that in the absence of formal reinforcement some soldiers will be patriotic, some presidents will be ecology minded, and some orphanage directors will care about children. The point, however, is that in such cases the rewarder is not *causing* the behaviors desired but is only a fortunate bystander. For an organization to *act* upon its members, the formal reward system should positively reinforce desired behaviors, not constitute an obstacle to be overcome.

It might be wise to underscore the obvious fact that there is nothing really new in what has been said. In both theory and practice these matters have been mentioned before. Thus in many states Good Samaritan laws have been installed to protect doctors who stop to assist a stricken motorist. In states without such laws it is commonplace for doctors to refuse to stop, for fear of involvement in a subsequent lawsuit. In college basketball additional penalties have been instituted against players who foul their opponents deliberately. It has long been argued by Milton Friedman and others that penalties should be altered so as to make it irrational to disobey the ecology laws, and so on.

By altering the reward system the organization escapes the necessity of selecting only desirable people or of trying to alter undesirable ones. In Skinnerian terms (as described in 11, p. 704), "As for responsibility and goodness—as commonly defined—no one . . . would want or need them. They refer to a man's behaving well despite the absence of positive reinforcement that is obviously sufficient to explain it. Where such reinforcement exists, 'no one needs goodness.' "

REFERENCES

1 Barnard, Chester I. *The Functions of the Executive* (Cambridge, Mass.: Harvard University Press, 1964).

2 Blau, Peter M., and W. Richard Scott. *Formal Organizations* (San Francisco: Chandler, 1962).

3 Fiedler, Fred E. "Predicting the Effects of Leadership Training and Experience from the Contingency Model," *Journal of Applied Psychology,* Vol. 56 (1972), 114–119.

4 Garland, L. H. "Studies of the Accuracy of Diagnostic Procedures," *American Journal Roentgenological, Radium Therapy Nuclear Medicine,* Vol. 82 (1959), 25–38.

5 Kerr, Steven. "Some Modifications in MBO as an OD Strategy," *Academy of Management Proceedings,* 1973, pp. 39–42.

6 Kerr, Steven. "What Price Objectivity?" *American Sociologist,* Vol. 8 (1973), 92–93.

7 Litwin, G. H., and R. A. Stringer, Jr. *Motivation and Organizational Climate* (Boston: Harvard University Press, 1968).

8 Perrow, Charles. "The Analysis of Goals in Complex Organizations," in A. Etzioni (Ed.), *Readings on Modern Organizations* (Englewood Cliffs, N.J.: Prentice-Hall, 1969).

9 Scheff, Thomas J. "Decision Rules, Types of Error, and Their Consequences in Medical Diagnosis," in F. Massarik and P. Ratoosh (Eds.), *Mathematical Explorations in Behavioral Science* (Homewood, Ill.: Irwin, 1965).

10 Simon, Herbert A. *Administrative Behavior* (New York: Free Press, 1957).

11 Swanson, G. E. "Review Symposium: Beyond Freedom and Dignity," *American Journal of Sociology,* Vol. 78 (1972), 702–705.

12 Webster, E. *Decision Making in the Employment Interview* (Montreal: Industrial Relations Center, McGill University, 1964).

How to Ruin Motivation with Pay

W. Clay Hamner

MERIT PAY—SHOULD IT BE USED?

Most behavioral scientists believe in the "law of effect," which states simply that behavior which appears to lead to a positive consequence tends to be repeated. This principle is also followed by most large organizations which have a merit pay system for their management team. Merit pay or "pay for performance" is so widely accepted by compensation managers and academic researchers that criticizing it seems foolhardy.

Despite the soundness of the principle of the law of effect on which merit pay is based, academic researchers have criticized the merit system as being detrimental to motivation rather than enhancing motivation as designed. These criticisms generally fall into one of two categories. The first group of researchers criticize the failure of the merit plan to increase the motivation of the work force because of mismanagement or lack of understanding of the merit program by managers. The second group of researchers criticize the use of merit pay because it utilizes externally mediated rewards rather than focusing on a system where individuals can be motivated by the job itself. This second criticism centers on the proposition that employees who enjoy their job (i.e., are intrinsically motivated) will lose interest in the job when a merit pay plan is introduced because they soon believe they are doing the job for the money and not because they enjoy their job. Therefore, for the first group of researchers, the recommendation is that compensation managers need to examine ways to improve the introduction of merit plans, while the second group of researchers, albeit fewer in number, would recommend that compensation managers need to deemphasize the merit pay plan system and concentrate on improving other aspects of the job.

The purpose of this presentation will be to examine the research behind both of these positions and then present recommendations which, it is hoped, will enable the compensation manager to utilize a "pay performance" plan as a method of improving the quality and quantity of job performance. Let's begin the discussion by examining possible reasons why merit pay systems fail.

REASONS WHY MERIT PAY SYSTEMS FAIL

As noted earlier, one group of researchers has concluded that the failure of merit pay plans is due not to a weakness in the law of effect, but to a weakness in its implementation by compensation managers and the line managers involved in the merit increase recommendations. For example, after reviewing pay research from General Electric and other companies, H. H. Meyer (1975) concluded that despite the apparent soundness of the simple principle on which merit pay is based, experience tells us that it does not work with such elegant simplicity. Instead, managers typically seemed to be inclined to make relatively small discriminations in salary treatment among individuals in the same job regardless of perceived differences in performance. As a matter of fact, Meyer notes, when discriminations are made, they are likely to be based on factors other than performance—such as length of service, future potential, or perceived need for "catch up," where one employee's pay seems low in relation to others in the group.

Michael Beer (see Beer & Gery, 1972), Director of Organizational Development at Corning Glass, explains why the implementation of the merit system has lost its effectiveness when he states that pay systems evolve over time and administrative considerations and tradition often override the more important considerations of behavioral outcomes in determining the shape of the system and its administration. Therefore, both of these researchers seem to say that it is not the merit pay theory that is defective. Rather, the history of the actual implementation of the theory is at fault. Let us look at the shortcomings—noted in the literature— that may cause low motivation to result from a merit pay program.

Pay Is Not Perceived as Being Related to Job Performance

Edward E. Lawler III, a leading researcher on pay and performance, has noted that one of the major reasons managers are unhappy with their wage system is that they do not perceive the relationship between how hard they work (productivity) and how much they earn. Lawler (1966), in a survey of 600 middle and lower level managers, found virtually no relationship between their pay and their rated performance. Of the managers studied, those who were most highly motivated to perform their jobs effectively were characterized by two attitudes: (1) they said that their pay was important to them and (2) they felt that good job performance would lead to higher pay for them.

There are several reasons why managers do not perceive their pay as being related to performance even when the company claims to have a merit pay plan. First, many rewards (e.g., stock options) are *deferred payments,* and the time horizon is so long that the employee loses sight of its relationship to performance. Second, the *goals* of the organization on which performance appraisals are based are either unclear, unrealistic, or unrelated to pay. W. H. Mobley (1974) found only 36 percent of the managers surveyed from a company using an MBO program saw goal attainment as having considerable bearing on their merit increase, while 83 percent of their bosses claim that they used the goal attainments to determine their pay increase recommendations. Third, the *secrecy* of the annual merit increases may lead managers to conclude that their recommended pay increase has no bearing on their past year's performance. R. L. Opsahl and M. D. Dunnette (1966) claimed that secrecy is due in part to a fear by salary administrators that they would have a difficult time mustering convincing arguments in favor of many of their practices. E. E. Lawler (1971) summarized his extensive research on secrecy of pay by stating that managers did not have an accurate picture of what other managers were earning. There was a general tendency for the managers to overstate the pay of managers at their own level (thereby reducing their own pay, relatively speaking) and at one level below them (again reducing their own pay, relatively speaking), while they tended to underestimate the pay of managers one level above them (thus reducing the value of future promotions).

Performance Ratings Are Seen as Biased

While many managers working under a merit program believe that the program is a good one, they are dissatisfied with the evaluation of their performance given them by their immediate superior. A merit plan is based on the assumption that managers can make objective (valid) distinctions between good and poor performance. Unfortunately, most evaluations of performance are subjective in nature, and consist of a "summary score" from a general (and sometimes dated) performance evaluation form. As H. H. Meyer (1975) notes, the supervisor's key role in determining pay creates a problem in that it reminds the employee very clearly that he or she is dependent on the supervisor for rewards. Therefore, the merit plan should, whenever possible, be based on objective measures (e.g., group sales, cost reduction per unit, goal obtainment, etc.) rather than subjective measures (e.g., cooperation, attitude, future potential, etc.).

As an aside, it should be noted that in the area of fair employment of minorities, both the courts (e.g., see *Rowe v. General Motors Corporation,* 1972) and the new EEOC (1974) guidelines recognize the potential of bias in subjective performance appraisals, and organizations must begin examining the validity of their performance ratings to see if they are, in fact, job related. My recent research has shown that, even when objective measures of job performance are clearly spelled out, supervisors have a tendency to rate blacks differently than whites and females differently than males even though their performance levels are identical (e.g., see Scott & Hamner, 1975; Hamner, Kim, Baird, & Bigoness, 1974). E. E. Lawler III feels that the complaints of managers and employees about the subjective nature of their performance evaluations may be a sign of a system of poor leadership. Lawler (1971) notes that many plans seem to fail not because they are mechanically defective, but because they are ineffectively introduced, there is a lack of trust between superiors and subordinates, or the quality of the supervisor is too low. He adds that no plan can succeed in the face of low trust and poor supervision, no matter how well-constructed it may be. L. W. Gruenfeld and P. Weissenberg (1966) reported support for this theory of poor leadership espoused by Lawler when they found that good managers are much more amenable than poor managers to the idea of basing pay on performance.

Rewards Are Not Viewed as Rewards

A third problem in administering a merit increase deals with management's inability to communicate accurately to the employee the information that they are trying to communicate through the pay raise. There is no doubt that the pay raise is more than money; it tells the employee "You're loved a lot," "You're only average," "You're not appreciated around here," "You'd better get busy," etc. Often management believes it is communicating a positive message to the employee, but the message being received by the employee is negative. This may have a detrimental effect on his or her future potential. Opsahl and Dunnette (1966) warn us that the relation between performing certain desired behaviors and attainment of the pay-incentive must be explicitly specified.

The reasons that the reward message may not be seen as a reward include the following (1) Conflicting reward schedules may be operating. (2) A problem of inequity among employees is perceived to exist. (3) The merit increase is threatening to the self-esteem of the employee. All three of these problems center on the fact that the pay increases are generally kept secret—thus causing the employees to draw erroneous conclusions—or on the fact that there is little or no communication in the form of coaching and counselling coming from the supervisor during the year, or following the performance appraisal. Instead, the employee is "expected to know" what the supervisor thinks about his or her performance. As Beer and Gery (1972) stated, the more frequent the formal and informal reviews of performance and the more the individual is told about reasons for an increase, the greater his preference for a merit increase and the lower his preference for a seniority system.

Conflicting Reward Schedules   Such schedules come about because of a defect in the merit plan itself. For example, individual rewards (e.g., the best manager will get a free trip to Hawaii) are set up in such a way that cooperation with other managers is discouraged, or perhaps a cost-reduction program is introduced at the expense of production, and one department (sales) suffers while another department (manufacturing) benefits in the short run. As Kenneth F. Foster, Manager of Composition at Xerox, has noted (see *Harvard Business Review,* July–August 1974), pay plans must be constantly changing because of general business conditions, shifts in management philosophy, competitive pressures, participant feedback, and modification in the structure and objectives of the organization. Nevertheless, these changes should be designed in such a way that the negative side effect of reduced cooperation does not result. For this reason, many companies are using a company-wide merit plan (e.g., the Scanlon Plan: see Frost, Wakeley, & Ruh, 1974) where there is a financial incentive to everyone in the organization based on the performance of the total organization.

Inequity   Inequity in pay can come about for one of two reasons. First, the employee perceives the merit increase to be unfair relative to his own past year's performance. That is, he is dissatisfied with the performance evaluation or else feels the performance evaluation is fair, but believes his supervisor failed to reward him in a manner consistent with his rating. A much more common problem is that while the employee may agree with the dollar amount of his pay, he perceives that others who are performing at levels below him are receiving as large an increase as he, or else those who are performing at his same level are receiving higher raises. For example, an employee who was rated as above average receives an 8 percent pay increase. He perceives this to be low since he believes that the average increase was 9 percent, when in fact it was 6½ percent. In order to avoid the feeling of inequity, which will contribute to dissatisfaction with pay and possible lower job performance, Lawler (1973) recommends that managers tell their employees how the salary raises were derived (e.g., 50 percent based on cost of living and 50 percent on merit) and tell them the range and mean of raises given in the organization for people at their job level. Lawler (1965) advocated the abandonment of secrecy policies: "There is no reason why organizations cannot make salaries public information."

Threat to Self-Esteem   H. H. Meyer, in an excellent paper, argues that the problem with merit pay plans may be more than a problem of equity. Drawing on his previous research (Meyer, Kay, & French, 1965), he concluded that 90 percent of the managers at General Electric rated themselves as above average. Bassett and Meyer (1968) and Beer and Gery (1972) found similar results. Meyer concludes that the inconsistency in the information of the merit raise with the employee's evaluation of his or her performance will be a threat to the manager's *self-esteem,* and the manager may cope with this threat by either denying the importance of hard work or disparaging the source. Meyer (1975) concludes:

> The fact that almost everyone thinks he is an above average performer probably causes most of our problems with merit pay plans. Since the salary increases most people get do not reflect superior performance (as determined by interpersonal comparisons, or as defined in the guide book for the pay plan), the effects of the actual pay increases on motivation are likely to be more negative than positive. The majority of the people feel discriminated against because, obviously, management does not recognize their true worth.

Managers of Merit Increases Are More Concerned with Satisfaction with Pay than Job Performance

Most studies which survey managers' satisfaction with their pay have shown high levels of dissatisfaction. Porter (1961) found that 80 percent of the managers surveyed from companies throughout the United States reported dissatisfaction with their pay. These same findings have been reported in surveys at General Electric (Penner, 1967) and a cross-section of managers from many companies (Lawler, 1965). Beer (Beer & Gery, 1972) points out that too often dissatisfaction with pay is assumed to mean dissatisfaction with amount. However, his research suggests that a change to a merit system with no increase in amount paid out by the company will increase satisfaction if the reasons for the increases are explained.

Opsahl and Dunnette (1966) noted that while there is a great deal of research on satisfaction with pay, there is less solid research in the area of the relationship between pay and job performance than any other field. Because of this failure to deal with the role of pay, Lawler (1966) notes that many managers have come to the erroneous conclusion that the experts in "human relations" have shown that pay is a relatively unimportant incentive.

In fact, Cherrington, Reitz, and Scott (1971) found that the magnitude of the relationship between satisfaction and performance depends primarily upon the performance-reinforcer contingencies that have been arranged (i.e., people who were appropriately reinforced were satisfied with their pay, while those people who were dissatisfied with their pay were those who were inappropriately rewarded). Likewise, Hamner and Foster (1974) found that the best performers working under a contingent (piece rate) pay plan were more satisfied than the poorer performers, but that there was no relationship between satisfaction and performance for those paid under a noncontingent (across the board) pay plan.

Managers need to be concerned with two questions. First, *is the merit raise being based on performance?* Numerous studies (e.g., see Lee, 1969; Belcher, 1974) show that pay is not closely related to performance in many organizations that claim to have merit raises. Typically, these studies show that pay is much more closely related to job level and seniority than performance. In fact, Belcher (1974) reports that low, zero, and even negative correlations between pay and supervisory ratings of performance occur even among managers where the correlation would be expected to be high.

Second, *who is doing the complaining?* Donald Finn, Compensation Manager at J. C. Penney, says we are often "hung up" as managers about the satisfaction of employees with our pay recommendations. He says:

> So who is complaining and why? If low producers are low earners, the pay plan is working—but there will be complaints. If a company wants an incentive plan in which rewards are commensurate with risk, it must be willing to accept a relatively broad range of earnings and corresponding degrees of manager satisfaction. (*Harvard Business Review*, July–August, 1974, pg. 8)

Beer agrees with Finn when he says:

> A merit system can probably be utilized effectively by management in motivating employees. This concept has been in disfavor lately, but our findings indicate that more might be done with money in motivating people, particularly those who are work and achievement oriented in the first place.
>
> While a merit system would seem to be less need satisfying to the security-oriented individual and, therefore, potentially less motivating, there is probably a net gain in installing a merit system. Those who are high in achievement oriented needs will be stimulated by such a system to greater heights of performance, while those high in security-oriented needs will become more dissatisfied and it is hoped, will leave. (Beer & Gery, 1972, p. 330)

Trust and Openness about Merit Increases Is Low

A merit system will not be accepted and may not have the intended motivational effects if managers do not actively administer a performance appraisal system, practice good human relations, explain the reasons for the increases and ensure that employees are not forgotten when eligibility dates come and go. The organization must provide an open climate with respect to pay, and an environment where work and effort are valued (Beer & Gery, 1972).

The Xerox Corporation has recognized the problem of trust and openness and states a philosophy that "If pay and satisfaction is to be high, pay rates must vary according to job demands in such a way that each perceived increment in a job demand factor will lead to increased pay" (*Xerox Compensation Planning Model,* June 1972). This same document at Xerox notes that organizations expect extremely high levels of trust on the part of their employees, in that:

(a) Only 72% of 184 employing organizations had a written statement of the firm's basic compensation policy covering such matters as paying competitive salaries, timing of wage and salary increases, and how raises are determined.

(b) Only 51% of these same organizations communicate their general compensation policies directly to all employees, while 21% communicate the policy only to managers.

(c) Contrarily, 69% of the firms do not provide their employees with wage and salary schedules or progression plans that apply to their own categories, thus indicating a low trust level toward employees.

(d) Over 50% of the firms do not tell their employees where this information is available.

(e) In only 48% of the firms do managers have access to salary schedules applying to their own level in the organization, and in only 18% of the companies do managers have knowledge of the salaries of other managers at their own level or higher levels. (*Xerox Compensation Planning Model,* June, 1972, pp. 68–69)

SOME ORGANIZATIONS VIEW MONEY AS THE PRIMARY MOTIVATOR, IGNORING THE IMPORTANCE OF THE JOB ITSELF

The first five shortcomings deal with the criticism of researchers that the failure of the merit plan is due to poor implementation, and not due to a weakness in the theory of the "law of effect." However, the sixth shortcoming under discussion now centers on the second criticism that employees who have intrinsically interesting jobs will lose interest in the job when a merit pay plan is introduced. An intrinsically motivating job can be defined as one that is interesting and creative enough that certain pleasures or rewards are derived from completing the task itself. Until recently, most theories dealing with worker motivation (e.g., Porter & Lawler, 1968) have assumed that the effects of intrinsic and extrinsic reinforcement (e.g., merit pay) are additive; i.e., a worker will be more motivated to complete a task which combined both kinds of rewards than a task where only one kind of reward is present.

Deci (1971, 1972a, b), among others (Likert, 1967; Vroom & Deci, 1970), criticizes behavioral scientists who advocate a system of employee motivation that utilizes externally mediated rewards, i.e., rewards such as money administered by someone other than the employee. In so doing, according to Deci, management is attempting to control the employee's behavior so he or she will do as told. The limitations of this method of worker motivation, for Deci, is that it only satisfies a person's "lower order" needs (Maslow, 1943) and does not take into account "higher order" needs for self-esteem and self-actualization.

Deci recommends that we should move away from a method of external control, and toward a system where individuals can be motivated by the job itself. He says that this approach will allow managers to focus on higher-order needs where the rewards are mediated by the recipient (intrinsically motivated). To motivate employees intrinsically, tasks should be designed which are interesting, creative, and resourceful, and workers should have some say in decisions which concern them "so they will feel like causal agents in the activities which they engage in" (Deci, 1972b, p. 219).

Deci has introduced evidence which reportedly shows that a person's intrinsic motivation to perform an activity decreases when he or she receives contingent monetary payment for performing an interesting task. Deci concludes from these findings that:

> Interpreting these results in relation to theories of work motivation, it seems clear that the effects of intrinsic motivation and extrinsic motivation are not additive. While extrinsic rewards such as money can certainly motivate behavior, they appear to be doing so at the expense of intrinsic motivation; as a result, contingent payment systems do not appear to be comparable with participative management systems. (1972b, pp. 224–225)

Deci brings out an important point: Managers should not use pay to offset a boring or negative task. However, like Herzberg before him, his results don't appear to completely support his conclusion about the effect of money as a motivator. Research by both Hamner and Foster (1974) and Calder and Staw (1975) has shown that the effect of intrinsic and extrinsic monetary rewards is additive and that even Deci's results themselves, on close examination, support this more traditional argument. In addition, I am not sure that merit pay plans are incompatible with a participative management system. The noted psychologist B. F. Skinner offers advice to managers on both of these last two arguments.

Skinner recommends that the organization should design feedback and incentive systems in such a way that the dual objective of getting things done and making work enjoyable are met. He says:

> It is important to remember that an incentive system isn't the only factor to take into account. How pleasant work conditions are, how easy or awkward a job is, how good or bad tools are—many things of that sort make an enormous difference in what a worker will do for what he receives. One problem of the production-line worker is that he seldom sees any of the ultimate consequences of his work. He puts on left front wheels day in and day out and he may never see the finished car . . . (1973, p. 39)

Skinner also suggested that people be involved in the design of the contingencies of reinforcements (in this case, merit pay plans) under which they live. This way the rewards come from the behavior of the worker in the environment, and not the supervisor. Both Kenneth F. Foster at Xerox and Joe W. Rogers, Chairman of the Board of Waffle House, agree. Foster, commenting on the McDonald pay plan said, "McDonald's management is to be commended for recognizing a number of important incentive reward axioms. Foremost, the reward system must be meaningful to the recipient. They must also see it as equitable and its financial outcomes and rewards as within their power to control" (*Harvard Business Review*, July–August 1974, p. 5). Rogers agreed, saying, "In the restaurant industry, a bonus system must be self-monitoring and deal only with the facts. All areas of judgment by a friendly or unfriendly superior should be absent in a bonus system. . . . Let people participate in the design of the new pay. Credibility with the participants is much more critical" (Ibid., p. 6).

Deci's recommendation that jobs be designed so that they are interesting, creative, and resourceful should be wholeheartedly supported by proponents of a merit pay plan. Skinner warns managers that too much dependency on force and a poorly designed monetary reward system may actually reduce performance, while designing the task so that it is automatically reinforcing can have positive effects on performance. He says:

> The behavior of an employee is important to the employer, who gains when the employee works industriously and carefully. How is he to be induced to do so? The standard answer was once physical force; men worked to avoid punishment or death. The by-products were troublesome, however, and economics is perhaps the first field in which an explicit change was made to positive reinforcement. Most men now work, as we say, "for money."
>
> Money is not a natural reinforcer; it must be conditioned as such. Delayed reinforcement, as in a weekly wage, raises a special problem. No one works on Monday morning because he is reinforced by a paycheck on Friday afternoon. The employee who is paid by the week works during the week to avoid losing the standard of living which depends on a weekly system. Rate of work is determined by the supervisor and special aversive contingencies maintain quality. The pattern is therefore still aversive. It has often been pointed out that the attitude of the production-line worker toward his work differs conspicuously from that of the craftsman, who is envied by workers and industrial managers alike. One explanation is that the craftsman is reinforced by more than monetary consequences, but another important difference is that when a craftsman spends a week completing a given set object, each of the parts produced during the week is likely to be automatically reinforcing because of its place in the completed object (Skinner, 1969, p. 18).

RECOMMENDATIONS FOR OVERCOMING FAILURES IN MERIT PAY SYSTEMS

In the discussion of the shortcomings of merit pay plans, my suggestions for overcoming these deficiencies have been implied or suggested. Let us briefly review and outline several of these suggestions as a point of departure for our discussion.

1 *Openness and trust should be stressed by the compensation manager.* As a minimum, employees should know the formula for devising the merit increases and should be told the range and mean of the pay increases for people at their job level. This alone should reduce some of the feeling of low self-esteem and inequity present in many organizations today.

2 *Supervisors should be trained in rating and feedback techniques.* Compensation managers should help personnel design and carry out training programs which emphasize the necessity of having consistency between performance ratings, other forms of feedback, and pay increases. In addition, managers should be trained to emphasize objective rather than subjective areas of job performance. Skinner sees one of the greatest weaknesses in the motivation of workers through reinforcement principles as due to poor training of managers. He says that what must be accomplished, and what he believes is currently lacking, is an effective training program for managers. "In the not too distant future, a new breed of industrial managers may be able to apply the principles of operant conditioning effectively" (*Organizational Dynamics,* 1973, p. 40).

3 *Components of the annual pay increase should be clearly and openly specified.* Compensation managers need to allocate a certain percentage for a cost-of-living increase (not to cover the total cost of living, however) and a percentage for merit. The percentage for merit should be an average and not a maximum, and the manager should be able to distribute this percentage in any way he or she deems appropriate. In other words, it should not be an either-or situation where the worker either gets the full amount of the merit increase or none at all. Any pay increase due to an adjustment for past inequities and pay increases due to promotions should come out of the payroll increase first, but should not be included in the stated average pay increase. Frequently, if the organization can afford a 10 percent increase in wages and benefits, it might take 2 percent of wages and benefits to use for the adjustments mentioned above, and then allocate an 8 percent average increase to cost of living (e.g., 4 percent) and merit (e.g., 4 percent). Therefore, the range of pay increases would be from 4 percent to 12 percent—not including adjustments—where the average for the department would be 8 percent. Along these same lines, I feel it is important to give the increases in percentages and not dollar amounts since managers have a tendency to "cheat" long-term good performers (i.e., high pay managers) when a dollar amount is used.

4 *Each organization should tailor its pay plan to the needs of the organization and individuals therein—with participation a key factor in the merit pay plan design.* One of the reasons the Scanlon plan has been so successful is that it combines participation with the company's ability to afford a merit increase. Workers understand how they get the increase they do and why it is the amount it is. In addition each company using a Scanlon approach has a unique pay plan designed especially for that organization by the members of the organization.

5 *Don't overlook other rewards.* Compensation managers should work with other staff people in the organization to improve the climate of the organization, the task design, and other forms of feedback to ensure that an employee has as much chance of success as possible.

ETHICAL IMPLICATIONS: EXCHANGE, NOT CONTROL

No discussion of effective uses of merit pay plans would be complete without a discussion of the compensation manager's ethical responsibilities in using pay as a motivator. There is no doubt that poorly designed reward structures can interfere with the development of spontaneity and creativity. Reinforcement systems which are deceptive and manipulative are an insult to everyone's integrity. The employee should be a willing party to any attempt to influence, with both parties benefiting from the relationship.

Nord (1974), referring to a well designed incentive plan, says:

> I would add that to the degree that such approaches increase the effectiveness of man's exchanges with his environment, the potential for expanding freedom seems undeniable. To me these outcomes seem highly humanistic, although, for some reason this approach is labeled anti-humanistic and approaches which appear to have less potential for human advancement are labeled humanistic.

I concur with Nord, and think the ethical responsibility of compensation managers is clear. The first step in the ethical use of monetary control in organizations is the understanding by managers of the determination of behavior (see Hamner, 1974). Since reinforcement is the single most important concept in the learning process, managers must learn how to design effective reinforcement programs that will encourage productive and creative employees. This presentation has attempted to outline the knowledge and research available for this endeavor.

REFERENCES

Bassett, G. L., & Meyer, H. H. Performance appraisal based on self review. *Personnel Psychology,* 1968, **21,** 421–430.

Beer, M., & Gery, G. J. Individual and organizational correlates of pay system preferences. In H. L. Tosi, R. House, & M. D. Dunnette (Eds.), *Managerial Motivation and Compensation.* East Lansing, Michigan: Michigan State University Press, 1972.

Belcher, D. W. *Compensation Administration.* Englewood Cliffs, N.J.: Prentice-Hall, 1974.

Blood, M. R. Applied behavioral analysis from an organizational perspective. Paper presented at the 82nd Annual Convention of the American Psychological Association, New Orleans, August 1974.

Calder, B. J., & Straw, B. M. The interaction of intrinsic and extrinsic motivation: Some methodological notes. *Journal of Personality and Social Psychology,* 1975, **31,** 599–605.

Case of Big Mac's pay plans. *Harvard Business Review,* July–August 1974, 1–8.

Cherrington, D. L., Reitz, H. J., & Scott, W. E. Effects of reward and contingent reinforcement on satisfaction and task performance. *Journal of Applied Psychology,* 1971, **55,** 531–536.

Deci, E. L. Effects of externally mediated rewards on intrinsic motivation. *Journal of Personality and Social Psychology,* 1971, **18,** 105–115.

Deci, E. L. Work: Who does not like it and why? *Psychology Today.* August 1972(a), **92,** 57–58.

Deci, E. L. The effects of contingent and noncontingent rewards and controls on intrinsic motivation. *Organizational Behavior and Human Performance.* 1972(b), **8,** 217–229.

Drucker, P. F. Beyond the stick and carrot: Hysteria over the work ethic. *Psychology Today,* November 1973, **87,** 89–93.

Employer survey finds most like their work. *Equinews,* March 18, 1974 (Vol. III, No. 6).

Equal Employment Opportunity Commission Guidelines (Rev. ed.). Washington, D.C.: U.S. Government Printing Office, 1974.

Frost, C. F., Wakeley, J. H., & Ruh, R. A. *The Scanlon Plan for Organization Development: Identity, Participation and Equity.* East Lansing: Michigan State University Press, 1974.

Gruenfeld, L. W., & Weissenberg, P. Supervisory characteristics and attitudes toward performance appraisals. *Personnel Psychology,* 1966, 143–152.

Hamner, W. Clay. Reinforcement theory and contingency management in organizational settings. In H. L. Tosi & W. C. Hamner (Eds.), *Management and Organizational Behavior: A Contingency Approach,* Chicago: St. Clair Press, 1974.

Hamner, W. Clay, Kim, J., Baird, L., & Bigoness, W. Race and sex as determinants of ratings by "potential" employees in a simulated work sampling task. *Journal of Applied Psychology,* 1974, **59,** 705–711.

Hamner, W. Clay, & Foster, L. W. Are intrinsic and extrinsic rewards additive? A test of Deci's cognitive evaluation theory. Paper presented at the National Academy of Management, Seattle, 1974.

Lawler, E. E. Managers' perceptions of their subordinates' pay and of their superiors' pay. *Personnel Psychology*, 1965, **18**, 413–422.

Lawler, E. E. The mythology of management compensation. *California Management Review*, 1966, **9**, 11–22.

Lawler, E. E. *Pay and Organizational Effectiveness*. New York: McGraw-Hill, 1971.

Lawler, E. E. *Motivation in Work Organization*. Monterey, Calif.: Brooks/Cole, 1973.

Lee, S. M. Salary equity: Its determination, analysis and correlates. Unpublished doctoral dissertation, University of Georgia, 1969.

Likert, R. *New Patterns of Management* (2nd ed.). New York: McGraw-Hill, 1967.

Maslow, A. H. A theory of human motivation. *Psychological Review*, 1943, **50**, 370–396.

Meyer, H. H. The pay for performance dilemma. *Organizational Dynamics*, 1975, **3**(3), 39–50.

Meyer H. H., Kay, E., & French, J. R. P. Split roles in performance appraisals. *Harvard Business Review*, January-February 1965, 123–129.

Mobley, W. H. The link between MBO and merit compensation. *Personnel Journal*, June 1974, 423–427.

Nord, W. R. Some issues in the application of operant conditioning to the management of organizations. Paper presented at the National Academy of Management, Seattle, 1974.

Opsahl, R. L., & Dunnette, M. D. The role of financial compensation in industrial motivation. *Psychological Bulletin*, 1966, **66**, 94–118.

Penner, D. D. A study of the causes and consequences of salary satisfaction. *Behavioral Research Service Report*, General Electric Company, 1967.

Porter, L. W. A study of perceived need satisfactions in bottom and middle management jobs. *Journal of Applied Psychology*, 1961, **45**, 1–10.

Porter, L. W., & Lawler, E. E. *Managerial Attitudes and Performance*. Homewood, Ill.: Irwin-Dorsey, 1968.

Rowe vs. General Motors Corporation, 457 F 2d. 348 (5th Cir. 1972).

Scott, W. E., & Hamner, W. Clay. The influence of variations in performance profiles on the performance evaluation process: An examination of the validity of the criteria. *Organizational Behavior and Human Performance*, 1975, **14**, 360–370.

Skinner, B. F. *Contingencies of Reinforcement*. New York: Appleton-Century-Crofts, 1969.

Skinner, B. F. Conversations with B. F. Skinner. *Organizational Dynamics*. Winter 1973, 31–40.

Vroom, V. H., & Deci, E. L. An overview of work motivation. In V. H. Vroom & E. L. Deci (Eds.), *Management and Motivation*. Baltimore: Penguin Press, 1970.

Xerox Compensation Planning Model. Rochester, N.Y.: Xerox Corporation, June 1972.

New Approaches to Total Compensation

E. E. Lawler III

The charge is often made that major innovations in personnel administration are few and far between. Furthermore, it is noted that even when innovations are suggested, adoption and dissemination are painfully slow. Although this charge can be made in most areas, it seems to apply to the area of compensation particularly well. In many respects, it is not surprising that innovations in compensation practice are rare. The field is a mature one and the costs associated with unsuccessful innovation are great. Possibly because the risks are so great, the innovation which takes place tends to concentrate on making small improvements in already existing technologies (e.g., adding to or reducing the number of factors in a job evaluation system, improving a fringe benefit, or adding a new one like dental insurance). Against this background of low innovation, four "new" approaches stand out. None of them represent radical changes, although each of them, in its own way, takes an old problem or practice and casts it in a new light. They all have been around for a few years and there is some evidence that under the right conditions they can work. Thus, although they are different, they are not completely untried or unproven.

The remainder of this chapter will be devoted to reviewing each of them in the hope that the discussion of their strengths, weaknesses, and applicability under different circumstances will lead to their further adoption and development. The oldest of the new approaches, the all-salaried work force, will be discussed first. Skill-based job evaluation systems will be discussed next. Finally, two approaches (cafeteria or flexible benefits and lump sum salary increases) to allowing individuals to determine parts of their compensation packages will be considered.

THE ALL-SALARIED WORK FORCE

Most organizations distinguish between their management and non-management employees in terms of the fringe benefits provided and whether employees are paid on an hourly or salaried basis. As a rule, hourly employees punch time clocks, lose pay when they are late, and have little, if any, sick leave or personal leave. Salaried employees, on the other hand, do not punch time clocks, do not lose pay if they are a little late, and have well-developed, often generous, leave programs. The idea of putting all employees on salary seems to be slowly growing in popularity. It is not a new idea in the sense of only recently being thought of and implemented. Some organizations have used it for decades (e.g., IBM). It is a new idea, however, as far as most organizations are concerned since they typically have not tried or, in some cases, even heard of the all-salaried approach. Given that the all-salary idea has been around since at least the 1930s, this is dramatic

Reprinted from E. E. Lawler III, *Pay and organization development*. Reading, Mass.: Addison-Wesley, 1981, pp. 61–79. Reprinted by permission.

testimony to the slowness with which innovations in compensation practice are adopted.

The presumed advantages of the all-salaried approach include increases in both organizational effectiveness and the quality of work life (Hulme and Bevan 1975). The all-salaried work force is supposed to increase organizational effectiveness by reducing administrative costs and producing more committed and loyal employees. It is supposed to increase the quality of work life of employees because it gives them more flexibility and treats them as mature and responsible adults.

There is some evidence that workers do prefer to be on salary. Typical of these data are the results of a survey I did with G.D. Jenkins in a New England factory. Such a plan was strongly favored by 55 percent of the work force but it was opposed by about 30 percent of the employees. A company president, in commenting on his own experiences, has pointed out one reason why employees do not like salary pay plans: "We took the right not to work away from our people by putting them on salary. When they chose to go hunting or fishing or drinking instead of coming to work, it didn't make sense to them to be paid for not working. They felt a little guilty, so they didn't enjoy the day off. They couldn't understand how the company could stay in business that way—which is a helluva good perception" (Sheridan 1975).

All-salary plans are also sometimes opposed by some employees because they feel other employees will take advantage of it (i.e., be absent more) and, as a result, they will have to do more work. Overall, however, most employees do prefer a salary plan to an hourly plan because it accords them more mature treatment and eliminates an inequity that is experienced when some, but not all, employees are on salary. In addition, when it grants the same fringe benefits and perquisites as those given to managers and white collar employees, it often means improved benefits. Thus it probably does represent an improvement in the quality of work life for most people.

The United Auto Workers (UAW) has raised the issue of all-salary plans with the big three auto manufacturers in past negotiations, and it has been implemented in one UAW contract (Kinetic Dispersion). Still, there has been little widespread union support for the idea. Some unions see all-salary plans as a strategy to prevent unionization (for example, at Boston Edison); in fact, all-salary plans have been implemented mostly by nonunion companies. IBM, for example, went to an all-salary plan in the 1950s, as did Gillette. Still, because most workers seem to prefer salary plans, there is good reason for unions to make them a negotiable issue.

There is no solid evidence to indicate that an all-salary pay plan contributes to organizational effectiveness. Although it is frequently argued that such a plan produces increased commitment to the organization, there is nothing but secondary evidence to support this claim. Typical of the kind of statements that are made is the following one by Frank Pluta of Kinetic Dispersion Corporation: "I don't think the men work any harder as a result, but there are some benefits to the company. There is a sense of loyalty. And the men come up with ideas to help keep things going a little better. There is an easy kind of relationship between the workers and supervisors. I can't say there has been a measurable gain in productivity, but the employees will help you to innovate, especially in a time of short-ages" (Sheridan 1975). This statement probably represents a valid assessment of how most employees react to all-salary plans. Still, it would be useful to have some solid data showing what benefits come about when employees are placed on salary plans. The major place where benefits are likely to show up is in turnover. To the extent that it makes working for a particular organization more attractive (something it should do since it is a desired approach), it should help to reduce turnover, and this can contribute to organizational effectiveness.

Critics of the all-salary idea argue that there is a real danger that it will lead to increased absenteeism and tardiness. They argue that when time clocks disappear and the threat of lost pay decreases, employees may think they have been granted a license to cheat the company. The counterargument to this is that workers will be less motivated to cheat because the company has trusted them (besides, who says you cannot cheat on a time clock?). Just because a time clock is not present does not mean that management cannot be concerned when people do not come to work or show up late. Management has not given up its right to notice and dismiss individuals who do not show up on time or are frequently absent. White collar workers show up even though they are not on time clocks, and there is little reason to believe they are more responsible than hourly employees.

Unfortunately, there is little firm evidence as to whether or not all-salary plans lead to higher absenteeism and tardiness rates. A number of companies (e.g., Gillette and Dow Chemical) have been quoted as saying that when they moved to an all-salary plan, absenteeism either went down or stayed the same (see Hulme and Bevan 1975). Others report that all-salary plans have led to a slight increase in absenteeism. There simply is not adequate evidence to indicate what the most common effect is. A good guess is that the effect depends very much on such other factors as the style of management, the nature of the job, and the attention given to absenteeism.

If the all-salary pay plan is the only thing management does to get employees involved in their work and to communicate to them that they are expected to be responsible, it probably will not decrease absenteeism and tardiness. Although such a plan gives workers a message that they are trusted, it has to compete with a lot of other messages that say they are not. This message is often a difficult one to get across and cannot stand a lot of competition, particularly when the desired behavior (coming to work) has to compete with other attractive alternatives (such as recreation and shopping). If, however, an all-salary plan is combined with more challenging jobs, greater decision-making latitude, and other changes in the reward system, it can be a useful base on which to build a better relationship between the organization and the individual. This in turn could reduce absenteeism. If all-salary pay is to help reduce absenteeism and tardiness, supervisors must take an active role in dealing with them. Rules must be made and enforced, and the few that abuse the privilege must be disciplined. As will be discussed later, this discipline does not have to come from the supervisor; it can come from the work groups, but it must come.

In summary, the all-salary pay system appears to be a promising approach that can increase both the quality of work life and organizational effectiveness. However, it is not likely to be universally accepted; nor should it be; since it is not likely to be universally effective. It is likely to be effective only if it is part of an overall management strategy and organization design that emphasizes employee participation, meaningful work, and mature treatment of employees.

SKILL-BASED JOB EVALUATION SYSTEMS

The idea of paying the person and not the job is a common one in many professional organizations (e.g., universities, law offices, and research and development labs). However, it has not been used for lower level jobs in most organizations. Its recent application to production and service jobs in some companies is therefore potentially important. It represents a fundamentally different approach to determining total compensation in these situations—one which seems to be applicable in a variety of situations and which fits with a more participative approach to management. Perhaps its greatest strength is that it communicates to the employee a concern for the development of his or her skills. This is in notable contrast to traditional job evaluation plans, which tend to communicate a concern for job descriptions, job evaluation, and market comparisons.

The plan at the Topeka plant of General Foods provides a good example of how a skill evaluation pay plan works. It is based on a starting rate given to new employees upon first entering the plant. After entry, employees are advanced one pay grade for each job they learn. Jobs can be learned in any sequence and all jobs earn equal amounts of additional pay. When all the jobs in the plant are mastered, the top or plant rate is obtained. Employees are given encouragement and support to learn new jobs, but it usually takes a minimum of two years for an employee to learn all the jobs. The members of an individual's work team decide when a job has been mastered. After individuals have learned all the jobs, they continue to rotate among the same jobs, but the only opportunity they have for additional pay lies in acquiring a specialty rate which is given to an individual who has gained expertise in a skilled trade, such as pipe fitting. In one plant which has a skill-based plan like the Topeka one, employees are also given the opportunity to learn about the economics of the business. When they can pass a test based on it, they receive additional pay, just as if they have mastered a new maintenance or production skill.

Analysis of the Topeka plant reports that the pay plan seems to be successfully contributing to both organizational effectiveness and a high quality of work life (Lawler 1978; Walton 1972, 1975). Organizational effectiveness seems to have come about because of the flexibility of the work force, the broader perspective of the work force on how the plant operates, and the low level of turnover. A high quality of work life seems to have been achieved because the plan reinforces a spirit of personal growth and development and produces wage rates that are perceived to be equitable. The latter point is supported by the data collected by Jenkins and myself. Several years after the plant opened we compared the attitudes toward pay of the Topeka employees with those of employees in other similar plants that did not have skill-based pay plans; the result was some rather dramatic differences. The Topeka plant had much higher levels of pay satisfaction, and the employees generally felt their pay was well and fairly administered. The plant also showed very low absenteeism and turnover rates. In this one case, a skill-based pay plan did seem to have contributed to both organizational effectiveness and a high quality of work life.

Despite their high degree of promise, skill-based pay plans are not without their problems. Even under such plans, for example, individuals run up against the top end of a pay range because they have learned all the jobs there are to learn. There is nowhere to go financially unless some type of bonus or other performance-based system is used. This "topping-out" effect may be a substantial problem as a plant matures and many people reach the top pay rate. Depending on the complexity of the plant or work situation, this may take anywhere from a few months to a few years. It may also become a more serious problem if a highly trained work force is developed whose skills cannot be used fully by the organization. So far, this does not seem to have become a problem in any of the skill-based plans. It has apparently been negated by the selective use of promotion and by the fact that not all employees want to learn all jobs. At Topeka, for example, some employees stopped learning jobs after they mastered five or fewer of them.

These plans also require a tremendous investment in training. This investment can take many costly forms, ranging from formal classroom education to having inexperienced individuals doing jobs to add to their skills. In order to control training costs in some complex production facilities, employees are limited to learning jobs in their immediate work area. That way no one employee is likely to ever learn all the jobs in the plant. This is done to limit the amount of training that has to be done and to be sure that individuals will be performing a job they know well. My interviews in several plants indicate that as long as there is a variety of jobs to be learned in the work area, the effectiveness of the skill-based approach is not harmed by this approach.

The desire of employees to learn new jobs can also cause problems if it is not managed well. Since the pay system rewards individuals for learning new jobs, it can lead to situations where an employee wants to move on to a new job as soon as he or she has mastered the previous one. If people are moved as soon as they learn a job, an organization can rapidly find itself in the position of having most tasks being performed by individuals who are just learning how to do them. The impact of this on organizational effectiveness can be quite negative.

Three approaches have been successfully used to see that most tasks are assigned to individuals who know how to perform them. The first is to specify a performance period for each task. Individuals are required to perform the job for a certain period of time *after* they have mastered the job. The second is to install an individual performance pay plan in combination with the skill-based plan. This has the effect of evaluating and rewarding individuals for learning the job and continuing to perform it well. The third approach is to install a plant level performance pay system. As will be discussed further in later chapters, this increases the motivation of people to see that the organization is functioning effectively and makes it less likely that individuals will end up performing jobs they cannot perform well. In essence, it creates a countervailing force to the one created by the skill-based system.

Another problem that has arisen with skill-based pay plans is setting pay rates. Most pay plans set pay rates in terms of the rates paid for similar jobs in the same community. This is difficult with skill-based plans, however, because the emphasis is on individuals, not on jobs. Because each organization has its own unique configuration of jobs that individuals learn, it is unlikely that individuals with similar skills can be found elsewhere. The situation is further complicated by the fact that an organization that has a skill-based plan is likely to be the only one in the community with such a plan. My interviews at the Topeka plant indicated that the employees had no clearly developed idea of whose pay their pay should be compared with. They did feel that their pay should be higher than that of people who did only one of the jobs they did, but beyond that, many had no clear position. A few did compare their pay to that of foremen in other plants because they felt they had as much responsibility as they, and, in some cases, more skills. Although the lack of community pay comparisons makes setting pay rates more difficult, it can help to reduce turnover because it tends to create situations in which individuals have no options that are nearly as attractive in terms of pay level and skill utilization.

Like the all-salary pay plan idea, skill-based plans are not likely to be effective in all situations. It is interesting to note that most of the plants where skill-based plans have been used successfully are essentially process production plants (for example, chemicals or bulk food). This seems to be a production technology where it is particularly advantageous to use skill evaluation plans. With process production, there is a definite advantage to having employees know a number of jobs and understand the total plant as a system. The latter is particularly important in process plants because jobs are so highly interrelated.

The type of production technology may also moderate the desire of employees to have a skill-based plan. As part of an experiment in worker participation in pay system design workers were asked to vote on whether or not they wanted a skill-based plan (Lawler and Jenkins 1976). They voted it down, giving as one reason that they were skilled machinists who wanted to learn their own jobs better. There might have been some advantages to the company if the machinists had wanted to learn other jobs—it would have created a more flexible work force. The advantages would have been limited though because of the nature of the workflow. The company manufactures products in a way that creates fairly independent jobs. The employees finally decided in favor of a system that would pay individuals more as they became more skilled at operating a single machine.

Overall, skill-based plans appear to be a promising approach to administering rewards in a way that will provide a high quality of work life and contribute to organizational effectiveness. They seem to be particularly appropriate in process production plants, in situations where skill acquisition and personal growth should be emphasized, and in situations where they fit the overall management style of the organization.

LUMP SUM SALARY INCREASES

Most organizations provide no flexibility for an employee as to when pay raises are received. Although many organizations speak in terms of annual salary increases, all but a few organizations give raises by adjusting the regular paychecks of employees. For example, if employees are paid weekly, their weekly paycheck is increased to reflect the amount of their annual salary increase. Similar changes are made for employees paid on a biweekly or monthly basis. This approach allows employees absolutely no flexibility with respect to when they receive their raises. They have to wait a full year to get the full amount of their annual increase. This approach often has the effect of perceptually burying a raise so that it is hardly visible to the recipient. Once the annual raise is divided up among regular paychecks and the tax deductions are made, very little change appears in an employee's take-home pay.

Recognizing these problems, a few organizations (e.g., Aetna, B.F. Goodrich, Timex, and Westinghouse) have started lump sum increase programs that are aimed at making salary increases more flexible and visible and, at the same time, communicating to their employees that they are willing to do innovative things in the area of pay administration. Under a lump sum increase program, employees are given the opportunity to decide when they will receive their annual increase. Just about any option is available, including receiving it *all* in one lump sum at the beginning of the year. Employees can also choose to have the increases folded into their regular paychecks, as has been done in the past. The following quote from a publication of an insurance company that has installed such a plan illustrates the philosophy behind it:

> The Lump Sum Increase Program (LSIP) is a payment option offering you the flexibility to tailor part of your total compensation to your specific needs. Under this program you can elect to receive all or part of any salary increase—whether merit, promotional, or a special adjustment—in the form of one lump sum payment (less a small discount for payment in advance). By making the full amount of your increase available as soon as it is effective, LSIP allows you to plan realistically for large expenditures without using retail credit plans having high interest rates.

Each year employees can make new choices. They are not bound by any of their past choices, and each year they have the opportunity to allocate not only the current year's raise but also the raises from some of the years since the program began. The number of raises that can be taken as a lump sum varies from two in some companies to all past raises in others. In some cases this can give individuals a considerable amount of flexibility in when they receive a significant portion of their total compensation.

In most plans, the money that is advanced to employees is treated as a loan. This means that if an employee quits before the end of the year, the portion of the increase which has not yet been earned has to be paid back. Also, because the money is advanced to individuals before they earn it, in some plans they are charged interest to offset the cash flow problem such payments cause the company.

Unfortunately, there is no research evidence on how effective the lump sum program is. All that can be reported so far is that most employees who are subject to it seem to be enthusiastic about it. Most employees, for example, seem to opt for a lump sum when they have the chance. One article estimates that from 40 to

95 percent of the employees in firms offering the plans have chosen a lump sum payment (Smith 1979). Lower acceptance rates seem to come when the money is treated as a loan and interest is charged. Employee acceptance of the idea is not surprising since it costs individuals very little and gives them the opportunity to shape their income to fit their unique needs and desires. In short, a lump sum program represents one way in which employees are treated more as individuals by the organizations that employ them and, as such, it improves the quality of work life.

There are some reasons to believe lump sum increases can also contribute to organizational effectiveness. For one thing, the costs involved to an organization are minimal. The administration of a lump sum increase plan does involve some extra costs because it requires extra bookkeeping and record keeping. There are also some situations where money is lost because employees quit and do not pay back the advances they receive. However, organizations need not lose interest income on the cash they advance since they can charge interest on it. Most organizations that have tried the plan so far have charged relatively low interest rates. These organizations realize that they might be able to invest their cash more profitably but they feel, nevertheless, that the lump sum program is worthwhile. One organization even decided to charge no interest.

What are the advantages to an organization that provides a lump sum increase plan? The major positive outcome should be that it makes working for the organization more attractive. All other things being equal, organizations that give employees choices about when they will receive their pay increases should have a competitive advantage in attracting and retaining employees. Like other practices that make organizations more attractive, the lump sum plan can pay off in a number of ways—better selection ratios, lower turnover, and lower absenteeism. These, in turn, can result in lower personnel costs and a more talented group of employees.

Giving lump sum increases also increases the visibility of the amount of a salary increase. A large raise tends to come across clearly as a large amount of money, and a small raise comes across as just what it is—a small increase. Increasing the saliency of the amount of a raise may or may not be functional for an organization; it depends on how well pay is administered by the organization. If pay is administered in an arbitrary and nonperformance-based manner, then it is hardly functional to highlight the size of an increase. On the other hand, if an organization does a good job of administering pay, then increasing the saliency of raises can be functional. When increases are based on performance, the lump sum approach has the potential of making pay a more effective motivator because pay will be more clearly tied to performance. If pay increases are equitably distributed, lump sum increases can make this clear, thereby increasing pay satisfaction and reducing the tendency of individuals to look for other jobs. On the other hand, if pay increases are inequitably distributed, lump sum increases can highlight this.

In summary, the lump sum increase approach is usually seen as an attractive benefit by employees, and it can magnify both the positive and the negative aspects of a pay plan. It can help an organization if pay increases are well administered, and it can hurt if pay increases are poorly administered. Therefore, it is a tool to be used only when an organization has a reasonable, well-functioning salary increase plan.

CAFETERIA BENEFIT PROGRAMS

The typical fringe benefit program provides equal amounts of such benefits as life insurance and health insurance to all organization members who are at similar levels in the organization. Typically, there is one fringe benefit package for hourly employees, one for salaried employees, and a third for the top levels of management. This approach emphasizes the differences between levels of the organization but fails to emphasize the significant differences among people who are at the same level. It also fails to give individuals any choice in the mixture of benefits and cash they will receive. For decades, research has clearly shown that the perceived value of benefits to employees varies widely from employee to employee (Nealey 1963). Such things as age, marital status, and number of children influence which benefits a person prefers. For example, young unmarried men prefer more time off the job whereas young married men prefer less time off. Likewise, older employees prefer greater retirement benefits while younger employees prefer more cash.

These findings are hardly surprising; people in different life situations have different needs. The fact that many people do not get the fringe benefits they want has some interesting implications for the effectiveness of fringe benefit programs. Essentially, it means that most fringe benefit programs fail to get a good return on the dollars they cost. These programs end up costing more than they buy; therefore, they do not contribute fully either to employee satisfaction or to employee desires to work for the organization. What organizations are doing is taking something of value (money), converting it to something of less value (benefits), and then trying to use this commodity in order to attract and retain employees.

One way to increase the perceived value of fringe benefits is simply to increase everyone's coverage on all benefits so that everyone has an ample amount of each benefit. Although this would contribute to improving the quality of work life, it is very costly. A less costly alternative is a cafeteria style or flexible benefits pay plan. This kind of plan involves telling employees just how much the organization is willing to spend on their total pay package and giving them the opportunity to spend this money as they wish. They can choose to take it all in cash or they can choose to take some cash and use the rest to buy the benefits they want. Although it has not been done, the cafeteria plan could contain a lump sum feature so that not only would employees have a choice of how much cash they would receive, they would have a choice of when they would receive it. A flexible benefits plan makes it clear to employees just how much the organization is spending to compensate them, and it assures that the money will be spent only on the benefits the employees want. Such a program can increase an employee's perception of the value of the pay package and this, in turn, can increase pay satisfaction. From the point of view of quality of work life, the cafeteria style plan clearly seems superior to the traditional pay and benefit approach. As might be expected, a survey in one company that has a flexible benefit program found a very high level of satisfaction with the plan and with the overall level of benefit coverage.

Although there is little supportive evidence, it seems likely that a cafeteria style plan can contribute to organizational effectiveness. It involves no additional direct compensation costs and it has the potential to decrease absenteeism and turnover and allow the organization to attract a more competent work force. Since individuals receive the benefits they want rather than the benefits someone else thinks they want, working for the organization becomes more attractive.

There are some practical problems with the cafeteria approach but they are far from insurmountable. Some managers feel that if employees are given the chance to choose their own pay and benefit package they will be irresponsible and choose only cash. If illness or other problems occur, the employees will not be protected and they may blame the organization. This concern can be dealt with on three levels. First, the research evidence indicates that most people will behave responsibly, given the choice (Lawler and Levin 1968; Nealey 1963; Schlachtmeyer and Bogart 1979). Second, it is not clear that employers should intervene if people take all cash. Controlling the kind of benefit package an employee selects is a form of control that places the employee in a dependent and passive position. Such control is also in direct opposition to providing a work life that allows freedom of choice. In addition, people may choose not to take health care coverage, but who is to say they are not covered by the spouse's policy? Finally, if an organization wants to be sure everyone has certain minimum amounts of coverage, it can simply give everyone a minimum benefit package and then allow employees to supplement it according to their needs.

Probably the most serious practical problem with the cafeteria approach stems from the fact that the cost and availability of many benefits, such as insurance plans, are based on the number of people who are covered by them. It is therefore difficult to price a benefit plan and to determine its availability in advance so that an employee can make an intelligent decision about participating in it. This is not likely to be a serious problem in large companies because a minimum number of participants usually can be guaranteed. Smaller companies may have to try to negotiate special argreements with insurance companies and others who underwrite aspects of the benefit package or they may simply have to take some risks when the plan first goes into effect. After some experience with the plan, however, an organization should be able to judge in advance the number of employees who will select different benefits, and thus be able to price them accordingly.

Up until the 1978 Revision of the Tax Code, there was also a tax liability problem with cafeteria compensation. Prior to 1978, the IRS indicated that if individuals took cash instead of benefits, those individuals who took the benefits might be liable for taxes on their previously tax-exempt benefits. This now seems to have been ruled out and, as a result, one obstacle to the spread of these plans has been eliminated. Finally, there are likely to be some additional administrative costs associated with flexible benefit plans. These may be rather heavy during start-up but, assuming computerization is adopted, should not continue to be heavy.

Despite the practical problems with cafeteria style plans, three organizations— the Systems Group of TRW Corporation, the Educational Testing Service, and American Can—have put them into effect. The largest and first plan is the one at TRW (Fragner 1975). It started with a series of surveys designed to estimate how many people would choose different benefit options. The plan, as it was finally put into practice in the fall of 1974, is far from a full cafeteria plan. It allows for a limited number of choices and requires everyone to take minimum levels of the important benefits. (The ETS and American Can plans allow for only slightly more choice). The TRW plan does, however, put all of the approximately 12,000 employees in the organization on the plan. It allows individuals to change their benefits plan every year and gives employees choices among significantly different benefits. Interestingly over 80 percent of the employees took advantage of this opportunity and changed their benefit packages when the plan first went into effect. At the present time, for example, the employees can choose among four hospital plans. It should be noted that the plan is supported by an extensive computer software program; and that its introduction was preceded by several years of developmental work.

The TRW project represents an important initial effort to make cafeteria compensation plans a reality. Unfortunately, little research has been reported on the effects of the TRW plan or, for that matter, on any cafeteria plan. My interviews at TRW indicate a high level of satisfaction with the plan and a belief on the part of management that it has aided in attracting and retaining skilled workers. One article on the American Can plan reports a survey showing that "more than 90 percent of American Can's salaried employees have had a positive reaction." Unfortunately, this is the only evaluation of the plan which is offered and not much information is known on how the data was collected. It is thus impossible to say with any certainty whether any of the hoped-for benefits (e.g., lower turnover) of the plan have been realized.

Flexible benefits would seem to be potentially effective in most organizations. They do not seem as limited in their applicability as are some of the other "new" approaches. In addition, there are certain types of organizations where they are likely to work particularly well. For example, large organizations, organizations with good data processing capability, and organizations with well-educated work forces seem particularly well suited to flexible benefit programs. At present, more organizations are needed that are willing to try plans which allow high levels of flexibility (e.g., taking all cash). A true test of the concept requires a full-blown test. There appear to be some forces that are likely to lead to the development of more flexible benefit plans. These include: better tax treatment, inflation, the rising costs of benefits, the increase in dual career families and their tendency to produce dual benefits, and a more educated work force that can make decisions and prefers individual treatment. Unions could also provide some impetus in encouraging more organizations to experiment in this area. So far, however, no union has tried to bargain for a cafeteria style plan, but there are reasons why they might begin to do so. First, these plans promise to make union members more satisfied; and second, unions are often in the position of having to bargain for benefits many of their members are not interested in. Cafeteria plans could eliminate this problem. Hopefully, more organizations will soon have full cafeteria plans in operation. Only if this happens will we be able to assess fully the degree to which they can contribute to organizational effectiveness and to the quality of work life.

SUMMARY AND CONCLUSIONS

Table 1 provides an overview of the four new approaches and lists the advantages and disadvantages of each. A major advantage of most of them is increased satisfaction and job attractiveness. Although this may not have an immediate direct impact on profit or organizational effectiveness, it is still a significant advantage since it can reduce absenteeism, turnover, and tardiness. These, in turn, have significant impacts on profits and organizational effectiveness.

Also shown in the summary are some of the situational factors that favor each of the new approaches. The importance of these situational factors cannot be emphasized too strongly. The potential advantages of these practices can be realized only if they are installed in a situation that is favorable to them.

Two situational factors, the management style of the organization and the condition of the present pay system, must be considered carefully. Figure 1 shows how management style and pay fairness affect the applicability of the four pay practices. It assumes that an effort is being made to use pay as a motivator and, therefore, a clear visible relationship between pay and performance is desired. Basically, it suggests that most of the new practices belong in organizations having a participative management style. In most cases, these practices have been

TABLE 1
SUMMARY OF NEW PRACTICES

	Major advantages	Major disadvantages	Favorable situational factors
All-salary:	Climate of trust; increased satisfaction and job attraction	Possible higher costs and absenteeism	Supervisors who will deal with absenteeism problems; a participative climate; an involved, responsible work force; well-designed jobs
Skill-based evaluation:	More flexible and skilled work force; increased satisfaction; climate of growth	Cost of training; higher salaries	Employees who want to develop themselves; jobs that are interdependent
Lump-sum salary increases:	Increased pay satisfaction; greater visibility of pay increases	Cost of administration	Fair pay rates; pay related to performance
Cafeteria benefits:	Increased pay satisfaction; greater attraction	Cost of administration	Well-educated, heterogeneous work force; large organization; good data processing

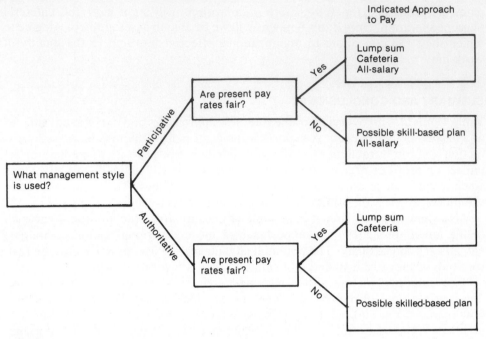

FIGURE 1
Applicability of new approaches to pay administration

implemented after a participative management style has been adopted, but a few organizations have experimented with using changes in pay administration practices as a way of moving the organization toward a more participative management style. Pay system changes have been used as an important change lever in a larger change program. It is also apparent that most of these practices are applicable only when a good basic pay structure is in place. All-salary plans and cafeteria benefit programs are not substitutes for a good basic salary system that sets fair salaries. They can, however, often lead to significant advantages when a good basic salary plan is in place.

REFERENCES

Fragner, B. N. 1975. Employees' "cafeteria" offers insurance options. *Harvard Business Review* **53**(6): 7–10.

Hulme, R. D., and Bevan, R. V. 1975. The blue collar worker goes on salary. *Harvard Business Review* **53**: 104–112.

Lawler, E. E. 1978. The new plant revolution. *Organizational Dynamics* **6**: 2–12.

Lawler, E. E., and Jenkins, G. D. 1976. *Employee participation in pay plan development.* Unpublished technical report to Department of Labor, Ann Arbor, Mich.

Lawler, E. E., and Levin, E. 1968. Union officers' perceptions of members' pay preferences. *Industrial and Labor Relations Review* **21**: 509–517.

Nealey, S. 1963. Pay and benefit preference. *Industrial Relations* **3**: 17–28.

Schlachtmeyer, A. S., and Bogart, R. B. 1979. Employee-choice benefits—Can employees handle it? *Compensation Review* **11**: 12–19.

Sheridan, J. H. 1975. Should your production workers be salaried? *Industry Week* **184**: 28–37.

Smith, C. A. 1979. Lump sum increases—A creditable change strategy. *Personnel* **56**: 59–63.

Walton, R. E. 1972. How to counter alienation in the plant. *Harvard Business Review* **50**: 70–81.

Walton, R. E. 1975. The diffusion of new work structures: Explaining why success didn't take. *Organizational Dynamics* **3**: 3–22.

QUESTIONS FOR DISCUSSION

1 Provide an example from your work experience (or from an organization with which you are familiar) of a reward system that did not fit well with other aspects of the organization's total human resources management program. In your opinion, were the organization's managers aware of these inconsistencies?

2 Suppose an organization desires to use a more participative approach (than it has in the past) in designing its reward system. What are some of the factors that it should take into account in implementing this increased participation that might affect subsequent performance motivation? Under what set of circumstances would an organization be well-advised *not* to try to increase the participation of its employees in designing (or redesigning) its reward system?

3 As a manager, how would you use a knowledge of the factors affecting reward allocation to distribute organizational rewards more effectively?

4 Given the causes of reward displacement discussed by Kerr, what problems might you anticipate in trying to remedy the situation by altering the reward system?

5 How do Kerr's remedies specifically deal with the causes of rewarding A while hoping for B? What other remedies might be suggested?

6 How would you implement each of Hamner's recommendations for overcoming failures in merit pay systems? What problems do you anticipate? What costs? What benefits?

7 Hamner's discussion focuses on the failure of merit pay systems. What other forms of reward (other than pay) might be subject to similar criticisms?

8 If you were the top executive of a newly formed organization deciding on compensation policies, on what criteria would you base a choice between the compensation approaches presented by Lawler? Why?

9 What implications do Kerr's observations suggest for each of the approaches to compensation listed by Lawler?

CHAPTER 6

SOCIAL INFLUENCES
ON MOTIVATION

Dating from the early work of Allport (1924), Mayo (1933), and Roethlisberger and Dickson (1939), a considerable body of research data has accumulated on the effects of the social aspects of an employee's work environment on motivation and behavior. In this chapter we first will consider group processes and their impacts; then we will examine the crucial process of organizational socialization. This discussion should serve to emphasize the fact that individuals seldom work in isolation and that they are continuously and often strongly affected by the social forces that exist in both the immediate and the larger organizational setting.

Defining precisely what constitutes a ''group'' is no easy task. The boundaries of group membership tend to be rather permeable, with new members joining and old ones leaving at a fairly consistent rate. Moreover, members of one group are generally also members of several additional groups, thereby dividing their time and loyalties. Because of problems such as these, we tend to discuss and define groups more in terms of processes than in terms of specific members and their personal characteristics. Thus, a typical definition of a group would include the notion of a collectivity of people who share a set of norms (or common viewpoints), who generally have differentiated roles, and who jointly pursue common goals. While it is not possible to specify the ''required'' size of such a collectivity, the number usually averages between four and seven.

Groups form for a variety of reasons. Some groups result simply from proximity. The day-to-day interactions with one's immediate coworkers tend to facilitate group formation. Other groups form for economic reasons. For example, where bonuses are paid to workers on the basis of *group* productivity, an incentive exists to band together for mutual gain. Still other groups form as the result of various social-psychological forces. Such groups can satisfy employees' social needs for interaction, reinforce feelings of self-worth, and provide emotional support in times of stress. Whatever the reason for their formation, they can be a potent factor in the determination of both individual job effort and individual job satisfaction.

Primarily as a result of the Hawthorne studies (Roethlisberger & Dickson, 1939) and the later research they stimulated, we have developed a fairly clear picture of some of the more common characteristics of a group. To begin with, as mentioned above, there are generally rather detailed norms, or shared beliefs, that are held by the group members and that guide their behavior. In addition, various members often have specific duties, or role prescriptions, for which they are responsible. Groups usually have acknowledged control procedures, such as ostracism, to minimize deviant behavior from their norms. They also develop their own systems or patterns of communications, which often include special or technical words (jargon). They tend to have an informal leader whose responsibility it is to enforce the norms and assure goal attainment. Finally, groups provide a useful source of support for their members. Employees who find little satisfaction in a dull, repetitive job may refrain from quitting because they really enjoy their co-workers, who provide comfort, support, and satisfaction on an otherwise meaningless job. Moreover, groups also provide support in a different sense where the group intends to regulate its rate of output. If one member restricts output, a very real possibility exists that he or she will be punished or even terminated by the organization. However, if all group members restrict output in unison, there is much less chance of "retribution" by the company.

From a motivational standpoint, perhaps the most important group process is the tendency toward conformity (Asch, 1958; Sherif, 1936). One of the basic prerequisites for continued group membership is adherence to group standards, norms, and so forth. Once a work group has determined an acceptable rate of output, for example, it tends to punish or reject members whose output is above ("rate-busters") or below ("goldbricks") this rate. If a company offers individual incentives for increased output but the group decides the new rate of output is too high (perhaps out of fear of working themselves out of a job), the group will exert force on its members not to increase output, despite the potential short-run monetary gain. On the other hand, however, if group support can be won for the new rate of output, conformity could then lead to increased output. The application of this latter example can be seen in such programs as the Lincoln Electric and the Scanlon plans, where workers have a significant voice in the determination of production rates and in the introduction of new production techniques. Under such plans, participation in program formulation *and* in the rewards from the new techniques appears to lead to group acceptance of the innovations, resulting in increased output.

In summary, then, research indicates that groups often serve useful functions for their members and must be taken into account as potential moderator variables in any program designed by the organization to increase employee effort and performance. It is important to recognize that from an organization's perspective, or the perspective of an individual manager, groups are neither "good" nor "bad" per se. From a motivational standpoint, groups have the potential to either facilitate or inhibit performance of their individual members. What kind of effect a particular group will have on its members will depend on a number of factors in the work situation in which the group operates. In any event, it is necessary to keep in mind that since most of us who work in organizations are social in nature, groups can exert very powerful influence. It is also necessary to note that the effects of a group on its members can change over time. Therefore, while a group may have had a negative impact on its members' performance or attitudes in the past, this does not imply that this must be the case in the future. Group effects can change direction, given a change in the influences from outside of a group as well as changes that may take place internally. Thus, the direction of the motivational impact a group can have on a set of individuals potentially can be altered in either a more positive or a more negative direction.

In the first reading in this chapter, Porter, Lawler, and Hackman review several mechanisms by which groups influence individual employees to produce (or not to produce). Included in this discussion is a consideration of how managers may try to change the work environment so that group processes are more compatible with organizational goals. The second article, by Sussmann and Vecchio, highlights the importance of social influence attempts as a major set of factors determining the motivation of individuals in work settings. A conceptual framework is provided, along with suggested hypotheses based on this way of viewing the motivational process. The reader will want to compare the ideas presented in this article with the social learning approach described by Kreitner and Luthans in Chapter 4. In the next article, Feldman examines how group norms develop and the role they have in influencing the motivation and behavior of group members. Again, like the preceding articles, this selection serves to emphasize the decidedly social nature of motivation in organizational circumstances. The final article in this chapter, by Rakestraw and Weiss, describes an elegantly designed experiment that demonstrates how social factors can influence the goals that individuals set for themselves in work-type situations and how the extent of such influence is moderated by the degree of one's experience with a task. This article relates directly to the goal-setting technique described in Chapter 3 and shows how that technique can be impacted by the surrounding social context.

REFERENCES

Allport, F. H. *Social psychology.* Boston: Houghton Mifflin, 1924.

Asch, S. E. The effects of group pressure upon the modification and distortion of judgments. In E. E. Maccoby, T. E. Newcomb, & E. L. Hartley (Eds.). *Readings in social psychology.* New York: Holt, 1958. (First published in 1939.)

Mayo, E. *The human problems of an industrial civilization.* New York: Macmillan, 1933.

Roethlisberger, F. J., & Dickson, W. J. *Management and the worker.* Cambridge, Mass.: Harvard University Press, 1939.

Sherif, M. *The psychology of social norms.* New York: Harper, 1936.

Ways Groups Influence Individual Work Effectiveness

Lyman W. Porter
Edward E. Lawler III
J. Richard Hackman

To analyze the diversity of group and social influences on individual work effectiveness, it may be useful to examine group effects separately on each of four summary classes of variables that have been shown to influence employee work behavior. These four classes of variables are:

1 The job-relevant knowledge and skills of the individual
2 The level of psychological arousal the individual experiences while working
3 The performance strategies the individual uses during his work
4 The level of effort the individual exerts in doing his work.

Below, we shall examine the ways in which work groups influence each of these four major influences on individual performance.

GROUP INFLUENCES BY AFFECTING MEMBER KNOWLEDGE AND SKILLS

Performance on many tasks and jobs in organizations is strongly affected by the job-relevant knowledge and skills of the individuals who do the work. Thus, even if an employee has both high commitment toward accomplishing a particular piece of work and well-formed strategy about how to go about doing it, the implementation of that plan can be constrained or terminated if he does not know how to carry it out, or if he knows how but is incapable of doing so. While ability is relevant to the performance of jobs at all levels in an organization, its impact probably is somewhat reduced for lower-level jobs. The reason is that such jobs often are not demanding of high skill levels. Further, to the extent that organizational selection, placement, and promotion practices are adequate, *all* jobs should tend to be occupied by individuals who possess the skills requisite for adequate performance.

Discussion in the previous chapter focused on how groups can improve the job-relevant knowledge and skills of an individual through direct instruction, feedback, and model provision. For jobs in which knowledge and skill are important determiners of performance effectiveness, then, groups can be of help. Nevertheless, the impact of groups on member performance effectiveness by improving member knowledge and skill probably is one of the lesser influences groups can have—both because employees on many jobs tend already to have many or all of the skills needed to perform them effectively and because there are other sources for improving skills which may be more useful and more potent than the work group, such as formal job training programs and self-study programs.

Slightly revised from L. W. Porter, E. E. Lawler, & J. R. Hackman, *Behavior in organizations.* New York: McGraw-Hill, 1975, pp. 411–422. Used by permission.

GROUP INFLUENCES BY AFFECTING MEMBER AROUSAL LEVEL

A group can substantially influence the level of psychological arousal experienced by a member—through the mere presence of the other group members and by those others sending the individual messages which are directly arousal-enhancing or arousal-depressing. The conditions under which such group-promoted changes in arousal level will lead to increased performance effectiveness, however, very much depend upon the type of task being worked on (Zajonc, 1965).

In this case, the critical characteristics of the job have to do with whether the initially *dominant task responses* of the individual are likely to be correct or incorrect. Since the individual's output of such responses is facilitated when he is in an aroused state, arousal should improve performance effectiveness on well-learned tasks (so-called performance tasks) in which the dominant response is correct and needs merely to be executed by the performer. By the same token, arousal should impair effectiveness for new or unfamiliar tasks (learning tasks) in which the dominant response is likely to be incorrect.

It has sometimes been argued that the *mere* presence of others should heighten the arousal of individuals sufficiently for the predicted performance effects to be obtained. However, the evidence now seems to indicate that the *mere* presence of others may not result in significant increases in arousal. Instead, only when the other group members are—or are seen as being—in a potentially evaluative relationship vis-à-vis the performer are the predictions confirmed (cf. Zajonc & Sales, 1966; Cottrell et al., 1968; Hency & Glass, 1968).

Groups can, of course, increase member arousal in ways other than taking an evaluative stance toward the individual. Strongly positive, encouraging statements also should increase arousal in some performance situations—for example, by helping the individual become personally highly committed to the group goal, and making sure he realizes that he is a very important part of the team responsible for reaching that goal. What must be kept in mind, however, is that such devices represent a double-edged sword: while they may facilitate effective performance for well-learned tasks, they may have the opposite effect for new and unfamiliar tasks.

What, then, can be said about the effects on performance of group members when their presence (and interaction) serves to *decrease* the level of arousal of the group member—as, for example, when individuals coalesce into groups under conditions of high stress? When the other members of the group are a source of support, comfort, or acceptance to the individual (and serve to decrease his arousal level), it would be predicted that performance effectiveness would follow a pattern exactly opposite to that described above: the group would impair effectiveness for familiar or well-learned performance tasks (because arousal helps on these tasks and arousal is being lowered) and facilitate effectiveness for unfamiliar or complicated learning tasks (because in this case arousal is harmful, and it is being lowered).

The relationships predicted above are summarized in Figure 1. As the group becomes increasingly threatening, evaluative, or strongly encouraging, effectiveness should increase for performance tasks and decrease for learning tasks. When

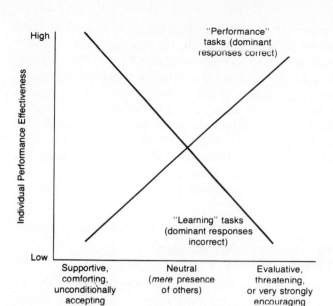

FIGURE 1
Individual performance effectiveness as a function of type of
task and experienced relationship to the group.

the group is experienced as increasingly supportive, comforting, or unconditionally accepting, effectiveness should decrease for performance tasks and increase for learning tasks. And when no meaningful relationship at all is experienced by the individual between himself and the group, performance should not be affected. While some of these predictions have been tested and confirmed in small group experimental settings, others await research.

Even that research which has focused on these relationships has not been designed or conducted in actual organizational settings, and the findings must be generalized with caution. It is clear, however, that individuals in organizations do use their group memberships as a means of achieving more comfortable levels of arousal. Individuals in high-pressure managerial jobs, for example, often find that they need to gather around themselves a few trusted associates who can and do provide reassurance and continuing acceptance when the going gets especially tough. This, presumably, should help reduce the manager's level of arousal and thereby increase the likelihood that he will be able to come up with *new and original* ways of perceiving and dealing with his immediate problem. If the theory is correct, however, this practice should not facilitate performance of the more "routine" (i.e., well-learned) parts of his job.

It is well known that overly routine jobs can decrease a worker's level of arousal to such an extent that his performance effectiveness is impaired. It seems quite possible, therefore, that the social environment of workers on such jobs can be designed so as to compensate partially for the deadening effects of the job itself and thereby lead to an increment in performance on well-learned tasks.

Finally, the supervisor probably has a more powerful effect on level of arousal of a worker than any other single individual in his immediate social environment. By close supervision (which usually results in the worker's feeling more or less constantly evaluated) supervisors can and do increase the level of arousal experienced by workers. While this may, for routine jobs, have some potential for improving performance effectiveness, it also is quite likely that the worker's negative reactions to being closely supervised ultimately will result in his attention being diverted from the job itself and focused instead on ways he can either get out from "under the gun" of the supervisor or somehow get back at the supervisor to punish him for his unwanted close supervision.

GROUP INFLUENCES BY AFFECTING LEVEL OF MEMBER EFFORT AND MEMBER PERFORMANCE STRATEGIES

The level of effort a person exerts in doing his work and the performance strategies he follows are treated together here because both variables are largely under the performer's *voluntary* control.

Direct versus Indirect Influences on Effort and Strategy   We have used a general "expectancy theory" approach to analyze those aspects of a person's behavior in organizations which are under his voluntary control. From this perspective, a person's choices about his effort and work strategy can be viewed as hinging largely upon (1) his *expectations* regarding the likely consequences of his choices and (2) the degree to which he *values* those expected consequences. Following this approach, it becomes clear that the group can have both a direct and an indirect effect on the level of effort a group member exerts at his job and on his choices about performance strategy.

The *direct* impact of the group on effort and strategy, of course, is simply the enforcement by the group of its own norms regarding what is an "appropriate" level of effort to expend on the job and what is the "proper" performance strategy. We previously discussed in some detail how groups use their control of discretionary stimuli to enforce group norms, and thereby affect such voluntary behaviors. Thus, if the group has established a norm about the level of member effort or the strategies members should use in going about their work, the group can control individual behavior merely by making sure that individual members realize that their receipt of valued group-controlled rewards is contingent upon their behaving in accord with the norm.

The *indirect* impact of the group on the effort and performance strategies of the individual involves the group's control of information regarding the state of the organizational environment outside the boundaries of the group. Regardless of any norms the group itself may have about effort or strategy, it also can communicate to the group member "what leads to what" in the broader organization, and thereby affect the individual's *own* choices about his behavior.

For example, it may be the case in a given organization that hard work (i.e., high effort) tends to lead to quick promotions and higher pay; the group can influence the effort of the individual by helping him realize this objective state of affairs. Similarly, by providing individual members with information about what performance strategies are effective in the organization, the group can indirectly affect the strategy choices made by the person. Whether high quality of output or large quantities of output are more likely to lead to organizational rewards, for example, is information that the group can provide the individual with to assist him in making his own choices about work strategy.

Moreover, groups can affect the *personal preferences and values* of individual members—although such influences tend to occur relatively slowly and over a long period of time. When such changes do occur, the level of desire (or the valence) individuals have for various outcomes available in the organizational setting will change as well. And as the kinds of outcomes valued by the individual change, his behavior also will change to increase the degree to which the newly valued outcomes are obtained at work. The long-term result can be substantial revision of the choices made by the individual about the effort he will expend and the performance strategies he will use at work.

It should be noted, however, that such indirect influences on members effort and performance strategy will be most potent early in the individual's tenure in the organization when he has not yet had a chance to develop through experience his own personal "map" of the organization. When the individual becomes less dependent upon the group for data about "what leads to what" and "what's good" in the organization, the group may have to revert to direct norm enforcement to maintain control of the work behavior of individual members.

In summary, the group can and does have a strong impact on both the level of effort exerted by its members and the strategies members use in carrying out their work. This impact is realized both directly (i.e., by enforcement of group norms) and indirectly (i.e., by affecting the beliefs and values of the members). When the direct and indirect influences of a group are congruent—which is often the case—the potency of the group's effects on its members can be quite strong. For example, if at the same time that a group is enforcing its *own* norm of, say, moderately low production, it also is providing a group member with data regarding the presumably *objective* negative consequences of hard work in the particular organization, the group member will experience two partially independent and mutually reinforcing influences aimed at keeping his rate of production down.

Effort, Strategy, and Performance Effectiveness   What, then, are the circumstances under which groups can improve the work *effectiveness* of their members through influences on individual choices about level of effort and about strategy? Again, the answer depends upon the nature of the job. Unless a job is structured so that effort level or performance strategy actually can make a real difference in work effectiveness, group influences on effort or strategy will be irrelevant to how well individual members perform.

Strategy: In general, groups should be able to facilitate member work effectiveness by influencing strategy choices more for complex jobs than for simple, straightforward, or routine ones. The reason is that on simple jobs, strategy choices usually cannot make much of a difference in effectiveness; instead, how well one does is determined almost entirely by how hard one works. On jobs characterized by high variety and autonomy, on the other hand, the work strategy used by the individual usually is of considerable importance in determining work effectiveness. By helping an individual develop and implement an appropriate work strategy—of where and how to put in his effort—the group should be able to substantially facilitate his effectiveness.

Effort: In the great majority of organizational settings, most jobs are structured such that the harder one works, the more effective his performance is likely to be. Thus, group influences on the effort expended by members on their jobs are both very pervasive and very potent determiners of individual work effectiveness. There are, nevertheless, some exceptions to this generalization; the success of a complicated brain operation, for example, is less likely to depend upon effort expended than it is upon the strategies used and the job-relevant knowledge and skills of the surgeon.

When either effort or strategy or both are in fact important in determining performance effectiveness, the individual has substantial personal control over how well he does in his work. In such cases, the degree to which the group facilitates (rather than hinders) individual effectiveness will depend jointly upon (1) the degree to which the group has accurate information regarding the task and organizational contingencies which are operative in that situation and makes such information available to the individual and (2) the degree to which the norms of the group are congruent with those contingencies and reinforce them.

Participation   One management practice which in theory should contribute positively to meeting both of the above conditions is the use of group participation in making decisions about work practices. Participation has been widely advocated as a management technique, both on ideological grounds and as a direct means of increasing work effectiveness. And, in fact, some studies have shown that participation can lead to higher work effectiveness (e.g., Coch & French, 1948; Lawler & Hackman, 1969). In the present framework, participation should contribute to increased work effectiveness in two different ways.

1 Participation can increase the amount and the accuracy of information workers have about work practices and the environmental contingencies associated with them. In one study (Lawler & Hackman, 1969), for example, some groups themselves designed new reward systems keyed on coming to work regularly (a task clearly affected by employee effort—i.e., trying to get to work every day). These groups responded both more quickly and more positively to the new pay plans than did groups which had technically identical plans imposed upon them by company management. One reason suggested by the authors to account for this finding was that the participative groups simply may have understood their plans better and had fewer uncertainties and worries about what the rewards were (and were not) for coming to work regularly.

2 Participation can increase the degree to which group members feel they "own" their work practices—and therefore the likelihood that the group will de-

velop a norm of support for those practices. In the participative groups in the study cited above, for example, the nature of the work-related communication among members changed from initial "shared warnings" about management and "things management proposes" to helping members (especially new members) come to understand and believe in "our plan." In other words, as group members come to experience the work or work practices *as under their own control or ownership,* it becomes more likely that informal group norms supportive of effective behavior vis-à-vis those practices will develop. Such norms provide a striking contrast to the "group protective" norms which often emerge when control is perceived to be exclusively and unilaterally under management control.

We can see, then, that group participative techniques can be quite facilitative of individual work effectiveness—but only under certain conditions:

1 The topic of participation must be relevant to the work itself. There is no reason to believe that participation involving task-irrelevant issues (e.g., preparing for the Red Cross Bloodmobile visit to the plant) will have facilitative effects on work productivity. While such participation may indeed help increase the cohesiveness of the work group, it clearly will not help group members gain information or develop norms which are facilitative of high work effectiveness. Indeed, such task-irrelevant participation may serve to direct the attention and motivation of group members *away from* work issues and thereby even lower productivity (cf. French, Israel, & As, 1960).

2 The objective task and environmental contingencies in the work setting must actually be supportive of more effective performance. That is, if through participation group members learn more about what leads to what in the organization, then it is increasingly important that there be real and meaningful positive outcomes which result from effective performance. If, for example, group members gain a quite complete and accurate impression through participation that "hard work around here pays off only in backaches," then increased effort as a consequence of participation is most unlikely. If, on the other hand, participation results in a new and better understanding that hard work can lead to increased pay, enhanced opportunities for advancement, and the chance to feel a sense of personal and group accomplishment, then increased effort should be the result.

3 Finally, the work must be such that increased effort (or a different and better work strategy) objectively can lead to higher work effectiveness. If it is true—as argued here—that the main benefits of group participation are (1) increased understanding of work practices and the organizational environment and (2) increased experienced "ownership" by the group of the work and work practices, then participation should increase productivity only when the *objective determinants of productivity are under the voluntary control of the worker.* There is little reason to expect, therefore, that participation should have a substantial facilitative effect on productivity when work outcomes are mainly determined by the level of skill of the worker and/or by his arousal level (rather than effort expended or work strategy used) or when outcomes are controlled by objective factors in the environment over which the worker can have little or no control (e.g., the rate or amount of work which is arriving at the employee's station).

IMPLICATIONS FOR DIAGNOSIS AND CHANGE

This section has focused on ways that the group can influence the performance effectiveness of individual group members. While it has been maintained throughout that the group has a substantial impact on such performance effectiveness, it has been emphasized that the nature and extent of this impact centrally depends upon the characteristics of the work being done.

To diagnose and change the direction or extent of social influences on individual performance in an organization, then, the following three steps might be taken.

1 An analysis of the task or job would be made to determine which of the four classes of variables (i.e., skills, arousal, strategies, effort) objectively affect measured performance effectiveness. This might be done by posing this analytical question: "If skills (or arousal, or effort, or strategies) were brought to bear on the work differently than is presently the case, would a corresponding difference in work effectiveness be likely to be observed as a consequence?" By scrutinizing each of the four classes of variables in this way, it usually is possible to identify which specific variables are objectively important to consider for the job. In many cases, of course, more than one class of variables will turn out to be of importance.

2 After one or more "target" classes of variables have been identified, the work group itself would be examined to unearth any ways in which the group was blocking effective individual performance. It might be determined, for example, that certain group norms were impeding the expression and use of various skills which individuals potentially could bring to bear on their work. Or it might turn out that the social environment of the worker created conditions which were excessively (or insufficiently) arousing for optimal performance on the task at hand. For effort and strategy, which are under the voluntary control of the worker, there are two major possibilities to examine: (a) that norms are enforced in the group which coerce individuals to behave in ineffective ways or (b) that the group provides information to the individual members about task and environmental contingencies in an insufficient or distorted fashion, resulting in their making choices about their work behavior which interfere with task effectiveness.

3 Finally, it would be useful to assess the group and the broader social environment to determine if there are ways that the "people resources" in the situation could be more fully utilized in the interest of increased work effectiveness. That is, rather than focusing solely on ways the group may be blocking or impeding performance effectiveness, attention should be given as well to any unrealized *potential* which resides in the group. It could turn out, for example, that some group members would be of great help to others in increasing the level of individual task-relevant skills, but these individuals have never been asked for help. Alternatively, it might be that the group could be assisted in finding new and better ways of ensuring that each group member has available accurate and current information about those tasks and environmental contingencies which determine the outcomes of various work behaviors.

The point is that the people who surround an individual at work can facilitate as well as hinder his performance effectiveness—and that any serious attempt to diagnose the social environment in the interest of improving work performance should explicitly address unrealized possibilities for enhancing performance as well as issues for which remedial action may be required.

What particular organizational changes will be called for on the basis of such a diagnosis—or what techniques should be used to realize these changes—will, of course, largely depend upon the particular characteristics of the organization and of the resources which are available there. The major emphasis of this section has been that there is *not* any single universally useful type of change or means of change—and that, instead, intervention should always be based on a thorough diagnosis of the existing social, organizational, and task environment. Perhaps especially intriguing in this regard is the prospect of developing techniques of social intervention which will help groups see the need for (and develop the capability of) making such interventions *on their own* in the interest of increasing the work effectiveness of the group as a whole.

REFERENCES

Coch, L., & French, J. R. P., Jr., Overcoming resistance to change. *Human Relations,* 1948, **1,** 512–532.

Cottrell, N. B., Wack, D. L., Sekerak, F. J., & Rittle, R. H. Social facilitation of dominant responses by the presence of an audience and the mere presence of others. *Journal of Personality and Social Psychology,* 1968, **9,** 245–250.

French, J. R. P., Jr., Israel, J., & As, D. An experiment on participation in a Norwegian factory. *Human Relations,* 1960, **19,** 3–19.

Hency, T., & Glass, D.C. Evaluation apprehension and the social facilitation of dominant and subordinate responses. *Journal of Personality and Social Psychology,* 1968, **10,** 446–454.

Lawler, E. E., & Hackman, J. R. The impact of employee participation in the development of pay incentive plans: A field experiment. *Journal of Applied Psychology,* 1969, **53,** 467–471.

Zajonc, R. B. Social facilitation. *Science,* 1965, **149,** 269–274.

Zajonc, R. B., & Sales, S. M. Social facilitation of dominant and subordinate responses. *Journal of Experimental Social Psychology,* 1966, **2,** 160–168.

A Social Influence Interpretation of Worker Motivation

Mario Sussmann
Robert P. Vecchio

When considering the topic of worker motivation, one is initially overwhelmed by the abundance of different theories and approaches that are present in the organizational literature (Adams, 1965; Campbell & Pritchard, 1976; Campbell,

From *Academy of Management Review,* 1982, **7,** 177–186. Reprinted by permission.

Dunnette, Lawler, & Weick, 1970; Lawler, 1973; Porter & Lawler, 1968; Vroom, 1964). However, the major theories of worker motivation (both mechanistic and cognitive) have largely ignored a fundamental issue concerning the origins of worker behavior. Specifically, this omission stems from an assumption that factors which appear to precede changes in behavior operate in a unilateral fashion: and workers (it is assumed) do not exercise an appreciable degree of personal volition, that is, they *do not decide to accept influence attempts*. This theoretical omission sidesteps the question of the process whereby influence attempts are accepted/rejected as well as the varieties of influence that exist. Rather than define "influence processes," one can instead attempt to define the "basis of acceptance." However, the latter view does not present the worker as an active participant in the determination of his or her behavior. Presented in this paper is a process view of social influence that specifies the manner and nature of socially induced changes in worker behavior.

An influence attempt is defined here as a social occasion wherein one individual exhibits behaviors, emits verbal utterances, and so on, with the intent of altering the behavior of another or others to a desired end. The scope of this discourse is restricted to work related behaviors (especially, but not exclusively, behaviors related to worker productivity). Of concern here are occasions of socially dependent influence. That is to say, influence that originates from outside the target person can be distinguished from influence that originates primarily from within the target person (e.g., the socially independent process of a competency motive or exploratory motive). Furthermore, it is recognized that influence is unlikely to be unilateral. Rather, it is most commonly a reciprocal process in that the target person's response to an influence attempt likely will alter the variety, frequency, intensity, and/or direction of future influence attempts.

For the moment, the focus is on the behavior (i.e., response to an influence attempt) of the person who occupies a "subordinate" position (i.e., in the formal, organizational sense of subordinate) because subordinate behavior traditionally has been the primary interest of theories of worker motivation. However, as will be illustrated, influence can be more broadly conceptualized so as to include the impact of subordinate behavior on supervisor behavior (specifically, supervisor's influence attempts).

SOCIAL INFLUENCE PROCESSES

Kelman's (1961) work on identifying qualitatively distinct processes of opinion change has particular relevance to the goals of this paper. These processes are termed compliance, identification, and internalization. If Kelman's terms are extended to work settings, it may be said that *compliance* is concerned with whether a worker accepts an influence attempt because of a desire to obtain a favorable outcome or to avoid an unfavorable outcome. *Identification* refers to whether a worker exhibits behaviors derived from another or others because these behaviors contribute to a person's self-image. The third type of influence process, *internalization*, refers to whether a worker accepts an influence attempt because the encouraged actions are congruent with a personal value system and/or are intrinsically rewarding to the individual.

French and Raven's (1959) view of social power suggests five major sources of influence: reward, coercive, legitimate, referent, and expert. Each of these five may be viewed as being relatively more closely aligned with one of the three processes proposed by Kelman. Specifically, French and Raven's reward and coercive power possesses a strong conceptual similarity with Kelman's notion of compliance. Also, the social power bases of referent power are most in allegiance with Kelman's process of identification. And, finally, legitimate power may be viewed as being potentially the power source for an internalization influence process. Therefore, French and Raven's analysis of social power may be viewed as overlapping with Kelman's typology such that French and Raven's power bases provide a more elaborate conceptual foundation for influence attempts. These influence attempts, in turn, are directed at (or, perhaps more properly, are translated into) specific psychological processes (Kelman, 1961) and succeed or fail in altering behavior as a function of individual and situational contingencies.

Etzioni (1975) has offered an approach that examines social power and worker response within the framework of a structurally oriented organizational analysis. Etzioni considered the influence-motivation problem as one of *compliance*, a term that indicates the relation between the influence agent's power and the influencee's involvement (by involvement is meant a cathectic-evaluative orientation of an actor to an object).

In Etzioni's typology of power, coercive power refers to the administration of pain or the threat to do so. Remunerative or utilitarian power refers to allocation of rewards such as pay, benefits, services, and commodities. Among two types of normative power, pure normative power refers to the allocation of symbolic rewards based on prestige, esteem, and ritualistic symbols, and social power refers to the apportionment of interpersonal rewards and acceptance. There also are four types of involvement: alienative (a negative and hostile orientation); calculative (based on the material gain in an economic relationship); and two types of moral involvement (devotion to ideas, groups, movements, organizations, leaders), with a distinction between "pure moral" commitment and "social" commitment, paralleling the distinction between pure normative and social power. In a proposal that anticipated contingency theories, congruent types of compliance are defined as occasions in which a type of power is paired with a corresponding type of involvement (coercive with alienative, renumerative-utilitarian with calculative, normative with moral); all other combinations are incongruent.

A comparison of Kelman's and Etzioni's typologies shows that Etzioni offers two types of relationship (coercive power and remunerative-utilitarian power) but Kelman writes only of compliance. On the other hand, Kelman's distinction between identification (social power, social commitment) and internalization (pure normative power—pure moral commitment) appears to be particularly useful because Kelman also postulates a cost difference between identification and internalization: the internalization process clearly is the one that does not require surveillance (in contrast with compliance) or the presence/salience (in contrast with identification) of the power agent and might be seen as the most effective and parsimonious means of control. Yet, an important difference remains: Kelman's three processes are located at the individual level of analysis, whereas Etzioni's compliance is defined as a relation between an individual process (involvement) and an organizational process (power).

INDIVIDUAL AND SITUATIONAL MODERATORS

Individual differences variables, one may reasonably assume, moderate the impact of influence attempts such that a given type of influence attempt will be more successful with a given group of individuals. Imagine, for example, the outcome of the use of coercive/reward power in order to bring about simple compliance. In such an instance, one would find that the influence attempt was or was not successful as a partial function of such predispositions as willingness to comply with incentives, intimidation, bribery, or threats. It would be suspected that animals, children, and those adults who possess little desire for autonomy would be most responsive to influence attempts that are designed to bring about simple compliance and that are based on coercive/reward power.

Some individual differences moderators that have been the focus of considerable organizational research include growth need strength (Hackman & Oldham, 1976), Protestant work ethic (Blood, 1969; Mirels & Garrett, 1971), and internal versus external locus-of-control (Rotter, 1966). It is suspected that these value system indices are likely to be most relevant for social influence attempts directed at an internalization process. That is to say, influence attempts that essentially are appeals to the target's value system will be differentially effective as a function of the target's value system.

A value system having implications across all three influence modes has been advanced by Kohlberg (1963, 1969). Kohlberg proposes that an individual passes through three identifiable stages of value maturity. At the first level, the preconventional, an individual is most concerned with the consequences of his or her behavior. At the second (conventional) level, an individual is most concerned with meeting the expectations of family, immediate group, or nation because it is valuable as an end in itself. The final, or postconventional, level is characterized by an individual's effort to define and apply these values or principles apart from external norms and potential sanctions.

It can be argued that Kohlberg's typology maps, aptly, into the social influence processes. Specifically, the more an influence attempt is based on simple reward/coercive power and seeks to evoke compliance, the more successful the influence attempt will be if it is directed towards individuals whose value system is best characterized as hedonistic/utilitarian. Influence attempts based on referent power should be most effective with individuals who have a strong desire for social conformity. And, finally, influence heavily directed toward appealing to an individual's values will be most effective with persons who are strongly concerned with value issues. It is worthy of note that a recent motivational study that employed the Kohlberg typology (Vecchio, 1981) reported support for the hypothesis that individual values moderate worker response to incentive schemes.

In addition to individual differences moderators, one might expect situational factors to play an important role in moderating the differential effectiveness of the various influence approaches. Situational attributes of possible importance include job autonomy and job challenge. Organizational level (a potentially significant situational factor) may be of particular importance to the influence process view of motivation. For example, one might find that different influence processes are used more frequently at different organizational levels, such that internalization influence attempts are used more frequently in higher organizational levels and compliance-based influence attempts are employed more commonly at lower organizational levels. Although such a finding would be of a purely descriptive nature, it should be possible to document the differential effectiveness of these influence processes at different levels.

At a still broader level of conceptualization, the organizational power types proposed by Etzioni offer a further framework for matching the type of influence attempt with situational attributes. That is to say, specific types of influence attempts may appear most appropriate (congruent) and be most effective within specific organizational power structures.

Up to this point, the importance has been shown of several situational and individual attributes as moderators of the relationship between influence attempts and individual motivation. However, the translation of individual motivation (often conceptualized as effort and/or strength of a behavioral intention) into performance requires the specification of individual and situational attributes that serve as moderators of the relationship between individual motivation and performance (Lawler, 1971; Porter & Lawler, 1968; Vroom, 1964). These specific attributes can be best summarized by the terms "ability" and "availability of the behavior."

The intersection of situational attributes, individual differences attributes, and influence attempts yields a complex and theoretically rich framework for hypothesizing specific interactions. However, before discussing such effects it is necessary to link the influence processes with clusters of relevant dependent variables. That is to say, not only is the presently proposed model deliberately explicit with respect to the impact of situational and individual differences moderators (and their interactions), but it also explicitly specifies theoretically relevant intermediate variables and it ties relevant dependent variables to associated processes. Therefore, it is suggested that each influence process is most directly relevant for only certain outcome/process variables.

RELEVANT VARIABLES

Before linking intermediary variables to their associated processes, one must consider the constructs and variables commonly investigated in the area of worker motivation. These constructs and variables have various conceptual commonalities that permit a simple clustering in the interest of parsimony.

The intermediary process variables may be defined as those dimensions that describe individuals' behaviors, intentions, and cognitive and emotional states within an organizationally-relevant setting. These process variables appear to describe the specific details of Etzioni's "involvement." Two trends have emerged within the literature for identifying these variables. For the first approach, clusters of these variables are identified and relationships with their antecedents, concomitants, and consequents are explored (Porter & Steers, 1973). Alternatively, many authors have dropped the strict dichotomy between overt behaviors and attitudinal, conative, and cognitive antecedents/concomitants. These authors tend (implicitly) to conceive of acts as including both overt and covert aspects, and they describe work behavior as a process involving a sequence of stages (Mobley, 1977; Mobley, Horner, & Hollingsworth, 1978; Mobley, Griffith, Hand, & Meglino, 1979; Porter & Lawler, 1968; Steers & Rhodes, 1978). The second approach has the potential advantage of emphasizing the importance of individual processes that mediate overt actions and observable outcomes. Thus, the second route of viewing behavior as a unit of overt and covert processes (by covert is meant those latent processes that can reasonably be deduced from overt behaviors) has been adopted for this paper.

Based on a review of the recent literature, three sets of intermediary process variables and a suspected sequence were derived. The first set of variables centers on the issue of the extent to which work events and attributes are related to the individual's value system. Therefore, these variables are termed *value-related*. This set is similar to Katz's (1964) motivational patterns of intrinsic satisfaction, goal internalization, and acceptance of organizational rules. Four variables were identified for this set: (a) importance of success versus failure at work for a person's self-esteem—a variable identified by Rabinowitz and Hall (1977) as one conceptualization of job involvement; (b) the extent to which one's job and/or work is a "central life interest" (Dubin, 1956)—a variable also interpreted by Rabinowitz and Hall (1977) as a manifestation of the "importance of self-esteem" conceptualization of job involvement; (c) the worker's expectation of pleasant/unpleasant feelings as a result of success versus failure (Lawler, 1969)— a variable best summarized as intrinsic motivation; and (d) the extent of belief in and acceptance of values pertinent to the work role—these values can consist of organizational goals, but they may be specific to a particular profession or occupation (Gouldner, 1957). As "acceptance of organizational goals and values," this variable is identical to the first component of "organizational commitment" (Porter, Steers, Mowday, & Boulian, 1974).

The second set, which includes two variables, represents the extent to which work role, occupation, and organizational membership mark the individual's self-image and the degree to which the individual derives satisfaction from interpersonal relations and primary-group relationships (Katz, 1964) in organizations. This set therefore may be labeled *identity-related*. More specifically, the variables in this set may be termed: (a) importance of the job or the work role for a person's self-concept; and (b) social attachment to the organization. Importance of the job for self-concept is the second conceptualization of job involvement as elaborated by Rabinowitz and Hall (1977). According to these authors, this variable also can be understood as the degree of psychological identification with work. Social attachment refers to the desire to remain within one's organization and to remain a member of the organization. It corresponds therefore to the third component of "organizational commitment" (Porter et al., 1974).

The third set of variables is comprised of utility-related aspects of the job—for example Katz's (1964) instrumental system and individual rewards. These aspects will be referred to with the inclusive variable label of "job outcome utility." This variable consists of extrinsic factors and is reflected in terms such as role attraction (Mobley, Hand, Baker, & Meglino, 1979) and valence of the work role (Vroom, 1964). Also, it is parallel to satisfaction with specific extrinsic facets of the job (Lawler, 1973). Subjective evaluations of job outcomes are thought to be a function not only of the absolute attractiveness of outcomes, but also of social comparisons (Adams, 1965; Katzell, 1964; Locke, 1969).

These three sets of variables—value-related, identity-related, and utilitarian—may be understood as antecedents of those *behavioral intentions* that are, in turn, related to overt behavior. Thus, the variable now considered corresponds to Fishbein's (1967) "behavioral intentions" (BI). This variable is used in Mobley's turnover model (Miller, Katerberg, & Hulin, 1979; Mobley, 1977; Mobley et al., 1978). In the Porter et al. (1974) "organizational commitment" scheme, this variable appears as "willingness to exert effort on behalf of the organiza tion." It must be noted that Porter et al.'s "willingness to exert effort" is far less specific than are such variables as intentions to quit, attend, and produce efficiently, which usually are criteria for prediction. Thus, willingness to exert effort might appear as an antecedent to specific intentions.

Lastly, the proposed process generates overt activity. Examples of this variable are production behavior, quitting, attending, and job performance (the latter is defined as production behavior projected on an evaluative dimension of effectiveness).

A SOCIAL INFLUENCE FRAMEWORK

The entire sequence, consisting of the influence attempts, the three sets of antecedent variables, BI, and overt behavior, is portrayed in Figure 1. Cardinal emphasis is placed on the concept that BI is determined by the three categories of antecedents identified herein. A major corollary of this contention is that in order to change motivation, one has to alter one, two, or all three of these categories. That is to say, motivation change is mediated by changes in the three sets of antecedent variables.

Logically, the question then must be asked as to how these antecedent variables can be modified. Kelman's (1961) aforementioned processes of influence appear to correspond closely to the character of the three BI-antecedent categories.

1 Compliance is defined by Kelman as acceptance of influence in order to gain specific rewards and to avoid punishments. It is a process wherein behavior is controlled by its contingencies; or, in the terminology of expectancy theory, by expectancies of differently valued outcomes. These notions are similar to the

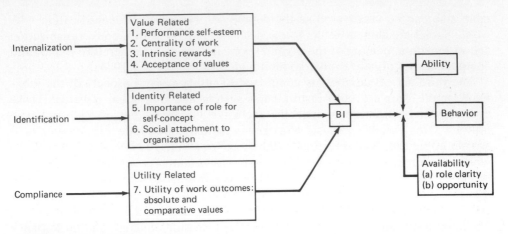

*Includes desire for competence, mastery.

FIGURE 1
Influence processes and sequence.

variable "utility of work outcomes." It is proposed here, therefore, that motivation is influenced through the mediary of *utility* by the process of *compliance*.

2 Identification refers to the process of accepting influence in order to engage in a satisfying role-relationship with another person or a group. It is behavior controlled by role acceptance, the involvement in the work role in terms of its importance for the self-concept, the commitment to a group, or the attractiveness of membership in an organization. Therefore, this variety of motivation is influenced through the mediary of *identity-related* variables (i.e., importance of the work role for the self-concept, and social attachment to the organization) by the process of *identification*.

3 Internalization refers to the acceptance of influence because it is congruent with a worker's value system and/or because it is intrinsically rewarding. With regard to the work behavior variables listed above, internalization can be understood to exert control through the importance of success and failure for self-esteem, the place of work as a central life interest, the importance of intrinsic rewards, and acceptance of organizational goals and values. Thus, in such cases, motivation is influenced through the mediary of *value-related* variables by the process of *internalization*.

The relationship between the Kelman influence processes and the dependent and process variables is shown at the left-hand side of Figure 1. The incorporation of the dependent and process variables within the Kelman scheme represents an important elaboration of Kelman's work. The proposed framework and inherent process may be summarized as follows: Among the three variables that influence overt behavior directly, BI is the motivational construct. Motivation, in turn, is a function of value-related, identity-related, and/or utility-related categories of person variables. These three categories are controlled by the interpersonal influence process of internalization, identification, and compliance, respectively.

A relationship exists between Kelman's interpersonal influence processes and

Etzioni's types of organizational power. Pure normative organizational power (Etzioni) parallels an internalization interpersonal influence process (Kelman), social power corresponds to identification, and utilitarian and coercive power correspond to Kelman's compliance. In the present framework, this paper proposes to distinguish between *positive* (reward based) and *negative* (punitive oriented) compliance, in order to provide the connections with utilitarian and coercive power. Figure 2 portrays this integration of structural (macro-level) with interpersonal and individual (micro-level) processes. On the left-hand side of Figure 2 are Etzioni's types of power, which at the level of interpersonal influence attempts appear as Kelman-type influence processes (second column). The dependent and process variables are clustered, as in Figure 1, with the difference that now the corresponding involvement labels are: pure moral commitment for the value-related variables, social commitment for the identity-related variables, and calculative involvement for the utility-related variables. A cluster is added to describe alienative involvement (consisting of responses such as fear, hostility, and estrangement). These clusters are then seen as antecedents of BI. The right-hand side of Figure 2 is identical to the right-hand side of Figure 1.

The *validity* of the proposed view of social influence is suggested by a consideration of popular methods of motivating workers. For example, O. B. Mod

FIGURE 2
An expanded motivation framework.

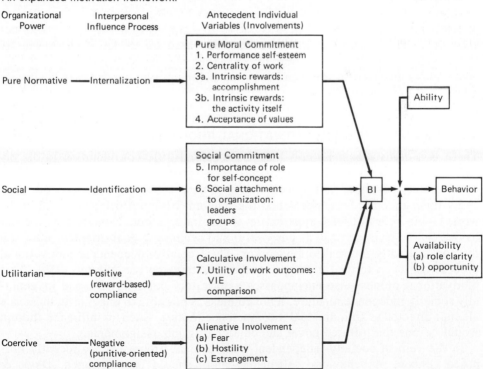

Solid arrows indicate congruent (appropriate) links.

and incentive-type schemes appear to be representative of influence attempts that are based on a simple compliance process. Such approaches seek to use extrinsic factors to bring about behavior change (with little or no attention given to appealing to higher order processes).

Identification-based motivational techniques are best represented by modeling techniques. For example, Goldstein and Sorcher (1974) proposed the use of behavioral modeling, which recently was tested by Latham and Saari (1979) and found to be an effective training technique. Also, studies reported by Burnaska (1976) and Kraut (1976) exemplify the social-learning theory approach to modifying work behavior (Davis & Luthans, 1980a).

Job enrichment, by contrast, appears to be directed toward altering the behavior of workers who are more seriously concerned with value-related issues (by offering opportunities for psychological rewards via job redesign). Job enrichment investigators have reported difficulty with respect to motivating individuals who are low on higher-order growth need strength (e.g., the case of the hard-core unemployed). This gives testimony to the validity of the proposition that an internalization influence attempt is most effective with only certain individuals (Hulin, 1971).

In summary, the major approaches to motivating workers (i.e., organizational intervention approaches) can be viewed as being aligned with each of the proposed influence processes. Although the effectiveness of the various intervention approaches is potentially *moderated* by individual and situational contingencies, the possibility exists that the simultaneous use of multiple approaches may result in relatively greater effectiveness (relative to employing a single motivational approach). This second, *additive* strategy is based on evidence—reviewed by Porras (1979) and Porras and Berg (1978)—that suggests that the number of OD techniques employed in intervention projects (or intervention mix) is positively related with effectiveness.

A SOCIALLY-INDEPENDENT MOTIVATIONAL PROCESS

There is a motivational process that has received little consideration in the organizational literature. This process has been ignored, perhaps, because it may be accurately described as a process that is somewhat socially independent. "Socially independent" here means that the relevant behavior originates within the worker with little (at least apparent) external inducement. Nonetheless, the behavior can be characterized as purposeful and seemingly goal-oriented, although the goal is totally internal to the worker. This socially independent motivational process has been termed a competence or mastery motive (White, 1959). This motivational process also encompasses exploratory behavior. Despite its generally socially independent nature, it nonetheless is possible to imagine an influence attempt directed at an individual's competence motive. Such an influence attempt would be one that offered novel and challenging job assignments.

In the vein of socially-independent motivational processes, the recently proposed concept of behavioral self-management should be mentioned (Davis & Luthans, 1980b; Luthans & Davis, 1979; Manz & Sims, 1980). Based on con-

cepts derived from cognitive behavior modification (Meichenbaum, 1977), behavioral self-management has been offered as a device for self-directing one's
own behavior in desired directions.

IMPLICATIONS

By extending and elaborating the proposed framework, it is possible to deduce
several implications for supervisory behaviors that would be directed toward
motivating workers. For this extension, it is necessary to introduce a feedback
loop from worker behavior to a supervisor or, more generally, an evaluator. In
this process (see Figure 3), the supervisor compares the observed behavior of
the worker with a standard or prior expectations. The supervisor then determines
whether a further influence attempt is warranted. If so, the supervisor decides
the nature of the influence attempt (compliance, internalization, and/or identification). From a purely descriptive standpoint, the framework represents a cyclical view of social influence, with the supervisor changing influence strategies
as a function of worker behavior. It might be argued that this view places a
substantial emphasis on worker behavior as a determinant of supervisor behavior.
At first glance, this seems like supervision turned upside-down in that the supervisor's influence attempts are "shaped" by the behavior of the worker. However, once the cycle begins, a reciprocal causation process is set in motion so
that the question of primary control of one person over the other becomes point-
less.

Taking the descriptive stance a bit further, it might be demonstrated empirically that different types of supervisors prefer different influence modes. For
example, highly authoritarian supervisors might prefer to use compliance influence modes; human-relations oriented supervisors might prefer to use identification influence modes. Also, supervisors might be observed to use different
modes of influence when operating in different levels of an organization.

From a prescriptive standpoint, the proposed influence framework suggests
that supervisors should be attentive to individual worker differences for preferred
inducements. For example, to increase worker motivation, a supervisor should
be sensitive to differences in subordinates' preferences for compliance-identifi-
cation-internalization inducement schemes. It might be possible to demonstrate

FIGURE 3
A social influence view of supervisor behavior.

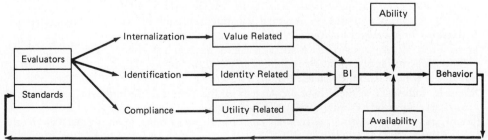

that more effective supervisors are aware of and make use of subordinate's inducement preferences when attempting to influence the latter's behavior. Such a finding would have important implications for a prescriptive application of the proposed framework.

The above-mentioned extension to supervisor behavior is consistent with the currently popular contingency view of leadership. Clearly, the framework's implications for supervision point to an optimal "matching" of (a) supervisor's preferred style of influence, (b) individual predisposition to respond to specific influence modes, and (c) situational variables that dictate what is socially-appropriate (i.e., normative) for the employment of specific influence modes. The view of the supervisor within the proposed framework, in essence, is best summarized as a view of the supervisor "as motivator."

SUMMARY

This paper has outlined a viewpoint that argues that worker motivation cannot be adequately understood without relating the concept of motivation to attempts on the part of organizational agents to "motivate" people. Such attempts usually take place by means of manipulating outcomes that are made contingent on the actions of individuals. The variables were identified that operate at the individual level (motivation), the interpersonal level (influence), and the organizational level (power). A framework was presented for tying these variables together, and concepts from both micro-level and macro-level approaches were integrated in a relatively meso-level approach. Also, specific testable predictions were generated from a proposed theoretical integration.

REFERENCES

Adams, J. S. Inequity in social exchange. In L. Berkowitz (Ed.), *Advances in experimental social psychology* (Vol. 2). New York: Academic Press, 1965, 267–299.

Blood, M. R. Work values and job satisfaction. *Journal of Applied Psychology*, 1969, 53, 456–459.

Burnaska, R. F. The effects of behavior upon managers' behaviors and employees' perceptions. *Personnel Psychology*, 1976, 29, 329–335.

Campbell, J. P., & Pritchard, R. D. Motivation theory in industrial and organizational psychology. In M. Dunnette (Ed.), *Handbook of industrial and organizational psychology*. Chicago: Rand-McNally, 1976, 63–130.

Campbell, J. P., Dunnette, M. D., Lawler, E. E., & Weick, K. E. *Managerial behavior, performance, and effectiveness*. New York: McGraw-Hill, 1970.

Davis, T. R. V., & Luthans, F. A social learning approach to organizational behavior. *Academy of Management Review*, 1980a, 5, 281–290.

Davis, T. R. V., & Luthans, F. A social learning approach to training and development: Guidelines for application. *Proceedings of the 12th Annual Meeting of the American Institute for Decision Sciences*, 1980b, 1, 399–401.

Dubin, R. Industrial workers' worlds: A study of the "central life interests" of industrial workers. *Social Problems*, 1956, 3, 131–142.

Etzioni, A. *A comparative analysis of complex organizations* (Rev. ed.). New York: Free Press, 1975.

Fishbein, M. (Ed.). *Readings in attitude theory and measurement*. New York: Wiley, 1967.

French, J. R. P., & Raven, B. The bases of social power. In D. Cartwright (Ed.), *Studies in social power*. Ann Arbor, Mich.: Institute for Social Research, 1959, 150–167.

Goldstein, A. P., & Sorcher, M. *Changing supervisory behavior*. New York: Pergamon Press, 1974.

Gouldner, A. W. Cosmopolitans and locals: Toward an analysis of latent social roles. *Administrative Science Quarterly*, 1957, 2, 281–292.

Hackman, J. R., & Oldham, G. R. Motivation through the design of work: Test of a theory. *Organizational Behavior and Human Performance*, 1976, 16, 250–279.

Hulin, C. L. Individual differences and job enrichment: The case against general treatments. In J. R. Maher (Ed.), *New perspectives in job enrichment*. New York: Van Nostrand, 1971, 159–191.

Katz, D. The motivational basis of organizational behavior. *Behavioral Science*, 1964, 9, 131–146.

Katzell, R. A. Personal values, job satisfaction, and job behavior. In H. Borow (Ed.), *Man in a world of work*. Boston: Houghton Mifflin, 1964, 314–363.

Kelman, H. C. Processes of opinion change. *Public Opinion Quarterly*, 1961, 25, 57–78.

Kohlberg, L. Moral development and identification. In H. Stevenson (Ed.), *Child psychology*, 62nd Yearbook of the National Society for the study of Education. Chicago: University of Chicago Press, 1963, 383–431.

Kohlberg, L. The cognitive-developmental approach to socialization. In D. A. Goslin (Ed.), *Handbook of socialization theory and research*. Chicago: Rand-McNally, 1969, 347–480.

Kraut, A. I. Developing managerial skills via modeling techniques: Some positive research findings—a symposium. *Personnel Psychology*, 1976, 29, 325–369.

Latham, G. P., & Saari, L. M. Application of social-learning theory to training supervisors through behavioral modeling. *Journal of Applied Psychology*, 1979, 64, 239–246.

Lawler, E. E., III. Job design and employee motivation. *Personnel Psychology*, 1969, 22, 426–435.

Lawler, E. E., III. *Pay and organizational effectiveness*. New York: McGraw-Hill, 1971.

Lawler, E. E., III. *Motivation in work organizations*. Monterey, Cal.: Brooks/Cole, 1973.

Locke, E. A. What is job satisfaction? *Organizational Behavior and Human Performance*, 1969, 4, 309–336.

Luthans, F., & Davis, T. R. V. Behavioral self-management —the missing link in managerial effectiveness. *Organizational Dynamics*, 1979, 8, 42–60.

Manz, C. C., & Sims, H. P. Self-management as a substitute for leadership: A social learning theory perspective. *Academy of Management Review*, 1980, 5, 361–367.

Meichenbaum, D. *Cognitive behavior modification: An integrative approach*. New York: Plenum, 1977.

Miller, E. E., Katerberg, R., & Hulin, C. L. Evaluation of the Mobley, Horner, and Hollingsworth model of employee turnover. *Journal of Applied Psychology*, 1979, 64, 509–517.

Mirels, H. L., & Garrett, J. B. The Protestant ethic as a personality variable. *Journal of Consulting and Clinical Psychology*, 1971, 36, 40–44.

Mobley, W. H. Intermediate linkages in the relationship between job satisfaction and employee turnover. *Journal of Applied Psychology*, 1977, 62, 237–240.

Mobley, W. H., Horner, S. O., & Hollingsworth, A. T. An evaluation of precursors of hospital employee turnover. *Journal of Applied Psychology*, 1978, 63, 408–414.

Mobley, W. H., Griffeth, R. W., Hand, H. H., & Meglino, B. M. Review and conceptual analysis of the employee turnover process. *Psychological Bulletin*, 1979, 86, 493–522.

Mobley, W. H., Hand, H. H., Baker, R. L., & Meglino, B. M. Conceptual and empirical analysis of military recruit training attrition. *Journal of Applied Psychology*, 1979, 64, 10–18.

Porras, J. I. The comparative impact of different OD techniques and intervention intensities. *Journal of Applied Behavioral Sciences*, 1979, 15, 156–178.

Porras, J. I., & Berg, P. O. The impact of organization development. *Academy of Management Review*, 1978, 3, 249–266.

Porter, L. W., & Lawler, E. E., III. *Managerial attitudes and performance*. Homewood, Ill.: Irwin, 1968.

Porter, L. W., & Steers, R. M. Organizational, work and personal factors in employee turnover and absenteeism. *Psychological Bulletin*, 1973, 80, 151–176.

Porter, L. W., Steers, R. M., Mowday, R. T., & Boulian, P. V. Organizational commitment, job satisfactions and turnover among psychiatric technicians. *Journal of Applied Psychology*, 1974, 59, 603–609.

Rabinowitz, S., & Hall, D. T. Organizational research and job involvement. *Psychological Bulletin*, 1977, 84, 265–288.

Rotter, J. B. Generalized expectancies for internal versus external control of reinforcement. *Psychological Monographs*, 1966, 80, (1, Whole No. 609).

Steers, R. M., & Rhodes, R. S. Major influences on employee attendance: A process model. *Journal of Applied Psychology*, 1978, 63, 391–407.

Vecchio, R. P. An individual differences interpretation of conflicting predictions generated by equity theory and expectancy theory. *Journal of Applied Psychology*, 1981, 66, 470–481.

Vroom, V. H. *Work and motivation*. New York: Wiley, 1964.

White, R. Motivation reconsidered: The concept of competence. *Psychological Review*, 1959, 66, 297–334.

The Development and Enforcement of Group Norms

Daniel C. Feldman

Group norms are the informal rules that groups adopt to regulate and regularize group members' behavior. Although these norms are infrequently written down or openly discussed, they often have a powerful, and consistent, influence on group members' behavior (Hackman, 1976).

From *Academy of Management Review*, 1984, **9**, 47–53. Reprinted by permission.

Most of the theoretical work on group norms has focused on identifying the types of group norms (March, 1954) or on describing their structural characteristics (Jackson, 1966). Empirically, most of the focus has been on examining the impact that norms have on other social phenomena. For example, Seashore (1954) and Schachter, Ellertson, McBride, and Gregory (1951) use the concept of group norms to discuss group cohesiveness; Trist and Bamforth (1951) and Whyte (1955a) use norms to examine production restriction; Janis (1972) and Longley and Pruitt (1980) use norms to illuminate group decision making; and Asch (1951) and Sherif (1936) use norms to examine conformity.

This paper focuses on two frequently overlooked aspects of the group norms literature. First, it examines *why* group norms are enforced. Why do groups desire conformity to these informal rules? Second, it examines *how* group norms develop. Why do some norms develop in one group but not in another? Much of what is known about group norms comes from post hoc examination of their impact on outcome variables; much less has been written about how these norms actually develop and why they regulate behavior so strongly.

Understanding how group norms develop and why they are enforced is important for two reasons. First, group norms can play a large role in determining whether the group will be productive or not. If the work group feels that management is supportive, groups norms will develop that facilitate—in fact, enhance—group productivity. In contrast, if the work group feels that management is antagonistic, group norms that inhibit and impair group performance are much more likely to develop. Second, managers can play a major role in setting and changing group norms. They can use their influence to set task-facilitative norms; they can monitor whether the group's norms are functional; they can explicitly address counterproductive norms with subordinates. By understanding how norms develop and why norms are enforced, managers can better diagnose the underlying tensions and problems their groups are facing, and they can help the group develop more effective behavior patterns.

WHY NORMS ARE ENFORCED

As Shaw (1981) suggests, a group does not establish or enforce norms about every conceivable situation. Norms are formed and enforced only with respect to behaviors that have some significance for the group. The frequent distinction between task maintenance duties and social maintenance duties helps explain why groups bring selected behaviors under normative control.

Groups, like individuals, try to operate in such a way that they maximize their chances for task success and minimize their chances of task failure. First of all, a group will enforce norms that facilitate its very survival. It will try to protect itself from interference from groups external to the organization or harassment from groups internal to the organization. Second, the group will want to increase the predictability of group members' behaviors. Norms provide a basis for predicting the behavior of others, thus enabling group members to anticipate each other's actions and to prepare quick and appropriate responses (Shaw, 1981; Kiesler & Kiesler, 1970).

In addition, groups want to ensure the satisfaction of their members and prevent as much interpersonal discomfort as possible. Thus, groups also will enforce norms that help the group avoid embarrassing interpersonal problems. Certain topics of conversation might be sanctioned, and certain types of social interaction might be openly discouraged. Moreover, norms serve an expressive function for groups (Katz & Kahn, 1978). Enforcing group norms gives group members a chance to express what their central values are, and to clarify what is distinctive about the group and central to its identity (Hackman, 1976).

Each of these four conditions under which group norms are most likely to be enforced is discussed in more detail below.

1 Norms Are Likely to Be Enforced if They Facilitate Group Survival A group will enforce norms that protect it from interference or harassment by members of other groups. For instance, a group might develop a norm not to discuss its salaries with members of other groups in the organization, so that attention will not be brought to pay inequities in its favor. Groups might also have norms about not discussing internal problems with members of other units. Such discussions might boomerang at a later date if other groups use the information to develop a better competitive strategy against the group.

Enforcing group norms also makes clear what the "boundaries" of the group are. As a result of observation of deviant behavior and the consequences that ensue, other group members are reminded of the *range* of behavior that is acceptable to the group (Dentler & Erikson, 1959). The norms about productivity that frequently develop among piecerate workers are illustrative here. By observing a series of incidents (a person produces 50 widgets and is praised; a person produces 60 widgets and receives sharp teasing; a person produces 70 widgets and is ostracized), group members learn the limits of the group's patience: "This far, and no further." The group is less likely to be "successful" (i.e., continue to sustain the low productivity expectations of management) if it allows its jobs to be reevaluated.

The literature on conformity and deviance is consistent with this observation. The group is more likely to reject the person who violates group norms when the deviant has not been a "good" group member previously (Hollander, 1958, 1964). Individuals can generate "idiosyncrasy credits" with other group members by contributing effectively to the attainment of group goals. Individuals expend these credits when they perform poorly or dysfunctionally at work. When a group member no longer has a positive "balance" of credits to draw on when he or she deviates, the group is much more likely to reject the deviant (Hollander, 1961).

Moreover, the group is more likely to reject the deviant when the group is failing in meeting its goals successfully. When the group is successful, it can afford to be charitable or tolerant towards deviant behavior. The group may disapprove, but it has some margin for error. When the group is faced with failure, the deviance is much more sharply punished. Any behavior that negatively influences the success of the group becomes much more salient and threatening to group members (Alvarez, 1968; Wiggins, Dill, & Schwartz, 1965).

2   Norms Are Likely to Be Enforced if They Simplify, or Make Predict-able, What Behavior Is Expected of Group Members   If each member of the group had to decide individually how to behave in each interaction, much time would be lost performing routine activities. Moreover, individuals would have more trouble predicting the behaviors of others and responding correctly. Norms enable group members to anticipate each other's actions and to prepare the most appropriate response in the most timely manner (Hackman, 1976; Shaw, 1981).

For instance, when attending group meetings in which proposals are presented and suggestions are requested, do the presenters really want feedback or are they simply going through the motions? Groups may develop norms that reduce this uncertainty and provide a clearer course of action, for example, make suggestions in small, informal meetings but not in large, formal meetings.

Another example comes from norms that regulate social behavior. For in-stance, when colleagues go out for lunch together, there can be some awkward-ness about how to split the bill at the end of the meal. A group may develop a norm that gives some highly predictable or simple way of behaving, for example, split evenly, take turns picking up the tab, or pay for what each ordered.

Norms also may reinforce specific individual members' roles. A number of different roles might emerge in groups. These roles are simply expectations that are shared by group members regarding who is to carry out what types of activ-ities under what circumstances (Bales & Slater, 1955). Although groups ob-viously create pressure toward uniformity among members, there also is a tend-ency for groups to create and maintain *diversity* among members (Hackman, 1976). For instance, a group might have one person whom others expect to break the tension when tempers become too hot. Another group member might be expected to keep track of what is going on in other parts of the organization. A third member might be expected to take care of the "creature" needs of the group—making the coffee, making dinner reservations, and so on. A fourth mem-ber might be expected by others to take notes, keep minutes, or maintain files.

None of these roles are *formal* duties, but they are activities that the group needs accomplished and has somehow parcelled out among members. If the role expectations are not met, some important jobs might not get done, or other group members might have to take on additional responsibilities. Moreover, such role assignments reduce individual members' ambiguities about what is expected spe-cifically of them. It is important to note, though, that who takes what role in a group also is highly influenced by individuals' personal needs. The person with a high need for structure often wants to be in the note-taking role to control the structuring activity in the group; the person who breaks the tension might dislike conflict and uses the role to circumvent it.

3   Norms Are Likely to Be Enforced if They Help the Group Avoid Em-barrassing Interpersonal Problems   Goffman's work on "facework" gives some insight on this point. Goffman (1955) argues that each person in a group has a "face" he or she presents to other members of a group. This "face" is analogous to what one would call "self-image," the person's perceptions to himself or herself and how he or she would like to be seen by others. Groups want to insure that no one's self-image is damaged, called into question, or embarrassed. Consequently, the group will establish norms that discourage topics of conversation or situations in which face is too likely to be inadvertently broken. For instance, groups might develop norms about not discussing romantic involvements (so that differences in moral values do not become salient) or about not getting together socially in people's homes (so that differences in taste or income do not become salient).

A good illustration of Goffman's facework occurs in the classroom. There is always palpable tension in a room when either a class is totally unprepared to discuss a case or a professor is totally unprepared to lecture or lead the discussion. One part of the awkwardness stems from the inability of the other partner in the interaction to behave as he or she is prepared to or would like to behave. The professor cannot teach if the students are not prepared, and the students cannot learn if the professors are not teaching. Another part of the awkwardness, though, stems from self-images being called into question. Although faculty are aware that not all students are serious scholars, the situation is difficult to handle if the class as a group does not even show a pretense of wanting to learn. Although students are aware that many faculty are mainly interested in research and consulting, there is a problem if the professor does not even show a pretense of caring to teach. Norms almost always develop between professor and students about what level of preparation and interest is expected by the other because both parties want to avoid awkward confrontations.

4   Norms Are Likely to Be Enforced if They Express the Central Values of the Group and Clarify What Is Distinctive about the Group's Identity   Norms can provide the social justification for group activities to its members (Katz & Kahn, 1978). When the production group labels rate-busting deviant, it says: "We care more about maximizing group security than about individual profits." Group norms also convey what is distinctive about the group to outsiders. When an advertising agency labels unstylish clothes deviant, it says: "We think of ourselves, personally and professionally, as trend-setters, and being fashionably dressed conveys that to our clients and our public."

One of the key expressive functions of group norms is to define and legitimate the power of the group itself over individual members (Katz & Kahn, 1978). When groups punish norm infraction, they reinforce in the minds of group members the authority of the group. Here, too, the literature on group deviance sheds some light on the issue at hand.

It has been noted frequently that the amount of deviance in a group is rather small (Erikson, 1966; Schur, 1965). The group uses norm enforcement to show the *strength* of the group. However, if a behavior becomes so widespread that it becomes impossible to control, then the labeling of the widespread behavior as deviance becomes problematic. It simply reminds members of the *weakness* of the group. At this point, the group will redefine what is deviant more narrowly, or it will define its job as that of keeping deviants *within bounds* rather than that of obliterating it altogether. For example, though drug use is and always has been illegal, the widespread use of drugs has led to changes in law enforcement over time. A greater distinction now is made between "hard" drugs and other controlled substances; less penalty is given to those apprehended with small amounts than large amounts; greater attention is focused on capturing large scale smugglers and traffickers than the occasional user. A group, unconsciously if not consciously, learns how much behavior it is capable of labeling deviant *and* punishing effectively.

Finally, this expressive function of group norms can be seen nicely in circumstances in which there is an inconsistency between what group members *say* is the group norm and how people actually *behave*. For instance, sometimes groups will engage in a lot of rhetoric about how much independence its managers are allowed and how much it values entrepreneurial effort; yet the harder data suggest that the more conservative, deferring, or dependent managers get rewarded. Such an inconsistency can reflect conflicts among the group's expressed values. First, the group can be ambivalent about independence; the group knows it needs to encourage more entrepreneurial efforts to flourish, but such efforts create competition and threaten the status quo. Second, the inconsistency can reveal major subgroup differences. Some people may value and encourage entrepreneurial behavior, but others do not—and the latter may control the group's rewards. Third, the inconsistency can reveal a source of the group's self-consciousness, a dichotomy between what the group is really like and how it would like to be perceived. The group may realize that it is too conservative, yet be unable or too frightened to address its problem. The expressed group norm allows the group members a chance to present a "face" to each other and to outsiders that is more socially desirable than reality.

HOW GROUP NORMS DEVELOP

Norms usually develop gradually and informally as group members learn what behaviors are necessary for the group to function more effectively. However, it also is possible for the norm development process to be short-cut by a critical event in the group or by conscious group decision (Hackman, 1976).

Most norms develop in one or more of the following four ways: explicit statements by supervisors or co-workers; critical events in the group's history; primacy; and carry-over behaviors from past situations.

1   Explicit Statements by Supervisors or Co-workers   Norms that facilitate group survival or task success often are set by the leader of the group or powerful members (Whyte, 1955b). For instance, a group leader might explicitly set norms about not drinking at lunch because subordinates who have been drinking are more likely to have problems dealing competently with clients and top management or they are more likely to have accidents at work. The group leader might also set norms about lateness, personal phone calls, and long coffee breaks if too much productivity is lost as a result of time away from the work place.

Explicit statements by supervisors also can increase the predictability of group members' behavior. For instance, supervisors might have particular preferences for a way of analyzing problems or presenting reports. Strong norms will be set to ensure compliance with these preferences. Consequently, supervisors will have increased certainty about receiving work in the format requested, so they can plan accordingly; workers will have increased certainty about what is expected, so they will not have to outguess their boss or redo their projects.

Managers or important group members also can define the specific role expectations of individual group members. For instance, a supervisor or a co-worker might go up to a new recruit after a meeting to give the proverbial advice: "New recruits should be seen and not heard." The senior group member might be trying to prevent the new recruit from appearing brash or incompetent or from embarrassing other group members. Such interventions set specific role expectations for the new group member.

Norms that cater to supervisor preferences also are frequently established even if they are not objectively necessary to task accomplishment. For example, although organizational norms may be very democratic in terms of everybody calling each other by their first names, some managers have strong preferences about being called Mr., Ms., or Mrs. Although the form of address used in the work group does not influence group effectiveness, complying with the norm bears little cost to the group member, whereas noncompliance could cause daily friction with the supervisor. Such norms help group members avoid embarrassing interpersonal interactions with their managers.

Fourth, norms set explicitly by the supervisor frequently express the central values of the group. For instance, a dean can set very strong norms about faculty keeping office hours and being on campus daily. Such norms reaffirm to members of the academic community their teaching and service obligations, and they send signals to individuals outside the college about what is valued in faculty behavior or distinctive about the school. A dean also could set norms that allow faculty to consult or do executive development two or three days a week. Such norms, too, legitimate other types of faculty behavior and send signals to both insiders and outsiders about some central values of the college.

2   Critical Events in the Group's History   At times there is a critical event in the group's history that established an important precedent. For instance, a group member might have discussed hiring plans with members of other units in the organization, and as a result new positions were lost or there was increased competition for good applicants. Such indiscretion can substantially hinder the survival and task success of the group; very likely the offender will be either formally censured or informally rebuked. As a result of such an incident, norms about secrecy might develop that will protect the group in similar situations in the future.

An example from Janis's *Victims of Groupthink* (1972) also illustrates this point nicely. One of President Kennedy's closest advisors, Arthur Schlesinger, Jr., had serious reservations about the Bay of Pigs invasion and presented his strong objections to the Bay of Pigs plan in a memorandum to Kennedy and Secretary of State Dean Rusk. However, Schlesinger was pressured by the President's brother, Attorney General Robert Kennedy, to keep his objections to himself. Remarked Robert Kennedy to Schlesinger: "You may be right or you may be wrong, but the President has made his mind up. Don't push it any further. Now is the time for everyone to help him all they can.'' Such critical events led group members to silence their views and set up group norms about the bounds of disagreeing with the president.

Sometimes group norms can be set by a conscious decision of a group after a particularly good or bad experience the group has had. To illustrate, a group might have had a particularly constructive meeting and be very pleased with how much it accomplished. Several people might say, ''I think the reason we got so much accomplished today is that we met really early in the morning before the rest of the staff showed up and the phone started ringing. Let's try to continue to meet at 7:30 a.m.'' Others might agree, and the norm is set. On the other hand, if a group notices it accomplished way too little in a meeting, it might openly discuss setting norms to cut down on ineffective behavior (e.g., having an agenda, not interrupting others while they are talking). Such norms develop to facilitate task success and to reduce uncertainty about what is expected from each individual in the group.

Critical events also can identify awkward interpersonal situations that need to be avoided in the future. For instance, a divorce between two people working in the same group might have caused a lot of acrimony and hard feeling in a unit, not only between the husband and wife but also among various other group members who got involved in the marital problems. After the unpleasant divorce, a group might develop a norm about not hiring spouses to avoid having to deal with such interpersonal problems in the future.

Finally, critical events also can give rise to norms that express the central, or distinctive, values of the group. When a peer review panel finds a physician or lawyer guilty of malpractice or malfeasance, first it establishes (or reaffirms) the rights of professionals to evaluate and criticize the professional behavior of their colleagues. Moreover, it clarifies what behaviors are inconsistent with the group's self-image or its values. When a faculty committee votes on a candidate's tenure, it, too, asserts the legitimacy of influence of senior faculty over junior faculty. In addition, it sends (hopefully) clear messages to junior faculty about its values in terms of quality of research, teaching, and service. There are important ''announcement effects'' of peer reviews; internal group members carefully reexamine the group's values, and outsiders draw inferences about the character of the group from such critical decision.

3 Primacy The first behavior pattern that emerges in a group often sets group expectations. If the first group meeting is marked by very formal interaction between supervisors and subordinates, then the group often expects future meetings to be conducted in the same way. Where people sit in meetings or rooms frequently is developed through primacy. People generally continue to sit in the same seats they sat in at their first meeting, even though those original seats are not assigned and people could change where they sit at every meeting. Most friendship groups of students develop their own ''turf'' in a lecture hall and are surprised/dismayed when an interloper takes ''their'' seats.

Norms that develop through primacy often do so to simplify, or make predictable, what behavior is expected of group members. There may be very little task impact from where people sit in meetings or how formal interactions are. However, norms develop about such behaviors to make life much more routine and predictable. Every time a group member enters a room, he or she does not have to "decide" where to sit or how formally to behave. Moreover, he or she also is much more certain about how other group members will behave.

4 Carry-over Behaviors from Past Situations Many group norms in organizations emerge because individual group members bring set expectations with them from other work groups in other organizations. Lawyers expect to behave towards clients in Organization I (e.g., confidentiality, setting fees) as they behaved towards those in Organization II. Doctors expect to behave toward patients in Hospital I (e.g., "bedside manner," professional distance) as they behaved in Hospital II. Accountants expect to behave towards colleagues at Firm I (e.g., dress code, adherence to statutes) as they behaved towards those at Firm II. In fact, much of what goes on in professional schools is giving new members of the profession the same standards and norms of behavior that practitioners in the field hold.

Such carry-over of individual behaviors from past situations can increase the predictability of group members' behaviors in new settings and facilitate task accomplishment. For instance, students and professors bring with them fairly constant sets of expectations from class to class. As a result, students do not have to relearn continually their roles from class to class; they know, for instance, if they come in late to take a seat quietly at the back of the room without being told. Professors also do not have to relearn continually their roles; they know, for instance, not to mumble, scribble in small print on the blackboard, or be vague when making course assignments. In addition, presumably the most task-successful norms will be the ones carried over from organization to organization.

Moreover, such carry-over norms help avoid embarrassing interpersonal situations. Individuals are more likely to know which conversations and actions provoke annoyance, irritation, or embarrassment to their colleagues. Finally, when groups carry over norms from one organization to another, they also clarify what is distinctive about the occupational or professional role. When lawyers maintain strict rules of confidentiality, when doctors maintain a consistent professional distance with patients, when accountants present a very formal physical appearance, they all assert: "These are the standards we sustain *independent* of what we could 'get away with' in this organization. This is *our* self-concept."

SUMMARY

Norms generally are enforced only for behaviors that are viewed as important by most group members. Groups do not have the time or energy to regulate each and every action of individual members. Only those behaviors that ensure group survival, facilitate task accomplishment, contribute to group morale, or express the group's central values are likely to be brought under normative control. Norms that reflect these group needs will develop through explicit statements of supervisors, critical events in the group's history, primacy, or carry-over behaviors from past situations.

Empirical research on norm development and enforcement has substantially lagged descriptive and theoretical work. In large part, this may be due to the methodological problems of measuring norms and getting enough data points either across time or across groups. Until such time as empirical work progresses, however, the usefulness of group norms as a predictive concept, rather than as a post hoc explanatory device, will be severely limited. Moreover, until it is known more concretely why norms develop and why they are strongly enforced, attempts to *change* group norms will remain haphazard and difficult to accomplish.

REFERENCES

Alvarez, R. Informal reactions to deviance in simulated work organizations: A laboratory experiment. *American Sociological Review*, 1968, 33, 895–912.

Asch, S. Effects of group pressure upon the modification and distortion of judgment. In M. H. Guetzkow (Ed.), *Groups, leadership, and men.* Pittsburgh: Carnegie, 1951, 117–190.

Bales, R. F., & Slater, P. E. Role differentiation in small groups. In T. Parsons, R. F. Bales, J. Olds, M. Zelditch, & P. E. Slater (Eds.), *Family, socialization, and interaction process.* Glencoe, Ill.: Free Press, 1955, 35–131.

Dentler, R. A., & Erikson, K. T. The functions of deviance in groups. *Social Problems*, 1959, 7, 98–107.

Erikson, K. T. *Wayward Puritans.* New York: Wiley, 1966.

Goffman, E. On face-work: An analysis of ritual elements in social interaction. *Psychiatry*, 1955, 18, 213–231.

Hackman, J. R. Group influences on individuals. In M. Dunnette (Ed.), *Handbook of industrial and organizational psychology.* Chicago: Rand McNally, 1976, 1455–1525.

Hollander, E. P. Conformity, status, and idiosyncrasy credit. *Psychological Review*, 1958, 65, 117–127.

Hollander, E. P. Some effects of perceived status on responses to innovative behavior. *Journal of Abnormal and Social Psychology*, 1961, 63, 247–250.

Hollander, E. P. *Leaders, groups, and influence.* New York: Oxford University Press, 1964.

Jackson, J. A conceptual and measurement model for norms and roles. *Pacific Sociological Review*, 1966, 9, 35–47.

Janis, I. *Victims of groupthink: A psychological study of foreign-policy decisions and fiascos.* New York: Houghton-Mifflin, 1972.

Katz, D., & Kahn, R. L. *The social psychology of organizations.* 2nd ed. New York: Wiley, 1978.

Kiesler, C. A., & Kiesler, S. B. *Conformity.* Reading, Mass.: Addison-Wesley, 1970.

Longley, J., & Pruitt, D. C. Groupthink: A critique of Janis' theory. In Ladd Wheeler. (Ed.), *Review of personality and social psychology.* Beverly Hills: Sage, 1980, 74–93.

March, J. Group norms and the active minority. *American Sociological Review*, 1954, 19, 733–741.

Schachter, S., Ellertson, N., McBride, D., & Gregory, D. An experimental study of cohesiveness and productivity. *Human Relations*, 1951, 4, 229–238.

Schur, E. M. *Crimes without victims*. Englewood Cliffs, N.J.: Prentice-Hall, 1965.

Seashore, S. *Group cohesiveness in the industrial work group*. Ann Arbor: Institute for Social Research, University of Michigan, 1954.

Shaw, M. *Group dynamics*. 3rd ed. New York: Harper, 1936.

Trist, E. L., & Bamforth, K. W. Some social and psychological consequences of the longwall method of coal-getting. *Human Relations*, 1951, 4, 1–38.

Whyte, W. F. *Money and motivation*. New York: Harper, 1955a.

Whyte. W. F. *Street corner society*. Chicago: University of Chicago Press, 1955b.

Wiggins, J. A., Dill, F., & Schwartz, R. D. On status-liability. *Sociometry*, 1965, 28, 197–209.

The Interaction of Social Influences and Task Experience on Goals, Performance, and Performance Satisfaction

Thomas L. Rakestraw, Jr.
Howard M. Weiss

Since the late 1960s there has been a renewed interest in the effects of task goals on performance and satisfaction. This interest can be traced to the empirical and theoretical work of Locke and his associates and the recognition by organizational researchers of the practical implications of Locke's work. In a series of papers (Locke, 1968, 1970; Locke, Cartledge, & Knerr, 1970) Locke presented what he described as "the foundations" of a theory of task performance and satisfaction. Central to the theory are the notions that task goals are the most immediate determinants of performance and that satisfaction with performance is a function of the discrepancy between performance and performance standards. In a program of laboratory research Locke found consistent support for the important influences of goals on performance (Locke, 1968; Locke *et al.* 1970). He repeatedly found that performance was positively related to goal difficulty and specificity, and performance satisfaction was a function of the discrepancy between goals and achievement.

In his 1968 paper Locke stated that he was not attempting "to specify the ultimate roots or causes of the particular goals or intentions an individual develops on a task" (Locke, 1968, p. 159). Since the research to that point focused only on the relationship between goals and intentions, once established, and subsequent behavior. Locke referred to his work as presenting only the foundations of a theory of task performance.

Although Locke's original work has stimulated a great deal of research, the major thrust of this research has focused on goal setting as a motivational tech-

From *Organizational Behavior and Human Performance*, 1981, **27**, 326–344. Copyright © 1981 by Academic Press, Inc. All rights of reproduction in any form reserved.

nique useful in organizations for increasing productivity. In general, this field work has supported Locke's laboratory findings of the effects of task goals on performance (Latham & Yukl, 1975). Research on goal setting as an intervention technique is of obvious practical importance. However, it is clear that individuals develop their own performance goals and intentions in the absence of formal goal setting procedures and that these goals are as important to the regulation of task performance as are goals which are externally assigned or determined by formal mechanisms. Since Locke presented his theory almost no attention has been paid to the natural processes of goal setting; the way individuals working on tasks come to set, for themselves, specific task goals. The ubiquity of these goals, coupled with their influence on performance and satisfaction, suggests the need for extending Locke's "foundations of a theory of task performance" with more research on the factors which affect the levels of these self-set goals.

Some things are known about the way individuals set their goals. Of particular relevance is the classic work on level of aspiration (Lewin, Dembo, Festinger, & Sears, 1944; Zander, 1971). The most consistent findings of this research are that goals are influenced by prior performance (see also Yukl & Latham, 1978) and are affected by success (upward adjustment) and failure (downward adjustment), and that the effects of success and failure generalize across tasks as a function of task similarity. In addition, aspiration levels have been shown to be responsive to normative information about the average performance levels of various reference groups, although this effect is not always found (Koulak & Peterson, 1969). Lewin believed that aspiration levels were chosen as a function of the probabilities and incentive values of success and failure and, more recently, Dachler and Mobley (1973) have shown that similar VIE constructs correlate with stated performance goals. Additionally, Locke *et al.* (1970) showed that goal choices correlated with subjects' anticipated satisfaction with reaching the goal.

In spite of the knowledge gained from classic aspiration research and recent attempts to tie together goal setting and VIE theory, it is clear that our understanding of factors influencing goal choice is nowhere near the level one might expect given the relationship between goals and task performance. This should be a particular concern of organizational researchers, since, in spite of the plethora of motivational techniques currently in use, so much of any workers' motivated behavior is ultimately self-controlled.

Particularly relevant to the setting of personal performance goals and standards, but inadequately studied, is the way goals are influenced by the observation of the achievements of other workers. The mounting body of evidence on the way models influence other forms of work-related behaviors and attitudes (Latham & Saari, 1979; Weiss, 1977, 1978; White & Mitchell, 1979) suggests that observational processes may be relevant to the way individuals develop personal standards and goals. Although neither he nor his associates have conducted research on this issue, Locke (1968) has alluded to the effects of others' achievements on the levels of goals set by observers.

Two lines of inquiry do suggest the relevance of social influences on this process without actually demonstrating that models influence goals or performance. First, as mentioned earlier, normative reference group information has sometimes, although not always, been shown to affect individual aspiration levels. However, this research has not focused on the effects of the actual observation of another individual's performance, a much more likely occurrence in organizations than encountering average performance levels. Second, research by Bandura and his associates (Bandura, 1976) has shown that children will reward themselves on tasks (with candy, toys, etc.) for achievement levels based upon the self-reinforcement patterns they observe in adult models. Bandura equates these self-reinforcement levels with task goals. However, in these studies only self-reinforcement levels are assessed. Model effects on observer intentions and actual observer-performance levels are not systematically measured.

These results are suggestive but not conclusive. Yet Bandura's research, the research on normative effects on aspiration levels and research on modeling influences on other organizationally relevant behaviors, indicates that the study of social influences, particularly observational processes, on goal setting behavior may be productive. It seems likely that under conditions where objective indices of success and failure are absent the performance achievements of other workers serving as role models will influence the goals and task performance of observers. The first purpose of this study was to examine, in a laboratory setting, these modeling influences on goal setting.

It also seems likely that the influence of models on observers' goals and performance will vary across situations. Research has shown that individuals will search for information provided by others under conditions of task uncertainty (Crawford, 1974). Marlatt (1971) has shown that the influence of models is more pronounced on unstructured than on structured tasks. Similarly, Weiss (1977, 1978) has shown that low-self-esteem workers, being more uncertain about appropriate role behaviors, are more likely to model co-workers. It seems that individuals generally turn to models under conditions of uncertainty, when the situation or their own personal experiences fail to provide appropriate guides for their behavior. Although no research has examined the effects of prior task experience on modeling, it seems reasonable to suggest that when individuals can look to their own experiences as sources of relevant information, the importance of models will decrease. In this regard, while discussing the substantial role that models play in the establishment of self-reinforcement standards, Bandura additionally states that individuals also use their previous behaviors as the reference against which to judge their performance. This is likely to be true in the setting of performance goals as well. That is, observational influences on performance goals are likely to be greatest under conditions of uncertainty, on new tasks and in the absence of adequate personal task experience. Under conditions of more task experience the effects of models are likely to be less pronounced. A second purpose of this study was therefore, to examine the interactive effect of model performance and task experience on goal setting behavior. Specifically, based upon the reasoning presented above, the following hypotheses were tested:

Hypothesis 1a Individuals who observe a high-performing model will themselves set higher performance goals than individuals who observe a low-performing model.

Hypothesis 1b The effects of the model's performance on observers' goals will be stronger among subjects without task experience prior to being exposed to the model than among subjects with task experience.

Obviously model influences on goals without accompanying effects on performance would be less than meaningful. However, Locke's research clearly shows that performance is linearly related to goal difficulty. As a result, it was expected that observational effects would also extend to performance differences between subjects viewing high- and low-performing models. Thus, hypotheses 2a and 2b were tested.

Hypothesis 2a Individuals who observe a high-performing model will themselves perform higher on the same task than will individuals who observe a low-performing model.

Hypothesis 2b The effects of the model's performance on observers' performances will be stronger among subjects without task experience prior to being exposed to the model than among subjects with task experience.

Finally, observational effects on performance satisfaction were also expected. As stated earlier, Locke's research has generally shown performance satisfaction to be a function of the discrepancy between performance and performance standards (Locke *et al.* 1970). Reasoning in a similar manner to Locke, Bandura (1976) has also argued that self-reinforcement is conditional upon matching self-presented standards of behavior. It then becomes logical to argue that where individuals are using the observed performance of others as a performance standard, performance satisfaction (positive self-reinforcement in Bandura's framework) will be a function of the discrepancy between self- and model's performance. Further, for the same reasons suggested earlier, this relationship should be weaker where previous task experience allows for an internal standard of performance. Based upon this reasoning, hypotheses 3a and 3b were examined.

Hypothesis 3a Performance satisfaction will be negatively related to the discrepancy between subjects' and model's task performance.

Hypothesis 3b This relationship will be stronger among subjects without task experience than among subjects with task experience.

METHOD

Overview

Subjects were told they were taking part in a study of training methods. All subjects were first given written instructions for a card sorting task, and at that time, approximately half of the subjects were allowed to work on the task. All subjects then viewed a "training film" which showed a male student working on the task while the experimenter described appropriate work methods. Approximately half of the subjects saw a film in which the student worker (model) achieved a high level of performance while the remaining subjects saw a film identical in all respects except that the student worker achieved a lower level of performance. After seeing the film all subjects worked on the task and their performance was recorded. Finally, a questionnaire was administered to assess task goal levels and satisfaction. This procedure produced a 2 (high-performing model vs low-performing model) × 2 (task experience vs no task experience) design with subjects' goals, task performance, and satisfaction serving as dependent variables.

Subjects

Subjects were 174 male introductory psychology students at Purdue University who participated in the study as partial fulfillment of a course requirement.

Task

Subjects worked on a card sorting task which had been previously used in the goal setting studies of Pritchard and Curts (1973) and White, Mitchell, and Bell (1977). The task required subjects to sort cards with specific patterns of punched holes onto vertical spikes on a sorting board. Printed across the top of each card is information about the sex (male, female), age (20 years or under, 21–22 years, 23 years or older), and state residency (resident, nonresident) of an individual. This information is also represented on each card by a set of three punched holes. Thus, on each card there is one of 12 configurations of holes corresponding to one of the 12 combinations of sex, age, and residency information. Subjects are also given a sorting board which has 12 sets of three metal spikes, corresponding to the 12 configurations of holes in the cards. They are required to sort each card into one of the 12 categories by placing it on the appropriate set of spikes.

One important variation was introduced to the card sorting task. This variation involved the use of a feedback board designed to provide subjects with continuous performance feedback as they worked on the task. Subjects received their cards in packets of 10. These packets were hung on a "feedback board" in two rows of six packets each and the board was placed directly in front of the subject. When working on the sorting task the subject removed the cards from the board, one packet at a time, beginning at the upper left-hand corner and proceeding across the first row and then through the second. Once a packet was removed, a number was revealed on the board which provided the subjects with cumulative, continuous feedback about how many cards he had sorted (i.e., removal of the third packet revealed the number 30, removal of the fifth packet revealed the number 50, etc.). The use of the feedback board was also designed to facilitate the unobtrusive communication of the model's performance level during the training film. (This will be described later.) When working on the task, subjects were given 5 min to sort as many cards as they could. This length of time was chosen so that the subjects' time per trial would be equal to the time the model on the "training film" (see below) was given to work on the task. The equivalence of subjects' and model's trial time was obviously necessary so that subjects could use the model's performance as an appropriate goal for their own performance. The comparatively simple nature of the card sorting task was such that a much longer trial time for the model, and therefore a much longer training film, would have strained the credibility of the film as a training device (long pauses between trainer comments, undue repetition, etc). While a subject trial time of 5 min is rather short, it was of sufficient duration to produce substantial variation in subjects' performance (range across all subjects of 30 to 92 with a SD of 12.5).

This task was chosen for a number of reasons. First, as Pritchard and Curts note, since a card cannot be sorted incorrectly (a card cannot fit on the wrong configuration of spikes), performance varies in terms of quantity only. Second, performance on this task is mainly a function of effort or motivation, producing a closer correspondence between goals or intentions and performance. Third, the task has been used successfully in other goal setting studies.

Independent Variables

Task Experience   Subjects in the task experience condition ($n = 85$) were given the opportunity to practice sorting the cards for 5 min before seeing the "training film." During this period, these subjects sorted an average of 46 cards. The initial familiarity with the task of subjects in the no task experience condition ($n = 89$) was restricted to the written set of instructions given to all subjects.

Model Performance   The model performance conditions were manipulated by using videotapes of a trained actor performing the card sorting task for two trials. The general procedure was similar to that used by Weiss and Shaw (1979) to examine model influences on task attitudes. Subjects were told that before working on the task they would see a "training film" which would provide instructional information to supplement the written material they had been given. They were told that the film would show a student working on the task while the voice of a trainer would provide instruction on how to do the task using the behavior of the worker in the film to provide illustrative examples. They were also told that the worker was a student who had been unobtrusively filmed through a one-way mirror while he worked on the task during an earlier phase of the research.

In reality, the training films that subjects saw were two videotapes designed to unobtrusively manipulate the two levels of model performance. In both tapes the "student worker" was the same drama major who was trained to display varying levels of performance and who was paid for his participation. Both tapes showed the model seated at a table with his back to the camera. The model and table were positioned so that both the sorting board and the feedback board were in plain view. The tapes began with the experimenter (off camera throughout) giving the model oral instructions for the card sorting task. Although the model's back was toward the camera, his face could occasionally be seen as he looked to the experimenter while receiving the instructions and later as he reached across the desk in front of him while sorting the cards.

After giving the instructions the experimenter told the model he had 5 min to work on the task and then left the room. Five minutes later the experimenter returned and reported the model's performance to him. The model then worked on the task for another 5 min after which the experimenter returned and again reported the model's performance.

In order to determine appropriate high- and low-model-performance levels, a group of similar subjects was pretested on the task. These subjects were able to sort, on the average, approximately 50 cards in a 5-min period. As a result, in the videotape of the low-achieving model, the student worker sorted 28 cards during the first trial and 40 cards during the second trial. By contrast, in the videotape of the high-achieving model, the student worker first sorted 68 cards and then 80 cards.

In addition to hearing the experimenter report the model's performance, the subjects were also able to observe the numbers on the feedback board. Thus the model (and the viewing subjects) received feedback about the model's performance in two ways: continuous feedback from the feedback board and final feedback from the experimenter. In both the low- and high-model performance films the model vocally expressed to the experimenter two statements of dissatisfaction after hearing his first trial performance and two statements of satisfaction after hearing his second trial performance so as to communicate to the subjects the importance of the performance level to the model.

In keeping with the training rationale for the film, while the model sorted the cards, the trainer's voice pointed out details concerning methods of task performance. This commentary included a description of the feedback board, the arrangements of categories on the sorting board and suggestions for sorting the cards more easily (e.g., ''some persons find it easier to first sort the cards into groups of males and females before placing them into their appropriate categories on the sorting board''). The training commentary was identical for both films.

Dependent Measures

Each subject's *performance* was assessed by simply counting the number of cards sorted by the subject after 5 min. Although the feedback board gave subjects a running account of their performance, as in the film the experimenter also reported to the subject the final count at the conclusion of the 5-min work period. In the post-task questionnaire, subjects were asked to report the number of cards they had sorted. The correlation of $r = .95$ between their actual and perceived performance levels indicates that there was very little ambiguity surrounding their performance.

Also in the post-task questionnaire, subjects were asked to indicate their *performance goals* for the trial they had just completed. Although assessing performance goals after performance obviously creates problems of causal interpretation, the decision to assess the goals retrospectively rather than measuring goals prior to performance was based upon two considerations. First, any sequence of collecting goal reports and performance data in the same study will produce problems of causal interpretation and it seemed more reasonable to protect the harder performance data from being contaminated by stated goal levels than vice versa. Second, in the research reported by Locke (1968) retrospective and non-retrospective collections of goal data were both employed and yielded substantially equivalent results. However, in order to shed additional light on the causal sequence involving observation of model performance, goal setting, and subject performance, a causal correlational analysis was conducted and is reported with the other results in the study.

Finally, *satisfaction with performance* was measured by asking each subject to respond to the question "How satisfied were you with your performance on the task?", using a 7-point scale ranging from "very dissatisfied" to "very satisfied." Subjects were also asked to respond to the question "To what extent did you enjoy working on the card sorting task?", using a 7-point scale that ranged from "did not enjoy the task at all" to "enjoyed the task very much." It should be noted that the correlation of $r = .08$ between the two measures suggests that the subjects were distinguishing between their satisfaction with the task and their satisfaction with their performance on the task.

Procedure

Each subject was seated in a small room containing a table, video monitor, and a headset with a microphone for communicating with the experimenter. On the table was a sorting board, a feedback board (with card packets), and a set of written instructions for the task. Subjects were advised by the experimenter that the study involved an evaluation of different training methods and different modes of presenting instructional material. As part of the training method they were going to see a "training film" on the monitor in front of them. All subjects were then given an opportunity to read the brief description of the task. Subjects in the task experience condition ($n = 85$) were told that before seeing the training film they would be given the opportunity to familiarize themselves with the task by practicing the task for five minutes. At the end of this period the experimenter entered the subject's room, counted the number of cards sorted and reported the performance to the subject. At this point, (without the practice period for subjects in the no experience condition, $n = 89$) all subjects were shown the "training film." Approximately half of the subjects ($n = 89$) were shown the film depicting the high-performing model and half ($n = 85$) were shown the film with the low-performing model. After seeing the "training film" subjects were instructed to work on the task for a 5-min period. At the end of the period the experimenter entered the subject's room, recorded and announced the subject's performance, and distributed the post-task questionnaire. In keeping with the training methods focus of the study, this questionnaire was ostensibly designed to assess subjects' reactions to the training film and the task. As such it contained numerous items asking about the clarity of the video and audio portions of the film, the instructional material presented in the film, whether the subjects thought the film was an effective training device, etc. Embedded in these "training evaluation" questions were the items measuring the subject's performance goals and satisfaction. Additional items were included to assess the effectiveness of the manipulations. After completing the post-task questionnaire, subjects were thoroughly debriefed and dismissed.

RESULTS

Manipulation Checks

Judging from subjects' responses to the post-task questionnaire, it appears that the experimental manipulations were very effective. With few exceptions, subjects were able to recall the exact number of cards sorted by the model. The correlation between their reports and the model's actual performance was $r = .99$. In addition, subjects in the high-model-performance condition perceived the model as exerting significantly more effort on both the first trial (respective means of 4.90 and 2.93 on a 7-point scale, $p < .001$) and second trial (means of 6.34 and 5.49, $p < .001$). Although only 23% of the subjects believed that the model had a goal on the first trial, a full 82% believed that he had a goal on the second trial. Reports of these goals indicate that they were significantly higher for subjects in the high-model-performance condition ($\bar{X} = 75.2$) than for subjects in the low-model-performance condition ($\bar{X} = 35.2$) (differences significant at $p < .001$). As desired, no differences between task experience conditions nor interactions between model and experience conditions were found for accuracy of recall of model performance, perceptions of model effort or beliefs about the model's goals. Finally, those subjects who practiced the task were able to recall their performance during this time period very accurately, as evidenced by the high correlation between their actual and reported performance ($r = .98$).

Goals

Hypothesis 1a stated that subjects viewing a high-performance model would set significantly higher performance goals than would subjects viewing a low-performance model. Hypothesis 1b further stated that this effect would be stronger among inexperienced than experienced subjects.

Results relevant to these hypotheses are presented in Tables 1 and 2. As hypothesized, model performance level had a significant ($F = 13.7, p < .001$) effect on subjects' goals, with subjects who observed the high-performance model setting higher goals ($\bar{X} = 55.4$) for themselves than did subjects who viewed the low-performance model ($\bar{X} = 46.4$). In addition, and not unexpectedly, subjects

TABLE 1
EFFECTS OF MODEL PERFORMANCE AND TASK EXPERIENCE ON
SUBJECTS' PERFORMANCE GOALS

Source	df	Ms$_e$	F
Model performance	1	3350.39	13.70*
Task experience	1	2777.07	11.36*
Model × experience	1	806.23	3.30**
Residual	165	244.52	

* $p < .10$.
** $p < .001$.

TABLE 2
CELL MEANS FOR SUBJECTS' PERFORMANCE GOALS

	No task experience	Task experience	Total
Low-performance model	40.1	52.7	46.4
High-performance model	53.5	57.3	55.4
Total	46.8	55.1	50.9

with task experience set significantly higher goals ($X = 55.1$) than did subjects without task experience ($\bar{X} = 46.8$).

An examination of Tables 1 and 2 suggests that the simple main effect for model performance may be a less than complete description of the data. First, a marginally significant interaction between model performance and task condition was found ($F = 3.30$, $p < .08$). The pattern of cell means (Table 2) indicates that model performance had a more pronounced effect among subjects without task experience than among subjects with task experience. To further explore this effect, separate point biserial correlations between model performance condition and subjects' goals were computed for subjects with and without task experience. Among subjects without task experience, model performance correlated $r = .42$ ($p < .001$) with subjects' goals. For subjects with task experience, this same correlation was only $r = 14$ (n.s.). These correlations were significantly different at the $p < .05$ level.

In sum, model performance had a significant effect on the task goals of observers with evidence to suggest that the effect was more pronounced among subjects without task experience.

Performance

Hypotheses 2a and b stated that the performance of the subjects who observed a high-performance model would be higher than the performance of subjects who observed a low-performance model (2a) and that this effect would be more pronounced among subjects without prior task experience (2b).

Before turning to the relevant results, it should be noted that as expected from the extensive body of goal setting literature, the correlation between subjects' stated goals and performance was positive and strong ($r = .57$, $p < .001$) across all conditions. Independent of how they were formed, goals correlated substantially with performance.

Tables 3 and 4 describe the effects of model performance and task experience on subjects' own performance. Not surprisingly, prior task experience had a significant positive effect on subjects' performance. More central to the issues of this paper are the effects of the model's performance. Here the results basically follow the pattern already described for observer goals. In this case, however, a significant interaction was found while a main effect for model performance was not obtained. An inspection of the cell means (Table 4) indicates that, as hy-

TABLE 3
EFFECTS OF MODEL PERFORMANCE AND TASK EXPERIENCE ON
SUBJECTS' PERFORMANCE

Source	df	Ms_e	F
Model performance	1	15.22	.10
Task experience	1	1292.94	8.81*
Model × experience	1	825.47	5.62**
Residual	170	146.82	

* $p < .05$.
** $p < .01$.

TABLE 4
CELL MEANS FOR SUBJECTS' PERFORMANCE

	No task experience	Task experience	Total
Low-performance model	53.8	63.7	58.6
High-performance model	58.7	59.9	59.3
Total	56.3	61.8	59.0

pothesized, the level of model performance had a significant positive effect on subjects' own performance only for subjects without task experience.

As with goals, to further examine the interaction of model performance and prior experience on observer performance, separate point biserial correlations between model performance condition and subject performance were computed for subjects with and without prior task experience. For subjects without task experience, this correlation was significant and positive ($r = .22$, $p < .05$). For subjects with prior experience this correlation was negative although not significant ($r = -.15$, n.s.). These correlations are significantly different ($p < .05$) from each other.

The pattern of results presented so far supports the hypothesized influence of a model's achievement level on observers' task goals and performance. However, this effect seems to hold only for subjects who had no task experience before observing the model.

Causal Analysis

Conceptually, we have hypothesized a specific causal sequence for the modeling effects demonstrated among subjects in the no task experience condition. In this sequence, derived from and compatible with the body of goal setting research, model achievement influenced observer performance level through the model's more immediate effect on goals and intentions, (see Fig. 1). However, assessing subjects' goals retrospectively obviously raises an alternative causal interpretation. One might argue that model achievement had a direct influence on subjects'

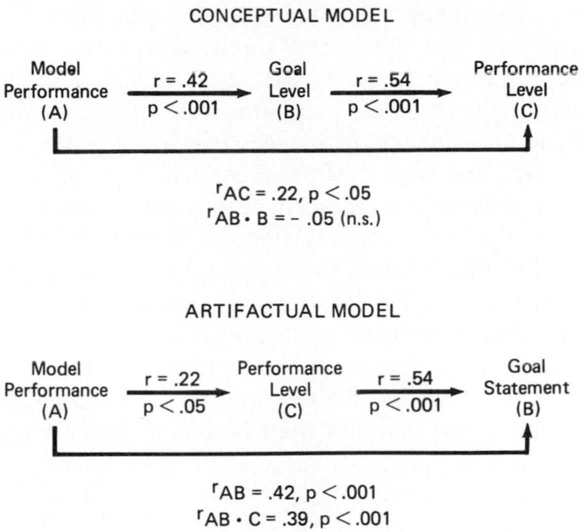

CONCEPTUAL MODEL

Model Performance (A) $\xrightarrow{\begin{array}{c} r = .42 \\ p < .001 \end{array}}$ Goal Level (B) $\xrightarrow{\begin{array}{c} r = .54 \\ p < .001 \end{array}}$ Performance Level (C)

$r_{AC} = .22, p < .05$
$r_{AB \cdot B} = -.05$ (n.s.)

ARTIFACTUAL MODEL

Model Performance (A) $\xrightarrow{\begin{array}{c} r = .22 \\ p < .05 \end{array}}$ Performance Level (C) $\xrightarrow{\begin{array}{c} r = .54 \\ p < .001 \end{array}}$ Goal Statement (B)

$r_{AB} = .42, p < .001$
$r_{AB \cdot C} = .39, p < .001$

FIGURE 1
Partial correlational analyses examining the alternative causal models.

performance without the mediating mechanism of goal setting. So, for example, the obviously higher effort and arousal of the model in the high-performance film may have increased the arousal of the subject, resulting in higher performance. Subjects may then have reported goals compatible with their performance levels, producing a relationship between model achievement and subjects' goals that was primarily artifactual (Fig. 1).

To investigate the alternative models a causal correlation analysis was performed for subjects in the no experience condition. The method used was one suggested by Simon (1954) and Blalock (1964) for examining the adequacy of prespecified three-variable causal chains. The adequacy of a model is assessed by examining the correlation between the first and third variables in the sequence with the hypothesized mediating variable partialed out. For adequate models this partial correlation should reduce to zero.

Results of this partial correlation analysis are presented in Fig. 1. Examination of the patterns of zero-order and partial correlations provides substantial support for the mediating influence of goals on the model performance–subject performance relationship, while providing no support for the alternative artifactual model. The artifactual model would predict that the correlation between model achievement condition and subjects' goals would have been substantially reduced when subjects' performance levels were partialed. However, as can be seen in Fig. 1, the partial correlation is virtually identical to the zero-order correlation.

On the other hand, the conceptual model would predict that the correlation between model and subjects' performance levels would have reduced to zero when the hypothesized mediating mechanism of subjects' goals were partialed. This, in fact, did occur. Partialing goal level reduced the zero-order correlation from $r = .22$ ($p < .05$) to a nonsignificant $r = -.05$.

It should be noted that, as one might expect, among subjects with prior experience, performance on the practice trial correlated significantly with later goals ($r = .36$, $p < .001$) and performance ($r = .41$, $p < .001$). Causal correlational analyses only partially supported the mediating role of goal level on the relationship between practice and final performance. Partialing goals reduced the correlation between practice and final performance from $r = .41$ to $r = .27$ ($p < .01$). Although the relationship was reduced, it was not eliminated. Nor would elimination of a relationship be expected. Although simple, the task does have some ability component and this is likely to produce some covariation between performance on the two trials even with motivational variance removed. It should also be noted that the correlation between goals and final performance was not substantially reduced when practice performance was partialed (the correlation changed from .56 to .48), indicating that the relationship between goals and final performance was not an artifactual result of their both correlating with practice performance.

Satisfaction

Hypotheses 3a and b stated that subjects' satisfaction with their performance would be a function of the discrepancy between their own performance and the model's performance (3a) and that this relationship would be stronger for subjects without prior experience on the task (3b). Results support hypothesis 3a but not 3b.

Across all conditions, absolute level of performance correlated with subjects' performance satisfaction ($r = .24$, $p < .001$). However, this correlation was significantly smaller ($t = 3.55$, $p < .05$) than the correlation between satisfaction and the discrepancy between one's own and the model's performance ($r = -.42$, $p < .001$) (comparisons were made between the absolute levels of these correlations) indicating that the more important influence on subjects' self-evaluations was how their performance levels compared to the standards provided by the model.

It is also interesting to note that this comparison was apparently more important to them than the discrepancy between their performance and their own goals, in that the latter discrepancy had a significantly smaller ($t = 2.32$, $p < .05$), although still highly significant, relationship with their own satisfaction ($r = .27$, $p < .001$).

Of particular interest, and in contrast to the findings on goals and performance, is that these satisfaction findings were not influenced by task experience. Subjects in both the prior experience and no prior experience conditions used the model's achievement as a standard of personal evaluation ($r = -.44$ and $r = -.40$ respectively, both $p < .001$). In addition, for subjects in the prior task experience condition, the correlation between their performance improvement and their performance satisfaction was $r = .30$ ($p < .01$). It seems that these subjects were using two standards of evaluation, their own and the model's achievements.

These results clearly indicate that the model provided a standard which the subjects used to evaluate their own performance levels. Further, although subjects with prior experience on the task were less likely to use the model to set their own goals, they still used the model's performance as an evaluative standard for judging the adequacy of their own achievement.

Of some parenthetical interest is the finding that the model had a much smaller, although still significant, effect on task satisfaction apart from performance satisfaction. Across all conditions the correlation between the discrepancy between self- and model performance and task satisfaction was $r = -.18, p < .01$. This correlation was basically unaffected by task familiarity. The smaller effect for models on task as opposed to performance satisfaction again attests to the independence of these constructs.

DISCUSSION

The substantial causal influence of goals on achievement and satisfaction has been repeatedly demonstrated in both laboratory and field settings. Yet our knowledge of the factors influencing the goals individuals naturally set when approaching tasks is nowhere near our understanding of the effects of these goals. This study demonstrated that the observed achievement of other workers can serve as a standard by which individuals set their goals and evaluate their performance, thereby significantly influencing their own levels of achievement. It also showed this modeling effect to be significantly moderated by task experience. Inexperienced subjects who viewed a high-performing model set higher performance goals and achieved greater levels of performance than inexperienced subjects who observed a lower-performing model. However, the goals and performance levels of subjects who were familiar with the task were less influenced by the model. Yet, subjects in all conditions, regardless of task familiarity or model achievement level used the model as a standard of self-evaluation. Model achievement influenced observers' performance satisfaction even under conditions where it had no influence on goals or performance.

The findings of this study, by providing additional information about the way individuals develop their own task goals and intentions, help to extend Locke's original "foundations of a theory of task motivation." Beyond that, they are of obvious relevance to an understanding of the processes of self-controlled motivation at work. Obviously, these laboratory results need to be replicated in the field before conclusions about the effects of social influences on work goals can be drawn with confidence. Yet goal setting is probably the research area which has best demonstrated the complementary nature of laboratory and field studies (Latham & Locke, 1979; Latham & Yukl, 1975). In addition, the results of this study are compatible with research demonstrating modeling influences on other organizationally relevant behaviors, perceptions, and attitudes (Latham & Saari, 1979; O'Reilly & Caldwell, 1979; Weiss, 1977, 1978; Weiss & Shaw, 1979; White & Mitchell, 1978). The consistent replication of Locke's laboratory research in field settings and increased recognition of the importance of social influences on organizational behaviors supports the probable influence of models on goals, performance, and satisfaction in field settings as well.

The moderating effect of task familiarity has additional organizational implications by suggesting that social influences on the development of goals and performance standards may be most pronounced for new workers or individuals approaching an unfamiliar task. Weiss (1977) has argued that new employees enter what is to them a fairly undifferentiated psychological environment and are actively seeking information about appropriate behaviors, attitudes, etc. Similarly, Katz (1980) has characterized the initial employment period as a time of uncertainty reduction. Under such conditions other workers can be an important source of information and individuals are likely to try to reduce uncertainty and determine appropriate behaviors, goal levels in this case, by attending to the behavior of co-workers. Crawford (1974) has shown that under conditions of response uncertainty individuals seek information from others. In this regard, Katz (1980) has suggested that new workers turn to the social environment for guidance. The results of this study certainly support the arguments about workers using social information under conditions of uncertainty. The results also indicate that as uncertainty is reduced through personal task experience social influences will diminish. However, the inability of task familiarity to moderate the performance satisfaction results suggests that social influences are not just an issue for new workers.

As described in the results, the argument that the model influenced the goals and subsequent performance of inexperienced subjects must be qualified by the retrospective reporting of subjects' goals. In spite of this, for a number of reasons, the hypothesized causal sequence of the model influencing performance through the mediating process of goal setting seems to be the most acceptable explanation of events. First, this causal sequence is clearly compatible with other research on the mediating role of intentions and the direct causal effect of goals on performance. Second, it is strongly supported by the causal correlation analyses conducted to examine alternative causal models. The partial correlation analysis supported the hypothesized causal sequence but did not support the alternative artifactual sequence of the model directly influencing observer performance with observers then reporting their goals to conform to their achievement levels. Nor does the partial correlational analysis support a causal sequence where the model influenced both observer goals and performance directly and independently. Thus, based upon both theory and data, it seems logical to conclude that model influences on observers' performance levels were mediated by the model's influences on the observers' performance intentions.

While modeling effects on observer goal setting, performance, and satisfaction have been demonstrated, continued research should be done on why this occurs. Lewin *et al.* (1944) theorized that goal choice is a function of the probabilities and incentive values of different aspiration levels. Similarly Locke *et al.* (1970) have argued that the anticipated or expected satisfaction of achieving various goal levels influence goal choice. What role do models play within these frameworks? Models may have their effect by increasing the observer's expectations or perceived probabilities of successfully reaching more difficult goal levels. They may also have their effect by increasing incentive values or anticipated satisfaction associated with varying levels of achievement. This latter issue is related to issues of competition, a state which may be aroused in situations like the present study, where the performance levels of others are known. Modeling in such instances occurs for reasons other than reduction of uncertainty, although the observed behaviors (imitation) in both cases may be quite similar. Possibly both mechanisms are operating as the achievement levels of models influence the performance intentions of observers.

Research which helps to delineate the way models influence goal choices will increase our understanding of both the role of goals and intentions in task motivation and general observational learning processes. That research should also help to increase our knowledge of self-control as it relates to performance in organizations.

REFERENCES

Bandura, A. Self reinforcement: Theoretical and methodological considerations. *Behaviorism*, 1976, **4**, 135–155.

Blalock, H. M., Jr. *Causal Influences in Non-Experimental Research*. New York: Norton, 1964.

Crawford, J. L. Task uncertainty, decision importance, and group reinforcement as determinants of communication processes in groups. *Journal of Personality and Social Psychology*, 1974, **29**, 619–627.

Dachler, H. P., & Mobley, W. H. Construct validation of an instrumentality-expectancy—Task goal model of work motivation: Some theoretical boundary conditions. *Journal of Applied Psychology*, 1973, **58**, 397–418. (Monograph)

Katz, R. Time and work: Toward an integrative perspective. In B. M. Staw & L. L. Cummings (Eds.), *Research in Organizational Behavior*, Vol. 2, Greenwich, Conn.: JAI Press, 1980.

Koulak, D., & Peterson, P. D. Level of aspiration: A function of anchor distance and direction. *Journal of Social Psychology*, 1969, **77**, 141–142.

Latham, G. P., & Locke, E. A. Goal setting: A motivational technique that works. *Organizational Dynamics*, 1979, **8**, 68–80.

Latham, G. P., & Saari, L. M. Applications of social learning theory to training supervisors through behavior modeling. *Journal of Applied Psychology*, 1979, **64**, 239–246.

Latham, G. P., & Yukl, G. A. A review of research on the application of goal setting in organizations. *Academy of Management Journal*, 1975, **18**, 824–845.

Lewin, K., Dembo, T., Festinger, L., & Sears, P. S. Level of aspiration. In J. McV. Hunt (Ed.), *Personality and the Behavior Disorders*, New York: Ronald Press, 1944.

Locke, E. A. Toward a theory of task motivation and incentives. *Organizational Behavior and Human Performance*, 1968, **3**, 157–189.

Locke, E. A. Job satisfaction and job performance: A theoretical analysis. *Organizational Behavior and Human Performance*, 1970, **5**, 484–500.

Locke, E. A., Cartledge, N., & Knerr, C. S. Studies of the relationship between satisfaction, goal setting, and performance. *Organizational Behavior and Human Performance*, 1970, **5**, 135–158.

Marlatt, G. A. Exposure to a model and task ambiguity as determinants of verbal behavior in an interview. *Journal of Consulting and Clinical Psychology*, 1971, **36**, 268–276.

O'Reilly, C. A., III, & Caldwell, D. F. Informational influence as a determinant of perceived task characteristics and job satisfaction. *Journal of Applied Psychology*, 1979, **64**, 157–165.

Pritchard, R. D., & Curts, M. I. The influence of goal setting and financial incentives on task performance. *Organizational Behavior and Human Performance*, 1973, **10,** 175–183.

Salancik, G. R., & Pfeffer, J. A social information processing approach to job attitudes and task design. *Administrative Science Quarterly*, 1978, **23,** 224–253.

Simon, H. A. Spurious correlation: A causal interpretation. *Journal of the American Statistical Association*, 1954, **49,** 467–479.

Weiss, H. M. Subordinate imitation of supervisor behavior: The role of modeling in organizational socialization. *Organizational Behavior and Human Performance*, 1977, **19, 89**–105.

Weiss, H. M. Social learning of work values in organizations. *Journal of Applied Psychology*, 1978, **63,** 711–718.

Weiss, H. M. Social influences on judgments about tasks. *Organizational Behavior and Human Performance*, 1979, **24,** 126–140.

White, S. E., & Mitchell, T. R. Job enrichment versus social cues: A comparison and competitive test. *Journal of Applied Psychology*, 1979, **64,** 1–9,

White, S. E., Mitchell, T. R., & Bell, C. H., Jr. Goal setting, evaluation apprehension and social cues as determinants of job performance and job satisfaction in a simulated organization. *Journal of Applied Psychology*, 1977, **62,** 665–673.

Yukl, G. A., & Latham, G. P. Interrelationships among employee participation, individual differences, goal difficulty, goal acceptance, goal instrumentality and performance. *Personnel Psychology*, 1978, **31,** 305–323.

Zander, A. *Motives and Goals in Groups*. New York: Academic Press, 1971.

QUESTIONS FOR DISCUSSION

1 What relationship exists between group aspiration level and individual performance on the job?

2 What motivationally relevant functions do groups serve in organizations? How could you use this information to increase employee motivation?

3 Under what circumstances would you expect competition among group members for rewards to result in higher performance than cooperation? When might cooperation lead to higher performance? Explain why such differences occur.

4 If you were a manager trying to increase performance among your subordinates, would you use group or individual incentives? Why?

5 Porter, Lawler, and Hackman use expectancy theory to explain how group processes influence individual motivation to perform. What other theories of motivation might be useful in explaining group influences? Explain.

6 Several articles (in previous chapter) have suggested that members should be carefully selected and trained so as to diminish differences between individual and organizational goals. What predictions might you make about decisions made in organizations which adopt this suggestion? What steps might an organization take to increase the effectiveness of decision making and yet maintain goal congruence?

7 Compare the relative costs and benefits to a supervisor of attempting to use each of Kelman's three interpersonal influence processes (compliance, identification, and internalization) to motivate subordinates.

8 To what extent could each of the social influence processes identified in the article by Sussmann and Vecchio be used by managers to motivate their *bosses* (as opposed to their subordinates)?

9 Explain how the concept of ''group norm'' relates to different theories of employee motivation (goal-setting, expectancy, social learning, etc.).

10 Suppose that a manager who has been newly appointed to head a particular organizational unit finds that he or she is confronted with a norm in that unit that can be summarized as follows: ''Don't make waves, but also don't exert yourself beyond a minimally adequate level of effort.'' How could the manager, utilizing a knowledge of motivational theory, proceed to attempt to change this norm?

11 How could the results of the study by Rakestraw and Weiss be combined with the points made in Feldman's article on group norms to provide a set of guidelines for a manager confronted with a group of newly hired employees? Would the guidelines be different if the group were composed of experienced employees?

12 If you were a motivational researcher, what would be the next hypothesis you would want to test to follow up directly the findings of Rakestraw and Weiss?

CHAPTER 7

CAREERS IN ORGANIZATIONS

The concept of careers and career management has received considerable attention in recent years. A central concern in this issue is how managers and organizations can facilitate careers and career development so that employees can develop to their fullest potential. This chapter does not attempt to review the issue of careers in a comprehensive fashion. Instead, our focus is on the more narrow issue of career motivation. That is, we are concerned here with how individuals decide to join a particular organization, as well as with how they choose to pursue their careers over time. Primary emphasis is therefore on the motivational bases underlying career decisions.

The first reading, by Wanous, focuses on the individual's decision to join a particular organization. This topic is generally known as "organizational entry." Following this, the article by London presents a model of career motivation. Finally, Schein considers the role played by cultural differences in career patterns. Unique to this third article is a consideration of what the concept of careers means in different regions of the world.

Throughout, consideration is given to what managers can learn that can help with career development programs in organizations. To be meaningful, the issue of career management must offer substance to organizations concerned with how best to utilize their human resources. With such knowledge, managers are in a better position to facilitate goal attainment for both employees and organizations.

Organizational Entry:
The Individual's Viewpoint

John P. Wanous

All organizational systems import various types of energy: people, money, raw materials, information, and so forth. This paper is concerned with *human* energy sources, in particular new employees in organizations. Fundamentally, the "organizational entry process" can be viewed in two ways: (1) from the individual's viewpoint, and (2) from the organization's perspective. This paper focuses exclusively on the individual's viewpoint during the entry process and has four objectives. The first is to define the individual's view of organizational entry in general, and then identify four components of this process. The second objective is to describe why new employees are an important group to study. The third is to review what we know about each of the topic areas in organizational entry. The final objective is to point out what remains to be done for a better understanding of newcomers in organizations.

WHAT IS ORGANIZATIONAL ENTRY?

Organizational entry concerns how individuals move from outside to inside a new organization. Viewed from the perspective of the individual who enters, the entry process begins outside the organization as people think about possible entry. The process continues throughout the phase where an effort is made to join, when there is an acceptance of the individual by the organization, and when the individual makes the final decision to enter.

The topic of organizational entry continues to be important even after entry itself. In particular, it is important to consider the "aftereffects" of the entry process on both the individual and the organization. An examination of these entry consequences does *not* include what some have called "organizational socialization" (Bakke, 1953; Schein, 1968) or the "personalizing process" (Bakke, 1953). Both of these processes occur *after* entry, but are *not* necessarily *direct* consequences of the entry itself. Organizational socialization refers to how individuals learn: (1) the basic values and goals of the organization, (2) the means for attaining them, (3) individual job responsibilities, (4) acceptable behavior patterns for effective job performance, and (5) other guiding principles for maintaining the organization (Schein, 1968). The personalizing process refers to how each individual leaves his or her "mark" on the organization. Together these describe the character of mutual-influence processes that are set in motion when newcomers enter organizations.

Organizational entry does not focus on these two active processes, but it does include that postentry behavior of newcomers which has been caused by the entry

From J. R. Hackman, E. E. Lawler III, & L. W. Porter, *Perspectives on behavior in organizations.* New York: McGraw-Hill, 1977, pp. 126–135. Used by permission of the author and publisher.

process itself. It can perhaps be best understood by listing four specific components, each of which has become a question for research.

1 How do individuals choose new organizations?

2 How accurate and complete is the information that "outsiders" have about new organizations?

3 What is the impact of organizational recruitment on the "matching" of individual and organization?

4 What are the consequences of matching or mismatching individuals and organizations?

NEW EMPLOYEES AS AN IMPORTANT TOPIC

Implied by the above questions is a view of organizational entry from the individual's viewpoint, not the organization's. Viewing entry from an organizational perspective changes the way such questions are asked. For example, the selection and testing research in industrial psychology is the "flip side" of the first area. Concern over getting lots of data about job applicants is the organizational analogue of the second question. For the third area, organizations have been concerned with making themselves appear attractive for recruitment purposes, but have not investigated the impact of this recruitment strategy on newcomers. Thus, one reason why the study of new employees has merit is that we know so little about it from the individual's viewpoint. The second reason is closely related. Because organizations and researchers have viewed new employees primarily as passive figures, they have tended to concentrate on abilities and skills in the context of predicting job performance. This emphasis overlooks the fact that individuals choose new organizations and that the satisfaction of the individual's need is a crucial element in keeping effective employees from leaving.

A third reason for the significance of this area is that turnover in most organizations tends to be highest during the first six months or so of work experience. This varies from situation to situation, but tends to be fairly characteristic of most business organizations. In many cases this is quite costly to an organization, when there is a "revolving-door" effect for certain jobs. That is, there can be high turnover for some entry-level jobs because the newcomers are "testing" the work environment to see if it will be satisfactory. If it is not, they often leave quickly; hence the revolving-door phenomenon. A fourth point is that people who join new organizations are probably more open to influence than they will be at any other time spent in that particular organization. For example, the formation of a "psychological contract" (Schein, 1968) may revolve around how well matched are personal versus organizational values.

MATCHING INDIVIDUAL AND ORGANIZATION: A GENERAL FRAMEWORK FOR ORGANIZATIONAL ENTRY

Most organizations are constantly involved in a "matching process" between the individual and the organization. On the one hand, newcomers to an organization come with their own *individual talent* (such as skills, abilities, and knowledge), as well as important *human needs*. On the other hand, the typical organization can be viewed as having *talent requirements* for various jobs as well as its own particular *climate characteristics*. Thus, there are two important "match-ups" which occur during the process of new employees entering an organization: (1) individual talent with organizational talent requirements, and (2) human needs with organizational climate. This general process of matching individual and organization is *continuous* because both people and jobs change over time, and because there is constant labor force movement (hires, promotions, quits, and fires).

It is fair to say that most organizations strongly emphasize the match between employees' talents and job demands. On the other hand, matching the needs of employees and the characteristics of jobs is typically underemphasized. In fact, rarely are efforts made to match newcomers to a specific job in a particular organization in terms of human needs and the job climate.

While both matches are probably important for motivation, performance, and job satisfaction, the match between an employee's talent and job-talent requirements probably has a more immediate and powerful effect on job performance than it does on job satisfaction or job tenure (Lofquist & Dawis, 1969). A poor match typically results in poor job performance. Sometimes, however, a mismatch of this first type can affect job tenure (i.e., absenteeism, turnover, or tardiness), especially when an individual is *over*-qualified for a job.

On the other hand, the match between human needs and organizational climate usually has a more immediate and potent effect on job satisfaction and tenure than on job performance. A poor matching can produce employees' dissatisfaction which results in tardiness, absenteeism, and turnover. There are exceptions to this, of course, because some individuals may use ineffective job performance as a way to "get back" at an organization for a job which is not psychologically rewarding (Argyris, 1964).

Two selection processes operate in the matching of people and jobs. One of these involves the organization selecting the individual and the other involves the individual selecting the organization. Research pertaining to the former abounds in industrial psychology, as it has been a major focus there. When the organization is selecting an individual the tendency has been to assess the *talents* of an applicant for placement on an appropriate type of job. On the other hand, when individuals select an organization they often look for a potentially satisfying climate in which to work (in a business organization), or study (in a university).

Thus, there has been a historical tendency for the matching of individual talent and organizational requirements to be associated with the organization's selection of individuals rather than vice versa. It is obvious that a complete treatment of organizational entry necessarily includes *both* match-ups, and should stress organizational selection of individuals as well as the individuals' choice of organizations. However, the present paper is intentionally slanted toward the relatively underresearched topics concerning organizational entry from the individual's viewpoint.

EXAMPLES OF RESEARCH ON ORGANIZATIONAL ENTRY

Although our present knowledge about organizational entry is highly asymmetrical, we do have a good start in all four of the areas listed above. Below are examples of what has been done to date.

How Do Individuals Choose New Organizations?

About one dozen studies of organizational choice can be found in today's literature. The procedures of each study vary. For example, one long-term study investigated how a group of forty-nine people studying for the master's degree at Carnegie-Mellon University chose their first full-time jobs (Vroom, 1966; Vroom & Deci, 1971). This study "tracked" the job expectations and goals these students held concerning the organizations they interviewed. For most students there was a very close correspondence between their *overall* ratings of "organizational attractiveness" and an *index* composed of their *specific expectations* (about each organization) multiplied by their *personal goals* for the job. When it came time to choose a particular job offer, 76 percent of them picked the organization which had been rated the highest on the index of "expectations × goals." This was felt to be strong confirmation of the "expectancy theory" of motivation (Vroom, 1964), upon which the study was based.

A number of other studies have also found that individuals tend to select those organizations which have the greatest personal attractiveness based on an index of their *expectations* multiplied by their *goals*. Perhaps the best way to characterize these studies is to distinguish among the various stages in the individual's choice of organization:

Stage 1: Initial Attractiveness of an Organization   Most studies indicate that people are attracted to those organizations which are rated highest on a psychological index based on *both* an individual's *expectations* about what the organization will be like *and* each person's own values or goals (Huber, Daneshgar, & Ford, 1971; Lawler, Kuleck, Rhode, & Sorenson, 1975; Vroom, 1966; Wanous, 1975a).

Stage 2: Effort to Join a Particular Organization   After deciding what organizations are most attractive, the field of possibilities is somewhat narrowed. From among those remaining, certain ones seem to be more highly sought out than others. An individual's greatest efforts to join a particular organization seem to be directed to those which not only are attractive, but which are seen as likely to offer an opening. In a nutshell, studies have shown that one's *expectations* of gaining entry *and* the *attractiveness* of an organization determine how hard most individuals try to join certain organizations (Glueck, 1974; Lawler et al., 1975; Wanous, 1975a).

Stage 3: Choice from among Organizations Offering Entry   In between stages 2 and 3 the initiative returns to the organization, which selects or rejects the individual. Every organization that one tries to enter will not necessarily offer admission.

Once again the range of possibilities is limited. From among those which do extend offers, most people choose the one which has the greatest attractiveness (Ford, Huber, & Gustafson, 1972; Huber et al., 1971; Lawler et al., 1975; Pieters, Hundert, & Beer, 1968; Soelberg, 1967; Vroom, 1966; Wanous, 1975a).

Although the art of organizational choice seems to be quite rational, and well understood, research has uncovered two interesting "twists." For example, the *act of choosing* seems to *distort* the perceptions of those engaged in the process. Immediately after deciding which organization to enter, most people tend to perceive it as even *more* attractive than before the choice. They also tend to perceive the rejected alternatives as even less attractive (Lawler et al., 1975; Soelberg, 1967; Vroom, 1966). This is an example of a basic human need to *justify* one's own choices, although it may not always occur (Sheridan, Richards, & Slocum, 1975).

The second "twist" to be found is that newcomers in organizations tend to be *less* satisfied with their choice than either before making it or immediately after choosing (Vroom & Deci, 1971; Wanous, 1975a). This result raises many questions, but especially those concerning the quality of information outsiders have when making choices and the impact of typical recruitment programs on such expectations. Both of these are taken up in the next two component areas of the organizational entry process.

How Accurate and Complete Is the Information of Outsiders about New Organizations?

Until recently, problems of misinformation were not considered serious enough to warrant much attention. The subsequent disappointment after entry clearly implies that some people were led to expect the wrong things about new organizations. The research to be discussed under topic 3 (see page 313) also points in the direction of inaccurate—especially inflated—expectations held by outsiders before entry.

A study of Harvard M.B.A. students (Ward & Athos, 1972) indicated that recruiters from various companies gave "glowing" rather than "balanced" descriptions, and glossed over details of organizational life. Research at an automotive manufacturer (Dunnette, Arvey, & Banas, 1973) examined two groups of employees: those who left within their first four years, and those who remained longer than four years. They found that most people's expectations were *not* realized in actual job situations. The problem of unfulfilled expectations was much more severe for those who "terminated early." Only such concrete expectations as pay levels were confirmed by actual experience, a finding documented by Wanous (1972b) earlier in a study of University of Minnesota graduating seniors.

The American Telephone and Telegraph study of newly entered managers (Bray, Campbell, & Grant, 1974) shows that expectations decline with increasing years in the same company. This study did not begin until after entry, but found that employees' expectations about the future continued to decline for the first seven years at AT&T work experience. This decline was about equal for both effective and ineffective performers.

A recent study of M.B.A. students in three New York City graduate business schools (Wanous, 1976) provides the most detailed information on the quality of information that outsiders have about new organizations. Students were asked to complete questionnaires about their school choices at three points in time: (1) outsiders—before entry, (2) newcomers—shortly after entry in the fall semester, and (3) insiders—during the spring after the first academic year. There was a *decline* from naive (inflated) expectations of outsiders to realistic (lower) beliefs on the part of insiders. Interestingly enough, the decline occurred only for those aspects "intrinsic" to the educational process itself (e.g., quality of teaching, school status, competition), and not for those "extrinsic" to learning (e.g., location, tuition, transfer credit, etc.). The Wanous (1976) study also looked at a smaller group of telephone operators who moved from outside to inside the Southern New England Telephone Company. As with the M.B.A. students, there was a decline for intrinsic job characteristics. Unlike the M.B.A. study, a decline also occurred for extrinsic factors, but it was not as strong as the decline for intrinsic job characteristics.

As the M.B.A. data from the Wanous (1976) study indicate, there may *not* be a problem of "total inaccuracy" on the part of outsiders. Nevertheless, those aspects considered intrinsic in this study, and in other studies (e.g., Dunnette, Campbell, & Hakel, 1967), are the ones *most* important to individuals. This poses a very serious and interesting problem for organizational recruitment. Namely, outsiders tend to have inaccurately inflated expectations about those organizational characteristics (i.e., the intrinsic ones) which are the hardest ones to describe because they are the most abstract. Even if an organization tried to describe itself accurately to new recruits, it would not be easy. The next section discusses a series of studies where a variety of organizations tried to recruit newcomers with as much realism as possible.

What Is the Impact of Organizational Recruitment on the "Matching" of Individual and Organization?

One way to deal with the inflated expectations of outsiders is to give recruits a "realistic job preview" (Wanous, 1975b, c) to "set" initial expectations at a realistic level and to help individuals make better organizational choices. Over the last twenty years six experimental studies in organizations have compared the effectiveness of a realistic job preview with a more "traditional" approach.

The basic difference between the two strategies is that the realistic one emphasizes *specific* facts which are typical of *both* desirable *and* undesirable aspects of the organization. The traditional approach tries to maximize the number of recruitees for each opening by "selling" the job in its most positive light. Recruitment by the traditional approach also tends to overlook the costs associated with high quit rates.

The six experiments involved a variety of techniques to present a realistic job preview: four studies used a booklet, one a film, and another a two-hour "practice session." They involved a variety of individuals and jobs: insurance salesmen, West Point cadets, telephone operators, and sewing machine operators. The first two groups were all male, while the latter were all female.

A number of criteria were used to assess the impact of these realistic job previews. First, was the ability to recruit newcomers impaired by the use of realism? Four of the six studies directly addressed this issue and three show no impairment at all (Wanous, 1973; Weitz, 1956; Youngberg, 1963). A fourth study (Farr, O'Leary, & Bartlett, 1973) found a slightly higher rate of job offer refusals for those seeing the realistic preview. Second, were initial job expectations really lowered due to the realistic preview? Two of the six directly addressed this issue, and the answer is clearly affirmative (Wanous, 1973; Youngberg, 1963). In fact, Wanous found that the preview was "selective," i.e., it lowered *only* those initial expectations that were discussed in the preview, and did not "spill over" to other aspects of the job.

A third question is whether realistic recruitment results in more positive attitudes on the part of newcomers. Two of the six studies did address this issue and both found such beneficial effects as higher satisfaction after three months (Youngberg, 1963) and fewer thoughts of quitting (Wanous, 1973). The fourth, and final, question is whether realism resulted in lower turnover. For many organizations this is the "bottom line" question concerning the effectiveness of realistic job previews. The typical way to assess it has been to compare the percentage of newcomers who "survive" (i.e., do *not* leave) with a similar percentage for those in the control group. The higher the survival percentage, the lower the turnover, and the more effective the preview. These results are listed below in chronological order, showing the realistic preview's percentage first, followed by the job survival rate of the control group.

- At Life and Casualty Insurance Company of Tennessee, 68 percent versus 53 percent over five months for life insurance agents (Weitz, 1956).
- At Prudential Insurance Company, 71 percent versus 57 percent over six months for life insurance agents (Youngberg, 1963).
- At West Point, 91 percent versus 86 percent over one year for first year cadets (Macedonia, 1969).
- At the Southern New England Telephone Company, 62 percent versus 50 percent over three months for telephone operators (Wanous, 1973).
- At Manhattan Industries, Inc., 88.9 percent versus 68.8 percent over six weeks for White sewing machine operators. No differences were found for Black operators, however.
- At West Point, 94 percent versus 88.5 percent over a three-month summer training period for first year cadets (Ilgen & Seely, 1974).

What Are the Consequences of Matching or Mismatching Individuals and Organizations?

Thus far we have seen that individuals *try* to "match" themselves to organizations, but they often make such decisions on the basis of incomplete and inaccurate information. A few organizations, however, have consciously tried to recruit newcomers using realistic job previews to effect better match-ups between human needs and organizational climate. The majority of organizations, whether businesses or universities, have not attempted systematic, realistic recruiting. Thus it is important to ask what the consequences are when mismatches between individuals and organizations occur.

Guiding this brief review are two assumptions. First, based on the "matching model" presented earlier, it is expected that the match between individual and organization will have a greater impact on job *satisfaction* and *tenure* than on actual job performance. Second, in most cases a good, or "close," match between an individual's needs and the organizational climate is desirable. The exceptions to these assumptions will be discussed last.

The match-up between individual and organization takes place in two related "levels": (1) the immediate job or task, and (2) general aspects of the climate other than the immediate job, such as pay, relationships with coworkers, the status of the organization, etc (Schneider, 1975). This distinction is similar to the one Herzberg et al. have drawn between job content and the job's context (Herzberg, Mausner, & Snyderman, 1959).

Studies of the relationship between job characteristics and individual differences are good examples of research falling into the first type of matching category. Early studies in the area of task (or job) characteristics sought to identify the most important ones which influence employees' motivation, performance, tenure and satisfaction (e.g., Herzberg et al., 1959). Recent studies have gone beyond the mere identification of important job characteristics to include the influence of individual differences (in desires or needs). Several recent studies have shown that matching *actual* job characteristics to *desired* characteristics leads to high levels of employee motivation and satisfaction but not necessarily to performance (Hackman & Lawler, 1971; Wanous, 1974).

Besides the individual's matchup to the immediate job, studies have examined the consequences of the match-up between individuals and the broader context of organizational climate. Most of these do, in fact, support the assumption that organizational climate has a greater impact on satisfaction than on actual job performance (Friedlander & Margulies, 1969; Lawler, Hall, & Oldham, 1974; Pritchard & Karasick, 1973).

A recent study by Schneider (1975) tried to relate the match-up (or "fit," as he called it) between individual and organization to both performance and tenure among 1,125 life insurance agents. Initially he was unable to find any sizable relationships. Further analysis revealed that some of the agencies studied had far "better" climates than others. That is, they were higher on supportiveness, concern, morale, and autonomy, and lower on conflict than other agencies. By then examining the match-up between individual and organization for both the "good" and "bad" agencies, he found differences which had been hidden when he examined all the agencies together. Among the "good" agencies the expected relationship was found (i.e., the closer matched individuals and organizations were, the higher the sales and the lower the turnover). On the other hand, in the "bad" (or "negative") climates the reverse was true. The *less* the individual was similar to the climate, the better were sales and turnover was lower. Although Schneider's study is one of the first to separate out the *type* of climate, it does suggest that a strict interpretation of matching individual to organization may have to be slightly modified. This is especially true for those organizations with basically "negative" climates.

WHERE DO WE GO FROM HERE?

For the future study of organizational entry the greatest single need is for an *integrated conceptual overview* of the entire process. The present paper should be considered as only suggestive in this regard. What needs to be done is to adopt a general "systems view" of this process by drawing on the relevant research from industrial, organizational, social, and vocational psychology, as well as from the relevant areas of other disciplines such as industrial sociology, labor economics, and industrial relations. In one way or another all these areas of research have something of relevance for the study of organizational entry.

Certainly, future efforts in this direction should look at organizational entry from *both* sides of the matching process, and should consider both organizational selection of individuals as well as organizational choice by individuals. The present paper did *not* do this because it was considered more urgent to emphasize the underdeveloped research areas.

The future may also hold different views of organizational entry depending on the *type* of organization concerned. Most of what we know today has been obtained from studies in business organizations, and less so from colleges, universities, or the military. The basic problem of matching individual and organization is common to all these organization types, but shows up in quite different ways. For example, some businesses experience high turnover in certain entry-level jobs. In university programs, however, students pay for the opportunity to study (rather than being paid for their services), and they can be influenced by the magnet of "sunk costs." That is, the length of time for getting a degree is predictable. Thus, the longer a student remains in a school, the greater is the investment in it, and the harder it is to leave before graduation. In the military, the situation is different still. Given the legal nature of commitment to such service, the major problem is to retain qualified personnel at reenlistment time.

REFERENCES

Argyris, C. *Integrating the individual and the organization.* New York: Wiley, 1964.

Bakke, E. W. *The fusion process.* New Haven: Labor and Management Center, Yale University, 1953.

Bray, D. W., Campbell, R. J., & Grant, D. L. *Formative years in business.* New York: Wiley, 1974.

Dunnette, M. D., Arvey, R. D., & Banas, P. A. Why do they leave? *Personnel,* 1973, **3**, 25–39.

Dunnette, M. D., Campbell, J. P., & Hakel, M. D. Factors contributing to job satisfaction and job dissatisfaction in six occupational groups. *Organizational Behavior and Human Performance,* 1967, **2**, 143–174.

Farr, J. L., O'Leary, B. S., & Bartlett, C. J. Effect of a work sample test upon self-selection and turnover of job applicants. *Journal of Applied Psychology*, 1973, **58**, 283–285.

Ford, D. L., Huber, G. P., & Gustafson, D. H. Predicting job choices with models that contain subjective probability judgments: An empirical comparison of five models. *Organizational Behavior and Human Performance*, 1972, **7**, 397–416.

Friedlander, F., & Margulies, N. Multiple impacts of organizational climate and individual value systems upon job satisfaction. *Personnel Psychology*, 1969, **22**, 171–183.

Glueck, W. F. Decision-making: Organizational choice. *Personnel Psychology*, 1974, **27**, 77–93.

Hackman, R. J., & Lawler, E. E., III. Employee reactions to job characteristics. *Journal of Applied Psychology*, 1971, **55**, 259–286.

Herzberg, F., Mausner, B., & Snyderman, B. *The motivation to work*. New York: Wiley, 1959.

Huber, G. P., Daneshgar, R., & Ford, D. L. An empirical comparison of five utility models for predicting job preferences. *Organizational Behavior and Human Performance*, 1971, **6**, 267–282.

Ilgen, D. R., & Seely, W. Realistic expectations as an aid in reducing voluntary resignations. *Journal of Applied Psychology*, 1974, **59**, 452–455.

Lawler, E. E., III, Hall, D. T., & Oldham, G. R. Organizational climate: Relationship to organizational structure, process, and performance. *Organizational Behavior and Human Performance*, 1974, **11**, 139–155.

Lawler, E. E., III, Kuleck, W. J., Rhode, J. G., & Sorenson, J. E. Job choice and post decision dissonance. *Organizational Behavior and Human Performance*, 1975, **13**, 133–145.

Lofquist, L. H., & Dawis, R. V. *Adjustment to work*. New York: Appleton-Century-Crofts, 1969.

Macedonia, R. M. Expectations—press and survival. Unpublished doctoral dissertation, New York University, Graduate School of Public Administration, 1969.

Pieters, G. R., Hundert, A. T., & Beer, M. Predicting organizational choice: A post hoc analysis. *Proceedings of the 76th Annual Convention of the American Psychological Association*, 1969, 573–574.

Pritchard, R. D., & Karasick, B. The effects of organizational climate on managerial job performance and job satisfaction. *Organizational Behavior and Human Performance*, 1973, **9**, 126–146.

Schein, E. H. Organizational socialization and the profession of management. *Industrial Management Review*, 1968, **9**, 1–16.

Schneider, B. Organizational climate: Individual preferences and organizational realities revisited. *Journal of Applied Psychology*, 1975, **60**, 459–465.

Sheridan, J. E., Richards, M. D., & Slocum, J. W. Comparative analysis of expectancy and heuristic models of decision behavior. *Journal of Applied Psychology*, 1975, **60**, 361–368.

Soelberg, P. Unprogrammed decision making. *Industrial Management Review*, 1967, **8**, 19–29.

Vroom, V. H. *Work and motivation*. New York: Wiley, 1964.

Vroom, V. H. Organizational choice: A study of pre and post decision processes. *Organizational Behavior and Human Performance*, 1966, **1**, 212–225.

Vroom, V. H., & Deci, E. L. The stability of post decisional dissonance: A follow-up study of the job attitudes of business school graduates. *Organizational Behavior and Human Performance*, 1971, **6**, 36–49.

Wanous, J. P. Occupational preferences: Perceptions of valence and instrumentality, and objective data. *Journal of Applied Psychology,* 1972, **56**, 152–155.

Wanous, J. P. Effects of a realistic job preview of job acceptance, job attitudes, and job survival. *Journal of Applied Psychology,* 1973, **58**, 327–332.

Wanous, J. P. Individual differences and reactions to job characteristics. *Journal of Applied Psychology,* 1974, **59**, 616–622.

Wanous, J. P. *Organizational entry: The transition from outsider to newcomer to insider* (Working Paper 75–14). New York University, Graduate School of Business Administration, 1975a.

Wanous, J. P. Tell it like it is at realistic job previews. *Personnel,* 1975b, **52**(4), 50–60.

Wanous, J. P. A job preview makes recruiting more effective. *Harvard Business Review,* 1975c, **53**(5), 16, 166–8.

Wanous, J. P. Organizational entry: From naive expectations to realistic beliefs. *Journal of Applied Psychology,* 1976, **61**, 22–29.

Ward, L. B., & Athos, A. G. *Student expectations of corporate life.* Boston: Division of Research, Graduate School of Business Administration, Harvard University, 1972.

Weitz, J. Job expectancy and survival. *Journal of Applied Psychology,* 1956, **40**, 245–247.

Youngberg, C. F. An experimental study of job satisfaction and turnover in relation to job expectations and self expectations. Unpublished doctoral dissertation. New York University Graduate School of Arts and Sciences, 1963.

Toward a Theory of Career Motivation[1]

Manuel London

The term motivation often is used to explain decisions and behaviors that cannot be explained by ability alone. Motivation is concerned with the direction, arousal, amplitude, and persistence of an individual's behavior (Campbell & Pritchard, 1976). Work motivation is a construct that generally refers to motivation to do one's current job. The term managerial motivation refers to the desire to engage in and meet managerial role requirements (e.g., exerting leadership, conducting routine administrative activities) (Miner, 1977). These constructs are limited in scope, however, in that they do not reflect the many individual characteristics and associated decisions and behaviors relevant to one's career. The term career motivation encompasses the terms work motivation and managerial motivation and goes further to include motivation associated with a wide range of career decisions and behaviors. These include searching for and accepting a job, deciding to stay with an organization, revising one's career plans, seeking training and new job experiences, and setting and trying to accomplish career goals.

[1]Douglas W. Bray contributed immeasurably to the identification, organization, and definition of the individual characteristic dimensions and domains. Joseph Fischer contributed to the development of the situational characteristics and career decisions and behaviors. Both made valuable comments on earlier drafts of the manuscript.

From *Academy of Management Review,* 1983, **8**, 620–630. Reprinted by permission.

Career motivation is defined as the set of individual characteristics and associated career decisions and behaviors that reflect the person's career identity, insight into factors affecting his or her career, and resilience in the face of unfavorable career conditions.

Career motivation should be understood in terms of the relationships among individual characteristics, career decisions and behaviors, and situational conditions. Several authors have pointed to the need for theoretical models linking these variables over time (Brousseau, 1983; Dubin, 1976; Raynor, 1978). Toward this end, this paper begins to develop a theory of career motivation by outlining an integrative, holistic framework for understanding psychological and organizational career-related variables and processes.

CAREER MOTIVATION COMPONENTS

Career motivation is conceptualized here as a multidimensional construct internal to the individual, influenced by the situation, and reflected in the individual's decisions and behaviors. The variables relevant to career motivation form a set of dimensions clustered a priori into domains. The dimensions are neither independent nor necessarily exhaustive of all possible important constructs. Each domain is not intended to be a sum of its dimensions. The dimensions support and extend the meaning of the domain and are likely to vary in importance to the domain. Each individual characteristic associated with career motivation corresponds to a situational characteristic and a career decision or behavior.

Individual Characteristics

The individual characteristic dimensions are needs, interests, and personality variables potentially relevant to a person's career. These dimensions are clustered into three domains: career identity, career insight, and career resilience. The dimensions comprising these domains were derived from work on personality and individual assessments (Bray, 1982, Bray, Campbell, & Grant, 1974; Murray, 1938). Career identity reflects the direction of career motivation; career insight and resilience reflect the arousal, strength, and persistence of career motivation. Some of the dimensions (e.,g., need advancement and commitment to managerial work) are most applicable to managers in hierarchical organizations. Additional dimensions may have to be developed for studying career motivation in other contexts. Many of the dimensions, however, are very general (e.g., self-esteem, risk taking tendency, adaptability, self-objectivity) and are applicable to many types of occupations as well as to other areas of life. Each of the three domains and their dimensions are described below:

Career Identity This is how central one's career is to one's identity. Career identity consists of two subdomains: work involvement and desire for upward mobility. Work involvement dimensions, which should be positively related to career identity, include job involvement, professional orientation, commitment to managerial work, and identification with the organization. Also, individuals who are high on career identity are likely to find career satisfaction to be more important than satisfaction from other areas of life (primacy of work).

The upward mobility subdomain includes the needs for advancement, recognition, dominance, and money. It also includes ability to delay gratification, which should be negatively related to desire for upward mobility.

Career Insight   This is the extent to which the person has realistic perceptions of him or herself and the organization and relates these perceptions to career goals. Goal flexibility and need change should be inversely related to career insight. Other relevant dimensions (goal clarity, path goal clarity, social perceptiveness, self-objectivity, realism of expectations, career decision making, and future time orientation) should be positively related to career insight.

Career Resilience   This is a person's resistance to career disruption in a less than optimal environment. To understand the meaning of career resilience more clearly, it should help to have a conception of its opposite—career vulnerability. This is the extent of psychological fragility (e.g., becoming upset and finding it difficult to function) when confronted by less than optimal career conditions (e.g., barriers to career goals, uncertainty, poor relationships with co-workers). Being high on career resilience (low on career vulnerability) does not mean that the person is insensitive to such environmental conditions, but rather that he or she will be able to cope more effectively with a negative work situation.

The dimensions under career resilience fall into three subdomains. One is self-efficacy, which includes the dimensions of self-esteem, need autonomy, adaptability, internal control, need achievement, initiative, need creativity, inner work standards, and development orientation. Another subdomain is risk taking, including risk taking tendency, fear of failure, need security, and tolerance of uncertainty and ambiguity. The third subdomain is dependency. This includes career dependency, need for superior approval, and need for peer approval. It also includes competitiveness, which should be negatively related to the other dependency dimensions. Individuals will be more resilient the higher they are on the self-efficacy and risk taking dimensions and the lower they are on the dependency dimensions. Those low on career resilience are likely to be motivated to avoid risk, be dependent on others, seek structure, and avoid situations in which organizational outcomes depend on their behavior. Those high on career resilience are likely to do the reverse—take risks, be independent of others, create their own structure, and thrive on situations in which outcomes are contingent on their behavior.

Thus, career motivation is not a unidimensional construct but a set of variables, whose dimensions do not necessarily encompass all relevant individual characteristics; nor are the dimensions meant to be orthogonal. Furthermore, the grouping of dimensions into domains is theoretical at this point. Research will be necessary to refine and extend the dimensions, derive more coherent domains, and consider interactions among the dimensions. Table 1 lists and defines the

TABLE 1
CAREER MOTIVATION VARIABLES

Individual characteristics	Situational characteristics[b]	Career decisions and behaviors[b]
Domain I: *Career identity*—how central one's career is to one's identity	*Career identity press*—work elements, such as importance of one's job, contribute to self-image	*Career identification*—establishing career plans, giving up something of value for one's career, etc.
Work involvement subdomain: *Job involvement*—interest in and satisfaction from one's current job	Encouragement of involvement subdomain: *Job challenge*—the job's skill variety, autonomy, significance, etc.	Work involvement subdomain: *Demonstrating job involvement*—working long hours; recommending the work to others
Professional orientation—identification with an area of specialization	*Encouragement of professionalism*—support for involvement in professional activities, others in organization are professionally oriented, etc.	*Professional behavior*—enhancing one's prestige in the profession, describing oneself as a professional rather than as an employee of the organization
Commitment to managerial work[a]—preference for managerial work compared to other types of work	*Importance of managing*—emphasis on managerial roles (e.g., status and level of responsibility)	*Managerial striving*—using and improving managerial skills; setting career goals aimed at managerial positions
Identification with the organization—how central the organization is to one's identity	*Press for organizational commitment*—value of inducements (e.g., salary, pension) for individual contributions (e.g., good performance, staying with the organization)	*Demonstrating organizational commitment*—staying with the organization; investing in it; describing oneself as an employee of the organization
Primacy of work[a]—satisfaction derived from one's career compared to other areas of life	*Work priority*—intrinsic value of job and career compared to nonwork activities	*Showing devotion to work*—sacrificing nonwork activities and responsibilities for work (e.g., relocating one's family, working overtime)
Desire for upward mobility subdomain:	Opportunities and rewards subdomain:	Desire for upward mobility subdomain:
Need advancement[a]—need to be promoted	*Advancement opportunities*—the value of, and opportunities for, advancement	*Striving for advancement*—furthering advancement possibilities (e.g., establishing a career path, requesting to be considered for promotion)
Need recognition—need to be appreciatively acknowledged	*Potential for recognition*—opportunities for recognition (e.g., through regular appraisal feedback, visible work)	*Seeking recognition*—attracting attention (e.g., volunteering for important assignments, communicating work results to higher management)
Need dominance—need to lead and direct	*Leadership opportunities*—opportunities to assume leadership roles	*Trying to lead*—requesting and assuming leadership roles

Financial motivation—need to make money	Potential for monetary gain—value of, and opportunities for, financial rewards	Striving for money—requesting a raise, changing jobs for a higher paying position, etc.
Ability to delay gratification[a]—willingness to wait for promotion and other career rewards (negatively related to desire for upward mobility)	Advancement controls[a]—time and experience requirements for promotion, salary increases, leadership opportunities, etc.	Accepting slow progress—not taking action to increase one's progress even when others are progressing faster
Domain II: Career insight—realistic perceptions of oneself and the organization and relating this to career goals	Support for career development—career information and guidance	Career planning—seeking career information and performance feedback; setting career goals
Goal clarity—clarity of career goals	Structure for goal setting—existence of career alternatives, procedures, and assistance for setting career goals	Establishing career goals—identifying specific career goals and making them concrete (e.g., putting them in writing)
Path goal clarity—clarity of means of achieving career goals	Path goal structure—existence of standard career paths; help in establishing a career path; extent career paths are realized	Establishing a career path—identifying how goals can be achieved and working toward them
Goal flexibility[a]—willingness to modify or alter career goals (negatively related to career insight)	Organizational flexibility—requirements and procedures for establishing and changing career goals; variety of alternatives	Changing goals—changing goals in response to changes in interests, circumstances, and influences
Need change—interest in new and different career experiences (negatively related to career insight)	Opportunity for change—amount of change in the organization, opportunities for voluntary change, and assistance in adapting to change	Making changes—initiating change; expressing enthusiasm for new experiences and boredom with old experiences
Social perceptiveness—sensitivity to organizational and interpersonal factors affecting career progress	Visibility of organizational processes—organizational processes (e.g., appraisals, personnel decisions) are explicit, observable, and veridical	Responsiveness to social conditions—altering behavior to fit the situation; seeking information and personal contacts to take advantage of organizational processes
Self-objectivity[a]—having an accurate view of one's strengths, weaknesses, and motives	Feedback processes—fairness and accuracy of performance and potential appraisal and review	Self-monitoring—keeping track of one's performance, trying to strengthen weaknesses that can be developed, and seeking assignments that use one's strengths
Realism of expectations[a]—Realism of expectations about career outcome (e.g., advancement, salary)	Realistic job information—completeness and accuracy of information about career opportunities	Forming and expressing realistic expectations—seeking information; comparing one's expectations to others

TABLE 1
CAREER MOTIVATION VARIABLES (CONTINUED)

Individual characteristics	Situational characteristics[b]	Career decisions and behaviors[b]
Career decision making—Tendency to be thorough and decisive in decision making	*Favorability of decision context*—existence of alternatives and information about them; time available for making decisions; revokability of decisions	*Decision making behavior*—seeking and evaluating alternatives and information; not waivering once alternatives are evaluated or regretting decisions after they are made
Future time orientation—tendency to anticipate the future and work toward future goals	*Organization's emphasis on long-term*—requirements for long term planning; changes expected in the future; rewards for long term accomplishments	*Instrumental behavior*—working harder on projects that will affect one's career than on routine tasks; planning for the future and acting on those plans
Domain III: *Career resilience*—the person's resistance to career disruption in a less than optimal environment. The opposite is *career vulnerability*—extent of psychological fragility (e.g., becomes upset and finds it difficult to function) when confronted by less than optimal career conditions.	*Organizational strength and support*—the clarity, harmony, and certainty of organizational processes and procedures. Other factors include openness of communication, integrity, stability, growth, and other indexes of organizational effectiveness. The opposite is *organizational stress*—the degree of ambiguity, conflict, and uncertainty within the organization.	*Increasing individual effectiveness*—demonstrating initiative, purposive action, and high performance. The opposite is *decreasing individual effectiveness*—demonstrating withdrawal, anxiety, and confusion (e.g., absenteeism, task avoidance, physical and/or psychological symptoms of stress, low performance).
Self-efficacy subdomain:	Encouragement of individual contribution and personal growth subdomain:	Self-efficacy subdomain:
Self-esteem—the extent to which the person has a positive self-image	*Positive reinforcement*—positive reinforcement and constructive feedback are given to employees	*Showing belief in oneself*—requesting difficult assignments; expressing one's ideas; constructively dealing with criticism
Need autonomy—need to be independent (also relevant to dependency subdomain)	*Encouragement of autonomy*—assignments are given to individuals not groups; individuals are encouraged to work alone; individual accomplishment is rewarded	*Striving for autonomy*—choosing to work alone; taking independent action; not asking for assistance
Adaptability—acceptance of and adjustment to job and organizational changes	*Organizational change*—frequency and extent of changes in task assignments, job structures, reporting relationships, work locations, policies, and regulations; assistance given by organization in adapting to change	*Demonstrating adaptability*—changing behaviors to meet changing demands; readily learning new procedures, rules, technology, etc.

Internal control—belief that one can influence career outcomes (e.g., promotional opportunities, job assignments)

Need achievement—need to do difficult jobs well (apart from trying to advance)

Initiative—need to take action to enhance one's career

Need creativity—need to create new methods, products, procedures, etc.

Inner work standards[a]—desire to do a good job even when something less will do

Development orientation[a]—desire to expand one's skill or knowledge

Risk taking subdomain:

Risk taking tendency—tendency to risk something of value (e.g., money, one's job, self-esteem) to gain something of value

Fear of failure—fear of not living up to one's expectations or those of others (negatively related to risk taking)

Need security[a]—value of secure employment (negatively related to risk taking)

Amount of individual control—how much discretion the individual has in determining work methods and work outcomes

Opportunity for achievement—difficulty and importance of one's job; time span for goal accomplishment

Opportunity for input—the extent to which employees' ideas are listened to and acted on; formal programs for input (e.g., MBO)

Support for creativity—rewards are given for creative ideas and solutions; change is frequent and there are few standard procedures and routine tasks

Demands for quality—incentives for high quality work; explicitness of performance standards

Support for development—tuition aid; in-house training programs; rewards for development

Risk taking potential subdomain:

Opportunity for and value of risk taking—how positively risk is viewed (aside from the outcome); the opposite is emphasis placed on stability and not "rocking the boat."

Consequences of failure—visibility of failure; a failure can be the "kiss of death" for advancement, bad reputations spread quickly and die slowly.

Job security—the organization's reputation as a long term employer; availability of jobs in the labor market

Taking control—working hard to obtain valued outcomes; requesting assignments, promotions, and raises

Striving to achieve—working hard on difficult tasks and seeking knowledge of the results; requesting projects that use one's skills and expertise

Taking action for self-benefit—letting career goals be known, requesting desired assignments, making the outcomes of one's work known to higher management

Creative behavior—searching for and offering innovative ideas and new procedures; applying a wide range of resources to one's job

Quality of work—attending to details; taking time to do the best job possible

Seeking development—taking courses, keeping up with developments in one's field; improving one's skills

Risk taking subdomain:

Taking risks—suggesting ideas contrary to those of others; taking a job with high rewards but little security; assuming responsibility for one's behavior

Response to failure (or potential failure)—withdrawing from difficult situations; working in groups to avoid individual accountability

Seeking security—keeping a secure job even though advancement possibilities and salary may be better elsewhere

TABLE 1
CAREER MOTIVATION VARIABLES (CONTINUED)

Individual characteristics	Situational characteristics[b]	Career decisions and behaviors[b]
Tolerance of uncertainty and ambiguity[a]—the degree to which one's work performance stands up under uncertain or unstructured situations	Organizational uncertainty and ambiguity—clarity, structure, and stability of work goals, methods, reporting relationships, policies, etc.; predictability of work outcomes	Seeking structure—setting schedules; organizing work loads; acting without direction
Dependency subdomain (negatively related to career resilience):	Interpersonal concern and cohesiveness subdomain:	Dependency subdomain:
Competitiveness—need to compete with one's peers (negatively related to dependency)	Competitive situations—employees are compared to each other for purposes of evaluation and reward	Competing—taking jobs or assignments for which rewards are based on competition; trying to advance faster and farther than one's peers
Career dependency—expecting the organization or supervisors to guide one's career	Paternalism—supervisors act as mentors or sponsors to selected subordinates, make plans for and decisions about subordinates' careers, and are held responsible for subordinates' career development.	Waiting for career direction—waiting for information about career development; expressing the belief that the organization has a career plan for each individual
Need supervisor approval[a]—emotional dependency on authority figures	Supervisor's consideration and control—supervisor develops friendships with selected subordinates and gives them more attention and latitude than others; sets goals and standards; monitors work	Deferent behavior—trying to impress one's supervisor; being influenced by the supervisor (e.g., expressing the same opinions)
Need for peer approval[a]—emotional dependency on co-workers	Group cohesiveness—co-workers develop friendly relationships and depend on each other for task accomplishment	Relying on others—seeking task assistance from co-workers; being socially involved with them; being influenced by them

[a]Based on management assessment center dimensions (Bray, 1982; Bray et al., 1974).
[b]Relationships to the individual characteristic in the row are hypothesized to be positive.

individual characteristic dimensions and domains and should serve as a resource for identifying relevant variables for psychological research on careers and for suggesting how a given variable fits into a vector of related variables.

Situational Variables

Many elements of a person's work environment are likely to be important to career motivation. These include staffing policies and procedures, leadership style, job design, group cohesiveness, career development programs, and the compensation system, to name a few. (For the sake of parsimony, situational variables applying only to the work organization are presented. They could be extended to include nonwork variables.)

Table 1 links the individual characteristic dimensions of career motivation to situational characteristics. For example, career identity should be associated with the extent to which work attributes, such as the importance of one's job to the organization, contribute to one's self-image (career identity press). Career insight should be related to the amount of career information and guidance supplied by the organization (support for career development). Career resilience should be associated with variables reflecting the organization's strength and support. Conversely, career vulnerability should be associated with the degree of ambiguity, conflict, and uncertainty in the organization (organizational stress). Each of the situational characteristics should be viewed as a continuum that may vary from low to high at different times.

Career Decisions and Behaviors

Career decisions and behaviors include generating alternative courses of action, seeking information about them, evaluating the information, setting goals, making decisions to behave in various ways, and carrying out the decisions. The processes of setting career goals and making career decisions are cognitive but are manifest in observable actions.

Career decisions and behaviors may be linked to the individual and situational characteristics. This idea is captured in Table 1 in a set of behavioral dimensions. For instance, career identity should be related to giving up something of value for one's career (demonstrating career identification). Career insight should be related to seeking career information and setting career goals (career planning). Career vulnerability should be associated with increased absenteeism, task avoidance, and symptoms of stress (decreasing effectiveness).

Although each dimension outlined in Table 1 is conceptually distinct, overlap among the dimensions is likely. For instance, career planning is relevant to several behavioral dimensions.

A CAREER MOTIVATION MODEL

One way to view career motivation is that it affects what will happen, or what a person hopes will happen, in the future. Career decisions and behaviors are guided by the outcomes that are desired and one's expectations for attaining them. This is known as prospective rationality (O'Reilly & Caldwell, 1981). Another view, compatible with the first, is that career decisions, behaviors, and situational conditions affect how one interprets the environment and one's psychological state. This is known as retrospective rationality (Salancik & Pfeffer, 1978). Although some individual characteristics may be quite stable, evolving during one's early life and supported by fairly consistent situational conditions, other dimensions are more sensitive to the environment. The level and importance of an individual characteristic to career decisions and behaviors will depend on the salience of different situational variables and their stability over time. The processes of prospective and retrospective rationality provide a basis for understanding the relationships among individual, situational, and behavioral variables associated with career motivation. These are general processes that may apply to other facets of life in addition to careers.

Prospective Rationality

This approach holds that choice processes are "based on a search for and use of information that allows the decision maker to form rational expectations about how good or bad the alternatives are likely to be" (O'Reilly & Caldwell, 1981, p. 598). Inferior information, misperceptions, or inaccurate interpretation of information may result in poor decisions and/or inappropriate or dysfunctional behaviors. Prospective rationality assumes that objective differences in organizations, jobs, and individuals account for variations in career decisions and behaviors.

Expectancy theory of work motivation provides an example of prospective rationality assumptions. The theory focuses on cognitions or expectancies of various outcomes and the extent to which the outcomes are valued by the individual (Vroom, 1964). The assumption is that people cognitively combine information to determine maximally beneficial alternatives and then direct their behavior in a way most likely to derive those alternatives (Staw, 1981). (See Naylor, Pritchard, & Ilgen, 1981, for a recent elaboration of this approach.)

Content theories of motivation focus on the needs, interests, and values people try to achieve (Campbell, Dunnette, Lawler, & Weick, 1970). These theories, exemplified by the work of Murray (1938), Maslow (1954), and Herzberg (1966), also assume prospective rationality in that they specify what an individual will try to achieve in the future.

Retrospective Rationality

This process begins with the idea that people spend much more time with the consequences of their actions and decisions than they spend contemplating future behaviors and beliefs (Salancik & Pfeffer, 1978). Individual characteristics, such as one's needs and one's self-concept, are cognitions that make sense out of past actions in a social environment (Pfeffer, 1980). The more ambiguous the environment, the more the worker will rely on social comparisons and past behavior to assess it. Individual characteristics are affected by the salience and relevance of information and by the general need to develop socially acceptable and legitimate rationalizations for actions.

Salancik and Pfeffer (1978) outlined three bases for retrospective rationality. One is social, another is environmental, and the third is behavioral. The social basis occurs when the job is so complex that the individual is uncertain how to react to it. Knowing how others evaluate the job suggests to the employee how he or she should react. Also, people are likely to agree with their co-workers so that they fit into the work environment. Moreover, people are influenced by what others say about them and by the advice given to them.

Individuals cognitively evaluate facets of the job environment. Objective characteristics of the organization affect the individual's perceptions of these characteristics. Judgments are a function of the positive and negative information a person has about the job.

Past behavior can be a determinant of individual needs states. It can serve as a source of information for constructing attitude statements (Bem, 1972). Also, it may influence future behavior in that individuals attempt to behave in ways that are consistent with the past, giving little thought to what might happen in the future (Staw, 1981). Retrospective rationality may be based partially on the need to justify one's behavior and the desire to appear competent in previous as opposed to future actions. There is considerable evidence that individuals try to maximize consistency between their behavior and their self-image (Baumeister, 1982). Moreover, they behave in ways that construct (create, maintain, and modify) their public self congruent to their ideal self and behave in ways that please the observer.

Retrospective rationality processes can serve as the basis for prospective rationality directed toward future actions. Cognitive social learning results in establishment of perceived self-competencies, expectancies, values, ways of encoding the environment, and self-regulatory mechanisms (Mischel, 1973). These, in turn, operate cognitively through different decision making heuristics to affect future actions. Deci (1980) provides a similar formulation by arguing that individuals' perceptions, or cognitive evaluations, of the environment develop from their experiences. These perceptions and evaluations shape behavioral choices. Thus, both retrospective and prospective rationality processes may affect career decisions and behaviors (Staw, 1981).

An Integrative Model

Figure 1 diagrams the proposed relationships among situational characteristics, individual characteristics, and career decisions and behaviors. The model emphasizes that career motivation is a multidimensional, dynamic process—not a unidimensional construct. The specific variables involved and their strength vary over time and for different individuals in different situations. Individual characteristics are not necessarily stable traits in all environmental contexts. Some are stable for a long time, others are activated and become strong for a short period, and still others have little effect or never fully evolve. The nature of the

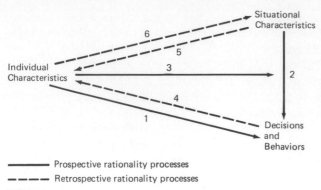

```
———————  Prospective rationality processes
— — — —  Retrospective rationality processes
```

FIGURE 1
An interactive model of career motivation components.

interactions in the model also varies. Different types of interactions arise at different times depending on the variables involved and their strength. The numbers in the diagram referring to the linkages do not imply order of occurrence or importance. Rather, the model represents continuous processes of direct and indirect relationships.

Linkages 1, 2, and 3 describe prospective rationality processes. Linkage 1 refers to the direct effects of individual characteristics on decisions and behaviors, as when a person behaves in a certain way almost regardless of the situation. For example, risk taking tendency will lead to choosing career alternatives with higher values and lower probabilities of occurrence.

> Proposition 1. Individual characteristics associated with career motivation will have a greater direct effect on career decisions and behaviors the more the individual characteristics are stable and integrated into the individual's self-concept. This is evident when a decision or behavior fits into a pattern of decisions and behaviors typical of the individual.

Linkage 2 represents the direct impact of the situation on career decisions and behaviors. These are cases in which the situation restricts or in other ways determines individual actions. For instance, an organization may require that a new manager attend a set of training programs or enroll in a graduate degree program. As another example, the more cohesive the work group, the more likely social influence processes will affect career decisions and behaviors.

> Proposition 2. Situational characteristics will have a greater effect on career decisions and behaviors the more the situational characteristics control or limit possible decisions and behaviors, define what decisions and behaviors are socially acceptable, and require justifying one's decisions and behaviors to others.

Linkage 3 represents the interactions that may occur between the individual and the situation as they affect career decisions and behaviors. The nature of the interactions that emerge will depend on the variables involved. Different theoretical approaches posit different independent and intervening variables. (For example, McClelland's, 1971, need achievement theory holds that individuals with high need achievement will choose moderately difficult tasks, whereas those with low need achievement will choose very easy or very difficult tasks.) Each individual characteristic dimension associated with career motivation may interact with its corresponding situational characteristic to affect career decisions and behaviors. (Corresponding variables are those in each row of Table 1.) In general, the strength of a main effect or interaction will depend on the strength of the independent variables (their stability, favorability, recency of occurrence, etc.). For instance, if the situation is such that the individual has discretion in determining work assignments, those high on the individual characteristic of internal control (the belief that one can influence career outcomes) are more likely to try to control their assignments than are those low on internal control. When there is little discretion in determining work assignments, internal control is not as likely to affect the individual's behavior.

The congruence or match between the individual and the situation is likely to affect what career decisions and behaviors will occur and their potential value to the individual and the organization. For example, consider an organizational environment low in encouragement of autonomy, discretion over career outcomes, opportunities for achievement, feedback on performance, and positive reinforcement for good performance. The resilient individual is likely to tolerate the situation for a while and, if it does not improve, look for better alternatives elsewhere. This may be negative for the organization if the individual is a valued employee. Alternatively, the individual may cease striving for autonomy, taking control, striving to achieve, and showing belief in himself or herself. This could lead to negative outcomes for the employee and the organization. As another example, consider the case of a vulnerable employee assigned to a supervisor who provides encouragement of autonomy, discretion over career outcomes, opportunities for achievement, performance feedback, and positive reinforcement. The subordinate is unlikely, at least initially, to be effective in this environment. Perhaps over time, he or she may become more resilient if the supervisor maintains this style of management.

> Proposition 3. Career decisions and behaviors will be more effective (e.g., have more positive outcomes for the individual and the organization) the greater the congruence between the individual and the situational characteristics.

The notion of individual/situational congruence must be viewed broadly, taking into account sets of individual characteristics and sets of situational characteristics. For example, the individual's internal control may not moderate the relationship between the amount of individual control available and the extent to which the person takes control if the individual's need achievement and need autonomy are low. Also, the effectiveness of a particular career decision or behavior will depend on a number of factors, including the individual's ability and the conditions in the organization. A person with low ability who tries to take control over his or her career outcomes may not do so effectively. An individual who establishes specific career goals and puts them in writing may be wasting his or her time if the organization is in a state of flux.

Linkages 4, 5, and 6 describe retrospective rationality processes. Linkage 4 deals with how past decisions and behaviors affect individual characteristics. The tendency to maintain consistency between one's behavior and self-concept underlies this linkage. For example, establishing plans for one's career is likely to enhance career identity as long as the plans are likely to be put into effect. As another example, turning down a lucrative job offer is likely to enhance loyalty to one's present employer unless the decision can be changed easily or attributed to factors beyond the individual's control.

> Proposition 4. Past career decisions and behaviors will have a greater effect on the individual characteristics associated with career motivation the more the decisions and behaviors have positive or negative consequences and the longer these consequences last.

Linkage 5 deals with how the current situation affects individual characteristics. For instance, receiving positive feedback for performance should lead to higher self-esteem and a greater sense of internal control, particularly when the task is such that the individual has control over the outcome. Increasing job challenge (e.g., by increasing the job's skill variety, task identity, feedback, autonomy, and significance) should positively affect job involvement unless such changes in task design are viewed as increased demands.

> Proposition 5. Situational characteristics will have a greater effect on the individual characteristics associated with career motivation the more the situational characteristics are viewed as positive or negative, the more recently they occurred, and the more they control possible career decisions and behaviors.

Linkage 6 is the process of interpreting the situation. A high self-esteem individual would be likely to attribute a lower-than-expected pay raise to external factors, such as the economy, if another justification is not provided by the supervisor. A low self-esteem individual would be likely to attribute a lower-than-expected raise to his or her own performance. To do otherwise in either case would be inconsistent with the individual's self-concept. However, if the pay raise is explained (e.g., everyone received the same percentage, or the individual's performance was lower than it should have been), then the causal attribution may not be affected by the individual's self-esteem.

> Proposition 6. Individual characteristics associated with career motivation will affect how the situation is perceived the more the situation initially is ambiguous, uncertain, and/or cognitively inconsistent.

The propositions and associated linkages provide a framework for investigating and understanding career motivation and for generating more specific hypotheses about the effects of the components of the model. Changes in the variables and their effects may be observed over time. It should be recognized that the proposed relationships do not occur in isolation from one another or in a fixed sequence. Also, Figure 1 is a simplified version of the relationships because the individual, situational, and behavioral components of the model are vectors of interrelated dimensions.

The propositions express the primary linkages among the components of the model. Other relationships also may occur, although they may emerge more clearly in one of the above proposed relationships because of the sequence of events. Career decisions and behaviors may have a direct effect on the situation, as when an individual's requesting and assuming leadership roles is recognized and results in increased leadership opportunities. Also, career decisions and behaviors may moderate relationships between individual and situational characteristics. For example, individuals may not acquire a sense of internal control from new organizational policies allocating increased power and responsibilities unless they have behaved in a way that demonstrates power. However, this may appear from analyses over time as a sequence of the effects of the situation on behavior and the effects of behavior on the individual's psychological state. Another possibility is that the situation may moderate relationships between individual characteristics and career decisions and behaviors, as when effective leadership behavior does not result in the feeling of internal control and need dominance unless a formal statement detailing reporting relationships and responsibilities has been issued by the organization. However, this may appear as a strong relationship between the situation and the individual characteristics and a weak relationship between the behavior and the individual characteristics, particularly if the behavior has been ongoing and the situational characteristic justifying the behavior is of recent occurrence.

Recognizing the complexity of the model, a manageable approach to testing the propositions would be to investigate the linkages by studying sets of dimensions. The model cannot be tested in one study, nor can it be tested by measuring a few variables. It requires an organismic, in-depth longitudinal program of research. This should involve three types of assessment: one focusing on the individual characteristics, another on the situation, and a third on the career decisions and behaviors. An assessment center is one way to measure the individual characteristic dimensions. Techniques for assessing the situational characteristics and career decisions and behaviors include interviews, observations, ratings, diaries, and network analysis. (See Lawler, Nadler, & Cammann, 1980, for a review of such methods.) The assessments should be repeated over time to test causal relationships among the components.

Implications of the Model

Traditional motivational strategies entail changing an element of the environment (e.g., the compensation system or the job design) to increase motivation and thereby enhance job performance. Another approach has been to hire people who have not only the requisite skills and abilities but also a psychological profile that is believed (but unfortunately seldom empirically demonstrated) to be job related. The idea that some individual characteristics may change over time and be affected by situational conditions introduces possibilities for new motivational strategies. Once there is a better understanding of how the situation activates different individual characteristics, it will be possible to affect motivation by changing the salience of different situational variables. Attention may be focused on different elements of the environment by changing them or perhaps merely discussing them or communicating information about them. For example, a company may offer its employees a voluntary, self-administered career management program that consists of several workbooks. Because this requires considerable work with no immediate benefit to one's career, the program may be completed by relatively few employees. Just knowing that the program exists, however, may focus the attention of many more employees on their career goals, factors that affect those goals, and their responsibility for their own careers. This could ultimately affect their career decisions and behaviors, although not necessarily in the way the program was intended.

How people interpret the environment has implications for motivational strategies. For instance, a given situational change may not affect motivation because it is not perceived as intended. Understanding which individual characteristics are relevant to interpreting different situations may suggest ways of controlling the process.

The multidimensional nature of career motivation suggests that motivational strategies will have to deal with broad sets of variables. For example, a new pay system may be designed and implemented along with a career development program, a supervisor-subordinate joint goal setting process, and new transfer and promotion policies as an integrated system. Such a system could be designed using knowledge about relationships among groups of situational characteristics, individual characteristics, and career decisions and behaviors. As another example, an employee communications program coupled with training to help subordinates set and carry out career goals may affect career insight variables. But these programs may have no effect if prior circumstances generated low career resilience. Consequently, programs to affect resilience dimensions (e.g., ways of providing constructive feedback while reducing the negative consequences of failure) also may be necessary.

SUMMARY

This paper outlines the components of career motivation and proposed relationships among them. The components consist of individual characteristics organized into three domains (career identity, career insight, and career resilience) with corresponding situational characteristics and career decisions and behaviors. The relationships among the components are based on prospective and retrospective rationality. Prospective rationality is the process by which individuals' career decisions and behaviors are affected by what they believe will happen in the future. The nature of the situation and the individual characteristics associated with career motivation affect career decisions and behaviors. Retrospective rationality holds that social learning and information processing influence individual characteristics. The importance of different individual characteristics will change with the salience of corresponding elements of the situation and one's decisions and behaviors. Testing the model requires an organismic, longitudinal assessment of each component. The results are likely to be valuable for designing new motivational strategies.

REFERENCES

Baumeister, R. R. A self-presentational view of social phenomena. *Psychological Bulletin*. 1982, 91, 3–25.

Bem, D. J. Self-perception theory. In L. Berkowitz (Ed.), *Advances in experimental social psychology* (Vol. 6). New York: Academic Press, 1972, 1–62.

Bray, D. W. The assessment center and the study of lives. *American Psychologist*, 1982, 37, 180–189.

Bray, D. W., Campbell, R. J., & Grant, D. L. *Formative years in business: A long-term AT&T study of managerial lives*. New York: Wiley, 1974.

Brousseau, K. R. Toward a dynamic model of job-person relationships: Findings, research, questions, and implications for work system design. *Academy of Management Review*, 1983, 8, 33–45.

Campbell, J. P., & Pritchard, R. D. Motivation theory in industrial and organizational psychology. In M. D. Dunnette (Ed.), *Handbook of industrial and organizational psychology*. Chicago: Rand McNally, 1976, 63–130.

Campbell, J. P., Dunnette, M. D., Lawler, E. E., III, & Welch, K. E., Jr. *Managerial behavior, performance, and effectiveness*. New York: McGraw-Hill, 1970.

Deci, E. L. *The psychology of self-determination*. Lexington, Mass.: Lexington Books, 1980.

Dubin, R. Theory building in applied areas. In M. D. Dunnette (Ed.), *Handbook of industrial and organizational psychology*. Chicago: Rand McNally, 1976, 17–39.

Herzberg, F. *Work and the nature of man*. Cleveland, Ohio: World Publishing, 1966.

Lawler, E. E., III., Nadler, D. A., & Cammann, C. *Organizational assessment: Perspectives on the measurement of organizational behavior and the quality of work life*. New York: Wiley, 1980.

Maslow, A. H. *Motivation and personality*. New York: Harper & Row, 1954.

McClelland, D. C. *Motivational trends in society*. Morristown, N. J.: General Learning Press, 1971.

Miner, J. B. *Motivation to manage: A ten-year update on the "studies in management education" research*. Atlanta, Ga.: Organizational Measurement Systems Press, 1977.

Mischel, W. Toward a cognitive social learning reconceptualization of personality. *Psychological Review*, 1973, 80, 252–283.

Murray, H. A. *Explorations in personality. A clinical and experimental study of fifty men of college age*. New York: Oxford University Press, 1938.

Naylor, J. C., Pritchard, R. D., & Ilgen, D. R. *A theory of behavior in organizations*. New York: Academic Press, 1980.

O'Reilly, C. A., III, & Caldwell, D. F. The commitment and job tenure of new employees: Some evidence of post decisional justification. *Administrative Science Quarterly*, 1981, 26, 597–616.

Pfeffer, J. A partial test of the social information processing model of job attitudes. *Human Relations*, 1980, 33, 457–476.

Raynor, J. O. Motivation and career striving. In J. W. Atkinson & J. O. Raynor (Eds.), *Personality, motivation, and achievement*. New York: Wiley, 1978, 199–219.

Salancik, G. R., & Pfeffer, J. A. A social information processing approach to job attitudes and task design. *Administrative Science Quarterly*, 1978, 23, 224–253.

Staw, B. M. The escalation of commitment to a course of action. *Academy of Management Review*, 1981, 6, 577–587.

Vroom, V. H. *Work and motivation*. New York: Wiley, 1964.

Culture as an Environmental Context for Careers

Edgar H. Schein

INTRODUCTION

Much has been written recently about the concept of 'career', but relatively little attention has been given to the cultural context within which careers occur. Yet even the idea of what a 'career' is depends on the culture in which it is embedded. We know that in different countries different notions exist about how one should pursue careers, how much emphasis one should give to career versus family concerns, and what makes careers legitimate. Moreover, there is growing evidence that organizational cultures also influence careers in specifying what is expected of career occupants (Schwartz and Davis, 1981; Schein, 1983; Dyer, 1982; Pettigrew, 1979).

In this paper I would like to explore several facets of culture as an environment for careers and to demonstrate that career research is inevitably culture-bound. I will draw primarily on my own consulting, clinical, and research experiences to analyse some of the issues that culture raises for career research and career development. Three separate areas will be discussed:

1 Cultural influences on the concept of career itself.

2 Cultural influences on the importance of career relative to personal and family issues.

3 Cultural influences on the bases of legitimacy of managerial careers.

CULTURAL INFLUENCES ON THE CONCEPT OF CAREER

The focus in this section is to distinguish what 'career' means to the members of a given culture from the meanings the word has come to have for career researchers. I was not aware of the issue until I encountered it in labelling some of my own work. My interest in career research began over twenty years ago with the application of the concept of 'coercive persuasion' to the problem of organizational socialization and management development (Schein, 1961). In the early 1970's I began to pull this research together into a book designed for the practicing manager and was searching for a title. A number of my colleagues advised me to avoid putting the word 'career' into the title, on the grounds that the word itself connoted only those professions and 'higher' occupations in which clear hierarchical progress was intrinsic, and in which membership implied middle class origins and advanced levels of education.

The sociological notion of *any* set of role transitions being, in a sense, a career, such as the 'career of the mental patient' (Goffman, 1959), was only gradually taking hold in our own society, so careers remained associated in the minds of

From *Journal of Occupational Behaviors*, 1984, **5**, 71–81. Reprinted by permission. © 1984 by John Wiley & Sons, Ltd.

many with middle class success syndromes. Use of the word would imply dis-interest in lower occupations where a rise in rank could never be expected, as in the occupations of taxi driver, janitor, semi-skilled production worker, and pros-titute. It is only recently, in other words, that the concept of career has been applied to all occupations as a neutral descriptive term such that we can now talk of linear, steady state, or even spiral careers (Driver, 1980), and think of a career as being a morally neutral vehicle for describing occupational progress, or the lack thereof (Van Maanen, 1977).

This experience made me aware of how dependent we are on the culture in which we live for definitions of even simple everyday terms like career. Cross-cultural variations were brought home to me when, in 1975, I was asked to attend a conference on 'career planning and development' sponsored by the International Labor Office. Participants were drawn from the U.S., Western European coun-tries, and Socialist countries such as the German Democratic Republic, Hungary, Poland, Bulgaria, and the Soviet Union. In constructing a summary presentation for this conference, differences in the cultural connotation of the word 'career' between the socialist and non-socialist countries became apparent. For the so-cialist countries, career implied personal ambition above and beyond what might be justified or good for the system, and 'careerism' would, therefore, be viewed as a personal fault in the sense of a display of excess ambition (Schein, 1976). We have a similar connotation in the U.S. when we say to someone, 'don't make a "career" of it', implying don't put excess effort into it.

One of the major cultural variations in the concept of career, then, is the extent to which it implies only personal ambition to rise in the occupational structure. In societies where such personal ambition is not valued, the concept of 'career' would have a very different meaning, or might not exist at all as a shared concept.

From the researcher's point of view, we need not only to distinguish between the various cultural connotations of 'ambition' and 'motivation', but also whether we are viewing career events from the perspective of the society or from the perspective of the career occupant. Thus, we need to distinguish what we have called the *external career*, which is the socially defined set of steps and require-ments for fulfilling a given occupation, as well as the degree of prestige asso-ciated with that occupation from what we have called the *internal career* which is the individual career occupant's view of his or her own steps and progress over time, as well as his or her own views of the importance of that career (Van Maanen and Schein, 1977). Cultural variation, then, should be studied with respect to both the external and internal career concepts, and may show up most dramatically in the interaction between the two as will be noted below.

To illustrate the distinction, the actual steps to becoming a doctor, as well as the prestige of being one (the external career), involving such matters as going to medical school, fulfilling internship and residency requirements, taking spe-cialty examinations, and working in various combinations of private practice and hospital staff, differ to some degree across cultures. Such differences in the external career would then also show up in the internal career in how an individual felt about being a doctor. The individual's own motivation, i.e., whether it was primarily altruistic, technical, or economic, would be judged against what the society and the occupation judged to be 'legitimate' criteria for being a doctor, and that judgement would, in turn, influence how successful the individual felt.

The occupational structure of every society evolves to fulfil the functions needed in that society. To the extent that those functions are different across societies, we can assume variations in how external careers are structured, how internal careers are perceived, and the nature of the interaction between the two. Beyond these societal influences it is clear that organizations also influence how careers are to be structured and how members feel about those careers. Organizations will reflect the broader culture in which they exist, but it is clear that they develop cultures of their own as a result of the personal biases of their founders and leaders, and their own histories (Pettigrew, 1979; Schein, 1981; Schwartz and Davis, 1981).

Companies vary in the degree in which they explicitly define career paths, the steps required for each path, the kinds of motives considered legitimate for pursuing them, and the prestige attached to them (the equivalent of external careers), leading to variations in how career occupants in those organizations perceive and feel about those careers (the equivalent of internal careers).

For example, in one company I work with there are three well defined career paths or ladders—a hierarchical one, a technical specialist one which includes the concept of 'individual contributor', and a less formally defined path toward inclusion and influence where one's 'centrality' can increase even if one's rank does not (Schein, 1971; Van Maanen and Schein, 1979). People have a sense of being on or off the path, of being on time or off time with respect to rates of movement (Lawrence, 1984), and clearly expect the company to manage major career movement.

In contrast, within another company in the same country, careers are defined as being 'owned' by individual career occupants. Top management announces loudly and clearly that there are no special paths, steps, or sequences, and that anyone can be fired at any time for non-performance or if they are found to be redundant. Individual career occupants have a sense of moving hierarchically, along functional and/or technical paths, and toward the centre of the organization, but those feelings are subjective and are not reflected in any expected or acknowledged external career events.

In summary, countries and organizations differ in the degree to which they specify explicitly the external career paths that are to be followed by members of a given occupation, the kinds of motives and ambitions that are considered legitimate for pursuit of careers, and the degree of prestige that is attached to different paths. Organizational cultures will reflect, in part, the broader societal cultures, and in a sense mediate between the larger culture and the occupational structure experienced by the individual. These differences strongly influence the way people feel about their careers, the kind of motivation that is considered to be appropriate for a career, how successful people will feel, and even how explicitly they experience having a career. Individual reactions, what we have called the 'internal career', are, therefore, a joint outcome of broad societal forces, specific occupational or oganizational forces, and each person's own experience.

CULTURAL INFLUENCES ON THE IMPORTANCE OF CAREER

The next issue is how members of a society or organization set their priorities between the demands of a career and other areas of their lives. Again, we must distinguish between the structural external issues such as the culture's view of work, the stage of economic development, the kind of occupational structure that exists, and the particular culture of the employing organization from the internal career issues of how much emotional energy and commitment a given person chooses to allocate to his or her career versus other life experiences. We have argued previously (Bailyn and Schein, 1976; Schein, 1978) the utility of distinguishing three settings or domains that draw the individual's attention and commitment—(1) the occupational setting; (2) the family setting; and (3) self-oriented settings.

Self-oriented activities refer to those hobbies, sports, friendship relations and other activities that are pursued primarily for purposes of self development and which sometimes take as much or more time away from family as does work (Schein, 1978). These three settings exert independent pulls on the person, but in practice they overlap, and it is the *degree* of overlap that is under the control of the individual role occupant.

At the external structural level, cultures differ in the extent to which they separate self, work, and family. In some of the Eastern cultures, for example, there is more unity to the concept of self, even though the physical domain where work and family are pursued may be totally non-overlapping (Redding and Martyn-Johns, 1979). Americans, on the other hand, clearly segregate these domains, as symbolized by jokes about 'leaving one's work at the office' or 'bringing one's work home'. There is a clear conceptual separation between work/career activities, family activities, and self-development activities. Time is viewed as a limited resource that must be allocated to one or another of those activities. Combining them, as when the spouse is taken on a business trip or a child is taken to the office on a Saturday, is viewed as creative and non-routine.

To some extent such separation is the result of industrialization. Factory work and urbanization produce more segregation of roles than does rural village life. But even within industrially advanced societies there are differences between, for example, Japan and the U.S. in the degree to which the domains are conceptually segregated. Furthermore, certain occupations structurally stimulate more or less segregation, as can be seen if one contrasts fishing, forestry, and the military with running a store or restaurant (Kanter, 1977).

Culture also affects career commitment in that societies, occupations, and organizations develop norms and values about the degree to which work is expected (1) to be seen as intrinsically satisfying versus instrumental only, (2) to be separated from family, and, beyond that, (3) to take priority over family (England, 1975; Hofstede, 1980). In his survey of one major multi-national company, Hofstede found that employees differ tremendously in how important it is that work leave enough time for personal and family life. For example, employees in Singapore, Hong Kong, Colombia, Mexico, and Peru placed little value on having enough time for family and personal life, employees in Japan,

Taiwan, and the Philippines were in the middle, while Australia, New Zealand, and Canada were at the high end.

If we think of occupational norms in the U.S., we can think of examples such as the military where it is expected from the outset that long periods of separation from family are part of the career, and that career assignments must always take precedence over family issues. On the other hand, wherever possible, military organizations enable families to move and create family enclaves on military bases to provide compensatory structures.

In the U.S. there are many occupational careers where two sets of norms pertain to this issue. One set of norms may clearly specify that career occupants must treat career demands as higher priority than personal and family demands. Examples one can think of are medicine, the military, airline pilots, and police, occupations where public safety and welfare are priority concerns. On the other hand, strong U.S. norms of individualism and individual choice support any given individual if he or she decides to leave such an occupation for 'family or personal reasons'. In other words, it is alright in our society to refuse careers which require too much personal and family sacrifice, but if such a career is accepted we expect full career commitment.

In fact, one of the most salient aspects of U.S. culture is its ideology of an open occupational structure where, in principle, everyone has equal access to any career, limited only by lack of talent. By the same token, everyone has the right to limit their career involvement so long as they are willing to take the consequences if the organization considers their involvement insufficient. In some older, more structured, and class bound societies in the world, one sees, in contrast, early tracking systems where career choices have to be made early in life and, once made, are relatively more binding. The degree of commitment to the career is then, itself, culturally constrained, and easy exit from the career for either party, employer or employee, is prevented by social pressure.

Given these external career considerations, one can formulate the hypothesis that variation within the internal career will be greater in those societies that have norms supporting freedom of entry into and exit from occupations and organizations. In other words, one might expect within a given occupation a greater range of work involvement in a country like the U.S. than in a country like Japan. Similarly, one might expect within the U.S. greater variation among organizations in the degree to which their organizational cultures demand high levels of work involvement.

Societies such as Japan, Korea, China, Singapore, Hong Kong, and Taiwan become especially interesting to study because they are rapidly developing economically, yet have very different norms about work versus family commitment. In the Hofstede survey, employees in Singapore and Hong Kong placed less value on time for personal and family life as an important characteristic of a job than did employees in Japan, Taiwan, and the Philippines. Such variations remind one that not only are there huge cultural differences within what is often labelled 'Eastern' cultures, but also that one cannot easily determine the different effects of cultural, economic, and organizational forces. Are the reported attitudes reflecting cultural differences or do they say more about variations in the treatment of employees in these different countries even though they are employed by the same company?

We have noted above that in some societies family relations are more honoured than they are in our own, suggesting that work might be considered less important in those societies. On the other hand, if they make less of a separation between work life and family life in the first place, and if *family* norms support a strong work ethic, then an individual's commitment to family does not necessarily conflict with strong commitment to work and career. Such conflict is much more likely to arise in the U.S. where the work ethic has been challenged, where self development and family development are posed as *counter* to the demands of work, and where the dual career family with two fully work-involved partners is becoming increasingly legitimized, if not yet very common.

What data we have on internal career indexes such as 'work involvement' (Bailyn and Schein, 1980) shows that certain careers, such as being a professor, an entrepreneur, a manager, or a consultant, do stimulate more work involvement than others, such as being a staff engineer or accountant. But there is considerable variation among individuals within a given occupation, reflecting both their personalities and the organizational culture in which they work. Some companies are clearly better able to elicit higher levels of work involvement among all of their employees than others. The identification of such *cultural* factors within companies has become a major preoccupation of organizational researchers (Ouchi, 1981; Pascale and Athos, 1981; Deal and Kennedy, 1982; Pfeffer, 1981; Peters and Waterman, 1982).

One sees work organizations in the U.S. adapting to this broader range of individual resolution of career versus family versus self conflicts with gradual changes in personnel policies on such matters as maternity and paternity leaves, part-time instead of full-time work, more time off, joint employment and rethinking of the nepotism rules, job sharing, extra support in helping spouses find work, supporting moves when necessary, and daycare for children (Schein, 1978; Bailyn, 1982).

In summary, cultures will differ in the degree to which the career is defined as clearly separate from personal and family life, and in the degree to which career commitment is expected to supercede personal and family commitment. Cultures will also differ in the degree to which the choice of an external career has to be made early and is considered binding on the individual. In those societies, and in organizations where choice can be made late and even re-made in adulthood, the more relevant cultural factors are the norms and values which pertain to how much one is supposed to value work versus family versus personal development. In the U.S. there is evidence that the basic assumptions about work, family, and self may be in transition, particularly as more issues are surfaced around the management of dual careers.

CULTURAL VALUES AS BASES OF LEGITIMACY OF ORGANIZATIONAL CAREERS

Cultures and organizations vary in what they regard to be acceptable and legitimate motives for entering a career, and in how success in those careers is measured. This issue was made salient to me by my own research on 'career anchors' (Schein, 1978). A career anchor is defined as the emerging self-image around which a person organizes his or her career decisions, integrating the self-perceived talents, motives, and values which the person recognizes during the first 5 to 10 years of a career. Career anchors can be elicited during workshops by pairing participants and having them conduct careful career history interviews of each other. Following such interviews we typically survey the workshop participants to determine how many people fall into some of the major career anchor categories such as (1) security/stability, (2) autonomy/independence, (3) technical/functional competence, (4) enterpreneurial creativity, (5) general management competence, (6) service or dedication to a cause, (7) pure challenge, or (8) total life style integration.

It was during the tabulation of such results in different countries that I became aware how culture affects what people consider to be 'legitimate' career anchors. For example, in contrasting workshop results in Australia and the U.S. with comparable groups of managers, I found opposing biases in what people are *willing to report*. In the U.S., managers admitted in private that they had security concerns, were thinking about early retirement, were losing some of their ambition, and were turning increasingly toward family and self concerns. But if asked to state publicly what their career anchors were, they tended to claim loudly that they lay in the managerial, entrepreneurial, or autonomy areas. They claimed to be motivated to continue rising to the top, admitting that if they did not publicly express such ambitions their careers would be compromised.

The Australian experience was the mirror opposite of the U.S. experience. In five consecutive workshops, done in different parts of Australia in the summer of 1980, the same phenomenon occurred. In reporting results, managers were quite vocal in claiming to be security/stability oriented and publicly denied any desire to increase their power or to continue climbing to the top. At the same time, I would be told informally after the meetings that what Mr So-and-So said when he claimed to be 'just security oriented' was 'laughable' in that he was seen as one of the most ambitious and ruthless men in the organization. But it was clearly understood that in public one had to deny power motives in Australia, just as one had to deny security motives in the U.S. So, if one listened only to the public statements of career motivation, one would overestimate the number of ambitious power seekers in the U.S. and underestimate the number of levelled off security seekers; in Australia one would overestimate the number of security seekers and underestimate ambition. What these managers believed about the values associated with the external career was, for many of them, incongruent with their internal career picture and, therefore, deliberately concealed. It was not 'legitimate' to have certain motives or feelings in a given cultural context.

These anecdotal findings suggest a whole area of cultural research that needs to be pursued concerning the bases of legitimacy for occupational activities, quite apart from one's actual underlying motives or career anchors. What kinds of reasons are accepted as valid 'apologies' or 'excuses' for what one is doing, and how do these vary by country and by organization?

I have already described the variations in apologies offered for personal am-

bition. In different societies, and in different organizations within a given society, norms develop around legitimate reasons for ambitious behaviour, ranging
from the U.S. extreme of pure personal drive to 'get ahead', 'succeed', 'make
a lot of money', 'gain power or position', to, at the other extreme, 'serve society', do what is expected of one by the employer or the peer group', or, as the
Australians so nicely put it, 'one must do one's job, but one mustn't be a tall
poppy', because 'tall poppies will be cut down'. Similar metaphors suggesting
that individuation in the career arena is not acceptable can be found in China
and Japan, presumably reflecting the basic assumptions of those cultures about
the overarching importance of the group relative to the individual (Inaba, 1981).

In the context of daily work behaviour, one can study what are taken to be
acceptable excuses for absence or not getting one's work done. Personal illness
has always been an acceptable excuse in the U.S., but it is interesting to note,
also, the cynicism toward such excuses reflected in our educational system where
written notes from parents, nurses, or doctors are required as validation. One
wonders whether such cynicism also operates in work organizations, in that the
excuse is accepted but treated as a lie, as when an employee admits to using
some 'sick leave' days to take a vacation, the boss knows that this is happening,
and yet condones it. It would be interesting to conduct a comparative study,
either across organizations or countries, on the validity of illness as an excuse
for not working, and on the degree of documentation required that one is ill.

Family crises, death or illness in the family, needs of spouses and children,
are the next category of apologies to consider. At one extreme, we have societies
and organizations where time off is granted immediately for any reasonable indication that an employee's family needs attention. At the other extreme, I once
encountered a company on the west coast of the U.S. with such a strong work
ethic that an employee went through the suicide and funeral of his wife without
missing work, and without telling anyone at work about it, because he believed
it would not be considered appropriate to intrude his 'private affairs' on the
company. Whether or not this person's behaviour reflects his organization's culture or his own extreme paranoia is, of course, important to consider, but I have
certainly encountered other U.S. organizations in which it is considered a sign
of weakness not to have one's family affairs completely under control and in
order. 'If he can't manage his own family, how can he manage a department?'
is said often enough in some organizations to make employees aware that family
problems are not a legitimate excuse. The dual career couple faces issues like
the above around child care. Does a given organization consider it legitimate for
an employee to stay home or go home if a child is ill 'because the spouse cannot
get time off?'

Legitimate reasons also have to be developed around 'refusals'—refusal to
accept a geographic move, a promotion, or a particular assignment. Health and
family reasons have always played a role in such refusals, but the behaviour one
observes in dual career couples reveals another layer of cultural norms that may
vary across societies and organizations. For example, when a company proposes
to a manager that he or she move to another location, and the move is refused
on the grounds that the spouse is in a job or profession that would be disrupted

by it, does the company accept this as a legitimate excuse or not? U.S. companies vary in the degree to which they would (1) coerce a decision by threatening to withhold future promotions unless the manager managed his or her own family situation somehow or another and moved as requested; (2) negotiate a settlement by offering to relocate the spouse and attempt to find equivalent employment in the new situation; or (3) capitulate and find an equivalent promotion possibility for the manager in the original location, thus permitting the spouse to continue his or her career uninterrupted.

What is interesting to consider, however, is to what extent the manager really could not go because of the spouse, or simply used the spouse as a culturally acceptable excuse. A similar example is the use of children's age and/or school location as a reason for not moving. In either case, the clear possibility exists that the individual personally did not want to move, but that the only reason the company would accept was 'the kids are in high school and should not be moved'. We know virtually nothing about the attitudes of different companies, industries, or countries toward the personal reasons people give in their efforts to negotiate with organizations, what kinds of reasons are respected, and how such areas of respect are culturally patterned.

A third way of getting at cultural definitions of legitimacy for organizational careers is to investigate criteria used for success. Often such criteria are parallel to what is considered legitimate motivation for entering the career, but sometimes they reflect additional cultural norms that need to be identified. We can infer success criteria from knowing the wider assumptions and values of different cultures. For example, U.S. managers are more likely to succeed if they are individualistic, ambitious, and result oriented, and Japanese managers are more likely to succeed if they are group oriented, respectful, loyal, and result oriented. But beyond case studies we have little systematic data on such criteria, except from several surveys of multi-national companies where company culture is, to a degree, held constant in order to study variations in national culture.

One recent survey done by Laurent (1981) in the European branch of a U.S. based multi-national company provides some provocative data. In this company, among other things, managers were asked to rate sixty different items on their importance in determining career success. These data revealed that some items were judged as 'most important' by virtually all managers who answered the survey, regardless of the country in which they worked: ambition and drive, leadership abilities, achieving results, skills in interpersonal relations and communication, being labelled as high potential, managerial skills, hard work, and ability to handle interfaces between groups.

In addition, virtually all managers agree that the following items were 'unimportant' in determining career success: opinions of colleagues, number of assessors, national differences in using evaluation criteria, rumours about individual's reputation, opinions of subordinates, and seniority. These lists, then, can be thought of as the consensus on what is important for success in the organizational culture. It should be noted that the U.S. origin of the company shows up in the item bias toward individualistic achievement criteria. If a company from another culture were studied, one might expect the list to look somewhat different.

When Laurent looked at individual country data, he found that criteria for career success differed across countries.

U.S. 'Achieving results' was checked significantly more often, even though everyone gave it a high rating in the first place, and no items were checked significantly less often.

France 'Adaptability to organizational change' was checked more often, while 'self confidence' and 'creative mind' were checked less often.

Germany 'Creative mind', 'age', 'health', and 'company policies about career development' were checked more often, while 'job visibility and exposure', 'being labelled as having high potential', and 'knowing how to please management' were checked less often.

United Kingdom 'Assessor's subjective judgement' was checked more often, while 'development opportunities within job' was checked less often.

Netherlands 'Type of educational background' was checked more often, no items were checked less often.

These data suggest that in each country particular features are valued more as criteria of success and that the career is perceived somewhat differently by managers in each of these countries.

SUMMARY AND IMPLICATIONS

I have tried to illustrate in each of three areas how culture serves as an environmental context for careers, and how all career findings are essentially culture bound. We cannot infer from one culture to another what the structure of external careers will be, nor can we infer how people will feel about their own careers.

The most important implication is that in the management of people it is crucial for managers to learn how to decipher the culture in which they are operating. However much a company may try to standardize its career pathing and career development programmes, such standardization is doomed to failure if it does not take into account (1) what a career means in the first place in a given country, (2) how important work and career are, (3) what kinds of reasons are acceptable for certain kinds of work and career behaviour, and (4) by what criteria career success is judged.

Secondly, it is essential to recognize that, within a given country, occupations and organizations also vary along these same cultural dimensions within the cultural envelope provided by the broader societal culture. Such variation will occur, especially in what kinds of occupational choices people will make in the first place, how they will view their internal careers, how work-involved they will be, what kinds of career anchors they will develop, and what kinds of career anchors they will espouse. Such variation will be especially significant in countries like the U.S. where the external career structure is governed by cultural norms of individual choice, equality of opportunity, and free mobility throughout life.

Finally, the kinds of variations described above present the career researcher with a whole new agenda of comparative research. Not only must we become more competent in describing the relevant cultural dimensions of societies, occupations, and organizations, but we must systematically compare career variables across cultural units to sort out whether observed regularities in career events reflect societal, occupational, organizational, or personality patterns.

REFERENCES

Bailyn, L. (1982). 'Resolving contradictions in technical careers; or, what if I like being an engineer?' *Technology Review*, **85**, 40–47.

Bailyn, L. with Schein, E. H. (1980). *Living with Technology*, MIT Press, Cambridge, MA.

Bailyn, L. and Schein, E. H. (1976). 'Life/career considerations as indicators of quality of employment'. In: Biderman, A. D. and Drury, T. F. (Eds) *Measuring Work Quality for Social Reporting*, Wiley (Sage), New York.

Deal, T. E. and Kennedy, A. A. (1982). *Corporate Cultures*, Addison-Wesley, Reading, MA.

Driver, M. J. (1980). 'Career concepts and organizational change'. In: Derr, C. B. (Ed.) *Work, Family and the Career*, Praeger, New York.

Dyer, W. G., Jr. (1982). 'Culture in organizations', Working paper, Sloan School of Management, MIT, Cambridge, MA.

England, G. W. (1975). *The Manager and His Values*, Ballinger, Cambridge, MA.

Goffman, E. (1959). 'The moral career of the mental patient', *Psychiatry*, **22**, No. 2.

Hofstede, G. (1980). *Culture's Consequences*, Sage Publications, Beverly Hills, CA.

Inaba, M. (1981). 'Organizational development—A critical and comparative view', *Yokohama Business Review*, **2** No. 2, 119–128.

Kanter, R. M. (1977). *Work and Family in the United States*, Russell Sage, New York.

Laurent, A. (1981). 'International study on career success and conceptions of management and organization', Working paper, INSEAD, Fountainebleau, France.

Lawrence, B. S. (1984). 'Age grading: The implicit organizational timetable', *Journal of Occupational Behaviour*, **5**, 23–35.

Ouchi, W. (1981). *Theory Z*, Addison-Wesley, Reading, MA.

Pascale, R. T. and Athos, A. G. (1981). *The Art of Japanese Management*, Simon & Schuster, New York.

Peters, T. J. and Waterman, R. H. (1982). *In Search of Excellence*, Harper Row, New York.

Pettigrew, A. M. (1979). 'On studying organizational cultures', *Administrative Science Quarterly*, **24**, 570–581.

Pfeffer, J. (1981). 'Management as symbolic action: The creation and maintenance of organizational paradigms'. In: Cummings, L. L. and Staw, B. M. (Eds) *Research in Organizational Behaviour*, Vol. 3, JAI Press, Greenwich, CT, pp. 1–52.

Redding, S. G. and Martyn-Johns, T. A. (1979). 'Paradigm differences and their relation to management, with reference to South-East Asia'. In: England, G. W., Neghandhi, A. R. and Wilpert, B. (Eds) *Organizational Functioning in a Cross-cultural Perspective*, Comparative Administration Research Institute, Kent State University Press, Ohio, pp. 103–125.

Schein, E. H. (1961). 'Management development as a process of influence', *Industrial Management Review*, **2**, 59–77.

Schein, E. H. (1971). 'The individual, the organization, and the career: A conceptual scheme', *Journal of Applied Behavioral Science*, **7**, 401–426.

Schein, E. H. (1976). 'Career development: Theoretical and practical issues for organizations'. In: *Career Planning and Development*, International Labor Office, Geneva, Switzerland.

Schein, E. H. (1978). *Career Dynamics*, Addison-Wesley, Reading, MA.

Schein, E. H. (1981). 'Does Japanese management style have a message for American managers?' *Sloan Management Regiew*, Fall, 55–68.

Schein, E. H. (1983). 'The role of the founder in creating organizational culture', *Organizational Dynamics*, Summer, 13–28.

Schwartz, H. and Davis, S. M. (1981). 'Matching corporate culture and business strategy', *Organizational Dynamics*, Summer, 30–48.

Van Maanen, J. (Ed.) (1977). *Organizational Careers: Some New Perspective*, John Wiley, New York.

Van Maanen, J. and Schein, E. H. (1977). 'Improving the quality of work life: Career development'. In: Hackman, J. R. and Suttle, J. L. (Eds) *Improving Life at Work*, Goodyear, Santa Monica, CA.

Van Maanen, J. and Schein, E. H. (1979). 'Toward a theory of organizational socialization'. In: Staw, B. (Ed.) *Research in Organizational Behavior*, Vol. 1, JAI Press, Greenwich, CT, pp. 209–264.

QUESTIONS FOR DISCUSSION

1 Before you entered your present job (or the university at which you are currently studying), what information about the organization (or university) did you seek? Judging from what you know now, how accurate and complete was that information? How could you have obtained more complete and relevant information?

2 Under what circumstances would it be undesirable to have a close match between individual needs and organizational climate?

3 What are the important questions about organizational entry that have yet to be answered? Where should research on this topic focus?

4 Critically evaluate the model of career motivation presented in this chapter. How does the model help us understand career motivation issues in organizations? What implications of the model follow for managers?

5 How do individual characteristics of employees combine with situational factors to determine career success? Explain.

6 Identify the major ways in which culture can influence careers in organizations. Provide examples to illustrate your point.

7 What do you believe represents career success in Japan? The People's Republic of China? Mexico? Canada?

8 What are the basic lessons from this chapter that can assist managers in improving human resources development and utilization? Explain.

CHAPTER 8

EMPLOYEE ABSENTEEISM
AND TURNOVER

This chapter focuses on what has widely been termed the "decision to partici-pate" (see Chapter 1). That is, we are concerned here with employees' decisions and actions that result in their either staying with or leaving an organization. The decision to leave can be either temporary, as in the case of absenteeism, or permanent, as in the case of turnover. In both situations, the consequences for both the employee and the organization can be significant.

The question of why employee absenteeism and turnover deserve attention can be answered in several ways. Perhaps the most direct answer lies in considering the costs and consequences associated with such behavior. With respect to em-ployee turnover, it is noted in the first article in this chapter that absenteeism in the U.S. costs approximately $26 billion annually. In Canada, the annual cost is estimated to be about $7 billion. Not only do employees lose income, but or-ganizations lose productivity. In view of the current economic problems facing industrialized countries and the increased competition in the marketplace, such losses can have a severe impact on the national economy.

Similar costs are associated with turnover. Turnover costs the organization in many ways, including increased selection and recruitment costs, increased train-ing and development costs, increased organizational disruption, and possible demoralization of those who remain. For the leavers themselves, there is a loss of seniority and nonvested benefits, possible loss of friendships, and possible disruption for their families if relocation is necessary for new jobs. Again, both the individual and the organization can lose in such situations.

On the other hand, it would be inaccurate to assume that such withdrawal is associated with negative consequences only. Several positive outcomes are also possible. With respect to absenteeism, temporary withdrawal can allow employ-ees some relief from a highly stressful or boring job. The employee may be better able to cope when he or she returns after a short hiatus. In addition, for those organizations that have a policy of job rotation, temporary absences often allow other employees to gain needed experience with different aspects of the work situation.

Employee turnover can also lead to positive outcomes on occasion. In some cases, turnover can lead to improved performance when those leaving either have burned out on the job or have such negative attitudes that they adversely affect output. In such cases, we would expect new employees to bring a fresh approach to the job situation. Moreover, turnover can in some cases prove beneficial where it reduces entrenched conflict that has built up over the years. The departure of someone whom others consider abrasive, for example, can relax tensions for those remaining. In addition, turnover can sometimes increase both mobility and morale by allowing room for internal growth and promotion. Finally, turnover can at times allow for increased innovation, as new people and new ideas enter the workplace.

Hence, absenteeism and turnover can be both functional and dysfunctional for individuals and organizations. As we shall see in several of the selections that follow, the question is not so much *why* turnover or absenteeism as *which* turnover or absenteeism. That is, which employees are leaving (or being absent) and which are remaining? Under which circumstances are people most likely to leave or be absent? And, finally, which actions can management initiate that will cause the more valued employees to want to remain?

In the first article, Steers and Rhodes identify the major influences on employee attendance. In particular, it is argued that managers must differentiate between attendance motivation, or the desire to come to work, and actual attendance. Next, Nicholson and Johns focus on the corporate culture that fosters or inhibits absence behavior. The final two selections in this chapter present models dealing with employee turnover. The article by Mobley focuses on the intermediate linkages between job satisfaction and turnover, while the article by Steers and Mowday attempts to present a comprehensive model of the dynamics underlying the turnover process. Together, these two models should provide for a broad examination of the major factors influencing an employee to remain attached to the organization or to sever this connection.

Major Influences on Employee Attendance: A Process Model[1]

Richard M. Steers
Susan R. Rhodes

Each year, it is estimated that over 400 million work days are lost in the United States due to employee absenteeism, or about 5.1 days lost per employee (Yolles, Carone, & Krinsky, 1975). In many industries, daily blue-collar absenteeism runs as high as 10% to 20% of the workforce (Lawler, 1971). A recent study by Mirvis and Lawler (1977) estimates the cost of absenteeism among non-managerial personnel to be about $66 per day per employee; this estimate includes both direct salary and fringe benefit costs, as well as costs associated with temporary replacement and estimated loss of profit. While such figures are admittedly crude, combining the estimated total days lost with the costs associated with absenteeism yields an estimated annual cost of absenteeism in the U.S. of $26.4 billion! Even taking the more conservative minimum wage rate yields an estimated annual cost of $8.5 billion. Clearly, the phenomenon of employee absenteeism is an important area for empirical research and management concern. . . .

A review of existing research indicates that investigators of employee absenteeism have typically examined bivariate correlations between a set of variables and subsequent absenteeism (Muchinsky, 1977; Nicholson, Brown, & Chadwick-Jones, 1976; Porter & Steers, 1973; Vroom, 1964). Little in the way of comprehensive theory-building can be found, with the possible exception of Gibson (1966). Moreover, two basic (and questionable) assumptions permeate the work that has been done to date. First, the current literature largely assumes that job dissatisfaction represents the primary cause of absenteeism. Unfortunately, however, existing research consistently finds only weak support for this hypothesis. Locke (1976), for example, points out that the magnitude of the correlation between dissatisfaction and absenteeism is generally quite low, seldom surpassing $r = .40$ and typically much lower. Moreover, Nicholson et al. (1976), in their review of 29 such studies, concluded that "at best it seems that job satisfaction and absence from work are tenuously related (p. 734)." Nicholson et al. also observed that the strength of this relationship deteriorates as one moves from group-based studies to individually-based studies. Similar weak findings have been reported earlier (Porter & Steers, 1973; Vroom, 1964). Implicit in these modest findings is the probable existence of additional variables (both personal and organizational) which may serve to moderate or enhance the satisfaction-attendance relationship.

The second major problem to be found in much of the current work on absenteeism is the implicit assumption that employees are generally free to choose whether or not to come to work. As noted by Herman (1973) and others, such is often not the case. In a variety of studies, important situational constraints were

[1]Support for this paper was provided by funds supplied under ONR Contract No. N00014-76-C-0164, NR 170-812.

found which influenced the attitude-behavior relationship (Herman, 1973; Ilgen & Hollenback, 1977; Morgan & Herman, 1976; Smith, 1977). Hence, there appear to be a variety of situational constraints (e.g., poor health, family responsibilities, transportation problems) that can interfere with free choice in an attendance decision. Thus, a comprehensive model of attendance must include not only job attitudes and other influences on attendance motivation but also situational constraints that inhibit a strong motivation-behavior relationship.

In view of the multitude of narrowly-focused studies of absenteeism but the dearth of conceptual frameworks for integrating these findings, it appears useful to attempt to identify the major sets of variables that influence attendance behavior and to suggest how such variables fit together into a general model of employee attendance. Toward this end, a model of employee attendance is presented here. This model incorporates both voluntary and involuntary absenteeism and is based on a review of 104 studies of absenteeism (see Rhodes & Steers, Note 4). . . .

THE CONCEPTUAL MODEL

The model proposed here attempts to examine in a systematic and comprehensive fashion the various influences on employee attendance behavior. Briefly stated, it is suggested that an employee's attendance is largely a function of two important variables: (1) an employee's motivation to attend; and (2) an employee's ability to attend. Both of these factors are included in the schematic diagram presented in Figure 1 and each will be discussed separately as it relates to existing research. First, we shall examine the proposed antecedents of attendance motivation.

FIGURE 1
A model of employee attendance.

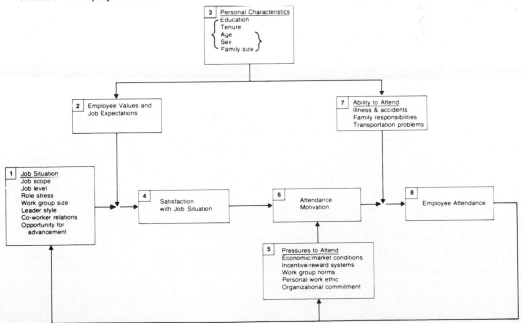

Job Situation, Satisfaction, and Attendance Motivation

A fundamental premise of the model suggested here is that an employee's motivation to come to work represents the primary influence on actual attendance, assuming one has the ability to attend (Herman, 1973; Locke, 1968). Given this, questions must be raised concerning the major influences on attendance motivation. Available evidence indicates that such motivation is determined largely by a combination of: (1) an employee's affective responses to the job situation; and (2) various internal and external pressures to attend (Vroom, 1964; Hackman & Lawler, 1971; Locke, 1976; Porter & Lawler, 1968). In this section, we will examine the relationship between an employee's satisfaction with the job situation and attendance motivation. The second major influence on attendance motivation, pressures to attend, will be dealt with subsequently.

Other things being equal, when an employee enjoys the work environment and the tasks that characterize his or her job situation, we would expect that employee to have a strong desire to come to work (Hackman & Lawler, 1971; Lundquist, 1958; Newman, 1974; Porter & Steers, 1973; Vroom, 1964). Under such circumstances, the work experience would be a pleasurable one. In view of this relationship, our first question concerns the manner in which the job situation affects one's attendance motivation. The job situation (box 1 in Figure 1), as conceived here, consists of those variables that characterize the nature of the job and the surrounding work environment. Included in the job situation are such variables as: (1) job scope; (2) job level; (3) role stress; (4) work group size; (5) leader style; (6) coworker relations; and (7) opportunities for advancement. In essence, available evidence suggests that variables such as these strongly influence one's level of satisfaction which, in turn, influences attendance motivation. . . .

The Role of Employee Values and Job Expectations

Considerable evidence suggests that the relationship between job situation variables and subsequent satisfaction and attendance motivation is not a direct one (Locke, 1976). Instead, a major influence on the extent to which employees experience satisfaction with the job situation is the values and expectations they have concerning the job (box 2). It has been noted previously that people come to work with differing values and job expectations; that is, they value different features in a job and expect these features to be present to a certain degree in order to maintain membership (Locke, 1976; Porter & Steers, 1973).

To a large extent these values and expectations are influenced by the personal characteristics and backgrounds of the employees (box 3). For example, employees with higher educational levels (e.g., a college degree) may value and expect greater (or at least different) rewards from an organization than those with less education (e.g., a private office, a secretary, a higher salary, greater freedom of action). Support for this contention can be found in Hedges (1973). Moreover, older and more tenured employees often value and expect certain perquisites because of their seniority (Baumgartel & Sobol, 1959; Cooper & Payne, 1965; Nicholson et al., 1976; Nicholson, Brown, & Chadwick-Jones, 1977; Hill & Trist, 1955; Martin, 1971).

Whatever the values and expectations that individuals bring to the job situation, it is important that these factors be largely met for the individual to be satisfied. In this regard, Smith (1972) found that realistic job previews created realistic job expectations among employees and led to a significant decline in absenteeism. Somewhat relatedly, Stockford (1944) found that absenteeism was higher among a sample of industrial workers whose previous training was not seen as relevant for their current positions than among a sample whose training was more closely aligned with the realities of the job situations (see also, Weaver & Holmes, 1972). Hence, based on the limited evidence that is available, it would appear that the extent to which an employee's values and expectations are met does influence the desirability of going to work.

Pressures to Attend

While satisfaction with the job situation thus apparently represents a major influence on attendance motivation, the relationship is indeed not a perfect one. Other factors can be identified which serve to enhance attendance motivation, probably in an additive fashion (Garrison & Muchinsky, 1977; Ilgen & Hollenback, 1977; Nicholson et al., 1976). These variables are collectively termed here "pressures to attend" and represent the second major influence on the desire to come to work. These pressures may be economic, social, or personal in nature and are represented in Figure 1 by box 5. Specifically, at least five major pressures can be identified: (1) economic and market conditions; (2) incentive/reward system; (3) work group norms; (4) personal work ethic; and (5) organizational commitment.

Economic and Market Conditions The general state of the economy and the job market place constraints on one's ability to change jobs. Consequently, in times of high unemployment, there may be increased pressure to maintain a good attendance record for fear of losing one's job. Evidence suggests that there is a close inverse relationship between changes in unemployment levels within a given geographical region and subsequent absence rates (Behrend, Note 1; Crowther, 1957). Moreover, as the threat of layoff becomes even greater (e.g., when an employee's own employer begins layoffs), there is an even stronger decrease in absenteeism (Behrend, Note 1).

However, when an employee knows that *he* or *she* is to be laid off (as opposed to a knowledge that layoffs are taking place in general), the situation is somewhat different. Specifically, Owens (1966) found that railway repair employees in a depressed industry who had been given notice of layoff because of shop closure had significantly higher absence rates prior to layoffs than a comparable group of employees who were not to be laid off. Owens suggests that, in addition to being a reflection of manifest anxiety, the increased absenteeism allowed employees time to find new positions. On the other hand, Hershey (1972) found no significant differences in absence rates between employees who were scheduled for layoffs and employees not so scheduled. Hershey argued that the subjects in his study were much in demand in the labor market and generally felt assured of finding suitable jobs. (Improved unemployment compensation in recent years may also have been a factor in minimizing absenteeism among those to be laid off.)

Hence, economic and market factors may be largely related to attendance motivation and subsequent attendance through their effects on one's ability to change jobs. When *general* economic conditions are deteriorating, employees may be less likely to be absent for fear of reprisal. However, when the *individual* employee is to be laid off, absence rates are apparently influenced by one's perceptions of his or her ability to find alternative employment. Where such alternatives are readily available, no effect of impending layoff on absenteeism is noted; when such alternatives are not readily available, absence rates can be expected to increase as employees seek other employment.

Incentive/Reward System   A primary factor capable of influencing attendance motivation is the nature of the incentive or reward system used by an organization. Several aspects of the reward system have been found to influence attendance behavior.

When perceptual measures of pay and pay satisfaction are used, mixed results are found between such measures and absenteeism. Specifically, three studies among various work samples found an inverse relationship between pay satisfaction or perceived pay equity and absenteeism (Patchen, 1960; Dittrich & Carrell, 1976; Smith, 1977), while six other studies did not find such a relationship (Hackman & Lawler, 1971; Newman, 1974; Nicholson et al., 1976; Lundquist, 1958; Garrison & Muchinsky, 1977; Nicholson et al., 1977). Three other studies found mixed results (Waters & Roach, 1971, 1973; Metzner & Mann, 1953). In short, it is difficult to draw any firm conclusions about pay and absenteeism from these perceptual measures.

In contrast, when actual wage rates or incentive systems have been studied, the results are somewhat more definitive. Lundquist (1958), Fried et al. (1972), Beatty and Beatty (1975), and Bernardin (1977) all found a direct inverse relationship between wage rate and absenteeism. The Bernardin study is particularly useful here because several potentially spurious variables (e.g., age, tenure) were partialled out of the analysis and because the results were crossvalidated. Moreover, the Lundquist study employed multiple absence measures with similar results. Other studies cited in Yolles et al. (1975) point to the same conclusion. However, studies by Fried et al. (1972) and Weaver and Holmes (1972), both using the less rigorous "total days absent" measure of absenteeism, did not support this relationship. In view of the objective nature of actual wage rates as opposed to perceptual measures, it would appear that greater confidence can be placed in them than in the perceptual studies mentioned above. Hence we would expect increases in salary or wage rates to represent one source of pressure to attend, even where the employee did not like the task requirements of the job itself.

Several factors must be kept in mind when considering the role of incentives or reward systems in attendance motivation. First, the rewards offered by the organization must be seen as being both attainable and tied directly to attendance. As

Lawler (1971) points out, many organizations create reward systems that at least up to a point reward *non*attendance. For instance, the practice of providing 12 days "sick leave" which employees lose if they fail to use only encourages people to be "sick" 12 days a year (see also: Morgan & Herman, 1976). In this regard, Garrison and Muchinsky (1977) found a negative relationship between job satisfaction and absenteeism for employees absent without pay but no such relationship for employees absent with pay. Hence there must be an expectancy on the part of the employee that attendance (and not absenteeism) will lead to desirable rewards. Moreover, the employees must value the rewards available. If an employee would prefer a three-day weekend to having additional pay, there is little reason to expect that employee to be motivated to attend. On the other hand, an employee with a strong financial need (perhaps because of a large family) would be expected to attend if attendance was financially rewarded.

Oftentimes, a major portion of an employee's income is derived from overtime work. Consequently, the effects of such overtime on absenteeism is important to note. Two studies found that the availability of overtime work among both male and female employees was *positively* related to absenteeism (Gowler, 1969; Martin, 1971), while two other studies found no such relationship (Buck & Shimmin, 1959; Flanagan, 1974). One could argue here that the availability of overtime with premium pay can lead to an incentive system that rewards absenteeism, not attendance. That is, if an employee is absent during regular working hours (and possibly compensated for this by sick leave), he or she can then work overtime later in the week to make up for the production lost earlier due to absenteeism. Clearly, such a reward system would operate differently than it was intended to. However, in view of the fact that all four relevant studies used either weak absence measures or unduly small samples, the influence of overtime availability on absenteeism must remain in the realm of conjecture pending further study.

Several attempts have been made to examine experimentally the effects of incentive or reward systems in work organizations. In one such study, Lawler and Hackman (1969; Scheflen, Lawler, & Hackman, 1971) experimentally introduced a bonus incentive plan to reward group attendance among a sample of part-time blue-collar employees. Two important findings emerged. First, the employees working under the bonus plan were found to have better attendance records than those not working under the plan. Moreover, the group that was allowed to participate in developing the bonus plan had higher attendance rates than the other experimental group that was given the bonus plan without an opportunity to participate in its design (see also, Glaser, 1976). Hence, both the adoption of a bonus incentive system to reward attendance and employee participation in the development of such a system appear to represent important influences on subsequent attendance.

A few studies have examined the role of punitive sanctions by management in controlling absenteeism. Results have been mixed. Two studies found that the use of stringent reporting and control procedures (e.g., keeping detailed attendance records, requiring medical verifications for reported illnesses, strict disciplinary measures) was related to lower absence rates (Baum & Youngblood, 1975; Seatter, 1961), while one found no such relationship (Rosen & Turner, 1971). Moreover, Buzzard and Liddell (Note 2) and Nicholson (1976) found that such controls did not influence average attendance rates, but did lead to fewer but longer absences. Such contradictory results concerning the use of punitive sanctions suggests that more effective results may be achieved through more positive reward systems than through punishment.

One such positive approach is the use of a lottery reward system, where daily attendance qualifies employees for an opportunity to win some prize or bonus. This approach is closely tied to the behavior modification approach to employee motivation (Hamner & Hamner, 1976). Four studies report such lotteries can represent a successful vehicle for reducing absenteeism (Nord, 1970; Tjersland, 1972; Pedalino & Gamboa, 1974; Johnson & Wallin, Note 3). However, in view of the very small magnitude of the rewards available for good attendance, it is possible here that results were caused more by the Hawthorne effect than the lottery itself. As Locke (1977) points out, in at least one of the lottery experiments (Pedalino & Gamboa, 1974), absenteeism in the experimental group declined even before anyone in the group had been, or could have been, reinforced. In addition, more conventional behavior modification techniques for reducing absenteeism, reviewed in Hamner and Hamner (1976), show only moderate results over short periods of time.

Finally, other approaches to incentives and rewards relate to modifying the traditional work week. For instance, Golembiewski et al. (1974) and Robison (Note 5) both reported a moderate decline in absenteeism following the introduction of "flexitime," where hours worked can be altered somewhat to meet employee needs. Moreover, while Nord and Costigan (1973) found favorable results implementing a four-day (4-40) work week, Ivancevich (1974) did not. Since both of these studies used similar samples, it is difficult to draw meaningful conclusions about the utility of such programs for reducing absenteeism.

Work Group Norms Pressure for or against attendance can also emerge from one's colleagues in the form of work group norms. The potency of such norms is clearly established (Cartwright & Zander, 1968; Shaw, 1976). Where the norms of the group emphasize the importance of good attendance for the benefit of the group, increased attendance would be expected (Gibson, 1966). Recent findings by Ilgen and Hollenback (1977) support such a conclusion. This relationship would be expected to be particularly strong in groups with a high degree of work group cohesiveness (Whyte, 1969). In his job attractiveness model of employee motivation, Lawler (1971) points out that members of highly cohesive groups view coming to work to help one's coworkers as highly desirable; hence, job attendance is more attractive than absenteeism. In this regard, several uncontrolled field experiments have been carried out (summarized by Glaser, 1976) which found that the creation of "autonomous work groups" consistently led to increased work group cohesiveness and reduced absenteeism. It should be remembered, however, that work group norms can also have a detrimental impact on attendance where they support periodic absenteeism and punish perfect attendance.

Personal Work Ethic A further influence on attendance motivation is the personal value system that individuals have (Rokeach 1973). Recent research on the "work ethic" has shown considerable variation across employees in the extent to which they feel morally obligated to work. In particular, several investigations have noted a direct relationship between a strong work ethic and the propensity to come to work (Goodale, 1973; Ilgen & Hollenback, 1977; Feldman, 1974; Searls et al., 1974). While more study is clearly in order here, it would appear that one major pressure to attend is the belief by individuals that work activity is an important aspect of life, almost irrespective of the nature of the job itself.

Organizational Commitment   Finally, somewhat related to the notion of a personal work ethic is the concept of organizational commitment (Porter, Steers, Mowday, & Boulian, 1974). Commitment represents an agreement on the part of the employees with the goals and objectives of an organization and a willingness to work towards those goals. In short, if an employee firmly believes in what an organization is trying to achieve, he or she should be more motivated to attend and contribute toward those objectives. This motivation may exist even if the employee does not enjoy the actual tasks required by the job (e.g., a nurse's aide who may not like certain distasteful aspects of the job but who feels he or she is contributing to worthwhile public health goals). Support for this proposition can be found in Steers (1977) and Smith (1977), where commitment and attendance were found to be related for two separate samples of employees. On the other hand, where an employee's primary commitments lie elsewhere (e.g., to a hobby, family, home, or sports), less internal pressure would be exerted on the employee to attend (Morgan & Herman, 1976). This notion of competing commitments is an important one often overlooked in research on absenteeism.

Ability to Attend

A major weakness inherent in much of the current research on absenteeism is the failure to account for (and partial out) involuntary absenteeism in the study of voluntary absenteeism. This failure has led to many contradictions in the research literature that may be explained by measurement error alone. [In fact, in a comparison of five absenteeism measures, Nicholson and Goodge (1976) found an average intercorrelation of $r = .24$ between measures, certainly not an encouraging coefficient.] Thus, if we are serious about studying absenteeism, a clear distinction must be made between voluntary and involuntary attendance behavior and both must necessarily be accounted for in model-building efforts.

Even if a person wants to come to work and has a high attendance motivation, there are many instances where such attendance is not possible; that is, where the individual does not have behavioral discretion or choice (Herman, 1973). At least three such unavoidable limitations on attendance behavior can be identified: (1) illness and accidents; (2) family responsibilities; and (3) transportation problems (box 7).

Illness and Accidents   Poor health or injury clearly represents a primary cause of absenteeism (Hedges, 1973; Hill & Trist, 1955). Both illness and accidents are often associated with increased age (Baumgartel & Sobol, 1959; de La Mare & Sergean, 1961; Cooper & Payne, 1965; Martin, 1971). This influence of personal characteristics on ability to attend is shown in box 3 of Figure 1. Included in this category of health-related absences would also be problems of alcoholism and drug abuse as they inhibit attendance behavior. [See Yolles et al. (1975) for a review of the literature on health-related reasons for absenteeism.]

Family Responsibilities   The second constraint on attendance is often overlooked; namely, family responsibilities. As with health, this limitation as it relates to attendance is largely determined by the personal characteristics of the individual (sex, age, family size). In general, women as a group are absent more frequently than men (Covner, 1950; Hedges, 1973; Kerr et al., 1951; Kilbridge, 1961; Isambert-Jamati, 1962; Flanagan, 1974; Yolles et al., 1975). This finding is apparently linked, not only to the different types of jobs women typically hold compared to men, but also to the traditional family responsibilities assigned to women (that is, it is generally the wife or mother who cares for sick children). Support for this assumption comes from Naylor and Vincent (1959), Noland (1945), and Beatty and Beatty (1975). Hence, we would expect female absenteeism to increase with family size (Ilgen & Hollenback, 1977; Nicholson & Goodge, 1976; Isambert-Jamati, 1962).

It is interesting to note, however, that the available evidence suggests that the absenteeism rate for women declines throughout their work career (possibly because the family responsibilities associated with young children declines). For males, on the other hand, unavoidable absenteeism apparently increases with age (presumably because of health reasons), while avoidable absenteeism does not (Nicholson et al., 1977; Martin, 1971; Yolles et al., 1975). In any case, gender and family responsibilities do appear to place constraints on attendance behavior for some employees.

Transportation Problems   Finally, some evidence suggests that difficulty in getting to work can at times influence actual attendance. This difficulty may take the form of travel distance from work (Isambert-Jamati, 1962; Martin, 1971; Stockford, 1944), travel time to and from work (Knox, 1961), or weather conditions that impede traffic (Smith, 1977). Exceptions to this trend have been noted by Hill (1967) and Nicholson and Goodge (1976), who found no relationship between either travel distance or availability of public transportation and absence. In general, however, increased difficulty of getting to work due to transportation problems does seem to represent one possible impediment to attendance behavior for some employees, even when the individual is motivated to attend.

Cyclical Nature of Model

Finally, as noted in Figure 1, the model as presented is a process model. That is, the act of attendance or absenteeism often influences the subsequent job situation and subsequent pressures to attend in a cyclical fashion. For example, a superior attendance record is often used in organizations as one indicator of noteworthy job performance and readiness for promotion. Conversely, a high rate of absenteeism may adversely affect an employee's relationship with his or her supervisor and coworkers and result in changes in leadership style and coworker relations. Also, widespread absenteeism may cause changes in company incentive/reward systems, including absence control policies. Other outcomes could be mentioned. The point here is that the model, as suggested, is a dynamic one, with employee attendance or absenteeism often leading to changes in the job situation which, in turn, influence subsequent attendance motivation.

CONCLUSION AND DISCUSSION

Our review of the research literature on employee absenteeism reveals a multiplicity of influences on the decision and ability to come to work. These influences emerge both from the individuals themselves (e.g., personal work ethic, demographic factors) and from the work environment (e.g., the job situation, incentive/reward systems, work group norms). Moreover, some of these influences are largely under the control of the employees (e.g., organizational commitment), while others are clearly beyond their control (e.g., health).

We have attempted to integrate the available evidence into a systematic conceptual model of attendance behavior. In essence, it is suggested that the nature of the job situation interacts with employee values and expectations to determine satisfaction with the job situation (Locke, 1976; Porter & Steers, 1973). This satisfaction combines in an additive fashion with various pressures to attend to determine an employee's level of attendance motivation. Moreover, it is noted that the relationship between attendance motivation and actual attendance is influenced by one's ability to attend, a situational constraint (Herman, 1973; Smith, 1977). Finally, the model notes that feedback from the results of actual attendance behavior can often influence subsequent perceptions of the job situation, pressures to attend, and attendance motivation. Hence, the cyclical nature of the model should not be overlooked.

The importance of the various factors in the model would be expected to vary somewhat across employees. That is, certain factors may facilitate attendance for some employees but not for others. For instance, one employee may be intrinsically motivated to attend because of a challenging job; this individual may not feel any strong external pressures to attend because he or she likes the job itself. Another employee, however, may have a distasteful job (and not be intrinsically motivated) and yet may come to work because of other pressures (e.g., financial need). Both employees would attend, but for somewhat different reasons.

This interaction suggests a substitutability of influences up to a point for some variables. For instance, managers concerned with reducing absenteeism on monotonous jobs may change the incentive/reward system (that is, increase the attendance-reward contingencies) as a substitute for an unenriched work environment. In fact, it has been noted elsewhere that most successful applications of behavior modification (a manipulation of behavior-reward contingencies) have been carried out among employees holding unenriched jobs (Steers & Spencer, 1977). Support for this substitutability principle can be found in Ilgen and Hollenback (1977), who found some evidence that various factors influence attendance in an additive fashion, not a multiplicative one. Thus, the strength of attendance motivation would be expected to increase as more and more major influences, or pressures, emerged.

In addition, differences can be found in the manner in which the various influences on attendance affect such behavior. That is, a few of the major variables are apparently fairly *directly* related to desire to attend (if not actual attendance). For instance, highly satisfied employees would probably want strongly to attend, while highly dissatisfied employees would probably want strongly not to attend. On the other hand, certain other factors appear to serve a *gatekeeper* function and do not covary directly with attendance. The most prominent gatekeeper variable is one's health. While sick employees typically do not come to work, it does not necessarily follow that healthy employees will attend. Instead, other factors (e.g., attendance motivation) serve to influence a healthy person's attendance behavior.

In conclusion, the proposed model of employee attendance identifies several major categories of factors that have been shown to influence attendance behavior. Moreover, the model specifies, or hypothesizes, how these various factors fit together to influence the decision to come to work. Throughout, the model emphasizes the psychological processes underlying attendance behavior and in this sense is felt to be superior to the traditional bivariate correlational studies that proliferate on the topic. It remains the task of future research to extend our knowledge on this important topic and to clarify further the nature of the relationships among variables as they jointly influence an employee's desire and intent to come to work. It is hoped that the model presented here represents one useful step toward a better understanding of this process.

REFERENCE NOTES*

1 Behrend, H. Absence under full employment. Monograph A3, University of Birmingham Studies in Economics and Society, 1951.
2 Buzzard, R. B., & Liddell, F. D. K. Coal miners' attendance at work. NCB Medical Service, Medical Research Memorandum No. 3, 1958.
3 Johnson, R. D., & Wallin, J. A. Employee attendance: An operant conditioning intervention in a field setting. Paper presented at American Psychological Association annual meeting, Washington, D. C., 1976.
4 Rhodes, S. R., & Steers, R. M. Summary tables of studies of employee absenteeism. Technical Report No. 13, University of Oregon, 1977. This report is available from the second author at the Graduate School of Management, University of Oregon, Eugene, OR 97403.
5 Robison, D. Alternate work patterns: Changing approaches to work scheduling. Report of a conference sponsored by National Center for Productivity and Quality of Working Life and the Work in America Institute, Inc., June 2, 1976, Plaza Hotel, New York.

REFERENCES

Baum, J. F., & Youngblood, S. A. Impact of an organizational control policy on absenteeism, performance, and satisfaction. *Journal of Applied Psychology*, 1975, **60**, 688–694.

*Reference Notes and References have been abridged.

Baumgartel, H., & Sobol, R. Background and organizational factors in absenteeism. *Personnel Psychology,* 1959, **12**, 431–443.

Beatty, R. W., & Beatty, J. R. Longitudinal study of absenteeism of hard-core unemployed. *Psychological Reports,* 1975, **36**, 395–406.

Bernardin, H. J. The relationship of personality variables to organizational withdrawal. *Personnel Psychology,* 1977, **30**, 17–27.

Buck, L., & Shimmin, S. Overtime and financial responsibility. *Occupational Psychology,* 1959, **33**, 137–148.

Cartwright, D., & Zander, A. *Group dynamics.* New York: Harper & Row, 1968.

Cooper, R., & Payne, R. Age and absence: A longitudinal study in three firms. *Occupational Psychology,* 1965, **39**, 31–43.

Covner, B. J. Management factors affecting absenteeism. *Harvard Business Review,* 1950, **28**, 42–48.

Crowther, J. Absence and turnover in the divisions of one company—1950–55. *Occupational Psychology,* 1957, **31**, 256–270.

de la Mare, G., & Sergean, R. Two methods of studying changes in absence with age. *Occupational Psychology,* 1961, **35**, 245–252.

Dittrich, J. E., & Carrel, M. R. Dimensions of organizational fairness as predictors of job satisfaction, absence and turnover. *Academy of Management Proceedings '76.* Thirty-Sixth Annual Meeting of the Academy of Management, Kansas City, Missouri, August 11–14, 1976.

Feldman, J. Race, economic class, and the intention to work: Some normative and attitudinal correlates. *Journal of Applied Psychology,* 1974, **59**, 179–186.

Flanagan, R. J., Strauss, G., & Ulman, L. Worker discontent and work place behavior. *Industrial Relations,* 1974, **13**, 101–123.

Fried, J., Wertman, M., & Davis, M. Man-machine interaction and absenteeism. *Journal of Applied Psychology,* 1972, **56**, 428–429.

Garrison, K. R., & Muchinsky, R. M. Attitudinal and biographical predictors of incidental absenteeism. *Journal of Vocational Behavior,* 1977, **10**, 221–230.

Gibson, J. O. Toward a conceptualization of absence behavior of personnel in organizations. *Administrative Science Quarterly,* 1966, **11**, 107–133.

Glaser, E. M. *Productivity gains through worklife improvement.* New York: The Psychological Corporation, 1976.

Golembiewski, R. T., Hilles, R., & Kagno, M. S. A longitudinal study of flex-time effects: Some consequences of an OD structural intervention. *Journal of Applied Behavioral Science,* 1974, **10**, 503–532.

Goodale, J. G. Effects of personal background and training on work values of the hardcore unemployed. *Journal of Applied Psychology,* 1973, **57**, 1–9.

Gowler, D. Determinants of the supply of labour to the firm. *Journal of Management Studies,* 1969, **6**, 73–95.

Hackman, J. R. & Lawler, E. E., III. Employee reactions to job characteristics. *Journal of Applied Psychology Monograph,* 1971, **55**, 259–286.

Hamner, W. C., & Hamner, E. P. Behavior modification on the bottom line. *Organizational Dynamics,* 1976, **4**(4), 2–21.

Hedges, J. N. Absence from work—A look at some national data. *Monthly Labor Review,* 1973, **96**, 24–31.

Herman, J. B. Are situational contingencies limiting job attitude-job performance relationships? *Organizational Behavior and Human Performance,* 1973, **10**, 208–224.

Hershey, R. Effects of anticipated job loss on employee behavior. *Journal of Applied Psychology,* 1972, **56**, 273–274.

Hill, J. M., & Trist, E. L. Changes in accidents and other absences with length of service. *Human Relations,* 1955, **8,** 121–152.

Ilgen, D. R., & Hollenback, J. H. The role of job satisfaction in absence behavior. *Organizational Behavior and Human Performance,* 1977, **19,** 148–161.

Isambert-Jamati, V. Absenteeism among women workers in industry. *International Labour Review,* 1962, **85,** 248–261.

Ivancevich, J. M. Effects of the shorter workweek on selected satisfaction and performance measures. *Journal of Applied Psychology,* 1974, **59,** 717–721.

Kerr, W., Koppelmeier, G., & Sullivan, J. Absenteeism, turnover and morale in a metals fabrication factory. *Occupational Psychology,* 1951, **25,** 50–55.

Kilbridge, M. Turnover, absence, and transfer rates as indicators of employee dissatisfaction with repetitive work. *Industrial and Labor Relations Review,* 1961, **15,** 21–32.

Knox, J. B. Absenteeism and turnover in an Argentine factory. *American Sociological Review,* 1961, **26,** 424–428.

Lawler, E. E., III. *Pay and organizational effectiveness.* New York: McGraw-Hill, 1971.

Lawler, E. E., III, & Hackman, J. R. Impact of employee participation in the development of pay incentive plans: A field experiment. *Journal of Applied Psychology,* 1969, **53,** 467–471.

Locke, E. A. Toward a theory of task motivation and incentives. *Organizational Behavior and Human Performance,* 1968, **3,** 157–189.

Locke, E. A. The nature and causes of job satisfaction. In M. D. Dunnette (Ed.), *Handbook of industrial and organizational psychology.* Chicago: Rand McNally, 1976. Pp. 1297–1349.

Locke, E. A. The myths of behavior mod in organizations. *Academy of Management Review,* 1977, **2,** 543–553.

Lundquist, A. Absenteeism and job turnover as a consequence of unfavorable job adjustment. *Acta Sociologica,* 1958, **3,** 119–131.

Martin, J. Some aspects of absence in a light engineering factory. *Occupational Psychology,* 1971, **45,** 77–91.

Metzner, H., & Mann, F. Employee attitudes and absences. *Personnel Psychology,* 1953, **6,** 467–485.

Mirvis, P. H., & Lawler, E. E., III. Measuring the financial impact of employee attitudes. *Journal of Applied Psychology,* 1977, **62,** 1–8.

Morgan, L. G., & Herman, J. B. Perceived consequences of absenteeism. *Journal of Applied Psychology,* 1976, **61,** 738–742.

Muchinsky, P. M. Employee absenteeism: A review of the literature. *Journal of Vocational Behavior,* 1977, **10,** 316–340.

Naylor, J. E., & Vincent, N. L. Predicting female absenteeism. *Personnel Psychology,* 1959, **12,** 81–84.

Newman, J. E. Predicting absenteeism and turnover. *Journal of Applied Psychology,* 1974, **59,** 610–615.

Nicholson, N. Management sanctions and absence control. *Human Relations,* 1976, **29,** 139–151.

Nicholson, N., Brown, C. A., & Chadwick-Jones, J. K. Absence from work and job satisfaction. *Journal of Applied Psychology,* 1976, **61,** 728–737.

Nicholson, N., Brown, C. A., & Chadwick-Jones, J. K. Absence from work and personal characteristics. *Journal of Applied Psychology,* 1977, **62,** 319–327.

Nicholson, N., & Goodge, P. M. The influence of social, organizational and biographical factors on female absence. *Journal of Management Studies,* 1976, **13,** 234–254.

Nicholson, N., Wall, T., & Lischeron, J. The predictability of absence and propensity to leave from employees' job satisfaction and attitudes toward influence in decision-making. *Human Relations,* 1977, **30**, 499–514.

Noland, E. W. Attitudes and industrial absenteeism: A statistical appraisal. *American Sociological Review,* 1945, **10**, 503–510.

Nord, W. Improving attendance through rewards. *Personnel Administration,* November 1970, 37–41.

Nord, W. R., & Costigan, R. Worker adjustment to the four-day week: A longitudinal study. *Journal of Applied Psychology,* 1973, **58**, 660–661.

Owens, A. C. Sick leave among railwaymen threatened by redundancy: A pilot study. *Occupational Psychology,* 1966, **40**, 43–52.

Patchen, M. Absence and employee feelings about fair treatment. *Personnel Psychology,* 1960, **13**, 349–360.

Pedalino, E., & Gamboa, V. V. Behavior modification and absenteeism: Intervention in one industrial setting. *Journal of Applied Psychology,* 1974, **59**, 694–698.

Porter, L. W., & Lawler, E. E. *Managerial attitudes and performance.* Homewood, Ill.: Irwin, 1968.

Porter, L. W., & Steers, R. M. Organizational, work, and personal factors in employee turnover and absenteeism. *Psychological Bulletin,* 1973, **80**, 151–176.

Porter, L. W., Steers, R. M., Mowday, R. T., & Boulian, P. V. Organizational commitment, job satisfaction, and turnover among psychiatric technicians. *Journal of Applied Psychology,* 1974, **59**, 603–609.

Rokeach, M. *The nature of human values.* New York: The Free Press, 1973.

Rosen, H., & Turner, J. Effectiveness of two orientation approaches in hard-core unemployed turnover and absenteeism. *Journal of Applied Psychology,* 1971, **55**, 296–301.

Scheflen, K. C., Lawler, E. E., III, & Hackman, J. R. Long-term impact of employee participation in the development of pay incentive plans: A field experiment revisited. *Journal of Applied Psychology,* 1971, **55**, 182–186.

Searls, D. J., Braucht, G. N., & Miskimins, R. W. Work values and the chronically unemployed. *Journal of Applied Psychology,* 1974, **59**, 93–95.

Seatter, W. C. More effective control of absenteeism. *Personnel,* 1961, **38**, 16–29.

Shaw, M. E. *Group dynamics.* New York: McGraw-Hill, 1976.

Smith, A. L. Oldsmobile absenteeism/turnover control program. *GM Personnel Development Bulletin,* February 1972.

Smith, F. J. Work attitudes as predictors of specific day attendance. *Journal of Applied Psychology,* 1977, **62**, 16–19.

Steers, R. M. Antecedents and outcomes of organizational commitment. *Administrative Science Quarterly,* 1977, **22**, 46–56.

Steers, R. M., & Spencer, D. G. The role of achievement motivation in job design. *Journal of Applied Psychology,* 1977, **4**, 472–479.

Stockford, L. O. Chronic absenteeism and good attendance. *Personnel Journal,* 1944, **23**, 202–207.

Tjersland, T. *Changing worker behavior.* New York: Manpower Laboratory, American Telephone and Telegraph, December, 1972.

Vroom, V. *Work and motivation.* New York: Wiley, 1964.

Waters, L. K., & Roach, D. Relationship between job attitudes and two forms of withdrawal from the work situation. *Journal of Applied Psychology,* 1971, **55**, 92–94.

Waters, L. K., & Roach, D. Job attitudes as predictors of termination and absenteeism: Consistency over time and across organizations. *Journal of Applied Psychology,* 1973, **57**, 341–342.

Weaver, C. N., & Holmes, S. L. On the use of sick leave by female employees. *Personnel Administration and Public Personnel Review*, 1972, **1**(2), 46–50.

Whyte, W. F. *Organizational behavior*. Homewood, Ill.: Irwin, 1969.

Yolles, S. F., Carone, P. A., & Krinsky, L. W. *Absenteeism in industry*. Springfield, Ill.: Charles C. Thomas, 1975.

The Absence Culture and the Psychological Contract—Who's in Control of Absence?

Nigel Nicholson
Gary Johns

Reviews of the literature (Muchinsky, 1977; Steers & Rhodes, 1978) suggest that two main themes have dominated research concerning absence from work. One of these themes involves the relationship between job satisfaction and absence; the other involves the association between personal characteristics and absence. For different reasons, each of these conventional themes or paradigms is slowly losing its dominance.

The job satisfaction paradigm is grounded in the plausible theory that people will absent themselves from social obligations that prove aversive or dissatisfying. However, recent meta-analyses of the relationship between job satisfaction and absence have now established the limitations of this approach. Correcting for unreliability in absence, but not satisfaction, Hackett and Guion (in press) estimated the population correlation across all satisfaction and absence measures to be $-.09$. The highest specific estimate they obtained (overall satisfaction with "attitudinal" absence) was $-.23$. McShane (1984), correcting for unreliability in both measures, found a population estimate of $-.21$ for satisfaction with work and frequency of absence, but all other combinations of satisfaction and absence measures yielded lower estimates, usually much lower. The utility of these relationships may be limited further when the research controls for nonattitudinal correlates of absence (Breaugh, 1981; Johns, 1978).

Significant relationships between absence and personal characteristics such as sex, age, and tenure seem to be more universal but extremely poorly understood. Evidently because no theory underlies the pursuit of these associations, they have not stimulated more sophisticated, informative research. Thus, no theoretical stream has emerged from this work.

Perhaps as a result of dissatisfaction with the traditional research themes, recent studies have invoked a variety of new theoretical approaches. Thus, absence has been portrayed usefully as a maintenance mechanism (Staw & Oldham, 1978), a stress reaction (Parkes, 1983), and an economic response for increasing nonwork time (Youngblood, 1984). This examination of the wide variety of

From *Academy of Management Review*, 1985, **10**, 397–407. Reprinted by permission.

meanings for absenteeism is to be applauded (Johns & Nicholson, 1982). However, recent research shares with the traditional research a common limitation—the portrayal of absence as an individual, "private" behavior that can be analyzed without regard for its social context. The present paper offers a complement to this individual differences approach using two concepts—the absence culture and the psychological contract.

DEFINING CULTURE AND CONTRACT

Very generally, culture can be defined as the way of life and shared meanings of a collective. Thus, some patterns of behavior are common to members of the culture, and these behaviors are interpreted similarly by them. The notion of an absence culture was first invoked by Hill and Trist (1953, 1955) to explain how absences of different types are associated with different phases in workers' job tenure. To learn the absence culture was to acquire a sufficiently sophisticated understanding of the operation of rules, norms, and sanctions to obviate the need for "trial and error" absence behavior. The consequence over time is a progressive substitution of sanctioned for unsanctioned absence as the worker learns the formal and informal "ropes" of the organization. Here, absence culture is defined as "the set of shared understandings about absence legitimacy . . . and the established 'custom and practice' of employee absence behavior and its control" (Johns & Nicholson, 1982, p. 136).

Evidently coined by Argyris (1960), the concept of psychological contract has been developed most fully by Schein (1980). He defines it as the set of unwritten reciprocal expectations between an individual employee and the organization. The contract is the essence of individual-organizational linkage, because employment entails an implicit exchange of beliefs and expectations about what constitutes legitimate actions by either party. Gibson (1966) has presented a theory of absence that considers the influence of both formal and psychological contracts. The present paper examines the details of these contractual relations and explains how they operate to influence absence.

In essence, then, culture is transmitted through the social context, and its imprint on employees is a mechanism for the reinforcement of the social order of the organization and its larger setting. The psychological contract emerges from interaction and communication, effectively dictating how culture is *acted out*. Thus, the contract is a psychological mechanism by which collective influence is translated into individual behavior.

NATURE OF THE ABSENCE CULTURE

Absence cultures can be imagined to operate in several ways. First, they may exert a very direct effect on the level and patterning of absence for a given collection of workers. This is easiest to conceive when the content of the culture involves a specific norm regarding the level of absence that is tolerated. Such norms may be responsible in part for the common observation of restricted variance in absence within collectives (departments, plants, or occupations) and greater variation between collectives (Chadwick-Jones, Nicholson, & Brown 1982).

Absence cultures also may operate directly but subtly through less obvious social information processing mechanisms (Salancik & Pfeffer, 1978). For instance, workers may observe the absence behavior of others and the reactions of various constituencies to this behavior and then adopt a pattern or level of absence that reflects these observations. This may occur even though the transmission mechanisms are transitory and the enforcement mechanisms negligible. This form of absence culture may be less tangible than that involving specific norms, but nonetheless it reflects social influence (Johns, 1984).

Finally, absence cultures may operate indirectly to facilitate or constrain the extent to which individual level variables effectively influence absence. Given some abstract, natural base rate at which job satisfaction or personal characteristics might be expected to influence absence, variations in culture may set the limits on the extent to which this influence is realized in a particular setting. For example, some cultures may contain norms that effectively dictate good attendance regardless of how satisfied one is with the job. Other cultures may signal that absence is a legitimate response to dissatisfaction. The ultimate task is to determine which cultures generate which effects.

The elements that contribute to the formation of an absence culture can be located in two spheres—in the values and beliefs of the larger society and its subcultures and in the unique set of beliefs that are shared by virtue of membership in a particular organization or subunit. This distinction is not predicated on theory. Rather, it is a simple reflection of the assumption that variation in absence is influenced by social consensus both inside and outside the workplace.

For clarification, it is worthwhile to contrast the concepts of absence culture and organizational climate. Schneider and Reichers (1983) cite research dealing with service, safety, and achievement climates, and in this context the notion of an absence climate makes perfect sense, with the terms ''climate'' and ''culture'' being interchangeable (Johns & Nicholson, 1982). On the other hand, climate research generally has ignored the larger social context in which climates exist and thus contain no analog to the societal dimension of an absence culture. Also, an absence culture is a collective concept, the product of conceptual or empirical aggregation. This stands in sharp contrast to positions that allow for individual level, unaggregated measures of ''psychological climate'' (James & Jones, 1974).

Societal Dimension of the Absence Culture

Steers and Rhodes (1984) note that there are rather striking cross-national differences in time lost because of absence, ranging from 1 percent in Switzerland, to 3 percent in the United States, to 14 percent in Italy. It is unlikely that these variations are a sole function of mean differences in job satisfaction or the differential distribution of demographic characteristics. Rather, it is probable that they reflect in part differences in social consensus concerning the legitimacy of absence as work and nonwork behavior.

The nature of the absence culture at the societal level involves two interrelated themes—beliefs about absence and assumptions about employment. If prevailing beliefs about absence set limits on the content of specific absence cultures, assumptions about employment set limits on the form that psychological contracts may take. General trends in these beliefs and assumptions that exist in Anglo-American society are noted here. Also important, however, is the hypothesized variation in these trends across social or occupational status boundaries. Fox (1974) introduced the notion of a "trust dynamic" to explain how beliefs, expectations, and obligations vary considerably across the social/occupational spectrum. In short, persons in high discretion roles (such as the professions) operate under high trust psychological contracts that reinforce the work ethic and internalized commitment to the organization. Those in low discretion roles are parties to a lower trust psychological contract that fosters a more detached view of organizational participation. Similarly, high discretion roles foster internal control; low discretion roles reinforce feelings of external control (Kohn, 1981).

Beliefs about Absence   The limited research evidence available suggests that the popular conception of absence is part Jekyll and part Hyde. On one hand, absence is seen predominantly as a function of medical problems beyond one's control. For example, Nicholson and Payne (1984) report a survey concerning the causes of absence conducted among householders, a research technique designed to reduce the self-serving reasons that might be provided to employers or doctors. Even under these conditions, minor physical ailments were reported to be the most frequent potential and actual cause of absence. However, Taylor (1974) has noted historical changes in the diagnoses given for sickness absence, such as a reduction in gastritis and an increase in back problems. Although these changes may reflect actual transitions in exposure to risks, they also reflect evolving social beliefs about what constitutes sensible reasons for absence. Thus, a fair amount of paramedical symbolism and ritual surrounds absence, and Rushmore and Youngblood (1979) found that medically-related absence was not random behavior but, instead, was related to work and nonwork motives.

There also is a darker side to the popular conception of absence, a side that equates absence with marginal or willfully deviant behavior. In general, of course, this attribution is more likely to stem from the observer than the actor. Thus, in detailed interviews Nicholson (1975) found that negative stereotypes of other people's absence were widely held. Similarly, a survey of 987 personnel managers (Scott & Markham, 1982) suggests that most absence management strategies are post hoc, reactive, and punishment-oriented, a common response to deviant behavior. Such strategies evidently are directed toward those who exhibit absence "proneness," a term with negative connotations similar to truancy or delinquency.

Despite these general trends, there is reason to suppose that beliefs about absence will vary systematically with occupational status and the level of trust associated with this status. First, *workers in low discretion roles are expected to have a limited, concrete conception of absence causation and to use the medical model in a quasi-legalistic fashion to legitimate behavior (H$_1$)*. Such responses should be less likely in higher discretion roles. Second, *those in low* *discretion roles are more likely to attribute absence to external causes; those in higher discretion roles are more likely to favor internal attributions (H_2).* In high status roles, the value placed on self-control (Kohn, 1981) may even lead role occupants to exhibit self-blame and guilt about legitimate organic ailments that lead to absence.

Assumptions about Employment   Assumptions about employment rights and obligations comprise the psychological contract. On one hand are the shared expectations that employees' time has been "purchased" and that the employer has the right to set and enforce work schedules. On the other are shared expectations that some absence from work is necessary, legitimate, and mutually beneficial for employer and employee. In recent decades there has been a gradual enlargement of the scope of allowable or legitimate absence causes (Taylor, 1974), a situation that finds expression in the obsessively detailed and complicated absence coding schemes prevalent in many organizations.

Again, however, these developments are moderated by occupational status and trust. The psychological contract probably is perceived as more inclusive by those in high discretion roles. Thus, it might be hypothesized that *managers and professionals view absence as work-related behavior, an aspect of individual performance, and a fundamental ethical challenge to the contract (H_3).* In contrast, wage earners in low discretion roles may have a more restricted view of their ethical obligations to go to work, especially when absence means a loss of pay. They are more likely to view absence as nonwork behavior and to see legitimation as a technical, rather than moral, matter (Gibson, 1966). In fact, the complex absence coding systems, which are most likely to be applied to hourly workers, set out the game rules for technical legitimation ("Put me down for one unpaid contractual domestic leave day"). Managers and professionals who wish to absent themselves may be forced to engage more esoteric constructs, such as executive stress reduction ("I'll be staying over in Honolulu another day to write my report").

Organizational Dimension of the Absence Culture

Organizations or their subunits may foster more or less distinctive beliefs about absence, assumptions about employment, and conceptions of self-control. The degree of this distinctiveness can be called cultural salience. Highly salient absence cultures tend to be homogeneous and directly impactful on the individual, and they often involve obvious norms regarding attendance behavior:

> In a Midwest university, professors in the management department came into work every weekday as well as Saturday mornings. Those who were absent on Saturday received much good-natured but not-so-subtle razzing on Monday morning (Johns, 1984, p. 378–379).

Less salient absence cultures invoke more subtle social influence and permit individual differences to have a greater impact on absence:

> Consider a work force composed of men and women of dissimilar ages and ethnic backgrounds who are operating under an individual piece-rate pay system. Work sta-

tions are far enough apart to discourage regular interaction but close enough for workers to see who is at work and to follow exchanges between the boss and co-workers. The company has a strict written absence policy, but supervisors have a high degree of discretion in its application (Johns, 1984, p. 379).

As these examples suggest, one consequence of high cultural salience should be the restriction of *variation in absence*. (It is worth noting that these examples happen to differ in the likely degree of trust inherent in the psychological contract.)

Important determinants of cultural salience include the organization's absence control system, its technology, and the social ecology of the setting.

Absence Control Systems   The employer's side of the psychological contract consists of expectations about attendance that are communicated and transformed by a variety of formal and informal agencies. Initially, the personnel function may communicate the literal provisions of the contract to the employee. Having learned the formal rules, the employee then moves to learning the unwritten "contextual" rules of organizational practice (Van Maanen, 1980). For example, workers may learn that they should *never* be absent on the day inventory is taken or that showing up on the first day of hunting season is considered deviant. The third stage of this process is the acquisition of knowledge about "operational" rules, the situationally specific consequences of rule following and rule breaking. For example, although the formal rules may be oriented toward limiting costly time lost, workers may find that their supervisors are most likely to retaliate against very frequent short term absence that disrupts day-to-day operations.

Compared with some other work behaviors, absence seems particularly susceptible to this translation from literal rules to more symbolic contextual and operational rules. Even at the blue-collar level, organizations are notoriously lax in systematically measuring and monitoring absence (Robertson, 1979; Scott & Markham, 1982). To complicate matters, most extant systems require organizational officials to make attributions about cause (Johns & Nicholson, 1982) that would test the wisdom of Solomon. The net result is a fair degree of scope for variations in cultural salience, limited by the constraints of technology and social ecology noted below. This may be especially true if the literal contract provisions are vague or unknown to employees and the psychological contract is high in trust. For example, many professors will be familiar with departmental absence cultures that are much less salient than that noted above for the Midwest management department.

Technology and Social Ecology   Broadly, technology denotes the way work relations are structured to meet organizational goals, whether the impetus is physical machinery or bureaucratic requirements. Social ecology refers to the physical distribution of workers with various personal characteristics in the workplace. Technology can influence social ecology, and conversely social ecology can lead to liaisons among employees that are identical in consequence to those fostered by the technology. In either case, cultural salience is closely associated with the degree of interdependence that is fostered among workers.

At the most abstract level, variables such as job cycle time, role discretion, task identity, and associated environmental stressors may create an imagery of work that strongly influences how employees view the world and their place in it (Berger, Berger, & Kellner, 1973). Thus, technological and bureaucratic experience may encourage them to see themselves as isolated, dispensable functionaries whose temporary absence is of no fundamental importance, or they may see themselves as people whose coordinated commitment and reliable attendance is vital to organizational success. To exacerbate matters, blue-collar technologies offer few incentives for employees to make their boss look good by showing up for work regularly. In white-collar settings, the reverse may be true, because each successive level has a fair degree of control over the promotion opportunities and other privileges of lower levels. The net effect may be a subjective norm among managers and professionals that favors good attendance (Gibson, 1966). Furthermore, in a given organization, it is hypothesized that *white-collar workers agree more than blue-collar workers concerning the amount of absence that is considered "normal" and "acceptable" (H_4).* This is predicated on the extensive socialization and chained interdependence that promote a common view of work responsibilities among managers and professionals.

More interesting than these gross variations in absence cultures between blue- and white-collar workers are variations within each class. Thus, despite Hypothesis 4, salient absence cultures certainly can be found at lower organizational levels if local conditions foster interdependence among workers. For example, at the blue-collar level, compelling pressures for conformity to norms of good attendance can occur if cohesive teams operate under a system that ties rewards to group performance (Chadwick-Jones et al., 1982). On the other hand, strong primary group interdependence can produce very different norms when rewards are not tied to performance and the organization employs standby cover for absentees. For instance, workers may "share out" sick days on a very systematic basis, a practice that may be reinforced by any consequent increase in lucrative overtime work (Gowler, 1969).

Finally, cultural salience can be influenced by friendship patterns, informal communication networks, selection and placement practices, and staffing arrangements. For example, in many industrial operations female employees are isolated in a few low scope, low paying "women's" jobs. This perfect confounding of sex, technology, and status may lead to the development of a salient culture that supports high levels of absence (Johns, 1978; Johns & Nicholson, 1982). In a similar vein, it is hypothesized that *so-called "inside" workers who work with others generally exhibit more salient absence cultures than do isolated "outside" workers who work autonomously (H_5).* Thus, inside postal workers should exhibit more salient absence cultures than letter carriers, and bus drivers should exhibit less salient absence cultures than bus mechanics.

A TYPOLOGY OF ABSENCE CULTURES

The present section develops specific implications of this material, using two of the key concepts developed earlier to generate predictions about the ways in which organizations or their subunits differ from one another in their absence cultures. This presumes that organizations or their subunits can be classified in two dimensions. The first is whether the psychological contract is high or low in trust (i.e., high or low discretion tasks, with accompanying expectations) at the level of investigation. The second is the salience of the culture at the same level (i.e., how homogeneous and impactful on the individual). Operationally, these two dimensions may be seen as different forms of cultural integration. Trust is a form of vertical integration, with low trust relations signifying low integration among organizational levels. Salience is a form of horizontal integration, with low salience signifying fragmentation across organizational subunits, including groups and/or individuals. Dichotomizing and counterposing these dimensions produces a matrix of four ideal organizational types. It may be hypothesized that a characteristic form of employee absence culture (Figure 1) exists for each type.

In essence, this matrix is derivative of, rather than isomorphic with, the details of the previous discussion. The trust inherent in the psychological contract influences the *content* of the absence culture, including beliefs about absence and related assumptions about employment. As noted earlier, this content is predictable in part from the social and occupational status of the employees in question. Cultural salience, on the other hand, determines the "press" of this cultural content and is more dependent on the unique combination of technology, social ecology, and absence control under which the employees work.

Type I cultures (low salience, high trust) are those in which people are given roles and responsibilities that bind them into the hierarchical system, but the organization of work itself inhibits the development of lateral relationships. The result is a *dependent* culture that is common in early states of industrial development and is frequently identified with paternalistic practices. Here, for example, delegation may be a mechanism of "divide and rule" that helps generate commitment to the authority structure. Voluntary absence is engaged as a form

FIGURE 1
A typology of organizational absence cultures.

		Cultural salience (Horizontal integration)	
		Low salience	High salience
Psychological contract	High trust	TYPE I DEPENDENT Deviant absence	TYPE II MORAL Constructive absence
(Vertical integration)	Low trust	TYPE III FRAGMENTED Calculative absence	TYPE IV CONFLICTUAL Defiant absence

of "deviance" in such a culture, with individuals varying in their absence according to how "guilt" at "cheating" the psychological contract can be assuaged by legitimation. To predict absence in this kind of culture the researcher needs to plot the differential access of employees to sources of legitimation and individual differences in motivation to conform to organizational rules. For example, it is *hypothesized that authoritarianism* (Adorno, Frenkel-Brunswick, Levinson, & Sanford, 1950) *and preference for bureaucracy* (Gordon, 1970) *are negatively related to absence in a Type I culture (H$_6$)*.

Type II cultures (high salience, high trust) achieve integration on both dimensions, vertically through maintaining high trust relations and laterally through cohesive and homogeneous cultural ties. Such cultures can be termed moral to denote the achievement of unitary identification with goals that would follow from this combination of features (Etzioni, 1961). The absence culture is one that is determined by internalized norms and standards. In such a culture voluntary absence is based on how individuals "read" their psychological contract with the organization. Absence thus is a "construction," constrained by how the contractual relationship is construed. It also is "constructive" as a means of meeting one's needs within organizationally approved parameters. To predict individual absence in such a culture, researchers might investigate how rights and obligations are differentially perceived and how certain forms of absence are perceived as serving the interests of both the individual and the organization. However, clinical prediction probably is superior to statistical prediction, because high cultural salience would greatly restrict inter-individual variation in absence. This was exactly the case in the Midwest management department cited earlier, where very little absence was observed.

Type III cultures (low salience, low trust) are *fragmented* insofar as the variables discussed above supply little basis for interdependence and cohesion, and the existence of low trust employment relations supplies little basis for integration between organizational and individual values. The piecework factory example cited earlier demonstrates a Type III culture. Workers are isolated and privatized, and their involvement with work is limited to a calculative exchange relationship, dominated by the economic exchange of time for money. The absence culture also will be dominated by calculation. Voluntary absence will be engaged in as a form of "gambling" in such a culture, based on the balance of profit and loss in pay and satisfaction, and calculations of personal consequences and their likelihood. To predict absence in a fragmented culture, a fruitful research approach is the calculation of individual differences in the subjective expected utilities of absence. Also, of the four cultural types, *individual measures of job satisfaction are most predictive of absence under a Type III culture (H$_7$)*.

In Type IV cultures (high salience, low trust) there are strong lateral ties among members of the shared salient employee culture, but the low trust dynamic of hierarchical relations divorces employees from employer interests. Employees share a culture that is alienated from and resistant to the employer, and therefore *conflictual*. In such a culture voluntary absence is likely to be regarded as an "entitlement," and as defiant of managerial injunctions, though staying within the letter of enforceable law. Predicting individual variation in voluntary absence behavior in such a culture involves examining what individuals feel is personally desirable and acceptable to their coworkers and, outside work, to their family and friends.

Predicting differences in *levels* of absence across the four cultural types is complicated because the trust dimension is influenced by existing absence control systems. However, it can be hypothesized that *more salient cultures have more extreme absence levels (high or low) and less variation among employees than less salient cultures (H_8)*. Also, in more salient absence cultures workers should be more motivated to monitor their own attendance behavior and that of co-workers. Thus, compared with low salience cultures, *workers in highly salient cultures are more accurate in recalling their own attendance histories and in recalling or predicting the attendance behavior of specific coworkers (H_9)* (Johns, 1984).

AN ABSENCE CULTURE IN TRANSITION

A study by Hammer, Landau, and Stern (1981) provides some support for the dynamics underlying the typology of absence cultures presented here. For present purposes, it represents something of a quasi-experimental case study of a change in an absence culture. Hammer et al. examined the absenteeism of employees in a furniture manufacturing plant before and after a change in plant ownership. During the data collection period, it was announced that the plant would be closed by its corporate owners. Subsequently, a plan was devised by which the employees assumed ownership of the plant. Data collection was terminated 12 months after the change of ownership.

Early in the data collection period, before the notice of closure, there was evidence of a Type III absence culture. Low trust was suggested by the status of the jobs sampled (production and office, all nonsupervisory) and by the presence of a detailed contract specifying attendance regulations. Although the exact degree of cultural salience was unclear, it probably was low in comparison to subsequent periods. In this initial phase of the study, voluntary absence was consistently higher than involuntary absence. This elevation of voluntary absence (reflected by no excuse or "personal reasons") seems indicative of a calculated, individualized pattern of behavior.

When the closure of the plant was announced, both voluntary and involuntary absence increased dramatically. Hammer et al. interpreted this increase as indicative of a personal stress reduction mechanism. However, a collective, cultural explanation seems more likely. Specifically, trust levels doubtless fell at the time of the announcement. Furthermore, it is reasonable to expect that cultural salience increased dramatically in line with the well-established relationship between threat and cohesion (Stein, 1976). This is a conflictual Type IV culture under which the typology predicts defiant absence. It is suspected that workers were using elevated absence levels to "send a message" about their unhappiness with a perceived violation of the psychological contract. After plans for employee ownership were announced, absence fell to its former level.

What effect could employee ownership be expected to have on the absence culture and absence behavior? Ownership suggests that conditions of elevated trust would develop as the success of the venture became clear. Although job content did not change, former workers had increased their status to worker/owners, and both workers and managers had cooperated to assume ownership. In addition, it is reasonable to expect heightened cultural salience because interdependence of interests was magnified by ownership. Jointly, these conditions point to a Type II absence culture in which the psychological contract would have to be constructively renegotiated to cope with the moral dilemma involved in damaging one's own interests and those of coworkers by being absent. In fact, this appears to be what happened. Absolute levels of absence did not differ from those observed before the change of ownership. However, the *explanations* provided for absence change dramatically, and now involuntary absence was invoked more often than voluntary absence. This occurred although the literal contract provisions regarding absence remained the same. In the words of Hammer et al.:

> Employee ownership did not affect the volume of absence but rather the way in which the absence was labeled or publicly identified .... Although employee ownership did not significantly alter the cost-benefit ratio of an absence to the individual, it clearly raised the costs of a publicly identifiable absence. Employees now took care to "legitimize" their absence by providing the record keeper with a specific reason that was acceptable under company policy or the union contract. In other words, they called in sick when they did not bother to do so earlier and perhaps when the physical impediment to work attendance was not overwhelming. The need to legitimize withdrawal can come from forces within the individual, such as cognitive dissonance arising when one is absent from one's own company, and from forces in the work environment, such as perceived co-worker pressure against unexcused absences (1981, pp. 571–572.)

IMPLICATIONS FOR RESEARCHERS AND MANAGERS

The concepts of absence culture and psychological contract have implications for researching and managing absence. Implications for researchers include the following:

1 Careful attention must be devoted to the issue of aggregation. Most current studies of absence are conducted in a single level of a single organization. Under these circumstances, the distribution of absences will be severely restricted. This is precisely what the general concept of an absence culture would predict, especially when that culture is highly salient. To complicate matters, most current research analyzes data at solely the individual level of analysis. This combination of tactics often results in the discovery of small and ephemeral relationships. The cultural approach taken here begins to suggest when an individual differences approach makes sense and when contrasts between aggregations (firms, occupations, organizational levels, shifts) would be more profitable. For example, recall that individual differences in job satisfaction are expected to be most predictive of absence under a Type III (fragmented) culture.

2 Contrasts among existing aggregations that differ in absence behavior are open to explanations that are not social or cultural. To validate a cultural explanation, researchers should ask subjects probing questions about absence that correspond to the process underlying that explanation. For example, if a social norm controls absence in a salient culture, workers should have an accurate awareness of the norm, agree with each other, and be sensitive to enforcement mechanisms.

3 Researchers have been remiss in describing the literal contract provisions, pay arrangements, and control systems that pertain to absence at their research sites. These factors provide grist for the emergent psychological contract and cultural salience, and researchers need to confront their potential impact in their reports. For instance, the loss of pay for absenteeism is a constraint that should reduce interindividual variation in absence. This reduced variation may have the appearance of a norm to new employees and effectively regulate their behavior despite individual differences in economic need.

4 If absence cultures and their related psychological contracts exist, they must be contingent in part on the *consequences* that workers and managers feel will result from absence (to individuals, groups, or the organization as a whole). Despite this, virtually all extant research has been restricted to the causes or control of absence. Goodman and Atkin (1984) have recently provided an excellent conceptual analysis of the potential consequences of absence.

Implications for managers include the following:

1 Control systems and literal contract provisions regarding absence often have a symbolic effect that is different from and much more powerful than their intended effect. Managers often will err if they assume that the ambient level of absence is the product of the objective nature of such systems and contracts. Before attempting changes to reduce absence, managers should identify the emergent culture and the emergent psychological contract that maintain absence levels.

2 Absence recording systems that require organizational members to make complex attributions about the causes for workers' absence can contribute greatly to the shaping of absence cultures. Most absence control systems are ultimately oriented toward how much employees are absent (time lost) rather than how often they are absent (frequency), because the former measure is more directly associated with costs. However, such systems may be subverted by supervisors who assign less favorable absence codes to disruptive high frequency absentees and more favorable codes to low frequency absentees, even though the latter may actually exhibit greater time lost. This practical response is not lost on the workers, who often will tailor their absence patterns to the boss's needs.

3 Most absence control systems appear to be post hoc, clinical, and individualized in nature, seriously taking effect only after a particular employee has exhibited substantial absence. This approach is at odds with many examples of absence cultures in which the bulk of absence may not be under the control of individual motives and goals. In concentrating on outliers and ignoring group dynamics, organizations may be reinforcing the ambient absence level that has been dictated by the culture.

4 Disregarding negative side effects, conventional systems that punish absence or reward attendance offer some promise of success only under Type III cultural conditions under which workers perceive themselves as independent agents in an economic exchange. Beyond this, if Hypothesis 8 is correct, serious attempts to reduce absence probably will enhance the salience of the absence culture while ensuring that its content involves a norm of good attendance. This suggests a movement toward a Type II culture (high salience, high trust), and it is common for occidental versions of "Japanese management" to cite absence reduction as one of their rationales. However, as the study by Hammer et al. (1981) suggests, the Type II culture may still contrive to modify the style rather than the level of absence.

In summary, the absence culture concept is deemed valuable because it provides a new perspective on researching and managing absence that recognizes how individual behavior may be constrained by the collective reality of organizations.

REFERENCES

Adorno, T. W., Frenkel-Brunswick, E., Levinson, D. J., & Sanford, R. N. (1950) *The authoritarian personality*. New York: Harper.

Argyris, C. (1960) *Understanding organizational behavior*. Homewood, IL: Dorsey.

Berger, P. L., Berger, B., & Kellner, H. (1973) *The homeless mind*. New York: Random House.

Breaugh, J. A. (1981) Predicting absenteeism from prior absenteeism and work attitudes. *Journal of Applied Psychology*, 66, 555–560.

Chadwick-Jones, J. K., Nicholson, N., & Brown, C. A. (1982) *Social psychology of absenteeism*. New York: Praeger.

Etzioni, A. (1961) *A comparative analysis of complex organizations*. Glencoe, IL: Free Press.

Fox, A. (1974) *Beyond contract: Work, power and trust relations*. London: Faber.

Gibson, R. O. (1966) Toward a conceptualization of absence behavior of personnel in organizations. *Administrative Science Quarterly*, 11, 107–133.

Goodman, P. S., & Atkin, R. S. (1984) Effects of absenteeism on individuals and organizations. In P. S. Goodman & R. S. Atkin (Eds.), *Absenteeism: New approaches to understanding, measuring, and managing employee absence* (pp. 276–321). San Francisco: Jossey-Bass.

Gordon, L. V. (1970) Measurement of bureaucratic orientation. *Personnel Psychology*, 23, 1–11.

Gowler, D. (1969) Determinants of the supply of labour to the firm. *Journal of Management Studies*, 6, 73–95.

Hackett, R. D., & Guion, R. M. (in press) A reevaluation of the absenteeism-job satisfaction relationship. *Organizational Behavior and Human Decision Processes*.

Hammer, T. H., Landau, J. C., & Stern, R. N. (1981) Absenteeism when workers have a voice: The case of employee ownership. *Journal of Applied Psychology*, 66, 561–573.

Hill, J.M.M., & Trist, E. L. (1953) A consideration of industrial accidents as a means of withdrawal from the work situation. *Human Relations*, 6, 357–380.

Hill, J.M.M., & Trist, E. L. (1955) Changes in accidents and other absences with length of service. *Human Relations*, 8, 121–152.

James, L. R., & Jones, A. P. (1974) Organizational climate: A review of theory and research. *Psychological Bulletin*, 81, 1096–1112.

Johns, G. (1978) Attitudinal and nonattitudinal predictors of two forms of absence from work. *Organizational Behavior and Human Performance*, 22, 431–444.

Johns, G. (1984) Unresolved issues in the study and management of absence from work. In P. S. Goodman & R. S. Atkin (Eds.), *Absenteeism: New approaches to understanding, measuring, and managing employee absence* (pp. 360–390). San Francisco: Jossey-Bass.

Johns, G., & Nicholson N. (1982) The meanings of absence: New strategies for theory and research. In B. M. Staw & L. L. Cummings (Eds.), *Research in organizational behavior* (Vol. 4, pp. 127–172). Greenwich, CT: JAI Press.

Kohn, M. L. (1981) Personality, occupation, and social stratification: A frame of reference. In D. J. Treiman & R. V. Robinson (Eds.), *Research in social stratification and mobility* (Vol. 1, pp. 267–297). Greenwich, CT: JAI Press.

McShane, S. L. (1984) Job satisfaction and absenteeism: A meta-analytic re-examination. *Canadian Journal of Administrative Sciences*, 1, 61–77.

Muchinsky, P. M. (1977) Employee absenteeism: A review of the literature. *Journal of Vocational Behavior*, 10, 316–340.

Nicholson, N. (1975) *Industrial absence as an indicant of employee motivation and job satisfaction*. Unpublished doctoral thesis, University of Wales, Cardiff.

Nicholson, N., & Payne, R. L. (1984) *The relationship between absence inducing events, susceptibility and causes.* Memo No. 598, Medical Research Council/Economic Science Research Council Social and Applied Psychology Unit, The University of Sheffield, United Kingdom.

Parkes, K. R. (1983) Smoking as a moderator of the relationship between affective state and absence from work. *Journal of Applied Psychology*, 68, 698–708.

Robertson, G. (1979) Absenteeism and labour turnover in selected Ontario industries. *Relations Industrielles*, 34, 86–107.

Rushmore, C. H. & Youngblood, S. A. (1979) Medically-related absenteeism: Random or motivated behavior? *Journal of Occupational Medicine*, 21, 245–250.

Salancik, G. R., & Pfeffer, J. (1978) A social information processing approach to job attitudes and task design. *Administrative Science Quarterly*, 23, 224–253.

Schein, E. H. (1980) *Organizational psychology* (3rd ed.). Englewood Cliffs, NJ: Prentice-Hall.

Schneider, B., & Reichers, A. E. (1983) On the etiology of climates. *Personnel Psychology*, 36, 19–39.

Scott, D., & Markham, S. (1982) Absenteeism control methods: A survey of practices and results. *Personnel Administrator*, 27(6), 73–84.

Staw, B. M., & Oldham, G. R. (1978) Reconsidering our dependent variables: A critique and empirical study. *Academy of Management Journal*, 21, 539–559.

Steers, R. M., & Rhodes, S. R. (1978) Major influences on employee attendance: A process model. *Journal of Applied Psychology*, 63, 391–407.

Steers, R. M., & Rhodes, S. R. (1984) Knowledge and speculation about absenteeism. In P. S. Goodman & R. S. Atkin (Eds.), *Absenteeism: New approaches to understanding, measuring, and managing employee absence* (pp. 229–275). San Francisco: Jossey-Bass.

Stein, A. (1976) Conflict and cohesion: A review of the literature. *Journal of Conflict Resolution*, 20, 143–172.

Taylor, P. J. (1974) Sickness absence: Factors and misconceptions. *Journal of the Royal College of Physicians*, 8, 315–334.

Van Maanen, J. (1980) Career games: Organizational rules of play. In C. B. Derr (Ed.), *Work, family and the career* (pp. 111–143). New York: Praeger.

Youngblood, S. A. (1984) Work, nonwork, and withdrawal. *Journal of Applied Psychology*, 69, 106–117.

Intermediate Linkages in the Relationship between Job Satisfaction and Employee Turnover

William H. Mobley

Reviews of the literature on the relationship between employee turnover and job satisfaction have reported a consistent negative relationship (Brayfield & Crockett, 1955; Locke, 1975; Porter & Steers, 1973; Vroom, 1964). Locke (1976) noted that while the reported correlations have been consistent and significant they have not been especially high (usually less than .40).

It is probable that other variables mediate the relationship between job satisfaction and the act of quitting. Based on their extensive review, Porter and Steers (1973) concluded the following:

> Much more emphasis should be placed in the future on the psychology of the withdrawal *process* . . . Our understanding of the manner in which the actual decision is made is far from complete (p. 173).

The present paper suggests several of the possible intermediate steps in the withdrawal decision process (specifically, the decision to quit a job). Porter and Steers (1973) suggested that expressed "intention to leave" may represent the next logical step after experienced dissatisfaction in the withdrawal process. The withdrawal decision process presented here suggests that thinking of quitting is the next logical step after experienced dissatisfaction and that "intention to leave," following several other steps, may be the last step prior to actual quitting.

A schematic representation of the withdrawal decision process is presented in Figure 1. Block A represents the process of evaluating one's existing job, while Block B represents the resultant emotional state of some degree of satisfaction-dissatisfaction. A number of models have been proposed for the process inherent in Blocks A and B—for example, the value-percept discrepancy model (Locke, 1969, 1976), an instrumentality-valence model (Vroom, 1964), a met-expectations model (Porter & Steers, 1973), and a contribution/inducement ratio (March & Simon, 1958). Comparative studies that test the relative efficacy of these and other alternative models of satisfaction continue to be needed.

Most studies of turnover examine the direct relationship between job satisfaction and turnover. The model presented in Figure 1 suggests a number of possible mediating steps between dissatisfaction and actual quitting. Block C suggests that one of the consequences of dissatisfaction is to stimulate thoughts of quitting.

Reprinted from *Journal of Applied Psychology*, 1977, **62**, 237–240. © 1977 American Psychological Association. Reprinted by permission.

Although not of primary interest here, it is recognized that other forms of withdrawal less extreme than quitting (e.g., absenteeism, passive job behavior) are possible consequences of dissatisfaction (see e.g., Brayfield & Crockett, 1955; Kraut, 1975).

Block D suggests that the next step in the withdrawal decision process is an evaluation of the expected utility of search and of the cost of quitting. The evaluation of the expected utility of search would include an estimate of the chances of finding an alternative to working in the present job, some evaluation of the desirability of possible alternatives, and the costs of search (e.g., travel, lost work time, etc.). The evaluation of the cost of quitting would include such considerations as loss of seniority, loss of vested benefits, and the like. This block incorporates March and Simon's (1958) perceived ease of movement concept.

If the costs of quitting are high and/or the expected utility of search is low, the individual may reevaluate the existing job (resulting in a change in job satisfaction), reduce thinking of quitting, and/or engage in other forms of withdrawal behavior. Research is still needed on the determinants of alternative forms of withdrawal behavior and on how the expression of withdrawal behavior changes as a function of time and of changes in or reevaluation of the environment.

If there is some perceived chance of finding an alternative and if the costs are not prohibitive, the next step, Block E, would be behavioral intention to search for an alternative(s). As noted by Arrow (b) in Figure 1, non-job-related factors may also elicit an intention to search (e.g., transfer of spouse, health problem, etc.). The intention to search is followed by an actual search (Block F). If no alternatives are found, the individual may continue to search, reevaluate the expected utility of search, reevaluate the existing job, simply accept the current state of affairs, decrease thoughts of quitting, and/or engage in other forms of withdrawal behavior (e.g., absenteeism, passive job behavior).

If alternatives are available, including (in some cases) withdrawal from the labor market, an evaluation of alternatives is initiated (Block G). This evaluation process would be hypothesized to be similar to the evaluation process in Block A. However, specific job factors the individual considers in evaluating the present job and alternatives may differ (see Hellriegel & White, 1973; and Kraut, 1975, for a discussion of this point). Independent of the preceding steps, unsolicited or highly visible alternatives may stimulate this evaluation process.

The evaluation of alternatives is followed by a comparison of the present job to alternative(s) (Block H). If the comparison favors the alternative, it will stimulate a behavioral intention to quit (Block 1), followed by actual withdrawal (Block J). If the comparison favors the present job, the individual may continue to search, reevaluate the expected utility of search, reevaluate the existing job, simply accept the current state of affairs, decrease thoughts of quitting, and/or engage in other forms of withdrawal behavior.

Finally, Arrow (e) gives recognition to the fact that for some individuals, the decision to quit may be an impulsive act involving few, if any, of the preceding steps in this model. The relative incidence and the individual and situational determinants of an impulsive versus a subjectively rational decision process presents yet another area of needed research.

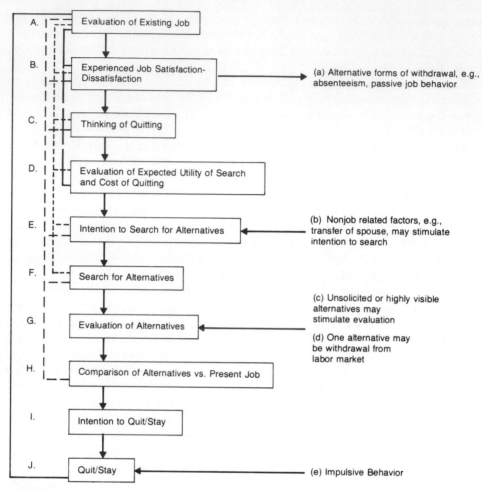

FIGURE 1
The employee turnover decision process.

The model being described is heuristic rather than descriptive. There may well be individual differences in the number and sequence of steps in the withdrawal decision process, in the degree to which the process is conscious, and as noted earlier, in the degree to which the act of quitting is impulsive rather than based on a subjectively rational decision process. One value of such an heuristic model is to guide thinking and empirical research toward a valid descriptive model that can account for such individual differences.

There is a lack of research evaluating all or even most of the possible steps in the withdrawal decision process. There have been a few studies that have tested one or two of the intermediate linkages proposed in the present note. Mobley (Note 1) found high negative correlations between satisfaction and frequency of thinking of quitting (Blocks B and C). Atkinson and Lefferts (1972), who dealt with the association between Blocks C and J, found that the frequency with which people thought about quitting their job was significantly related to actual termination. Kraut (1975), looking at the associations among Blocks B, I, and J, found significant correlations between expressed intention to stay and subsequent employee participation. These correlations were much stronger than relationships between expressed satisfaction and continued participation. Finally, Armknecht and Early's (1972) review is relevant to the relationships between Blocks D and/or F and Block J. They concluded that voluntary terminations are closely related to economic conditions.

Each of these studies fails to look at a complete withdrawal decision process. Such research would appear to be sorely needed. Several researchable questions that follow from the withdrawal decision process described in the present note were mentioned earlier. Additional questions include the following. Do individuals evaluate the expected utility of search? If so, what are the determinants and consequences of this evaluation? What are the consequences and determinants of behavior in the face of an unsuccessful search? In such cases, do individuals persist in search, reevaluate their existing jobs, reevaluate the cost of search, or engage in other forms of withdrawal? Is the process and/or content for evaluating alternative jobs the same as for evaluating the present job? Does satisfaction with the present job change as a function of the availability or evaluation of alternatives?

Attention to these sorts of questions rather than a continued replication of the direct relationship between job satisfaction and turnover would appear to be warranted. Particularly useful would be the longitudinal analysis of the variables and linkages suggested by the model. Such research would be responsive to Porter and Steers' (1973) conclusion that more emphasis should be placed on the psychology of the withdrawal decision process.

REFERENCE NOTE

1 Mobley, W. H. *Job satisfaction and thinking of quitting* (Tech. Rep. 75–3). Columbia: University of South Carolina, College of Business Administration, Management and Organizational Research Center, 1975.

REFERENCES

Armknecht, P. A., & Early, J. F. Quits in manufacturing: A study of their causes. *Monthly Labor Review*, 1972, **11**, 31–37.

Atkinson, T. J., & Lefferts, E. A. The prediction of turnover using Herzberg's job satisfaction technique. *Personnel Psychology*, 1972, **25**, 53–64.

Brayfield, A. H., & Crockett, W. H. Employee attitudes and employee performance. *Psychological Bulletin*, 1955, **52**, 396–424.

Hellriegel, D., & White, G. E. Turnover of professionals in public accounting: A comparative analysis. *Personnel Psychology*, 1973, **26**, 239–249.

Kraut, A. I. Predicting turnover of employees from measured job attitudes. *Organizational Behavior and Human Performance*, 1975, **13**, 233–243.

Locke, E. A. What is job satisfaction? *Organizational Behavior and Human Performance*, 1969, **4**, 309–336.

Locke, E. A. Personnel attitudes and motivation. *Annual Review of Psychology,* 1975, **26**, 457–480.

Locke, E. A. The nature and consequences of job satisfaction. In M. D. Dunnette (Ed.), *Handbook of industrial and organizational psychology.* Chicago: Rand-McNally, 1976.

March, J. G., & Simon, H. A. *Organizations.* New York: Wiley, 1958.

Porter, L. W., & Steers, R. M. Organizational, work, and personal factors in employee turnover and absenteeism. *Psychological Bulletin,* 1973, **80**, 151–176.

Vroom, V. H. *Work and motivation.* New York: Wiley, 1964.

Employee Turnover in Organizations

Richard M. Steers
Richard T. Mowday

Our progress toward a better understanding of employee turnover in organizations can be traced by examining the various reviews that have appeared over time. A careful reading of these reviews reveals that, while some progress has been made, much remains to be learned concerning turnover and its outcomes in work organizations.

We have attempted in Exhibit 1 to summarize several of the more important findings of the various reviews of the turnover literature. Several of these reviews have pointed to the importance of job attitudes as a factor in turnover (Brayfield and Crockett, 1955; Herzberg *et al.,* 1957; Porter and Steers, 1973). In addition, some evidence exists that personality and biodemographic data can predict turnover to some extent (Schuh, 1967). The importance of economic factors has also been shown (Stoikov and Raimon, 1968). Finally, several of the more recent reviews have pointed to the wide diversity of factors (e.g., personal factors, job characteristics, reward systems, supervisory and group relations) that combine to influence the decision to stay or leave (Lefkowitz, 1971; Porter and Steers, 1973; Price, 1977; Mobley *et al.,* 1979; Muchinsky and Tuttle, 1979).

Beyond simple reviews, however, several investigators have attempted to propose conceptual models of the turnover process based on existing literature (March and Simon, 1958; Vroom, 1964; Price, 1977; Mobley, 1977). Although the details of the models differ, turnover is generally thought to be a function of negative job attitudes combined with an ability to secure employment elsewhere. Mobley (1977) goes further here in suggesting several intermediate linkages that intercede between attitudes and actual turnover, noting in particular the importance of behavioral intentions (after Fishbein, 1967).

Despite this long history of research on employee turnover, several issues remain unanswered. At least nine shortcomings of many of the existing models can be identified that need to be taken into account in any comprehensive model of voluntary employee turnover:

From R. M. Steers and R. T. Mowday, "Employee turnover and post-decision accommodation processes." In L. L. Cummings and B. M. Staw (Eds.). *Research in Organizational Behavior.* Greenwich, Conn.: JAI Press, 1981, pp. 237–249. Reprinted by permission.

EXHIBIT 1
SUMMARY OF EMPIRICAL REVIEWS OF TURNOVER LITERATURE

Investigator(s)	Focus	Major findings	Formal model presented
Brayfield and Crockett (1955)	Effects of job satisfaction on turnover	Significant if modest relation between dissatisfaction and turnover	No
Herzberg *et al.* (1957)	Comprehensive review	Significant if modest relation between dissatisfaction and turnover	No
March and Simon (1958)	Comprehensive review	Turnover largely influenced by desirability of leaving plus ease of movement	Yes
Vroom (1964)	Limited review	Turnover influenced by force to remain vs. force to leave	Yes
Schuh (1967)	Personality and biodemographic predictors of turnover	Modest evidence that vocational interest inventories and scaled biographical information blanks predicted some turnover	No
Stoikov and Raimon (1968)	Economic factors in turnover	Money and labor market factors have sizable influence on industry-wide turnover rates	No
Lefkowitz (1971)	Comprehensive review	Turnover influenced by job expectations, satisfaction, work environment, compensation, job itself, and supervisory style	No
Porter and Steers (1973)	Comprehensive review	Satisfaction modestly related to turnover; major influences on turnover can be found in person, job, work environment, and organization-wide factors; importance of met expectations	Partial
Pettman (1973, 1975)	Test of March and Simon model	Modest support for model based on review of literature	Yes

(Continued)

EXHIBIT 1 (CONTINUED)
SUMMARY OF EMPIRICAL REVIEWS OF TURNOVER LITERATURE

Investigator(s)	Focus	Major findings	Formal model presented
Price (1977)	Comprehensive review	Turnover influenced by dissatisfaction plus opportunity to leave; also considers organizational outcomes of turnover	Yes
Forrest et al. (1977)	Effort to integrate psychological and economic influences on turnover	Based on Vroom model, both psychological and economic factors shown to influence turnover	Yes
Mobley (1977; Mobley et al., 1979)	Comprehensive review	Model of intermediate linkages between satisfaction and actual turnover presented (1977); review of literature (1979) supports expanded version of model	Yes
Muchinsky and Tuttle (1979)	Comprehensive review	Major influences on turnover can be found in attitudes, person, work, and biographical sheets; support for met expectations proposition	No

1 Many current models ignore the role of available information about one's job or prospective job in an individual's participation decision. Recent research on realistic job previews clearly demonstrates how prior knowledge concerning the actual job environment can ultimately affect turnover (Wanous, 1977).

2 The extent to which an individual's expectations and values surrounding a job are met by one's organizational experiences have also been shown to be an important factor in turnover (Porter and Steers, 1973; Muchinsky and Tuttle, 1979). These factors have likewise received scant attention in comprehensive models of employee turnover.

3 The role of job performance level as a factor influencing desire or intent to leave has also been overlooked. High job performance may heighten one's expectations concerning organizational rewards, while poor performance may cause lower attitudes concerning the intrinsic worth of the job. In both cases, performance must be recognized in the turnover process (Marsh and Manari, 1977).

4 Most models of turnover focus exclusively on one job attitude (namely, job satisfaction) and ignore other attitudes (like organizational commitment) that may also be relevant. In view of recent studies indicating that commitment (rather than satisfaction) represents a better predictor of turnover (Porter, Steers, Mowday, and Boulian, 1974; Mowday, Steers, and Porter, 1979), this omission appears serious.

5 Current models ignore a host of nonwork influences on staying or leaving. When one's spouse is transferred—or when one's spouse cannot transfer—the employee's mobility is affected.

6 Current models assume that once an employee has become dissatisfied, the wheels are set in motion for eventual termination. This assumption ignores the fact that the employee may be able to change his or her current work situation (perhaps through bargaining with the supervisor, threats to quit, etc.). Ironically, March and Simon (1958) did point to this factor over two decades ago, but most subsequent efforts have dropped it from consideration.

7 It would be useful if models of employee turnover would clarify the role of available alternative job opportunities, both in terms of which factors influence such availability and in terms of the consequences for employees of having no alternatives.

8 Current models of turnover assume a one-way flow process and ignore important feedback loops that serve to enhance or ameliorate one's desire to leave.

9 Very little thought has been given to how people accommodate the participation decision. What happens to those who want to leave but cannot or to those who choose to stay when their friends and associates are leaving? Alternatively, how do people adjust psychologically to the act of leaving one organization and joining a second? This accommodation process is perhaps the most fruitful area for future research on the turnover process since it has significant implications for the attitudes and behavior of both stayers and leavers.

Clearly, there is a need for more comprehensive process models of employee turnover that take such factors as these into account. Such a model is presented here in the hopes that it will stimulate more comprehensive, multivariate efforts to study employee turnover and its outcomes. The model is largely inductive in nature and has been developed from the existing literature on the topic.

A MODEL OF EMPLOYEE TURNOVER

We shall build upon earlier theoretical and empirical work and propose a largely cognitive model of employee turnover that focuses on the processes leading up to the decision to participate or withdraw. This model is meant to summarize and integrate earlier work and to extend such efforts by incorporating the points mentioned above. The model is schematically represented in Exhibit 2. It will provide a basis for the subsequent discussion on accommodation of the participation decision. In order to clarify the dynamics of the model, it will be described in three sequential parts: (1) job expectations and job attitudes; (2) job attitudes and intent to leave; and (3) intent to leave, available alternatives, and actual turnover. Relevant research will be cited as we proceed.

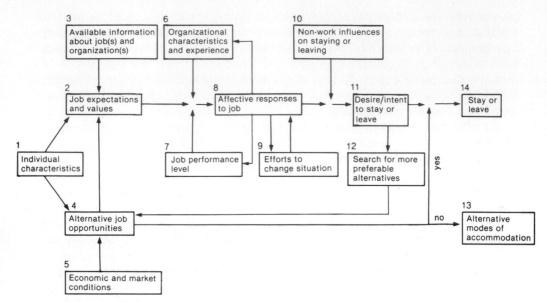

EXHIBIT 2
A model of voluntary employee turnover.

Job Expectations and Job Attitudes

Job Expectations and Values   A model of employee turnover could start in many places. We could begin with the nature of the job or work environment, the job market and economic factors, and so forth. We chose to begin with the individual and his or her expectations and values since it is the individual who must ultimately decide whether to stay or leave. All individuals have expectations upon entering a new organization. These expectations may involve beliefs about the nature of the job, the rewards for satisfactory performance, the availability of interpersonal contacts and interactions, and so forth. It would be expected that each employee would have a somewhat different set of expectations depending upon his or her own values and needs at the time.

These expectations (shown in box 2 of Exhibit 2) are believed to be influenced by three categories of variables: (1) individual characteristics; (2) available information about job and organization; and (3) alternative job opportunities. Several individual characteristics (see box 1) can influence job expectations and ultimately turnover. These include one's occupation, education, age, tenure, family responsibilities, family income level, personal work ethic, previous work experiences, and personality (Federico *et al.,* 1976; Mangione, 1973; Mobley *et al.,* 1978; Waters *et al.,* 1976; Porter and Steers, 1973; Hines, 1973; Mowday *et al.,* 1978). As a result of such factors, people determine consciously or unconsciously what they expect from a job; what they feel they must have, what they would like to have, and what they can do without.

A second influence on the determination of job expectations is the available information about the job and organization both at the time of organizational choice and during reappraisal periods throughout one's career (box 3). The basic argument here follows from the literature on "realistic job previews" (Wanous, 1977). It has been fairly consistently found that when people are provided with more complete or more accurate information about prospective jobs, they are able to make more informed choices and, as a result, are more likely to develop realistic job expectations that are more easily met by the organization. Modest support for the ultimate impact of unmet expectations on turnover can be found in studies reviewed by Porter and Steers (1973), Wanous (1977), Muchinsky and Tuttle (1979), and Mobley *et al.* (1979).

Such information about one's job or organization can also be important later in one's career. That is, if an accountant, for example, joins one of the major CPA firms in the hopes of eventually becoming a partner but later learns that the probability of attaining such status is minimal, the accountant may change his or her expectations and may decide to set off on a different course (e.g., corporate accounting).

A third influence on job expectations is the extent to which an individual has alternative job opportunities (box 4). Simply put, the greater the number of attractive job alternatives, the more demanding an individual may be when evaluating his or her current job or job offer. Pfeffer and Lawler (1979) found availability of alternative jobs was negatively related to job attitudes among a large sample of university faculty. However, Mowday and McDade (1979) found that the mere availability of alternative jobs was a less important influence on job attitudes than the relative attractiveness of the alternatives. In addition, they found that the influence of attractive alternative jobs on attitudes changed over time. In a longitudinal analysis, attractiveness of alternative jobs was negatively related to organizational commitment on the first morning a new employee reported for work. After one month on the job, however, attractiveness of alternative job offers the individual did not take advantage of was positively related to organizational commitment. Hence, on the first day at work, information about alternative jobs may be very salient since information about the chosen job is limited. After a period of time at work, however, the individual must justify his or her choice of the job and this may result in more positive attitudes for those who have given up an opportunity to take a relatively attractive alternative job.

Given the salience of alternative jobs during the early employment period, it is not surprising to discover that expectation levels of employees are quite high at the point of organizational entry (Porter and Steers, 1973). Once in a given job for a period of time, however, expectations tend to become more realistic as one develops greater behavioral commitments that make it less attractive to go elsewhere (Salancik, 1977). (We shall say more about the role of alternative job opportunities shortly.)

Affective Responses to Job   The next link in our proposed model relates job expectations and values to subsequent job attitudes (box 8). Following the literature on job attitudes, it is proposed that affective responses (including job satisfaction, organizational commitment, and job involvement) result from the interactions of three factors: (1) job expectations (2) organizational characteristics and experiences; and (3) job performance level. (A discussion of the relative impact of the various affective responses on turnover goes beyond the scope of this paper—see Hom *et al.,* 1979; Cooper and Payne, 1978; Porter *et al.,* 1974).

The major thrust of the argument here deals with the interaction between job expectations (box 2) and organizational characteristics and experiences (box 6). Again, following from the literature on realistic job previews (Wanous, 1977), the more one's experiences in the organization are congruent with what one expects, the greater the propensity that an individual would be satisfied and would wish to remain with the organization (Muchinsky and Tuttle, 1979; Porter and Steers, 1973; Vroom, 1964). Such experiences have also been shown to be related to organizational commitment (Buchanan, 1974; Steers, 1977).

It should be noted here that the impact of expectations on subsequent job attitudes is a point open to dispute. Locke (1976) has argued that when expectations are not met, the reaction by individuals is surprise, not dissatisfaction. Instead, he argues that it is the extent to which valued attributes (instead of expected attributes) are present in a job that influences satisfaction. Although values and expectations are conceptually distinct, available evidence suggests that they are highly related in practice. [Bray, Campbell, and Grant (1974) found the two to be correlated at $r = .87$]. Perhaps employees develop higher expectations about those aspects of the job that are most highly valued and, hence, both concepts may be related to subsequent attitudes (see also Ilgen and Dugoni, 1977).

Other aspects of organizational life that could influence the extent to which one's expectations are met include the organization's pay and promotion policies, one's actual job duties, coworker relations, work group size, supervisory style, organization structure and opportunities for participation in decision making, geographic location, and organizational goals and values (Marsh and Manari, 1977; Ilgen and Dugoni, 1977; Dansereau *et al.,* 1974; Koch and Steers, 1978; Waters *et al.,* 1976; Krackhardt, McKenna, Porter, and Steers, 1978). Variables such as these, when taken together, constitute a form of experienced organizational reality that signal the individual as to whether his or her expectations are being (or are likely to be) met.

In addition, recent research suggests that job performance level (box 7) may also influence job attitudes and ultimate turnover. Poor performance has been shown to lead to poor attitudes about the job, possibly in an attempt to rationalize the poor performance ("This is a crummy job anyway."). Poor performance has also been shown to lead to increased anxiety and frustration (Cooper and Payne, 1978). Finally, two recent studies have shown that poor job performance represented an important influence on voluntary turnover (Marsh and Manari, 1977; Wanous, Stumpf, and Bedrosian, 1978).

The resulting job attitudes, in turn, influence several other aspects of behavior. First, attitudes can feed back and influence both organizational experiences (box 6) and job performance (box 7), as shown in Exhibit 2 (see, for example, Forrest *et al.,* 1977). Poor job attitudes often color an employee's perceptions of organizational actions (e.g., promotion decisions, pay raises, supervisory behavior). Support for this position can be found in the recent attribution theory literature (Salancik and Pfeffer, 1978) and in studies of selective exposure to information (Janis and Mann, 1977).

Poor attitudes may in fact lead supervisors to take certain (punitive) actions which, in turn, lead to further reduced job attitudes. Likewise, negative affective responses to one's level of job performance can lead to further reductions in performance level (a "who cares?" attitude). This degenerative, self-reinforcing cycle can significantly enhance an employee's desire and interest to leave.

In addition, poor job attitudes may cause individuals to engage in efforts to change the situation (box 9). It is logical to assume that before actually deciding to leave, an individual would in many cases attempt to change or eliminate those aspects of the work situation that are compelling the individual to leave. Such efforts may take the form of attempted intraorganizational transfer (March and Simon, 1958) or, alternatively, attempts to act on the work environment. Efforts to change the situation by acting on the environment can include attempts to restructure one's job or job responsibilities, changing the payoffs for continued participation, unionization efforts, threatening to leave, or forcing someone else to leave. Through mechanisms such as these, the work environment hopefully becomes more tolerable, thereby improving one's job attitudes and desire to stay. On the other hand, where an employee finds it impossible to alter the situation, poor job attitudes would be expected to remain the same (or possibly decrease), thereby strengthening one's resolve to leave. The potential effects of efforts to change the situation (whether successful or unsuccessful) on intent to leave and actual turnover represents a major area in need of serious study.

Job Attitudes and Intent to Leave

The second phase of the model focuses on the linkage between one's job attitudes and one's desire and intent to stay or leave. In brief, it is suggested that desire/intent to leave is influenced by: (1) affective responses to job; and (2) nonwork influences on staying or leaving.

Following from the work of Fishbein (1967) and others on attitude theory, it is assumed that one's affective responses to the job lead to behavioral intentions. In the case of employee turnover, we would expect reduced levels of job satisfaction and organizational commitment (box 8) to result in an increased desire or intent to leave (box 11; Mobley, 1977; Price, 1977; Steers, 1977; Koch and Steers, 1978). Such an assertion is common throughout the literature on turnover.

What is often overlooked in determining desire/intent to leave, however, is a constellation of nonwork influences on staying or leaving (box 10). There are many instances in which one may not like a particular job but still does not desire or seek termination. Such instances include situations where (1) an individual tolerates an unpleasant job (e.g., an apprenticeship) because of its instrumentality for future career considerations (e.g., a master craftsman); (2) a spouse is limited geographically to a certain region and alternative employment is scarce; (3) an individual's central life interests lie outside of work; and (4) family considerations (Dubin, Champoux, and Porter, 1975; Porter and Steers, 1973; Schneider and Dachler, 1978).

In fact, following a review of relevant work, Sussman and Cogswell (1971, p. 485) suggested that "there is a direct relationship between the supply and demand of workers in any occupational system and the consideration of noneconomic factors in job movement; the greater the demand for workers in any occupational system the greater is the consideration given to familial concerns such as work aspirations of spouses, special needs of children, community activities, linkages with kin, friends, and voluntary associations; physical and social environments." Included here too would be Fishbein's (1967) notation of subjective normative beliefs, or how those around an individual would feel about his or her leaving. These nonwork factors are often overlooked in turnover research but may, in fact, explain a greater proportion of the turnover variance than job attitudes.

Parenthetically, it should be noted here that in our proposed model, we have combined desire and intent to leave. This has been done for the sake of parsimony and because we wished to focus our attention on the processes leading up to one's behavioral intentions. It was felt that these early influences were perhaps the least understood segment of the participation decision. It should be noted that more elaborate distinctions between desire to leave and intent to leave are presented by Mobley (1977; Mobley, Horner, and Hollingsworth, 1978) and Fishbein (1967). Fishbein introduces the term "attitude toward the act," which is similar to our use of "desire to leave." Fishbein and others (e.g., Horn et al., 1979) argue that an individual's feelings toward the act of quitting (desires) represent a more immediate determinant of intent to leave than feelings about the job.

Intent to Leave, Available Alternatives, and Turnover

Finally, the third segment of the proposed model focuses on the link between behavioral intent to leave and actual turnover. Following from the earlier work of March and Simon (1958), it is argued that employee turnover is ultimately determined by a combination of behavioral intent to leave (box 11) and the availability of alternative job opportunities (box 4). Although research support for this contention is mixed, much of the discrepancy appears to result more from inadequate methodology than from any repudiation of the basic hypothesis (Pettman, 1973; Schwab and Dyer, 1974; Schneider, 1976; Dansereau, Cashman, and Graen, 1974).

Intent to leave apparently influences actual turnover in at least two ways. First, it may lead fairly directly to turnover (Muchinsky and Tuttle, 1979). Some people decide to leave their jobs even when alternative jobs are not available. Recent changes in the social welfare system aimed at providing unemployed people with minimal support levels may serve to enhance this direct relationship by providing an economic cushion to leavers.

Intent to leave may further influence actual turnover in an indirect fashion by causing the individual to initiate search behavior for more preferable alternative jobs (box 12). Research suggests that less satisfied people are more likely to be sensitive to job market changes (March and Simon, 1958). Such search behavior serves to open up to an individual a greater number of job possibilities, thereby increasing the likelihood of leaving.

In addition, however, alternative job opportunities (box 4) are also influenced by individual characteristics (box 1) and economic and market conditions (box 5). Individual characteristics such as age, sex, and occupation often constrain one's opportunities for jobs (Porter and Steers, 1973). Moreover, economic and market conditions also influence the availability of jobs (Forrest, Cummings, and Johnson, 1977).

If an individual has no (or few) alternative job opportunities, he or she would be less likely to leave the organization. Instead, however, the individual may engage in alternative forms of withdrawal or accommodation in order to reduce the anxiety or frustration that results from not being able to leave (box 13). These alternatives may include absenteeism, drug abuse or alcoholism, sabotage, slowdowns, and so forth. Or, alternatively, they may take the form of rationalizing why it is in one's best interest to remain after all, as we shall see in the next section. In any case, where an individual wishes to leave but is unable to do so, some form of accommodation process can be expected. Where the individual wishes to leave and is able to do so, the probability of actual turnover (box 14) is markedly increased (Dansereau et al., 1974; Mobley et al., 1978; Woodward, 1976).

With regard to the availability of alternative job opportunities, we can see a further feedback loop in operation. Specifically, when an employee is presented with a new and attractive alternative position, perhaps because of changes in market conditions, his or her expectations on the current job are likely to be increased, making it more difficult for the organization to meet these expectations. As a result, job attitudes may suffer which cause heightened desire and intent to leave. This, in turn, sensitizes the individual to the possibility of changing jobs. Again, this self-reinforcing cycle can ultimately hasten the decision to leave.

Relationship to Earlier Methods

As noted above, the model suggested here attempts to summarize and integrate much of the earlier theorizing on the topic of employee turnover. Even so, while many aspects of the model have appeared earlier, other aspects are somewhat unique.

To begin with, the role of available information about the prospective job and organization is explicitly recognized (box 3). Second, job performance level as a factor in affective responses to the job is also noted (box 7). Third, like Mobley et al.'s (1979) model, but unlike others, several attitudes (not simply job satisfaction) are considered as they related to turnover (box 8). Fourth, major emphasis is placed on a series of nonwork factors that have been shown to influence desire to leave and/or actual termination (box 10). Fifth, recognition is also given to the fact that when an employee is dissatisfied he or she may engage in attempts to change the situation or work environment prior to deciding upon termination (box 9). Finally, special emphasis is given to the accommodation processes used by individuals who leave a positive situation or remain in a negative one (box 13), as well as those used by individuals left behind when someone else leaves.

REFERENCES

Bray, D. W., Campbell, R. J., & Grant, D. L. *Formative years in business.* New York: Wiley-Interscience, 1974.

Brayfield, A. H., & Crockett, W. H. Employee attitudes and employee performance. *Psychological Bulletin,* 1955, **52**, 396–424.

Buchanan, B. Building organizational commitment: The socialization of managers in work organizations. *Administrative Science Quarterly,* 1974, **19**, 533–546.

Cooper, C., & Payne, R. *Stress at work,* London: Wiley, 1978.

Dansereau, F., Cashman, J., & Graen, G. Expectancy as a moderator of the relationship between job attitudes and turnover. *Journal of Applied Psychology,* 1974, **59**, 228–229.

Dubin, R., Champoux, J. E., & Porter, L. W. Central life interests and organizational commitment of blue-collar and clerical workers. *Administrative Science Quarterly,* 1975, **20**, 411–421.

Federico, J. M., Federico, P., & Lundquist, G. W. Predicting women's turnover as a function of extent of met salary expectations and biodemographic data. *Personnel Psychology,* 1976, **29**, 559–566.

Fishbein, M. Attitude and the prediction of behavior. In M. Fishbein (Ed.), *Readings in attitude theory and measurement.* New York: Wiley, 1967.

Forrest, C. R., Cummings, L. L., & Johnson, A. C. Organizational participation: A critique and model. *Academy of Management Review,* 1977, **2**, 586–601.

Herzberg, F., Mausner, B., Peterson, R. O., & Capwell, R. *Job attitudes: Review of research and opinions.* Pittsburgh: Pittsburgh Psychological Services, 1957.

Hines, G. H. Achievement motivation, occupations, and labor turnover in New Zealand. *Journal of Applied Psychology,* 1973, **58**, 313–317.

Hom, P. W., Katerberg, R., & Hulin, C. L. Comparative examination of three approaches to the prediction of turnover. *Journal of Applied Psychology,* 1979, **64**, 280–290.

Ilgen, D., & Dugoni, I. Initial orientation to the organization: Its impact on psychological processes associated with the adjustment of new employees. Paper presented at the National Meeting of the Academy of Management, Kissimee, Florida, 1977.

Janis, I. L., & Mann, L. *Decision making.* New York: Free Press, 1977.

Koch, J. L., & Steers, R. M. Job attachment, satisfaction, and turnover among public employees. *Journal of Vocational Behavior,* 1978, **12**, 119–128.

Krackhardt, D., McKenna, J., Porter, L. W., & Steers, R. M. Goal-setting supervisory behavior and employee turnover: A field experiment. Technical Report No. 17, Graduate School of Management, University of Oregon, 1978.

Lefkowitz, J. Personnel turnover. *Progress in Clinical Psychology,* 1971, 69–90.

Locke, E. A. The nature and consequences of job satisfaction. In M. D. Dunnette (Ed.), *Handbook of industrial and organizational psychology.* Chicago: Rand McNally, 1976.

Mangione, T. W. Turnover: Some psychological and demographic correlates. In R. P. Quinn & T. W. Mangione (Eds.), *The 1969-1970 survey of working conditions.* Ann Arbor: University of Michigan, Survey Research Center, 1973.

March, J. G., & Simon, H. A. *Organizations.* New York: Wiley, 1958.

Marsh, R., & Manari, H. Organizational commitment and turnover: A predictive study. *Administrative Science Quarterly,* 1977, **22**, 57–75.

Mobley, W. H. Intermediate linkages in the relationship between job satisfaction and employee turnover. *Journal of Applied Psychology,* 1977, **62**, 237–240.

Mobley, W. H., Griffeth, R. W., Hand, H. H., & Mezlino, B. M. Review and conceptual analysis of the employee turnover process. *Psychological Bulletin,* 1979, **86**, 493–522.

Mobley, W. H., Horner, S. O., & Hollingsworth, A. T. An evaluation of precursors of hospital employee turnover. *Journal of Applied Psychology,* 1978, **63,** 408–414.

Mowday, R. T., & McDade, T. W. Linking behavioral and attitudinal commitment: A longitudinal analysis of job choice and job attitudes. Paper presented at the Annual Meeting of the Academy of Management, Atlanta, 1979.

Mowday, R. T., Porter, L. W., & Stone, E. F. Employee characteristics as predictors of turnover among female clerical employees in two organizations. *Journal of Vocational Behavior,* 1978, **12,** 321–332.

Mowday, R. T., Steers, R. M., & Porter, L. W. The measurement of organizational commitment. *Journal of Vocational Behavior,* 1979, **14,** 224–247.

Muchinsky, P. M. & Tuttle, M. L. Employee turnover: An empirical and methodological assessment. *Journal of Vocational Behavior,* 1979, **14,** 43–77.

Pettman, B. O. Some factors influencing labour turnover: A review of the literature. *Industrial Relations Journal,* 1973, **4,** 43–61.

Pfeffer, J., & Lawler, J. The effects of job alternative, extrinsic rewards, and commitment on satisfaction with the organization: A field example of the insufficient justification paradigm. Unpublished manuscript. School of Business Administration, University of California, Berkeley, 1979.

Porter, L. W., & Steers, R. M. Organizational, work, and personal factors in employee turnover and absenteeism. *Psychological Bulletin,* 1973, **80,** 151–176.

Porter, L. W., Steers, R. M., Mowday, R. T., & Boulian, P. V. Organizational commitment, job satisfaction, and turnover among psychiatric technicians. *Journal of Applied Psychology,* 1974, **59,** 603–609.

Price, J. I. *The study of turnover.* Ames, Iowa State University Press, 1977.

Salancik, G. R. Commitment and control of organizational behavior. In B. M. Staw and G. R. Salancik (Eds.), *New directions in organizational behavior.* Chicago: St. Clair Press, 1977.

Salancik, G., & Pfeffer, J. A social information processing approach to job attitudes and task design. *Administrative Science Quarterly,* 1978, **23,** 224–253.

Schneider, B., & Dachler, H. P. Work, family and career considerations in understanding employee turnover intentions. Technical Report No. 19, Department of Psychology, University of Maryland, 1978.

Schneider, J. The "greener grass" phenomenon: Differential effects of a work context alternative on organizational participation and withdrawal intentions. *Organizational Behavior and Human Performance,* 1976, **116,** 303–333.

Schuh, A. J. The predictability of employee tenure: A review of the literature. *Personnel Psychology,* 1967, **20,** 133–152.

Schwab, D. P., & Dyer, L. D. Turnover as a function of perceived ease and desirability: A largely unsuccessful test of the March and Simon participation model. Paper presented at the Annual Meeting of the Academy of Management, Seattle, 1974.

Steers, R. M. Antecedents and outcomes of organizational commitment. *Administrative Science Quarterly,* 1977, **22,** 46–56.

Stoikov, V., & Raimon, R. L. Determinants of differences in the quit rate among industries. *American Economic Review,* 1968, **58,** 1283–1298.

Sussman, M. B., & Cogswell, B. E. Family influences on job movement. *Human Relations,* 1971, **24,** 477–487.

Vroom, V. H. *Work and motivation.* New York: Wiley, 1964.

Wanous, J. P. Organizational entry: Newcomers moving from outside to inside. *Psychological Bulletin,* 1977, **84,** 601–618.

Wanous, J. P., Stumpf, S. A., & Bedrosian, H. Job survival of new employees. Unpublished paper, New York University, 1978.

Waters, I. K., Roach, D., & Waters, C. W. Estimate of future tenure, satisfaction, and biographical variables as predictors of termination. *Personnel Psychology,* 1976, **29,** 57–60.

Woodward, N. The economic causes of labour turnover: A case study. *Industrial Relations Journal,* 1975–1976, **6,** 19–32.

QUESTIONS FOR DISCUSSION

1 What managerial implications follow from the Steers and Rhodes model of employee absenteeism?

2 Combining the materials from the two articles on absence behavior, how would you design a work environment aimed at minimizing voluntary absenteeism?

3 Absenteeism in several Asian countries (such as Japan) is substantially lower than that in most western countries (including those in North America and Europe). What factors explain these differences?

4 Using Mobley's model of the individual's decision to leave an organization, how would you as a manager determine a subordinate's intent to leave? How would you increase the likelihood that individuals who have considered leaving will end up staying?

5 If you as a manager had a high rate of turnover among your employees, how would you determine the cause of this high turnover?

6 Considering the biases and moderators affecting the attribution process, what cautions would you give a manager who is attempting to decide why a particular subordinate left the organization?

7 What are the underlying assumptions of the theory of cognitive dissonance? Is a cognitive dissonance theory a need theory of motivation? Explain.

8 Steers and Mowday provide information on the possible attitudinal and behavioral consequences of decisions to participate. How could you use this information to make more effective personal career choices?

CHAPTER 9

MANAGING
MARGINAL PERFORMANCE

Earlier in the book, we focused on the use of rewards or positive reinforcement in organizations. The present chapter deals with the use of punishment and sanctions associated with managing marginal employees. Thus, in this chapter we are dealing with the issue of how organizations attempt to motivate individuals to stop engaging in a particular type of behavior that is not desired by the organization and to replace that behavior with a more desired type of behavior. Historically, punishment (e.g., sanctions and disciplinary measures) is a topic that has been relatively ignored in the organizational behavior literature, but it is a fairly common occurrence in organizational settings. Therefore, it is an important topic to consider in an overall perspective on motivation at work.

The reasons the use of punishment and sanctions in organizations has not received extensive attention by organizational scholars and researchers are reviewed in the article by Arvey and Ivancevich. Primarily, these reasons revolve around the fact that utilization of aversive stimuli is often unpleasant for the organization and for individuals in the organization, managers and supervisors as well as employees. In addition, the effects of this use are frequently difficult to ascertain. Typically, it is far easier for both organizational scholars and managers to talk about how the use of positive reinforcement can direct individuals toward certain types of desired behavior than it is to show how the use of punishment or sanctions will have the same intended effect. It is reasonably clear that such aversive stimuli often can succeed in preventing undesired behavior, but what is not clear is what behavior will replace that which has been stopped. Frequently, what is produced is a number of possible undesired or unintended consequences, such as more clever attempts on the part of the individual who has received punishment to avoid detection of negative behavior in the future. Also, it is possible that the individual on the receiving end may subsequently engage in other types of undesired behavior such as eventual retaliation against the person administering the sanctions. While all of these and other possible complications can occur when punishment is used, it is nevertheless a category of behavior which does occur in organizations and which is strongly linked to a number of motivational issues. In short, the use of sanctions and disciplinary measures is often necessary in organizations, but the major problem is that their use may not result in the motivation of the organizationally deemed "correct" behavior.

TYPES OF BEHAVIOR SUBJECT TO THE USE OF SANCTIONS

As can be seen in Exhibit 1, it is useful to look at the different types of behavior that are subject to punishment and sanctions in organizations. We can think in terms of two dimensions of behavior. One dimension is whether the behavior is a short-term or acute type of incident or a long-term or chronic type of conduct. The other dimension is whether the behavior is in the realm of personal conduct or whether it involves direct job performance. The motivational context might be quite different for one combination versus another. For example, a short-term acute incident of personal conduct is different from, say, consistent, long-term, relatively low-quality or marginal performance. In the former case, there may have been special circumstances that would be unlikely to occur again, and hence the supervisor or organization would be faced with the issue of taking action with respect to some behavior which could not be ignored yet which might not be expected to recur. In the latter case, the situation may involve a consistent level of job performance which is not so unacceptably low that it clearly calls for dismissal from the organization, but which is at the margin of acceptable performance and therefore may involve some persistent motivational factors. Clearly, the response of the organization would probably vary considerably depending on which combination of circumstances had occurred.

Of course, it must also be pointed out that incidents or examples of personal conduct can in fact interact with job performance, but there is no necessarily direct link. For example, consistent tardiness, a type of personal conduct, could clearly be a factor in producing a regular low level of job performance. However, as we have indicated, there is no necessarily direct connection between the two types of behavior. That is, an employee could be tardy on a fairly consistent basis and yet produce at an extremely high level of job performance. Thus, the

EXHIBIT 1
TYPES OF EMPLOYEE BEHAVIOR SUBJECT TO PUNISHMENT AND SANCTIONS

	Short-term behavior (acute incident)	Long-term behavior (chronic)
Personal conduct/behavior	Example: Intoxicated at work	Example: Consistent tardiness
Job performance (quality & quantity)	Example: Failure to meet specific deadline	Example: Consistent low-quality performance

organization would be faced with the problem of whether to take action in response to the tardiness, even though the performance was excellent.

Just as there can be interaction (though no necessary link) between personal conduct and job performance, there also can be relationships between short-term behavior and long-term behavior. In any particular short-term or potentially one-time incident, the organization would need to make decisions about whether such behavior is likely to occur again. If the acute incident is ignored, the problem may occur again. If it did, more severe sanctions would therefore be necessary than if the problem were being dealt with for the first time. On the other hand, an acute incident dealt with in an overly severe manner might have side effects on a person's behavior. Such punishment and its side effects might not be necessary because, in fact, the incident may have been only a one-time occurrence. These are only some of the issues that are faced by organizations and supervisors in attempting to relate aspects of behavior to particular types and degrees of punishment and sanctions.

TYPES OF SANCTIONS

As is pointed out in the opening article in this chapter, there are two basic types of sanctions that organizations can employ. The first type is providing an aversive stimulus, that is, supplying something to the individual that is negative from that person's perspective. Applications of aversive stimuli, as O'Reilly and Weitz observe in the final article in this chapter, involve a range of possible actions: informal sanctions such as an oral warning, formal sanctions that involve written actions that are inserted into an employee's records, and, finally, the ultimate sanction of dismissal from the organization. The other major type of punishment or sanction is the removal of positive stimuli. Typical examples would involve the removal or reduction of particular perquisites or privileges that a person has previously received. Another example of this type of sanction would be a change of job assignment or job location from a more interesting or attractive job or location to a less attractive one. Either type of punishment—the provision of aversive stimuli or the removal of rewards—potentially can be effective in stopping or inhibiting a particular type of conduct or level of performance. However, as discussed earlier, the correct or desired behavior may not necessarily replace the punished behavior. The article by Arvey and Ivancevich discusses a set of variables, such as the timing and intensity of the sanction, that governs the potential effectiveness of punishment for producing desired consequences. Obviously, there are a number of factors that any organization or supervisor needs to consider in attempting to determine what sanctions to employ and when to employ them.

DECISIONS IN THE USE OF SANCTIONS

In the use of punishment in organizations, the supervisor faces a number of decisions. First, does the behavior of the subordinate or other individual warrant recognition? That is, is it severe enough or important enough that the supervisor should take note that it has occurred? Second, the supervisor is faced with attempting to determine the cause of the behavior. The supervisor needs to determine whether the cause of the individual's behavior was something that the person could have prevented, or whether it was due to external circumstances largely beyond the person's control. This is the problem of making the correct attribution for the behavior. If the behavior is attributed to something that could have been prevented by the subordinate, then the supervisor is likely to take some corrective action. However, if the supervisor makes an attribution to causes beyond the person's control, then ordinarily some action other than punishment or sanctions would be called for. The crucial problem facing the supervisor is obviously to make the correct attribution. A third decision facing the supervisor is determining the action that should be taken. That is, he or she has to consider the type of action to be taken (e.g., whether it should be a warning or a penalty), how severe or intense the action should be, when it should be scheduled, and other questions regarding the nature of the action to be taken. A fourth problem concerns what expectation the supervisor should create regarding the individual's future behavior. In other words, what standards of future behavior should be set forth by the supervisor?

Still another issue faced by the supervisor is anticipating the likely effects of the use of sanctions. Is it expected that there will be a change in performance? In attitude toward the job? In attitude toward the supervisor? Furthermore, what will be the impact not only on the employee but also on the peer group? In essence, the supervisor needs to consider the broader consequences beyond the impact on just the individual directly involved. Others in the organization may be strongly affected by the particular use of sanctions on a specific employee. The ripple effect may benefit the organization, as in instances where others think that the punishment was correct and that the organization was being effective. However, in other cases the attitudes of peers and others may be negative if the punishment is not seen as fair or justified. These extended consequences often are not considered at the time that sanctions are invoked.

In summary, it can be seen that any use of sanctions or punishment in an organization has the potential for achieving a particular desired result, that is, the prevention or elimination of a particular undesired behavior, but their use also involves a number of other considerations that may have broader consequences both for the recipient of the sanctions and for those administering them. The motivational analysis of punishment situations is not a simple matter.

OVERVIEW

The first article in this chapter, by Latham, Cummings, and Mitchell, examines what is meant by "poor performance" and why poor performance occurs. It then proposes means to correct such problems in organizations. Next, Arvey and Ivancevich review the literature on punishment. Finally, O'Reilly and Weitz examine the use of warnings and dismissals in managing marginal performance.

Behavioral Strategies to Improve Productivity

Gary P. Latham
Larry L. Cummings
Terence R. Mitchell

America is in trouble. The competitive spirit has caught on around the world, and we no longer lead in productivity gains—indeed, some people argue that we are dangerously close to being out of the game. According to statistics from the Bureau of Labor Statistics, the United States ranked sixth among seven leading industrial nations in productivity increases from 1968 to 1978. The rankings from the study appear in the box below.

Top decision-making executives are beginning to recognize the importance of using the organization's human resources to improve productivity. The many approaches to developing human resources range from improving work methods to improving quality of work life. Before selecting a particular tactic, a systematic appraisal of the causes of good and poor performance is necessary. The three stages in our proposed process for improving productivity through the utilization of human resources are: strategies for *identifying* poor performance, strategies for *deciding* what causes poor performance, and strategies for *coping* with poor performance.

IDENTIFYING POOR PERFORMANCE

How should managers go about identifying problems? How do they do so? The answers to these two questions may not be the same. Basically, an ideal approach to identifying problems can be called a rational approach. By contrast, we can describe the way managers actually do identify performance problems as a condi-

---

PRODUCTIVITY INCREASES OF THE TOP SEVEN COUNTRIES (1968–1978)

Rank	1968–1978 Productivity Increases
1. The Netherlands	93.7%
2. Japan	89.1
3. West Germany	63.8
4. France	61.8
5. Italy	60.1
6. United States	23.6
7. United Kingdom	21.6

Source: Bureau of Labor Statistics, United States Department of Labor, 1979.

Reprinted by permission of the publisher from *Organizational Dynamics*, Winter, 1981, **8**(3), 5–23.

tionally rational approach that is subject to the limitation of managers as information processors and decision makers. Emerging evidence indicates that the processes actually used by managers in identifying and formulating performance problems are not always completely rational. Hopefully, a better understanding of what managers actually do can lead to the development and implementation of strategies that will bring them closer to what they should do.

TYPICAL EVALUATION PROCEDURES

This section describes the two most prevalent criteria for evaluating performance in today's organizations—performance outcomes and personality traits. We then describe (1) the judgment processes underlying the use of rational procedures in identifying performance problems and (2) several limitations involved in using these rational processes.

Performance Outcomes

Senior-level management, stockholders, and consumers are generally concerned with performance outcomes, or results, as measures of an individual's or organization's productivity level. That is, they are concerned with such cost-related measures as profits, costs, product quantity and quality, returns on investment, and so forth. The person who scores well on these measures is presumed to be highly motivated toward performance improvement. The person who has received adequate resources (including training) to do the job, but who performs poorly on these measures, is presumed to be poorly motivated.

Performance outcomes may be an excellent gauge of an organization's health or effectiveness, but they are generally inadequate, by themselves, in measuring an individual employee's job effectiveness. Indeed, they can even be demotivating, if not destructive, for both employee and employer. Here's why:

• First, cost-related measures are often affected by factors over which an individual employee has little or no control. One individual's performance is often affected by the performance of others. It not only is unfair, but may be illegal, to distribute organizational rewards and punishments (for example, promotions, transfers, demotions, dismissals, or bonuses) on the basis of measures over which an employee has minimal control.

• Second, these measures often fall short because they omit important aspects of a person's job. When a superintendent in one district, for example, lends equipment to a superintendent in another district, profits may increase for the company while costs increase for the superintendent who lent the equipment. A superior's poor memory and an incomplete accounting system that merely "keeps score" may identify a "winner" and a "loser" rather than two team players who contributed to the company's overall profits.

• Third, these measures can encourage a results-at-all-costs mentality that can run counter to corporate ethics or policies—not to mention legal requirements.

Moreover, a results-at-all-costs mentality can run counter to the organization's overall productivity. In the above example, lending equipment hurt the lender's monthly cost sheet, but it significantly increased the organization's profits. The reverse might have been true if the lender had adhered to a "my own results at all costs" philosophy.

• Fourth, it is difficult to formulate cost-related measures for most white-collar jobs. Such measure of a log-cutter's effectiveness, for example, might be the number of trees cut divided by the number of hours worked. But what cost-related measures exist for the jobs of an engineer or a newspaper reporter?

• Finally, and most important from a performance-improvement standpoint, economic measures or performance outcomes fail to give the employee information about what he or she needs to do to maintain or increase productivity. Telling a baseball player that he just struck out, for example, will not come as a surprise to him. What the player needs to know is what he must *do* to get to first base or possibly hit a home run.

Personality Traits

For one or more of the above reasons, 90 percent of today's organizations measure an employee's effectiveness—at least at lower levels—primarily in terms of traits or distinguishing human qualities that those in the organizational hierarchy believe are desirable, not in terms of cost-related outcomes. These trait measures generally include commitment, creativity, loyalty, initiative, and the like. The problem with traits, from a productivity standpoint, is twofold. First, telling a person to "be a better listener" or to "show more initiative" may be excellent advice, but it doesn't tell the person what to do to implement this advice. Before such discussions can motivate the employee to behave appropriately, traits must be defined explicitly.

Second, trait measures are looked upon unfavorably by the courts when decisions based on them adversely impact people in a protected class. This is because, in the words of one court decision, traits are susceptible to partiality and to the personal taste, whim, or fancy of the evaluator. [*Wade v. Mississippi Cooperative Extension Service,* 372 F. Suppl. 126 (1974), 7EDP 9186].

Rationally Identifying Performance Problems

These two approaches to assessing performance represent the most popular techniques currently used in industry. Notice that both tell the subordinate very little about what he or she has done wrong and how to correct it. Also, evaluations in terms of cost or traits are far removed from what the employee actually does.

In this section we will describe some less frequently used procedures that are based on more rational models. They represent attempts to describe more specifically what the subordinate is doing incorrectly. The heart of these rational approaches is to base evaluations on comparisons. Three different types of comparison can be used to detect performance problems and establish ways to assess or identify such performance problems. The key is to discover a performance gap. The three approaches differ on what components they compare to discover the gap.

Discrepancy between Goals and Achievement

Identifying a performance problem may require comparing a goal with actual performance. For example, one could compare the number of cars sold by a salesperson in a given month with the agreed-upon goal for cars to be sold that month. When fewer are sold than planned, a performance gap exists. This approach, of course, is the one taken by performance improvement programs such as management by objectives (MBO), work planning and review, and other results-oriented management strategies. As an approach to identifying performance problems, it works best when several important conditions are present:

1 Performance goals can be defined in measurable terms.
2 The goals are not contradictory: that is, one performance goal is not attained at the expense of another (for example, increasing quantity of performance at the expense of quality).
3 The employee's performance can be measured in units identical to the way in which the goal is expressed (for example, number of cars sold versus number of cars that were supposed to be sold).

In many cases these three conditions cannot be met. For example, a salesperson being urged to develop sustained, long-term relationships with customers may actually be compensated for short-term, quarterly sales results. When performance is multidimensional, as it is in most if not all complex jobs, identifying gaps between performance goals and actual performance may lead to the identification of performance areas that are being emphasized to the detriment of other, equally important areas.

Finally, while it may be feasible to establish quantifiable goals, it may not be possible to measure an individual's performance in relation to these goals. For example, while it may be necessary to reduce scrap by 15 percent, scrap may be affected in many ways by one or more groups as well as by people within a group. Thus documenting an individual's performance on the basis of performance outcomes can prove difficult.

Comparisons among People, Units, or Organizations

Perhaps because of this difficulty, managers often compare individuals, divisions, or organizations with one another. This can be achieved without setting specific, measurable performance goals for any individual, division, or organization. Because the comparison is made on the basis of performance relative to others, those who rank lowest are identified as those who have performance problems.

However, combining different dimensions of job performance and measuring achievement on each dimension frequently poses a problem. For example, even though two managers may agree that individuals X and Y are "poor" supervisors relative to others, such comparisons are not particularly helpful in diagnosing the causes of poor performance. As we shall note later, these two managers may well attribute high or low performance to quite different causes even though they agree on the overall performance ranking. And this is unfortunate, because such attributions can be crucial in deciding what to do to sustain high performance and/or improve low performance.

Comparisons across Time

Single individuals, units, or organizations can be compared with themselves across time. This type of comparison implies that the definition of poor performance is declining performance (and increasing performance is good). As long as the same dimensions of performance are compared across time this approach avoids both problems identified earlier. Of course, performance still must be measurable in units that are meaningful and understandable to the employee in question. But managers' agreement on goals and performance ranking is not necessary with this approach.

However, this approach is susceptible to naïve application and gross myopia. Frequently, increasing performance may not indicate success or even survival (for example, when the competition is improving even more rapidly). It is also possible that decreasing performance may not be dysfunctional (for example, when an individual's performance decrement is necessary to prevent overload and possible detrimental stress). Actually, a short-term performance decline may even be necessary to ensure long-run survival and continued productivity.

In summary, each of these three approaches to identifying performance problems assumes that performance is measurable. Each assumes that some standard for assessment exists or can be derived. In the first case, the standard consists of well-defined, quantifiable goals. In the second, the standard is the performance of another individual, unit, or organization. In the third, the standard is previous performance.

However, there are problems with these procedures. A manager may have biased or inadequate information or the information processing may require technical assistance. In addition, there are human limitations to the efficient use of these procedures. We need to know what these are and how to overcome them before we can discuss the practical implications of determining and coping with the causes of poor performance.

Human Limitations

Personal characteristics of the evaluator and/or the subject may influence the diagnosis in such a way that it becomes less rational and systematic and more intuitive. The personal characteristics that might influence evaluations include these:

● First, managers are frequently willing to accept the first satisfactory identification of a performance problem rather than pursue the best possible and most accurate identification because a long pursuit may not be cost effective. A completely rational analysis may not even be humanly possible when managers are confronted with many performance symptoms and a wide array of possible causes for poor performance. Also, because the managerial world involves frequent interruptions, rapid reordering of priorities, political subtleties, and considerable time pressures, the complex comparison processes may not be feasible in day-to-day managerial situations.

• Second, goals and the assessment of performance problems are not always the impetus for managerial action. In fact, they frequently become "after the fact" rationalizations or justifications for what has already occurred. This displacement of goals and performance definitions is common when managers justify a salary increase or promotion decision (which has already been made on other than performance grounds) by appealing to selective cases of high performance that were not carefully documented or defined beforehand. In other words, goals and definitions of desirable performance are derived from observations of performance rather than being established prior to instruction, guidance, and other managerial actions aimed at producing high performance.

• Third, performance problems and performance goals and definitions are subject to varying interpretations on the basis of managers' values, beliefs, and experiences. Seldom does an organization allow a single manager with a single goal to define a problem solely from his or her perspective. Rather, managers with varying and possibly conflicting values and objectives use political, bargaining, and negotiating skills to evolve performance definitions. With these forces set in motion, the analytical, systematic, and logical processes of comparison required by the three rational perspectives become less feasible. At a minimum, the realities of multiple parties with multiple objectives result in more diffuse and less certain definitions of performance and performance problems.

• Fourth, performance goals and problems are not static, frozen, or rigid; they tend to shift, to be unstable and dynamic. In growing organizations, particularly at the top, expected performance dimensions shift over time, occasionally in unpredictable ways. This instability and dynamism mean that rational approaches would require continuous comparisons that adjust for changing environmental inputs. Such a requirement is clearly unfeasible and unrealistically costly. To fixate on single, static performance measures can embed a manager in a quagmire of rigidity and frozen action. In order to maintain needed flexibility, wise managers usually resist complete rationality and thorough systematization.

When we combine these all-too-human characteristics, an effective manager seems to be a person who is flexible, dynamic, possessed of limited information-processing capacity, and willing to compromise and bargain—but who, most of all, is subject to major constraints in identifying performance gaps and establishing performance goals. Does this mean that careful analysis of performance problems is impossible? That systematic approaches to enhancing performance are impossible? That meaningful goals cannot be set? That there is little to help managers correct performance deficiencies? Clearly, the answer to these questions is an emphatic "no!" It is equally clear, however, that if normative, purely rational comparative perspectives on identifying performance problems are to be helpful, we must understand and account for the underlying realities of decision making on performance problems.

Thus we now move to a discussion of several new findings about how managers go about the difficult and complex task of deciding what causes a performance problem once it has been identified. The point is, of course, to do something about it—a move that logically arises from assumptions about its presumed cause. However, causes and assumptions about causes are not obvious in the world of performance appraisal.

DECISIONS ON CAUSES OF POOR PERFORMANCE

What happens when a manager or supervisor observes or is informed about a subordinate's poor performance? That is, given the manager's knowledge of the problem, how does he or she proceed to remedy it?

Until recently, the literature on this question has been rather sparse and tends to be descriptive or based on personal experience. There seems to be agreement that certain violations merit an immediate punitive response. For example, theft, falsification of records, fighting with the supervisor, or flagrant insubordination usually result in severe reprimands, probation, and/or termination. This kind of response is often dictated by company policy, leaving the supervisor very little discretion about how to respond.

However, most cases of performance deficiencies are not so clear-cut. What usually happens is that a subordinate misses a deadline, is tardy or absent occasionally, won't work overtime when needed, engages in horseplay, does sloppy work, or commits some other, less extreme violation of expected behavior. The supervisor or manager's task is more complex in these situations because there are few clear prescriptions or rules on how to proceed.

When there's no clear policy, the supervisor probably first tries to determine why the behavior occurred—soliciting information from a variety of sources, including the person involved. Then the information must be processed, sorted, and evaluated, and eventually some cause or causes ascribed. The poor performance might, for example, be attributed to a low skill level, a lack of motivation, poor instruction, or insufficient support services.

After the cause is determined, the supervisor usually selects some course of action aimed at the perceived cause. If, for example, the subordinate's poor performance is perceived to stem from low motivation, the supervisor might resort to the formal discipline procedure or orally reprimand the employee. If, on the other hand, the reason is seen as insufficient information or support, the supervisor might institute changes in the work setting; if low-level ability is seen as the cause, training might be instituted.

Two key points about this process need to be highlighted. First, it is a two-stage process encompassing a diagnostic phase in which the supervisor determines the cause of poor performance and a decision phase in which a response is selected from a set of alternatives. Second, we must recognize that the process entails active information processing by the supervisor. Therefore, simply having good performance appraisal instruments or prescribed disciplinary procedures is not enough. To understand what is happening and how poor performance can be handled more effectively, we must understand this evaluation process more fully.

A Model for Diagnosing and Responding to Poor Performance

We have designed a model to represent the two-stage process described above. The foundation for its development comes from a variety of sources and more detailed discussions can be found elsewhere. However, we must emphasize that the assumptions and hypotheses built into the model were largely generated by social psychological research on attribution theory rather than from literature on industrial discipline or performance appraisal. A brief review of attribution theory and its relevance to performance appraisal issues will contribute to a better understanding of the following material.

Attribution theory is essentially a theory about people's naïve assumptions about the causes of their own and others' behavior. All of us try to figure out why we did things and/or why other people did what they did. The process of determining the causes of behavior is called an attribution process—we attribute our behavior or other people's behavior to various causes. Engaging in this process gives order and understanding to our prediction of our own and others' actions.

The contributions of attribution theory to the problem of performance evaluation are threefold. First, research on the attributional process has shown that people are fairly systematic in their diagnoses of behavior. We know a fair amount about what sort of information is processed and how it is processed. Second, we have learned that a number of both rational and less rational activities go on. Some of these "errors" in the attributional process are built into our model.

FIGURE 1
A model of supervisory responses to poorly performing subordinates.

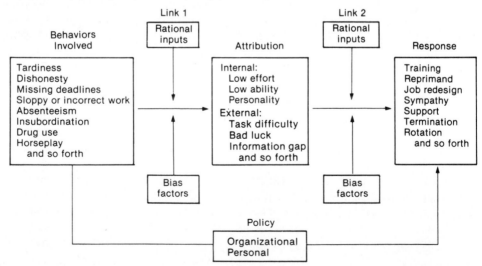

Third, one major, exceptionally helpful distinction has been the idea that causes of behavior fall into two major classes—internal and external. Internal causes concern people—their abilities, effort, personality, and mood. External causes concern the setting—task difficulty, available information, interpersonal pressures. Obviously, whether a supervisor makes an internal or external attribution about the causes of poor performance is critical to understanding what response will be selected.

The model is presented in Figure 1. The two main stages are labeled links 1 and 2. Link 1 refers to the process of making an attribution, and link 2 refers to the process of choosing an appropriate response. At both stages there are some rational factors and some biases that affect the supervisor's judgments. The rest of this section briefly describes these "moderators" in more detail.

Attribution Factors

The most obvious rational factors on which attributions are based are distinctiveness, consistency, and consensus. *Distinctiveness* refers to the extent to which a subordinate has performed poorly on other tasks. The less distinctive the performance, the more likely the attribution is external. *Consistency* refers to the extent to which the employee has previously performed poorly on this particular task. The greater the consistency, the more internal the attribution. Finally, *consensus* refers to the extent to which other subordinates perform this task poorly. The lower the consensus, the more internal the attribution.

Let's take an example. Suppose a subordinate fails to turn in a budget report on time. The supervisor recalls that (1) this subordinate is always tardy in submitting any report, (2) he/she is always late with financial reports, and (3) none of the other subordinates are late. Therefore, the supervisor is likely to attribute this poor performance to something about the subordinate (for example, ability or motivation). If, on the other hand, (1) the subordinate has never before missed a deadline for any task, (2) he or she has always submitted financial reports on time, and (3) everybody had trouble getting their reports in this particular month, then an external attribution—that is, something about the financial situation this month (or perhaps too much work)—is probable.

In addition to these rational informational cues, other factors can affect attribution—many of which introduce bias into the process. First, and probably most important, is the actor/observer bias. It has been well documented that people think their own behavior stems from external forces while others' behavior stems from internal factors. That is, someone else's behavior is salient to the outside observer, but the environment is salient to the actor. Therefore, the subordinate (actor) is likely to blame external events for his or her behavior, while the supervisor (observer) is likely to blame internal factors. The same result arises from self-serving biases that lead people to attribute successes to themselves and failures to forces beyond their control. This difference in attributions is likely to lead to conflict, disagreement, and hard feelings.

Other sources of error in this attribution phase are possible. Anything that increases the distance (psychologically and physically) between the supervisor and the subordinate is likely to increase actor/observer and self-serving errors. For example, the less the supervisor likes the subordinate, the less experience the supervisor has with the subordinate's job and the more power the supervisor has, the more likely the supervisor is to make internal attributions for poor performance.

Decision and Response

The second link in the model is the decision phase—the supervisor must select a response. Obviously, if an internal attribution has been made, the response is likely to be directed at the subordinate (reprimand, for example, or training), but if an external attribution is made, a response directed at the task would be more appropriate (provide more support, for example, or change the task). Again, some rational and some less rational factors affect this response.

On the rational side is the fact that supervisors at this point usually do some sort of cost/benefit analysis. That is, they weigh the pros and cons of various responses. They consider the probability that a given response will change the subordinate's behavior, have a positive or negative impact on other employees, make the supervisor feel good, adhere to company policy, and so on. These considerations are clearly important to the decision.

But less obvious factors may enter in. For example, there's considerable evidence that the consequences of the poor performance affect the supervisor's response. If the missed deadline for the financial report results in a lost contract, the supervisor is much more likely to be vindictive and punitive than if nothing negative occurs, even though the subordinate may have had no control over the outcome.

Another source of bias might be the subordinate's apologies, excuses, and external explanations. Even though the supervisor has accurately diagnosed that a subordinate performed poorly because of low motivation, he or she is less likely to be punitive and severe if the subordinate apologizes and promises it will never happen again.

A final source of bias springs partly from the actor/observer error. Supervisors are less likely to look for ways in which a task can be changed than for ways in which the person can change; it is somehow easier to tell someone to "be different" than to try to change the environment.

If one summarizes the implications of these two phases, the following conclusions emerge. First, supervisors are likely to see subordinates' poor performance as internally caused. Second, there is likely to be disagreement about the attribution. Third, there are forces that combine with the internal attribution to push the supervisor toward a personal, punitive response. However, apologies and social or organizational constraints may make it difficult to actually use such responses. Thus we are faced with a situation in which a supervisor may unknowingly make some errors in judgment about the causes of poor performance, and then feel frustrated because of certain social or organizational prohibitions about the responses he or she feels are required.

One final point needs to be mentioned. The attributional process is not used when there's a personal or organizational policy to deal with the specific type of poor performance (for example, three unexcused absences in a month requires a written reprimand). We have represented this situation in our model by a line that goes directly from the behavior to the response.

This model has a number of implications for both theory and practice. But perhaps the most important point to recognize is that the supervisor is an active processor of information and that a variety of both relevant (for example, past performance) and nonrelevant (for example, similarity) cues affect his or her judgment about a subordinate. Thus there are rational and nonrational components in (1) the definition of poor performance, (2) the manager's interpretation of its cause, and (3) the response made to it. Before turning to a discussion of ways to improve the process, we will briefly describe the process from the subordinate's perspective.

COPING WITH POOR PERFORMANCE: THE SUBORDINATE'S PERSPECTIVE

What happens when an employee is confronted with data indicating a serious performance problem? Frequently a sequence of psychological and behavioral events occur—so that the employee will:

• *Deny it*. In many cases the first reaction is a cognitive adjustment of denial. The facts are disputed, the actuality or reality is denied or interpreted in a more favorable light, or a different mission than the one intended by the evaluator is claimed. People resort to this defense mechanism quickly and frequently because it protects them, at least momentarily, from loss of esteem, confidence, and face. Moreover, if others accept the denial (which may be backed by equivocal evidence and ambiguous goals), the performer does not need to spend time and energy in actually correcting or improving his or her performance. On the surface, denial appears to be a reasonable, first-shot strategy for coping with a performance problem. It is a subordinate's natural reaction. Managers should expect it, be prepared to confront it, and encourage movement beyond this stage of coping.

• *Hide it*. If denial doesn't work, many problem performers will move from a cognitive adjustment to explicit behavior aimed at hiding, covering, or burying observable symptoms of the substandard performance. Such behavior may be aimed at shielding the symptoms from the boss's view; in professional occupations, considerable effort may be exerted to hide poor performance from other evaluators—for example, peers, public regulators, or agency inspectors. Unfortunately, such a response is not infrequent in publicly sensitive professions, such as nuclear inspection, medical practice, public accounting, and even presidential affairs. This coping strategy represents a recognition that denial is either not possible (that is, there is too much evidence that confirms poor performance) or too risky (that is, if the evidence were public, previous denial would appear dishonest and stupid).

● *Justify it.* Let's elevate the coping process one more step. If the performance problem cannot be denied (it *did* happen) and cannot be hidden (the boss knows or perhaps peers and even the public know), then *what?* Typically, at this stage, the problem performer will attempt to justify or rationalize behavior. Most frequently he or she will try to diminish the significance of the performance problem. Phillip Caldwell, Ford Motor Company chairman, when confronted by a *Wall Street Journal* reporter who compared Ford's recent financial losses to Chrysler corporation's evolving collapse, reportedly responded, "Ford is a strong company and intends to remain a secure leader in world automotive production and technology." [*The Wall Street Journal,* April 16, 1980] In other words, it could be worse. When compared with Chrysler, Ford's performance problems appear minuscule. Caldwell *could* well have said, "Ford intends to survive on its own, and that's better than Chrysler." Of course, the art of justification in the face of declining performance depends on the creative and selective use of comparisons. Ford looks quite different when compared with the Toyota Motor Company or Nissan Motor Company.

● *Allocate it.* The plot thickens. What happens if denial is denied the poor performer? If substandard performance is public knowledge? If comparisons with even poorer performers are impossible or unbelievable? Frequently, individuals and organizations will then allocate responsibility for the poor performance to someone else or to an external agent (for example, a competitor engaging in unfair acts, the government, or an unpredictable, adverse twist of nature)—that is, an external attribution. This stage involves aggressive fault-finding and emotional assertions of blame.

Why These Strategies?

Why are these reactions to performance problems so prevalent? Our analysis suggests at least two fundamental reasons. The first focuses on the nature of performance environments and the way in which performance goals are typically articulated. The second is that, until recently, managerial and behavioral science knowledge had not produced a valid and realistic technology for changing and improving human performance—that is, one supported by theory, evidence, and experience. But more on this later.

These four coping strategies are most likely to occur and to undermine the supervisor's ability to deal with poor performance when one or more of the following three conditions exist:

1 When statements of desired performance are ambiguous.

2 When public admission of poor performance is punished (for example, is politically dangerous).

3 When commitments to specific performance goals are avoided in order to maintain future flexibility and accessibility to opportunism.

Our final section suggests some ways to deal with these processes.

COPING THROUGH CONSTRUCTIVE PERFORMANCE IMPROVEMENT

Coping with the poor performer involves at least four basic steps. First, what are the critical elements of the job that the worker must perform effectively? As noted earlier, some methods of identifying poor performance also lead to definitions of desired performance. But some do not. So in order to improve performance, we must go beyond merely identifying undesirable performance to specify what is better performance. In the process we can also reduce uncertainty and ambiguity. The second step is to make sure that managers are able to recognize effective performance when they see it. Rating errors must be recognized and reduced; inaccurate appraisals lead to employees' discouragement and apathy. Third, one must set specific goals for the employee. It has repeatedly been shown that specific goals that are difficult but attainable lead to effective outcomes. Finally, one must ensure that the consequences of goal attainment are positive for the employee, or the goals will not be accepted. What we are suggesting is that (1) a clearer, better definition of performance can be made, (2) rating errors and biases can be recognized and reduced, (3) goals can be set in behavioral or other terms that are fair, agreed upon, and assessable, and (4) commitment to these goals can be attained.

Defining Effectiveness

To motivate someone to improve productivity, it is first necessary to specify what the person must start doing, stop doing, or continue doing. That is, productivity must be defined in terms of what an individual employee is to do on the job. Traditionally, performance outcomes or personality traits have been used to evaluate performance; we have already evaluated the shortcomings of those measures. Recent literature places the emphasis on defining effectiveness on the basis of behavior, and we feel this procedure has promise.

Behavioral Measures

Measures of performance based on behavior can be related more directly to what the employee actually does, and they are more likely to minimize irrelevant factors that are not under the control of the employee than are cost-related measures or personality traits. Behavioral measures developed from a systematic job analysis can serve as indicators of such performance outcomes as units produced/work hours, attendance, accidents, and so forth. Great performance outcomes, such as high profits, do not come about through osmosis; someone must do something to create them. Behavioral measures based on a thorough job analysis indicate precisely what is being done by an employee to warrant recognition, discipline, transfer, promotion, demotion, or termination. Thus behavioral measures not only define personality traits (for example, initiative) explicitly, but also encompass performance-related outcomes. For example, reducing costs by 10 percent, selling

52 cars in a month, and turning in a report on time are observable behaviors. What makes behavioral measures desirable from a productivity standpoint is that they measure the individual on things over which he or she has control and, most important, specify what the person must do or not do to attain these outcomes.

Developing accurate behavioral measures of performance begins with a thorough job analysis that identifies the strategies that one must take to impact an organization's bottom line. One of the most frequently used and straightforward job analysis procedures for developing behavioral measures is the critical incident technique (CIT). The CIT involves interviewing people who are aware of the aims and objectives of the job in question, who frequently observe job incumbents on the job, and who are capable of differentiating between competent and incompetent performance. The interviewees are asked to describe examples of effective and ineffective behavior that they observed in the past 12 months—behavior that was critical to doing the job effectively. The emphasis on the past 12 months ensures that the information obtained is applicable to the organization's current needs. For example, some behaviors that were effective for an engineer in the 1960s may no longer be effective in the 1980s.

In describing effective/ineffective incidents, an interviewee is asked to explain the circumstances surrounding a specific incident in which the behavior was demonstrated, exactly what was done, and how the behavior was effective or ineffective. Critical incidents that are similar, if not identical, are grouped together to form one behavioral item. For example, incidents in which a supervisor encouraged subordinates to work effectively with one another were used to develop the item: "Orally praises a subordinate for voluntarily helping another employee on any aspect of the job." Behavioral items that are similar are grouped together to form one criterion or yardstick for defining and measuring an employee's effectiveness. For example, items dealing with supervisory involvement with employees might be called "Interactions with Subordinates." Each behavioral item is rated on a scale of five points—with a particular rating dependent upon the frequency with which an employee engages in a behavior. Such scales are referred to as behavior observation scales (BOS). These scales possess several important advantages for improving performance. First, substantial input from employees goes into their development. Thus employees usually understand and are committed to the measures.

Second, BOS explicitly spell out behaviors an employee needs to perform a given job. As a job description, BOS can also be used as a realistic preview for job candidates by showing them what they will be expected to do on the job. Such previews are an effective means of reducing turnover because they give candidates enough knowledge to ascertain whether they would have the desire and ability to satisfactorily perform the job duties on a regular basis.

Third, the BOS facilitate fair appraisals because they let both supervisor and employee know what will be observed on the job. Through the job analysis, the BOS contain a representative sampling of the behaviors that are critical to performing effectively in the organization.

Finally, BOS facilitate explicit performance feedback because they encourage meaningful discussions between supervisor and employee about the latter's strengths and weaknesses. Generalities are avoided in favor of specific overt behaviors that the employee is encouraged to demonstrate on the job or for which he or she is praised. Explicit feedback using BOS combined with the setting of specific goals (to be discussed shortly) has repeatedly been shown to be effective in bringing about and/or maintaining positive behavior change.

However, while BOS are a preferred strategy for assessing performance, they are subject to human errors both in their development and in their administration. It is important to minimize these errors. What strategies are available?

Minimizing Rating Errors

Human judgment enters into every criterion of employee effectiveness, regardless of whether the criterion is an economic, trait, or behavioral measure. If feedback based on the measures is to serve as a motivator rather than a demotivator, careful observation is necessary. Unfortunately, most organizations assume that the careful construction of performance measures obviates the need to train supervisors how to observe, record, and evaluate objectively what they have seen. Because observers are usually unaware of their own rating errors, training is necessary or employees may be erroneously promoted, demoted, transferred, or terminated. Common rating errors may be based on contrast effects, halo, similar-to-me, leniency, and attributional biases.

• The *contrast effects* error results from a rater's tendency to evaluate an employee in relation to others rather then on the job requirements. A typical outcome of this error occurred recently in an organization where an "average" manager in an exceptionally good department was laid off. An equally "average" manager who was doing exactly the same job, but in a poor department, was given additional responsibility and was subsequently promoted. Thus even though these two individuals had comparable job performance, one benefited from the mediocrity of peers, while the other suffered because of outstanding peers.

• *Halo* error involves an overgeneralization from one aspect of a person's job performance to all aspects of the person's performance. For example, a person who is outstanding at inventory control may be rated inaccurately as outstanding in credit management, customer relations, and other aspects of the job in which performance is less than outstanding.

• The *similar-to-me* error involves the tendency to judge those people who are similar to the rater in attitudes and background more favorably than those who are dissimilar, regardless of whether the similarity is job-related.

• Raters who rate everyone at the high or the low end of the scale are guilty of *leniency* errors.

• Finally, as we mentioned before, there are a number of judgment errors based on *attributional biases*. Supervisors tend to see the causes of poor performance as internal and to blame subordinates for failure to see this. Supervisors also tend to be biased by apologies or other irrelevant information (for example, outcomes).

What makes these errors insidious is that they appear to be well-developed rating habits resistant to change. People may continue to make them even after receiving lectures and warnings on why the errors must be avoided. They continue to make them after receiving information on how to spot potential rating errors (for example, when one person is rated favorably on everything or when one evaluator rates everyone at the low end of an appraisal scale).

The only training program that is effective in minimizing rating error is one that incorporates three learning principles basic to bringing about a relatively permanent behavior change—that is, active participation, knowledge of results, and practice.

This means, first, that an effective program that reduces rating errors must allow trainees to rate individuals during the training process. (Simply giving a lecture or showing a film on how to serve a tennis ball is unlikely to increase the skill level of a novice tennis player.)

Second, the training program must provide immediate feedback on the accuracy of the trainee's rating. Discussion can then focus on what the trainee did correctly or incorrectly.

Finally, the training program must allow sufficient time for the trainee to practice the correct behavior. The literature tells of many unsuccessful five-minute to one-hour training programs that increased manager's observation skills only temporarily.

The probability of stimulating the employee's productivity is greatly decreased, and the probability of a discrimination charge is significantly increased if supervisory observations are inadequate, biased, or reported inaccurately.

One training program that is effective in reducing rating errors and increasing observer accuracy allows the trainees to view job applicants on videotape. They rate a job applicant on the basis of a job description distributed before they observe the applicant. The trainer then tells the trainees the correct rating. The discussion that follows focuses on (1) what the applicant was observed doing in the film to justify the rating, (2) examples of where each trainee has seen a given rating error in both on-the-job and off-the-job settings, and (3) ways to minimize the occurrence of each rating error.

Goal Setting

Once effective or ineffective performance can be described and defined and supervisors have been trained to recognize and record it accurately, the issue of improving performance can be addressed directly. Most current theories of performance motivation incorporate setting goals or specifying exactly what the individual should do on the job.

Goal setting is effective because it clarifies exactly what is expected of an individual. As several engineers have commented to us, "by receiving a specific goal from the supervisor we are able to determine for the first time what that *@?% really expects from us." Moreover, the process of working against an explicit goal injects interest into the task. It gives challenge and meaning to a job. When they attain their goals, people experience feelings of accomplishment and recognition (from self and/or supervisors and others).

When goals are set, the following points should be taken into account:

1 Setting specific goals leads to higher performance than adopting an attitude of "do your best." A specific score on each BOS should be specified as well as the key behavior or behaviors that the employee needs to work on to improve or maintain the score.

2 Employee participation in setting goals generally leads to higher goals than when the goal is unilaterally set by a supervisor.

3 The higher the goal, the higher the performance.

4 Performance feedback is critical to maintaining employee interest in the job, revising goals, and prolonging effort to attain them. Feedback reinforces goal setting.

5 If employees are evaluated on performance rather than goal attainment, they will continue to set high goals whether the goals are attained or not. High goals lead to higher performance levels than do easy goals. If employees are evaluated on goal attainment rather than actual performance, they are likely to set low goals or reject higher goals imposed by supervisors.

6 The employee must have some latitude in influencing performance. Where performance is rigidly controlled by technology or work flow, as on the typical assembly line, goal setting is likely to have little effect.

7 Workers must not feel threatened by the prospect of job cuts—affecting their own jobs or the jobs of others—resulting from their increased performance under the goal-setting procedure. Most people are careful to avoid putting themselves or others out of work by being too productive.

These principles are basic to most management by objectives (MBO) programs. The primary difference between what we are saying here and what has been advocated by MBO enthusiasts is that the latter often emphasize the use of cost-related measures (for example, number of sales); we are arguing for the use of behavioral measures for *counseling/development/motivational purposes*. We have no objection to the use of MBO as a vehicle for planning where the organization, department, or individual should focus attention and efforts over the next three months, year, or five years. Nor do we have any objection to the inclusion of these objectives with behavioral measures. Cost-related objectives can clarify the context or situation in which the employee's behavior will be appraised. But it should not be surprising if the two sets of measures lead to different conclusions. As pointed out previously, environmental factors or organizational constraints beyond the employee's control may be preventing him or her from attaining satisfactory cost-related outcomes. BOS are helpful here because they alert the manager to look for organization-related obstacles if the employee is doing everything correctly. In instances where the cost-related outcomes are satisfactory despite unsatisfactory employee behavior, the satisfactory cost-related outcomes may be short-lived because other employees, subordinates, and/or clients may respond adversely to this behavior. After all, cost-related outcomes occur because people in the organization—virtually always more than one person—"did something." Accounting for what each person *did* is one of the purposes of developing behavioral measures. Finally, cost-related and behavioral measures may not correlate with each other because of recording errors on the part of the appraiser. This is why the training of raters is so important.

Ensuring Goal Acceptance

A straightforward aid in understanding why an employee does or does not accept a goal is to draw up lists showing the good and bad consequences of desirable and undesirable behavior.

Head the first list "desirable behaviors." In a column to the right of that, list all positive consequences the employee gains from engaging in each desirable behavior and in a third column list all the negative consequences for each. One desirable behavior for a mechanic, for example, might be working ten hours instead of six. A positive consequence for him would be earning two additional hours of straight-time pay and two hours of overtime pay. Undesirable consequences of this behavior might be fatigue or arriving home late for dinner.

Head another list "undesirable behaviors" and repeat the process of showing positive and negative consequences of undesirable behavior. The results can provide the basis for an in-depth analysis of the consequences when you discuss them with the employees in question. This approach can provide a rational way to gain insight and develop hypotheses about why people behave the way they do. More important, it gives you the information you need to motivate subordinates to do what you want them to do by pointing up what consequences need to be changed in order to change their behavior. The approach is straightforward and costs little; however, the cost of changing the consequences sometimes exceeds the benefits of changing the behavior, in which case a change may not be advisable. The advantage of this approach is that one can estimate the costs knowing, with a high degree of certainty, that if the consequences are changed, the behavior involved will change accordingly.

Emery Air Freight successfully used this approach. The company was losing nearly $1 million annually because people on airport loading docks were shipping small packages separately rather than placing those with the same destination in one container that would be carried at lower rates by air carriers. Management found containers were being used 45 percent of the time when they should have been used 90 percent of the time. Instead of setting up a training program, management examined the positive consequences employees would enjoy if they loaded shipments properly. This analysis revealed that such behavior had no consequences of any kind (either positive or negative) at the time. Moreover, most employees believed they were performing efficiently.

The program required each employee to fill out a behavioral checklist similar in concept to BOS. Goals were set for each job—for example, to ship small packages with the same destination in a single container. All improvements in employee performance were reinforced by supervisory praise regardless of whether company goals were attained. Failure to attain a goal was assuaged by praise for honesty in reporting that failure. Thus was behavior shaped toward desired goals through praise, a positive consequence.

It is important to note that the positive consequences of engaging in a given behavior must be perceived immediately by the employee. If the consequences aren't immediate, their effectiveness decreases because the employee doesn't clearly see the connection between the consequences and the behavior. Even worse, delayed positive consequences may inadvertently reinforce inappropriate behaviors. For example, a new division manager in a start-up operation may initially perform at a high level. The organization may want to reward the manager with a salary increase. Unfortunately, final approval of salary increase may take months. By that time the manager's high level of performance may have diminished as a result of numerous frustrations, including the lack of reward. When the salary increase finally comes through, the manager is, in effect, being reinforced for mediocre performance.

In summary, a straightforward approach to coping with poor performance and enhancing productivity includes these four steps:

1 *Define performance behaviorally.* The manager must identify and define specific behavior or behaviors required of the employee on the job. The behavior must be pinpointed so that it can be reliably observed and recorded. Thus "Showing initiative" is not pinpointed—but "Calling on a customer without being asked by anyone" is. The ability to specify behavior in observable terms is the first skill managers must acquire before they can change or maintain an employee's performance.

2 *Train managers to reduce rating errors.* Rating errors are observers' errors in judgment that occur in a systematic manner. These errors are insidious because observers are usually unaware that they are making them. And even if they are aware of the error, they are frequently unable to correct themselves. The end result can be an employee who is erroneously promoted, demoted, transferred, or terminated.

3 *Set specific goals.* Involving the employee in goal setting has two advantages: First, it increases an employee's understanding of what the job must accomplish, and second, it can lead to the setting of higher goals than those the supervisor would set unilaterally. The higher the goal, the higher the performance.

4 *Establish positive consequences for goal attainment.* If goals are to be accepted, the employee must perceive that goal attainment will lead to positive consequences.

CONCLUSION

What prescriptions flow from our analysis of reducing performance gaps and improving productivity? The process depicted here suggests several guidelines for managerial action:

1 Adopt a flexible posture toward identifying performance problems. At times, any one of the three comparisons we have described may be appropriate but, where possible, clear and specific behavioral goals can be used for comparisons across both people and time. Beyond the comparison processes, the limitations of people as information processors and decision makers must be recognized and accommodated when attempting to spot performance gaps.

2 Understand and use the knowledge of how people identify *causes* of poor performance. Paying attention to attributional processes will make it easier to focus on ways to improve problem diagnosis and the problem-solving process.

3 Do not expect that people will always attack performance problems with constructive, proactive steps aimed at productivity improvement. It may be necessary to assist managers through the usual coping strategies that so frequently hinder direct confrontation and improvement of substandard performance. That is, pushing beyond denial, cover-up, and blame allocation for performance gaps may be necessary before performance problems can be confronted and solved.

4 Follow the steps toward constructive performance improvement; define desired outcomes behaviorally, set goals carefully, implement evaluation training to reduce assessment errors, encourage feedback, and make positive rewards for performance improvement.

Clearly, our analysis and prescriptions go well beyond the components of traditional performance appraisal systems and techniques. It is our belief that performance definition, diagnosis, appraisal, and improvement need to be firmly anchored in what is currently known about people as observers of performance, as evaluators, and as facilitators of change. Such an orientation provides the best opportunity for advancing beyond generally unproductive and unrealistic techniques and strategies and for improving productivity by developing an organization's human resources.

SELECTED BIBLIOGRAPHY

A summary of how managers frequently formulate and identify performance problems can be found in H. Mintzberg's *The Nature of Managerial Work* (Prentice-Hall, 1980).

A review of court cases pertaining to performance appraisal can be found in a book by G. P. Latham and K. N. Wexley, *Increasing Productivity Through Performance Appraisal* (Addison-Wesley, 1981).

A discussion of attribution theory and how it applies to the leadership setting appears in S. G. Green and T. R. Mitchell's "Attributional Processes of Leaders in Leader-Member Interactions" (*Organizational Behavior and Human Performance,* Vol. 23, 1979) and in a chapter by T. R. Mitchell, S. G. Green, and R. E. Wood, "An Attributional Model of Leadership and the Poor Performing Subordinate: Development and Validation," in Vol. 3 of L. L. Cummings and B. M. Staw's edited work, *Research in Organizational Behavior* (JAI Press, 1981).

A training program to increase accuracy in appraisal and decrease rating error can be found in the book, *Increasing Productivity Through Performance Appraisal,* (Addison-Wesley, 1981) by G. P. Latham and K. N. Wexley.

A summary of work on goal setting can be found in an earlier issue of *Organizational Dynamics,* "Goal Setting: A Motivational Technique That Works" (*Organizational Dynamics,* Autumn 1979) written by G. P. Latham and E. A. Locke.

Typical workplace offenses and managerial actions in cases of industrial discipline are discussed by II. N. Wheeler in "Punishment Theory and Industrial Discipline" (*Industrial Relations*, May 1976).

Punishment in Organizations: A Review, Propositions, and Research Suggestions[1]

Richard D. Arvey
John M. Ivancevich

Despite its unpleasant connotations, the use of punishment or threat of punishment is a relatively common phenomenon in organizational and industrial settings. The topic of punishment, however, has received essentially no attention from organizational researchers. Although research in other applied settings has revealed that punishment is effective in reducing or eliminating undesirable behavior, organizational researchers and behavioralists have focused entirely on "positive" reward systems for modifying and changing employee behavior [Komaki, Barwick, & Scott, 1978; Pedalino & Gamboa, 1974; Stephens & Burroughs, 1978]. Although there are a number of procedures that can have the effect of decreasing the frequency of undesirable behavior (e.g., extinction, satiation, and physical restraint). Johnston states that there is "no indication from any data that any of these procedures provides an effect which is as immediate, enduring, or generally effective as that produced by the proper use of punishment" [1972, pp. 1050–1051].

We shall review some of what is known about punishment in laboratory and applied settings, and apply this knowledge to managerial practices in organizational settings. Specifically, we shall (1) define punishment and trace some of its historical treatments; (2) review and discuss some issues and questions concerning objections to punishment; (3) review the research literature to delimit certain variables that influence the effectiveness of punishment; (4) generate a number of propositions and hypotheses about when and how punishment procedures will be effective in organizational settings, and (5) discuss a variety of research issues associated with the study of punishment within organizational contexts.

DEFINITION OF PUNISHMENT

Although there are differences among psychologists concerning a definition of punishment, we will adopt Kazdin's concise definition, which captures the con-

[1]We wish to thank James Terborg and Robert Pritchard for their comments on earlier drafts of this paper.

From *Academy of Management Review*, 1980, **5**, 123–132. Reprinted by permission.

cept effectively: "Punishment is the presentation of an aversive event or the removal of a positive event following a response which decreases the frequency of that response" [1975, pp. 33–34]. There is a key point embedded within this definition. A relationship or contingency exists between some defined response and some aversive consequences or stimuli (e.g., a leader's sarcastic remarks for poor performance, or an organizational fine for tardiness). That is, the random or noncontingent administration of adversive stimuli on behavior does not represent punishment. (However, we make no strong claim that punishment operates only through strict behavioristic principles. Instead, we feel that there may be important cognitive elements that operate to influence directly or mediate the punishment process. For more discussion and criticism of behavior modification principles applied to organizations, see Locke [1977] and Babb and Kopp [1978]).

Punishment can occur under two kinds of circumstances. The first involves the presentation of an aversive event after a response. Psychologists often define a primary aversive event as a stimulus that is inherently aversive (e.g., electric shock, loud noises), whereas a conditioned or secondary aversive event involves a stimulus that becomes aversive through repeated pairing with an already aversive event. Many of the aversive events in organizational contexts are of this second type (e.g., reprimands, nods, gestures). A conditioned aversive stimulus may serve two distinct purposes. First, the stimulus may punish or decrease the response that led to it. Second, it may warn of or forecast some impending aversive consequence if a response is performed. . . .

A second punishment circumstance involves the *removal* of positive outcomes or reinforcers after a response has been made. For example, punishment may take the form of the withdrawal of privileges, being ignored, or not being considered for promotion.

HISTORICAL PERSPECTIVES

Solomon [1964] has documented the controversies surrounding the punishment concept. Some of these controversies were first initiated by Skinner in 1938, and his position was further articulated in his book *Walden Two* [1948], in which he declared punishment to be ineffective or only temporary, and to produce undesirable side effects. Skinner's arguments were quite persuasive for most psychologists. Solomon claimed, however, that "the scientific bases for the conclusions therein were shabby, because, even in 1938, there [were] conflicting data which demonstrated the great effectiveness of punishment in controlling instrumental behavior" [1964, p. 248]. It was not until the 1960s that punishment was recognized by researchers as an effective but extremely complex method for suppressing or eliminating behavior. In a literature review of laboratory findings, Church [1963] focused on a variety of variables that appeared to influence the effectiveness of punishment in laboratory settings. Azrin and Holz [1966] provided another review of the effect of punishment in laboratory settings. Researchers also began to study punishment as a procedure to suppress or eliminate predominantly deviant or pathological behaviors among human subjects. Punishment has been used effectively to modify such conditions as homosexuality [Feldman & MacCullock, 1965], self-mutilating behaviors [Bucher & Lovaas, 1968; Harris & Ersner-Hersfield, 1978], alcoholism [Balke, 1965], and other behaviors. Summaries of the effectiveness of punishment on human behavior are provided by Johnston [1972], and Rimm and Masters [1974]. Parke [1972] has reviewed the effects of punishment on children's behavior. Kazdin [1975] provides an excellent review of the use of punishment in applied settings in his book on behavior modification.

Notably lacking in all of these literature reviews and interpretations are references on the use of punishment in organizational settings. Typically, discussions of punishment applied in organizations focus on what is wrong with using this method of behavioral control. Most of these discussions are laced with moral overtones and opinions concerning the use of punishment, and lack scientifically based research results.

One effort to scientifically study organizationally applied punishment is offered by Wheeler [1976]. He analyzed over 300 arbitration cases from the standpoint of the particular punitive philosophy involved in disciplinary actions (i.e., corrective, authoritarian, or humanitarian) and made an effort to integrate punishment theory with the disciplinary practices used within organizations. Moreover, he provided several suggestions for future research concerning punishment in organizational contexts. Hamner and Organ [1978] include a chapter on punishment in their recent organizational behavior book. They present arguments for and against the use of punishment and some of the factors that determine when punishment is effective. However, their presentation is based entirely on research carried out in nonorganizational contexts.

Thus, it is quite clear that punishment techniques have been studied and applied effectively in clinical, laboratory, and school settings, but the study of the phenomenon in organizational contexts has remained essentially dormant. The primary theme found in the organizational behavior and management literature is that punishment is not a high priority choice for managerial application. The presumed negative consequences of its use are usually presented so convincingly that intelligent persons would not include the approach in their repertoires. This literature base is, however, nonempirical in that only a miniscule number of studies of the success or failure of punishment in organizational settings have been conducted. It is worthwhile to speculate about why this is so, particularly in view of the fact that most practicing managers have extensive experience with punishment and that most organizations incorporate punishment as an enforcer in their behavior control policies (e.g., absence-control systems).

BELIEFS ABOUT THE EFFECTS OF PUNISHMENT

In general, punishment has not been viewed favorably by organizational psychologists for several reasons. *First,* it is thought that the use of punishment by an employer will result in *undesirable emotional side effects* (e.g., anxiety, aggressive acts or feelings toward the punishing agent, or passivity or withdrawal). In addition, employees might attempt to escape or avoid (e.g., turnover, absentee-ism) or show aggression toward (e.g., sabotage) the punishing agent.

The empirical evidence concerning these presumed effects is particularly weak. Johnson [1972] reports that of the numerous studies he reviewed, only one [Powell & Azrin, 1968] demonstrated these problems. Instead, his review revealed that there were indications of unexpected *improvement* in subject behavior as a result of punishment instead of withdrawal or passive responses. Kazdin's [1975] review likewise does not support the hypothesis of emotional side effects or resulting acts of aggression.

Parke [1972] suggests that undesirable side effects of punishment might occur mainly in situations where the punishing agents are indiscriminately punitive. In addition, acts of aggression may occur when the aversive event is particularly harsh and no alternative behavior is available. However, the evidence collected in nonorganizational settings simply does not support the contention of significant undesirable side effects. Before any definitive conclusions about undesirable side effects of punishment in organizations are reached, evidence must be gathered within work settings to support or refute these notions.

Second, the use of punishment is thought to be *unethical* and *nonhumanitar-ian.* Some people argue that punishment in organizations is old-fashioned and reflects a "tribal mentality" and reverts to the retributive justice theme of "an eye for an eye." This thinking confuses the notion of punishing to achieve justice ("paying back") in contrast to punishing to change or modify behavior. The first perspective views punishment as "past oriented" whereas the second perspective views punishment as having "future oriented" effects. Clearly, punishment has different connotations under the two perspectives. Retribution punishment may indeed be unethical, whereas punishment that is intended to be corrective and ultimately operate to the advantage of the person punished may not be considered unethical.

Punishment, however, does involve the systematic administration of aversive or undesirable stimuli. As Rimm and Masters [1974] have indicated, we must con-sider carefully the potential harm that might accompany some aversive stimuli. It is also clear that one must also consider the potential harm that can occur if *noth-ing* is done. As an extreme example, Rimm and Masters [1974] suggest that it is more humane to use punishment techniques to modify self-destructive behavior than to do nothing or "extinguish" these behaviors. Thus, punishment must be viewed carefully in the context in which it appears. Is it more humane for a super-visor to ignore a disruptive employee, hoping that the behavior will extinguish, than to administer immediate and consistent punishment of the disruptive re-sponses in order to effect an immediate behavior change?

Moreover, as Bandura [1969], and Hamner and Organ [1978] succinctly point out, punishment is a frequent and naturally occurring event in all our lives that shapes a large part of our behavior. The use of aversive stimuli has always oc-curred in organizational settings and probably always will. Perhaps it is more ethical to study this process and apply it correctly and with a touch of humanity than to ignore or deny its value. As Skinner argues in *Beyond Freedom and Digni-ty* [1971], the environment plays an important role in controlling behavior. Therefore, it makes sense for us to understand and arrange environmental circumstances to achieve some kind of managed systematic control.

Third, punishment is said to *never really eliminate* undesirable responses. The effects of punishment are said to be only temporary, the undesirable response returning full force when the threat of punishment is removed [Hamner and Organ, 1978]. A rebuttal to this claim is that the recovery rate of the punished response is potentially under the control of the punishing agent. "Actually, it [recovery] is potentially just as controllable as the 'recovery' of an experimenter-reinforced response to base-line levels when extinction is begun" [Johnston, 1972, p. 1047]. That is, the kinds of punishment schedules used (e.g., intermittent or continuous), the kinds of discriminative stimuli or cues in the punishment setting that are available, and the alternative kinds of positive reinforcement contingencies for new behaviors (or no behaviors) that take the place of punished responses will influence the recovery rate. It is apparent from the reviews of Johnston [1972] and Kazdin [1975] that the effects of punishment need not always be temporary and that the recovery rate of the punished response depends on various parameters of punishment often under the control of a punishing agent (managers or organizations).

VARIABLES THAT INFLUENCE THE EFFECTIVENESS OF PUNISHMENT

What, then, are some of the variables that influence the effectiveness of punishment? Moreover, how might specific variables influence the effectiveness of punishment in organizational contexts? Our intent here is to present those variables that seem to be the most salient in influencing punishment rather than attempt to be totally comprehensive.

Timing of Punishment

An aversive stimulus can be introduced at different times during the applications of punishment. It can be introduced *while* the punished response is being emitted, immediately *after* the punished response, or sometime after the response. Trenholme and Baron [1975] and reviews by Johnston [1972], Parke [1972], and Church [1963] indicate that, in general, the effectiveness of punishment is enhanced when the aversive event is delivered close in time to the punished response. Punishment of the response while it is in progress is also effective but care should be exercised that the aversive stimulus does not last longer than the punished response, otherwise the behavior emitted just before the termination of the aversive stimuli will be reinforced and strengthened. (This process is called negative reinforcement.)

In organizational settings, the implications of attempting to deliver punishment promptly are obvious. Managers or employers should apply the aversive event(s) as soon as the undesirable behavior occurs. Supervisors who wait a week or so before taking punitive action may not be as effective in eliminating the undesirable response as those who act immediately. Despite the importance of punishing deviant behavior when it occurs, one cannot always do so.

Proposition 1: Punishment is more effective in organizational contexts if the aversive stimuli or events are delivered immediately after the undesirable response occurs than if the delivery is delayed.

Intensity

Laboratory experiments and research with children have consistently shown that punishment achieves greater effectiveness when the aversive stimulus is relatively intense [Azrin & Holz, 1966; Parke & Walters, 1967; Johnston, 1972]. The implication of these findings is that in order for punishment to be effective in organizations, it should start out at a relatively high level. Under conditions where the aversive stimulus is relatively weak, subjects may adapt to the stimulus level and continue to emit the punished behavior [Weinstein, 1969]. Hamner and Organ point out, however, that in many organizations, disciplinary procedures are set up so that punishment may begin at a very mild level and increase in intensity. "This may be much less effective (and ultimately less humanitarian) than moderately severe punishment of early instances of the offense" [1978, p. 78].

Taking the opposite view, Parke [1972] has called attention to the notion that high-intensity punishment may create a level of anxiety and impose a situation where adaptive learning (e.g., learning to discriminate between a correct and incorrect response) will not occur. In an organizational context, this might occur where an employee learning to perform a complex task (e.g., shutting down a computer) anticipates a high-intensity punishment if a response is incorrect (e.g., destroying internal computer tapes). The anxiety created by this situation may inhibit the learning process.

In addition, while aversive stimuli of high intensity levels may be the most effective in suppressing undesirable behavior, these aversive stimuli may also have the effect of suppressing other *desirable* responses. The available research appears to suggest that perhaps moderate intensity levels may be the most functional in organizational settings. Defining what are low, moderate, and high intensity levels of aversive stimuli may be difficult in organizational contexts. However, for purposes of research, these stimuli should be scaleable.

Proposition 2: Moderate levels of punishment are more effective than low or high intensity levels.

Relationships with Punishing Agents

Should the person administering punishment have a relatively close and warm relationship with the person being punished, or should the relationship be cold and distant? Research on children indicates that parents who are warm and affectionate in their relationships with their children achieve greater effectiveness when they apply punishment procedures [Parke, 1978]. The effect could be partially due to their concomitant withdrawal of affection with the administration of an aversive stimulus in the punishment situation.

The implication for organizational settings is that punishment may be most effective where supervisors have established close relationships with respect from and for employees. Hamner and Organ [1978] suggest that punishment might be most effective when it is dispensed in an impersonal manner where the focus is on the act and not the person. Field research is needed, however, to determine whether punishment is effective because of the withdrawal of managerial affection or attention, or because of the specific aversive stimulus presented.

> Proposition 3: Punishment procedures are more effective where the agent administering the punishment has relatively close and friendly relationships with the employee being punished.

Schedule of Punishment

The effects of punishment depend also on the schedule of punishment. The schedule of punishment is as important in correcting deviant behavior as the nature of the aversive event. Punishment could occur after *every* response (continuous schedule), after a variable or fixed period of time since the undesired behavior occurred (variable or fixed interval schedules), or after a variable or fixed number of responses have occurred (variable or fixed ratio schedules). Thus, some managers may be consistent in punishing employees after each undesirable behavior, whereas other managers may be inconsistent by punishing employees only after several infractions of a rule or policy have occurred. The laboratory-based research is fairly consistent in showing that punishment is most effective if administered on a continuous schedule—that is, after each response [Johnston, 1972; Parke, 1972; Azrin & Holz, 1966]. Some support is offered for this relationship in organizations by Gary [1971]. In this study, employees who were disciplined consistently for absenteeism demonstrated less absenteeism than employees who received discipline haphazardly or not at all.

The notion of consistency may be viewed from several perspectives. Are managers consistent in punishing the same undesired behavior *over time*? Also, are supervisors consistent in punishing undesirable behavior *across employees*? Rosen and Jerdee [1974] have demonstrated that individuals are highly inconsistent in applying punishment across employees. Managers are apt to vary their enforcement of punishment of the same response depending on the tenure and skill levels of the employee.

Finally, we need to ask whether *different* managers are consistent in their applications of punishment across employees. Obviously, differential enforcement of punishment and differential intensities (penalties) will influence subordinates' perceptions of equity and fairness. It seems intuitively correct to us that an effective supervisor is not necessarily one who doesn't punish, but instead one who punishes *fairly* and *equitably*. These terms demand further clarification; however, it is beyond the scope of this paper to present a discussion of distributive justice, equity theory, and the like. The reader is referred to Walster and Walster [1975] and Deutsch [1975] for further discussion.

Another consideration that may influence a manager's consistency in administering punishment is his or her attributions concerning the cause of the specific behavior being punished [Jones & Davis, 1965]. A manager who perceives the behavior as being externally caused and beyond the control of the employee may choose *not* to administer punishment. However, employees may have little or no knowledge concerning the cause of the behavior, and therefore view the manager as inconsistent in the administration of punishment. Attribution theory has important implications in the study of punishment.

There are also situations in which particular schedules of punishment may *not* have the desired effects. For example, an aversive event can become a signal or cue for other later events—that is, it may become a discriminative stimulus. The punishing stimulus may become a sign that *no* punishment will occur for a period of time or signal that a positive reward will occur if the response occurs. Under these circumstances, we would expect an *increase* in the punished response. For example, employees may realize that once one of them is fined for being tardy, there will be no further fines for at least a week and subsequently increase the number of occasions they arrive late for work. Alternatively, the aversive stimulus could signal that no rewards are forthcoming, or that additional punishment will occur if the widespread behavior occurs. Under these situations, we would expect a *decrease* in the punished response. As Johnston states:

> The important thing to remember is that the punishing stimulus itself always occurs in the presence of and is always followed by other stimuli. To the extent that these patterns occur regularly, the punishing stimulus can come to reliably signal the presence or absence of these other stimulus conditions. The exact nature of these other stimuli (punishing, reinforcing, etc.) can have considerable impact on the actual effects of the punishing stimulus [1972, p. 1043].

As one example of this phenomenon, Schmidt [1969] punished responses on a task according to either a variable interval or fixed interval schedule. Once subjects learned that punishment would be administered only after a fixed period of time, they continued to respond on the task until close to when they would be punished and then stopped. On the other hand, punishment administered on a variable schedule was more effective in suppressing the punished response, especially when the punishment (loss of money) was greater.

Based on what is already known about the importance of schedules of punishment, the following propositions seem warranted:

> Proposition 4: Punishment of undesired behavior is more effective within organizations if:
> (a) Punishment consistently occurs after *every* undesirable response.
> (b) Punishment is administered consistently across different employees by the same manager.
> (c) Different managers are consistent in their applications of punishment for the same undesirable response.

Provision of Rationale

The administration of punishment could be more effective when a clear rationale is provided for the punishment process. Parke [1972] has noted the important role played by cognitive variables in the operation of punishment. Providing clear, unambiguous reasons concerning why the punishment occurred, and notice of future consequences if the response recurs has been shown to be particularly effective in enhancing the effects of punishment in research with children [Parke, 1972]. Cognitive structure also appears to mediate some of the previously discussed variables influencing punishment. For example, Aronfreed [1965] found that the addition of reasoning to *late*-timed punishment increased its effectiveness. Moreover, Parke [1972] showed that when a rationale for punishment was provided, low-intensity punishment was just as effective as intense punishment in influencing behavior.

> Proposition 5: Punishment is more effective when clear reasons are communicated to employees concerning why the punishment occurred, what the contingency is, and what the consequences of the behavior are in the future.

Alternative Responses Available

It appears that the effect of punishment is greatly enhanced if subjects have an alternative desirable response available. Moreover, if employees receive positive reinforcement for performing this alternative response, punishment is even more effective. This effect is due to two factors: (1) the employee does *not* perform the punished response (avoidance), and (2) another response is rewarded. Thus, punishment procedures that build-in explanations of alternative correct responses and reinforcement of these responses should have greater effectiveness than punishment processes that do not include alternative response options.

> Proposition 6: To the extent that alternative desirable responses are available to employees and these responses are reinforced, punishment is enhanced.

HOW TO STUDY PUNISHMENT IN ORGANIZATIONS

The six propositions just stated have been offered to suggest that punishment may be effective in eliminating or suppressing deviant behavior in organizational settings. As indicated above, there is a paucity of research concerning punishment in organizational settings, possibly owing to a lack of knowledge concerning *how* to study punishment in the context of organizations. What seems to be needed are some guidelines and suggestions concerning variables and research methods that might be utilized to test the propositions.

Dependent Variables

What should be used as the dependent variables in studying punishment in organizational settings? The most obvious dependent variable is the measurement of the behavior being punished. That is, researchers should specify, record, and measure the precise behavior that is punished. If punishment is effective, a decrease in frequency or rate of that particular behavior should result. One mistake managers make is to assume that punishment will drastically alter a large range of employee behaviors. That is, they rely too much on the possibility of generalization of punishment to other behaviors. As Johnston states, "it is inappropriate simply to expect or hope for punishing effects to occur with . . . other responses in the same situation" [1972, p. 1048].

What kinds of behaviors might be candidates for study as dependent variables in organizational settings? Wheeler [1976] reviewed 339 cases appearing in the *Labor Arbitration Report* between 1970 and 1974 and classified the cases relating to discharge and discipline according to the type of offense or undesirable behavior. The categories and frequencies that emerged were as follows:

1 Absenteeism, tardiness, leaving early (30 cases).
2 Dishonesty, theft, falsification of records (43 cases).
3 Incompetence, negligence, poor workmanship, violation of safety rules (37 cases).
4 Illegal strikes, strike violence, deliberate restriction of production (31 cases).
5 Intoxication, bringing intoxicants into the plant (18 cases).
6 Fighting, horseplay, trouble-making (34 cases).
7 Insubordination, refusal of job assignment, refusal to work overtime, fights or altercations with supervisor (98 cases).
8 Miscellaneous rule violations (48 cases).

Although additional variables might be studied, these variables outlined by Wheeler [1976] seem to be likely candidates. We should not, however, neglect the possible use of performance and satisfaction as dependent variables. It could be that punishment has organizationally undesirable effects if it is administered in a manner that violates a number of the propositions presented above. That is, if aversive events are administered noncontingently, are delayed, and given with no explanation, we would expect not only little change in the specific response presumably being punished, but also possible *decreases* in satisfaction and performance. Moreover, increases in other undesirable behaviors (sabotage, work stoppage) might be observed.

Measurement of these dependent variables may be difficult in organizational settings. However, many organizations keep records of rule infractions (when they are observed) that may be one information source in detecting the frequency or rate of response occurrence. More use of unobtrusive observers may also be a method for obtaining accurate measurement of deviant behaviors. For example, Komaki, Barwick, and Scott [1978] used trained observers to determine the frequency of safe and unsafe behaviors. These observers were present 4 days a week for 55 minutes during each observational period. No complaints were noted about the presence of these observers. Possibly a similar measurement process could be used to determine the rates of particular undesirable job behaviors. (It would, however, have to be made clear to employees that the observers would not inform the management about who was exhibiting undesirable behavior.)

Managerial, peer, and self ratings may be additional measurement tools. For example, managers might be asked to evaluate their employees in terms of their "disruptiveness," "insubordination," and so forth, on psychometrically developed graphic rating scales. Rating scales might also be used to measure employee satisfaction and performance.

Independent Variables

Several problems confront the researcher attempting to study punishment in organizations. One of the most salient problems is determining what constitutes an aversive event or stimulus to employees. Managers have control over numerous potential punishing stimuli that range from overt and formal actions such as discharge and financial penalties to less overt behavior such as assignment of employees to undesirable tasks, subtle verbal statements, and ridicule.

Organizational psychologists have developed a reasonably well-defined taxonomic system of positive reinforcers that are available and used in organizational systems (e.g., recognition, praise, bonuses). What is needed is the development of a taxonomy of aversive stimuli in organizational settings. That is, what supervisory actions result in aversive situations for employees? One strategy for developing a taxonomy is to ask employees to relate situations where they felt punished in organizational settings and indicate the role their supervisors or managers played in the situation. A critical-incident method might be employed. The resulting incidents might be sorted and categorized in an effort to develop some sort of classification system. An important issue here would be the generality of the punishers. In order to serve as an effective behavior control mechanism in organizations, punishers should reduce the frequency of many kinds of behaviors across many organizations. Of course, a limitation of this critical-incident method is that it is basically retrospective. Even with this limitation, it is a start in the development of a taxonomic system.

A number of interesting side issues are worth considering here. For example, what is aversive to one employee may not be aversive to another. Moreover, what a manager perceives as a reward may actually be perceived as a punishment by an employee. A manager might assign a *challenging* task to an employee as a reward for a job well done. However, the employee may not desire a more challenging task, find it too demanding of time and effort [Tornow, 1971], and feel punished. In contrast, a manager may perceive that he or she is punishing an employee (e.g., ignoring the employee), whereas the employee may not feel that the event is aversive. In short, there may be wide discrepancies among managers' and employees' perceptions concerning when and what aversive stimuli are delivered. Furthermore, occupational and gender differences concerning the interpretation and perceptions of aversive stimuli would be useful information to managers.

Once basic aversive events have been identified in organizational contexts, it would be desirable to measure the "dimensions" of the stimuli. That is, researchers should attempt to record and quantify such properties as the timing of stimuli, the intensity, and the schedule of presentation. In addition, efforts should be made to quantify the degree of reasoning used in the punishment situation, the kind of relationship between the employee and punishing agent, and the alternative responses available. These measures could be used as independent variables in research studies.

Precise measurement of these dimensions may be impossible. Several strategies for providing valid measures may be available, however:

1 Just as observers have been carefully trained to observe, record, and evalu-

ate specific behaviors in work-sampling procedures [Campion, 1972], so might observers be trained to *observe and record behaviors* along the dimensions specified above. That is, observers might be able to identify the length of time between the response and aversive stimulus, the schedule of punishment, the intensity of the punishment and so forth.

2 Employees might be given a *case study* where a specific rule infraction is portrayed and then be asked to evaluate how their own managers might react to the given infractions along the various dimensions. Thus, a "standard" response is given and the employees are asked to indicate how their managers react or punish the response. The amount of agreement among employees who share the same supervisor could be calculated as one estimate of reliability.

3 *Rating methods* might be also used, which would entail employees describing their manager's punishment behavior on a variety of rating dimensions.

Thus, there appears to be a variety of possible measurement strategies available to researchers.

RESEARCH DESIGNS

At first blush, it appears as if planned experiments dealing with punishment might be out of the question because of ethical considerations. However, there seem to be several situations where an experimental method might be appropriate. Many organizations sponsor training workshops for managers that focus on how to discipline employees. It would be possible to incorporate an experimental design into these workshops by forming experimental and comparison groups of managers. The experimental group could be introduced to some of the principles of punishment presented above and pre- and post-measures of employee behavior would be collected (for both experimental and comparison groups). Manipulation checks might be obtained through employee questionnaires. For example, Bauum and Youngblood [1975] report the results of a study in college classrooms where two kinds of attendance policies (compulsory, noncompulsory) were manipulated. Results showed that significantly higher attendance and higher performance levels as measured by examination scores were achieved by students in the compulsory-attendance classrooms. No differences in satisfaction between the treatment groups were observed. This kind of experimentation could be implemented in organizational settings without too much difficulty.

Field studies of punishment are a must if managers are to receive an accurate picture of the effects of punishment. Regression analyses could be used to assess the relationship between the punished response and such independent variables as timing, schedule, and intensity. Organizations might be identified, in the same or different industries, that clearly differ in their punishments policies and procedures and efforts made to assess corresponding differences in the frequency and rates of undesirable behaviors.

A FINAL WORD

The application of punishment within organizational settings is generally a neglected area of inquiry in the field of management. Punishment has such a negative connotation that most researchers would not recommend its application. However, public denial is not sufficient reason to dismiss punishment as a potential management approach for modifying and controlling behavior.

There is agreement among some researchers that punishment may be a very effective procedure in accomplishing behavior change. Although punishment is a complex process influenced by a number of variables, continuing to ignore punishment as a practical managerial strategy will not enhance our understanding of the procedure. Only rigorous research and an open dialogue will provide the insight needed to understand the effectiveness of punishment in organizational settings. The question is not so much whether punishment is good or bad. It exists and is found quite frequently in organizational settings. The question should be: How may punishment best be used to accomplish behavior change?

REFERENCES

Aronfreed, J. *Punishment learning and internalization: Some parameters of reinforcement and cognition.* Paper read at biennial meeting of Society for Research in Child Development, Minneapolis, 1965.

Azrin, N. N., & Holz, W. C. Punishment. In W. K. Honig (Ed.), *Operant behavior: Areas of research and application.* New York: Appleton-Century-Crofts, 1966, pp. 380–447.

Babb, H. W., & Kopp, D. G. Application of behavior modification in organizations: A review and critique. *Academy of Management Review,* 1978, *3,* 281–293.

Balke, B. G. The application of behavior therapy to the treatment of alcoholism. *Behavior Research and Therapy,* 1965, *3,* 75–85.

Bandura, A. *Principles of behavior modification.* New York: Holt, Rinehart, & Winston, 1969.

Bauum, J. F., & Youngblood, S. A. Impact of an organizational control policy on absenteeism, performance, and satisfaction. *Journal of Applied Psychology,* 1975, *60,* 688–694.

Bucher, B., & Lovaas, O. I. Use of aversive stimulations in behavior modification. In M. R. Jones (Ed.), *Miami symposium on the prediction of behavior, 1967: Aversive stimulation.* Coral Gables, Fla.: University of Miami Press, 1968.

Campion, J. E. Work sampling for personnel selection. *Journal of Applied Psychology,* 1972, *56,* 40–44.

Church, R. M. The varied effects of punishment on behavior. *Psychological Review,* 1963, *70,* 369–402.

Deutsch, M. Equity, equality, and need: What determines which value will be used as the basis of distributive justice? *The Journal of Social Issues,* 1975, *31,* 137–150.

Feldman, M. P., & MacCulloch, M. J. The application of anticipatory avoidance learning to the treatment of homosexuality: I. Theory, technique and preliminary results. *Behavior Research and Therapy,* 1965, *2,* 165–183.

Frakes, F. V. Acquisition of disliking for persons associated with punishment. *Perceptual and Motor Skills,* 1971, *33,* 251–255.

Gary, A. L. Industrial absenteeism: An evaluation of three methods of treatment. *Personnel Journal,* 1971, *50,* 352–353.

Hamner, W. C., & Organ, D. W. *Organizational behavior: An applied psychological approach.* Dallas, Tex.: Business Publications, 1978.

Harris, S., & Ersner-Hershfield, R. Behavioral suppression of seriously disruptive behavior in psychotic and retarded patients: A review of punishment and altercations. *Psychological Bulletin,* 1978, *85,* 1352–1375.

Johnston, J. M. Punishment of human behavior. *American Psychologist,* 1972, *27,* 1033–1054.

Jones, E. E., & Davis, R. E. From acts to dispositions. In L. Berkowitz (Ed.), *Advances in experimental social psychology.*

Kazdin, A. E. *Behavior modification in applied settings.* Homewood, Ill.: Dorsey, 1975.

Komaki, J., Barwick, K. D., & Scott, L. R. A behavioral approach to occupational safety: Pinpointing and reinforcing safe performance in a food manufacturing plant. *Journal of Applied Psychology,* 1978, *63,* 434–445.

Locke, E. A. The myths of behavior mod in organizations. *The Academy of Management Review,* 1977, *2,* 543–553.

Parke, R. D., & Walters, R. H. Some factors determining the efficacy of punishment inducing response inhibition. *Monographs of the Society for Research in Child Development,* 1967, *32* (Serial No. 109).

Parke, R. D. Some effects of punishment on children's behavior. In W. W. Hartup (Ed.), *The young child: Reviews of research* (Vol. 2). Washington D.C.: National Association for the Education of Young Children, 1972.

Pedalino, E., & Gamboa, V. U. Behavior modification and absenteeism: Intervention in one industrial setting. *Journal of Applied Psychology,* 1974, *59,* 694–698.

Powell, J., & Azrin, N. The effects of shock as a punisher for cigarette smoking. *Journal of Applied Behavior Analysis,* 1968, *1,* 63–71.

Rimm, D. C. & Masters, J. C. *Behavior therapy: Technique and empirical findings.* New York: Academic Press, 1974.

Rosen, B., & Jerdee, T. H. Factors influencing disciplinary judgments. *Journal of Applied Psychology,* 1974, *59,* 327–331.

Schmidt, D. R. Punitive supervision and productivity: An ental analog. *Journal of Applied Psychology,* 1969, *53,* 118–123.

Skinner, B. F. *The behavior of organisms.* New York: Appleton-Century-Crofts, 1938.

Skinner, B. F. *Beyond freedom and dignity.* New York: Knopf, 1971.

Skinner, B. F. *Walden two.* New York: Macmillan, 1948.

Solomon, R. L. Punishment. *American Psychologist,* 1964, *19,* 239–253.

Stephens, T. A., & Burroughs, W. A. An application of operant conditioning to absenteeism in a hospital setting. *Journal of Applied Psychology,* 1978, *63,* 518–521.

Tornow, W. W. The development and application of an input/outcome moderator test on the perception and reduction of inequity. *Organizational Behavior and Human Performance,* 1971, *6,* 614–638.

Trenholme, I. A., & Baron, A. Immediate and delayed punishment of human behavior by loss of reinforcement. *Learning and Motivation,* 1975, *6,* 62–79.

Walster, E., & Walster, G. W. Equity and social justice. *Journal of Social Issues,* 1975, *31,* 21–44.

Weinstein, L. Decreased sensitivity to punishment. *Psychonomic Science,* 1969, *14,* 264.

Wheeler, H. N. Punishment theory and industrial discipline. *Industrial Relations,* 1976, *15,* 235–243.

Managing Marginal Employees: The Use of Warnings and Dismissals

Charles A. O'Reilly III
Barton A. Weitz

A central theme in the study of organizations has been that of effectiveness. Researchers and practitioners alike have sought to determine what structures and actions promote effective performance and minimize ineffective performance (e.g., Mahoney and Weitzel, 1969; Cummings and Schwab, 1973; Steers, 1975; Evan, 1976; Goodman et al., 1979).

The quest for effective performance on the individual level in organizations has centered primarily on recruiting, selecting, and training the best person for the job (Guion, 1976; Hinrichs, 1976), designing jobs that are satisfying and motivating as well as productive (Hackman and Oldham, 1976; Aldag and Brief, 1978), and supervising or managing employees in a way that ensures high levels of performance (Cummings and Schwab, 1973; Stogdill, 1974; Vroom, 1976). These efforts may be characterized as being focused on inputs. Researchers and practitioners have given less attention to the problem of dealing with employees who are hired, trained, and managed, yet remain ineffective or marginal performers. Compared to the voluminous research on selection (Guion, 1976), motivation (Campbell and Pritchard, 1976), and leadership (Vroom, 1976), the research devoted to the management of marginal employees is small although there have been studies by Steinmetz (1969) and Huberman (1975). Miner and Brewer (1976; 1002) note this when they observe that

> . . . there are . . . long-standing problem areas such as chronic disciplinary cases that have attracted practically no research and give little evidence of doing so in the future.

This lack of attention to the unpleasant task of managing marginal performance is unfortunate because some evidence exists that documents the positive benefits of discipline (Berkowitz, 1969; Booker, 1969; Huberman, 1975; Heizer, 1976). For example, a survey of one hundred firms showed that 44 percent used the threat of discipline to correct problems and considered it effective (Miner and Brewer, 1976: 1021). McDermott and Newhams (1971), in a study of fifty-three discharged workers who had been reinstated, found that performance improved after sanctions. Baum and Youngblood (1975) found that a control policy based on legal compliance significantly improved both attendance and performance without any change in levels of employee satisfaction. Franke and Karl (1978: 636), in a statistical analysis of the original Hawthorne experiments, indicate that managerial discipline "seems to have been the major factor in increased rates of output." This evidence generally confirms what appears to be an ignored fact; discipline that is

Abridged from C. A. O'Reilly & B. A. Weitz, Managing marginal employees: The use of warnings and dismissals. *Administrative Science Quarterly,* **25,** 467–484; by permission of *The Administrative Science Quarterly.* © 1980 by Cornell University.

not punitive but is used to ensure compliance with established rules of conduct is usually accepted and supported by employees (Odiorne, 1971; Wheeler, 1976).

BACKGROUND

Almost every experienced supervisor has been faced with the necessity of dealing with a marginal employee at some time during his or her career. This is not to suggest that the problem is commonplace (Mulder, 1971); rather, as Anderson (1976), in a study of over 1,600 manufacturing employees discovered, the marginal employee is typically one of a small number of employees who cause the most problems. This study suggests that it is this minority, not the majority, of employees with whom the supervisor must be concerned. A supervisor's failure to identify and deal with marginal employees may result in not only lowered performance on the part of these employees but also diminished motivation and effectiveness of the entire work group."

Some evidence is available from the few studies undertaken to identify the characteristics of marginal employees (Mulder, 1971; Anderson, 1976) that a variety of problems may result in the labeling of an employee as "marginal" or "ineffective." A Bureau of National Affairs survey of 185 firms reported in Megginson (1977: 471), showed that absenteeism and tardiness were considered serious disciplinary problems in 79 percent of the firms. Productivity was considered a serious problem in only 11 percent of the firms. Several authors have suggested employee problem areas from alcoholism to insubordination to emotional disorders (Miner and Brewer, 1976; Megginson, 1977; Glueck, 1978). While some problems are generally acknowledged as intolerable offenses (e.g., dishonesty, physical attacks), little is known about how supervisors actually identify marginal employees. It is possible, and perhaps likely, that supervisors vary widely in their reasons for labeling employees as marginal; they may each establish their own subjective standards for evaluating performance, standards that may vary among subordinates as well as across supervisors. Employees considered marginal by some supervisors might be considered acceptable by others.

The problem of how supervisors deal with marginal employees once they are identified must also be considered. It has been shown that clear differences in style exist (Thomas, 1976). For instance, some supervisors are more assertive in dealing with conflict while others attempt to be accommodating (Burke, 1970; Ruble and Thomas, 1976). Some supervisors, particularly inexperienced ones, may rely too heavily on dismissal as a solution to conflict (Parisi, 1972). In addition to differences across supervisors, there are differences in the way individual supervisors deal with different employees (Booker, 1969; Steinmetz, 1969; Wohlking, 1975).

There are four main types of sanctions used in dealing with marginal employees: (1) informal oral warnings, (2) formal written warnings, (3) suspension or loss of pay, and (4) dismissal. Some evidence exists suggesting that these sanctions may be differentially applied by supervisors. Wohlking (1975), for example, presents data suggesting that some supervisors do not resort to disciplinary actions as often as they could. In a study of arbitration reports, Wheeler (1976) reported that corrective punishments (e.g., warnings) were applied in over 50 percent of cases involving infractions such as absenteeism and intoxication, while more severe sanctions (e.g., termination) were applied in cases involving infractions such as dishonesty, illegal strikes, and insubordination.

Several authors have noted that dismissal of employees may be becoming more difficult due to legal constraints (Fisher, 1973; McAdams, 1978). Miner and Brewer (1976) spend considerable time delineating some of the difficulties and costs associated with firing an employee. Nevertheless, the right to dismiss an employee remains a carefully guarded management prerogative, and dismissal may be an effective sanction under certain circumstances.

Conceptual Framework and Propositions

The conceptual framework for this exploratory study is shown in Figure 1. This model postulates that variations will exist among supervisors in what they perceive as employee problems and in how they manage marginal employees. Those attitudes and behaviors associated with how supervisors approach and deal with marginal employees are characterized here as *style facets*. The figure also suggests that the problems perceived and strategies used in coping with the problems may be related. It is expected that variations in supervisors along these dimensions will be associated with differential use of sanctions such as warnings and dismissals. In addition, the model proposes a positive correlation between the use of sanctions and employee performance. Based on the conceptual framework shown in the figure, the following exploratory research questions are proposed:

Proposition 1a: Differences in perception of employee problems will be associated with variations in the use of sanctions. Proposition 1b: Differences in supervisor style facets will be associated with variations in the use of sanctions. Proposition 1c: Differences in the perception of employee problems will be associated with variations in supervisor style facets.

The research questions investigated here are based on similarities and differences among supervisors in identification and response to specific problems rather than in general conflict handling. Proposition 1a, for example, suggests the idea that clearly observable problem behaviors may be more likely to result in sanctions than behaviors that are harder to witness. Proposition 1b suggests, for instance, that supervisors who are more assertive in dealing with marginal employees may be more likely to apply sanctions than those who are less assertive. Proposition 1c suggests that certain employee problems, such as gross negligence of duties, may be associated with certain supervisor style facets, such as a propensity for confrontation. The general expectation underlying Proposition 1 is that supervisors will vary in perception of problems, ways used to deal with problems (style facets), and the use of sanctions.

Proposition 2: Supervisors who apply sanctions more frequently will have higher performing units than supervisors who apply sanctions less frequently.

Sanctions (e.g., informal warnings, formal warnings, and dismissals) may improve performance in several ways. First, sanctions may act to alert directly the

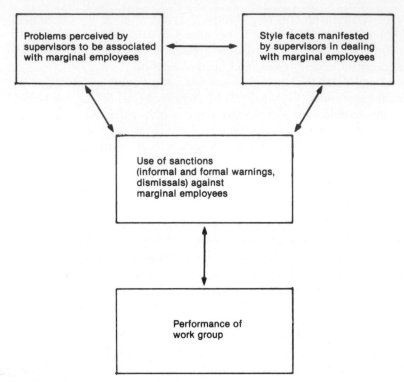

FIGURE 1
Interrelationship of perception of problems, style facets, sanctions, and performance.

marginal employee to his or her low performance and result in a change in behavior (e.g., improve attendance or increase output). Second, the sanction may be a signal to others in the work group as to expected levels of performance and standards of behavior, not in a punitive sense but in terms of social learning. Third, performance may be increased when the sanction is perceived as legitimate by other organizational members; the sanction may remove a source of inequity from the group and thus increase motivation and morale. In their reanalysis of the Hawthorne experiment, Franke and Karl (1978: 636) speculate that improvement in the relay assembly test room resulted from "the positive example of the two new workers, as well as from the aversive effects of management's disposal of two of the original workers." Rather than increased production resulting from a release from supervision, it appears that it occurred from its reassertion. Sayles and Strauss (1977: 115) quote an assembly line worker as saying,

> If a fellow is just a slacker, the foreman should straighten the man out for the sake of everybody . . . you don't like to do your best while the other guy goofs off, loafs . . . it burns you.

Heizer (1976: 119) provides a similar example in which a manager described an incident involving a dismissal and reported that the "remaining employees wondered why I had waited so long but unofficially agreed with my action."

Thus, when sanctions are perceived as legitimate by members of the organization and applied in an appropriate fashion, they may improve the performance of both the focal employee and the group. Discipline may act as a negative reinforcement to the former (Luthans and Kreitner, 1975) and improve feelings of equity for the latter (Weick, Bougon, and Maruyama, 1976). In cases where dismissal occurs, overall performance may be improved both through elimination of a marginal performer and through increased motivation of others.

DATA

Since there is a lack of data in identification and management of marginal employees, a data base was needed. The first phase of this investigation consisted of a series of structured interviews with twenty line managers and personnel officers in a large retail chain. These supervisors were asked how they characterized and dealt with marginal employees. Based on these interviews, a comprehensive questionnaire was constructed to gather information on the identification and management of marginal employees. This questionnaire was pilot-tested on five experienced retail sales managers. The pilot test allowed us to correct unclear wording, identify potential omissions, and ensure the accuracy and relevance of all items. The questionnaire was then screened for accuracy and completeness by two personnel managers familiar with procedures used for formally disciplining and terminating ineffective employees.

The questionnaire, a cover letter from the researchers explaining the purpose of the research and guaranteeing confidentiality of responses, a letter from the employer encouraging employees to participate, and a return envelope were sent to 169 managers from eight stores in a large retail chain. Each manager was a first-level supervisor of a department. After one follow-up mailing, responses were obtained from 141 supervisors (a response rate of 83 percent). Table 1 presents the means, standard deviations, and ranges for a series of demographic variables describing the sample. All managers were at the same hierarchical level and, excepting differences in the type of department supervised, performed the same set of tasks.

Each manager provided data on previous use of sanctions (informal warnings, formal warnings, and discharges), supplied demographic information, and responded to a series of questions measuring (1) perception of employee problems, (2) style facets, and (3) use of sanctions.

Problems characteristic of marginal employees were identified, through a critical-incident approach, during interviews with line and staff managers. A composite list of these problems was formed containing fourteen examples of problems that employees might present to a supervisor. Survey respondents indicated, on a seven-point Likert scale ranging from very infrequently to very frequently, the frequency with which these problems were encountered. Although an opportunity was provided for respondents to include additional problems, no further problems were added. The fourteen items were factor analyzed using a principal-components analysis and a varimax rotation. The items and factor loadings are presented in Table 2. Two dimensions were found. Based on the factor loadings, an interpre-

TABLE 1
141 RETAIL SALES MANAGERS: DEMOGRAPHICS, USE OF SANCTIONS, PERFORMANCE

	Mean	S.D.	Range
Demographics			
1 Tenure with organization (years)	4.0	5.9	0–32
2 Tenure as manager (years)	3.9	4.9	0–27
3 Age	30–34	under 25–over 50	
4 Education	2 years of college	High school– post grad	
5 Number of subordinates	8.4	3.7	0–27
Use of sanctions			
6 Number employees dismissed (present employment)	0.4	1.0	0–8
7 Number employees dismissed (lifetime)	0.9	1.5	0–8
8 Number formal warnings issued (present employment)	1.1	1.2	0–5
9 Number informal warnings issued (present employment)	2.7	2.3	0–15
Performance			
10 Performance rating (N = 113)	4.8	2.4	1–10

TABLE 2
MEANS, STANDARD DEVIATIONS, AND VARIMAX LOADINGS FOR FOURTEEN TYPES OF PROBLEMATIC BEHAVIOR (N = 141)

			Varimax loadings	
Problem*	Mean	S.D.	1 (Conduct)	2 (Sales orientation)
1. Fails to keep sales area tidy	3.6	1.6	.49	
2. Poor personal appearance	2.0	1.3		.40
3. Low sales productivity	3.0	1.6	.43	.55
4. Not courteous to customers	2.6	1.6		.70
5. High absenteeism	2.9	1.9	.51	
6. Doesn't assist in stocking	2.8	1.6	.48	
7. Conducts personal business during work hours	2.8	1.8	.66	
8. Doesn't follow supervisor's directions	2.7	1.6	.42	.51
9. Bad attitude toward job	2.8	1.6		.80
10. Lacks selling skills	2.9	1.7		.52
11. Takes long breaks	3.0	1.6	.69	
12. Doesn't cooperate with fellow workers	2.6	1.7	.48	.49
13. Leaves sales area unattended	2.2	1.6	.57	.43
14. Not punctual	2.8	1.7	.70	
Unique variance accounted for			46%	7%

*Responses were scored on a seven-point scale (1 = very infrequently to 7 = very frequently) tation suggests that supervisors generally see two independent problem areas—problems of personal conduct centered on attendance and punctuality (items 1, 5, 6, 7, 11, 13, and 14) and problems of sales orientation such as low sales productivity, a bad attitude, and lack of courtesy toward customers (2, 3, 4, 8, 9, and 10). . . .

Use of sanctions was assessed in two ways. First, respondents indicated the number of times they had, while employed by the firm, given informal oral warnings, given formal written warnings, or dismissed an employee. Respondents also indicated their beliefs about sanctions by specifying the number of informal and formal warnings that should be given before an employee was dismissed and the number of weeks that should elapse between a first warning and eventual dismissal.

In addition to questionnaire data, performance data on each of the first level managers were obtained from company files. Each was responsible for the sales of a department, and extensive sales and cost data were available comparing unit performances over time, both across similar departments and against projected goals. Managers were also rated on job knowledge and supervisory ability. These evaluations, completed by second- and third-level managers, were each summarized by the personnel office into a single overall rating. The overall score, on a ten-point scale, was used in this study. The performance rating was a summary measure of each manager's performance based predominantly on an assessment of the unit's annual costs and sales data. Performance ratings were available for 113 of the 169 managers surveyed. . . .

DISCUSSION

In general, the results . . . are consistent with the model shown in Figure 1. Supervisors appear to vary in their perceptions of employee problems and in their responses to marginal employees. Both the problems encountered and styles used are associated with types of sanctions employed. The evidence suggests, however, that associations between problems and sanctions may not be as consistent as associations between style facets and sanctions. The results do indicate that certain problems are associated with certain style facets. Importantly, the findings also show that supervisors who use sanctions more often also have higher performance ratings than those who use them less often.

Certain limitations must be kept in mind when interpreting the results of this study. First, the data are cross-sectional. While the performance ratings and use of sanctions constitute an objective record of previous behavior, the questionnaire responses are perceptual assessments. For this reason, causal inferences cannot be drawn safely. In addition, the sample (first-level retail managers) may not be representative of other managerial groups. These supervisors may be able to observe subordinate behavior and performance more closely than supervisors in situations where methods and goals are less clearly defined (e.g., Ouchi and Maguire, 1975). It should also be noted (Table 1) that the use of sanctions by supervisors is not great. Most supervisors have not dismissed many employees. This finding, supported by interview data, is consistent with previous evidence sug-

gesting that sanctions are not used frequently or against a wide range of subordinates but are typically concentrated on the occasional difficult employee. Finally,
company policies in the organization studied proscribed certain staffing options
such as transfer or retraining, which might be used in other firms as ways to deal
with marginal employees. Thus, differences affecting supervisor response to marginal employees may exist across organizations.

Sanctions and Performance

Despite these caveats, the existence of significant positive relationships among
use of sanctions and performance raises some interesting and important issues.
While previous research and theory have largely ignored the necessity for supervisors to deal with difficult employees, it is clear that, on occasion, supervisors do
have to do so. When authors deal with these issues at all, they tend to use the
literature on operant conditioning as a basis for recommendations (e.g., Megginson, 1977). This research usually demonstrates that negative reinforcement is a
less effective and predictable way to change behavior than positive reinforcement
or a simple lack of any conditioning response (e.g., Luthans and Kreitner, 1975).
The implication is that sanctions are likely to be an ineffective response to employee problems.

   The results here can be interpreted as directly contrary to this position. More
frequent use of sanctions is associated with increased performance. Several explanations can be offered. First, the performance ratings used in this study are largely
reflective of unit performance, not individual performance. Supervisors must deal
with the behaviors of individuals in a social context, not the isolated behavior of a
single person. Hence, generalizing to a social context from operant conditioning
theory, a theory of individual behavior, may be inappropriate (e.g., Roberts, Hulin, and Rousseau, 1978). Furthermore the disadvantages of negative reinforcement may be reduced if the sanction results in removal of the individual from the
group such that no opportunity exists for the repeated occurrence of an undesired
behavior; dismissal prohibits recurrence.

   A more powerful explanation for the positive relationship between sanctions
and performance can be found in social learning theory (Bandura, 1977). Individuals in groups look to others to learn appropriate behaviors and attitudes. In organizations, standards become institutionalized through the adoption of roles, standard operating procedures, and group norms (e.g., Zucker, 1977). Violation of
these institutionalized standards by an individual may result in feelings of uncertainty and inequity on the part of other group members and a loss of group cohesion. In addition, those individuals whose attitudes and behaviors are in violation
of group norms may cause problems for the group as well as for the supervisor.
Tolerance of such behavior by the supervisor may further threaten the group.
Hence, while employees may understandably resist frequent or unjustifiable authoritarian behavior on the part of a supervisor, actions by the supervisor that are
seen as maintaining legitimate group standards may reinforce productive group
norms, instill feelings of equity, and result in increased performance through so-

cial learning. Failure to invoke sanctions may result in loss of control by the supervisor and unproductive behavior on the part of employees.

Sanctions and Supervisor Style Facets

Evidence [from this study] suggests that there are differences in how supervisors characteristically choose to deal with marginal employees. A central distinction involves a willingness to confront difficult employees and take action. Supervisors who are more direct and who express less difficulty with firing are also more likely to apply sanctions. This evidence is consistent with previous studies demonstrating that some individuals are more likely to confront situations involving conflict than others (e.g., Burke, 1970; Thomas, 1976). These findings are also consistent with a study by O'Reilly and Weitz (1980) linking conflict-handling style to both the style facets reported here and the use of sanctions. The study showed that more assertive managers were more direct in their confrontation of problems and expressed less difficulty with firing. Managers who were more cooperative gave fewer warnings and had difficulty dismissing problem employees.

Unfortunately, in the present investigation causal relationships between use of sanctions and supervisor style facets cannot be determined. However, two arguments can be offered; either supervisors have characteristic styles that predispose them to use sanctions more frequently, or supervisors tend to adopt certain styles as they become more experienced. Both explanations, as well as one of reciprocal causation, are plausible. If the position taken by theorists who propose that conflict-handling styles are learned predispositions is correct, then it may be that supervisors learn through experience how to deal with marginal employees.

Those who are successful in learning how to confront marginal employees may then be more willing to use sanctions in future circumstances. Some qualitative evidence obtained during interviews supports this position. One highly successful manager described his willingness to fire employees as "an acquired taste." A second successful manager indicated that it was very important for a manager to learn early that the problem encountered was that of the employee, not the supervisor. Less successful managers often described dealing with marginal employees as a traumatic event, one to be avoided if possible.

Sanctions and Problems

Several issues are raised by the nature of the problems characterizing marginal employees (Table 2) and the relationships of these problems to use of sanctions . . . First, little data have been gathered on how supervisors characterize or identify employees as marginal. The prescriptive literature lists a variety of problems that might be encountered by a supervisor, but little data are available to suggest what problems are actually encountered by individual supervisors (e.g., Miner, 1975; Glueck, 1978). At the company level, problems such as absenteeism, dishonesty, intoxication, and insubordination are often mentioned (e.g., Parisi, 1972; Miner and Brewer, 1976), but these lists provide little insight into how often managers actually encounter these problems. Wheeler (1976), for instance, analyzes 339 incidents resulting in arbitration over a five-year period. While the data are useful, they do not indicate how many of these problems were handled by supervisors before going to arbitration, nor do they indicate whether similar problems are encountered in firms not covered by collective bargaining contracts.

The findings reported in this study suggest that, in the organization studied, instances of gross insubordination, intoxication, or dishonesty were not widely encountered. Instead, supervisors dealt with the more common problems listed in Table 2. Furthermore, it appears that the set of fourteen problems may be aggregated into two categories of problems—those of conduct and those of performance. These categories are conceptually similar to the behavior and output control categories suggested by Ouchi and Maguire (1975). To the extent that the problems encountered in this study are representative, it appears that supervisors use these two categories when defining marginal employees. Both categories are shown to be correlated with use of sanctions and supervisor style facets, suggesting that employees are assessed on two independent dimensions: to avoid being perceived as a problem, employees must give supervisors the impression that they are motivated and committed to the job and they must perform satisfactorily.

CONCLUSIONS

A central premise underlying this study is that supervisors are likely to encounter employees who, for a variety of reasons, are seen as marginal. It was postulated that supervisors would vary in how they chose to manage these employees and in their willingness to use sanctions. It was further postulated that failure to apply sanctions when required would be associated with lower performance. In general, these patterns were corroborated.

Given the exploratory nature of this study, firm conclusions are not warranted. A number of factors that might affect the use and impact of sanctions are not adequately explored here. For instance, it may be that the interdependence of work flows within groups will mediate the relationship between sanctions and performance. The task of selling in a retail store requires little task interdependence. In highly interdependent task groups, however, it may be that a marginal employee will be quite disruptive to group performance, especially if coordination is through mutual adjustment and feedback. Fry, Kerr, and Lee (1979: 6), in a study of athletic teams, suggest this when they observe that

> considerable day-to-day initiation of structure by the hierarchical leader (i.e., coach) will be useful under high interdependence conditions

These authors examined the performance of sport teams that varied in the degree of task interdependence among members and found that under conditions of high interdependence a directive leader behavior was most effective. A similar conclusion may be drawn from the path-goal literature, where initiating structure, which might include the use of sanctions, is seen as being more effective when the task is ambiguous to the subordinate. Thus, the efficacy of sanctions may be moderated by characteristics of technology or task design.

An additional point concerning the use of sanctions in a social context needs to be raised. Given a social learning theory perspective, it should be emphasized that the impact of sanctions on observers is dependent upon how group members interpret the sanction use. Conclusions drawn by observers will be related to subsequent attitudes and behaviors (Mitchell and Wood, 1980). As Pfeffer (1981) has suggested, it is the symbolic value of the action taken by the supervisor that may be most important. It is important that group members interpret the use of a sanction as beneficial to their own ends. This suggests the need for supervisors to be sensitive to group perceptions of their behavior and to be aware of factors such as equity norms and group cohesiveness that may color interpretation of their actions. Punitive behavior has been shown to be highly salient to subordinates (Curtis, Smith, and Smoll, 1979); therefore, sanctions may be of great symbolic significance.

Clearly the present study does not begin to explore these issues. It does, however, suggest that sanctions may play an important part in the development and maintenance of productivity norms and that the appropriate application of sanctions may be supported by group members. Further study is clearly needed to examine the full impact of sanctions in work settings.

REFERENCES

Aldag, Ray and Art Brief (1978), Task Design and Employee Motivation. Glenview, IL: Scott, Foresman.

Anderson, Claire (1976), The Marginal Worker: A Search for Correlates. Doctoral dissertation, School of Business, University of Massachusetts.

Bandura, Albert (1977), Social Learning Theory. Englewood Cliffs, NJ: Prentice-Hall.

Baum, John, and Stuart Youngblood (1975), "Impact of an organizational control policy on absenteeism, performance, and satisfaction." Journal of Applied Psychology, **60:** 688–794.

Berkowitz, Leonard (1969), "Social motivation." In Gardner Lindzey and Eliott Aronson (eds.), The Handbook of Social Psychology, vol. 3: 50–135. Reading, MA: Addison-Wesley.

Booker, Gene (1969), "Behavioral aspects of disciplinary action." Personnel Journal, **48:** 525–529.

Burke, Ronald (1970), "Methods of managing superior-subordinate conflict: Their effectiveness and consequences." Canadian Journal of Behavior Science, **2:** 124–135.

Campbell, John P., and Robert Pritchard (1976), "Motivation theory in industrial and organizational psychology." In Marvin Dunnette (ed.), Handbook of Industrial and Organizational Psychology: 63–130. Chicago: Rand-McNally.

Cummings, Larry, and Donald Schwab (1973), Performance in Organizations: Determinants and Appraisal. Glenview, IL: Scott, Foresman.

Curtis, Bill, Ronald Smith, and Frank Smoll (1979), "Scrutinizing the skipper: A study of leadership behaviors in the dugout." Journal of Applied Psychology, **64:** 391–400.

Evan, William (1976), "Organization theory and organizational effectiveness: An exploratory analysis." In S. Lee Spray (ed.), Organizational Effectiveness: Theory, Research, and Application: 15–28. Kent, OH: Kent State University Press.

Fisher, Robert (1973), "When workers are discharged: An overview." Monthly Labor Review, **96:** 4–17.

Franke, Richard, and James Karl (1978), "The Hawthorne experiments: First statistical interpretation." American Sociological Review, **43:** 623–643.

Fry, Louis, Steven Kerr, and Cynthia Lee (1979), "Athletic teams as research samples: A test of the moderating effects of task interdependence on the relationship between leader behavior and subordinate attitudes." Presented to the International Meeting of the Institute of Management Sciences, Honolulu, June.

Glueck, William (1978), Personnel: A Diagnostic Approach. Dallas: Business Publications.

Goodman, Paul, Johannes Pennings, and Associates (1979), New Perspectives on Organizational Effectiveness. San Francisco: Jossey-Bass.

Guion, Robert (1976), "Recruiting, selection, and job placement." In Marvin Dunnette (ed.), Handbook of Industrial and Organizational Psychology: 777–828. Chicago: Rand-McNally.

Hackman, J. Richard, and Greg Oldham (1976), "Motivation through the design of work: Test of a theory." Organizational Behavior and Human Performance, **16:** 250–279.

Heizer, Jay (1976), "Transfers and terminations as staffing options." Academy of Management Journal, **19:** 115–120.

Hinrichs, John (1976), "Personnel training." In Marvin Dunnette (ed.), Handbook of Industrial and Organizational Psychology: 829–860. Chicago: Rand-McNally.

Huberman, John (1975), "Discipline without punishment lives." Harvard Business Review, **53:** 6–18.

Luthans, Fred, and Robert Kreitner (1975), Organizational Behavior Modification. Glenview, IL: Scott Foresman.

Mahoney, Thomas, and William Weitzel (1969), "Managerial models of organizational effectiveness." Administrative Science Quarterly, **14:** 357–365.

McAdams, Tony (1978), "Dismissal: A decline in employer autonomy?" Business Horizons, **19:** 67–72.

McDermott, Thomas, and Thomas Newhams (1971), "Discharge-reinstatement: What happens thereafter." Industrial and Labor Relations Review, **24:** 526–540.

Megginson, Leon (1977), Personnel and Human Resources Administration. Homewood, IL: Irwin.

Miner, John (1975), The Challenge of Managing. Philadelphia: Saunders.

Miner, John, and J. Frank Brewer (1976), "The management of ineffective performance." In Marvin Dunnette (ed.), Handbook of Industrial and Organizational Psychology: 995–1030. Chicago: Rand-McNally.

Mitchell, Terry, and Robert Wood (1980), "Supervisor's responses to subordinate poor performance: A test of an attributional model." Organizational Behavior and Human Performance, **25:** 123–138.

Mulder, Frans (1971), "Characteristics of violators of formal company rules." Journal of Applied Psychology, **55:** 500–502.

Odiorne, George (1971), Personnel Administration by Objectives. Homewood, IL: Irwin.

O'Reilly, Charles, and Barton Weitz (1980), "Conflict handling styles and managers' use of sanctions." Working paper, School of Business Administration, University of California, Berkeley.

Ouchi, William, and Mary Ann Maguire (1975), "Organizational control: Two functions." Administrative Science Quarterly, **20:** 559–569

Parisi, Aurora (1972), "Employee terminations," In John Famularo (ed.), Handbook of Modern Personnel Administration: 1–14. New York: McGraw-Hill.

Pfeffer, Jeffrey (1981), "Management as symbolic action: The creation and maintenance of meaning." In Larry Cummings and Barry Staw (eds.), Research in Organizational Behavior, vol. 3 (forthcoming). Greenwich, CT: JAI Press.

Roberts, Karlene, Charles Hulin, and Denise Rousseau (1978), Developing an Interdisciplinary Science of Organizations. San Francisco: Jossey-Bass.

Ruble, Thomas, and Kenneth Thomas (1976), "Support for a two-dimensional model of conflict behavior." Organizational Behavior and Human Performance, **16:** 143–155.

Sayles, Leonard, and George Strauss (1977), Managing Human Resources. Englewood Cliffs, NJ: Prentice-Hall.

Steers, Richard (1975), "Problems in the measurement of organizational effectiveness." Administrative Science Quarterly, **20:** 546–558.

Steinmetz, Lawrence (1969), Managing the Marginal and Unsatisfactory Worker. Reading, MA: Addison-Wesley.

Stogdill, Ralph (1974), Handbook of Leadership. New York: Free Press.

Thomas, Kenneth (1976), "Conflict and conflict management." In Marvin Dunnette (ed.), Handbook of Industrial and Organizational Psychology: 889–935. Chicago: Rand-McNally.

Vroom, Victor (1976), "Leadership." In Marvin Dunnette (ed.), Handbook of Industrial and Organizational Psychology: 1527–1551. Chicago: Rand-McNally.

Weick, Karl, Michel Bougon, and Geoffrey Maruyama (1976), "The equity context." Organizational Behavior and Human Performance, **15:** 32–65.

Wheeler, Hoyt (1976), "Punishment theory and industrial discipline." Industrial Relations, **15:** 235–243.

Wohlking, Wallace (1975), "Effective discipline in employee relations." Personnel Journal, **54:** 489–493.

Zucker, Lynne (1977), "The role of institutionalization in cultural persistence." American Sociological Review, **42:** 726–742.

QUESTIONS FOR DISCUSSION

1 Why do you think there has not been more research on punishment? Does this imply any cautions for application of punishment in organizations?

2 What are the arguments *for* using punishment to control behavior in organizations?

3 How might you use punishment to decrease the absenteeism of a particular employee? Be specific about measurement of absenteeism and timing, intensity, scheduling, and type of punishment.

4 Do you think that punishment is an appropriate method for controlling behavior? If so, what type of behavior, and in what setting, calls for punishment, and how should it be administered?

5 Knowing that your methods of perception of subordinates' behavior and your personal managerial style will influence your decisions to use sanctions in the work environment, how would you make sure that your decisions are beneficial for your organization?

6 O'Reilly and Weitz present research evidence which suggests that there is a significant positive relationship between use of sanctions by leaders and work unit performance. What relationship would you propose exists between use of sanctions and satisfaction? Does your answer vary if you consider just the individual sanctioned rather than the work unit? Why?

7 What actions would you take in the case of subordinates who (*a*) conducted personal business during working hours, (*b*) lacked sales skill, and (*c*) did not cooperate with other employees? Analyze your answers by using either the Mitchell and Green model or the O'Reilly and Weitz model. What inferences can you make about yourself from this analysis?

8 How might a manager confront a subordinate's denial of poor performance and "encourage movement beyond the stage of coping"?

9 How do the suggestions for constructive performance improvement given by Latham, Cummings, and Mitchell compare with those of Locke concerning goal-setting (Chapter 3)?

CHAPTER 10

JOB DESIGN AND
QUALITY OF WORK

Early managerial approaches to job design (discussed in Chapter 1) focused primarily on attempts to simplify an employee's required tasks insofar as possible in order to increase production efficiency. It was felt that, since workers were largely economically motivated, the best way to maximize output was to reduce tasks to their simplest forms and then reward workers with money on the basis of units of output—a piece-rate incentive plan. In theory, such a system would simultaneously satisfy the primary goals of both the employees and the company. Evidence of such a philosophy can be seen in the writings of Taylor and other scientific management advocates.

This approach to simplified job design reached its zenith from a technological standpoint in assembly-line production techniques such as those used by automobile manufacturers. (Piece-rate incentive systems have been largely omitted here, however.) On auto assembly lines, in many cases, the average length of "work cycle" (i.e., the time allowed for an entire "piece" of work) ranges from 30 seconds to 1½ minutes. This means that workers repeat the same task an average of at least 500 times per day. Such a technique, efficient as it may be, is not without its problems, however. As workers have become better educated and more organized, they have begun demanding more from their jobs. Not only is this demand shown in recurrent requests for shorter hours and higher wages, but it is also shown in several undesirable behavior patterns, such as increased turnover, absenteeism, dissatisfaction, and sabotage.

While organizational psychologists and practicing managers have long sought ways of reducing such undesirable behavior, only recently have they begun to study it rigorously in connection with the task performed. As pointed out by Porter (1969, p. 415), ". . . at best, prior to the last few years, task factors have been underemphasized, if considered at all, in attempts to reveal the motivational and cognitive explanations for job behaviors." This omission has been largely alleviated by a series of recent investigations into ways to attack the problem of job redesign as it affects motivation, performance, and satisfaction. Somewhat surprisingly, many of the new "solutions" bear a striking resemblance to the old craft type of technology of pre-assembly-line days.

Considerable evidence has come to light recently in support of positive behavioral and attitudinal consequences of such job enrichment efforts (Ford, 1969; Lawler, 1973; Maher, 1971; Myers, 1970; Special Task Force, HEW, 1973; Vroom, 1964). In general, such efforts have tended to result in (1) significantly reduced turnover and absenteeism; (2) improved job satisfaction; (3) improved quality of products; and (4) some, though not universal, improvements in productivity and output rates. On the negative side, the costs often associated with such programs are generally identified as (1) increased training time and expense and (2) occasionally, additional retooling costs where dramatic shifts toward group assembly teams have been instituted.

A major thrust of many of the contemporary efforts at job redesign research represents a blend of two central factors. On the one hand, researchers are concerned with studying the motivational processes associated with redesigning jobs. On the other hand, they are equally concerned with the practical applications of such knowledge as it affects attempts to improve the work environment. In this sense, investigations in this area have generally represented applied research in the truest sense.

HERZBERG'S TWO-FACTOR THEORY

One of the earliest researchers in the area of job redesign as it affects motivation was Frederick Herzberg (Herzberg, Mausner, & Snyderman, 1959). Herzberg and his associates began their initial work on factors affecting work motivation in the mid-1950s. Their first effort entailed a thorough review of existing research to that date on the subject (Herzberg, Mausner, Peterson, & Capwell, 1957). On the basis of this review, Herzberg carried out his now famous survey of 200 accountants and engineers, from which he derived the initial framework for his theory of motivation. The theory, as well as the supporting data, was first published in 1959 (Herzberg, Mausner, & Snyderman, 1959) and was subsequently amplified and developed in a later book (Herzberg, 1966).

On the basis of his survey, Herzberg discovered that employees tended to describe satisfying experiences in terms of factors that were intrinsic to the content of the job itself. These factors were called "motivators" and included such variables as achievement, recognition, the work itself, responsibility, advancement, and growth. Conversely, dissatisfying experiences, called "hygiene" factors, resulted largely from extrinsic, non-job-related factors, such as company policies, salary, coworker relations, and supervisory style (see Exhibit I). Herzberg argued, on the basis of these results, that eliminating the causes of dissatisfaction (through hygiene factors) would not result in a state of satisfaction. Instead, it would result in a neutral state. Satisfaction (and motivation) would occur only as a result of the use of motivators.

Models	Basic Components of the Model
Two-Factor Theory (Herzberg)	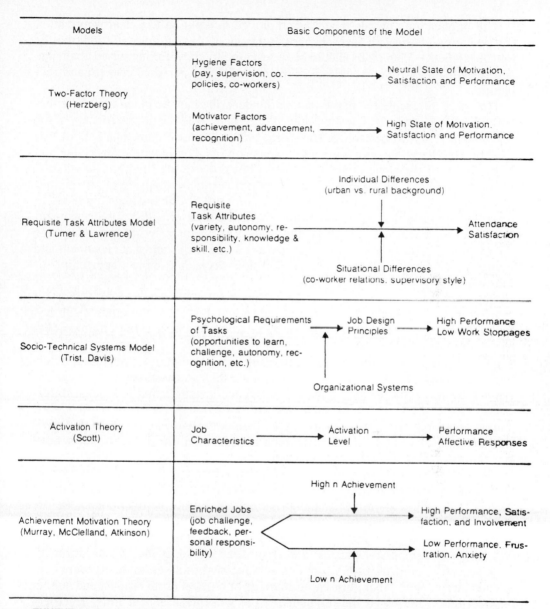
Requisite Task Attributes Model (Turner & Lawrence)	
Socio-Technical Systems Model (Trist, Davis)	
Activation Theory (Scott)	
Achievement Motivation Theory (Murray, McClelland, Atkinson)	

EXHIBIT 1
Conceptual models of the motivational properties of tasks. (From R. M. Steers and R. T. Mowday. The motivational properties of tasks. Academy of Management Review, 1977, **2**, 645–658. Reprinted by permission.)

The implications of this model of employee motivation are clear: motivation can be increased through basic changes in the nature of an employee's job (that is, job enrichment). Thus, jobs should be redesigned to allow for increased challenge and responsibility, opportunities for advancement and personal growth, and recognition.

Herzberg differentiated between what he described as the older and less effective job redesign efforts, known as job *enlargement,* and the newer concept of job *enrichment* (Paul, Robertson, & Herzberg, 1969). The term "job enlargement," as used by Herzberg, means a *horizontal* expansion of an employee's job, giving him or her more of the same kinds of activities but not altering the necessary skills. "Job enrichment," on the other hand, means a *vertical* expansion of an employee's job, requiring an increase in the skills repertoire which ostensibly leads to increased opportunities. As Paul et al. (1969, p. 61) described it, job enrichment "seeks to improve both efficiency and human satisfaction by means of building into people's jobs, quite specifically, a greater scope for personal achievement and recognition, more challenging and responsible work, and more opportunity for individual advancement and growth."

Since its inception, Herzberg's theory has been subject to several important criticisms. For example, it has been noted (King, 1970) that the model itself has five different theoretical interpretations and that the available research evidence is not entirely consistent with any of these interpretations. Second, a number of scholars believe the model does not give sufficient attention to individual differences (although Herzberg himself would dispute this) and assumes that job enrichment benefits all employees. Research evidence suggests that individual differences are, in fact, an important moderator of the effects of job enrichment. Finally, research also has generally failed to support the existence of two independent factors (motivators and hygiene factors). Even so, the model has enhanced our understanding of motivation at work.

One of the most significant contributions of Herzberg's work was the tremendous impact it had on stimulating thought, research, and experimentation in the area of motivation at work. This contribution should not be overlooked. Before 1959, little research had been carried out on *work* motivation (with the notable exception of Viteles, 1953, and Maier, 1955), and the research that did exist was largely fragmentary. Maslow's work on need hierarchy theory and Murray's, McClelland's, and Atkinson's work on achievement motivation theory were concerned largely with laboratory-based findings or clinical observations, and neither had seriously addressed the problems of the workplace at that time. Herzberg filled this void by specifically calling attention to the need for increased understanding of the role of motivation in work organizations.

Moreover, he did so in a systematic manner and in language that was easily understood by a large body of managers. He advanced a theory that was simple to grasp, was based on some empirical data, and—equally important—offered specific action recommendations for managers to improve employee motivational levels. In doing so, he forced organizations to examine closely a number of possible misconceptions concerning motivation. For example, Herzberg argued that money should not necessarily be viewed as the most potent force on the job.

Moreover, he stated that other "context" factors in addition to money which surround an employee's job (such as fringe benefits and supervisory style) should not be expected to affect motivation markedly either. He advanced a strong case that managers must instead give considerable attention to a series of "content" factors (such as opportunities for achievement, recognition, and advancement) that have an important bearing on behavior. According to Herzberg, it is these content factors, and not money or other context factors, that are primarily related to work motivation. These contributions are often overlooked in the heated debates over the validity of the empirical data behind the theoretical formulations.

Herzberg, in addition, probably deserves a good deal of credit for acting as a stimulus to other researchers who have advocated alternative theories of *work* motivation. A multitude of research articles have been generated as a result of the so-called "Herzberg controversy." Some of these articles (e.g., Bockman, 1971; Whitset & Winslow, 1967) strongly support Herzberg's position, while others (e.g., House & Wigdor, 1967; Vroom, 1964) seriously question the research methodology underlying the theory. Such debate is healthy for any science. The serious student of motivation should consider Herzberg's theory—and any other theory—to be one attempt at modeling work behavior. As such, the theory should be dissected and/or modified in a continuing effort to develop comprehensive and accurate predictors of human behavior on the job. In other words, it appears that a fruitful approach to this "controversial" theory would be to learn from it that which can help us develop better models, rather than to accept or reject the model totally.

ADDITIONAL EARLY MODELS OF JOB DESIGN

In addition to Herzberg's model, several other early models of job design can be identified (see Exhibit 1). These are (1) the requisite task attributes model, (2) the sociotechnical systems model, (3) activation theory, and (4) achievement motivation theory. While a detailed examination of these models is beyond the scope of this chapter (see Steers & Mowday, 1977, for a review), we can briefly review how these various models differ in their approach to the motivational properties of tasks.

The *requisite task attributes model*, proposed by Turner and Lawrence (1965), argued that an enriched job (that is, a job characterized by variety, autonomy, responsibility, etc.) would lead to increased attendance and job satisfaction. The model was similar to Herzberg's in that it viewed job enrichment as a motivating variable. It differed from Herzberg's in that Turner and Lawrence included absenteeism as a dependent variable. Moreover, Turner and Lawrence acknowledged the existence of two sets of important moderators in the job scope–outcome relationship. First, it was found in their study that workers from urban settings were more satisfied with low-scope jobs than workers from rural settings. Second, it was found that situational factors (such as supervisory style and coworker relations) also moderated the impact of job scope on satisfaction and absenteeism. This acknowledgment of the role of individual and situational variables represents a significant contribution to our understanding of the ways in which job redesign affects employee attitudes and behavior. In fact, much of the subsequent work on the topic has taken the lead from the work of Turner and Lawrence.

A second and popular model, advanced by Trist and Davis, is known as the *sociotechnical systems model.* This model suggests that an appropriate starting point for understanding job design is to consider the psychological requirements of tasks in order for them to be motivating. These principles include the need for a job to provide (1) reasonably demanding content, (2) an opportunity to learn, (3) some degree of autonomy or discretion in decisions affecting the job, (4) social support and recognition, and (5) a feeling that the job leads to a desirable future.

On the basis of these principles, job design principles are derived which suggest, in brief, that enriched jobs meet these psychological requirements. As a consequence, enriched jobs would be expected to lead to such outcomes as high job performance and low labor stoppages. An important aspect of the sociotechnical model is that it clearly acknowledges the role of the social context (or organizational system) in which job redesign attempts are made. That is, the model argues that such changes cannot be successfully implemented without acknowledging and taking into account various social and organizational factors that also influence people's desire to perform on the job (reward system, work group norms, supervisory relations, etc.). Hence, the sociotechnical systems approach attempts to be a truly systematic (that is, comprehensive) approach to work design.

Activation theory focuses on the physiological processes involved in job redesign (Scott, 1966). Activation, defined as the degree of excitation of the brain stem reticular formation, has been found in laboratory experiments to have a curvilinear relationship to performance. Research has demonstrated that performance suffers at very low or very high levels of activation. Hence, jobs that are dull or repetitive may lead to low levels of performance because they fail to activate. On the other hand, more enriched jobs should lead to a state of activation with a resulting increase in performance. While many questions remain concerning the empirical support for activation theory, it does suggest how job design can affect employees physiologically, a relationship ignored in previous research.

Finally, *achievement motivation theory,* proposed by Murray (1938) and refined by McClelland and Atkinson, also examines the process by which changes in the job situation influence behavior. The focus of this approach, however, is on employee personality, specifically, an employee's need for achievement. In essence, achievement motivation theory posits that employees with a high need for achievement will be more likely to respond favorably to enriched jobs than employees with a low need for achievement. Enriched jobs cue, or stimulate, the achievement motive, typically leading to higher levels of performance, involvement, and satisfaction. For employees with a low need for achievement, however, an enriched job may be threatening; that is, they may feel overchallenged. As a result, they may experience increased frustration and anxiety and exhibit lower performance. Findings by Steers and Spencer (1977) support this conclusion.

In conclusion, we have seen that several models of job design exist. Each model tends to focus on one aspect of the job situation (e.g., personality, social context, or physiological response) and, therefore makes a useful contribution by expanding our understanding of the relevant variables that must be included in a comprehensive model of work design. As the readings in this chapter will demonstrate, when one or more features of these models are implemented and job designs are actually changed, opinions about their efficacy for improving "quality of work life" are mixed. Results overall tend to be positive, but not uniformly so, and it is clear that the kinds of approaches discussed later in the chapter are not simple and do not constitute any type of panacea. In other words, there are a number of complexities involved in job design changes that are intended to improve the quality of work life. Nevertheless, these kinds of efforts have the *potential* for bringing about beneficial effects on the way the employee relates to the work situation, to supervision, and to the organization.

OVERVIEW

The readings that follow present a more comprehensive approach to quality-of-work-life (QWL) issues than those reviewed above. In the initial article, by Hackman, the concept of job design is examined in some detail, with particular attention to job design as a change strategy. The job characteristics model is presented, along with supporting evidence. Moreover, several principles for enriching jobs are reviewed. Finally, guidelines for instituting job redesign are suggested.

In the second article, Gyllenhammar, the president of Volvo, describes several efforts made by the Swedish industrial concern to improve the quality of work life. Included here is a description of the famous Kalmar experiment.

The third article, by Lawler, examines several techniques used in the workplace to enhance employee involvement. Several aspects of work design are considered as they relate to organization effectiveness. Finally, the article by Walton updates much of the QWL literature by focusing on how organizations can develop personnel policies that center on commitment instead of control. Implications for management are discussed.

REFERENCES

Bockman, V. M. The Herzberg controversy. *Personnel Psychology,* 1971, **24**, 155–189.

Ford, R. N. *Motivation through the work itself.* New York: American Management Association, 1969.

Herzberg, F. *Work and the nature of man.* Cleveland: World Publishing, 1966.

Herzberg, F., Mausner, B., Peterson, R. O., & Capwell, D. F. *Job attitudes: Review of research and opinion.* Pittsburgh: Psychological Services of Pittsburgh, 1957.

Herzberg, F., Mausner, B., & Snyderman, B. *The motivation to work.* New York: Wiley, 1959.

House, R. J., & Wigdor, L. A. Herzberg's dual-factor theory of job satisfaction and motivation. *Personnel Psychology,* 1957, **20**, 369–390.

King, N. Clarification and evaluation of the two-factor theory of job satisfaction. *Psychological Bulletin,* 1970, **74**, 18–31.

Lawler, E. E., III. *Motivation in work organizations.* Monterey, Calif.: Brooks/Cole, 1973.

Maher, J. R. (Ed.) *New perspectives in job enrichment*. New York: Van Nostrand Reinhold, 1971.

Maier, N. R. F. *Psychology in industry,* 2d ed. Boston: Houghton Mifflin, 1955.

Murray, H. A. *Explorations in personality*. New York: Oxford University Press, 1938.

Myers, M. S. *Every employee a manager*. New York: McGraw-Hill, 1970.

Paul, W. J., Robertson, K. B., & Herzberg, F. Job enrichment pays off. *Harvard Business Review,* 1969, **47**(2), 61–78.

Porter, L. W. Effects of task factors on job attitudes and behavior. *Personnel Psychology,* 1969, **22,** 415–418.

Scott, W. E. Activation theory and task design. *Organizational Behavior and Human Performance,* 1966, **1**, 3–30.

Special Task Force to the Secretary of Health, Education, and Welfare. *Work in America.* Cambridge, Mass.: M.I.T. 1973.

Steers, R. M., & Mowday, R. T. The motivational properties of tasks. *Academy of Management Review,* 1977, **2**, 645–658.

Steers, R. M., & Spencer, D. G. The role of achievement motivation in job design. *Journal of Applied Psychology,* 1977, **62**, 472–479.

Turner, A. N., & Lawrence, P. R. *Industrial jobs and the worker*. Boston: Harvard University, Graduate School of Business Administration, 1965.

Viteles, M. S. *Motivation and morale in industry*. New York: Norton, 1953.

Vroom, V. H. *Work and motivation*. New York: Wiley, 1964.

Whitset, D. A., & Winslow, E. K. An analysis of studies critical of the motivation-hygiene theory. *Personnel Psychology,* 1967, **20**, 391–416.

Work Design

J. Richard Hackman

Every five years or so, a new behavioral science "solution" to organization-al problems emerges. Typically such a solution is first tried out—with great success—in a few forward-looking organizations. Then it is picked up by the man-agement journals and the popular press and spreads across the country. And finally, after a few years, it fades away as disillusioned managers, union lead-ers, and employees come to agree that the solution really does not solve much of anything.

It looks as if the redesign of work is to be the solution of the mid-1970s. The seeds of this strategy for change were planted more than two decades ago, with the pioneering research of Charles Walker and Robert Guest (1952), Frederick Herzberg and his associates (Herzberg, Mausner, and Snyderman, 1959; Herz-berg, 1966), Louis Davis (1957, 1966), and a few others. Successful tests of work redesign were conducted in a few organizations and were widely reported. Now, change programs involving work redesign are flooding the nation, stories on "how we profited from job enrichment" are appearing in management journals, and the labor community is struggling to determine how it should respond to the tidal wave that seems to be forming (Gooding, 1972).

The question of the moment is whether the redesign of work will evolve into a robust and powerful strategy for organizational change—or whether, like so many of its behavioral science predecessors, it will fade into disuse as practitioners experience failure and disillusionment in its applications. The answer is by no means clear.

Present evidence regarding the merits of work redesign can be viewed as opti-mistic or pessimistic, depending on the biases of the reader. On the one hand, numerous published case studies of successful work redesign projects show that work redesign can be an effective tool for improving both the quality of the work experience of employees and their on-the-job productivity. Yet it also is true that numerous failures in implementing work redesign have been experienced by orga-nizations around the country—and the rate of failure shows no sign of diminish-ing. Reif and Luthans (1972), for example, summarize a survey, conducted in the mid-1960s, in which only four of forty-one firms implementing job enrichment described their experiences with the technique as "very successful." Increas-ingly, other commentators are expressing serious doubts about whether job en-richment is really as effective as it has been cracked up to be (Fein, 1974; Gom-berg, 1973; Hulin and Blood, 1968).

Unfortunately, existing research findings and case reports are not very helpful in assessing the validity of the claims made by either the advocates or the skeptics of work redesign. In particular, an examination of the literature cited in Hackman (1975a) leads to the following conclusions:

From J. R. Hackman & J. L. Suttle (Eds.), *Improving Life at Work*. Glenview, Ill.: Scott, Foresman, 1977. © 1977 by Scott, Foresman and Company. Reprinted by permission.

1 Reports of work redesign successes tend to be more evangelical than thoughtful; for example, little conceptualizing is done that would be useful either as a guide to implementation of work redesign in other settings or as a theoretical basis for research on its effects.

2 The methodologies used in evaluating the effects of changes in work design often are weak or incomplete. Therefore, findings reported may be ambiguous and open to alternative explanations.

3 Although informal sources and surveys suggest that the failure rate for work redesign projects is moderate to high, few documented analyses are available of projects that failed. This is particularly unfortunate because careful analyses of failures often are among the most effective tools for exploring the applicability and the consequences of this or any other organizational change strategy.

4 Most published reports focus almost exclusively on assessing the positive and negative effects of specific changes in work content. Conclusions are then drawn about the general worth of work redesign as a change strategy. Yet there is an *interaction* between the content of the changes and the organizational context in which they are installed; identical job changes may have quite different effects in different organizational settings (or when installed using different processes). Existing literature has little to say about the nature or dynamics of such interactions.

5 Rarely are economic data (that is, direct and indirect dollar costs and benefits) analyzed and discussed when conclusions are drawn about the effects of work redesign projects, even though many such projects are undertaken in direct anticipation of economic gains.

In sum, it appears that despite the abundance of writing on the topic, there is little definite information about why work redesign is effective when it is, what goes wrong when it is not, and how the strategy can be altered to improve its general usefulness as an approach to personal and organizational change.

This paper attempts to advance current understanding about such questions. It reviews what is known about how the redesign of work can help improve life in organizations and attempts to identify the circumstances under which the approach is most likely to succeed. It reviews current practice for planning and installing work redesign and emphasizes both the pitfalls that may be encountered and the change strategies that have been shown to be especially effective. And, at the most general level, it asks whether this approach to organizational change is indeed worth saving, or whether it should be allowed to die.

WHAT IS WORK REDESIGN?

Whenever a job is changed—whether because of a new technology, an internal reorganization, or a whim of a manager—it can be said that work redesign has taken place. The present use of the term is somewhat more specialized. Throughout this paper, work redesign is used to refer to any activities that involve the alteration of specific jobs (or interdependent systems of jobs) with the intent of increasing both the quality of the employees' work experience and their on-the-job productivity. This definition of the term is deliberately broad, to include the great diversity of changes that can be tried to achieve these goals. It subsumes such terms as *job rotation, job enrichment,* and *sociotechnical systems design,* each of which refers to a specific approach to or technique for redesigning work.

There are no simple or generally accepted criteria for a well-designed job, nor is there any single strategy that is acknowledged as the proper way to go about improving a job. Instead, what will be an effective design for one specific job in a particular organization may be quite different from the way the job should be designed or changed in another setting. There are, nonetheless, some commonalities in most work redesign experiments that have been carried out to date. Typically changes are made that provide employees with additional responsibilities for planning, setting up, and checking their own work; for making decisions about methods and procedures; for establishing their own work pace within broad limits; and sometimes for relating directly with the client who receives the results of the work. Often the net effect is that jobs which previously had been simplified and segmented into many small parts (in the interest of efficiency from an engineering perspective) are put back together again and made the responsibility of individual workers (Herzberg, 1974).

An early case of work redesign (reported by Kilbridge, 1960) is illustrative. The basic job involved the assembly of small centrifugal pumps used in washing machines. Prior to redesign, the pumps were assembled by six operators on a conveyor line, with each operator performing a particular part of the assembly. The job was changed so that each worker assembled an entire pump, inspected it, and placed his own identifying mark on it. In addition, the assembly operations were converted to a batch system in which workers had more freedom to control their work pace than they had had under the conveyor system. Kilbridge reports that after the job had been enlarged, total assembly time decreased, quality improved, and important cost savings were realized.

In another case, the responsibilities of clerks who assembled information for telephone directories at Indiana Bell Telephone Company were significantly expanded (Ford, 1973). Prior to the change, a production line model was used to assemble directory information. Information was passed from clerk to clerk as it was processed, and each clerk performed only a very small part of the entire job. There were a total of twenty-one different steps in the workflow. Jobs were changed so that each qualified clerk was given responsibility for all the clerical operations required to assemble an entire directory—including receiving, processing, and verifying all information. (For large directories, clerks were given responsibility for a specific alphabetical section of the book.) Not only did the new work arrangement improve the quality of the work experience of the employees, but the efficiency of the operation increased as well—in part because clerks made fewer errors, and so it was no longer necessary to have employees who merely checked and verified the work of others.

In recent years, work redesign increasingly has been used as part of a larger change package aimed at improving the overall quality of life and productivity of people at work. A good example is the new General Foods pet food manufacturing plant in Topeka, Kansas (Walton, 1972, 1975b). When plans were developed for the facility in the late 1960s, corporate management decided to design and manage the plant in full accord with state-of-the-art behavioral science knowledge. Non-traditional features were built into the plant from the beginning—including the physical design of the facilities, the management style, information and feedback systems, compensation arrangements, and career paths for individual employees. A key part of the plan was the organization of the work force into teams. Each team (consisting of from seven to fourteen members) was given nearly autonomous responsibility for a significant organizational task. In addition to actually carrying out the work required to complete that task, team members performed many activities that traditionally had been reserved for management. These included coping with manufacturing problems, distributing individual tasks among team members, screening and selecting new team members, and participating in organizational decision-making (Walton, 1972). The basic jobs performed by team members were designed to be as challenging as possible, and employees were encouraged to further broaden their skills in order to be able to handle even more challenging work. Although not without problems, the Topeka plant appears to be prospering, and many employees experience life in the organization as a pleasant and nearly revolutionary change from their traditional ideas about what happens at work.

The Uniqueness of Work Redesign as a Strategy for Change

The redesign of work differs from most other behavioral science approaches to changing life in organizations in at least four ways (Hackman, 1975b). Together, these four points of uniqueness make a rather compelling case for work redesign as a strategy for initiating organizational change.

1 Work Redesign Alters the Basic Relationship between a Person and What He or She Does on the Job   When all the outer layers are stripped away, many organizational problems come to rest at the interface between *people* and the *tasks* they do. Frederick Taylor realized this when he set out to design and manage organizations "scientifically" at the beginning of this century (Taylor, 1911). The design of work was central to the scientific management approach, and special pains were taken to ensure that the tasks done by workers did not exceed their performance capabilities. As the approach gained credence in the management community, new and more sophisticated procedures for analyzing work methods emerged, and industrial engineers forged numerous principles of work design. In general, these principles were intended to maximize overall production efficiency by minimizing human error on the job (often accomplished by partitioning the work into small, simple segments), and by minimizing time and motion wasted in doing work tasks.

It turned out, however, that many workers did not like jobs designed according to the dictates of scientific management. In effect, the person-job relationship had been arranged so that achieving the goals of the organization (high productivity) often meant sacrificing important personal goals (the opportunity for interesting, personally rewarding work). Taylor and his associates attempted to deal with this difficulty by installing financial incentive programs intended to make workers want to work hard toward organizational goals, and by placing such an elaborate set of supervisory controls on workers that they scarcely could behave otherwise. But the basic incongruence between the person and the work remained, and people-problems (such as high absenteeism and turnover, poor quality work, and high worker dissatisfaction) became increasingly evident in work organizations.

In the past several decades, industrial psychologists have carried out a large number of studies intended to overcome some of the problems that accompanied the spread of scientific management. Sophisticated strategies for identifying those individuals most qualified to perform specific jobs have been developed and validated. New training and attitude change programs have been tried. And numerous motivational techniques have been proposed to increase the energy and commitment with which workers do their tasks. These include development of human relations programs, alteration of supervisory styles, and installation of complex piece-rate and profit-sharing incentive plans. None of these strategies have proven successful. Indeed, some observers report that the quality of the work experience of employees today is more problematic than it was in the heyday of scientific management (cf., *Work in America,* 1973).

Why have behavioral scientists not been more successful in their attempts to remedy motivational problems in organizations and improve the quality of work life of employees? One reason is that psychologists (like managers and labor leaders) have traditionally assumed that the *work itself was inviolate*—that the role of psychologists is simply to help select, train, and motivate people within the confines of jobs as they have been designed by others. Clearly, it is time to reject this assumption and to seek ways to change both people and jobs in order to improve the fit between them.

The redesign of work as a change strategy offers the opportunity to break out of the "givens" that have limited previous attempts to improve life at work. It is based on the assumption that the work itself may be a very powerful influence on employee motivation, satisfaction, and productivity. It acknowledges (and attempts to build on) the inability of people to set aside their social and emotional needs while at work. And it provides a strategy for moving away from extrinsic props to worker motivation and to move instead toward *internal* work motivation that causes the individual to do the work because it interests him, challenges him, and rewards him for a job well done.

2 Work Redesign Directly Changes Behavior—and It Tends to Stay Changed People do the tasks they are given. How well they do them depends on many factors, including how the tasks are designed. But no matter how the tasks are designed, people do them.

On the other hand, people do *not* always behave in ways that are consistent with their attitudes, their levels of satisfaction, or what they cognitively know they should do. Indeed, it is now well established that one's attitudes often are *determined* by the behaviors one engages in—rather than vice versa, as traditionally has been thought (Bem, 1970; Kiesler, Collins, and Miller, 1969). This is especially true when individuals perceive that they have substantial personal freedom or autonomy in choosing how they will behave (Steiner, 1970).

Enriching jobs, then, may have twin virtues. First, behavior is changed; and second, because enriched jobs usually bring about increased feelings of autonomy and personal discretion, the individual is likely to develop attitudes that are supportive of his new on-the-job behaviors (cf. Taylor, 1971). Work redesign does not, therefore, rely on changing attitudes first (for example, inducing the worker to care more about the work outcomes, as in zero defects programs) and hoping that the attitude change will generalize to work behavior. Instead, the strategy is to change the *behavior,* and to change it in a way that gradually leads to a more positive set of attitudes about the work, the organization, and the self.

Moreover, after jobs are changed, it usually is difficult for workers to slip back into old ways. The old ways simply are inappropriate for the new tasks, and the structure of those tasks reinforces the changes that have taken place. Thus, one need not worry much about the kind of backsliding that occurs so often after training or attitude modification activities, especially those that occur off-site. The task-based stimuli that influence the worker's behavior are very much on-site, every hour of every day. And once those stimuli are changed, behavior is likely to stay changed—at least until the job is again redesigned.

3   Work Redesign Offers—and Sometimes Forces into One's Hands—Numerous Opportunities for Initiating Other Organizational Changes   When work is redesigned in an organization so that many people are doing things differently than they used to, new problems inevitably surface and demand attention. These can be construed solely as *problems,* or they can be treated as *opportunities* for further organizational change activities. For example, technical problems are likely to develop when jobs are changed—offering opportunities to smooth and refine the work system as a system. Interpersonal issues also are likely to arise, almost inevitably between supervisors and subordinates and sometimes between peers who now have to relate to one another in new ways. These issues offer opportunities for developmental work aimed at improving the social and supervisory aspects of the work system.

Because such problems are literally forced to the surface by the job changes, all parties may feel a need to do something about them. Responses can range from using the existence of a problem to justify that "job enrichment doesn't work," to simply trying to solve the problem quickly so the work redesign project can proceed, to using the problem as a point of entry for attacking other organizational issues. If the last stance is taken, behavioral science professionals may find themselves pleasantly removed from the old difficulty of selling their wares to skeptical managers and employees who are not really sure there is anything wrong. Eventually a program of organizational change and development may evolve that addresses organizational systems and practices that, superficially at least, seem unrelated to how the work itself is designed (Beer and Huse, 1972).

4   Work Redesign, in the Long Term, Can Result in Organizations That Rehumanize Rather than Dehumanize the People Who Work in Them   Despite the popular inflation of the work ethic issue in recent years, there is convincing evidence that organizations can and do sometimes stamp out part of the humanness of their members—especially people's motivations toward growth and personal development (cf. Kornhauser, 1965).

Work redesign can help individuals regain the chance to experience the kick that comes from doing a job well, and it can encourage them to once again *care* about their work and about developing the competence to do it even better. These payoffs from work redesign go well beyond simple job satisfaction. Cows grazing in the field may be satisfied, and employees in organizations can be made just as satisfied by paying them well, by keeping bosses off their backs, by putting them in pleasant work rooms with pleasant people, and by arranging things so that the days pass without undue stress or strain.

The kind of satisfaction at issue here is different. It is a satisfaction that develops only when individuals are stretching and growing as human beings, increasing their sense of competence and self-worth. Whether the creation of opportunities for personal growth is a legitimate goal for work redesign activities is a value question deserving long discussion; the case for the value of work redesign strictly in terms of *organizational* health easily can rest on the first three points discussed above. But personal growth is without question a central component of the overall quality of work life in organizations, and the impact of work redesign on the people who do the work, as human beings, should be neither overlooked nor underemphasized. . . .

DESIGNING WORK FOR INDIVIDUALS

A model specifying how job characteristics and individual differences interact to affect the satisfaction, motivation, and productivity of individuals at work has been proposed by Hackman and Oldham (1976). The model is specifically intended for use in planning and carrying out changes in the design of jobs. It is described below and then is used as a guide for discussion of diagnostic procedures and change principles that can be used in redesigning the jobs of individuals.

The Job Characteristics Model

The basic job characteristics model is shown in Figure 1. As illustrated in the figure, five core job dimensions are seen as creating three critical psychological states that, in turn, lead to a number of beneficial personal and work outcomes. The links among the job dimensions, the psychological states, and the outcomes are shown to be moderated by individual growth need strength. The major classes of variables in the model are reviewed briefly below.

Psychological States   The three following psychological states are postulated as critical in affecting a person's motivation and satisfaction on the job:

1 Experienced meaningfulness: The person must experience the work as generally important, valuable, and worthwhile.

2 Experienced responsibility: The individual must feel personally responsible and accountable for the results of the work he performs.

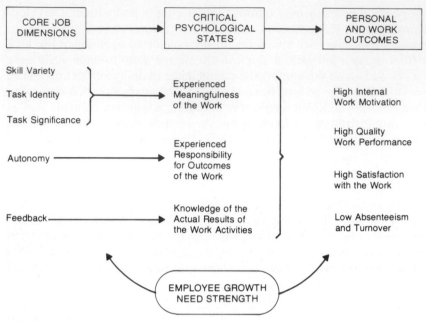

FIGURE 1
The job characteristics model of work motivation.

3 Knowledge of results: The individual must have an understanding, on a fairly regular basis, of how effectively he is performing the job.

The more these three conditions are present, the more people will feel good about themselves when they perform well. Or, following Hackman and Lawler (1971), the model postulates that internal rewards are obtained by an individual when he *learns* (knowledge of results) that he *personally* (experienced responsibility) has performed well on a task that he *cares about* (experienced meaningfulness). These internal rewards are reinforcing to the individual and serve as incentives for continued efforts to perform well in the future. When the person does not perform well, he does not experience reinforcement, and he may elect to try harder in the future so as to regain the rewards that good performance brings. The net result is a self-perpetuating cycle of positive work motivation powered by self-generated rewards. This cycle is predicted to continue until one or more of the three psychological states is no longer present, or until the individual no longer values the internal rewards that derive from good performance.

Job Dimensions   Of the five job characteristics shown in Figure 1 as fostering the emergence of the psychological states, three contribute to the experienced meaningfulness of the work, and one each contributes to experienced responsibility and to knowledge of results.

The three job dimensions that contribute to a job's *meaningfulness* are skill variety, task identity, and task significance.

Skill variety—the degree to which a job requires a variety of different activities that involve the use of a number of different skills and talents.

When a task requires a person to engage in activities that challenge or stretch his skills and abilities, that task almost invariably is experienced as meaningful by the individual. Many parlor games, puzzles, and recreational activities, for example, achieve much of their fascination because they tap and test intellectual or motor skills. When a job draws on several skills of an employee, that individual may find the job to be of very high personal meaning even if, in any absolute sense, it is not of great significance or importance.

Task identity—the degree to which the job requires completion of a whole and identifiable piece of work—that is, doing a job from beginning to end with a visible outcome.

If an employee assembles a complete product or provides a complete unit of service, he should find the work more meaningful than if he were responsible for only a small part of the whole job, other things (such as skill variety) being equal.

Task significance—the degree to which the job has a substantial impact on the lives or work of other people, whether in the immediate organization or in the external environment.

When an individual understands that the results of his work may have a significant effect on the well-being of other people, the experienced meaningfulness of the work usually is enhanced. Employees who tighten nuts on aircraft brake assemblies, for example, are much more likely to perceive their work as meaningful than are workers who fill small boxes with paper clips—even though the skill levels involved may be comparable.

The job characteristic predicted to prompt employee feelings of personal *responsibility* for the work outcomes is autonomy, which is defined as follows:

Autonomy—the degree to which the job provides substantial freedom, independence, and discretion to the individual in scheduling the work and in determining the procedures to be used in carrying it out.

To the extent that autonomy is high, work outcomes will be viewed by workers as depending substantially on their *own* efforts, initiatives, and decisions, rather than on the adequacy of instructions from the boss or on a manual of job procedures. In such circumstances, individuals should feel strong personal responsibility for the successes and failures that occur on the job.

The job characteristic that fosters *knowledge of results* is feedback, which is defined as follows:

Feedback—the degree to which carrying out the work activities required by the job results in the individual obtaining direct and clear information about the effectiveness of his performance.

It often is useful to combine the scores of a job on the five dimensions described above into a single index reflecting the overall potential of the job to prompt self-generated work motivation in job incumbents. Following the model diagrammed in Figure 1, a job high in motivating potential must be high on at least one (and hopefully more) of the three dimensions that lead to experienced meaningfulness, *and* high on autonomy and feedback as well. The presence of these dimensions creates conditions for all three of the critical psychological states to be present. Arithmetically, scores of jobs on the five dimensions are combined as follows to meet this criterion:

$$\begin{array}{l} \text{Motivating} \\ \text{Potential} \\ \text{Score (MPS)} \end{array} = \left[\dfrac{\dfrac{\text{Skill}}{\text{Variety}} + \dfrac{\text{Task}}{\text{Identity}} + \dfrac{\text{Task}}{\text{Significance}}}{3} \right] \times \text{Autonomy} \times \text{Job Feedback}$$

As can be seen from the formula, a near-zero score of a job on either autonomy or feedback will reduce the overall MPS to near-zero; a near-zero score on one of the three job dimensions that contribute to experienced meaningfulness cannot, by itself, do so.

Individual Growth Need Strength   Growth need strength is postulated to moderate how people react to complex, challenging work at two points in the model shown in Figure 1: first at the link between the objective job dimensions and the psychological states, and again between the psychological states and the outcome variables. The first link means that high growth need individuals are more likely (or better able) to *experience* the psychological states when their objective job is enriched than are their low growth need counterparts. The second link means that individuals with high growth need strength will respond more positively to the psychological states, when they are present, than will low growth need individuals.

Outcome Variables   Also shown in Figure 1 are several outcomes that are affected by the level of self-generated motivation experienced by people at work. Of special interest as an outcome variable is internal work motivation (Lawler and Hall, 1970; Hackman and Lawler, 1971). This variable taps directly the contingency between effective performance and self-administered affective rewards. Typical questionnaire items measuring internal work motivation include: (1) "I feel a great sense of personal satisfaction when I do this job well"; (2) "I feel bad and unhappy when I discover that I have performed poorly on this job"; and (3) "My own feelings are *not* affected much one way or the other by how well I do on this job" (reversed scoring).

Other outcomes listed in Figure 1 are the quality of work performance, job satisfaction (especially satisfaction with opportunities for personal growth and development on the job), absenteeism, and turnover. All of these outcomes are predicted to be affected positively by a job high in motivating potential.

Validity of the Job Characteristics Model

Empirical test of the job characteristics model of work motivation is reported in detail elsewhere (Hackman and Oldham, 1976). In general, results are supportive, as suggested by the following overview:

1 People who work on jobs high on the core job characteristics are more moti-vated, satisfied, and productive than are people who work on jobs that score low on these characteristics. The same is true for absenteeism, although less strongly so.

2 Responses to jobs high in objective motivating potential are more positive for people who have strong needs for growth than for people with weak growth needs. The moderating effect of individual growth need strength occurs both at the link between the job dimensions and the psychological states and at the link between the psychological states and the outcome measures, as shown in Figure 1. (This moderating effect is not, however, obtained for absenteeism.)

3 The job characteristics operate *through* the psychological states in influenc-ing the outcome variables, as predicted by the model, rather than influencing the outcomes directly. Two anomalies have been identified, however: (a) results in-volving the feedback dimension are in some situations less strong than results obtained for the other dimensions (perhaps in part because individuals receive feedback at work from many sources—not just the job), and (b) the linkage be-tween autonomy and experienced responsibility does not operate exactly as speci-fied by the model in affecting the outcome variables (Hackman and Oldham, 1976). . . .

Principles for Enriching Jobs

The core job dimensions specified in the job characteristics model are tied directly to a set of action principles for redesigning jobs (Hackman, Oldham, Janson, and Purdy, 1975; Walters and Associates, 1975). As shown in Figure 2, these princi-ples specify what types of changes in jobs are most likely to lead to improvements in each of the five core job dimensions, and thus to an increase in the motivating potential of the job as a whole.

   Principle #1: Forming Natural Work Units   A critical step in the design of any job is the decision about how the work is to be distributed among the people who do it. Numerous considerations affect that decision, such as technological con-straints, level of worker training and experience, efficiency from an industrial or

FIGURE 2
Principles for changing jobs.

CHANGE PRINCIPLES	CORE JOB DIMENSIONS
Combining Tasks	Skill Variety
Forming Natural Work Units	Task Identity
Establishing Client Relationships	Task Significance
Vertical Loading	Autonomy
Opening Feedback Channels	Feedback

systems engineering perspective, and equity of individual work loads. Work designed on the basis of these factors usually is distributed among employees rationally and logically. The problem is that the logic used often does not include the needs of employees for personally meaningful work.

Consider, for example, a typing pool consisting of one supervisor and ten typists who do all the typing for one division of an organization. Jobs are delivered in rough draft or dictated form to the supervisor, who distributes them as evenly as possible among the typists. In such circumstances the individual letters, reports, and other tasks performed by a given typist in one day or week are randomly assigned. There is no basis for identifying with the work or with the person or department for whom it is performed, or for placing any personal value on it.

By contrast, creating natural units of work increases employee "ownership" of the work and improves the chances that employees will view their work as meaningful and important rather than as irrelevant and boring. In creating natural units of work, one must first identify the basic work items. In the typing pool example, that might be "pages to be typed." Then these items are grouped into natural and meaningful categories. For example, each typist might be assigned continuing responsibility for all work requested by a single department or by several smaller departments. Instead of typing one section of a large report, the individual will type the entire piece of work, with knowledge of exactly what the total outcome of the work is. Furthermore, over time the typist will develop a growing sense of how the work affects co-workers or customers who receive the completed product. Thus, as shown in Figure 2, forming natural units of work increases two of the core dimensions that contribute to experienced meaningfulness—task identity and task significance.

Because it is still important that work be distributed so that the system as a whole operates efficiently, work loads must be arranged so that they are divided equitably. The principle of natural work units simply requires that these traditional criteria be supplemented so that, as far as possible, the tasks that arrive at an employee's work station form an identifiable and meaningful whole.

Principle #2: Combining Tasks   The very existence of a pool made up entirely of persons whose sole function is typing reflects a fractionalization of jobs that sometimes can lead to such hidden costs as high absenteeism and turnover and extra supervisory time. The principle of combining tasks is based on the assumption that such costs often can be reduced by taking existing and fractionalized tasks and putting them back together again to form a new and larger module of work. At the Medfield, Massachusetts plant of Corning Glass Works, for example, the job of assembling laboratory hot plates was redesigned by combining a number of tasks that had been separate. After the change, each hot plate was assembled from start to finish by one operator, instead of going through several separate operations performed by different people.

Combining tasks (like forming natural work units) contributes in two ways to the experienced meaningfulness of the work. First, task identity is increased. The hot plate assembler, for example, can see and identify with a finished product ready for shipment, rather than with a nearly invisible junction of solder. Moreover, as more tasks are combined into a single worker's job, the individual must use a greater variety of skills in performing the job, further increasing the meaningfulness of the work.

Principle #3: Establishing Client Relationships Jobs designed according to traditional criteria often provide workers with little or no contact with the ultimate user of their product or service. As a consequence, workers may have difficulty generating high commitment and motivation to do the job well.

By establishing direct relationships between workers and their clients, jobs often can be improved in three ways. First, feedback increases because additional opportunities are created for the employees to receive direct praise or criticism of their work outputs. Second, skill variety may increase, because of the need to develop and exercise one's interpersonal skills in managing and maintaining the relationship with the client. Finally, autonomy will increase to the degree that individuals are given real personal responsibility for deciding how to manage their relationships with the people who receive the outputs of their work.

Creating client relationships can be viewed as a three-step process: (1) identifying who the client actually is; (2) establishing the most direct contact possible between the worker and the client; and (3) establishing criteria and procedures so that the client can judge the quality of the product or service received and relay his judgments directly to the worker. Especially important (and, in many cases, difficult to achieve) is identification of the specific criteria by which the work output is assessed by the client, and ensuring that both the worker and the client understand these criteria and agree with them.

Principle #4: Vertical Loading In vertical loading, the intent is to partially close the gap between the "doing" and the "controlling" aspects of the job. Thus, when a job is vertically loaded, responsibilities and controls that formerly were reserved for management are given to the employee as part of the job. Among ways this might be achieved are the following:

- Giving job incumbents responsibility for deciding on work methods and for advising or helping to train less experienced workers;
- Providing increased freedom in time management, including decisions about when to start and stop work, when to take breaks, and how to assign work priorities;
- Encouraging workers to do their own troubleshooting and to manage work crises, rather than calling immediately for a supervisor;
- Providing workers with increased knowledge of the financial aspects of the job and the organization, and increased control over budgetary matters that affect their work.

Vertically loading a job inevitably increases *autonomy*. And, as shown in Figure 1, this should lead to increased feelings of personal responsibility and accountability for the work outcomes.

Principle #5: Opening Feedback Channels   In virtually all jobs there are ways to open channels of feedback to individuals, to help them learn not only how well they are performing their jobs but also whether their performance is improving, deteriorating, or remaining at a constant level. Although there are various sources from which information about performance can come, it usually is advantageous for a worker to learn about his performance directly as he does the job—rather than from management on an occasional basis.

Job-provided feedback is more immediate and private than supervisor-supplied feedback, and it increases workers' feelings of personal control over their work. Moreover, it avoids many of the potentially disruptive interpersonal problems that can develop when a worker can find out how he is doing only from direct messages or subtle cues from the boss.

Exactly what should be done to open channels for job-provided feedback varies from job to job and from organization to organization. Often the changes involve simply removing existing blocks that isolate the individual from naturally occurring data about performance, rather than generating entirely new feedback mechanisms. For example:

• Establishing direct client relationships (discussed above) often removes blocks between the worker and natural external sources of data about the work.

• Quality control efforts often eliminate a natural source of feedback, because all quality checks are done by people other than the individuals responsible for the work. In such situations, any feedback that workers do receive may be belated and diluted. Placing most quality control functions in the hands of workers will dramatically increase the quantity and quality of data available to them about their performances.

• Tradition and established procedure in many organizations dictate that records about performance be kept by a supervisor and transmitted up (not down) the organizational hierarchy. Sometimes supervisors even check the work and correct any errors themselves. The worker who made the error never knows it occurred and is therefore denied the very information that could enhance both internal work motivation and the technical adequacy of his performance. In many cases, it is possible to provide standard summaries of performance records directly to the workers. This would give the employees personally and regularly the data they need to improve their effectiveness.

• Computers and other automated machines sometimes can be used to provide individuals with data now blocked from them. Many clerical operations, for example, are now performed on computer consoles. These consoles often can be programmed to provide the clerk with immediate feedback in the form of a CRT display or a printout indicating that an error has been made. Some systems even have been programmed to provide the operator with a positive feedback message when a period of error-free performance has been sustained.

The principles for redesigning jobs reviewed above, although illustrative of the kinds of changes that can be made to improve the jobs of individuals in organizations, obviously are not exhaustive. They were selected for attention here because of the links (Figure 2) between the principles and the core job dimensions in the motivational model presented earlier. Other principles for enriching jobs (which, although often similar to those presented here, derive from alternative conceptual frameworks) are presented by Ford (1969), Glaser (1975), Herzberg (1974), and Katzell and Yankelovich (1975). . . .

GUIDELINES FOR INSTALLING PLANNED CHANGES IN JOBS

We move now to exploration of issues that arise in the actual installation of changes in the design of work. The material presented below is based on observations and interviews conducted by the author and his associates over the past three years in numerous organizations where work redesign activities were being planned, implemented, or evaluated.

In general, we have found job enrichment to be failing at least as often as it is succeeding. And the reasons for the failures, in many cases, appear to have more to do with the way planned changes are *implemented* in organizations than with the intrinsic merit of the changes. Again and again we have seen good ideas about the redesign of work die because the advocates of change were unable to gain acceptance for their ideas or because unexpected roadblocks led to early termination of the change project.

Our findings are summarized below as six prescriptive guides for implementing changes in jobs. Each guide includes a discussion of pitfalls that frequently are encountered in work redesign projects, as well as ingredients that were common to many of the more successful projects we observed.

Guide 1: Diagnose the Work System Prior to Change

It now is clear that work redesign is not effective in all organizational circumstances. Yet rarely is a systematic diagnosis carried out beforehand to determine whether meaningful change is feasible, given the jobs being considered, the people who will be involved, and the social, organizational, or cultural environment in which the work is performed. As a result, faulty initial assumptions often go uncorrected, and the change project may be doomed before it is begun.

The choice of the job to be changed, for example, often seems to be almost random. Perhaps a manager will decide that a given job seems right for enrichment. Or he will settle on a job because it is peripheral to the major work done in the organization—thereby minimizing the risk of severe disruption if something should go wrong. Or a job will be selected because everything seems wrong with it—the work is not getting done on time or correctly, employees are angry about everything from their pay to the cleanliness of the restrooms, grievances are excessive, and so on. The hope, apparently, is that somehow redesigning the job will fix everything all at once.

Yet it must be recognized that some jobs, given existing technological constraints, are about as good as they ever can be. Work redesign in such situations is at best a waste of time. Other jobs have so much wrong with them that is irrelevant to how enriched they are that job enrichment could not conceivably bring about a noticeable improvement—and instead might add even more complexity to an already chaotic situation. When such matters are overlooked in planning for work redesign, the result often is a change effort that fails simply because it is aimed at an inappropriate target.

Similarly, differences in employee readiness to handle contemplated changes in jobs only infrequently are assessed before a project is installed. Line managers often express doubts that employees can handle proposed new responsibilities or skepticism that employees will enjoy working on an enriched job. Sometimes, as planning for work redesign proceeds, managers become convinced of the contrary. But only rarely are change projects designed with full cognizance that employees are likely to differ in their psychological readiness for enriched work.

Even less frequently is explicit assessment made of the readiness of managers to deal with the kinds of problems that inevitably arise when a major organizational change is made. In one case, the management team responsible for a job enrichment project nearly collapsed when the first serious change-related problem emerged. Time and energy that were needed for the project were spent instead working on intrateam issues that had been flushed out by the problem. And another "job enrichment failure" occurred while the managers talked and talked. An adequate diagnosis of the readiness of the management team for change-management would have increased the likelihood that the problematic intrateam issues would have been dealt with *before* the work redesign activities were initiated.

The commitment of middle and top management to job enrichment also rarely received diagnostic attention in the organizations we observed. Whether organizational change activities must begin at the top—or whether work redesign is a strategy for change that can spread from the bottom up—remains an important and unresolved question (Beer and Huse, 1972). It is almost always true, however, that middle and top management can terminate a project they find unsatisfactory, whether for good reasons or on a whim. In one case, a high-level executive agreed to serve as sponsor for a project without really understanding what the changes would involve. When difficulties in implementation developed, the executive concluded that he had been misled—and the project found itself out from under its protective umbrella and in serious organizational jeopardy. In another case, a single vice-president was counted on to protect a fledgling project from meddling by others who favored alternative approaches to organizational change. When the vice-president departed the organization to attend a several-month executive development program, his temporary replacement terminated job enrichment activities and substituted a training program more to his own liking. In both cases, an early assessment of the attitudes of key top managers would have revealed the need to develop a broader and better informed base of high-level support for the projects.

A number of organizations we studied did conduct diagnoses of the work system before changes were installed. Almost invariably these studies identified problems or issues that required attention prior to the beginning of the job changes. Such diagnoses are not easy to make. They involve the raising of anxieties at a time when most participants in a project are instead seeking comfort and assurance that everything will turn out all right. Moreover, the tools and methodologies required for undertaking such diagnoses only now are beginning to become available (cf. Hackman and Oldham, 1975; Jenkins, Nadler, Lawler, and Cammann, 1975; Sirota and Wolfson, 1972). Our observations suggest, however, that the diagnostic task may be one of the most crucial in a work redesign project.

Guide 2: Keep the Focus on the Work Itself

Redesigning a job often appears seductively simple. In practice, it is a rather challenging undertaking. It requires a good deal more energy than most other organizational development activities, such as attitude improvement programs, training courses, and objective-setting practices (Ford, 1971).

There are many reasons why it is so hard to alter jobs. At the purely bureaucratic level, the entire personnel-and-job description apparatus often must be engaged to get the changes approved, documented, and implemented. If the organization is unionized, the planned changes often must be negotiated beforehand—sometimes a formidable task. Simple inertia often tempts managers to add lots of window dressing to make things appear different, rather than actually to change what people do on their jobs. Finally, when even one job in an organization is changed, many of the interfaces between that job and related ones must be dealt with as well. In even moderately complex work systems, this is no small matter.

Because of these and other forces against change, work redesign projects frequently are carried out that have very little impact on the work itself. A project carried out in the stock transfer department of a large bank is illustrative (Frank and Hackman, in press). At the end of the project the informal word among managers was, "We tried job enrichment and it failed." But our research data (which measured the objective characteristics of jobs before and after the change) showed that, although all manner of things did change as part of the job enrichment project, the work itself was not among them. Our correlational analyses of data collected in that organization showed that there were very positive relationships between the amount of skill variety, autonomy, and feedback in various jobs and the satisfaction, motivation, performance, and attendance of the job incumbents. These across-job relationships were present prior to the change project and they were there afterwards. But it was also true that those people who held the "good" jobs before the change also held them afterward, and those people whose jobs originally were routine, repetitive, and virtually without feedback had essentially identical jobs after the work was "redesigned." Workers had been formed into small groups, supervision had been changed, names of jobs and work units had been altered, and a general stirring about had taken place. But the *jobs* were not changed much, and the effect (after about six months) was a slight deterioration in worker satisfaction and motivation. This deterioration, apparently, was due more to the failure of the project to live up to expectations than to the changes that had actually taken place.

It is easy, apparently, for those responsible for work redesign activities to delude themselves about what is actually being altered in such projects, and thereby to avoid the rather difficult task of actually changing the structure of the work people do. One way of ensuring that a project stays focused on the work is to base change activities firmly on a theory of work design.

No doubt some theories are better than others. Our observations suggest, however, that the specific details of various theories may not be as important as the fact that *some* theory is used to guide the implementation of change. In addition to keeping the changes focused on the original objective of restructuring the work, a good theory can help identify the kinds of data needed to plan and evaluate the changes and can alert implementors to special problems and opportunities that may develop as the project unfolds.

The theory must, however, be appropriate for the changes that are contemplated. Therein lies one of the major difficulties of the stock transfer project described above. The project originally was designed on the basis of motivation-hygiene theory, which deals exclusively with the enrichment of jobs performed by individuals. The changes that actually were made, however, involved the creation of enriched *group* tasks. Because the theory did not address the special problems of designing work for groups (how to create conditions that encourage members to share with one another their special task-relevant skills), those responsible for implementation found the theory of limited use as a guide for planning and installing the changes. Gradually the theory dropped from their attention. Without the benefit of theory specified guidelines for change, the project became increasingly diffuse and eventually addressed many issues that had little or nothing to do with the work. All this is not to imply that these other issues were unrelated to the change or were improper. However, they cannot be made as substitutes for changes in the work itself.

Guide 3: Prepare Ahead of Time for Unexpected Problems

When substantial changes are made in jobs, shock waves may be created that reverberate throughout adjacent parts of the organization. If insufficient attention is given to such spin-off effects of job changes, they may backfire and create problems that negate (or even reverse) expected positive outcomes.

The site of the backfire varies from case to case. In one company, employees who prepared customer accounts for computer processing were given increased autonomy in scheduling their work and in determining their own work pace. This resulted in a less predictable schedule of data input to the computer system. Because the data processing department had not been involved in the project until the changes were already made, serious computer delays were encountered while data processing managers struggled to figure out how to respond to the new and irregular flow of work. The net result was an increase in antagonism between computer operations and the employees whose jobs had been enriched—and a decrease in the promptness of customer service.

In another company work was redesigned to give rank-and-file employees a number of responsibilities that previously had been handled by their supervisors. The employees (who dealt with customers of the company by telephone) were given greater opportunities for personal initiative and discretion in dealing with customers, and initially seemed to be prospering in their new responsibilities. But later observations revealed a deterioration in morale, especially in the area of supervisor-subordinate relationships. Apparently the supervisors had found themselves with little work to do after the change (because the employees were handling much of what the supervisors had done before). When supervisors turned to higher management for instructions, they were told to "develop your people—that's what a manager's job is." The supervisors had little idea what "developing your people" involved, and many of them implemented that instruction by looking over the employees' shoulders and correcting each error they could find. Resentment between the supervisor and the employee groups soon developed, and more than overcame any positive benefits that had accrued from the changes in the job (Lawler, Hackman, and Kaufman, 1973).

Problems such as those described above often can be avoided by developing contingency plans ahead of time to deal with the inevitable spin-off problems that crop up whenever jobs are changed. Such plans can be advantageous in at least two ways. First, employees, managers, and consultants all will share an awareness that problems are likely to emerge elsewhere in the work system as the change project develops. This simple understanding may help keep surprise and dismay at manageable levels when the problems do appear and so may decrease the opportunity for people to conclude prematurely that "the project failed."

Second, preplanning for possible problems can lead to an objective increase in the readiness of all parties to deal with those problems that do emerge. Having a few contingency plans filed away can increase the chances that change-related problems will be dealt with before they get out of hand—and before they create a significant drain on the energy and morale needed to keep the change project afloat.

Not all contingency plans can be worked out in detail beforehand. Indeed, they probably should not be. Until a project is underway one cannot know for sure what the specific nature of the most pressing needs and problems will be. But one can be ready to deal with common problems that may appear. For example, the training department can be alerted that some training may be required if managers find themselves in difficulty supervising the employees after the work is redesigned. And those responsible for the reward system can be asked to engage in some contingency planning on the chance that the new work system may require nontraditional compensation arrangements. One does not *begin* with these matters. But one is well advised to anticipate that some of them will arise, and to be prepared to deal with them when and if they do.

Guide 4: Evaluate Continuously

When managers or consultants are asked whether a work redesign project has been evaluated, the answer nearly always is affirmative. But when one asks to see the evaluation, the response frequently is something like, "Well, let me tell you . . . only one week after we did the actual job changes this guy who had been on the lathe for fifteen years came up to me, and he said . . ." Such anecdotes are interesting, but they provide little help to managers and union officials as they consider whether work redesign is something that should be experimented with further and possibly diffused throughout the organization. Nor is it the stuff of which generalizable behavioral science knowledge is made.

Sometimes hard data are pointed to, such as financial savings resulting from reductions in personnel in the unit where the work redesign took place. Such data can validly document an improvement in worker productivity, but they are of little value in understanding the full richness of what has happened, or why. And, of great importance in unionized organizations, they are hardly the kind of data that will engage the enthusiasm of the bargaining unit for broader application of work redesign.

There are many good reasons why adequate evaluations of work redesign projects are not done—not having the capability to translate human gains into dollars and cents, not being able to separate out the influence of the job changes on measured productivity and unit profitability from the many other factors that influence these outcomes, having an organization-wide accounting system that cannot provide data on the costs of absenteeism, turnover, training, and extra supervisory time, not really trusting measures of job satisfaction, and so on.

These reasons can be convincing, at least until one asks what was done to try to overcome the problems and gets as a response, "Well, we really didn't think we could get the accountants to help out, so. . . ." And one is left with several unhappy hypotheses: (1) nobody knows how to do a decent evaluation—nor how to get help in doing one; or (2) management does not consider systematic evaluation an essential part of the change activity; or (3) the desire of the people responsible for the program to have it appear successful is so strong that they cannot afford the risk of an explicit evaluation.

In a retailing organization, for example, job enrichment was sold to top management by a single individual. And soon the program came to be known throughout the organization as "Joe's program." Joe, understandably, developed a considerable personal interest in managing the image of the program within the organization. When offered the chance for a systematic evaluation of the project to be conducted at no cost to the organization, Joe showed considerable initial hesitation, and finally declined the offer. Later discussions revealed that although he recognized the potential usefulness of the information he would gain from an outside evaluation, that benefit was more than countered by the risk of losing his personal control over the image of the project that eventually would emerge.

Because of the pressure on lower-level managers and consultants to make job enrichment programs at least *appear* successful, it often is necessary for top management or union leaders to insist that serious and systematic evaluations of such programs take place. For such evaluations to be valid and useful, management must attempt to create an organizational climate in which the evaluation is viewed as an occasion for *learning*—rather than as an event useful mainly for assessing the performance and competence of those who actually installed the changes.

Such a stance permits interim disappointments and problems to be used as times for reconsideration and revision of the change project, rather than as a cause for disillusionment and abandonment. And it encourages those responsible for managing the change to learn as they go how most effectively to design, install, and manage enriched jobs. This is a matter of considerable importance, because there is no neat package for redesigning work in organizations and there probably never will be.

Taking a learning orientation to work redesign is, however, a costly proposition. It is expensive to collect trustworthy data for use in monitoring a project throughout its life, and to experiment actively with different ways of changing jobs. It is painful to learn from failure, and to try again. Yet such costs may actually be among the better investments an organization contemplating work redesign can make. Paying such costs may be the only realistic way for the organization to develop the considerable knowledge and expertise it will need to reap the full benefits of work redesign as a strategy for change.

Guide 5: Confront the Difficult Problems Early

Individuals responsible for work redesign projects often find it tempting to get the project sold to management and union leadership, and only then to begin negotiations on the difficult problems that must be solved before the project can actually be carried out. This seems entirely reasonable. If such problems are raised *before* the project is agreed to, the chances are increased that it will never get off the ground. It appears, nevertheless, that in the long run it may be wiser to risk not doing a project for which the tough issues cannot be resolved beforehand than to do one under circumstances that require compromise after compromise to keep the project alive after it has begun.

Vigilance by those responsible for the change is required to ensure that the tough issues are not swept under the rug when the project is being considered. Among such issues (that too often are reserved for later discussion) are:

• The nature and extent of the commitment of management and union leaders, including the circumstances under which a decision may be made to terminate the project. It is especially important to make sure that both management and union leadership realize that problems will emerge in the early stages of a project, and that a good deal of energy may be required to protect and nurture the project during such down phases.

• The criteria against which the project ultimately will be evaluated and the means by which the evaluation will be done, including measures that will be used. Given that there are serious measurement difficulties in assessing any work redesign project, it is important to make sure that all parties, including management and union sponsors, are aware of these difficulties and are committed at the outset to the evaluation methodology.

• The way that learnings gained in the project (whether they are "successful tactics we discovered" or "roadblocks we unexpectedly encountered") will be made available to people who can use them as guides for future action, in the same or in other organizations.

Guide 6: Design Change Processes That Fit with Change Objectives

Most work redesign projects provide employees with increased opportunities for autonomy and self-direction in carrying out the work of the organization. Employees are allowed to do their work with a minimum of interference, and they are assumed to have the competence and sense of responsibility to seek appropriate assistance when they need it. The problem is that far too often the process of *implementing* job enrichment is strikingly incongruent with that intended end state.

It appears unrealistic to expect that a more flexible, bottom-loaded work system can be created using implementation procedures that are relatively rigid and bureaucratic, and that operate strictly from the top down. Yet again and again we observed standard, traditional, organizational practices being used to install work redesign. More often than not employees were the last to know what was happening, and only rarely were they given any real opportunity to actively participate in and influence the changes. In many situations they were never told the reasons why the changes were being made.

What happens during the planning stages of a work redesign project is illustrative of such incongruence between means and ends. Typically, initial planning for work redesign (including decision-making about what jobs will be changed) is done privately by managers and consultants. Diagnostic work, if performed at all, is done using a plausible cover story—such as telling employees that they are being interviewed "as part of our regular program of surveying employee attitudes." (The rationale is that employee expectations about change should not be raised prematurely; the effect often is that suspicions are raised instead.) Eventually managers appear with a fully determined set of changes that are installed in traditional top-down fashion. If employees resist and mistrust the changes, managers are surprised and disappointed. As one said: "I don't understand why they did not respond more enthusiastically. Don't they realize how we are going to make their work a lot more involving and interesting?" Apparently he did not see the lack of congruence between the goals being aspired to and the means being used, between "what we want to achieve" and "how we're going to achieve it."

As an alternative approach, managers might choose to be public and participative in translating from theory through diagnosis to the actual steps taken to modify jobs. Such an approach could be advantageous for a number of reasons.

First, when diagnostic data are collected and discussed openly, everyone who will be affected by the changes has the chance to become involved in the redesign activities and knowledgeable about them, and so everyone is less threatened. In one organization, managers initially were very skeptical about employee participation in planning for job changes. After employees had become involved in the project, however, a number of managers commented favorably on the amount of energy employees contributed to the planning activities and on the constructive attitudes they exhibited.

Second, the quality of the diagnostic data may be improved. If employees know that changes in their own work will be made partly on the basis of their responses to the diagnostic instruments, they may try especially hard to provide valid and complete data.

Third, chances are increased that learnings will emerge from the project that can be used to develop better action principles of work redesign for future applications. The involvement of people from a diversity of organizational roles in diagnostic and change-planning activities should facilitate attempts to piece together a complete picture of the change project—including the reasons that various changes were tried, what went wrong (and what went right), and what might be done differently next time.

Fourth, expectations about change will be increased when employees are involved in diagnostic and change-planning processes. Rather than being something to be avoided, therefore, heightened employee expectations can serve as a positive force for change. For example, such expectations might counter the conservatism that inevitably creeps into changes planned and implemented downwards through several hierarchical levels in an organization.

Despite these potential advantages, it is not easy to carry off a fully participative work redesign project. Nor do openness and employee participation guarantee success. Indeed, some experienced commentators have argued explicitly against employee participation in planning job changes, because (1) participation may contaminate the change process with "human relations hygiene" (Herzberg, 1966), (2) employees are not viewed as competent to redesign their own jobs, or (3) job design is viewed solely as a management function (Ford, 1969).

Our observations of work redesign projects turned up few projects in which employee participation was actively used in the change process. And the ideas for change that employees proposed in these cases did focus mainly on the removal of roadblocks from the work and on the improvement of hygiene items. This is consistent with the predictions of Ford (1969) that employee suggestions usually deal more with the context of work than with its motivational core.

The circumstances under which employees participated in work redesign activities in these organizations, however, were far from optimal. Often employees simply were asked, "What would you suggest?" and given little time to consider their responses. In no case were employees provided with education in the theory and strategy of job redesign before being asked for suggestions. And in all cases we studied, employees had no real part in the final decision-making about what changes actually would be made. They were contributors to the change process, but not partners in it.

To develop and utilize the *full* potential of employees as resources for change would be an exciting undertaking, and a major one. It could require teaching employees the basics of motivation theory, discussing with them state-of-the-art knowledge about the strategy and tactics of work redesign, and providing them with training and experience in planning and installing organizational innovations. Such an approach would be costly, perhaps too much so to be practical. But it would have the advantage of encouraging employees to become full collaborators in the redesign of their own work, thereby creating a process for improving jobs that is consistent with the ultimate objectives of the change. Moreover, and of special importance to the quality of work life in organizations, the approach would provide employees with greatly increased opportunities for furthering their own personal growth and development—and at the same time would significantly increase their value as human resources to the organization.

REFERENCES

Bakan, P., Belton, J. A., & Toth, J. C. Extraversion-introversion and decrement in an auditory vigilance task. In *Vigilance: A symposium,* edited by D. N. Buckner and J. J. McGrath. New York: McGraw-Hill, 1963.

Beer, M., & Huse, E. F. A systems approach to organization development. *Journal of Applied Behavioral Science,* **8** (1972): 79–101.

Bem, D. J. *Beliefs, attitudes, and human affairs.* Monterey, Calif.: Brooks/Cole, 1970.

Berlyne, D. E. Arousal and reinforcement. *Nebraska Symposium on Motivation,* **15** (1967)

Best, F. Flexible work scheduling: Beyond the forty-hour impasse. In *The future of work,* edited by F. Best, Englewood Cliffs, N.J.: Prentice-Hall, 1973.

Blood, M. R., & Hulin, C. L. Alienation, environmental characteristics, and worker responses, *Journal of Applied Psychology,* **51** (1967): 284–290.

Calame, B. E. Wary labor eyes job enrichment. *Wall Street Journal,* February 26, 1973, p. 12.

Davis, L. E. Toward a theory of job design. *Journal of Industrial Engineering,* **8** (1957): 19–23.

Davis, L. E. The design of jobs. *Industrial Relations,* **6** (1966): 21–45.

Davis, L. E. Developments in job design. In *Personal goals and work design,* edited by P. B. Warr, London: Wiley, 1975.

Davis, L. E., & Trist, E. L. Improving the quality of work life: Sociotechnical case studies. In *Work and the quality of life,* edited by J. O'Toole. Cambridge, Mass.: MIT Press, 1974.

Dunnette, M. D., Campbell, J. P., & Hakel, M. D. Factors contributing to job satisfaction and dissatisfaction in six occupational groups. *Organizational Behavior and Human Performance,* **2** (1967): 143–174.

Emery, F. E., & Trist, E. L. Socio-technical systems. In *Systems thinking,* edited by F. E. Emery, Middlesex, England: Penguin, 1969.

Engelstad, P. H. Socio-technical approach to problems of process control. In *Design of jobs,* edited by L. E. Davis and J. C. Taylor, Middlesex, England: Penguin, 1972.

Fein, M. Job enrichment: A reevaluation. *Sloan Management Review,* **15** (1974): 69–88.

Fiss, B. *Flexitime in federal government.* Washington, D. C.: Government Printing Office, 1974.

Ford, R. N. *Motivation through the work itself.* New York: American Management Association, 1969.

Ford, R. N. A prescription for job enrichment success. In *New perspectives in job enrichment,* edited by J. R. Maher, New York: Van Nostrand-Reinhold, 1971.

Ford, R. N. Job enrichment lessons from AT&T. *Harvard Business Review,* January-February, 1973, pp. 96–106.

Frank, L., & Hackman, J. R. A failure of job enrichment: The case of the change that wasn't. *Journal of Applied Behavioral Science,* in press.

Friedlander, F., & Brown, L. D. Organization development. *Annual Review of Psychology,* **25** (1974): 313–341.

Glaser, E. M. *Productivity gains through worklife improvement.* New York: The Psychological Corp., 1975.

Gomberg, W. Job satisfaction: Sorting out the nonsense. *AFL-CIO American Federationist,* June 1973.

Gooding, J. *The job revolution.* New York: Walker, 1972.

Graen, G. B. Testing traditional and two-factor hypotheses concerning job satisfaction. *Journal of Applied Psychology,* **52** (1968): 343–353.

Gulowsen, J. A measure of work group autonomy. In *Design of jobs,* edited by L. E. Davis and J. C. Taylor. Middlesex, England: Penguin, 1972.

Hackman, J. R. *Improving the quality of work life: Work design.* Washington, D.C.: Office of Research, ASPER, U.S. Dept. of Labor, 1975(a).

Hackman, J. R. On the coming demise of job enrichment. In *Man and work in society,* edited by E. L. Cass and F. G. Zimmer. New York: Van Nostrand-Reinhold, 1975(b).

Hackman, J. R., & Lawler, E. E. Employee reactions to job characteristics. *Journal of Applied Psychology Monograph,* **55** (1971): 259–286.

Hackman, J. R., & Oldham, G. R. Development of the job diagnostic survey. *Journal of Applied Psychology,* **60** (1975): 159–170.

Hackman, J. R., & Oldham, G. R. Motivation through the design of work: Test of a theory. *Organizational Behavior and Human Performance,* **16** (1976): 250–279.

Hackman, J. R., Oldham, G. R., Janson, R., & Purdy, K. A new strategy for job enrichment, *California Management Review,* Summer 1975, pp. 57–71.

Herbst, P. G. *Autonomous group functioning.* London: Travistock, 1962.

Herzberg, F. *Work and the nature of man.* Cleveland: World, 1966.

Herzberg, F. The wise old turk, *Harvard Business Review,* September-October 1974, pp. 70–80.

Herzberg, F., Mausner, B., & Snyderman, B. *The motivation to work.* New York: Wiley, 1959.

Hinton, B. L. An empirical investigation of the Herzberg methodology and two-factor theory, *Organizational Behavior and Human Performance,* **3** (1968): 286–309.

House, R. J., & Wigdor, L. Herzberg's dual-factor theory of job satisfaction and motivation: A review of the evidence and a criticism. *Personnel Psychology,* **20** (1967): 369–398.

Hulin, C. L. Individual differences and job enrichment. In J. R. Maher (Ed.), *New perspectives in job enrichment.* New York: Van Nostrand-Reinhold, 1971.

Hulin C. L., & Blood, M. R. Job enlargement, individual differences and worker responses. *Psychological Bulletin,* **69** (1968): 41–55.

Jenkins, G. D., Jr., Nadler, D. A., Lawler, E. E. III, & Cammann, C. Standardized observations: An approach to measuring the nature of jobs. *Journal of Applied Psychology,* **60** (1975): 171–181.

Katzell, R. A., & Yankelovich, D. *Work, productivity and job satisfaction.* New York: The Psychological Corporation, 1975.

Kiesler, C. A., Collins, B. E., & Miller, N. *Attitude change.* New York: Wiley, 1969.

Kilbridge, M. D. Reduced costs through job enrichment: A case. *The Journal of Business,* **33** (1960): 357–362.

King, N. A clarification and evaluation of the two-factor theory of job satisfaction. *Psychological Bulletin,* **74** (1970): 18–31.

Kornhauser, A. *Mental health of the industrial worker.* New York: Wiley, 1965.

Lawler, E. E. III, Hackman, J. R., & Kaufman, S. Effects of job redesign: A field experiment. *Journal of Applied Social Psychology,* **3** (1973): 49–62.

Lawler, E. E. III, & Hall, D. T. The relationship of job characteristics to job involvement, satisfaction, and intrinsic motivation. *Journal of Applied Psychology,* **54** (1970): 305–312.

Oldham, G. R. The motivational strategies used by supervisors: Relationships to effectiveness indicators. *Organizational Behavior and Human Performance,* **15** (1976): 66–86.

Paul, W. J., Jr., Robertson, K. B., & Herzberg, F. Job enrichment pays off. *Harvard Business Review,* March-April 1969, pp. 61–78.

Reif, W. E., & Luthans, F. Does job enrichment really pay off? *California Management Review,* Fall 1972, pp. 30–37.

Rice, A. K. *Productivity and social organization: The Ahmedabad experiment.* London: Tavistock, 1958.

Scott, W. E. Activation theory and task design. *Organizational Behavior and Human Performance,* 1 (1966): 3–30.

Scott, W. E. The behavioral consequences of repetitive task design: Research and theory. In *Readings in organizational behavior and human performance,* edited by L. L. Cummings and W. E. Scott. Homewood, Ill.: Irwin-Dorsey, 1969.

Scott, W. E., & Rowland, K. M. The generality and significance of semantic differential scales as measures of 'morale'. *Organizational Behavior and Human Performance,* 5 (1970): 576–591.

Sirota, D., & Wolfson, A. D. Job enrichment: Surmounting the obstacles. *Personnel,* July-August 1972, 8–19.

Special Task Force to the Secretary of the U.S. Dept. of Health, Education, and Welfare. *Work in America.* Boston, Mass.: MIT Press, 1973.

Steiner, I. D. Perceived freedom. In *Advances in experimental social psychology,* edited by L. Berkowitz. Vol. 5. New York: Academic Press, 1970.

Taylor, F. W. *The principles of scientific management.* New York: Harper, 1911.

Taylor, J. C. Some effects of technology in organizational change. *Human Relations,* 24 (1971): 105–123.

Thayer, R. E. Measurement of activation through self-report. *Psychological Reports,* 20 (1967): 663–678.

Thayer, R. E. Activation states as assessed by verbal report and four psychophysiological variables. *Psychophysiology* 7 (1970): 86–94.

Trist, E. L., Higgin, G. W., Murray, H., & Pollock, A. B. *Organizational choice.* London: Tavistock, 1963.

Turner, A. N., & Lawerence, P. R. *Industrial jobs and the worker.* Boston: Harvard Graduate School of Business Administration, 1965.

Vernon, H. M. *On the extent and effects of variety in repetitive work.* Industrial Fatigue Research Board Report No. 26, London: H. M. Stationary Office, 1924.

Vroom, V. *Work and motivation.* New York: Wiley, 1964.

Walker, C. R., & Guest, R. H. *The man on the assembly line.* Cambridge, Mass.: Harvard University Press, 1952.

Walters, R. W. A long-term look at the shorter work week. *Personnel Administrator,* July-August 1971.

Walters, R. W. & Associates. *Job enrichment for results.* Reading, Mass.: Addison-Wesley, 1975.

Walton, R. E. How to counter alienation in the plant. *Harvard Business Review,* November-December 1972, pp. 70–81.

Walton, R. E. The diffusion of new work structures: Explaining why success didn't take. *Organizational Dynamics,* Winter 1975, pp. 3–22(a).

Walton, R. E. From Hawthorne to Topeka and Kalmar. In *Man and work in society,* edited by E. L. Cass and F. G. Zimmer. New York: Van Nostrand-Reinhold, 1975(b).

Whitsett, D. A., & Winslow, E. K. An analysis of studies critical of the motivator-hygiene theory. *Personnel Psychology,* 20 (1967): 391–415.

Worthy, J. C. Organizational structure and employee morale. *American Sociological Review,* 15 (1950): 169–179.

How Volvo Adapts Work to People

Pehr G. Gyllenhammar

In any industrialized country today, more than half the working population still works in companies with less than 50 employees. At the same time, however, very large organizations are growing even larger—too large to be comfortable for employees. Inside a large modern company too often the individual feels lost, unimportant in the overall scheme, merely a replaceable cog in the industrial system, with little or no control over his or her own life until he or she retires.

Inside government, too, as departments grow to cope with social problems and the growth itself creates new and different ills, the same anonymity occurs. In some countries the government employs directly or indirectly, at least one-third of the working population.

Much of our growth resulted from the discovery that a larger unit could get access to resources—notably capital—that were unavailable to smaller units. We found ways to produce in large factories more efficiently than we could in small workshops where a small team of employees was the basic manufacturing unit. We found ways to move our goods to more distant markets. We began to move people as well, creating new demands for products and an international flow of attitudes and values, as well as what we at Volvo refer to as "technology transfer."

In these circumstances, it is not surprising that the idea that if a little bigness is good, a lot of it must be better, seems to have flourished. This concept has given rise to such phenomena as conglomerates, 1,000-desk offices, and mile-long factories and assembly lines.

Like other good things, economy of scale turns out to have subtle limits. We begin to find today the symptoms of a new industrial illness. We invent machines to eliminate some of the physical stresses of work, and then we find that psychological tensions cause even more health and behavior problems. People don't want to be subservient to machines and systems. They react to inhuman conditions in very human ways: by job-hopping, absenteeism, apathetic attitudes, antagonism, and even malicious mischief.

From the employee's viewpoint this behavior is perfectly reasonable. The younger he or she is, the stronger his or her reactions are likely to be. The people entering the work force today have received more education than ever before in history. Society has educated them to regard themselves as mature adults, capable of making their own choices. By offering them jobs in our overorganized industrial units we offer them jobs where they have virtually no choices. For eight hours a day managers regard them as children, ciphers, or potential problems—and manage or control them accordingly.

Today a new element enters the picture—permanent unemployment. Technical advances in the industrial world have been so rapid that just at a time when more

From *Harvard Business Review*, July–August 1977, 102–113. Copyright © 1977 by the President and Fellows of Harvard College; all rights reserved.

people are entering the job market, we can produce more with less people. Employees whose jobs are threatened in the name of "progress" cluster together under union or government umbrellas to protect the status quo. The featherbedding that follows not only hastens the demise of their organizations but also creates polarized "them and us" attitudes that make it impossible for management to propose retraining, work reorganization, and diversification that might help create new jobs and new business. The more employees try to protect their endangered jobs, the more planners and managers find reason to design people out of the industrial system.

If the industrial society succeeds in putting people to one side, what will happen to them and thus to society itself? A humane answer to this crucial question depends on the cultural and economic framework in which industry operates and on the commitment of the people making the decisions that will affect employment in the future. Instead of doing away with jobs, they will have to ask themselves how to make the jobs meaningful to the people as well as to the organization.

Managers need to find ways to capture the personal involvement of each employee. Management cannot be based on power. In any show of power, the employees today will "win" and management will "lose," though the inevitable result is that everyone loses. Instead of an adversary game, I hope we can rewrite the rules to make business the kind of game in which everybody wins.

THE SWEDISH WAY

For reasons of its own, Sweden has spent a great deal of time and energy in the last few years looking at some of these problems and trying to find ways to make work more livable and life more workable. We have stringent new laws for job security and work safety. A 1977 law calls for full consultation with employees and full participation by their representatives in decision making from board level to the shop floor. Employee organizations have the right to all financial information about a company. More important than the laws are the attitudes of managers who, in spite of the discomforts of change, seem to share the conviction that greater employee participation is good and necessary.

Sweden has a unique demography, with a population less than that of Los Angeles spread over an area larger than the state of California. The country is more dependent on its success in world markets than are many larger countries. The population is fairly homogeneous, mainly Nordic. This coherence gives rise to a culture in which social change can sweep more swiftly than it can in countries that have more heterogeneous populations and cultures within their borders.

Industrially, Sweden's situation is quite different from that of the United States, for example. While the United States has a pool of unemployed that, in effect, buffers staffing problems, Sweden has relatively full employment and is to some extent dependent on "guest workers" from other countries. Like other industrialized nations, though, Sweden and the United States share a similar need to involve people in their work to achieve better productivity.

Sweden has its labor laws, a body of practice, a union/employer structure, and an entire industrial culture based on cooperative rather than contentious models.

Blue-collar union membership is approaching 90%, and wage agreements are worked out from a national viewpoint. The United States model is based more on arm's length negotiations, with different unions having different demands and union membership comprising considerably less than half the work force (though the membership is high in manufacturing industries).

Factories in both countries have fairly efficient unions and clear-cut ways for managers and unions to communicate with relatively strike-free results. Both countries experience employee absenteeism, but a major difference between the two is that Swedish companies had the problem sooner and have treated it as a more serious matter. Many U.S. companies, on the other hand, consider the problem less important as there are available people waiting hopefully for jobs. These distinct experiences of employee absenteeism underlie the differences between Swedish and American attitudes toward employee participation.

THE VOLVO EXPERIENCE

Just as Sweden's situation differs from that of the other countries, so Volvo's differs from that of other companies. The events at Volvo's factories need to be seen in that perspective. By today's international standards, Volvo is a medium-sized company, but in its home country, it is a large company. Ranking between sixtieth and seventieth in the list of non-U.S. companies, Volvo's share of the world automotive market has doubled in the last ten years to about 2.5%. Deriving 70% of its sales from outside Sweden, Volvo accounts for between 8% and 9% of Sweden's total export.

Like other auto manufacturers, at its inception Volvo had a production system that was technically oriented and planned in detail, and it used the Methods Time Measurement system (MTM). When labor unrest became visible in 1969, it became necessary for us to adapt the way we controlled production to new attitudes in the work force.

In 1972, to increase exports and build further volume and profit in the noncar divisions, Volvo went through a major reorganization. We cut headquarters staff from 1,800 to 100 people. Each major product group became an independent division, and all major market units became independent profit centers within the divisions. The new organization took on a more international flavor, recognizing the fact that more than 100 countries provided its income. To balance the income from the dominant car activities, we made major investments in trucks, buses, and industrial equipment.

Although Sweden's labor costs have become the highest in the world, Volvo remains a profitable company. In recent years, the company's cash flow as a percentage of sales was one of the three highest in the automotive industry. The corporate strategy today is to add strength and reduce vulnerability by diversifying within the transportation field.

When we started thinking about reorganizing the way we worked, the first bottleneck seemed to be production and technology. We couldn't really reorganize the work to suit the people unless we also changed the technology that chained people to the assembly line. But in an industry like ours such changes are risky and irreversible. Volvo's Kalmar plant, for example, is designed for a specific point: car assembly in working groups of about 20 people. If it didn't work, it would be a costly and visible failure, in both financial and social terms. We would lose credibility with our own people as well as with those who are watching from outside.

It was also clear that technical changes would be fruitless if they were not accompanied by organizational changes and evolution toward a climate of cooperation and partnership. So the second major change over the last five years has been Volvo's investment of tens of millions of dollars to improve the physical working environment for employees. That was simply part of the cost of achieving cleaner, more pleasant surroundings. This is our responsibility as an employer. It demonstrates in concrete, visible ways that we value the people who work for Volvo.

But this investment does not create better jobs. It only helps give us the conditions in which people can work together to organize their jobs in more human ways. The third part of our change strategy, then, concerned the jobs themselves. In some cases we have built entirely new factories, where work can be organized more flexibly. In other cases we have tried to mechanize unpleasant jobs and change or enrich those that can't be automated.

In addition to physical change and job redesign, the change process requires participation from the employees and a consultation structure that permits their voices to be heard. Therefore, the fourth element of our change strategy, one that grows increasingly important as we make progress on the other three fronts, is personal development. Volvo wants individuals to have a chance to learn more and to enhance their personal lives and careers through opportunities available within the company.

In both Sweden and Volvo, the structure for consultation already existed. Throughout the company we have a hierarchy of works councils with representatives from both management and the employees. Some of these councils, one per plant, have been required by law since 1948. Others, like the Corporate Works Council, were created to meet our own needs for consultation. Given these councils, the physical changes quite naturally led to improvements in the work itself and to greater individual involvement.

INNOVATION AT THE WORKPLACE

A new factory presents a unique opportunity to try out entirely new approaches to work design, and many of the changes Volvo has adopted in the last five years were first tried at the Kalmar factory in the south of Sweden.

Kalmar: The Catalyst

In designing the Kalmar plant, we decided to break up the inexorable assembly line to which the people are subservient and to use instead individual carriers that move under control of the employees. An assembly line is essentially a set of conveyors going through a warehouse full of materials. The materials, not the employees, are the focus of the system. People are continually having to run after their work as it moves past their stations. We thought perhaps people could do a better job if the product could stand still while they worked on it.

Another problem in factory life is that there is an antisocial atmosphere built into the production line. People want to have some social contact, a chance to look at each others' faces now and then. But in an assembly line, people are physically isolated from each other. If they do manage to get together to discuss something, people in the traditional auto plant typically have to yell over the sound of machines. Furthermore, people performing jobs of very short duration (perhaps 30 to 60 seconds) seldom get a chance to stop between tasks to think or talk.

We believed the human-scaled work group would be more effective. If work were patterned according to people, rather than the other way around, we thought people could act in cooperation, discuss more, and decide among themselves how to organize the work. In essence, our approach is based on stimulation rather than restriction. If one views the employees as adults, then one must assume they will respond to stimulation. If one views them as children, then the assumption is that they will need restriction. The intense emphasis in most factories on measurement and control seems to be a manifestation of the latter viewpoint.

The design for Kalmar incorporated pleasant, quiet surroundings, arranged for group working, with each group having its own individual rest and meeting areas. The work itself is organized so that each group is responsible for a particular, identifiable portion of the car—electrical systems, interiors, doors, and so on. Individual cars are built up on self-propelling "carriers" that run around the factory following a movable conductive tape on the floor. Computers normally direct the carriers, but manual controls can override the taped route. If someone notices a scratch in the paint on a car, he or she can immediately turn the carrier back to the painting station. Under computer control again, the car will return later to the production process wherever it left off.

Each work group has its own buffer areas for incoming and outgoing carriers so it can pace itself as it wishes and organize the work inside its own area so that its members work individually or in subgroups to suit themselves. Most of the employees have chosen to learn more than one small job; the individual increase in skills also gives the team itself added flexibility.

To gain a sense of identification with its work, a group must also take responsibility for its work. The myriad inspection stations with "watchdog" overtones that characterize most factories have been abandoned at Kalmar. Instead, each team does its own inspection. After a car passes about three work group stations, it passes through a special inspection station where people with special training test each car. A computer-based system takes quality information reports from these stations and, if there are any persistent or recurring problems, flashes the results to the proper group station, telling them also how they solved similar problems the last time. The computer also informs the teams when their work has been particularly problem-free.

When we started at Kalmar, we made the assumption that the productivity could equal that of any comparable traditional plant. Today we have not one but five new plants, organized in a nontraditional way, all scaled for 600 employees or less. These new plants cost a little bit more to build than traditional factories of similar size, but they are already showing good productivity. We believe productivity will continue to increase because the people who work in them have better jobs. One of the most important measures of our success came in autumn 1976 when we received the results of a union survey of all Kalmar employees. Almost all of them were in favor of the new working patterns; one result of the survey has been to increase our focus on working groups at other plants.

Torslanda: Breaking Down Bigness

At Kalmar where there is a maximum of 600 employees, organized in groups that control the auto carrier system, change was part of the design. At a place like our 8,000-employee Torslanda factory, just outside Gothenburg, introducing change is quite a different matter. Built in 1964, at the zenith of the technical era, Torslanda is tied to a large-scale assembly line. Furthermore, it remains the source of our "bread-and-butter" production, the mother factory for the cars that are the company's primary product. This means, too, that we can't make sweeping changes that might disrupt production, as we might be able to do in a new place where we were adding capacity.

While to a large extent central management spurred the Kalmar plan, most of the changes in the last five years at Torslanda have been locally generated. For this we must give considerable credit not only to the managers there but also to the 55 works council groups and subgroups, to a number of active union officials, and to the more than 8,000 employees themselves.

A factor that seems to permeate our experience, at Torslanda and throughout the company in Sweden, is the serious, mature attitude of union officials, who have often initiated or supported changes that caused them short-term inconveniences and required adjustments in such basic items as wage structures. Group working, for example, means that the basis for incentive or bonus payments shifts from individual production to group production; yet it is the union as much as the company that has made group working a primary goal for Torslanda.

Although the consultation structure has always been strong at Torslanda, real changes in the work itself began to come to light as the planning for Kalmar got under way. Torslanda was in some ways the cradle for Kalmar. The carrier was developed by people borrowed from Torslanda; its tilting device, which eliminates the need to work in pits on cars overhead, was tested at Torslanda, and 20 of the tilters replace pits in assembly there today.

One of the first change steps at Torslanda was to make the four main departments (pressing, body work, painting, and assembly) as autonomous as possible. Each department has its own problems and its own style. In 1973, for example, the body shop formed a working group to consider problems of noise and dust. The working group enlisted some architects from the Gothenburg School of Applied Art, and from their suggestions employees selected schemes for cutting noise, eliminating dirt, and brightening their environment. It took several years to implement all the proposals but today the body shop is one of the brightest spots in the corporation.

Starting change and keeping it going is a challenge in a place like Torslanda. Most of the works councils, consultation groups, and project groups have money to spend on such things as improving their working conditions. Changes to cut the dust or noise require little outside impetus. Changes of work structure that can take place within a single working group also occur naturally. But we have discovered that most real changes of work structure affect other groups, at least indirectly. So the problem has been to draw the boundaries for single working groups wherever we could and to make them as clear-cut as possible.

Job rotation was the opening wedge. It started around 1964 in the upholstery department for practical reasons—to eliminate the muscular aches and pains the employees got from doing the same operation over and over. Some of the employees, however, disliked the change of pace, and reactions were mixed for several years. In 1966, when the upholstery employees themselves helped plan a rotation system, the results were much better. Each employee learned the work for all 15 stations; and each checked and corrected his or her own work. The employees noticed a sharp drop in the aches and pains, and new signs of team spirit began to show up. Eventually they took responsibility for planning their own work as well as for checking it. Employee turnover and absenteeism in the group dropped, and the upholstery quality improved.

The evolution of this group from 1964 to 1968 has many of the characteristics of other successful changes that have occurred in more recent years. People often resist change at first, and this is overcome only when there has been sufficient time and contact among members for a real group to begin crystallizing. This contact is difficult to achieve on a rapidly moving assembly line with short-cycle tasks. As the upholstery example shows, a group creates itself; it cannot be created by someone else. And the process does not take place overnight.

Once a real group does exist, though, it can take on other tasks well beyond its original purpose. As later groups also learned, rotating jobs was often more satisfying than continually performing single short-cycle task, even though it entailed a lot of job-hopping. If group members could enlarge jobs, taking in neighboring tasks, they could turn a two-minute station time into four, or eight, or ten minutes, and have more satisfaction in handing on a fairly finished product. Enrichment, whereby the group took on supervision, control, and planning, usually came later when the group was quite well formed.

Although we had a good example in the upholstery group on hand, and a deep interest in job content, job rotation at Torslanda nonetheless crept on very slowly. By the end of 1970 about 3% of our 3,000 assembly people were rotating jobs. We hit 10% in 1971, 18% in 1972, and then began to see momentum when 30% of the assembly people were rotating by the end of 1973. Today it is well over 60%, with employees showing more interest in job enlargement or job enrichment, and we know that interest will grow until we gradually reach the point where employees make the natural demand for change in jobs. There will be a few people, however, especially older ones, who don't want to change at all.

In the body and paint shops it was fairly natural for the employees to be organized in groups, and enrichment occurred in different forms in different areas. Assembly in the shops, though, is still paced by the speed of the line. In late 1976, we began a new kind of work within Torslanda to replace the traditional line. Two groups, each with nine people, do final assembly in docks. The nine group members do everything including chassis assembly, body work, mating the chassis and body, final trimming, and checkout. The dock employees have production meetings every week to discuss their situation, which includes the usual technical problems that occur with new equipment.

It takes each group about an hour to make a car. Thus the production costs remain competitive, and we think the additional investment for the dock equipment and more material-handling support (such as fork-lift drivers, who already have fairly interesting jobs) is justified. We are convinced that improved working conditions and work content result in lower employee turnover and absenteeism, and thus in less expense to the company as well as the community.

We wouldn't invest in dock assembly if we couldn't see economic as well as social justification for it. We can already see that it is possible to cut the standard assembly line production time sharply. When work is split as in normal MTM, each employee has unused time between tasks. With larger job cycles more work is done in total, and the work is more satisfying for the person doing it.

Does It Work outside Sweden?

Volvo management realizes that the easy acceptance of joint union and company projects is uniquely Swedish. Our emphasis on improving work content was also early in terms of the current worldwide trend. When we bought a controlling interest in the Dutch auto manufacturer DAF in 1975, we found the company was experiencing some of the same problems we had observed at the beginning of the 1970s and was thinking about similar solutions. The association with Volvo simply added impetus to a trend that was already there.

The factory at Born in the Netherlands, which now manufactures our smaller model 343 car, employs about 3,700 people, about a third of whom are not Dutch. When absenteeism and employee turnover rose in 1973, a steering committee of managers and technical people set out to improve work on the assembly line. Starting with a relatively difficult mixture of people, 12 employees of both sexes, all ages, and varied nationalities, they explored job enlargement. Involvement grew rapidly as members taught each other their jobs. By the end of 1973, most people had learned from 3 to 11 of the 12 jobs, and then they could work in longer cycles. The foreman together with the group took the planning task formerly done by the foreman's supervisor.

While management was officially reviewing and evaluating these results during most of 1974, similar activities started spontaneously in other parts of the plant. In early 1975, a new steering committee, including employee representatives, set up discussion groups regarding job enlargement and problem solving. Today about 150 groups, each containing 15 or so people, involving more than 80% of the blue-collar employees, meet regularly, about once a month. Also, managers at Born are planning management development courses, concentrating on interpersonal relations and communications, for people starting at the foreman level.

One outgrowth of the Born activities is a new assembly hall, where the conveyor belt, which the employees control, is divided into small overhead conveyors with intermediate buffers between them. The conveyor idea is now being studied at Torslanda. The managers consult the employees regarding all new equipment or layouts; they have published a "letter of intent" setting out their desire to improve the work structure not just as a project but as an ongoing process. There is at Born now a useful strategy for the future.

At Volvo's own Ghent factory in Belgium, which is less troubled by absenteeism and employee turnover, the reexamination of work structure happened somewhat later than at Born, but managers there are pleased by recent progress. In April 1974, influenced by changes in the Belgian social climate, growing demand from employees for better conditions, and the rapid progress in most of Volvo's Swedish plants, the management at Ghent decided there was a need to make the individual more central to the production process.

Ghent managers initiated a program focusing on a better arrangement of the relief people (a ratio of 1 relief person to 14 employees instead of the former 1 to 25) and installation of buffer areas. Storage now provides 20-minute production coverage; fixed stations and group working replace the pits in the assembly factory and the merry-go-rounds in the body assembly shop. In the upholstery area the line was abandoned entirely in favor of group working. Today an employee assembles an entire seat and takes responsibility for the quality.

In the second phase at Ghent, managers saw that those areas where factory employees gave some input to the change process were obviously running more smoothly than those that had been changed entirely by managers and engineers. Now top managers are looking for better ways to keep in touch with employees, and management education has a higher priority today at Ghent. A "group working" project team is investigating further changes. Ghent managers say the results so far are convincing.

WORK TEAMS AND MANAGEMENT

At every level, management of group working is a different phenomenon. I think the change is healthy. Instead of giving orders the manager has to listen, argue, motivate, and often compromise. This process takes longer. Decisions are slower. But it works out better in the long run because, once they are made, the decisions are accepted and implemented rapidly.

We have learned something else from the group working at Torslanda and other factories. The success or failure of an idea is often attributable to whose idea it was, rather than to any intrinsic goodness or badness of the idea. If it is the union's idea, or if it comes from a work group, an innovation has a good chance of working. If it is a management idea, its chances are slimmer. (In the United States it seems to be the other way around.)

So the function of management at Volvo is not so much having ideas as creating an environment, a climate where the people who matter will be able to have ideas and try them out. Joint consultation on an informal basis—best exemplified in group working—gives the best chance for a group to develop ownership of an idea and, therefore, find good reasons to make sure it succeeds.

In this environment leadership is crucial. Participation actually demands better leadership, as well as more self-discipline from everyone involved. Some foreigners talk about Sweden as if management control, in the traditional sense, may be lost in the new industrial environment. Outsiders also worry that participation by employees will lead to reduced efficiency for corporations. Examples of reduced efficiency, however, and there will be some, are more likely to be due to poor management than to changes in the system.

I don't believe the new values and the new laws call for "permissiveness." Instead, I think managers have to be stronger and more disciplined. It is the weak people in management who have difficulties dealing with employee representatives. Until the manager can earn the respect of employees, there will be mutual suspicion, and too little information will flow between them. Leaders who have the strength and self-confidence to respect their employees and the strength to talk about their own mistakes will earn respect. Once the employees trust and respect a manager, real progress is possible. That kind of strength is the focus for selection, training, and development of Volvo managers.

The new climate we have achieved at Volvo clearly demands a different type of leadership at all levels. Foremen, who had been the focus of our production achievements in the past, are now faced with a new situation. The new approach means that they risk being squeezed between higher management and the plant employees. Also, today, foremen carry the heaviest responsibility in implementing changes.

For decades we told them, in essence, that they had two main functions. The first was to supervise the pace of the work, to keep the line moving. The second was to give technical advice and assistance wherever necessary. Thus most of the people promoted to foremen's positions had been skilled employees who could solve technical problems. To keep people working, they became disciplinarians, expert at saying "thou-shalt-not."

Suddenly we asked foremen to develop a rather different set of skills. We wanted them to be "good managers of people." Instead of people receiving discipline from the supervisor, the new climate emphasizes self-discipline. We redefined the foreman's role rapidly, and this created problems during the change. The problems were exacerbated by the fact that formal training for foremen was traditionally less important than on-the-job training, so they tended to be reluctant to take courses at first.

Yet in the new circumstances foremen needed considerable training to regard themselves as information-gatherers, as aides to the employees, as teachers and consultants, rather than as bosses. And in many cases the attitude change was only partial, stimulated and, at the same time, hampered because it was forced by pressure from employees and management, rather than from the foremen's own convictions. The situation is better today, but it was a problem at first because of the speed with which we implemented changes and the fact that we did not consult with foremen enough in planning for the changes.

VOLVO'S GUIDELINES

OUR EXPERIENCES WITH CHANGE IN OUR VARIOUS PLANTS HAVE PRODUCED A FEW RULES OF THUMB THAT MAY BE HELPFUL TO OTHERS:

- Each unit should be free to develop individually, without detailed control or interference from headquarters.
- An active and positive top management attitude toward change is a prerequisite for positive results. However, when this attitude turns into a drive from above to install programs, projects, and plans, management tends to fail.
- Headquarters is most effective when its role is sanctioning investments for new approaches and challenging local managers to take more radical initiatives and risks.
- Our positive achievements seem related to the extent our managers understand that the change process will sooner or later affect several organizational levels, regardless of where it started.
- We encounter problems if we formalize change and request targets, minutes, and figures too early. Change requires time and freedom of action. When people view it as a continuing search-and-learning process of their own, the chances of lasting effects are increased.
- The initiative for change should be a line responsibility, with specialists as supporters rather than initiators. Changes line managers initiate seldom have lasting effects. Managers can, however, act as sounding boards and catalysts, carrying know-how from one place to another.
- Progress seems to be fastest when a factory or company starts by forming a joint management and union steering committee to look at its own problems.
- Steering committee members should be the strongest possible people, sharing commitment to change.
- The fastest way to get ideas flowing seems to be to set up discussion groups in each working area. A working area in this sense (and in a group-working sense) should probably contain fewer than 25 people.
- Groups that have money to spend on their own facilities and a mandate to list their own problems seem to achieve cohesion and cooperation most rapidly. It need not cost the corporation more money to apportion facilities or safety budgets to the groups themselves than to experts.
- A new plant, a new product, or a new machine is an opportunity to think about new working patterns.
- An investment in one new facility or one group area often results in spontaneous changes in related facilities or groups. These can be encouraged by alert managers.
- Most factories have a number of tasks that need not be done on assembly lines. Once a few have been found and changed, others will reveal themselves.
- So that the change suggestions will emerge from inside, changes of work organization must be integrated with a structure of employee consultation.

In a sense top management can act as an enzyme, a catalyst, to speed up the process of change—but it has not been an easy process even in Sweden where the social and political values supported the directions we chose. In the mid-1960s there weren't many managers who could uphold what we're doing now.

Today's managers have moved a long way from the attitude they held ten years ago for several reasons. Because people had such bad experiences with existing systems, there was force from the bottom. And because we insisted on change, there was also force from the top. Furthermore, if a middle manager wakes up every morning wondering whether he will have to replace or do without 15% to 20% of his work force, he will grow more willing to change.

Numbers are important, and the manager has to produce the numbers. The pressure builds up, resulting in change much more rapid than the normally conservative culture of a corporation would permit.

We have no "management development" chief at Volvo. The task is too important to put into a specialist department. Instead, I consider it one of my most important duties. This view is increasingly shared by line managers throughout the company. Their foremen, supervisors, managers, and employees are resources for which they are accountable, just as they are accountable for investments in buildings and machines.

In this atmosphere of employee participation and rapid change, management is an exacting task. If you don't manage tautly, you can drift into inefficiency that endangers the entire venture. It is the manager's job to create an atmosphere of urgency. But tight management need not be authoritative. Today's manager must be able to talk to people, and to listen as well. If the manager is alert to every opportunity for improvement and full of zest for his job, this communicates itself to others.

Participation demands more work, not less, from everybody. Idle people become bored and sloppy, so it is an important part of the manager's job to be taking the temperature all the time, injecting some of his or her own alertness whenever he or she senses signs of apathy or boredom. As other companies have learned—and so have we—the manager who is reluctant or just gives lip service to the idea of participation can hold back employee-based changes that are actually in the best interests of both the corporation and its employees.

Creating High-Involvement Work Organizations

Edward E. Lawler III

The 1970s saw the successful construction, start-up, and operation of a significant number of new plants that are different from traditional plants in some important ways. These plants are different in how they are designed and man-

Adapted from E. E. Lawler III, The new plant revolution. *Organizational Dynamics*, Winter 1978, 3–12. © Edward E. Lawler III, 1980. Used with permission.

aged, and in the high level of involvement that seems to characterize their work-forces. The list of companies with these new plants reads like an excerpt from *Fortune's* 500. They include General Foods, PPG Industries, Procter & Gamble, Sherwin-Williams, TRW, Rockwell, General Motors, Mead Corporation, and Cummins Engine. Many of these organizations have started not one high-involvement plant, but two, three, four, or more. At this point no one knows precisely how many organizations have initiated new high-involvement plants, or how many of them exist. A good guess would be that more than twenty large organizations have at least one, and that, overall, more than a hundred are currently in operation.

It is possible that these high-involvement plants are merely an intriguing novelty which, although successful, can teach us little about how to create more effective work organizations. On the other hand, it is possible that they represent a broadly applicable approach to management that can teach us a great deal about how we can create more effective organizations and that, as such, they are a very important social invention which warrants careful study. Before we can determine just how applicable this approach is, we need to briefly review the characteristics of these plants and then to consider what has been learned about their effectiveness.

CHARACTERISTICS OF THE PLANTS

One of the most interesting aspects of the plants is the number of innovations common to all or almost all of them. These innovations are most interesting because of their potential for diffusion to other organizations. A review of the innovations will indicate how specific areas of management are handled in the high-involvement plants and how they differ from traditional plants.

Employee Selection

The traditional approach to employee selection has largely gone by the board. Instead of the personnel departments carefully screening, testing, and selecting among applicants, a process is used that includes helping the job applicant make a valid decision about taking the job and getting production employees more involved in the selection decision.

The selection process places a great deal of emphasis on acquainting applicants with the nature of the jobs they are expected to fill and the nature of the managerial style that will be used in the plant. They can then decide whether the particular job situation is right for them. Before start-up, a group interview is held by the managers and workers who will interact with new employees so they can decide together whether the job applicants will fit the management approach that will be used in the organization. After the plant becomes operational this approach to selection continues and work-team members are given the responsibility for selecting new members of their teams. In some cases, the personnel department does some initial screening of applicants and, where appropriate, administers tests and checks references.

Design of the Plant and Physical Layout

Many of the plants make an effort to have at least a few members of the workforce on board early enough to participate in decisions about the layout of machinery, equipment, and the recreational and personal areas of the plant. Often employees from existing plants—many of whom will be reassigned to the new plant—are asked to participate in the design. The idea is to capture the employees' ideas and implement them to improve the design of the plant. In some cases, experts in sociotechnical system design are also called in to make certain that the physical layout is congruent with the desired social system.

Frequently a strong egalitarian approach is taken to how the work and nonwork areas in the new plants are laid out. Rather than having separate areas in which managers eat and spend their nonwork time, everyone uses the same eating, restroom, and recreational facilities. In many plants the entrances and parking areas are common to all employees. In other words, employees all receive a clear message that at least in terms of the physical facilities and typical perquisites of office, a relatively egalitarian system exists at the plant level.

Security

Most plants are publicly committed to no-lay-off policies. So far, all of them I am aware of have been able to live up to their policies by using part-time employees during busy periods and by doing maintenance and other nonproductive work during slow periods. This policy is important because it assures people that they will not produce themselves out of a job and it shows that the company is willing to make a commitment to all employees.

Job Design

In all the plants, an attempt is made to see that employees have jobs that are challenging, motivating, and satisfying. In some cases this is done through individually based job-enrichment approaches that emphasize personal responsibility for a whole piece of meaningful work. In most cases, however, it is accomplished through the creation of autonomous work groups or teams (see, e.g., Poza & Markus, 1980).

Typically, teams are given the responsibility for the production of a whole product or a significant part of one. They are self-managing in the sense that they make decisions about who performs which tasks on a given day, they set their own production goals, and they are often also responsible for quality control, purchasing, and discipline. Most teams emphasize the desirability of job rotation for their members, and team members are expected to learn all the jobs that fall within the purview of the team.

In some plants an effort has even been made to mix interesting tasks with routine jobs. For example, one plant made the maintenance jobs part of the same team as warehousing so that no one would spend all of his or her time on the relatively boring warehousing tasks. The end result of the use of work teams usually is that the people participating feel responsible for a large work area, experience a sense of control, and develop an understanding of a large segment of the production process.

Pay System

Most plants have taken a different approach to establishing base pay levels for employees. Instead of using a traditional job-evaluation approach which scores jobs on their characteristics in order to determine the pay rates for every job in the plant, they evaluate the skills of each individual. Typically, everyone starts at the same salary. As employees learn new skills, their salaries go up. When this system is combined with job rotation, workers doing relatively low-level jobs may be quite highly paid because they are capable of performing a large number of other, more skilled tasks (see Lawler, 1981).

This approach has two main advantages: It tends to create a flexible, highly trained workforce that can adapt to most changes in product demand and staffing since ready replacements are available. It also promotes the development of the work team because it gives employees a broader knowledge of how the plant operates. This is important because it enables individuals to participate in more decisions and it aids identification with the goals of the plant.

In about half the new plants with which I am familiar, decisions about whether or not an individual has mastered a new job well enough to deserve a salary increase are left to the members of his or her team. This approach to pay decisions reinforces the participative management style that is very important to the way high-involvement plants are managed.

A few (but not most) of the plants have moved toward one of two approaches to tying pay to performance. Some have introduced a merit salary increase component into their skill-based pay systems. A few others have introduced plantwide profit-sharing or gain-sharing plans after they have operated long enough to develop a stable performance history. It is possible that as more of them mature and establish stable base periods for the measurement of productivity gains, more of them will adopt these plans. This seems likely, since organizationwide sharing of productivity gains is congruent with the team concept of management and the general participative, egalitarian principles that underlie the design of these plants.

Organizational Structure

One of the really striking features of these plants is their structural hierarchy. All the plants have located the plant manager only a few levels above the production workers. In some cases, the foreman's role has been eliminated completely. In others, the foremen report directly to the plant manager, and such traditional intermediate levels as general foreman and superintendent have been eliminated.

Where there are no foremen, several teams usually report to a single supervisor, and the teams are envisaged as being self-managed. Most of the time they elect a team leader who is then responsible for communicating with the rest of the organization. This person undertakes the kinds of lateral relations with other functional and line departments that consume so much of the time and constitute such an important responsibility for the typical first-line supervisor (see Walton & Schlesinger, 1979).

High-involvement plants also deemphasize functional-area responsibility. Rather than being organized on a functional basis (maintenance, production, and so on), they tend to be organized on a product or an area basis. Thus individuals have the responsibility for the production of something rather than for general maintenance or engineering. This system provides more meaningful job structures and creates a feeling of commitment to the product rather than to a function.

Because of the way they are structured, most plants have fewer staff and indirect-labor people assigned to them. Since many of the typical staff functions are handled by the work teams, not as many support people are needed. For example, since some scheduling is done by the teams, fewer people are needed in this support group.

Approach to Training

All the new plants place a heavy emphasis on training, career planning, and the personal growth and development of employees. This is usually backed up with extensive in-plant training programs and strong encouragement for employees to take off-the-job training, usually paid for by the organization.

There have been some interesting innovations in in-company training. For example, in some plants employees may take courses in the economics of the plant's business and are rewarded with higher pay when they complete such courses. On-the-job training by other employees is also very common and is necessary to implement the concept of multi-skilled employees. Regular career-planning sessions are also scheduled. In some plants, employees present a personal career-development plan to their team members; in others, the process is handled by someone in management. As a result of the strong emphasis on training, workers develop the feeling that personal development and growth are desirable goals.

Management Style

Most of the practices I have cited are in integral part of what it means to practice participative management. Operationally, this translates into pushing decisions as far down in the organization as possible. As we have seen, in high-involvement plants, production-line employees make purchasing decisions and even personnel-selection decisions. When decisions cannot be pushed down, it is typical for inputs to be gathered from everyone in the organization before the final decision is made. For example, a number of plants have delayed establishing personnel policies until the workforce has been hired and everyone has had the chance to have a say on what these policies should be.

Summary and Conclusions

Overall, these new plants are clearly different from traditional plants in a number of important ways. Almost no aspect of the organization has been left untouched.

The reward systems, the structure, the physical layout, the personnel-management system, and the nature of the jobs have all been changed—and in significant ways. Because so many particulars have been altered, in aggregate they amount to a new kind of organization.

I must stress, however, that most plants are still regarded by both employees and management as being in an evolutionary stage. They are being modified and altered continually on the basis of experience and changes in local conditions. Thus, although it is clear that a common set of practices is being tried by these organizations, every plant and organization that adopts them is simultaneously adapting them in ways that make the management system and overall design of each unique.

It is instructive to compare these high-involvement plants to the approach to management that is commonly used in Japan. In many respects they are similar. For example, both use groups and emphasize job security. But it would be wrong to consider them to be essentially equivalent. The high-involvement plants differ in some important ways. Two of the most important are in their pay systems and their management style. Japanese organizations do not use skill-based pay and gain sharing. In addition, their management style seems to be best described as a mixture of paternalism and consultation. They simply are not as participative as the high-involvement plants. For example, they use quality-control circles but assign them a recommendations role, not a decision-making role, and they do not expect them to deal with pay decisions, hiring decisions, and normal operating decisions.

EFFECTIVENESS OF THE PLANTS

There are almost no hard data on how effective most of the new-design plants are. In a few cases, the plants have been measured by outsiders, who report positive results. For example, the Topeka plant of General Foods has been studied by Richard Walton and by Douglas Jenkins and myself. Both studies reported low absenteeism, low turnover, low production costs, and high employee satisfaction. I have had the chance to study five other plants in considerable detail. I would rate four of these as highly successful since they have negligible turnover and absenteeism and their financial performance is from 10 percent to 40 percent better than comparable plants. Finally, survey data clearly show that these plants do have highly involved and highly motivated employees.

Unfortunately, the plants which have been studied are the exception as far as public data on organizational effectiveness are concerned. Comparable data simply are not available on most plants. There is, however, a good deal of circumstantial evidence that most, if not all, are highly successful in terms of productivity, costs, and the quality of worklife. Although this is not hard proof of success, it is known that Procter & Gamble has closed its plants to researchers and others because it believes that it now enjoys a competitive advantage and does not want to share it.

It is also significant that most corporations that have tried one plant have gone on to try others (for example, Procter & Gamble, TRW, and General Motors). It would seem that they must be meeting with favorable results. Finally, it is interesting that the demand from other companies to visit high-involvement plants is great. Some of those that allow visitors even charge for tours and still report waiting lists. Apparently the word has gotten around that these plants have obtained impressive results, and people want to see for themselves. Overall, it is too early to make a valid analysis of the long-term success of most plants. Although a few have been around for some time (seven years), most were set up only in the past two or three years. It is not too early, however, to identify some of the problems that characterize these plants.

Unrealistic Expectations

The innovative employee-selection process used in many of the plants has often combined with the initial enthusiasm of the managers involved to create very high expectations on the part of the workforce. Because of the stress that the selection interviews place on challenging work and autonomy, employees not unreasonably conclude that things will be totally different from the way they are in a typical plant. They expect their work to be interesting all the time, and they expect to be in total control of their worklives. When these expectations are not met, it has created problems. Typically, workers have either quit or stayed on and complained about the inconsistency between what they were told the work would be like and what it turned out to be like.

The irony is that even where this is a problem, the work situations have, in fact, offered more autonomy and interesting work than usual. Unfortunately, this has been offset by the failure to fulfill the employees' high expectations. The solution seems to be to counsel employees to have more realistic expectations and to listen sympathetically to all problems. Realistic expectations are not easy to achieve in a new plant. Often management itself does not really know what will evolve and there is no existing work model for future employees to look at in order to ground their expectations in reality.

Individual Differences

People differ in their needs, skills, abilities, values, and preferences. A great deal of research has shown that not everyone responds positively to the kinds of innovations that are being tried in these plants (see Lawler, 1974). Some simply prefer the more traditional ways of doing things. In most plants the selection process screens out many of the people who do not fit the new-design approach, but some always manage to slip through. There are applicants who are not even aware of their strong orientation toward more traditional approaches, and the group-interview method may fail to identify this preference. The failure of the group approach is not surprising; group interviews are not known for their validity. The result of this mismatch in most plants has been a limited amount of turnover and the need to work with some individuals in a more traditional manner.

In some ways the problem of finding workers who fit the management style of the organization is probably less severe in the case of high-involvement plants than it is in traditional ones. Compared with the available opportunities, a large number of workers seem to want to work in this kind of situation. Plants that have advertised for employees who want to work in a participative environment have found themselves swamped with applicants.

Role of First-Level Supervision

Probably the most frequent and most difficult problem involves the role of the first-level supervisor (see Walton and Schlesinger, 1979). In some plants, relatively traditional foremen are in place; in others, there is no first-level supervisor present in work groups, the assumption being that these groups will be self-managing or that they will elect a leader or straw boss. In still other situations, individuals have been put in as acting first-level supervisors and told to work themselves out of a job within a year or a year and a half of the start-up.

In almost all instances, first-level supervisors and elected leaders have complained about a lack of role clarity and confusion about what decisions they could and could not make. Typically, they are uncomfortable with ordering and directing people, because they feel things should get done on a participative basis. But in many cases they do not know how to function as participative managers. Often they lack the skills to help the group become a functioning team, make decisions, and work through issues. They also have a great deal of difficulty in deciding which decisions should be made on a participative basis and which should not. Foremen have ended up asking for participation on issues when they already had all the information and technical expertise that were needed to make the decision. Conversely, and perhaps more frequently, because many supervisors come from a traditional background, they make decisions unilaterally when they should involve the work team.

Perhaps the best way to delineate the problem is to point out that there is no clear-cut description of the correct behavior for a first-level supervisor in these plants. Therefore, there is no adequate training program or selection method to fit a person to this position. Training is on a hit-or-miss basis, and the failure rate for those chosen is often high. Several organizations are trying to solve this problem by developing appropriate training programs, but to the best of my knowledge, no adequate program exists. The best approach seems to be extensive on-the-job training in which a clear job definition is developed and a good deal of one-on-one counseling is provided.

Permissiveness versus Participation

One of the hardest issues that managers in new plants confront is differentiating between permissiveness and participation. In most plants, workers have raised issues that seemed to the managers concerned to go "too far." For example, in one case employees wanted to install a color television set in a work area. The managers considered this undesirable but had a great deal of difficulty dealing with the issue. They felt that if they said no they would be violating the participative spirit of the plant. They finally did refuse, because they felt that it would harm productivity and that it represented an example of permissiveness rather than participative management.

The difficulty this group of managers had is typical of the problems experienced in other plants when workers have requested unusual personnel rules and work procedures. Unfortunately, the difference between what constitutes a reasonable request for the abandonment of a rule or policy and what constitutes an unreasonable request is often unclear. There probably is no way to deal with this kind of issue in advance, but it is clear that when such issues arise, how they are dealt with can greatly influence the future of the plant. Arbitrary turndowns of such requests can destroy the participative spirit of the plant, just as quick acceptance of every suggestion for eliminating rules, regulations, and discipline can.

Finally, it is crucial that management not abdicate its responsibility for what occurs in the plant. Regardless of how the decision is made, management is accountable in the eyes of people outside the plant. This means that it has the responsibility for seeing that the process for making the decisions is a good one and that the tough issues are dealt with (e.g., favoritism in allocating raises, discipline). Sometimes this means that members of management must actually intervene in order to assure that decisions are being made appropriately. It also means that when participation is not appropriate, management must make the decision.

Office Personnel

Most new plants have had a great deal of difficulty coming up with innovative ways to treat their office and clerical employees. As a result, these employees often feel relatively unappreciated and deprived when they look at what is happening in the production areas. They often do exactly the same jobs they would do in a more traditional plant. Although they may be supervised in a more participative manner, their life simply is not that different, even though they are often told they are in a "new type of organization." What is needed, of course, are innovative approaches to organizing, training, and paying people in office situations. Some attempts have been made to improve matters—for example, by rotating employees between shipping and office jobs (an effort which was abandoned). The best solution at the moment seems to be to treat these employees as a team with all this implies.

Personnel Function

The personnel function is usually much more important in new plants than in traditional ones, and indeed, it is often the one staff function that is more heavily staffed than in a traditional plant. It tends to become a real stress point and requires a very different set of skills from those possessed by the traditional personnel manager. Since many of the typical personnel tasks are assigned to the work teams (for example, selection and pay administration), they are subtracted from the duties of the personnel manager. However, the personnel manager cannot simply ignore these areas, but instead must work with the line organization to facilitate the accomplishment of these tasks. The personnel manager must have good interpersonal skills and must function as a key resource on how the new practices should be implemented.

The personnel manager needs to be an expert in job design, pay systems, training, and so on, so that other employees will have someone to consult when they need advice. In many cases, the personnel manager ends up with a difficult and frustrating job. The skill demands are much different and often much greater than those required in a typical plant. The personnel manager may be asked to solve problems that have never been tackled before and that have no established solutions.

Establishing Standards

Adequate standards in such areas as production and performance are difficult to establish in any organization, and particularly difficult to establish in new organizations, because they lack a track record. Thus it is not surprising that high-involvement plants seem to have trouble developing criteria upon which to base such things as pay raises and promotions. The normal problems that are part of any start-up operation are compounded for them because in these plants employees are typically asked to set the standards for their peers. Unless these employees receive a great deal of help, they find it hard to develop objective, challenging yardsticks for measuring their co-workers, particularly when such matters as compensation are involved. This is hardly surprising, since they usually have little prior experience and it is easier to be a good guy and set relatively low standards. Some plants deal with this problem by having employees develop written tests of job knowledge and set minimum time periods that must elapse before raise applications will be considered.

Regression under Pressure

At some point in the history of most plant start-ups, whether high-involvement or not, intense pressure for production develops. The pressure stems from the need to get the plant on-line in accordance with a predetermined production schedule. This period has proved to be particularly crucial in the life of most plants. Managers tend to revert to traditional management practices in times of crisis. They jump in and try to take charge.

Needless to say, such an act can be very damaging to the successful start-up of a high-involvement plant. It communicates to everyone that the new principles of management apply only when things are going well. Not all plants get through this period with their commitment to participative management intact. In one instance, at least, start-up problems led the plant manager to declare that the participative-management program was officially abandoned. The problems in this plant stemmed from the fact that no preparation had been made to deal with the necessity for making some decisions, particularly technical ones, in a non-participative way. The plant also suffered from a severe learning-overload problem. People were trying to learn a new approach to management as well as a complex new production process. It was simply too much to learn in a very short period of time. What is needed, of course, is either a realistic learning schedule or a workforce that has a good background in either the technology or the management system.

Timing of Start-Up Decisions

At present, no clear timetable exists of when various activities should begin in the start-up of a new-design plant (see Lawler & Olsen, 1977). Thus every organization that has launched such a plant has wrestled with issues like: When should the pay system be developed? When are personnel policies to be set? When should the first employees be hired? When should autonomous work groups be established?

Factors such as the type of technology and the skills of the employees need to be taken into account in drawing up an implementation schedule. Where the technology will change during the growth of the plant, it may be best to think in terms of an intermediate organization design, something to be abandoned once the technology has stabilized. Some projects have gotten into trouble because they tried to proceed immediately to the final organization-design stage, despite the fact that it was not appropriate to do so during the start-up period. For example, efforts have been made to set up autonomous work groups as soon as production began even though the nature of the technology did not permit stable group membership at that time.

Interface with the Rest of the Organization

In one sense, high-involvement plants are foreign bodies inside larger organizations. They differ in a number of important ways from the organizations that created them and to which they are responsible. For every new plant—successful or not—this has created a number of interface problems. The most public attention has been devoted to the case of a Topeka dog food plant, but problems are by no means restricted to that situation (Walton, 1975). High-involvement plants are living demonstrations of a different way to operate, and as such they automatically raise the question of whether the rest of the organization needs to change.

Various vested interests inevitably feel threatened and challenged by this question. Managers on the corporate staff, for example, may feel threatened because many issues for which they have stock answers are dealt with in an individualized manner at the plant level. Such an approach can jeopardize their job security by fostering demands for change from other parts of the organization.

Some managers may feel threatened because the plants operate without managers in the same or similar positions. In addition, managers in other plants may be concerned that they will have to change their whole approach to management if the new plants succeed. Finally, other managers may feel that their upward mobility in the organization will be hindered if the managers in the new plants do well and their operations are highly profitable.

At this time, no organization has solved the interface issue, but some are trying intriguing approaches; the most successful seem to revolve around an emphasis on decentralization and communications (Walton, 1977). On the one hand, companies using this approach stress that it is okay to be different. On the other hand, they are dealing with the communications issue by a number of devices, including seminars, task forces to study and design new plants, and frequent visits by managers from other locations to the high-involvement plants.

DIFFUSION OF NEW APPROACHES

Despite their visibility and importance, at this point only a minute fraction of the population of the United States works in high-involvement plants. What does the future hold? It seems clear that more new plants like the ones mentioned in this article will be started in the next few years. Diffusion of these practices to many new plants seems almost certain because of the success of the existing ones and because knowledge about how to do it is rapidly growing.

But what about older plants? Many of the practices mentioned here are also being tried in established locations, although few have tried the kind of total-system approach that is characteristic of the new plants. This is a crucial difference. Can the total approach be applied successfully to existing plants? Can it provide a much-needed model for how organizations can be made more effective? The jury is still out on this one, but there is reason to believe that it has tremendous potential.

The high-involvement model is a seemingly successful total-system approach to the management of plants. It translates vague terms like "participative management" and "concern for human resources" into actual policies and practices. Thus, there is something substantial to disseminate. Many organizations' new plants are being used for training people who can apply their concepts elsewhere. Interestingly, all the managers I have interviewed in new plants have said that they did not want to go back to a more traditional approach. Finally, in a number of cases, pressure for dissemination is building up because of the success of the new plants. After all, it is hard to ignore plants which are more effective.

Perhaps the most difficult problem in applying the high-involvement model to existing plants stems from the fact that it is successful precisely because it is an internally consistent total approach to management. It is impossible in most existing organizations to install all the practices which are characteristic of the high-involvement model in a short period of time. This means that a transition period is needed during which new practices are being installed and costs are being incurred but no results are seen because enough new practices are not in place. In many respects installation would be a great deal easier if a few changes could be made and positive results shown, but this seems unlikely since people respond to their total environment, and with a few changes they are not likely to experience a significantly different management system. The challenge at this point, therefore, is one of devising effective implementation strategies for a system of management which seems to have great potential. If this can be done

I have no doubt that we will see many older plants slowly but successfully convert to the high-involvement model.

REFERENCES

Lawler, E. E. The individualized organization: Problems and promise. *California Management Review*, 1974, **17**(2).

——. *Pay and organization development*. Reading, Mass.: Addison-Wesley, 1981.

——, & Olsen, R. N. Designing reward systems for new organizations. *Personnel*, 1977, **54**(5), 48–60.

Poza, E. J., Markus, M. L. Success story: The team approach to work restructuring. *Organizational Dynamics*, Winter 1980, 3–25.

Walton, R. E. The diffusion of new work structures: Explaining why success didn't take. *Organizational Dynamics*, Winter 1975, 3–22.

——. Successful strategies for diffusing work innovations. *Journal of Contemporary Business*, Spring 1977, 1–22.

—— & Schlesinger, L. A. Do supervisors thrive in participative work systems? *Organizational Dynamics*, Winter 1979, 25–38.

From Control to Commitment in the Workplace

Richard E. Walton

The larger shape of institutional change is always difficult to recognize when one stands right in the middle of it. Today, throughout American industry, a significant change is under way in long-established approaches to the organization and management of work. Although this shift in attitude and practice takes a wide variety of company-specific forms, its larger shape—its overall pattern— is already visible if one knows where and how to look.

Consider, for example, the marked differences between two plants in the chemical products division of a major U.S. corporation. Both make similar products and employ similar technologies, but that is virtually all they have in common.

The first, organized by businesses with an identifiable product or product line, divides its employees into self-supervising 10- to 15-person work teams that are collectively responsible for a set of related tasks. Each team member has the training to perform many or all of the tasks for which the team is accountable, and pay reflects the level of mastery of required skills. These teams have received assurances that management will go to extra lengths to provide continued employment in any economic downturn. The teams have also been thoroughly briefed on such issues as market share, product costs, and their implications for the business.

Not surprisingly, this plant is a top performer economically and rates well on all measures of employee satisfaction, absenteeism, turnover, and safety. With its employees actively engaged in identifying and solving problems, it operates with fewer levels of management and fewer specialized departments than do its sister plants. It is also one of the principal suppliers of management talent for these other plants and for the division manufacturing staff.

In the second plant, each employee is responsible for a fixed job and is required to perform up to the minimum standard defined for that job. Peer pressure keeps new employees from exceeding the minimum standards and from taking other initiatives that go beyond basic job requirements. Supervisors, who manage daily assignments and monitor performance, have long since given up hope for anything more than compliance with standards, finding sufficient difficulty in getting their people to perform adequately most of the time. In fact, they and their workers try to prevent the industrial engineering department, which is under pressure from top plant management to improve operations, from using changes in methods to "jack up" standards.

A recent management campaign to document an "airtight case" against employees who have excessive absenteeism or sub-par performance mirrors employees' low morale and high distrust of management. A constant stream of formal grievances, violations of plant rules, harassment of supervisors, wildcat walkouts, and even sabotage has prevented the plant from reaching its productivity and quality goals and has absorbed a disproportionate amount of division staff time. Dealings with the union are characterized by contract negotiations on economic matters and skirmishes over issues of management control.

No responsible manager, of course, would ever wish to encourage the kind of situation at this second plant, yet the determination to understand its deeper causes and to attack them at their root does not come easily. Established modes of doing things have an inertia all their own. Such an effort is, however, in process all across the industrial landscape. And with that effort comes the possibility of a revolution in industrial relations every bit as great as that occasioned by the rise of mass production the better part of a century ago. The challenge is clear to those managers willing to see it—and the potential benefits, enormous.

APPROACHES TO WORK-FORCE MANAGEMENT

What explains the extraordinary differences between the plants just described? Is it that the first is new (built in 1976) and the other old? Yes and no. Not all new plants enjoy so fruitful an approach to work organization; not all older plants have such intractable problems. Is it that one plant is unionized and the other not? Again, yes and no. The presence of a union may institutionalize conflict and lackluster performance, but it seldom causes them.

At issue here is not so much age or unionization but two radically different strategies for managing a company's or a factory's work force, two incompatible views of what managers can reasonably expect of workers and of the kind of partnership they can share with them. For simplicity, I will speak of these profound differences as reflecting the choice between a strategy based on imposing *control* and a strategy based on eliciting *commitment*.

The "Control" Strategy

The traditional—or control-oriented—approach to work-force management took shape during the early part of this century in response to the division of work into small, fixed jobs for which individuals could be held accountable. The actual definition of jobs, as of acceptable standards of performance, rested on "lowest common denominator" assumptions about workers' skill and motivation. To monitor and control effort of this assumed caliber, management organized its own responsibilities into a hierarchy of specialized roles buttressed by a top-down allocation of authority and by status symbols attached to positions in the hierarchy.

For workers, compensation followed the rubric of "a fair day's pay for a fair day's work" because precise evaluations were possible when individual job requirements were so carefully prescribed. Most managers had little doubt that labor was best thought of as a variable cost, although some exceptional companies guaranteed job security to head off unionization attempts.

In the traditional approach, there was generally little policy definition with regard to employee voice unless the work force was unionized, in which case damage control strategies predominated. With no union, management relied on an open-door policy, attitude surveys, and similar devices to learn about employees' concerns. If the work force was unionized, then management bargained terms of employment and established an appeal mechanism. These activities fell to labor relations specialists, who operated independently from line management and whose very existence assumed the inevitability and even the appropriateness of an adversarial relationship between workers and managers. Indeed, to those who saw management's exclusive obligation to be to a company's shareowners and the ownership of property to be the ultimate source of both obligation and prerogative, and claims of employees were constraints, nothing more.

At the heart of this traditional model is the wish to establish order, exercise control, and achieve efficiency in the application of the work force. Although it has distant antecedents in the bureaucracies of both church and military, the model's real father is Frederick W. Taylor, the turn-of-century "father of scientific management," whose views about the proper organization of work have long influenced management practice as well as the reactive policies of the U.S. labor movement.

Recently, however, changing expectations among workers have prompted a growing disillusionment with the apparatus of control. At the same time, of course, an intensified challenge from abroad has made the competitive obsolescence of this strategy clear. A model that assumes low employee commitment and that is designed to produce reliable if not outstanding performance simply cannot match the standards of excellence set by world-class competitors. Especially in a high-wage country like the United States, market success depends on a superior level of performance, a level that, in turn, requires the deep commitment, not merely the obedience—if you could obtain it—of workers. And as painful experience shows, this commitment cannot flourish in a workplace dominated by the familiar model of control.

The "Commitment" Strategy

Since the early 1970s, companies have experimented at the plant level with a radically different work-force strategy. The more visible pioneers—among them, General Foods at Topeka, Kansas; General Motors at Brookhaven, Mississippi; Cummins Engine at Jamestown, New York; and Procter & Gamble at Lima, Ohio—have begun to show how great and productive the contribution of a truly committed work force can be. For a time, all new plants of this sort were non-union, but by 1980 the success of efforts undertaken jointly with unions—GM's cooperation with the UAW at the Cadillac plant in Livonia, Michigan, for example—was impressive enough to encourage managers of both new and existing facilities to rethink their approach to the work force.

Stimulated in part by the dramatic turnaround at GM's Tarrytown assembly plant in the mid-1970s, local managers and union officials are increasingly talking about common interests, working to develop mutual trust, and agreeing to sponsor quality-of-work-life (QWL) or employee involvement (EI) activities. Although most of these ventures have been initiated at the local level, major exceptions include the joint effort between the Communication Workers of America and AT&T to promote QWL throughout the Bell System and the UAW-Ford EI program centrally directed by Donald Ephlin of the UAW and Peter Pestillo of Ford. In the nonunion sphere, the spirit of these new initiatives is evident in the decision by workers of Delta Airlines to show their commitment to the company by collecting money to buy a new plane.

More recently, a growing number of manufacturing companies has begun to remove levels of plant hierarchy, increase managers' spans of control, integrate quality and production activities at lower organizational levels, combine production and maintenance operations, and open up new career possibilities for workers. Some corporations have even begun to chart organizational renewal for the entire company. Cummins Engine, for example, has ambitiously committed itself to inform employees about the business, to encourage participation by everyone, and to create jobs that involve greater responsibility and more flexibility.

In this new commitment-based approach to the work force, jobs are designed to be broader than before, to combine planning and implementation, and to include efforts to upgrade operations, not just maintain them. Individual responsibilities are expected to change as conditions change, and teams, not individuals, often are the organizational units accountable for performance. With management hierarchies relatively flat and differences in status minimized, control and lateral coordination depend on shared goals, and expertise rather than formal position determines influence.

People Express, to cite one example, started up with its management hierarchy limited to three levels, organized its work force into three- or four-person groups, and created positions with exceptionally broad scope. Every full-time employee is a "manager": flight managers are pilots who also perform dispatching and safety checks; maintenance managers are technicians with other staff responsibilities; customer service managers take care of ticketing, security clearance, passenger boarding, and in-flight service. Everyone, including the officers, is expected to rotate among functions to boost all workers' understanding of the business and to promote personal development.

Under the commitment strategy, performance expectations are high and serve not to define minimum standards but to provide " stretch objectives," emphasize continuous improvement, and reflect the requirements of the marketplace. Accordingly, compensation policies reflect less the old formulas of job evaluation than the heightened importance of group achievement, the expanded scope of individual contribution, and the growing concern for such questions of "equity" as gain sharing, stock ownership, and profit sharing. This principle of economic sharing is not new. It has long played a role in Dana Corporation, which has many unionized plants, and is a fundamental part of the strategy of People Express, which has no union. Today, Ford sees it as an important part of the company's transition to a commitment strategy.

Equally important to the commitment strategy is the challenge of giving employees some assurance of security, perhaps by offering them priority in training and retraining as old jobs are eliminated and new ones created. Guaranteeing employees access to due process and providing them the means to be heard on such issues as production methods, problem solving, and human resource policies and practices is also a challenge. In unionized settings, the additional tasks include making relations less adversarial, broadening the agenda for joint problem solving and planning, and facilitating employee consultation.

Underlying all these policies is a management philosophy, often embodied in a published statement, that acknowledges the legitimate claims of a company's multiple stakeholders—owners, employees, customers, and the public. At the center of this philosophy is a belief that eliciting employee commitment will lead to enhanced performance. The evidence shows this belief to be well-grounded. In the absence of genuine commitment, however, new management policies designed for a committed work force may well leave a company distinctly more vulnerable than would older policies based on the control approach. The advantages—and risks—are considerable.

THE COSTS OF COMMITMENT

Because the potential leverage of a commitment-oriented strategy on performance is so great, the natural temptation is to assume the universal applicability of that strategy. Some environments, however, especially those requiring intricate teamwork, problem solving, organizational learning, and self-monitoring, are better suited than others to the commitment model. Indeed, the pioneers of the deep commitment strategy—a fertilizer plant in Norway, a refinery in the United Kingdom, a paper mill in Pennsylvania, a pet-food processing plant in Kansas—were all based on continuous process technologies and were all capital and raw material intensive. All provided high economic leverage to improvements in workers' skills and attitudes, and all could offer considerable job challenge.

Is the converse true? Is the control strategy appropriate whenever—as with convicts breaking rocks with sledgehammers in a prison yard—work can be completely prescribed, remains static, and calls for individual, not group, effort? In practice, managers have long answered yes. Mass production, epitomized by the assembly line, has for years been thought suitable for old-fashioned control.

But not any longer. Many mass producers, not least the automakers, have recently been trying to reconceive the structure of work and to give employees a significant role in solving problems and improving methods. Why? For many reasons, including to boost in-plant quality, lower warranty costs, cut waste, raise machine utilization and total capacity with the same plant and equipment, reduce operating and support personnel, reduce turnover and absenteeism, and speed up implementation of change. In addition, some managers place direct value on the fact that the commitment policies promote the development of human skills and individual self-esteem.

The benefits, economic and human, of worker commitment extend not only to continuous-process industries but to traditional manufacturing industries as well. What, though, are the costs? To achieve these gains, managers have had to invest extra effort, develop skills and relationships, cope with higher levels of ambiguity and uncertainty, and experience the pain and discomfort associated with changing habits and attitudes. Some of their skills have become obsolete, and some of their careers have been casualties of change. Union officials, too, have had to face the dislocation and discomfort that inevitably follow any upheaval in attitudes and skills. For their part, workers have inherited more responsibility and, along with it, greater uncertainty and a more open-ended possibility of failure.

Part of the difficulty in assessing these costs is the fact that so many of the following problems inherent to the commitment strategy remain to be solved.

Employment Assurances

As managers in heavy industry confront economic realities that make such assurances less feasible and as their counterparts in fiercely competitive high-technology areas are forced to rethink early guarantees of employment security, pointed questions await.

Will managers give lifetime assurances to the few, those who reach, say, 15 years' seniority, or will they adopt a general no-layoff policy? Will they demonstrate by policies and practices that employment security, though by no means absolute, is a higher priority item than it was under the control approach? Will they accept greater responsibility for outplacement?

Compensation

In one sense, the more productive employees under the commitment approach deserve to receive better pay for their better efforts, but how can managers balance this claim on resources with the harsh reality that domestic pay rates have risen to levels that render many of our industries uncompetitive internationally? Already, in such industries as trucking and airlines, new domestic competitors have placed companies that maintain prevailing wage rates at a significant disadvantage. Experience shows, however, that wage freezes and concession bargaining create obstacles to commitment, and new approaches to compensation are difficult to develop at a time when management cannot raise the overall level of pay.

Which approach is really suitable to the commitment model is unclear. Traditional job classifications place limits on the discretion of supervisors and encourage workers' sense of job ownership. Can pay systems based on employees' skill levels, which have long been used in engineering and skilled crafts, prove widely effective? Can these systems make up in greater mastery, positive motivation, and work-force flexibility what they give away in higher average wages?

In capital-intensive businesses, where total payroll accounts for a small percentage of costs, economics favor the move toward pay progression based on deeper and broader mastery. Still, conceptual problems remain with measuring skills, achieving consistency in pay decisions, allocating opportunities for learning new skills, trading off breadth and flexibility against depth, and handling the effects of "topping out" in a system that rewards and encourages personal growth.

There are also practical difficulties. Existing plants cannot, for example, convert to a skill-based structure overnight because of the vested interests of employees in the higher classifications. Similarly, formal profit- or gain-sharing plans like the Scanlon Plan (which shares gains in productivity as measured by improvements in the ratio of payroll to the sales value of production) cannot always operate. At the plant level, formulas that are responsive to what employees can influence, that are not unduly influenced by factors beyond their control, and that are readily understood, are not easy to devise. Small stand-alone businesses with a mature technology and stable markets tend to find the task least troublesome, but they are not the only ones trying to implement the commitment approach.

Yet another problem, very much at issue in the Hyatt-Clark bearing plant, which employees purchased from General Motors in 1981, is the relationship between compensation decisions affecting salaried managers and professionals, on the one hand, and hourly workers, on the other. When they formed the company, workers took a 25% pay cut to make their bearings competitive but the managers maintained and, in certain instances increased, their own salaries in order to help the company attract and retain critical talent. A manager's ability to elicit and preserve commitment, however, is sensitive to issues of equity, as became evident once again when GM and Ford announced huge executive bonuses in the spring of 1984 while keeping hourly wages capped.

Technology

Computer-based technology can reinforce the control model or facilitate movement to the commitment model. Applications can narrow the scope of jobs or broaden them, emphasize the individual nature of tasks or promote the work of groups, centralize or decentralize the making of decisions, and create performance measures that emphasize learning or hierarchical control.

To date, the effects of this technology on control and commitment have been largely unintentional and unexpected. Even in organizations otherwise pursuing a commitment strategy, managers have rarely appreciated that the side effects of technology are not somehow "given" in the nature of things or that they can be actively managed. In fact, computer-based technology may be the least deterministic, most flexible technology to enter the workplace since the industrial revolution. As it becomes less hardware-dependent and more software-intensive and as the cost of computer power declines, the variety of ways to meet business requirements expands, each with a different set of human implications. Management has yet to identify the potential role of technology policy in the commitment strategy, and it has yet to invent concepts and methods to realize that potential.

Supervisors

The commitment model requires first-line supervisors to facilitate rather than direct the work force, to impart rather than merely practice their technical and administrative expertise, and to help workers develop the ability to manage themselves. In practice, supervisors are to delegate away most of their traditional functions—often without having received adequate training and support for their new team-building tasks or having their own needs for voice, dignity, and fulfillment recognized.

These dilemmas are even visible in the new titles many supervisors carry—"team advisers" or "team consultants," for example—most of which imply that supervisors are not in the chain of command, although they are expected to be directive if necessary and assume functions delegated to the work force if they are not being performed. Part of the confusion here is the failure to distinguish the behavioral style required of supervisors from the basic responsibilities assigned them. Their ideal style may be advisory, but their responsibilities are to achieve certain human and economic outcomes. With experience, however, as first-line managers become more comfortable with the notion of delegating what subordinates are ready and able to perform, the problem will diminish.

Other difficulties are less tractable. The new breed of supervisors must have a level of interpersonal skill and conceptual ability often lacking in the present supervisory work force. Some companies have tried to address this lack by using the position as an entry point to management for college graduates. This approach may succeed where the work force has already acquired the necessary technical expertise, but it blocks a route of advancement for workers and sharpens the dividing line between management and other employees. Moreover, unless the company intends to open up higher level positions for these college-educated supervisors, they may well grow impatient with the shift work of first-line supervision.

Even when new supervisory roles are filled—and filled successfully—from the ranks, dilemmas remain. With teams developed and functions delegated, to what new challenges do they turn to utilize fully their own capabilities? Do those capabilities match the demands of the other managerial work they might take on? If fewer and fewer supervisors are required as their individual span of control extends to a second and a third work team, what promotional opportunities exist for the rest? Where do they go?

EXHIBIT
WORK-FORCE STRATEGIES

	Control	Transitional	Commitment
Job design principles	Individual attention limited to performing individual job.	Scope of individual responsibility extended to upgrading system performance, via participative problem-solving groups in QWL, EI, and quality circle programs.	Individual responsibility extended to upgrading system performance.
	Job design deskills and fragments work and separates doing and thinking.	No change in traditional job design or accountability.	Job design enhances content of work, emphasizes whole task, and combines doing and thinking.
	Accountability focused on individual.		Frequent use of teams as basic accountable unit.
	Fixed job definition.		Flexible definition of duties, contingent on changing conditions.
Performance expectations	Measured standards define minimum performance. Stability seen as desirable.		Emphasis placed on higher, "stretch objectives," which tend to be dynamic and oriented to the marketplace.
Management organization: structure, systems, and style	Structure tends to be layered, with top-down controls.	No basic changes in approaches to structure, control, or authority.	Flat organization structure with mutual influence systems.
	Coordination and control rely on rules and procedures.		Coordination and control based more on shared goals, values, and traditions.
	More emphasis on prerogatives and positional authority.		Management emphasis on problem solving and relevant information and expertise.
	Status symbols distributed to reinforce hierarchy.	A few visible symbols change.	Minimum status differentials to de-emphasize inherent hierarchy.

Compensation policies	Variable pay where feasible to provide individual incentive. Individual pay geared to job evaluation. In downturn, cuts concentrated on hourly payroll.	Typically no basic changes in compensation concepts. Equality of sacrifice among employee groups.	Variable rewards to create equity and to reinforce group achievements: gain sharing, profit sharing. Individual pay linked to skills and mastery. Equality of sacrifice.
Employment assurances	Employees regarded as variable costs.	Assurances that participation will not result in loss of job. Extra effort to avoid layoffs.	Assurances that participation will not result in loss of job. High commitment to avoid or assist in reemployment. Priority for training and retaining existing work force.
Employee voice policies	Employee input allowed on relatively narrow agenda. Attendant risks emphasized. Methods include open-door policy, attitude surveys, grievance procedures, and collective bargaining in some organizations. Business information distributed on strictly defined "need to know" basis.	Addition of limited, ad hoc consultation mechanisms. No change in corporate governance. Additional sharing of information	Employee participation encouraged on wide range of issues. Attendant benefits emphasized. New concepts of corporate governance. Business data shared widely
Labor-management relations	Adversarial labor relations; emphasis on interest conflict.	Thawing of adversarial attitudes; joint sponsorship of QWL or EI; emphasis on common fate.	Mutuality in labor relations; joint planning and problem solving on expanded agenda. Unions, management, and workers redefine their respective roles.

Union-Management Relations

Some companies, as they move from control to commitment, seek to decertify their unions and, at the same time, strengthen their employees' bond to the company. Others—like GM, Ford, Jones & Laughlin, and AT&T—pursue cooperation with their unions, believing that they need their active support. Management's interest in cooperation intensified in the late 1970's, as improved work-force effectiveness could not by itself close the competitive gap in many industries and wage concessions became necessary. Based on their own analysis of competitive conditions, unions sometimes agreed to these concessions but expanded their influence over matters previously subject to management control.

These developments open up new questions. Where companies are trying to preserve the non-union status of some plants and yet promote collaborative union relations in others, will unions increasingly force the company to choose? After General Motors saw the potential of its joint QWL program with the UAW, it signed a neutrality clause (in 1976) and then an understanding about automatic recognition in new plants (in 1979). If forced to choose, what will other managements do? Further, where union and management have collaborated in promoting QWL, how can the union prevent management from using the program to appeal directly to the workers about issues, such as wage concessions, that are subject to collective bargaining?

And if, in the spirit of mutuality, both sides agree to expand their joint agenda, what new risks will they face? Do union officials have the expertise to deal effectively with new agenda items like investment, pricing, and technology? To support QWL activities, they already have had to expand their skills and commit substantial resources at a time when shrinking employment has reduced their membership and thus their finances.

THE TRANSITIONAL STAGE

Although some organizations have adopted a comprehensive version of the commitment approach, most initially take on a more limited set of changes, which I refer to as a "transitional" stage or approach. The challenge here is to modify expectations, to make credible the leaders' stated intentions for further movement, and to support the initial changes in behavior. These transitional efforts can achieve a temporary equilibrium, provided they are viewed as part of a movement toward a comprehensive commitment strategy.

The cornerstone of the transitional stage is the voluntary participation of employees in problem-solving groups like quality circles. In unionized organizations, union-management dialogue leading to a jointly sponsored program is a condition for this type of employee involvement, which must then be supported by additional training and communication and by a shift in management style. Managers must also seek ways to consult employees about changes that affect them and to assure them that management will make every effort to avoid, defer, or minimize layoffs from higher productivity. When volume-related layoffs or concessions on pay are unavoidable, the principle of "equality of sacrifice" must apply to all employee groups, not just the hourly work force.

As a rule, during the early stages of transformation, few immediate changes can occur in the basic design of jobs, the compensation system, or the management system itself. It is easy, of course, to attempt to change too much too soon. A more common error, especially in established organizations, is to make only "token" changes that never reach a critical mass. All too often managers try a succession of technique-oriented changes one by one: job enrichment, sensitivity training, management by objectives, group brainstorming, quality circles, and so on. Whatever the benefits of these techniques, their value to the organization will rapidly decay if the management philosophy—and practice—does not shift accordingly.

A different type of error—"overreaching"—may occur in newly established organizations based on commitment principles. In one new plant, managers allowed too much peer influence in pay decisions; in another, they underplayed the role of first-line supervisors as a link in the chain of command; in a third, they overemphasized learning of new skills and flexibility at the expense of mastery in critical operations. These design errors by themselves are not fatal, but the organization must be able to make mid-course corrections.

RATE OF TRANSFORMATION

How rapidly is the transformation in work-force strategy, summarized in the *Exhibit*, occurring? Hard data are difficult to come by, but certain trends are clear. In 1970, only a few plants in the United States were systematically revising their approach to the work force. By 1975, hundreds of plants were involved. Today, I estimate that at least a thousand plants are in the process of making a comprehensive change and that many times that number are somewhere in the transitional stage.

In the early 1970s, plant managers tended to sponsor what efforts there were. Today, company presidents are formulating the plans. Not long ago, the initiatives were experimental; now they are policy. Early change focused on the blue-collar work force and on those clerical operations that most closely resemble the factory. Although clerical change has lagged somewhat—because the control model has not produced such overt employee disaffection, and because management has been slow to recognize the importance of quality and productivity improvement—there are signs of a quickened pace of change in clerical operations.

Only a small fraction of U.S. workplaces today can boast of a comprehensive commitment strategy, but the rate of transformation continues to accelerate, and the move toward commitment via some explicit transitional stage extends to a still larger number of plants and offices. This transformation may be fueled by economic necessity, but other factors are shaping and pacing it—individual leadership in management and labor, philosophical choices, organizational competence in managing change, and cumulative learning from change itself.

SUGGESTED READINGS

Irving Bluestone, "Labor's Stake in Improving the Quality of Working Life," *The Quality of Working Life and the 1980s,* ed. Harvey Kolodny and Hans van Beinum (New York: Praeger, 1983).

Robert H. Guest, "Quality of Work Life—Learning from Tarrytown," HBR July-August 1979, p. 76.

Janice A. Klein, "Why Supervisors Resist Employee Involvement," HBR September-October 1984, p. 87.

John F. Runcie, " 'By Days I Make the Cars'," HBR May-June 1980, p. 106.

W. Earl Sasser and Frank S. Leonard, "Let First-Level Supervisors Do Their Job," HBR March-April 1980, p. 113.

Leonard A. Schlesinger and Janice A. Klein, "The First-Line Supervisor: Past, Present and Future," *Handbook of Organizational Behavior,* ed. Jay W. Lorsch (Englewood Cliffs, N.J.: Prentice-Hall, 1983).

Richard E. Walton, "Work Innovations in the United States," HBR July-August 1979, p. 88; "Improving the Quality of Work Life," HBR May-June 1974, p. 12; "How to Counter Alienation in the Plant," HBR November-December 1972, p. 70.

Richard E. Walton and Wendy Vittori, "New Information Technology: Organizational Problem or Opportunity?" *Office: Technology and People,* No. 1, 1983, p. 249.

Richard E. Walton and Leonard A. Schlesinger, "Do Supervisors Thrive in Participative Work Systems?" *Organizational Dynamics,* Winter 1979, p. 25.

QUESTIONS FOR DISCUSSION

1 How might variations in job design affect employee motivation? Explain using (*a*) Maslow's need hierarchy and (*b*) expectancy theory.

2 Why might individual differences among employees play an important role in the impact of job characteristics on motivation?

3 What are the possible negative consequences of job redesign for the worker and the organization?

4 Do you think that it is possible to increase both organizational productivity and worker satisfaction? What are some common determinants of productivity and satisfaction?

5 How might the implementation of an innovative work design differ in a new organization as opposed to implementation in an existing organization?

6 What guidelines would you give to top management which is considering a change to a more innovative work design?

7 Do you agree with the view that there is an ideological incompatibility between labor-management QWL efforts and the collective bargaining adversary relationship? Why or why not?

8 Which do you think is a more potent motivator of worker productivity—(*a*) more money and shorter hours or (*b*) increased QWL? Explain.

9 What lessons can North Americans derive from the results of the Volvo experiments? How would variations in culture affect these lessons?

CHAPTER 11

MOTIVATION IN OTHER CONTEXTS

Throughout this book, we have examined the topic of employee motivation as it relates to various aspects of the work environment. We began by considering several competing theories of work motivation. Then we examined several specific facets of motivation, such as the use of reward systems, the influence of groups, the use of punishment, and job redesign. Throughout, we have focused on salient features of the motivational process.

In the present chapter, we attempt to fill in several voids in an effort to round out our discussion of employee motivation. Three issues are considered here. First, we examine potential differences in motivational processes between public and private organizations. Perry and Porter attempt in the first selection to assess the present understanding of the motivational context in public organizations. In doing so, they try to identify aspects of public organizations that make them somewhat unique, compared with other types of organizations, and to see how these differences can affect work motivation.

The second paper, by Pearce, examines volunteer organizations. The volunteer organization is also unique, and it motivates its employees quite differently from the way so-called private organizations do. In examining volunteer organizations, special attention is given to intrinsic motivation and the psychology of insufficient justification.

Finally, Schein examines an approach to managing organizations that has been called "Japanese management style." This approach posits that North American organizations can learn much from Japanese companies in terms of employee motivation. Schein reviews this assertion and takes issue with it, arguing that variations in national cultures require managerial approaches that fit these cultures. Lessons for the manager are reviewed.

These three articles, when taken together, cover new ground in the study of work motivation. It is hoped that the materials presented here will round out the study of motivational processes in organizations and will facilitate a better understanding of how contextual variations influence employee behavior and attitudes.

Factors Affecting the Context for Motivation in Public Organizations[1]

James L. Perry
Lyman W. Porter

The need to get "more for less" has been a major issue within public sector organizations during the 1970s and, if recent developments provide any clues, it promises to remain near the top of managers' agendas throughout the coming decade. Many public managers probably identify the most recent efforts to get more for less with fads that, by now, are represented by familiar "buzz" words— zero-based budgeting (ZBB), cutback management, sunset, total performance measurement, and total pay comparability. The current concern about governmental efficiency, however, also has helped to focus renewed attention on some of the basic and enduring responsibilities of public managers, among them the motivation of employees.

At the outset, it is important for the reader to be aware that although the general terms "public employees" and "public organizations" are used, the public sector encompasses many different types of organizations and roles. Some of the generalizations in the present review, therefore, may not extend to all public organizations or public sector jobs. Based on the types of organizations studied in the research from which the present evidence is drawn, the generalizations are appropriate for civil servants and civil service jobs in medium to large governmental agencies, but they may apply to public employees in other contexts also. The research agenda proposed here should help to delimit better the proper scope of any generalizations.

THE CONTEXT FOR MOTIVATION

As a hypothetical construct, motivation usually stands for that which "energizes, directs, and sustains behavior." In shorthand terms, it is the degree and type of effort that an individual exhibits in a behavioral situation. However, care needs to be taken not to equate motivation simply with sheer amount of effort. It also has to do with the direction and quality of that effort.

Any comprehensive look at the motivational bases of behavior in organizational settings must of necessity focus on the several sets of variables that influence motivation. A classification system (Porter & Miles, 1974) found useful identifies four major categories of variables: (1) individual characteristics, (2) job characteristics, (3) work environment characteristics, and (4) external environment characteristics. If motivation is to be affected, one or more of these variables must be changed or affected. Let us look briefly at each category of variables and the special facets of motivational tasks in public organizations.

[1]This is a revised version of a paper presented at the Public Management Research Conference, 1979, Brookings Institution, Washington D.C.

From *Academy of Management Review*, 1982, **7**, 89–98. Reprinted by permission.

Individual Characteristics

Although it is obvious that certain characteristics (such as attitudes) can be changed after one joins an organization, the focus here is on individual characteristics *brought to* the work situation. Presently there is a very limited understanding of special considerations that involve the "raw materials" in public sector motivational processes. Of course, one reason for this deficiency is simply the belief that, if government is different from other management contexts, it is distinguished by the nature of work or the environment within which the work occurs, not by the individuals whom it attracts or employs. Given this prevailing belief, only a few studies provide an indication of the motivational characteristics of public employees. Guyot (1961) compared middle managers in the federal government and in business on their needs for achievement, affiliation, and power. He concluded, quite surprisingly, that both popular and academic images of civil servants were distorted. Government middle managers had higher needs for achievement and lower needs for affiliation than did their business counterparts, but their needs for power were roughly the same.

Few researchers have attempted to replicate Guyot's results. However, two relatively recent studies by Rawls and his associates (Rawls & Nelson, 1975; Rawls, Ulrich, & Nelson, 1975), using samples of students about to enter management careers, again uncovered differences in individual characteristics. They found that students about to enter the nonprofit sector (primarily government) were significantly more dominant and flexible, had a higher capacity for status, and valued economic wealth to a lesser degree than did entrants to the profit sector. No significant differences existed between the groups on need for power and need for security. Thus, the collective findings of the three studies cited above exhibit a fairly high degree of consistency, considering the limitations on the comparisons that may be made among them, regarding the needs of public employees and how these needs differ from individuals in other sectors.

An independent issue related to individual characteristics involves the types of individual needs that are satisfied by the activities that occur in government organizations. Several studies (Paine, Carrol, & Leete, 1966; Rhinehart, Barrell, DeWolfe, Griffin, & Spaner, 1969; Rainey, 1979a, 1979b) indicate that public managers experience significantly lower levels of satisfaction than do their counterparts in business. Among the areas in which the differences are significant is satisfaction with promotion. This finding can be contrasted with the strong need for achievement found among entrants to government organizations. However, these studies utilized deficiency scores to measure satisfaction; thus levels of satisfaction then could simply reflect more stringent norms or expectations among government managers.

Job Characteristics

The second major set of variables that can be changed or modified to affect motivation involve what the person *does* at work—that is, the nature of the job or the collection of tasks that comprise the job. Although the unique features of government structures are generally believed, as indicated earlier, to have little impact on individual characteristics affecting public sector motivational processes, organizational structures and goals unique to government clearly influence the design of jobs in the public sector. Yet, just as the understanding of individual characteristics is deficient, motivation-relevant characteristics of public sector jobs also are not well documented in the research literature. Among the job characteristics that have been identified to be important, however, are the measurability of individual performance, degree of goal clarity, and degree of job challenge.

A frequent point of departure for many scholars attempting to identify unique aspects of public employment is the nature, both from aggregate and disaggregate perspectives, of public sector jobs. For example, Rainey, Backoff, and Levine (1976), Newman and Wallendar (1978), and Fottler (1981) have concluded that demands on higher level public managers to maintain constituencies, deal with competing external interests, and seek funding in a political environment probably differentiate their roles from managers in other economic sectors. This view is reinforced by the results of a study (Porter & VanMaanen, 1970) that compared time management and task accomplishment for public and private managers. Similarly, from an aggregate perspective, government is perceived primarily as a service provider rather than a goods producer. And, in fact, government is enormously more labor intensive than are other sectors of the American economy because it is oriented toward the provision of personal services. The implications of this phenomenon are significant for the dimension of jobs that Thompson (1967) terms the *types of assessments* levied against individuals, that is, the extent to which individuals are likely to be evaluated by maximizing or satisficing criteria. Because government organizations are predominantly service providers, with additional burdens of accountability and public responsiveness, the problems of creating performance criteria and implementing evaluation schemes are complex and difficult. The difficulties place a special burden on public managers in designating what performance shall be evaluated.

A related aspect of performance appraisal in many public organizations is what Buchanan (1975a) terms *goal crispness*. Buchanan argues that governmental organizations pursue diffuse and conflicting goals, quite unlike the tangible and relatively more specific goals of business organizations. Thus, public managers are usually confronted by a two-pronged dilemma with respect to the motivational properties of public sector jobs: (1) jobs for which performance criteria cannot be readily defined or measured and (2) conflicting criteria for superior performance.

Quite surprisingly, the consequences of these characteristics of governmental jobs do not appear to spill over into other job dimensions and, therefore, they do not further complicate motivational processes. For example, Rainey (1979a) hypothesized that the greater vagueness and intangibility of governmental goals would lead to public middle managers expressing higher mean scores on role conflict and role ambiguity. He found, however, no significant differences between government and business managers. Thus, performance in public sector jobs generally may be more difficult to assess, and the task goals of public jobs might inherently conflict, but these phenomena apparently do not produce cor-

responding role-related conflicts. Managers develop means for coping with problematic job characteristics such as assessing jobs in terms of standard operating
procedures (Cyert & March, 1963) that simplify and avoid the difficulties of
performance measurement in public service organizations.

A recent report by the National Center for Productivity and Quality of Working
Life (1978) suggests that two other job dimensions, job content and job challenge, satisfy the needs of employees relatively well. Most public employees
responding to a series of attitude surveys rated the content of their jobs as good
(managers—84 percent; nonmanagers—64 percent), and few disagreed with a
statement that their jobs made good use of their skills and abilities (managers—
14 percent; nonmanagers—23 percent). Buchanan (1974a) reports results on first-
year job challenge comparing business and public managers that seemingly con-
tradict the latter result. Industrial managers in his sample scored higher, reporting
significantly greater *first-year* job challenge. Buchanan focused, however, on
first-year job challenge, and it is quite plausible that differences might exist
between the National Commission results and his more restrictive and retrospective concept. He offers several reasons for the lower level of first-year job challenge among government managers. One reason is that bureaucratic roles, particularly at training levels, might be difficult to infuse with excitement. This
could be exacerbated by the gap that exists between the routineness of the first
job and the idealism that might have drawn the manager to the public service.
Buchanan notes that first-year job challenge might also be negatively affected by
government's efforts to assure representation and to train unemployed individuals. These policies might unwittingly contribute to overstaffing and the dilution
of training positions.

Work Environment Characteristics

Variables dealing with work environment characteristics that can be changed or
modified to impact motivation can be placed into two subcategories: immediate
work environment characteristics and organizational actions. Clearly, the two
most critical factors in an employee's immediate work environment are: the peer
group and the supervisor. Organizational actions, insofar as they affect motivation, can be classified into (a) provision of system rewards, (b) provision of
individual rewards, and (c) creation of an organizational climate.

More insights have been developed about important motivational aspects of
the work situation in public organizations than about the preceding two catego-
rizations of variables, individual and job characteristics. A number of these insights relate to organizational climate and emanate from Buchanan's work (1974a,
1974b, 1975a, 1975b) on organizational commitment. Among the work situation
characteristics affecting motivation is the phenomenon of *goal crispness*, discussed earlier in conjunction with job characteristics. The diffuseness of, and
contradictions among, public organizational goals may be viewed as work environment characteristics as well as job characteristics. In either instance, they
complicate the task of developing attachments to government organizations and
generating spontaneous goal directed activities.

Goal crispness is only one of several work environment characteristics relevant to motivation in the public sector. Buchanan (1974a, 1975b) identifies at least three other work environment characteristics that influence a manager's leverage in motivating employees: personal significance reinforcement, stability of expectations, and reference group experiences.

Personal significance reinforcement, a related aspect of goal crispness, involves the extent to which individuals perceive that they make contributions to organizational success. As Buchanan argues, it is especially difficult for many public agencies to instill employees with a sense of personal significance. One reason is that it is often difficult for public employees to observe any link between their contributions and the success of their organizations. The absence of this linkage is the result of a variety of factors, among them the sheer size of many governments, the pluralistic composition of policy implementation networks, and the lack of clear-cut performance indicators or norms. Developing the attitude among employees that they are valued members of an organization is a difficult job even in the best circumstances. However, the task becomes increasingly demanding when attitudes of personal significance must be developed within a large scale organization in which there might be little acceptance or recognition of general standards of performance. The problems of stimulating a sense of personal significance among employees are compounded by the constitutional separation of the executive and legislative branches of government, which occasionally produces legislative-administrative conflicts that destroy attitudes of personal significance.

Goal crispness and personal significance reinforcement perhaps are the most important, but not the only, work situation characteristics affecting motivation.

A third factor, stability of expectations, is directly related to the frequency with which the dominant coalitions (Thompson, 1967) of governments change. This variable involves whether employees perceive that their organizations have a stable commitment to the mission or programs that they pursue. Of course, even "planned" changes in political leadership seriously jeopardize the development of this stability. If the directions of programs or missions change frequently enough, employees are likely to question the need to put forth maximum effort on what they come to perceive as transitory programs. The end result of such instability is that an organization "will find it more difficult to command the same intensity of loyalty that other organizations enjoy" (Buchanan, 1974a, p. 43).

Another significant work environment characteristic that influences motivation is the diversity of values and characteristics of work groups. Work or similar task related groups exercise a certain amount of control over their members' attitudes. Heterogeneous or representative groups, more typical of government than of the private sector, will, in Buchanan's terms, "rarely develop intensely favorable attitudes toward their agencies or foster climates in which commitment to the agency is a group norm" (Buchanan, 1975b). This phenomenon, by reducing cohesion and consensus within the work group, diminishes the likelihood or, at the very least, increases the difficulty of eliciting spontaneous goal directed behaviors from employees.

Another interpersonal dimension of the work situation, an aspect of the immediate work environment, with significant implications for motivation is the quality of supervision. The National Center for Productivity (1978), drawing on a nonrandom sample of previous attitudinal studies, reported employee perceptions of lower supervisory quality in the public than in the private sector. One exception to this generalization was that, among managers, public sector supervisors were rated more highly than private supervisors on human relations skills. Public supervisors, in contrast to their private counterparts, suffered primarily in terms of their subordinates' evaluation of their technical competence. The quality-of-supervision differences reported by the National Center for Productivity might have a variety of causes. The evaluations of technical competence could reflect greater predominance of manager-professional conflicts in government organizations. They also might reflect less investment in training or less success in recruiting supervisory personnel. In any event, the quality of supervision is a critical element in motivational processes.

As a whole, these special work environment considerations in public organizations appear likely to constrain motivational levels significantly even when individual and job characteristics are conducive to employee motivation. Factors such as goal crispness and the quality of supervision are too integral to eliciting superior employee performance to argue otherwise. Although the accumulated research evidence permits some generalizations about the underlying processes, it does not offer any prescriptions for better managing these work environment characteristics.

External Environment Characteristics

The fourth major category of variable that can affect employee motivation is the external environment (or environments). In particular, it is changes or the anticipation of changes in the external environment that can have powerful impacts on individuals' behavior in work organizations. This category of variables, however, in contrast with the first three, is not one which any given organization can directly control. Nevertheless, that does not leave the organization helpless. It can monitor the external environment and, based on such monitoring, it can proceed to make changes internally within the organization that can influence employee motivation.

External environments can be usefully subdivided (arbitrarily, to be sure) into several major categories: socionormative, political, demographic, economic, and technological. Focus will be on the first two categories, because it is believed that they contain the variables that have the greatest differential effects on employee motivation in public sector organizations.

Socionormative Changes   Public sector organizations cannot help but be impacted by what Clark Kerr has termed the "fourth period of great evolutionary change" in the labor force in the United States with respect to "its composition, its character, and the rules for its conduct" (1979, p. ix). The quest for personal self-fulfillment is regarded by Kerr, along with other social observers such as

Daniel Yankelovich and Amitai Etzioni, as especially significant for the work environment—any work environment, including that of the public sector. As Kerr puts it, "We have a crisis of aesthetics, not ethics—tastes have changed, and the indulgence of psychic satisfactions has increased" (1979, p. xi).

These broad socionormative changes can directly affect motivation, by altering the orientations of those who enter public organizations, but they also might influence motivation indirectly, by modifying the attitudes and values of those whom public organizations serve. To the extent that the general public holds unfavorable attitudes about public employment and public bureaucracies, motivation-relevant employee perceptions, such as self-worth and personal significance, can be expected to be affected. Furthermore, compounding any motivational difficulties that might be associated with society's attitudes about public employment—attitudes that tend to fluctuate widely over time (White, 1932; Janowitz & Wright, 1956)—is the complexity of public attitudes about government. As Katz and his colleagues (Katz, Guteck, Kahn, & Barton, 1975) have observed, for example, there appear to be marked inconsistencies between the public's ideological and pragmatic attitudes. One manifestation of this inconsistency (so evident in the public's response to Proposition 13) is that, at an ideological level, private enterprise is perceived as more effective than government agencies, but, at a pragmatic level, government interventions into areas like pollution control and auto safety regulation are strongly supported by the public. The continued existence of these types of inconsistencies in the socionormative environment will challenge those who attempt to sharpen the goals of public organizations and may diminish managers' ability to motivate individuals who seek guidance from stable and consistent, rather than ambiguous, public expectations.

Political Changes The implications of these changes for motivation perhaps are the most difficult to characterize because they influence motivation less directly than do socionormative or demographic changes, and, in recent years, they collectively have followed no easily discernible patterns. Some of the more long-standing political trends no doubt affect employee motivation only in very general ways. Counted among these trends might be the recent (the post-Eisenhower period) instability in the American Presidency, steadily declining public trust in major political institutions, and, perhaps partially as an outgrowth of the latter trend, increasingly frequent legislative intervention into day-to-day administrative details. Except for legislative interventionism, which actually or potentially might have an impact on the task structure of government jobs, the political changes above influence motivation primarily by altering the climate—the "psychological feel"—within an organization.

Other, more discrete political changes of recent years unquestionably will affect motivation in measurable, but yet to be explored ways. Legislative mandates for citizen participation, spanning the eras of the Great Society and New Federalism, have contributed to the dispersion of power and authority in administrative systems. This most recent manifestation and reassertion of the tenets of representative democracy (Kaufman, 1969) most certainly has affected key variables bearing on motivation. Similar consequences could be expected to flow from other current political developments: the "new" populism (including Ralph Nader, Common Cause, and Jimmy Carter), the ebb of the electorate toward greater conservatism (often equated with less government), and an era of relative scarcity within the political economy.

EFFICACY OF MOTIVATIONAL TECHNIQUES

Most organizations employ one or more methods to elicit role compliance and goal directed behaviors from their employees. These motivational techniques usually are intended to maximize benefits to the organization, but their relative utility varies considerably. The list of motivational techniques presently used by employers is extensive: monetary incentives, goal setting, flexitime, job enlargement, job enrichment, behavior modification, participation, award and recognition plans, discipline, and counseling. However, as a recent review (Locke, Feren, McCaleb, Shaw, & Denny, 1980) illustrates, most research has focused on four basic (but not mutually exclusive) motivational methods: monetary incentives, goal setting, job design, and participation. In fact, most motivational methods are derived from these basic techniques.

Monetary Incentives

Locke et al. (1980) concluded from their review of field studies of monetary incentives that significant performance improvements resulted from the use of these techniques. The median performance increase found in the field studies they reviewed was 30 percent. This median increase, however, may overestimate the value of money as an incentive, because monetary incentives typically are accompanied by some form of methods analysis, goal setting, or other technique that contributes to motivating performance. Until quite recently, monetary incentives, with the exception of output-oriented merit increases, have not been adopted widely in the public sector. A 1973 survey (National Commission on Productivity and Work Quality, 1975) of 509 local governments reported that 42 percent of the respondents used merit increases, only 6 percent employed performance bonuses, and 1 percent used shared savings or piecework systems. On the basis of a very limited amount of information, government's success with monetary incentives prior to the Federal Civil Service Reform Act of 1978 (CSRA) has, at best, been mixed. For example, the National Commission on Productivity stated:

> Some reported output-oriented merit increases were, in fact longevity increases or focused more on personal characteristics rather than output. Indeed, even truly output-oriented merit increases often became routine and are taken for granted by employees after they have been in operation for a while (1975, p. 44).

It should be noted, however, that CSRA is intended to remedy these types of shortcomings associated with the use of monetary incentives in the federal government. Whether or not the reforms achieve this goal is a matter for future inquiry.

At a conceptual level, the designs of monetary incentives must clearly deal with some of the motivational considerations discussed earlier. Perhaps the most important consideration is the values of employees. As noted previously, there is some indication that individuals entering the public sector value economic wealth to a lesser degree than do entrants to the profit sector. If this is indeed true, the motivational potential of monetary incentives might be limited in contrast to experiences elsewhere. It is quite possible, however, that greater emphasis on monetary incentives will begin to attract individuals who value economic wealth more highly. This development might lessen the attraction of the public service to more idealistic types. These concerns may be moot considering that even with the addition of monetary incentives public managers probably will receive much lower monetary rewards than will managers in other economic sectors (Fogel & Lewin, 1974; Smith, 1976).

The successful use of monetary incentives in government also is threatened by the extent to which performance differences can be measured with precision and an equitable formula can be developed that ties rewards to performance. Definition and measurement of performance criteria obviously will affect the acceptability and results of such incentive systems. The extent to which competing goals of an agency are mirrored in performance criteria also will complicate incentive systems.

Goal Setting

Goal setting essentially involves establishing observable standards for employee performance and offering feedback to the employee about the extent to which the standards have been achieved. Techniques for goal setting, like monetary incentives, come in a variety of formats, including performance targets, management by objectives, and work standards. Goal setting techniques have been used widely in government, and the early conceptual and practical development of some techniques, like MBO, owe a great deal to governmental experience (Sherwood & Page, 1976).

From their review of 17 field studies of goal setting, Locke et al. (1980) attribute a 16 percent median improvement in performance (with a range of 2 percent to 57.5 percent) as a result of goal setting. They also emphasized that feedback about progress vis-à-vis goals is essential for goal setting to regulate performance effectively. One reported use of goal setting in the Bureau of Census (Hornbruch, 1977), which gave regular feedback about performance against work standards, achieved a 52 percent improvement in output.

The design of goal setting techniques for public organizations must take into account a myriad of considerations that might moderate their success. The most important of these obviously is the vague and conflicting nature of governmental goals. An important issue is whether goal setting techniques will encourage more concrete goal explication, or whether there are countervailing influences that assure that government goals will remain inherently vague and conflicting. Although examples supporting the belief that goal setting can indeed improve employee understanding of tasks and objectives might readily be obtained, the practical difficulty of creating concrete and precise goal statements in many situations is not altered. Also, there is the problem that attempting to make goals more concrete (crisp) may run the risk of making them more trivial. Given these considerations, it might be necessary to create highly flexible, decentralized goal setting techniques so that the task characteristics of the focal agency receive adequate attention. It also might be necessary to state goals in terms of organizational inputs or activities rather than outputs because of the difficulty of measuring achievement.

The vagueness of the goals of public organizations is perhaps the most challenging problem confronting the success of goal setting, but it is not the only issue with which public managers and policy makers must be concerned. The diversity of internal and external constituencies will increase the effort that must be devoted to goal setting and could possibly increase the likelihood of political attacks upon administrators. It may be necessary to protect administrators from these inefficiencies or risks of goal setting techniques to assure that they will fully support their use.

Although the difficulties of implementing goal setting successfully in public organizations appear substantial, these difficulties must be weighed against several considerations. First, goal setting often is an important prerequisite of effective performance appraisal and monetary incentives. Second, goal setting offers one of the primary routes to personal significance reinforcement because it creates a mechanism by which individuals can observe their contributions to organizational success. Third, goal setting is an attractive alternative to monetary incentives, which in the long run either could fail for lack of adequate financial rewards or might detract from public interest values. Fourth, goal setting might be an efficient alternative to monetary incentives in that it offers a high rate of return for quite limited investments. This is an important factor in light of declining budgets and resource scarcity. Thus, because goal setting is an integral aspect of other motivational techniques and possibly is more efficient than other methods, it may be more likely to be incorporated effectively by public organizations.

Job Design

Job design involves the structuring of various aspects of the job content (Hackman, 1977). For example, job design might involve increasing job responsibilities, the variety of tasks, or employee autonomy. Although job design has been popular since the early 1960s, the 1973 Urban Institute survey for the National Commission on Productivity (1975) reported that only 73 of 509 local government organizations had used some form of job rotation, redesign, or teamwork technique.

Evaluating the effectiveness of job design is more difficult than evaluating the effectiveness of other motivational techniques because it usually is implemented in conjunction with feedback and other structural changes (Locke et al., 1980). As Locke et al. suggest, if the performance contributions of the goal setting component of job design programs are controlled, job design might have no further effects on performance. Thus, the contributions of job design to public sector performance are somewhat problematic. Many cases of successful job design are described in the National Commission report (1975), but no rigorous evaluation of applications of the technique is available. Furthermore, the primary thrust of job design has been toward changing job content, but, as already indicated, this is not a widespread source of dissatisfaction among public employees. This indicates that there might be only a selective need for job design, possibly confined to those situations in which a direct cause-effect relationship exists between satisfaction with job content and service quality or output, or in cases in which an employee is being underutilized.

Another threat to the success of job design involves the ability of managers to alter variables significantly—variables such as self-direction or responsibility—when these aspects of the job are controlled by legislators or program constituents. At the very least, this problem might restrict the applicability of job design to jobs embedded both vertically and horizontally within an organization. One selective use for which job design might clearly pay dividends is in training positions. The problem of first-year job challenge is clearly amenable to solution by the use of job design.

Participation

Participation involves some type of shared or joint decision making between superiors and subordinates at the work group, program, or organizational level. A few instances of its use in state and local governments are described in the National Commission report (National Commission on Productivity and Work Quality, 1975). Of course, collective bargaining, already widespread in the public sector, is one variant of participation.

Because of the limited understanding of the effects of participation, it is extremely difficult to judge its probable efficacy as a motivational tool in government. At a superficial level, questions might be raised about participation's consequences for "who governs," but this does not appear to be a significant impediment to the instrumental use of participation. Intuitively, one might expect that participation would contribute positively to motivational considerations like perceptions of personal significance and quality of supervision. Its utility for moderating the effects of other variables, such as work group diversity, is less clear.

CONCLUSIONS

This paper has reviewed a diverse set of topics focused around motivational processes in public organizations. Now is proposed an agenda for research, composed primarily of questions that have been raised implicitly in this paper. The issues enumerated below are illustrative of those that might be addressed.

1 *The individual-organization match*. Considerable research attention has been addressed to how organizations choose individuals, but much less attention has been paid to the reverse: how individuals choose organizations and how organizations attract individuals. Insufficient research attention also has been given to a related aspect of the individual-organization match: How the attitudes, beliefs, and interests that an individual brings to organizational settings impact motivation. An understanding of these questions seems particularly important in light of research evidence that indicates that public organizations attract somewhat different types of individuals than do private organizations. The practical payoff from such a line of inquiry might be to increase the extent to which individuals entering government are satisfied with their organization and the extent to which the organization is able to secure effective behaviors from its members.

2 *Measurability of individual performance.* One of the most immediately pressing needs for research attention involves the measurability of individual performance in typical public sector jobs. For example, it might be necessary to make some conceptual advances before a public manager's "ability to deal with competing external interests" can be adequately measured. Because the performance of many public employees probably will be measured despite the lack of availability of generally accepted criteria, research on performance appraisal methods most appropriate for such circumstances also is needed.

3 *Goal clarity.* A better understanding of the sources of goal clarity (or lack of it) is needed so that remedies can be designed or a certain degree of murkiness in the goals of public organizations may have to be generally accepted. It is necessary to develop a better understanding of the ways in which the political environment reduces goal crispness and displaces goal directed activity. Research on how people adapt to situations in which goals are inherently unclear might contribute to developing methods for encouraging effective behaviors in such situations.

4 *Job security.* Differences between job security practices are a source of continuing, and often unfavorable, comparison between the public and private sectors. As noted earlier, the findings of several studies suggest that the security needs of public employees do not differ from those of private employees. However, knowledge about the motivational effects of the use of job security as a system wide reward in public organizations is minimal. Research might focus on developing a better understanding of the motivational "costs" and "benefits" of current public job security practices and designing alternative means for protecting political neutrality.

5 *Moderators of motivation techniques.* Another research issue might be the identification of key moderators of the effectiveness of the various motivational techniques. For example, Locke et al. (1980) indicated in their review that although participation had demonstrated only about a 1 percent *median* performance increase in a group of 16 field studies, half of the field experiments exhibited positive results, one as high as 47 percent. The critical research question is: Did the eight field sites in which participation was successful share characteristics that were absent in those sites where participation failed? This search for the factors that moderated the effectiveness of participation could be generalized to all the motivational techniques and should be a central concern of evaluative studies in public organizations.

Generally, the literature on motivation tends to concentrate too heavily on employees within industrial and business organizations. The comparative perspective used in the present study has been valuable for showing the limitations of knowledge about the context for motivation in public organizations. With approximately 20 percent of the American work force employed in the public sector, it clearly is important to develop better insights about what accounts for motivational variance in public organizations. Exploration of the questions proposed here should contribute measurably to a better understanding of the variables that play an especially important part in public sector motivational processes.

REFERENCES

Buchanan, B., II. Building organizational commitment: The socialization of managers in work organizations. *Administrative Science Quarterly*, 1974a, 19, 533–546.

Buchanan, B., II. Government managers, business executives, and organizational commitment. *Public Administration Review*, 1974b, 35, 339–347.

Buchanan, B., II. Red tape and the service ethic: Some unexpected differences between public and private managers. *Administration and Society*, 1975a, 6, 423–438.

Buchanan, B., II. To walk an extra mile: The whats, whens, and whys of organizational commitment. *Organizational Dynamics*, 1975b, 4, 67–80.

Cyert, R. M., & March, J. G. *A behavioral theory of the firm.* Englewood Cliffs, N.J.: Prentice-Hall, 1963.

Fogel, W., & Lewin, D. Wage determination in the public sector. *Industrial and Labor Relations Review*, 1974, 27, 410–432.

Fottler, M. D. Management: Is it really generic? *Academy of Management Review*, 1981, 6, 1–12.

Guyot, J. F. Government bureaucrats are different. *Public Administration Review*, 1961, 22, 195–202.

Hackman, J. R. Work design. In J. R. Hackman & J. L. Suttle (Eds.), *Improving life at work.* Santa Monica, Cal.: Goodyear, 1977, 96–162.

Hornbruch, F. W., Jr. *Raising productivity.* New York: McGraw-Hill, 1977.

Janowitz, M., & Wright, D. The prestige of public employment. *Public Administration Review*, 1956, 16, 15–21.

Katz, D., Guteck, B. A., Kahn, R. L., & Barton, E. *Bureaucratic encounters.* Ann Arbor, Mich.: Survey Research Center, Institute for Social Research, University of Michigan, 1975.

Kaufman, H. Administrative decentralization and political power. *Public Administrative Review*, 1969, 29, 3–15.

Kerr, C. Introduction: Industrialism with a human face. In C. Kerr & J. M. Rostow (Eds.), *Work in America: The decade ahead.* New York: Van Nostrand, 1979, ix–xxvii.

Locke, E. A., Feren, D. B., McCaleb, V. M., Shaw, K. N., & Denny, A. T. The relative effectiveness of four methods of motivating employee performance. In K. D. Duncan, M. M. Gruneberg, & D. Wallis (Eds.), *Changes in working life.* London: Wiley, Ltd. 1980, 363–383.

National Center for Productivity and Quality of Working Life. *Employee attitudes and productivity differences between the public and private sector*. Washington, D.C.: U.S. Civil Service Commission, 1978.

National Commission on Productivity and Work Quality. *Employee incentives to improve state and local government productivity*. Washington, D.C.: U.S. Government Printing Office, 1975.

Newman, W. H., & Wallendar, H. W., III. Managing not-for-profit enterprises. *Academy of Management Review*, 1978, 3, 24–31.

Paine, F. T., Carrol, S. J., Jr., & Leete, B. A. Need satisfactions of managerial personnel in a government agency. *Journal of Applied Psychology*, 1966, 50, 247–249.

Porter, L. W., & Miles, R. P. Motivation and management. In J. W. McGuire (Ed.), *Contemporary management: Issues and viewpoints*. Englewood Cliffs, N.J.: Prentice-Hall, 1974, 545–570.

Porter, L. W., & VanMaanen, J. Task accomplishment and the management of time. In B. M. Bass (Ed.), *Managing for accomplishment*. Lexington, Mass.: Lexington, 1970, 180–192.

Rainey, H. G. Perceptions of incentives in business and government: Implications for civil service reform. *Public Administration Review*, 1979a, 39, 440–448.

Rainey, H. G. Reward expectancies, role perceptions, and job satisfaction among government and business managers: Indications of commonalities and differences. *Proceedings of the Thirty-Ninth Annual Meeting of the Academy of Management* 1979b, 357–361.

Rainey, H. G. Backoff, R. W., & Levine, C. H. Comparing public and private organizations. *Public Administration Review*, 1976, 36, 223–244.

Rawls, J. R., & Nelson, O. T., Jr. Characteristics associated with preferences for certain managerial positions. *Psychological Reports*, 1975, 36, 911–918.

Rawls, J. R., Ulrich, R. A., & Nelson, O.T., Jr. A comparison of managers entering or reentering the profit and nonprofit sectors. *Academy of Management Journal*, 1975, 18, 616–622.

Rhinehart, J. B., Barrell, R. P., DeWolfe, A. S., Griffin, J. E., & Spaner, F. E. Comparative study of need satisfaction in governmental and business hierarchies. *Journal of Applied Psychology*, 1969, 53, 230–235.

Sherwood, F. P., & Page, W. J., Jr. MBO and public management. *Public Administration Review*, 1976, 36, 5–12.

Smith, S. P. Pay differences between federal government and private sector workers. *Industrial and Labor Relations Review*, 1976, 29, 179–197.

Thompson, J. D. *Organizations in action*. New York: McGraw-Hill, 1967.

White, L. D. *Further contributions to the prestige value of public employment*. Chicago: University of Chicago Press, 1932.

Making Sense of Volunteer Motivation:
The Sufficiency of Justification Hypothesis

Jone L. Pearce

Many have become familiar with Deci's (1975) thesis concerning the influence of extrinsic rewards on individuals' intrinsic motivation to engage in activities, and the subsequent questions raised about the applicability of his ideas in the organizational context. Here it is suggested that there is some evidence for sufficiency of justification effects among volunteers working in organizations, and that these effects are not dependent on Deci's (1975) problematic intrinsic/extrinsic dichotomy of organizational rewards. Further, these processes have significant practical motivational implications.

Deci (1975) defines intrinsic motivation as the motivation to engage in activities for which there is no apparent reward except the activity itself. These activities are done for their own sake and not because they lead to an extrinsic reward. These include play activities such as solving puzzles and painting pictures, as well as challenging work which requires resourcefulness and creativity.

Building on the earlier work of the de Charms (1968) and Heider (1958), Deci suggests that when individuals are extrinsically rewarded (e.g., are "paid") for doing tasks that they were previously intrinsically motivated to do, there is a change in the preceived locus of causality. When they were intrinsically motivated individuals perceived that they were acting in order to feel competent and self-determining. But when externally mediated rewards are introduced, they began to believe that they are doing the activity in order to get the reward, so the perceived locus of causality for the activity becomes external, reducing their intrinsic motivation. Thus individuals experiencing "oversufficient justification" for their actions (that is, either the intrinsic or the extrinsic rewards, separately, would have provided sufficient motivation) respond by devaluing the less tangible intrinsic rewards.

Deci (1975) also applies this sufficiency of justification argument to situations in which individuals have neither sufficient intrinsic nor extrinsic rewards for engaging in a task: "If a person performs an act which is inconsistent with one of his internal states (e.g., an attitude, a feeling, a motive) he will experience dissonance and be motivated to reduce that dissonance. If he has 'sufficient external justification,' the behavior will be easily rationalized, thereby reducing the dissonance almost immediately. For example, if he were forced to behave by a strong threat or if he were given a sizeable reward to behave, he would rationalize that he did it because of the threat or the reward. This would quickly reduce the dissonance (Deci, 1975, p. 164)." However, he argues that if an individual has insufficient extrinsic reason for engaging in a task that has little intrinsic value, he or she would reduce experienced cognitive dissonance by finding that the task was more intrinsically rewarding after all.

This article was prepared especially for this book.

At this point it is reasonable to ask why people would do something for which they did not have "sufficient reason." In fact, individuals will often try out actions that they may not have a very strong motivation for doing. This is particularly the case for organizational volunteers, who are usually recruited by friends or family members, and often "try out" a volunteer job to see if they like it. That is, their initial motivation may be simply to silence a pestering friend, but this is usually not sufficient justification for continuing the work month after month.

To summarize, there are two "parallel processes" supporting a negative relationship between intrinsic and extrinsic motivation. If both intrinsic and extrinsic rewards are abundant, individuals will reduce their experienced intrinsic motivation for engaging in a task because of experienced "oversufficient justification." In addition, if they somehow engage in behaviors for which both intrinsic and extrinsic rewards are insufficient (insufficient justification) they will rationalize their actions to themselves as resulting from intrinsic enjoyment of the actions themselves. Deci reports the results of laboratory experiments to support these sufficiency of justification effects for motivation as well as attitudes such as "liking the activity."

If the sufficiency of justification hypothesis is accurate, it has important practical implications. Most prominently, if intrinsic motivation is low, then withdrawal of extrinsic rewards would result in cessation of the desired behaviors. In an organizational context, if the employee is only putting forth effort because she expects rewards or punishments from her supervisor, as soon as the supervisor's "back is turned" we would expect her to relax. Similarly, if extrinsic rewards are added to tasks for which individuals are already sufficiently motivated—as for example, volunteer social service work or playing sports—the intrinsic motivation to do the work will be reduced.

Deci (1975) himself attempted to generalize his propositions to workplace motivation. He suggested that contingent payment plans—e.g., piece rates and other pay-for-performance plans—would appear to be "more controlling" to workers and so would be expected to result in reduced experienced intrinsic motivation. However, Deci (1975) acknowledged that his discussion of organizational motivation was based on his "hunch" and that more research that directly examined the relative effects of extrinsic organizational rewards was needed.

Staw (1976) systematically reviewed and applied the research on intrinsic and extrinsic rewards in work motivation. He suggested that intrinsic rewards are devalued when employees experience oversufficient justification, or enhanced when they experience insufficient justification, because the intrinsic rewards are less tangible. Yet his review, as well as that of Notz (1975), found mixed support for these ideas in work settings. Although reduced intrinsic motivation has been produced in laboratory experiments, none of the field studies (e.g., Dermer, 1975; Eden, 1975) reported this effect.

Guzzo (1979) suggests that one reason may be the questionable theoretical status of the intrinsic and extrinsic dichotomy of organizational rewards. In analyzing the major definitional distinctions between these reward types, he argued that each was flawed. For example, one definition holds that intrinsically rewarded activities are those that are done "for their own sake"; Guzzo notes that "Behavior apparently occurring 'for its own sake' may be due to very tangible, visible rewards which happen to be received sporadically" (Guzzo, 1979, p. 76). Empirical support for confusion about categorizing work rewards as either intrinsic or extrinsic is provided by Dyer and Parker (1975) who surveyed members of the Industrial and Organizational Psychology Division of the American Psychological Association (presumed experts in organizational motivation) and found little consistency in their identification of intrinsic and extrinsic organizational rewards.

The earlier field studies finding support for sufficiency of justification processes in organizational settings were concerned with attitudes, not motivation, and so make no reference to an intrinsic/extrinsic dichotomy of organizational rewards. The best example is Staw's (1974) study of cadets' attitudes toward ROTC before and after the draft lottery. After the lottery those with high lottery numbers were assured they would not be drafted and would now be hypothesized to experience insufficient justification for participation in ROTC. Those with high numbers without committing contracts dropped out, while committed cadets with high draft numbers developed more favorable attitudes toward ROTC than did cadets with low draft numbers.

There are two features of this study of note for the present discussion—first, there is no need to assume that these cadets were more intrinsically motivated, since their participation was enforced by a contract, only that those cadets with a less retrospectively compelling justification for participation developed more positive attitudes toward the organization. Second, it is difficult to find actual cases of organizational motivation in which there is psychologically experienced insufficient justification—those cadets with insufficient motivation who were not legally bound to remain left. This appears to result from the relatively longer duration of organizational membership compared to participation in most laboratory studies, and, perhaps, that many organizational members join institutions expecting rewards, and if these rewards prove insufficient they leave if they can.

It is noteworthy that Festinger's (1961) and Aronson's (1966) original formulations of their psychology of insufficient justification also focused on attitudes, not motivation, and did not require that insufficient rewards would necessarily result in increased liking for the activity itself. For example, Festinger (1961, p. 10) stated,

> It is plausible to suppose that the extra preference which the organism develops in order to reduce dissonance may be focused on any variety of things. Let me explain this by using the experiment I have just described as an illustration. Those animals who were never fed in the mid-box, and thus experienced dissonance, could have developed a liking for the activity of running down the alley to the mid-box, they could have developed a preference for some aspect of the mid-box itself, or they could have developed a preference for any of the things they did or encountered subsequent to leaving the mid-box.

Thus, there is some evidence for the effects of sufficiency of justification processes on organizational members' attitudes but no available support for its possible effects on intrinsic (or any other kind of) job motivation. Since Deci's (1975) ideas have great potential importance for understanding workplace motivation, the following field study was conducted to help clarify the role of sufficiency of justification effects in organizational motivation.

VOLUNTEER MOTIVATION

There is a kind of organizational worker who might be expected to provide a naturally occurring "subject" for the study of sufficiency of justification effects in work motivation—the volunteer. Much organizational work is performed by those not paid for their labor—the United States Census Bureau reported that 15,455,000 Americans over the age of 14 had volunteered during the single week of April 7–13, 1974 (ACTION Pamphlet 4000-17). Further, there is substantial anecdotal evidence that some volunteers experience insufficient justification for their activities. For example,

> They [volunteers] probably decide they are doing it for a good reason so they assume a positive attitude about it. If you are paid you probably don't question it, you assume you are doing it for a living. Volunteers don't know why they are working; they don't know the answer. I guess they assume they do it because they want to do good. These assumptions lead to different ways of doing things. Not that paid people aren't cheerful; it's just that it's not needed (Pearce, 1978, p. 174).

The practical problems of designing reward systems for volunteers that are not based on pay dominates the writings for volunteer leaders (e.g., Naylor, 1967). As noted above, features of volunteer recruitment, as well as their lack of financial compensation, suggest that potential insufficient justification is a very real practical problem for organizational volunteers.

Organizational volunteers provide several additional features that make them particularly appropriate to the study of sufficiency of justification effects in work motivation. First, volunteers do not experience the withdrawal of a reward, so that results cannot be explained away as the result of experienced frustration or inequity, as is possible for Staw's (1974) cadets. Second, organizational volunteers that perform the same work as employees do can be selected, providing a sufficient (or oversufficient) justification comparison. There are a surprisingly large number of tasks completed by both volunteers and paid employees; examples include firefighting, leading tours, clerical work, and so forth.

The study is presented in detail in Pearce (1983a). Here it will be briefly noted that the sample included four matched sets of organizations, in which organizations staffed entirely by volunteers were paired with organizations staffed entirely by employees working on the same or very similar tasks. These are two small newspapers (one university-student staffed and the other a community newspaper), two poverty relief agencies (a voluntary Christian food distribution center and a local municipal welfare department), two family planning clinics, and two municipal fire departments (one rural New England all-volunteer force and a suburban employee-staffed department).

The two types of variables were taken from a single questionnaire. The Motivation Scales were developed to be free of the confounding among intrinsic and extrinsic organizational rewards noted by Guzzo (1979). Respondents were asked to rate the importance of nine work rewards that are available to both volunteers and employees. A factor analysis of the responses produced three scales—Intrinsic Motivation (e.g., "an interesting job"), Social Motivation (e.g., "working with people I like"), and Service Motivation (e.g., "identification with the mission of the organization"). In addition to work motivation, the job attitudes of Job Satisfaction, Intent to Leave (used by other researchers) were included. The additional variable of Job Praiseworthiness was added as a possible closer approximation to an experienced insufficient justification-influenced attitudes. The data were analyzed as volunteer/employee by organization-type (2 × 4) Analyses of Variance for each of the three motivation and the three attitude scales.

For the motivation scales there was no statistically significant difference in the Intrinsic Motivation of volunteers and employees. However, the volunteers were significantly more likely to report that they worked for Social and Service rewards than were the employees. Additionally, there was a significant Service Motivation interaction, reflecting the relatively greater service motivation of all poverty relief, family planning and firefighting workers, than among the volunteer and employee newspaper workers.

Volunteers reported substantially more positive attitudes than did comparable employees — greater Job Satisfaction, less Intent to Leave, and greater reported Job Praiseworthiness. There were significant interaction effects indicating less Job Satisfaction among all newspaper and poverty relief workers than among volunteer and employee family planners and firefighters.

In summary, volunteers doing the same work as employees reported greater social and service reward motivation—but not greater intrinsic motivation. They also reported substantially more positive work attitudes.

Before discussing the implications of these results for the presence of sufficiency of justification effects in organizational motivation, several limitations of this study need to be addressed. First, as in all of the field studies of sufficiency of justification in workplace motivation, these results do not offer definitive proof that sufficiency of justification is the sole cause of these motivation and attitude differences. Alternative explanations include (1) the possibility that different "types" of individuals become volunteers or employees, (2) volunteer or employee jobs "lose" workers in different ways, or (3) other possibly different expectations individuals bring to "spare time" volunteer work and holding a "job."

Regarding differences in who is attracted to the two kinds of work, there were no differences in age or sex (and virtually all of the volunteers had worked as employees, and many of the employees had worked as volunteers) between these volunteers and employees. Differences in volunteer and employee retention is, however, a real threat to the interpretation of the attitude differences. It is much less costly for dissatisfied volunteers to quit than it is for employees who derive their incomes from their jobs. In other words there is probably substantially less time between the volunteer's decision to leave and actual departure, than it is for employees who may want to obtain another source of income before quitting. However, dissatisfied employees who remain working because they depend on their salaries would not necessarily be less likely to report reduced social and service motivation than do volunteers, since these rewards are equally available to both groups. Finally, these self-reported motivations and attitudes toward work are consistent with sufficiency of justification but are presented with no claim that they are the only, or even the most important, psychological differences between volunteer and employed workers.

IMPLICATIONS

The most interesting finding from this study is that sufficiency of justification effects were produced for social and service motivation, but not for intrinsic motivation, the particular motivation proposed by Deci (1975) and Staw (1976) to be affected by extrinsic rewards. In fact, it appears that their original formulation was overly narrow. In the natural work setting with its many possible attractions or "rewards," the insufficiently and oversufficiently rewarded have many choices. Why should workers necessarily emphasize the interestingness of their jobs? Why not attend to the fact that saving lives from fire and keeping the poor from starving are services to others? If Festinger (1961) could assume that rats running mazes might find numerous possible targets for increased "liking," certainly human workers can choose from a wide variety of targets.

In fact, workers may enhance the sufficiency of the justification for their efforts in any number of ways, with the choices dependent on the nature of the work and the individual values or preferences of the worker. The tasks sampled for this report are all services to others, and most workers have opportunities to develop friendships with those they work with over the years. In contrast, most laboratory experiments offer few opportunities for meaningful social contact, and solving puzzles cannot reasonably be seen as a service to others. In these settings there really was nothing else that they could use to increase the justification for their efforts. These studies have been useful for directly identifying sufficiency of justification processes (something that is virtually impossible in natural work settings), yet generalizations to the workplace must be done with care. The psychological processes may be applicable, but the particular rewards that are valued or targets for positive attitudes are too dependent on idiosyncratic individuals and their settings to be reliably generalized.

These results also suggest that the sufficiency of justification effects, although operating in workplaces, may be of less practical utility now that the target of enhancement or devaluation cannot be assumed to be intrinsic motivation. It had been argued that extrinsic rewards led to less intrinsic motivation, and that if intrinsic motivation was critical in certain settings (say, perhaps, because worker surveillance was difficult) care needed to be taken in the administration of extrinsic rewards (although both Deci and Staw stopped short of recommending that employees not be paid for their work!). These results suggest that we may not be able to predict reliably what that target of sufficiency of justification cognitions may be. For example, professional athletes who experience oversufficient justification may still believe that playing the sport itself is fun, but may devalue the social rewards, or grow to dislike working conditions such as extensive travel, associated with their work. If we cannot be sure what may be devalued under oversufficient, or enhanced under insufficient reward conditions, the practical utility of the theory is reduced. Not only do we receive no guidance concerning what the motivations or attitudes of these individuals might be, what individuals choose to devalue may not be as important as intrinsic motivation.

Staw's (1976) and Deci's (1975) suggestions concerning why the intrinsic rewards changed—grew stronger with insufficient justification and weaker with oversufficient justification—are now difficult to justify. With the break-down of this neat dichotomy of organizational rewards, their ideas about the mechanism directing the choice of target for enhancement or devaluation is called into question. Staw suggested it was because intrinsic rewards were less tangible than extrinsic rewards. Are social and service rewards also relatively less tangible? Deci argued that extrinsic rewards led individuals to assume they were working for these external payoffs, reducing their experienced internal control. Do social and service rewards enhance or detract from experienced competence and self-control?

Both of these kinds of rewards are extrinsic (provided to the individual by someone else), as well as having some of the traditional self-reward features of intrinsic rewards. Many theorists have argued that social rewards involve reciprocity (Gouldner, 1960; Rubin, 1973); that is, most will not find it socially rewarding to continue to interact with someone who is nonresponsive or does not "reciprocate." Therefore, social rewards cannot be completely "self-administered." Service rewards may allow a greater degree of independence from the actions of others, but, again, they are usually thought of as having some connection to others. Individuals find that they must ask, were the others served? Was the service of value? Did the activities make a difference? Answers to these questions often depend on information provided by others, and so are to some extent externally controlled.

Yet neither social nor service rewards are administered solely at the discretion of management, as pay and benefits often are. Social rewards are notoriously independent from management control (Whyte, 1955; Nadler, Hackman & Lawler, 1979). Similarly, rewards based on a perception that one has been of service to others are also dependent on the individual's interpretation of the situation. This is not to say that managers may not influence social groupings and their normative expectations, or effectively persuade workers of the societal value of their work, only that it is the individual who ultimately decides whether or not to be influenced. Without the intrinsic/extrinsic dichotomy, arguments about the relative self-control or tangibility of various organizational rewards become more difficult to make.

It can be speculated that, at least in organizational contexts, sufficiency of justification effects may be directly dependent on the relatively unique features of pay, rather than on any general characteristics of extrinsically mediated rewards. All work examples of oversufficient justification provided by Deci (1975) concerned pay; examples of other extrinsic rewards, for example, retirement benefits, influencing intrinsic motivation simply would not "ring true" to most readers. Is it plausible that interest in the job itself would be reduced by increased employer pension fund contributions? It is the direct psychological power of pay itself that can influence attitudes and the value of other rewards, not its character as part of a class of externally controlled rewards. I have argued elsewhere (Pearce, 1983b) that pay has a psychological influence beyond its simple role as a secondary reinforcer, that pay has come to assume great symbolic importance as a surrogate of our worth and social status in modern society. It may be comforting to have a theoretically neat way of conceiving of the interrelationships among organizational rewards, yet the empirical evidence suggests that the intrinsic/extrinsic reward dichotomy and the proposed mechanisms for the interrelationships between the two types of rewards are simply not applicable to organizational rewards. These arguments may, in fact, have been masking the very special psychological role of pay at work that leads to sufficiency of justification effects. Clearly, more research addressing the role of pay on the cognitions, motivations, and attitudes of organizational members is needed.

If pay does have such power to affect perceived sufficiency of justification for organizational work, what practical implications does this have? Three suggestions are offered:

1 These results suggest that those (quite effective) criticisms of Deci's extrinsic/intrinsic dichotomy of rewards do not necessarily lead to a rejection of his arguments against contingent pay plans. He suggested that these plans, such as piece rate incentives, would be seen by workers as excessively "controlling" and would lead to negative motivational consequences, despite their positive short-term performance effects. Here it is suggested that these plans, as pay plans, not as extrinsic rewards, may well lead to reduced feelings of self-control and competence. Deci's cautions concerning these programs may still be valid, since these results suggest that sufficiency of motivation can be influenced by pay, if not by "extrinsic rewards."

2 Since these results support the idea that decisions have been justified after-the-fact in organizations, they suggest a different way of thinking about employee and volunteer recruitment. Too often, potential workers are seen as super-rational creatures that gather information about the possible benefits of organizational membership (information that is assumed to be clear and unambiguous) who then decide whether or not to join based on this analysis. In fact, many decisions in organizations may be seen as "trials," and evaluated afterwards. These would be the decisions that are not too costly to retract—and certainly "trial organizational behavior" is easier for volunteers than employees. In fact, the ease of experimentation for volunteers may help account for the tremendous variability in their actions—their frequent unpredictability in attendance and job performance. This also suggests that recruitment programs for volunteers should not waste expensive resources on determining what the "real" motivation of potential volunteers may be, but more profitably focus on influencing perceived rewards once the volunteer has joined.

3 Finally, these results suggest more attention may be necessary to the ongoing "sense-making" processes of organizational members. Workers appear to continually evaluate their own attitudes and motives "as they go along." Differences in the attractiveness of rewards appear to be based, not only on individual differences in preferences (e.g., you like challenge, I like congenial co-workers), but also on the available mix of rewards. Organizational rewards may not be properly thought of as concrete "objective" things that individual workers independently decide to either value or not, but more appropriately, as perceptions subject to substantial interpretation. This implies that managers and supervisors would want to take an active role in analyzing, and influencing, the on-going motivational sense-making in their organizations.

In summary, the present study has provided support for the argument that relative sufficiency of justification can influence perceived work motivation, but it has also undercut the most valuable feature of its application to work motivation—that intrinsic motivation to perform one's job will suffer when extrinsic rewards are abundant. These results suggest that pay, as an organizational reward, can have a powerful effect on motivation and attitudes, and that many organizational rewards are subject to substantial after-the-fact interpretation.

In conclusion, organizational volunteers have provided a particularly useful "laboratory" for these analyses, because so much of their behavior is "voluntary" in the traditional sense—not subject to the determination of powerful external constraints. Psychological processes that are often more subtle or masked in organizations staffed by employees are more visible to researchers and members alike in voluntary organizations. It is hoped that this study can demonstrate the usefulness of studying organizational behavior in other, less traditional, settings.

REFERENCES

Aronson, E. (1966) The psychology of insufficient justification: An analysis of some conflicting data. In S. Feldman (Ed.), *Cognitive consistency*. New York: Academic Press, pp. 109–133.

de Charms, R. (1968) *Personal causation: The internal affective determinants of behavior*. New York: Academic Press.

Deci, E. L. (1971) Effects of externally mediated rewards on intrinsic motivation. *Journal of Personality and Social Psychology, 18,* 105–115.

Deci, E. L. (1975) *Intrinsic motivation*. New York: Plenum.

Dermer, J. (1975) The interrelationship of intrinsic and extrinsic rewards. *Academy of Management Journal, 18,* 125–129.

Dyer, L., & Parker, D. F. (1975) Classifying outcomes in work motivation research: An examination of the intrinsic-extrinsic dichotomy. *Journal of Applied Psychology, 60,* 455–458.

Eden, A. (1975) Intrinsic and extrinsic rewards and motives: Replication and extension with kibbutz workers. *Journal of Applied Social Psychology, 5,* 348–361.

Festinger, L. (1961) The psychological effects of insufficient rewards. *American Psychologist, 16,* 1–11.

Gouldner, A. W. (1960) The norm of reciprocity: A preliminary statement. *American Sociological Review, 25,* 161–179.

Guzzo, R. A. (1979) Types of rewards, cognitions, and work motivation. *American Management Review, 4,* 75–86.

Heider, F. (1958) *The psychology of interpersonal relations.* New York: Wiley.

Nadler, D., Hackman, J. R., & Lawler, E. E. III (1979) *Managing organizational behavior.* Boston: Little, Brown.

Naylor, H. H. (1967) *Volunteers today.* New York: Association Press.

Notz, W. W. (1975) Work motivation and the negative effects of extrinsic rewards. *American Psychologist, 30,* 884–891.

Pearce, J. L. (1978) *Something for nothing: An empirical examination of the structures and norms of volunteer organizations.* Unpublished dissertation, Yale University.

Pearce, J. L. (1983a) Job attitude and motivation differences between volunteers and employees from comparable organizations. *Journal of Applied Psychology, 68,* 646–652.

Pearce, J. L. (1983b) Labor that is worth nothing: The paradox of volunteers. In M. S. Moyer (Ed.), *Managing voluntary organizations.* Toronto: York University.

Rubin, Z. (1973) *Liking and loving: An invitation to social psychology.* New York: Holt, Rinehart and Winston.

Staw, B. M. (1974) Attitudinal and behavioral consequences of changing a major organizational reward: A natural field experiment. *Journal of Personality and Social Psychology, 29,* 742–751.

Staw, B. M. (1976) *Intrinsic and extrinsic motivation.* Morristown, N.J.: General Learning Press.

Whyte, W. F. (1955) *Money and motivation.* New York: Harper.

Does Japanese Management Style Have a Message for American Managers?[1]

Edgar H. Schein

One of the greatest strengths of U.S. society is our flexibility, our ability to learn. When we see a problem, we tinker with it until we have it solved, and we seem to be willing to try anything and everything. One of our greatest weaknesses, on the other hand, is our impatience and short-run orientation. This leads to fads, a preoccupation with instant solutions, a blind faith that if we put in enough effort and money anything is possible, and an inability or unwillingness to see the long-range consequences of some of the quick fixes which we try. Complicated solutions which require long-range planning, resolute implementation, and patience in the face of short-run difficulties are harder for us to implement.[1]

[1]The author would like to acknowledge the Centre D'Etudes Industrielle, Geneva, Switzerland for its support in developing the ideas on culture. This paper was developed from a project supported by the Chief of Naval Research, Psychological Sciences Division (Code 452), Organizational Effectiveness Research, Office of Naval Research, Arlington, VA 22217 (under contract N00014-80-C0905; NR 170-911). Special thanks go to Gibb Dyer who helped to develop the ideas on how to analyze cultures.

The tension between flexibility and fadism can be seen clearly in the current preoccupation with Japanese management. Two recent books, Ouchi's *Theory Z* and Pascale and Athos's *The Art of Japanese Management,* are currently on the *New York Times* best sellers list. Why this sudden interest and what are the implications for management theory? I would like to examine some of the theses of these two books and to put those theses into a historical perspective. From this perspective I will draw some tentative conclusions about cultural themes in the U.S. and the implications for U.S. management.

Some Historical Perspective: Indoctrination

In 1961 I published an article called "Management Development as a Process of Influence" which attempted to show that many of the socialization methods used by some of our largest corporations (such as IBM and General Electric) were essentially similar to processes of indoctrination which one could observe in many other settings.[2] Such socialization methods were under strong attack by W.H. Whyte (in *The Organization Man*) and others who saw in them a tendency to create "men in grey flannel suits" who would cease to think for themselves and just parrot the corporate line, thus reducing the innovative and creative capacity of the organization and the individuality of the employee.[3] Ironically, the companies which had built such indoctrination centers (such as IBM at Sands Point, N.Y. and General Electric at Crotonville, N.Y.) were very proud of the spirit and common way of thinking which they could induce in their employees and managers. Such spirit was viewed as one of the key sources of strength of these enterprises.

But the pendulum swung hard during the 1960s, and it became the fashion to move away from producing conformity toward stimulating self-actualization.[4] "Indoctrination" either moved underground, was relabeled, or was replaced by "development" programs which emphasized opportunities for the integration of individual goals with organizational goals. Models of development shifted from the engineering model of "molding or shaping people to fit the organization" to more agricultural models of permitting people to flourish according to their innate potential; the obligation of the organization was to provide sunshine, nutrients, water, and other environmental supports. (Little is said in this model about pruning, transplanting, and uprooting, by the way.) The IBM songbook was put away, and managers who used to be proud of their ability to motivate people by inspiring them through common rituals and activities were made to feel ashamed of using "manipulative" tactics.

In the 1970s we discovered the concepts of "organizational culture" and have begun to rethink the issue once again.[5] Even if a company does not deliberately and consciously indoctrinate its new employees, its important beliefs, values, and ways of doing things will, in any case, powerfully socialize anyone who remains in the organization and wishes to move upward and inward in it.[6] Such socialization processes and their effects in producing either conformity or innovation have been described and analyzed, and the tactics which stimulate innovation have received special attention.[7]

Now, with the "discovery" that some Japanese companies are effective because of their ability to involve and motivate people, and the assertion that such involvement results from socialization tactics which induce a high degree of loyalty and conformity, we may be headed back toward the ideology of indoctrination which we so forcefully put aside a mere twenty years ago.

Human Relations and Participation

A similar pendulum swing can be identified with respect to two other human relations values: whether or not one should treat people wholistically and whether or not one should make decisions from the bottom up by participation and consensus mechanisms. Many Americans have grown up with a tradition of bureaucracy, of strong bosses, of hiring people as "hands" to provide certain activities in return for certain pay and benefits. But most students of industrial relations systems note that there has been a historical trend in such systems from a period of autocracy through a period of paternalism toward the present more consultative and participative models.[8] In the paternalistic phase American companies have treated employees very wholistically: building company towns; funding company sports activities; providing country clubs, counseling services, day care centers, medical facilities, uniforms, and so on. Indeed, one of Ralph Nader's most powerful films deals with the town of Kannapolis, N.C., where the Cannon Mills Co. not only provides lifetime employment but owns all of the housing, uses its own security force as the town police force, and provides all the services needed by the town. What alarmed Nader was the possibility that the citizens of this town were not developing any skills in self-government, which would leave them very vulnerable if the company should move or cease to be totally paternalistic.

We may also recall that one of the major results of the now historic studies of the Hawthorne plant of the Western Electric Company was the recognition that employees were whole people who brought their personal problems with them in their place of work. In the 1930s the company launched a counseling program which involved company-employed counselors to help employees deal with any personal problems on a totally confidential basis.[9] Though it has been a tradition in our military services not to fraternize with the men (presumably because it might be difficult to be objective when individuals must be sent into dangerous situations), there is no such tradition in industry generally. Office parties, company picnics, and other forms of fraternization have been considered legitimate and desirable in many organizations and by many managers, though they are clearly not as institutionalized in the U.S. as they are in Latin America and Japan.

The human relations training programs for foremen which were rampant in the 1940s were clearly aimed at teaching managers to treat their employees as whole people, to consider their needs, to fight for them when necessary, and to build strong loyalty and team spirit. The leadership and sensitivity training which flourished in the 1960s was similarly aimed at truly understanding the needs and talents of subordinates, peers, and bosses, so that appropriate levels of participation could be used in solving increasingly complex problems in organizations.[10] The writings of McGregor on Theory Y showed the importance of trust and faith in people; the writings of Argyris showed the necessity of permitting people in organizations to function as adults instead of reducing them to dependent children.[11] Likert argued cogently for System 4, as a more participative form of organization in which consensus management plays a big role; and Maslow first introduced the idea of Theory Z, a self-actualizing organization.[12]

Many managers saw the point immediately, and either felt reinforcement for what they were already doing or began to retrain themselves and their organization toward some of the new values and technologies of participative decision making. But as a total ideology this approach clearly has not taken hold. Many organizations discovered:

That high morale did not necessarily correlate with high productivity;

That autocratic systems could outproduce democratic systems (at least in the short run);

That high productivity even when achieved by autocratic methods could build high morale;

That the costs in terms of time and effort which participation entailed were often not affordable in certain kinds of environments.

Human Relations Japanese Style

Now the pendulum appears to be swinging once again on the issue of paternalism, managing the whole worker, and creating worker involvement through participation. We are told that the Japanese are extremely paternalistic and wholistic in their approach to employees, that they tend to employ people for life, and that supervisors take care of the personal as well as the work needs of subordinates (sometimes even helping an employee find a wife). The Japanese use bottom-up consensual decision making and encourage high levels of trust across hierarchical and functional boundaries.

THEORY Z

Ouchi has for some time been arguing that the essential differences between American (Theory A) and Japanese (Theory J) management systems lie in some key *structural* issues and *cultural* values which make it possible for certain kinds of management styles to flourish. Specifically, he points out that major Japanese companies:

Employ their key people for "life" (i.e., until forced retirement at the age of fifty-five to sixty);

Rotate them through various functions;

Promote them very slowly and according to more of a seniority than merit system;

Place responsibility on groups rather than on individuals (a value of the Japanese culture).

These determinants make it possible for Japanese companies:

To treat their employees as total people;
To build the kind of trust that facilitates bottom-up consensual decision making; and
To control employees in a subtle, indirect manner.

In contrast, Ouchi points out, the bureaucratic model often associated with pure American management methods emphasizes:

Employment contracts which last only as long as the individual is contributing;
Specialization of function with rotation reserved only for people on a general manager track;

Little concern for the total person;
Rapid feedback and promotion;
Explicit formal control systems;
Individual responsibility (a strong cultural value in the U.S.);
Individual top-down decision making.

The crucial insight which Ouchi provides is to identify another model, which he calls Theory Z, which is found in many American companies, which fits into our culture, and which combines certain features of the A and J models. Such companies have:

Lifetime employment;
Slower rates of promotion;
Somewhat more implicit, less formal control systems;
More concern for the total person;
More cross-functional rotation and emphasis on becoming a generalist;
Some level of participation and consensual decision making;
A continued emphasis on individual responsibility as a core value.

Though he does not give much evidence in his book, Ouchi has shown in other papers that a U.S. company which approximates the Theory Z criteria generated higher morale, higher loyalty, and generally more healthy, positive feelings at all levels of the hierarchy than did a comparable Theory A company. What is missing, however, is convincing evidence that those companies which fit the Theory Z model are more *effective* than comparable companies which operate more on the Theory A bureaucratic model. Furthermore, Ouchi acknowledges that the Theory Z companies he has studied generate less professionalism, have a harder time integrating mavericks into their ranks because they generate strong conformity pressures (leading them to be sexist and racist), and may only be adaptive for certain kinds of technological or economic environments. In fact, the only way a Theory Z company can manage the instabilities which are inherent in running a successful business in a turbulent environment is to limit lifetime employment to a small cadre of key people and to keep a large percentage of the labor force in a temporary role which resembles more closely the bureaucratic A model. In order to survive, it may be necessary for Theory Z companies to subcontract much of their work or to rely on a set of satellite companies to absorb the instabilities. (The latter is the typical Japanese pattern.)

Implications of Theory Z

After describing how this notion of an industrial "clan" can facilitate certain kinds of long-range involvement on the part of employees. Ouchi argues strongly that U.S. companies should think seriously about becoming more like clans, and lays out a program of how to do it. Neither the argument that a company, should be more like Z, nor the proposed steps for how to get there are at all convincing, however. The theoretical sophistication which is displayed in the analysis of types of organizational control is followed by naive and superficial prescriptions about how one might think about a change program designed to help a company to become more like a clan (if, indeed, this is even possible). In effect, the manager is invited to be more open and trusting and to involve his or her people more. Little attention is given to the issue of why a given organization would be less trusting and participative in the first place, and to the problem of taking managerial values from a culture in which they fit very well to one in which the fit is not at all clear.

But Ouchi makes a strong sales pitch, and it is here that our tendency to embrace the quick fix may get us into trouble. If someone tells us that Theory Z is closer to the Japanese model, and that the Japanese are getting a lot of mileage out of their model, do we all get on the bandwagon and give our employees tenure, push decision making down the hierarchy, and slow down promotions? Do we turn everyone into a generalist, throw out formal control systems, and treat each person as a total human being? If we do, will our productivity shoot right back up so that we can regain our once dominant economic position? Sounds too simplistic, does it not? Unfortunately that is just what it is, because it takes into account neither the uniqueness of Japanese culture nor the uniqueness of U.S. culture, nor the technological and environmental conditions which ultimately will dictate whether an A, a Z, or some other form will be the most effective in a given situation. What the Ouchi book leaves out, unfortunately, are criteria which might help a manager to decide whether or not a Z, an A, or some other form is appropriate.

On the positive side, the analysis focuses on the importance of the human factor, and Ouchi's seven criterion categories are certainly an important grid for assessing the options for managing people. The identification of the clan mechanism as a way of organizing and controlling people brings us back to what many companies know intuitively—"we are one big family in this organization"—and legitimizes the kind of indoctrination which used to be more common. We can see more clearly that between autocracy and democracy there lies a full range of choices, and that a high degree of paternalism is not necessarily incompatible with bottom-up consensual, participative decision making. The manager can also see that the way people feel about an organization can be explicitly managed even if the relationship to long-range effectiveness is not completely clear. As Etzioni noted long ago, a person can be involved in an organization in a variety of ways, ranging from the "alienated prisoner" or calculative employee to the participating member who is fully and morally involved.[13] Two serious questions to consider are whether U.S. economic organizations can claim moral involvement (as some Japanese firms apparently do) and whether such levels of involvement are even desirable in our culture.

The Ouchi analysis closes with a useful reminder that what ties the Japanese company together is a *company philosophy,* some dominant values which serve as criteria for decisions. What permits bottom-up consensual decision making to occur is the wide sharing of a common philosophy which guarantees a similarity of outlook with respect to the basic goals of the organization. Ouchi provides some case examples and displays a method by which a company can determine its own philosophy.

INTEGRATING THE SEVEN S's

Pascale and Athos make their argument at a different level of analysis, though they also stress the importance of managing *people* as key resources and the importance of superordinate goals, sense of spirit, or company philosophy. Ouchi is more the social scientist, presenting a theoretically grounded sociological argument for a structural approach to human resource management. Pascale and Athos are less theoretical and more didactic. They are the teachers/consultants, distilling some of the wisdom from the analysis of the Japanese experience, and they try to transmit the wisdom through a more down-to-earth writing style. The managerial reader will learn more from this book, while the social scientist will learn more from the Ouchi book.

   As already indicated, Ouchi has seven basic criteria for distinguishing A from J. Pascale and Athos (with due apologies for the gimmicky quality of the scheme) draw on a formulation developed by the McKinsey Co. which includes the following seven basic variables:

   1 Superordinate goals,
   2 Strategy,
   3 Structure,
   4 Systems,
   5 Staff (the concern for having the right sort of people to do the work),
   6 Skills (training and developing people to do what is needed), and
   7 Style (the manner in which management handles subordinates, peers, and superiors).

Within this structure, Pascale and Athos identify what they term the "soft S's" and the "hard S's," and explain that the superordinate goals are critical in tying everything together. They argue that Japanese companies are effective because of their attention to such integration and their concern for those variables which have to do with the human factor, the soft S's. These are the factors which American managers allegedly pay too little attention to: staff, skills, and, most importantly, style. The hard S's (which complete the Seven S model) are: strategy, structure, and systems.

   Through a detailed comparison of the Matsushita Corp. and ITT under Geneen, the authors bring out the essential contrast between Japanese attention to the soft S's and Geneen's more "American" preoccupation with very tight controls, autocratic decision making, and concern for the bottom line. Yet the Geneen story also illustrates that a system which is as internally consistent as ITT's was, can be very effective. Its weakness lay in its inability to survive without the personal genius of a Geneen to run it.

The Japanese Style

Following this dramatic contrast, Pascale and Athos analyze the Japanese management style and explain how a culture which values "face" and is collective in its orientation can breed managerial behavior which makes the most of ambiguity, indirection, subtle cues, trust, interdependence, uncertainty, implicit messages, and management of process (instead of attempting to develop complete openness, explicitness, and directness in order to minimize ambiguity and uncertainty). "Explicit communication is a cultural assumption; it is not linguistic imperative," they remind us.[14]

The lesson for American managers here is diametrically opposite in the two books. Ouchi's proposal for how to get to Theory Z is to be more open; Pascale and Athos imply (from their positive case examples of U.S. managers who use indirection, implicit messages, and nondecision as strategies) that we might do well to learn more of the arts of how to be less open. Though we in the U.S. often imply that to worry about "face" is a weakness and that it is better to "put all the cards on the table," in fact, there is ample evidence that Americans no less than Japanese respond better to helpful face-saving hints than to sledgehammers. "When feedback is really clear and bad, it's usually too late."[15] "The inherent preferences of organizations are clarity, certainty, and perfection. The inherent nature of human relationships involves ambiguity, uncertainty, and imperfection. How one honors, balances, and integrates the needs of both is the real trick of management."[16]

The analysis of face-to-face communication, drawn from an article by Pascale called "Zen and the Art of Management," is full of valuable insights on the subtleties of how and why indirection, tact, and concern for face are not merely niceties but necessities in human relations. It is crucial to recognize, of course, the distinction between *task* relevant information (about which one should be as open as possible in a problem-solving situation) and *interpersonal* evaluative information (about which it may be impossible to be completely open without running the risk of permanently damaging relationships).[17] Sensitivity training in which people attempted to tell each other what they thought of each other only worked in so-called "stranger groups," where people did not know each other before and knew that they would not have to work or live with each other after the program.[18]

Interdependence

Pascale and Athos supplement their analysis of face-to-face relations with an excellent analysis of groups and the dilemmas of interdependence. Noting that the American tradition is one of independence and that the Japanese tradition (based on their limited space and the technology of rice farming) is one of interdependence, they show how groups and meetings can work in this context by members being more restrained, self-effacing, and trusting. As Ouchi points out, getting credit in the *long-run,* instead of worrying (as Americans often do) about being recognized immediately for any and all accomplishments, is made possible by the knowledge of lifetime employment, i.e., if people have to work with each other for a long time, true contribution will ultimately be recognized. Both books indicate that such group relationships combined with lack of specialization of careers give the Japanese company the ability to integrate better across key functional interfaces, because everyone has more empathy and understanding for other functions.

Superior-Subordinate Relationships

Long-term relationships and a culture in which everyone knows his or her place in the status hierarchy lead to a different concept of superior-subordinate relationships in Japan. The boss is automatically more of a mentor, teaching through subtle cues rather than blunt feedback, exercising great patience while the subordinate learns how to interpret cues and to develop his or her own skills, and reinforcing the basic company philosophy as a conceptual source that helps subordinates to decide what to do in any given situation. This point is critical, because it highlights one of the most important functions of superordinate goals or organizational philosophy. If everyone understands what the organization is trying to do and what its values are for how to do things, then every employee who truly understands the philosophy can figure out what his or her course of action should be in an ambiguous situation. No directives or explicit control systems are needed because the controls are internalized.

Individualism and Authority

Pascale and Athos take the issues of power and authority into the cultural realm in a more subtle fashion than does Ouchi, who merely labels J companies as having collective responsibility and A and Z companies as having individual responsibility. But we must ask what individual or collective responsibility means in each culture. Can we assume that the American model of individual rights, independence, equal opportunity under the law, and related values and norms is in any sense the opposite of or even on the same dimension with the Japanese notion of group responsibility? Is the issue simply that the group would be sacrificed for the individual in the U.S., while the individual would be sacrificed for the group in Japan?

   A more appropriate formulation is to assume that in every culture and in every individual there is a core conflict about how self-seeking or self-effacing to be for the sake of one's group or organization. At the extremes where either nationalism or anarchy is involved, the conflict is easier to reduce, but in a pluralistic society (such as in the U.S.) it is a genuine dilemma. (This is exemplified in U.S. sports organizations which try to create a team while maximizing the individual talents of the players.) In a recent analysis of individualism, Waterman has indicated that in political and social science writings there have always been two versions of individualism: one which focuses on selfishness and takes advantage of the group and one which focuses on self-actualization in the interest of maximizing for both the individual and the group the talents latent in the members.[19] Those writers who argue for a humanistic solution to organizational problems are espousing the second definition which assumes that integration is possible.

In my experience the effective organization is neither individualistic nor collective; rather, it attempts to create norms and procedures which extol stardom and teamwork equally. The manager's job (just like the good coach's) is to find a way to weld the two forces together. The Japanese solution to this dilemma appears to be aided immensely by the fact that basic traditions and cultural values strongly favor hierarchy and the subordination of the individual to those above him or her. However, this solution has potentially negative consequences, because it reduces the creative talent available to the organization. One might suspect, however, that the effective organization in Japan finds ways of dealing with this dilemma, and that the highly talented individual is not as pressured to conform as the less talented individual.[20]

The Japanese company in the Ouchi model could be expected to be more innovative on those tasks which require group solutions, while the American company could be expected to be more innovative on those tasks that require a high level of individual expertise and creativity. Company effectiveness would then depend on the nature of the tasks which face it, its ability to diagnose accurately what those tasks are, and its flexibility in transforming itself, what I have termed an "adaptive coping cycle."[21] Whatever its human virtues and in spite of its ability to integrate better, a Theory Z organization might have *more* trouble both in seeing changes in its environment and in making the necessary transformations to adapt to those changes. Because of its strong commitment to a given philosophy and the pressure for everyone to conform, it is more likely to produce rigid paradigms for dealing with problems.

Implications for U.S. Management

Both books call for a reexamination of U.S. paradigms of how to organize and how to manage. While one can only applaud this challenge and use the models which the books present to gain perspective for such reexamination, one must be concerned about the glibness of the lessons, recommendations, and advice given the meager data base on which they are based. Neither book makes much of an effort to decipher what may be happening in our own culture and society which would explain our tendency toward Theory A (if, indeed, it can be shown that such a tendency exists). Why do we have difficulty with some of the solutions which the Japanese apparently find natural and easy, and, most importantly, what are the strengths in the U.S. system which should be preserved and built upon?

For example, Ouchi is quick to point out the negative consequences of the American tendency to try to *quantify* everything. Most of us would agree that for managing the human system of the organization, quantification may be more of a trap than a help, but one might also argue that our *desire* to quantify reflects some of the best traditions of western science and rationalism. The trick is to learn what to quantify and to know why quantification is helpful. In the design of quality control circles or in the setting of sales targets, it may be crucial to state a goal in quantifiable form in order to measure progress toward the goal. On the other hand, attempting to quantify managerial traits as part of a performance appraisal system may distort communication and reduce the effectiveness of the whole system, because people would begin to feel like "mere numbers." The effective manager in any cultural system would be the one who knows what to quantify.

Many of the formal control systems which have become associated with the concept of bureaucracy (and which are seen by Ouchi, Pascale, and Athos as dysfunctional relative to the more indirect controls associated with the Japanese style) imply that all organizations face similar control problems. One might suspect, however, that controlling the design and building of a large aerospace system might require more formal control mechanisms than the control of an R&D organization in a high technology industry. Ouchi's comparison of formal bureaucratic with informal clan mechanisms misses the point that Galbraith made so effectively: as any organization evolves, it develops organizational structures which are needed *at that stage* to deal with its information processing and control problems. A geographically dispersed organization dealing with local variants of a given market has different problems than a high technology company which has standard products that work more or less in any market. Galbraith's analysis reveals at least six or seven variants of control systems from simple rules to complex matrix structures.[22]

But the most important issue to examine before we race into new organizational paradigms is whether or not we even have the right explanation for Japanese success. Neither Ouchi nor Pascale and Athos present much evidence to justify the premise that the Japanese organizations cited are successful because of the management system described. In addition, no evidence is shown that such organizations are, indeed, the most successful ones in Japan. For example, it may well be that both Japanese productivity and management style are the reflection of some other common historical, economic, and/or sociocultural factor(s) in Japan.[23] Neither book tells us enough about the following important issues:

The role of postwar reconstruction;
The opportunity to modernize the industrial base;
The close collaboration between industry and government;
The strong sense of nationalism which produces high levels of motivation in all workers;
That lifetime employment is possible for roughly one-third of the employees in some Japanese organizations because of the system of temporary employment for the rest of the employees and the existence of satellite companies which absorb some of the economic fluctuations;
That all employees retire fairly early by U.S. standards (in their mid- to late fifties);
That many of the best companies are family dominated and their strong company philosophies may be a reflection of founder values which might be hard to maintain as these companies age;
That the cultural traditions of duty, obedience, and discipline strongly favor a paternalistic clan form of organization.

Neither book refers to the growing literature which compares managerial style and beliefs in different countries and which contradicts directly some of the books' assertions about U.S. and Japanese management approaches.[24] For example, although both books extol the virtues of Japanese indirection, subtlety, and ability to live with uncertainty and ambiguity, Hofstede found in a sample of forty countries that U.S. managers reported the highest levels of tolerance of ambiguity, while Japanese managers reported some of the lowest levels. On many dimensions U.S. and Japanese managers are surprisingly similar in their orientation which suggests that the real answer to organizational effectiveness may be to find those combinations of strategy, structure, and style which are either "culture free" or adaptable within a wide variety of cultures.

KNOWING WHAT IS CULTURAL

If we are to have a theory of organizations or management which is culture free or adaptable within any given culture, we must first know what culture is. This is surprisingly difficult because we are all embedded in our own culture. What can we learn from Japanese managers if we cannot decipher how their behavior is embedded in their culture? Can we attempt to adapt managerial methods developed in other cultures without understanding how they would fit into our own?

The first and perhaps the most important point is that we probably *cannot really understand another culture* at the level of its basic world view. The only one we can really understand is our own. Even understanding our own culture at this level requires intensive analysis and thought. One cannot suddenly become aware of something and understand it if one has taken it completely for granted. The true value of looking at other cultures is, therefore, to gain perspective for studying one's own culture. By seeing how others think about and do things, we become more aware of how we think about and do things, and that awareness is the first step in analyzing our own cultural assumptions and values. We can use analyses of Japanese management methods and their underlying cultural presumptions to learn about the hidden premises of U.S. managerial methods and our own cultural presumptions.

If we can grasp and become aware of our own premises and values, we can then examine analytically and empirically what the strengths and weaknesses of our own paradigm may be. This process of self-analysis is subtle and difficult. Not enough research has been done on managerial practices in our own culture; thus, the methods of analysis and tentative conclusions presented below should be treated as a rough first cut at analyzing our own cultural terrain.[25]

LEVELS OF CULTURE

In thinking about culture, one should distinguish surface manifestations from the essential underlying premises which tie together the elements of any given culture. As shown in Figure 1, there are at least three interconnected levels:

1 *Artifacts and creations* are the visible manifestations of a culture (which include its language, art, architecture, technology, and other material outputs) and its visible system of organizing interpersonal relationships, status levels, sex roles, age roles, etc. Though this level is highly visible, it is often not decipherable

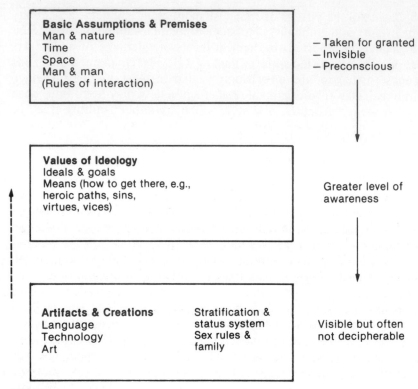

FIGURE 1
The levels of culture.

in the sense that the newcomer to the culture cannot figure out "what is really going on." what values or assumptions tie together the various visible manifestations.

2 *Values and ideology* are the rules, principles, norms, values, morals, and ethics which guide both the ends of a given society (group) and the means by which to accomplish them. Values and ideological statements usually define *what* national goals, intergroup relationships, and interpersonal relationships are appropriate to strive for; they are taught to children and reinforced in adults. Generally the level of culture we first encounter is *how* to achieve the goals (i.e., the appropriate rules of conduct which govern relationships between nations, groups, and individuals within the society). This is also where differences are felt most strongly because of the penalties associated with behaving inappropriately. This level of culture, although partly conscious and partly unconscious, can be revealed if people reflect analytically about their own behavior.

3 *Basic assumptions and premises* are the underlying and typically unconscious assumptions about the nature of truth and reality, the nature of human nature, "man's" relationship to nature, "man's" relationship to "man," the nature of time, and the nature of space.[26] These assumptions create the cultural core or essence, provide the key to deciphering the values and artifacts, and create the patterning that characterizes cultural phenomena. It is also this level, however, which is hardest to examine, because it is taken for granted and, hence, outside of awareness.

If we analyze U.S. culture and managerial assumptions in terms of some of the categories around which basic assumptions are built, what perspective does this provide, and how does this help us to learn from Japanese managerial practices?

SOME KEY ASSUMPTIONS OF U.S. CULTURE

"Man's" Relationship to Nature: Proactive Optimism

It is a premise of most western societies (particularly of the U.S.) that nature can and should be conquered, that "man" is ultimately perfectible, and that anything is ultimately possible if we put enough effort into it. "Where there's a will there's a way," buttressed by "Every day we do difficult things; the impossible just takes a little longer," sets the tone for how we approach tasks. We feel constrained by the environment only if we do not have the knowledge or technology to control or alter it, and then we proactively seek whatever knowledge or technology is necessary to overcome the obstacle.

Such proactive optimism underlies the values surrounding equality of opportunity in that we take it for granted that anyone might be able to accomplish anything. If given the opportunity. In other words, man is ultimately perfectible, as the thousands of self-help books in airport book shops proclaim. The notion of accepting one's "fate" (limiting one's aspirations by one's social position or some other nontechnological constraint) is simply not part of the underlying ideology, however much empirical data might argue to the contrary.[27]

Given this core assumption, what kinds of organizational forms are possible in the U.S.? Can an industrial clan (a Theory Z organization) with its intrinsic conservative orientation survive in a cultural environment which emphasizes change, progress, innovation, and novelty? Or would this cultural orientation begin to erode the very core of such an organization—the stability which produces the comfort?

Similarly, can a culture which encourages people to find better ways to do things independently, to resist arbitrary authority if it interferes with pragmatic problem solving, and to value individual accomplishment produce an integrated system like the Pascale/Athos S model? Perhaps the most notable characteristic of U.S. managerial practice is that we are never satisfied and are forever tinkering to find a better way. This will always undermine efforts toward integration. For many U.S. managers, integration equals stagnation; I have observed repeatedly that as soon as a system becomes routine, managers begin to think about "reorganization." Perhaps we deeply mistrust stability and are culturally "pot stirrers."

"Man's" Relationship to "Man": Individualistic Egalitarianism

Every society or group must resolve the issue between individualism and collectivism. The underlying U.S. assumption appears to be that the individual always does and should do what is best for himself or herself, and is constrained only by respect for the law and the rights of others. The rule of law implies that there are no philosophical and moral principles which can ultimately determine when another's rights have been violated, and, therefore, the legislative and judicial process must decide this on a case-by-case basis through a confronting, problem-solving process judged by a jury of peers. Buried in these assumptions is a further assumption that the world can only be known through successive confrontations with natural phenomena and other people; that the nature of truth resides in empirical experience, not in some philosophical, moral, or religious system; and that the ultimate "philosophy," therefore, might as well be one of pragmatism. Ambition, maximizing one's opportunities, and fully utilizing one's capacities become the moral imperatives.

These assumptions, in turn, are related to the western rational scientific tradition which emphasizes experimentation; learning from experience; open debate of facts; and a commitment to truth, accuracy, measurement, and other aids to establish what is "real." The openness and pluralism which so many commentators on America emphasize are closely related to the assumption that truth can only be discovered through open confrontation and can come from anyone. The lowest level employee has as good a chance to solve a key problem as the president of the company, and one of the worst sins is *arbitrary* authority ("Do it because I am the boss, even if you think it is wrong" or "If I'm the boss, that makes me right").

Yet teamwork is an important value in U.S. sports and organizational life. It is not clear to me how to reconcile the need for teamwork with the assumptions of individualism, and neither Ouchi nor Pascale and Athos offer much guidance on how consensual methods (such as those advocated) can be fitted to the notions of individual responsibility which U.S. managers take for granted. One of the greatest fears that U.S. managers have of groups is that responsibility and accountability will become diffused. We need to be able to identify who is accountable for what even when the realities of the task make shared responsibility more appropriate. According to Ouchi, and Pascale and Athos, the Japanese deliberately blur individual responsibility and adapt their decision making to such blurring. If that is so, their version of the consensus method may have little to teach us.

Participatory methods can work in the U.S., but they must be based on a different premise: the premise that teamwork and participation are *better* ways to *solve problems,* because knowledge, information, and skills are distributed among a number of people. We must, therefore, involve those people who have relevant information and skills. But the goal in terms of U.S. assumptions is better problem solving and more efficient performance, not teamwork, consensus, or involvement per se. Unless Japanese consensus methods are built on the same premise of effective problem solving, they are in many senses culturally irrelevant.

Similarly, the Japanese concern for the whole person may be based on premises and assumptions which simply do not fit our core assumptions of individualism and self-help. U.S. managers are scared of paternalism and excessive involvement with subordinates, because they see them as "invasions of privacy." If an individual is taken care of by an organization, he or she may lose the ability to fight for himself or herself. Our whole system is based on the assumptions that one must "be one's own best friend" and that the law is there to protect each and every one of us. Dependency, security orientation, and allowing others to solve our problems are viewed as signs of failure and lack of ambition, and are considered to be undeserving of sympathy. On the other hand, if it is necessary to take care of the whole family in an overseas transfer in order to enable the primary employee to function effectively, then we do it. Pragmatism, necessity, and efficiency override issues of what would be more humane, because of the underlying belief that we cannot philosophically agree on basic standards of what is "best" for everyone. What is best for people must be decided on the basis of negotiation and experience (ultimately expressed in laws, safety codes, and quality of work-life standards).

A culture based on such premises sounds harsh and cold, and the things we are told we should do to "humanize" organizations sound friendly and warm. But cultures are neither cold nor warm, because within any given culture both warmth and coldness have their own meaning. We may not like certain facets of our culture once we discover their underlying premises, and we may even set out to change our culture. However, we cannot produce such change simply by pointing to another culture and saying that some of the things they do *there* would be neat *here*. We have not yet begun to understand our own culture and the managerial paradigms which it has created. This paper is a beginning attempt to stimulate such self-understanding, and such understanding is a prerequisite for any "remedial" action.

REFERENCES

1 See P. Slater, *The Pursuit of Loneliness* (Boston, MA: The Beacon Press, 1970).
2 See: E. H. Schein. "Management Development as a Process of Influence," *Industrial Management Review* (now *Sloan Management Review*), May 1961, pp. 59–77; E. H. Schein, *Coercive Persuasion* (New York: Norton & Co., 1961).
3 See W. H. Whyte, Jr., *The Organization Man* (New York: Simon & Schuster, 1956).
4 See: C. Argyris, *Integrating the Individual and the Organization* (New York: John Wiley & Sons, 1964); A. H. Maslow, *Motivation and Personality* (New York: Harper & Row, 1954); D. M. McGregor. *The Human Side of Enterprise* (New York: McGraw-Hill, 1960).
5 See: S. Silverzweig and R. F. Allen, "Changing the Corporate Culture," *Sloan Management Review*, Spring 1976, pp. 33–49; A. M. Pettigrew, "On Studying Organizational Cultures," *Administrative Science Quarterly* (1979): 570–581; H. Schwartz and S. M. Davis, "Matching Corporate Culture and Business Strategy," *Organizational Dynamics*, Summer 1981, pp. 30–48.
6 See: E. H. Schein, "The Individual, the Organization, and the Career: A Conceptual Scheme," *Journal of Applied Behavioral Science* (1971): 401–426; E. H. Schein, *Career Dynamics: Matching Individual and Organizational Needs* (Reading, MA: Addison-Wesley, 1978).
7 See: J. Van Maanen and E. H. Schein, "Toward a Theory of Organizational Socialization," in *Research in Organizational Behavior* (Vol. 1) B. Staw, ed. (Greenwich, CT: JAI Press, 1979).
8 See, for example, F. Harbison and C. A. Myers, *Management in the Industrial World* (New York: McGraw-Hill, 1959).

9 See: W. J. Dickson and F. J. Roethlisberger, *Counseling in an Organization: A Sequel to the Hawthorne Researches* (Boston: Division of Research, Harvard Business School, 1966); H. W. Johnson, "The Hawthorne Studies: The Legend and the Legacy," in *Man and Work in Society,* E. L. Cass and F. G. Zimmer, eds. (New York: Van Nostrand Reinhold, 1975).

10 See E. H. Schein and W. G. Bennis, *Personal and Organizational Change through Group Methods* (New York: John Wiley & Sons, 1965).

11 See: McGregor (1960); Argyris (1964).

12 See: R. Likert, *The Human Organization* (New York: McGraw-Hill, 1967); A. H. Maslow, *The Farthest Reaches of Human Nature* (New York: The Viking Press, 1971).

13 See A. Etzioni, *Complex Organizations* (New York: Holt, Rinehart, and Winston, 1961).

14 See R. T. Pascale and A. G. Athos, *The Art of Japanese Management: Applications for American Executives* (New York: Simon & Schuster, 1981), p. 102.

15 Ibid., p. 106.

16 Ibid., p. 105.

17 See E. H. Schein, *Process Consultation* (Reading, MA: Addison-Wesley, 1969).

18 See Schein and Bennis (1965).

19 See A. S. Waterman, "Individualism and Interdependence," *American Psychologist* (1981): 762–773.

20 See J. McLendon, *Rethinking Japanese Groupism: Individual Strategies in a Corporate Context* (unpublished paper, Harvard University, 1980).

21 See E. H. Schein, *Organizational Psychology,* 3d. ed. (Englewood Cliffs, NJ: Prentice-Hall, 1980).

22 See J. Galbraith, *Designing Complex Organizations* (Reading, MA: Addison-Wesley, 1973).

23 See: W. M. Fruin, "The Japanese Company Controversy," *Journal of Japanese Studies* (1978):267–300; B. S. Lawrence, *Historical Perspective: Seeing through Halos in Social Research* (unpublished paper, M.I.T., 1981).

24 See: G. Hofstede, *Culture's Consequences: International Differences in Work-Related Values* (Beverly Hills, CA: Sage Publications, 1980); G. W. England, *The Manager and His Values* (Cambridge, MA: Ballinger, 1975).

25 Some excellent efforts in this direction can be found in: W. H. Newman, "Cultural Assumptions Underlying U.S. Management Concepts," in *Management in an International Context,* J. L. Massie and Luytjes, eds. (New York: Harper & Row, 1972); J. J. O'Toole, "Corporate Managerial Cultures," in *Behavioral Problems in Organizations,* C. L. Cooper, ed. (Englewood Cliffs, NJ: Prentice-Hall, 1979); England (1975).

26 See F. R. Kluckhohn and F. L. Stodtbeck, *Variations in Value Orientations* (Evanston, IL: Row, Peterson, 1961).

27 See J. M. Evans, *America: The View from Europe* (Stanford, CA: The Portable Stanford, 1976).

QUESTIONS FOR DISCUSSION

1 What is the primary lesson of the article by Perry and Porter on public organizations? Explain.

2 Briefly summarize the more salient differences between public and private organizations as they relate to employee motivation.

3 Are volunteer organizations public or private? What makes them unique?

4 Summarize how managers in volunteer organizations have to approach the problem of motivation differently from the way managers in other organizations do.

5 What conclusions do you draw concerning the principle of insufficient justification? Explain.

6 In his review of the book by Pascale and Athos about Japanese management, Schein explains that the uncertainty and ambiguity of face-saving among the Japanese may be more applicable to human relations than Americans' openness and honesty. Do you agree with this assertion? What implications does this notion have for theories of motivation and commitment which incorporate a need for clear information about the organization, job roles and tasks, and consequences of behavior?

7 Schein poses two central questions to frame his summation discussion of perspectives on Japanese management: (*a*) Why do we have difficulty with some of the solutions which the Japanese apparently find natural and easy? and (*b*) What are the strengths in the U.S. system which should be preserved and built upon? What would be your answers to these questions?

PART FOUR

MOTIVATION THEORY IN PERSPECTIVE

WORK AND MOTIVATION: SOME CONCLUDING OBSERVATIONS

The concept of the organization has long symbolized the efficient, effective, and rational allocation of resources for task accomplishment. Thus, many attempts have been made by managers and researchers to define the optimal balance of financial, physical, and human resources as they help determine the growth and development of business, governmental, and educational institutions. The present volume has focused on the human aspects associated with such concerns. Specifically, we have reviewed in a systematic fashion the current level of knowledge concerning motivational processes as they affect work behavior.

Before attempting to summarize the current status of motivation theory and research, however, we should review briefly what we know about the nature of work itself. After all, if one objective of an increased knowledge of motivational processes is to improve both work attitudes and work performance, then we must be aware of the functions served by work activities in a modern society.

THE MEANING OF WORK

Work is important in the lives of individuals for several reasons. First, there is the notion of reciprocity, or exchange. Whether we are talking about a corporate executive, an assembly-line worker, or a Red Cross volunteer, each worker receives some form of reward in exchange for his or her services. These rewards may be primarily extrinsic, such as money, or they may be purely intrinsic, such as the personal satisfaction that comes from providing the service. In either case, a worker has certain personal expectations concerning the type and amount of reward he or she should receive for services rendered. The extent to which such expectations are met would presumably affect in large measure the inclination of the worker to continue at the current level of performance and, indeed, might even ultimately affect the decision concerning whether to remain with the organization.

Second, work generally serves several social functions. The workplace provides opportunities for meeting new people and developing friendships. In fact, many employees appear to spend more time interacting with their coworkers than they do with their own families!

Third, a person's job is often a source of status, or rank, in society at large. For example, a carpenter who is trained in a specific craft is generally considered to be on a higher social plane than an unskilled ditchdigger. And a bank president would generally he accorded higher status than a carpenter. A point not to be overlooked here is the fact that work, or more precisely what one does at work, often transcends the boundaries of the work organization. The bank president in our example can have status in the *community* because of his or her position within the organization. Thus, work can be simultaneously a source of social differentiation as well as a source of social integration.

Fourth, and an aspect of work of special concern to the study of motivation, is the personal meaning that work has for the individual. From a psychological standpoint, it can be an important source of identity, self-esteem, and self-actualization. It can provide a sense of fulfillment by giving an employee a sense of purpose and by clarifying his or her value to society. Conversely, however, it can also be a source of frustration, boredom, and feelings of meaninglessness, depending on the characteristics of the individual and on the nature of the task. People tend to evaluate themselves according to what they have been able to accomplish. If they see their job as hampering the achievement of their full potential, it often becomes difficult for them to maintain a sense of purpose at work. Such feelings can then lead to a reduced level of job involvement, decreased job satisfaction, and a lowered desire to perform. Hence, the nature of the job—and the meaning it has for the employee—can have a profound impact on employee attitudes and work behavior.

As our society has increased in both complexity and affluence, so, too, have the problems associated with such developments. Alcoholism and drug abuse at work are prevalent, as are problems of turnover and absenteeism. Moreover, by several indications, worker productivity appears to be declining in many areas. Managers have often tried to explain away such problems by reverting to the old scientific management, or Theory X, assumptions about human nature—namely, that people are basically lazy and have little desire to perform well on a job. However, a more realistic explanation for such problems may be found by looking at the type of work most employees are asked to perform.

Consider, for example, the case of younger workers just entering the job market. With higher educational levels as well as greater expectations concerning their work, many young workers have shown a strong aversion toward many of the more traditional (and well-paying) jobs at both the blue- and the white-collar levels. However, these same workers are largely in agreement with the notion that one should "work hard" on a job (Yankelovich, 1972). How are these two points reconciled? Perhaps the answer lies in the nature of the tasks. That is, rather than simply rebelling against the traditional (hard) work ethic, many younger workers appear to be demanding greater substance in the *nature* of their job activities. In this sense, it is a qualitative revolt, not a quantitative one. What they object to, it seems, is being placed on jobs which are essentially devoid of intrinsic worth.

Other examples could be cited (minority-group workers, women employees, and even corporate executives). In all cases, a common denominator appears to be a reduced level of employee motivation to perform a job or even to remain with an organization. If we are to understand more clearly the nature and extent of such work-related problems and, better still, if we are to be able to find appropriate solutions to these problems, we must begin by understanding the very basic role played by motivation as it affects job behavior.

IMPORTANCE OF MOTIVATION IN WORK BEHAVIOR

Review of Major Variables

Perhaps the most striking aspect of the study of work motivation is the all-encompassing nature of the topic itself. Consider again our definition of motivation: that which energizes, directs, and sustains behavior. Following such a definition, it becomes readily apparent how many divergent factors can affect in some way the desire of an employee to perform. In Chapter 1, a conceptual framework, or model, was proposed (after Porter & Miles, 1974) to assist us in organizing these factors for detailed study and analysis throughout this book (see Exhibit 3 in Chapter 1).

By way of review, the model suggested that variables affecting motivation can be found on three levels in organizational settings. First, some variables are unique to the individual himself or herself (such as attitudes, interests, and specific needs). Second, other variables arise from the nature of the job (such as degree of control over the particular job and level of responsibility). Third, still other variables are found in the larger work situation, or organizational environment. Factors falling into this third category would include such things as peer group relations, supervisory practices, systemwide rewards, and organizational climate. In addition, it was emphasized in the model that a systems perspective is necessary. That is, instead of viewing these variables as three static lists of items, consideration has to be given to how they affect one another and change over time in response to circumstances. The individual is thus seen as potentially being in a constant state of flux vis-à-vis his or her motivational level, depending on the nature, strength, and interactive effects of these three groups of variables.

Let us consider briefly how some of the more important findings reviewed in this book relate to this conceptual framework, beginning with those variables unique to the individual. Only highlights of the major findings will be mentioned here. An analysis of the data presented throughout this volume reveals that several *individual* characteristics can represent a significant influence on employee performance. For instance, there is fairly consistent evidence that individuals who have higher needs for achievement generally perform better than those who have lower needs for achievement (as shown, for example, in Chapter 2). Moreover, other evidence indicates that individuals who have strong negative attitudes toward an organization are less inclined to continue their involvement in organizational activities. Locke and his associates (Locke, Cartledge, & Knerr, 1970) present laboratory evidence and Latham and Yukl (1975) review field evidence indicating that personal aspiration level on a task (the level of performance for which an individual is actually trying) can be an accurate predictor of subsequent performance. Finally, investigations by Adams (1965) and others found that *perceived* inequity in an organizational exchange situation is associated with changes (up or down) in performance levels. While many other examples could be cited, these kinds of findings generally support the proposition that personal characteristics unique to an individual can have an important impact on his or her work behavior.

A similar pattern emerges when we consider *job-related* characteristics. Evidence presented by Hackman (1976), Steers and Porter (1974), and others indicates that variations in the nature of the task itself can influence performance and satisfaction (see Chapter 10). For example, several studies have found that "enriching" an employee's job by allowing him or her more variety, autonomy, and responsibility can result in somewhat improved performance. However, many of these findings are not overly strong. Stronger evidence concerning the impact of job- or task-related variables emerges when we simultaneously consider the role of individual differences in such a relationship. That is, when variations across individuals are also taken into account, evidence indicates that certain task attributes are more strongly related to performance only for specific "types" of people, such as those with a high need for achievement. For other persons, such attributes appear to have diminished effects. In other words, it appears that not everyone wants *to the same degree* to have an enriched job, nor does everyone necessarily perform better when assigned to one. Recognition must be given, therefore, to the background characteristics of individual employees when considering job design changes.

Finally, let us review *work environment* effects on motivation and performance. Articles presented in Chapter 6 focused on these effects and reviewed much of the research on environmental impact, and they noted the importance of such variables as group influences, leadership styles, and organizational climate in the determination of employee performance. Again, however, we must consider the interactive dynamics between such factors and other individuals and job-related factors. Thus, it is possible that high group cohesion (a work environment characteristic) may be a much more potent influence on behavior for a person with a high need for affiliation (an individual characteristic) than for a person with a low need for affiliation. Persons with high needs for achievement may be less influenced by the degree of group cohesion and more interested in potential economic rewards. Moreover, a job that lacks enrichment (a job-related characteristic) may be eased somewhat by a supervisor who shows a good deal of consideration toward his or her subordinates (another work environment characteristic).

The important point, then, is that when we consider the variables involved in work motivation, we must take a strong, integrative approach. We must study *relationships* between variables rather than focus on one specific topic. Only then can we achieve a greater understanding of the complexities of the motivational process.

REVIEW OF MAJOR THEORIES

A central purpose of any theory is to organize in a meaningful fashion the major sets of variables associated with the topic under study. In fact, one test of the usefulness of a theory or model is the degree to which it can account for a wide diversity of variables while simultaneously integrating them into a cohesive— and succinct—unifying framework. Such a theory of work motivation would ideally account for variables from the three major areas discussed above (individual, job, and work environment), as well as consider the implications of interactive effects among these areas. Unfortunately, such a totally unifying theory does not appear to exist at this time. What does exist is a set of different theories that address themselves to one or more of these sets of variables, none of which, however, is completely and thoroughly comprehensive (both in terms of hypothesized interaction effects among the variables and in terms of accounting for a diverse array of evidence).

In the absence of a "master" theory, it may be well to review briefly the several major theories that were discussed in the early chapters of the book. In this way, we can see to what extent they do deal with different sets of variables and thus compare their relative explanatory power. As was stated at the end of Chapter 1, however, many of the theoretical approaches are complementary rather than contradictory. Thus it is often not just a matter of choosing which is the "best" theory, but rather one of deciding which approaches are, *relatively speaking,* the most helpful for understanding particular aspects of employee work behavior.

The need theories of Maslow, Alderfer, and Murray and McClelland (see Chapter 2), while not entirely ignoring job-related and work environment variables, are primarily individual theories of motivation. Strong emphasis is placed on the characteristics of the individual, and these models represent highly developed statements concerning the role played by personal need strengths in the determination of work behavior. While the influences of the job and work environment are not central themes, it is easy to see how such factors could play a major role in these models. For example, for employees with a strong need for self-actualization, providing a work environment that would promote fulfillment of this need should increase their propensity to remain with the organization and respond positively to organizational objectives. A similar argument could be advanced for creating an achievement-oriented work environment under the Murray-McClelland model for individuals with a high need for achievement. Even so, although a good deal of speculation is possible concerning how such job and environmental variables might affect personal need satisfaction and performance, it should be recognized that such considerations are dealt with relatively lightly in these models.

The next category of theories to be discussed were the cognitive models (Chapter 3). Here we examined several related theories, including equity theory, expectancy/valence theory, goal-setting theory, and attribution theory. It was noted that equity theory centers on the relationship between individual characteristics—attitudes toward inputs and outcomes, tolerance for feelings of inequity, and the like—and work environment characteristics (especially systemwide reward practices). This process-oriented approach does place considerable stress on the individual's *perceptual* reactions to environmental variables, and in that sense the theory considers interactive effects. The approach does not, however, provide a comprehensive framework for integrating the major sets of variables affecting motivation at work, and in particular it fails to consider many of the other impacts of these variables (besides producing feelings of equity or inequity).

Expectancy/valence theory can be examined in terms of how it deals with the three major sets of variables—individual, job, and work environment. To begin with, the theory is specific in dealing with the role of individual differences. It recognizes individual variations in need strengths by acknowledging that not everyone values the same rewards equally; people attach different valences to potential outcomes. People also differ in their perceptions of how equitable a given level of rewards is (in relation to their own standards of comparison). Moreover, the model particularly emphasizes that individuals have differing beliefs, or expectancies, that certain actions on their part will ultimately lead to desired rewards. Expectancy/valence theory also encompasses job-related variables by pointing to how these factors can affect future expectancies and by arguing that job attributes can at times serve as sources of intrinsically valued rewards. The more sophisticated versions of the model have also included the notion of role clarity; that is, performance can often be improved by specifying more carefully the direction of behavior. Finally, expectancy/valence theory focuses fairly explicitly on several work environment influences on performance, particularly those relating to reward structures. Throughout, this model stresses the necessity of analyzing relationships between variables as a prerequisite to an understanding of the motivational *process*. It does, however, place heavy (some would say too heavy) emphasis on individuals' cognitions about how their own behavior will or will not lead to particular outcomes potentially available in the work situation. Whether individuals actually engage in the kinds of thought processes implied by the theory is the major issue to be raised with this conceptual approach.

Similar conclusions can be drawn about goal-setting and attribution theories, although these two models are generally thought to be more narrow in scope than expectancy/valence theory. Even so, it should be noted that all four of these models place considerable emphasis on individual thought processes as employees attempt to make sense out of their work environment and decide how they wish to participate in work activities.

Of all the theoretical approaches considered in this book, reinforcement theory (Chapter 4) is the one that places by far the heaviest emphasis on the work environment cluster of variables. For those who advocate this approach, the response of the work environment—including its various elements such as the work group, the supervisor, and company reward practices—is *the* controlling factor in affecting employee behavior (assuming a given level of ability). The notion of individual differences, and particularly the notion of individual needs and attitudes, is virtually ignored by this approach. Rather, as stressed earlier in the book, the reinforcement approach to explaining behavior is epitomized by the aphorism, "Behavior is a function of its consequences." Thus, it is clear that this kind of orientation to understanding motivated behavior in the organizational setting deliberately focuses on, basically, only one set of variables—the reaction of the environment to specific behaviors.

In summary, each of these theories has something to offer in the attempt to explain motivation in the work situation. Also, as we have emphasized several times, various parts of the theories are, in many ways, complementary. For example, individuals who have particularly strong needs (e.g., for achievement) may also be inclined to make equity comparisons with regard to how their peers are being rewarded in relation to the types and amounts of rewards that they themselves are receiving. In addition, they are also likely to be sensitive to what it is that they do that results in "good" responses (from supervisors, peers, the organization, etc.) and thus are likely to form ideas (i.e., "expectancies") that a certain action (behavior) on their part will, or will not, result in a "good response" (i.e., a reward) next time. In other words, it seems clear that each of the major approaches to motivation provides an important *perspective* from which to view motivation, and—and this is *crucial*—these perspectives are not necessarily contradictory but rather provide a comprehensive viewpoint that permits an increased and (it is hoped) sophisticated understanding. If there is any utility to studying motivational theories, it is exactly this fact: One can obtain more meaning about the events and situations that one observes or takes part in if one knows something about the theories than if one is not familiar with them. In this sense, improved knowledge about motivational processes is requisite not only for management but also for the employees themselves if all members are to contribute more effectively to the goals of the organization and simultaneously receive greater personal satisfaction.

IMPLICATIONS FOR MANAGEMENT

As we have found, the level of understanding concerning work motivation has increased considerably in the past several decades. However, when we survey current practice in this area, we soon discover that there is a sizable discrepancy in a number of organizations between such practice and many of the more advanced theories of motivation. Why does such a discrepancy exist? There are several possible explanations.

First, many managers still hold conservative beliefs about how much employees really want to contribute on a job. They still tend to view motivation as largely a "carrot-and-stick" process, despite the fact that current research has demonstrated that employees by and large want active involvement in organizational activities.

Second, owing primarily to increased automation and machine-placed technology, some managers apparently feel that motivation is no longer a critical issue, since production control is often largely out of the employee's hands. Such a position ignores, however, the impact that turnover, absenteeism, strikes, output restrictions, and the like have on productivity, even with machine-paced technology. And, of course, the potential effects of motivation levels on performance are greatly increased as we move toward a more service-oriented economy (and, indeed, as one considers the *management* sector of organizations; if motivation differences have an impact anywhere, it is among *managers* themselves).

Third, considering the attitudes of some labor union leaders, we find that a few such leaders apparently still feel that increasing motivational and performance levels might ultimately lead to fewer jobs. Such attitudes in the past have led to the strengthening of the status quo insofar as potential changes in the performance environment were concerned.

It is our contention that such reasoning is somewhat superficial and is, to a large extent, unfounded. The creation of a stimulating, productive, and satisfying work environment can be beneficial for both management and workers if honest concern is shown for all parties involved. If everyone is to derive some benefit from such an evironment, however, the problems of the *employee* must be clearly recognized and taken into account. The pivotal role in this process belongs to managers (and, particularly, to upper-level managers) because of their influence in determining the characteristics of the performance environment. If improvements are to be made, management must take the first step. Assuming such an orientation, several implications for managerial practices can be drawn from the material presented here. While this list is not intended to be all-inclusive, we do feel that it points to several of the more important conclusions to be drawn:

1 Perhaps one of the most important lessons to be learned from the data reviewed here is that if managers truly want to improve performance and work attitudes, they must take an active role in *managing* motivational processes at work. Managing motivation is conscious, intentional behavior; it is not something that just happens. Any organization desiring to improve attitudes or work behavior must therefore accept responsibility for active involvement and participation if such changes are to be successful.

2 Any attempt by managers to improve the motivational levels of their subordinates should be prefaced by a self-examination on the part of the managers themselves. Are they aware of their major strengths *and* their major limitations? Do they have a clear notion of their own wants, desires, and expectations from their jobs? Are their perceptions of themselves consistent with the perceptions others have of them? In short, before managers attempt to deal with others, they should have a clear picture of their own role in the organizational milieu.

3 The importance of recognizing individual differences across employees has been pointed to time and again throughout the studies reviewed here. Managers should be sensitive to variations in employees' needs, abilities, and traits. Similarly, they should recognize that different employees have different preferences (valences) for the rewards available for good performance. Research has shown, for example, that money as a reward is much more important to some than to others. A greater awareness of such variations allows managers to utilize most efficiently the diversity of talents among their subordinates and, within policy limitations, to reward good performance with those things most desirable to the employees.

4 Somewhat relatedly, it is important that employees (i.e., anyone in the organization) see a clear relation between successful performance on their part and the receipt of their desired rewards. It therefore becomes incumbent upon management to be able to identify superior performers and reward them accordingly. When this is done, employee expectations generally increase, and this in turn should lead to greater effort toward goal attainment. Such an implication raises questions about the use of non-merit-based compensation systems and of seniority as a major factor in promotions. Where rewards are not based upon performance, we would expect motivational levels to be markedly reduced.

5 A further factor to consider is the nature of the tasks which employees are asked to perform. Questions should be raised by management concerning the feasibility of providing employees with jobs that offer greater challenge, diversity, and opportunities for personal need satisfaction. Managers might begin by putting themselves in the place of their subordinates and asking themselves what they would get out of doing such a job. Similarly, questions should be raised as to whether employees understand exactly what is expected of them. Research has shown that increasing role clarity on a job generally increases the likelihood of improving task performance.

6 In a broader sense, managers could give increased attention to the quality of the overall work environment. How are group dynamics affecting performance? Are the current styles of leadership effective, or would other styles be preferable? In short, is the "climate" within the work group such that it would facilitate task accomplishment or do obvious barriers exist that can be remedied?

7 In many cases greater efforts could be made to assess worker attitudes on a continual basis. In the past, attitude surveys have received little attention outside of personnel departments, or sometimes they have been used as a tool of last resort when managers noted a decline in performance. A more effective strategy might be to monitor job attitudes and use such information as a motivational barometer to identify potential trouble spots. It is essential for managers to become intelligent consumers of behavioral data so that they can act more from a position of knowledge and understanding than from one of uncertainty or ignorance.

8 Finally, if employee motivational levels—and consequently performance—are to be increased, it becomes especially important to involve the employees themselves in a cooperative venture aimed at improving output, for after all they too have a stake in what happens to the organization. Thus, one key factor in motivating employees is to engage them more fully in the processes aimed at attaining organizational effectiveness. Without employee cooperation and support, a great deal of managerial energy can be wasted.

In summary, it is our belief that theories of motivation, like research in the behavioral sciences in general, are useful for practicing managers and employees and are not solely for academicians. Their value lies primarily in their capacity to sensitize managers and researchers to specific factors and processes that can have an important bearing on the behavior of people at work. In this sense, theories and research data in the area of motivation are one more tool available to managers—and to employees—in the performance of their jobs.

REFERENCES

Hackman, J. R. Work design. In J. R. Hackman & J. L. Suttle (Eds.), *Improving life at work*. Santa Monica, Calif.: Goodyear, 1977.

Latham, G. P., & Yukl, G. A. A review of research on the application of goal setting in organizations. *Academy of Management Journal,* 1975, **18**, 824–845.

Locke, E. A., Cartledge, N., & Knerr, C. S. Studies of the relationship between satisfaction, goal-setting, and performance. *Organizational Behavior and Human Performance,* 1970, **5**, 135–158.

Porter, L. W., & Miles, R. E. Motivation and management. In J. W. McGuire (Ed.), *Contemporary management: Issues and viewpoints*. Englewood Cliffs, N.J.: Prentice-Hall, 1974.

Steers, R. M., & Porter, L. W. The role of task-goal attributes in employee performance. *Psychological Bulletin,* 1974, **81**, 434–452.

Yankelovich, D. *The changing values on campus: Political and personal attitudes on campus*. New York: Washington Square, 1972.